DATE DUE

NOV 15 1978	JUN 20 1984
NOV 15 1978	
NOV 9 1978 B R	
NOV 9 1978	MAR 14 1986
NOV 21 1979	OCT 25 1989
NOV 6 1979	NOV 30 1989
NOV 6 1979	NOV 30 1989
JAN 8 1980	DEC 22 1989
NOV 26 1980	
DEC 7 1980	
JAN 7 1981	
JUN 10 1981	
JUN 15 1981	
MAY 2 1984	
JUN 8 1984	
JUN 18 1984	
JUN 19 1984	

Riot, Rout, and Tumult

RIOT, ROUT, and TUMULT

Readings in American Social and Political Violence

edited by
Roger Lane and
John J. Turner, Jr.

Contributions in American History,
Number 69

GREENWOOD PRESS
WESTPORT, CONNECTICUT • LONDON, ENGLAND

Library of Congress Cataloging in Publication Data
Main entry under title:

Riot, rout, and tumult.

   (Contributions in American history ; no. 69
ISSN 0084-9219)
   Bibliography: p.
   Includes index.
   1. Violence—United States—Addresses, essays,
lectures. I. Lane, Roger. II. Turner, John J.
HN90.V5R56   301.6'33'0973   77-84752
ISBN 0-8371-9845-3

Library of Congress Catalog Card Number: 77-84752
ISBN: 0-8371-9845-3
ISSN: 0084-9219

First published in 1978

Greenwood Press, Inc.
51 Riverside Avenue, Westport, Connecticut 06880

Printed in the United States of America

10   9   8   7   6   5   4   3   2   1

HN
90
.V5
R56

for
ALFRED BAKER LEWIS
and ELIZABETH F. TURNER

CONTENTS

PREFACE

This volume comprises essays and articles arranged in rough, chronological order that span our entire national experience. Years of teaching, discussion, and debate over the many issues involved in the study of American violence have convinced us of the need for such a collection. Neither authors nor editors can present a fundamental agreement on all of the many issues involved; the subject is too close to the deepest emotions as well as beliefs of social scientists to command any consensus at this stage. But at the same time, there are recurring patterns and issues both in the experience itself and in the reflections of some of our most insightful observers. And we have stressed these as they appear, thus integrating the book without attempting to dictate any single viewpoint or analysis.

There is much that we have necessarily had to leave out—not only violent behavior such as ordinary crime, which is generally not "political and social," but behavior such as Indian-white conflict, which is. We believe nonetheless that these pieces, selected for readability as well as scholarly insight, provide a significant perspective on some of the most important political and social problems that have marked the American experiment from its beginning.

We are indebted to a number of individuals who have made this volume possible. A special word of thanks is due to Dr. Lisle A. Rose for his early encouragement and support of our project. We are grateful to Adeline Taraborelli and Eileen Burton for their careful physical preparation of the manuscript, to series editor Jon L. Wakelyn for his counsel, and to Sandra Soderberg and James T. Sabin of Greenwood Press for seeing the project through.

Roger Lane

John J. Turner, Jr.

INTRODUCTION

This volume of readings is addressed to a number of issues, including the central problem in American political history: how to account for the extraordinary stability of governmental institutions in the most violent nation in the Western world. The Constitution of the United States is the oldest such instrument now in force, and its record of unbroken operation is the longest in history. The American people meanwhile have earned a fierce reputation for lawlessness and bloodshed; our rates of homicide, of industrial strife, and of interracial violence far exceed any in comparably developed nations.

Virtually every major American social theorist has attempted to explain the secret of political stability in America. One of the most popular of these explanations, first articulated by Frederick Jackson Turner in 1893, stressed the importance of an open frontier, and of cheap land, as providing among other things a "safety valve" for the discontented, who often chose to go west rather than stay and fight "the system." Others have stressed the simple fact of American abundance, which has worked in a variety of ways to soften potentially explosive conflicts between economic classes, traditionally thought the most important source of revolutionary discontent. Perhaps most influential over the years have been explanations that derive ultimately from the visiting French artistocrat Alexis de Tocqueville, who observed nearly a century and a half ago that by foreign standards Americans were an ideologically homogeneous people, with the overwhelming majority committed to middle-class values, to the Constitution, private property, and ordered liberty.

All of these explanations, however, are primarily addressed to one-half of the paradox—the maintenance of stability—and not to the other—the persistence and intensity of violence. The riots, routs, and tumults that have marked our history testify that it is not simply mutual satisfaction that has held our political and legal system together. Discontented or impatient groups have challenged or bypassed authority continually over the past two hundred years. The phenomenon, moreover, has been nearly universal; no region, group, or class has held a monopoly on the use of illegal force to try to gain or maintain a position. The use of violence has in fact been so pervasive that no account of American politics can ignore it. Indeed, the resort to force occurs often enough, and with sufficient success, so that it should be thought of not as "outside the system" but as part of it, if system is defined not simply in terms of the formal lines of authority but of all channels of expression, the whole complex of maneuver, threat, repression, and concession by which issues are in fact decided in this country.

The study of violence has always been hampered by the mixed feelings of social scientists and other observers. On the one hand, many feel so powerful a distaste for illegality and bloodshed that they are reluctant to admit their importance in winning place and advantage in our society. Others tend to romanticize violence. It is especially easy to forget how pain, terror, and loss really feel when concrete sensations are dulled by time. We often applaud a ferocity in our ancestors that we would fear in our contemporaries, and it is possible for historians to refer to the mob activities of the Revolutionary era, for example, including tarring, feathering, and maiming, as "almost charmingly benign." Strong feelings about violence may be especially obtrusive in situations in which an author looks to the past for lessons or justification to apply directly to modern issues. Wishful thinking, in many cases, overrides objective judgment in the determination of when or whether illegal force has proved an appropriate tactic in various historical situations.

This and other issues are complicated by the fact that so little is known about the most fundamental causes of violence. Psychologists and psychoanalysts cannot agree as to what extent agression is "innate" or "instinctive" in human beings, or what part it plays in the normal range of emotional expression. Political scientists and sociologists are no more united as to the importance of conflict and deviance in society. And historians are hampered by the nature of their evidence. Many questions about incidents of violence in the past cannot be answered, simply because those who described them at the time did not consider or even concealed the relevant evidence. Students as well as historians should ask a reporter's sharp questions of any account: How many people were involved? If there was a crowd, what was its composition in terms of age, sex, and class, perhaps also of race or political party? Were the "citizens" really teen-aged gangsters? Was the "labor" trouble really ethnic in origin? Were the supposed aims of the group really clear to all of those active? The answers to these and similar questions may be revealing, or surprising; too often it turns out that they are simply not available, and no certain conclusions can be drawn.

The accounts and articles in this volume support no single point of view and lead to no single conclusion about the place of social and political violence in our history. But there are several themes or topics that keep recurring across time: the role and nature of mob activity, the relations among races, the relative importance of and interplay between economic and other issues that divide Americans. These themes in turn should help in formulating an opinion about a number of issues, many of them of critical concern today. What are the circumstances under which violence has "worked" or "failed" in the past, in terms of its objectives? What has been the relative importance and intensity of various forms of conflict? How have the majority, and the authorities, reacted to various forms of direct action?

Some of the explanation for the apparent paradox of stability despite disorder results simply from the fact that "law and order" are not indentical but separable and sometimes even antithetical. Often, that is, the law is bypassed or flouted in the name of some group's perception of what a proper "order" is or ought to be. Most political and social violence in this country has in fact been directed not against but in support of existing power relations. The legal authorities themselves have often condoned or even aided illegal efforts to maintain the status quo against perceived threats from Catholics, workingmen, or blacks, for example.

Direct action, too, may simply be a means of venting frustration or expressing high spirits without any clearly formulated political goals. Or it may be directed at modest changes that might otherwise have been met through perfectly peaceful legal action. Thus although all of it may be regarded as in some ways subversive of the rule of law, relatively little of the violence that has marked our history has been undertaken in the name of any fundamental change. Indeed, our most distinctive characteristics, even those thought of as stabilizing forces, may serve to fuel hostilities. Material abundance, although it may sometimes soften the edge of desperation, may also create an atmosphere of competitive expectation that leads to frustration and violence. Even ideas such as "democracy" and "equality" may be used to justify intergroup aggression, as when a minority seeks to defend or extend its rights in the face of predominantly hostile opinion, or when a majority acts to suppress dissent. Most social violence throughout our history can be and has been sanctified in the name of some appeal to Americanism and its values.

It may be, however, that the relatively unproductive character of American civil violence is not an explanation but only a symptom of a deeper explanation for the paradox. Perhaps stability and disorder have been not only something less than opposites, but in some ways related to and even dependent upon each other.

Clearly, much of the violence in our history is a direct result of the enormous diversity of the American population. If Americans have historically been less conscious than other peoples of the horizontal lines that divide classes, and if today in an age of modern communications we tend to eat similar breakfast foods, it still cannot be argued that homogeneity is natural to us. If not in terms of class, then in terms of race, region, and religion, of occupation, association, and origin, we are surely the most diverse of modern nations. That diversity has not been easy for us to come to terms with, and we have often found it simpler to attack each other, under stress, than the institutions that govern us all. But perhaps this diversity has ironically proved, in complex fashion, a kind of bulwark against radical change.

The authors of the Constitution, certainly, after several years of political experience during and after the Revolution, were acutely aware of the differences among this "fractious people." And they sought to design a formal system that would not only account for but use these differences to assure that none of the many interest groups in the new nation could oppress the others. The famous system of checks and balances was explicitly designed to harness conflict, to pit groups and branches of government against each other, to make a strong majority on any issue difficult to achieve. It was intended to prevent rapid or drastic action, to make compromise ultimately essential. And despite later developments such as the party system and the great growth of executive power, it is still true that by comparison with others the American political system requires great energy and much battling to produce even small results.

It may be also that the diversity of American society has had the same muting effect on group hostility as upon the formal operations of government. If the incidence of such hostility has been great, its consequences have been kept small. The many lines that divide our society may also serve after all to unite it. If, for example, the lines of economic class are regarded as horizontal, and those of ethnic or racial division as vertical, then the nation as a whole may be visualized as a great cross-hatched web of groups and associations in which hostility along any single one of the lines is hard to sustain. Just as the working class has often found it difficult to make common cause against employers because it is composed of many mutually suspicious elements—Catholic and Protestant, black and white, Greek and Turk—so ethnic groups find it equally difficult to unite across their own differences of class or association. Conversely, or positively, few groups find themselves totally isolated; ties of party, religion, or other interest have kept farmers and city folk, workingmen and capitalists, from confronting each other along simple lines of implacable division.

The most explosive situations are those in which, as in many cases of black-white conflict, the lines of economic interest and association run parallel with, reinforcing rather than crosscutting, those of race. But even here blacks have found enough support among whites with common interests or sympathies to stop our racial outbreaks well short of massacre.

Intergroup conflict has been persistent throughout American history, but by the standards of late nineteenth-century Russia, or late twentieth-century Bangladesh, it has not been truly genocidal.

This situation, however, cannot be simply taken for granted. No one would deny that our political system has weathered, indeed was partly designed to weather, fairly high levels of domestic turbulence; and the government now commands enormous force with which to quell outbreaks of disorder. But the paradox of stability and violence always implies the question: Will it last? Many observers, including several authors represented in this volume, suggest that problems new in degree or kind, problems wholly unanticipated by James Madison or any other major statesman, now pose serious internal threats to American society. The mechanisms that have contained violent conflict in the past, it is argued, may well be overwhelmed in the future. The implicit debate between this viewpoint and one that rests on the proved resilience of the system that has adapted to two centuries of challenge and change is perhaps the most important of those that run throughout the book.

For most, however, on either side, the issue is not one of stark physical survival, but rather continued existence as a tolerably free and democratic society. Beyond the purely practical questions of tactics, then, are those that involve the achievement of justice and the maintenance of rule by law. Although we have come in recent years to value our national diversity more than ever, as a source of pride and energy, we have not yet solved the problem of peaceful accommodation and justice between groups. We have yet to determine the point at which private resistance to authority is justified or when official use of force becomes repression or when violent confrontation finally subverts the peaceful constitutional mechanisms we have so long upheld. It is hoped that the readings that follow may contribute to an understanding of problems of this character.

Riot, Rout, and Tumult

James Madison

THE FEDERALIST, NUMBER 10

The tenth in the series of Federalist papers, the famous essays published in 1787-88 in support of ratification for the proposed Constitution of the United States, has been cited often as the most important American contribution to political science. The prevailing wisdom was, as it had been for centuries, that popular or republican governments were especially unstable, subject to sudden changes in the composition of the majority, unless the state was so small and its population so homogeneous that there were few differences to divide its citizens. The experience of the individual states prior to adoption of the Constitution seemed to many to confirm this view, as various minority interests complained of arbitrary oppression by popular majorities. But James Madison, author of the tenth essay, argued that a "well-constructed Union" would be less subject to instability or majority tyranny than any one of them alone. The very number of contending "factions" in the United States would preserve stability by tending to prevent any one from imposing its will completely.

Madison's insights, taken more broadly, may be applied to the politics of violence and protest as well as to the constitutional process. The Tenth Federalist *did not anticipate all of the causes that have divided Americans since the Revolution, and not all of the "factional" differences have lost their cutting edge in the manner predicted. But it is a useful place with which to begin the study of the paradox of violence and stability in America, and to judge whether the conditions of the past will continue to operate in the future.*

From *The Federalist* . . . (Hallowell, Me., 1857), 42–48.

Among the numerous advantages promised by a well-constructed Union, none deserves to be more accurately developed than its tendency to break and control the violence of faction. The friend of popular governments never finds himself so much alarmed for their character and fate as when he contemplates their propensity to this dangerous vice. He will not fail, therefore, to set a due value on any plan which, without violating the principles to which he is attached, provides a proper cure for it. The instability, injustice, and confusion introduced into the public councils have, in truth, been the mortal diseases under which popular governments have everywhere perished, as they continue to be the favorite and fruitful topics from which the adversaries to liberty derive their most specious declamations. The valuable improvements made by the American constitutions on the popular models, both ancient and modern, cannot certainly be too much admired; but it would be an unwarrantable partiality to contend that they have as effectually obviated the danger on this side, as was wished and expected. Complaints are everywhere heard from our most considerate and virtuous citizens, equally the friends of public and private faith and of public and personal liberty, that our governments are too unstable, that the public good is disregarded in the conflicts of rival parties, and that measures are too often decided, not according to the rules of justice and the rights of the minor party, but by the superior force of an interested and overbearing majority. However anxiously we may wish that these complaints had no foundation, the evidence of known facts will not permit us to deny that they are in some degree true. It will be found, indeed, on a candid review of our situation, that some of the distresses under which we labor have been erroneously charged on the operation of our governments; but it will be found, at the same time, that other causes will not alone account for many of our heaviest misfortunes; and, particularly, for that prevailing and increasing distrust of public engagements and alarm for private rights which are echoed from one end of the continent to the other. These must be chiefly, if not wholly, effects of the unsteadiness and injustice with which a factious spirit has tainted our public administrations.

By a faction I understand a number of citizens, whether amounting to a majority or minority of the whole, who are united and actuated by some common impulse of passion, or of interest, adverse to the rights of other citizens, or to the permanent and aggregate interests of the community.

There are two methods of curing the mischiefs of faction: the one, by destroying the liberty which is essential to its existence; the other, by giving to every citizen the same opinions, the same passions, and the same interests.

It could never be more truly said than of the first remedy that it was worse than the disease. Liberty is to faction what air is to fire, an ailment without which it instantly expires. But it could not be a less folly to abolish liberty, which is essential to political life, because it nourishes faction than it would be to wish the annihilation of air, which is essential to animal life, because it imparts to fire its destructive agency.

The second expedient is as impracticable as the first would be unwise. As long as the reason of man continues fallible, and he is at liberty to exercise it, different opinions will be formed. As long as the connection subsists between his reason and his self-love, his opinions and his passions will have a reciprocal influence on each other; and the former will be objects to which the latter will attach themselves. The diversity in the faculties of men, from which the rights of property originate, is not less an insuperable obstacle to a uniformity of interests. The protection of these faculties is the first object of government. From the protection of different and unequal faculties of acquiring property, the possession of different degrees and kinds of property immediately results; and from the influence of these on the sentiments and views of the respective proprietors ensues a division of the society into different interests and parties.

The latent causes of faction are thus sown in the nature of man; and we see them everywhere brought into different degrees of activity, according to the different circumstances of civil society. A zeal for different opinions concerning religion, concerning government, and many other points, as well of speculation as of practice; an attachment to different leaders ambitiously contending for pre-eminence and power; or to persons of other descriptions whose fortunes have been interesting to the human passions, have, in turn, divided mankind into parties, inflamed them with mutual animosity, and rendered them much more disposed to vex and oppress each other than to co-operate for their common good. So strong is this propensity of mankind to fall into mutual animosities that where no substantial occasion presents itself the most frivolous and fanciful distinctions have been sufficient to kindle their unfriendly passions and excite their most violent conflicts. But the most common and durable source of factions has been the various and unequal distribution of property. Those who hold and those who are without property have ever formed distinct interests in society. Those who are creditors, and those who are debtors, fall under a like discrimination. A landed interest, a manufacturing interest, a mercantile interest, a moneyed interest, with many lesser interests, grow up of necessity in civilized nations, and divide them into different classes, actuated by different sentiments and views. The regulation of these various and interfering interests forms the principal task of modern legislation and involves the spirit of party and faction in the necessary and ordinary operations of the government.

No man is allowed to be a judge in his own cause, because his interest would certainly bias his judgment, and, not improbably, corrupt his integrity. With equal, nay with greater reason, a body of men are unfit to be both judges and parties at the same time; yet what are many of the most important acts of legislation but so many judicial determinations, not indeed concerning the rights of single persons, but concerning the rights of large bodies of citizens? And what are the different classes of legislators but advocates and parties to the causes which they determine? Is a law proposed concerning private debts? It is a question to which the creditors are parties on one side and the debtors on the other. Justice ought to hold the balance between them. Yet the parties are, and must be, themselves the judges; and the most numerous party, or in other words, the most powerful faction must be expected to prevail. Shall domestic manufactures be encouraged, and in what degree, by restrictions on foreign manufactures? are questions which would be differently decided by the landed and the manufacturing classes, and probably by neither with a sole regard to justice and the public good. The apportionment of taxes on the various descriptions of property is an act which seems to require the most exact impartiality; yet there is, perhaps, no legislative act in which greater opportunity and temptation are given to a predominant party to trample on the rules of justice. Every shilling with which they overburden the inferior number is a shilling saved to their own pockets.

It is in vain to say that enlightened statesmen will be able to adjust these clashing interests and render them all subservient to the public good. Enlightened statesmen will not always be at the helm. Nor, in many cases, can such an adjustment be made at all without taking into view indirect and remote considerations, which will rarely prevail over the immediate interest which one party may find in disregarding the rights of another or the good of the whole.

The inference to which we are brought is that the *causes* of faction cannot be removed and that relief is only to be sought in the means of controlling its *effects.*

If a faction consists of less than a majority, relief is supplied by the republican principle, which enables the majority to defeat its sinister views by regular vote. It may clog the administration, it may convulse the society; but it will be unable to execute and mask its violence under the forms of the Constitution. When a majority is included in a faction, the form of popular government, on the other hand, enables it to sacrifice to its ruling passion or interest both the public good and the rights of other citizens. To secure the public good and private rights against the danger of such a faction, and at the same time to preserve the spirit and the form of popular government, is then the great object to which our inquiries are directed. Let me add that it is the great desideratum by which this form of government can be rescued from the opprobrium under which it has so long labored and be recommended to the esteem and adoption of mankind.

By what means is this object attainable? Evidently by one of two only. Either the existence of the same passion or interest in a majority at the same time must be prevented, or the majority, having such coexistent passion or interest, must be rendered, by their number and local situation, unable to concert and carry into effect schemes of oppression. If the impulse and the opportunity be suffered to coincide, we well know that neither moral nor religious motives can be relied on as an adequate control. They are not found to be such on the injustice and violence of individuals, and lose their efficacy in proportion to the number combined together, that is, in proportion as their efficacy becomes needful.

From this view of the subject it may be concluded that a pure democracy, by which I mean a society consisting of a small number of citizens, who assemble and administer the government in person, can admit of no cure for the mischiefs of faction. A common passion or interest will, in almost every case, be felt by a majority of the whole; a communication and concert result from the form of government itself; and there is nothing to check the inducements to sacrifice the weaker party or an obnoxious individual. Hence it is that such democracies have ever been spectacles of turbulence and contention; have ever been found incompatible with personal security or the rights of property; and have in general been as short in their lives as they have been violent in their deaths. Theoretic politicians, who have patronized this species of government, have erroneously supposed that by reducing mankind to a perfect equality in their political rights, they would at the same time be perfectly equalized and assimilated in their possessions, their opinions, and their passions.

A republic, by which I mean á government in which the scheme of representation takes place, opens a different prospect and promises the cure for which we are seeking. Let us examine the points in which it varies from pure democracy, and we shall comprehend both the nature of the cure and the efficacy which it must derive from the Union.

The two great points of difference between a democracy and a republic are: first, the delegation of the government, in the latter, to a small number of citizens elected by the rest; secondly, the greater number of citizens and greater sphere of country over which the latter may be extended.

The effect of the first difference is, on the one hand, to refine and enlarge the public views by passing them through the medium of a chosen body of citizens, whose wisdom may best discern the true interest of their country and whose patriotism and love of justice will be least likely to sacrifice it to temporary or partial considerations. Under such a regulation it may well happen that the public voice, pronounced by the representatives of the people, will be more consonant to the public good than if pronounced by the people themselves, convened for the purpose. On the other hand, the effect my be inverted. Men of factious tempers, of local prejudices, or of sinister designs, may, by intrigue, by corruption, or by other means, first obtain suffrages, and then betray the interests of the people. The question resulting is, whether small or extensive republics are most favorable to the election of proper guardians of the public weal; and it is clearly decided in favor of the latter by two obvious considerations.

In the first place it is to be remarked that however small the republic may be the representatives must be raised to a certain number in order to guard against the cabals of a few; and that however large it may be they must be limited to a certain number in order to guard against the confusion of a multitude. Hence, the number of representatives in the two cases not being in proportion to that of the two constituents, and being proportionally greatest in the small republic, it follows that if the proportion of fit characters be not less in the large than in the small republic, the former will present a greater option, and consequently a greater probability of a fit choice.

In the next place, as each representative will be chosen by a greater number of citizens in the large than in the small republic, it will be more difficult for unworthy candidates to practice with success the vicious arts by which elections are too often carried; and the suffrages of the people being more free, will be more likely to center on men who possess the most attractive merit and the most diffusive and established characters.

It must be confessed that in this, as in most other cases, there is a mean, on both sides of which inconveniences will be found to lie. By enlarging too much the number of electors, you render the representative too little acquainted with all their local circumstances and lesser interests; as by reducing it too much, you render him unduly attached to these, and too little fit to comprehend and pursue great and national objects. The federal Constitution forms a happy combination in this respect; the great and aggregate interests being referred to the national, the local and in particular to the State legislatures.

The other point of difference is the greater number of citizens and extent of territory which may be brought within the compass of republican than of democratic government; and it is this circumstance principally which renders factious combinations less to be dreaded in the former than in the latter. The smaller the society, the fewer probably will be the distinct parties and interests composing it; the fewer the distinct parties and interests, the more frequently will a majority be found of the same party; and the smaller the number of individuals composing a majority, and the smaller the compass within which they are placed, the more easily will they concert and execute their plans of oppression. Extend the sphere and you take in a greater variety of parties and interests; you make it less probable that a majority of the whole will have a common motive to invade the rights of other citizens; or if such a common motive exists, it will be more difficult for all who feel it to discover their own strength and to act in unison with each other. Besides other impediments, it may be remarked that, where there is a consciousness of unjust or dishonorable purposes, communication is always checked by distrust in proportion to the number whose concurrence is necessary.

Hence, it clearly appears that the same advantage which a republic has over a democracy in controlling the effects of faction is enjoyed by a large over a small republic—is enjoyed by the Union over the States composing it. Does the advantage consist in the substitution of representatives whose enlightened views and virtuous sentiments render them superior to local prejudices and to schemes of injustice? It will not be denied that the representation of the Union will be most likely to possess these requisite endowments. Does it consist in the greater security afforded by a greater variety of parties, against the event of any one party being able to outnumber and oppress the rest? In an equal degree does the increased variety of parties comprised within the Union increase this security. Does it, in fine, consist in the greater obstacles opposed to the concert and accomplishment of the secret wishes of an unjust and interested majority? Here again the extent of the Union gives it the most palpable advantage.

The influence of factious leaders may kindle a flame within their particular States but will be unable to spread a general conflagration through the other States. A religious sect may degenerate into a political faction in a part of the Confederacy; but the variety of sects dispersed over the entire face of it must secure the national councils against any danger from that source. A rage for paper money, for an abolition of debts, for an equal division of property, or for any other improper or wicked project, will be less apt to pervade the whole body of the Union than a particular member of it, in the same proportion as such a malady is more likely to taint a particular county or district than an entire State.

In the extent and proper structure of the Union, therefore, we behold a republican remedy for the diseases most incident to republican government. And according to the degree of pleasure and pride we feel in being republicans ought to be our zeal in cherishing the spirit and supporting the character of federalists.

Michael Wallace

THE USES OF VIOLENCE IN
AMERICAN HISTORY

For nearly a generation after World War II, the United States enjoyed a period of comparative freedom from large-scale domestic turbulence. Many concluded not only that this country, in its prosperous maturity, was immune to further upheaval but that in the past, also, with the significant exception of the Civil War, a superior economy and democratic institutions had protected Americans from serious intergroup conflict. Following the urban riots and student protests of the 1960s, however, social scientists were forced to reexamine both assumptions. And as often happens, their view of the present and the future helped to reshape their view of the past, and vice versa.

The article that follows, written in 1970, provides a survey not only of the kinds of violence that have marked American history but of their social and political uses. Its wide scope serves as a preview of many of the events and movements described elsewhere in this collection. And its perspective, while not always or necessarily contrary to the one employed in the Introduction, is at any rate different. Michael Wallace attempts here not merely to analyze and describe but to advise and even to warn both those who would uphold existing power arrangements and those who would challenge them.

Students of European collective violence once agreed that it was irrational. Recently, scholars like George Rudé, Eric Hobsbawm, E.P. Thompson and

From *The American Scholar* 41, Number 1, Winter, 1970–71, 81–102. Copyright © 1970 by the United Chapters of Phi Beta Kappa. By permission of the publishers.

Charles Tilly have argued that it was in fact purposive, a technique of protest, a demand for change. In this country we have experienced no such debate, partly because we have developed, as has been said, a case of "historical amnesia." We have not argued about the nature of our violent past because we have forgotten we had one. True, when we do consider instances of violence it is assumed that they are pointless and irrational, as the McCone Commission did in its interpretation of the Watts uprising. But this attitude has never inspired an interpretive school or the formation of a revisionist critique.

But *why* have we forgotten about our violence? Two answers seem important here: first, Americans have accepted the Horatio Alger myth, never doubting that ours was a society in which all groups had the opportunity to advance and prosper peacefully. For a variety of reasons—abundance of resources, a frontier safety valve, absence of feudal institutions or class divisions, the two-party system—ours was an open, fluid system. Rising groups easily entered the great middle class; ethnic differences softened and ran together in the great melting pot. The outs had no need for revolutionary violence; the ins, no need for forceful repression. Thus when violence did appear, it had to be dismissed as an inexplicable aberration. Second, with the exception of the Civil War and Reconstruction, only a tiny fraction of our violence has been directed against the state. Perhaps because we have been conditioned by the European experience to consider only anti-state violence truly significant, we have been prone to dismiss the American varieties.

But if we shift our focus on violence and look at its place in relations between groups rather than in relation to the state, violence assumes a much larger significance in our history. It has been one of the widely employed methods used by groups competing for places in the structure of power. Americans have often eschewed the normal electoral processes and have taken their quarrels into the streets. In the main, violence has been used most frequently and effectively by dominant groups seeking to preserve their power and less frequently and less effectively by subordinate groups seeking to protest or improve their situation. The great bulk of our violence, at least until the 1960s, has been *repressive,* rather than expressive or insurrectionary. Much of our violence has also been informal and private, committed by citizens against other citizens. The state was often not a participant, and when it did become intimately involved in the struggles of groups, as in our economic history, it usually played a secondary, assisting role; thus it aroused relatively little violence against itself.

The pattern of violent encounter in three areas—racial, economic and ethnic—supports these propositions. We find in our racial history the violent suppression of blacks by whites; in our economic history, the violent suppression of labor by capital; and in our ethnic history, the violent suppression of recent immigrant groups by more established ones.

Let us begin with racial violence in general and slavery in particular. Violence was a basic device used to change or preserve the system. Blacks used it in full-scale revolts, in individual breaks for freedom, or in attacks on hated masters. Whites used it to repress real or imagined threats to their supremacy. Compared to some other slave societies, slave-initiated violence was relatively slight. The great bulk of the violence came from the masters.

When slaves used violence, they were rigorously dealt with. In reprisal for an uprising in New York City in 1712, eighteen of the rebels were put to death: some were hanged, some were burned at the stake, and one was sentenced to be "burned with a slow fire that he may continue in torment for eight or ten hours, and continue burning in the said fire until he be dead and consumed to ashes." In 1811 five hundred slaves marched on New Orleans, burning plantations, but they were routed, and the heads of sixteen leaders were cut off and stuck up on poles at intervals along the Mississippi. In 1831 Nat Turner and his followers killed at least fifty-seven whites, but were immediately the victims of a countermassacre by roving bands of militia and vigilante groups in which at least one hundred blacks were killed. Twenty others went to the gallows. Thus were the perils of resistance made clear.

It was not necessary for blacks actually to use violence to bring on murderous repression. Although the Vesey conspiracy left whites unharmed in 1822, mass executions quickly followed. Twenty-two blacks were hanged on one day, their bodies left to dangle for hours; dozens more were scheduled for execution but the court stopped when thirty-five were dead, explaining that "the terror of example we thought would be sufficiently operative by the number of criminals sentenced to death." In 1860 some fires in Texas towns produced rumors of an uprising. In Fort Worth, two lists of "black Republicans, abolitionists or higher law men of every class" were prepared: "List no. 1, all suspected persons; no. 2, black list, to be exterminated by immediate hanging." Extermination proceeded through the summer, and an estimated seventy-five were killed, most of them blacks.

This violence is not surprising: under slavery, a system for subordinating and exploiting black people, the use of violence to terrorize and repress was logical. In the North, egalitarian pretensions made repression hypocritical but did not prevent it. Segments of the white communities which felt threatened by the growth and progress of blacks often resorted to violence to contain such advances. Most large cities in the Northeast— Philadelphia, New York, Providence and others— experienced race riots before the Civil War. The riots in Columbia, Pennsylvania, in 1834, although not notably violent, offer an example of how ends not easily achieved within the political process were achieved outside it. The black population of the town had grown with the influx of runaway slaves; many were employed in the lumber yards and several had amassed considerable property; black institutions were established and flourishing. In August of

1834, a recession year and a time of antiblack violence throughout the country, a crowd of whites assaulted the black district, breaking up houses and beating blacks. A few days later the working men of the town met and resolved that

the practice of others in employing Negroes to do that labor which was formerly done entirely by whites, we consider deserving our severest animadversions; . . . Must the poor honest citizens that so long have maintained their families by their labor, fly from their native place that a band of disorderly Negroes may revel with the money that ought to support the white man and his family?

The whites boycotted those who employed blacks and petitioned the town "to devise some means to prevent the further influx of colored persons to this place." These efforts were unavailing and were again supplemented with violence: two more riots saw black homes destroyed and blacks beaten.

This pattern prevailed in the Northwest as well: the frontier, far from liberalizing race relations, worsened them. In Cincinnati, when black population and enterprise grew, upper- and lower-class whites demanded that the local government "take measures to prevent the increase of negro population." In 1829, blacks were given several weeks to leave town or to post a five-hundred-dollar bond for good behavior as required under a dormant law; when these measures proved ineffective, hundreds of whites descended on the black district, beating and destroying, and over a thousand blacks fled the city for Canada.

Racial violence in this period culminated in a wave of wartime draft riots, the worst of which occurred in New York in 1863. These were complicated affairs, involving class and political antagonisms, but a critical aspect was racial. White workers feared the potential challenge of the liberated slaves and resented the continued competition of native blacks in key occupations. During the New York riots blacks were stomped, clubbed, shot or hanged; longshoremen and hotel workers were prime targets. The violence was successful: many blacks were fired by terrified employers, and the black population of the city dropped twenty percent between 1860 and 1865.

The next major period of racial upheaval—Reconstruction—was the most violent period of civil disorder in American history, and violence was fundamental to its outcome. The Northern armies had shattered the Southern social structure and undermined the ruling group, the white plantation owners. Had the North fostered an alliance between the black freedman and the lower-class white by expropriating the plantation owners' land, a social revolution might have been realized. For a multitude of reasons this was not done, but the critical one for our purposes is that the lower-class whites identified with their caste, not their class. In matters of race, after all, they belonged to a dominant group, not a subordinate one. But emancipation had endangered the caste system itself. The story of Reconstruction, then, is the use of violence by normally dominant whites of all classes to repress the challenge of the black freedman, and the use of force by Northern armies, for a time, to protect them. We may take as the Southern whites' rallying cry the demand of an Alabama newspaper that "We must render this either a white man's government, or convert the land into a negro man's cemetery."

White violence in the counterrevolutionary campaign took several forms. The commonest, numbering perhaps in the thousands, involved small-scale assaults against individual blacks who refused to accept the traditionally subordinate role. Black militia leaders, voters, Republicans, Union League organizers, school teachers, pupils, blacks who married whites, quit jobs, or simply were known as local leaders of their race, were systematically terrorized or killed. Somewhat less frequently, guerrilla operations became massive attacks on whole groups of blacks. Thus, in New Orleans in 1866, radicals challenged the 1864 Constitution, which restricted suffrage to whites, by reconvening the Convention. The city's whites, led by the police, mounted a furious assault on the convention hall, firing at the blacks and their white allies within. By the time federal troops arrived, at least thirty-eight were dead and a hundred and forty-six wounded. In Memphis, in 1866, white mobs led by local officials and police burned down black schools, churches and homes, raped and sexually humiliated black women, and shot down black men on sight. Forty-six blacks died and seventy-five to a hundred were wounded. At Laurens, South Carolina, in October, 1870, thirteen were killed and over a hundred wounded; in Texas it was estimated that over a thousand were killed during 1868–70. In Louisiana, General Philip Sheridan estimated that between 1866 and 1875, thirty-five hundred were killed and wounded, mostly blacks. Twenty-five to thirty were killed in 1871 in Meridian, Mississippi, fifty to eighty died at Ellenton, South Carolina, and an estimated eighty perished in the 1875 riots in and around Yazoo City, Mississippi.

Southern blacks did not sit passively while they were slaughtered. They organized in militia companies at the behest of Reconstruction governors and often were employed at election time to intimidate whites or to protect black and Republican voters. Otis Singletary tells us that "Republicans were victorious directly in proportion to their military preparedness." But there were many inherent weaknesses in the militia, and the white radical governors never really dared to employ them fully. They cited the danger of race war, although race war was going on all around them. Had they realized clearly the necessity of relying on armed blacks and mobilized accordingly, the story of Reconstruction might have been different.

Blacks also organized informally to defend themselves, but the odds in weapons and military experience were against them, and resistance often led to slaughter. In Millican, Texas, in 1868, for example, blacks, hearing that a comrade had been lynched, marched on the town in armed formation, led by a black preacher, and attempted to hang the guilty white. Other whites came to his rescue and, in the ensuing shoot-out, twenty blacks and four whites died and at least seventy-five were wounded.

As Reconstruction moved toward an end, whites resorted more and more to insurrectionary violence and directly attacked the Reconstruction states. In September, 1874, in New Orleans, the White League, a paramilitary organization of over twenty-five thousand men, including the largest property holders of the state, demanded that radical Governor William Kellogg resign. He refused and ordered his Adjutant General, James A. Longstreet of Confederate fame, to rally the militia, largely black, and join with the police to defend the government; he then took refuge in the federal Customs House. The White League forces put up barricades in the street, captured city hall and the telegraph office, routed Longstreet's forces, took the state house and effected a *coup d'etat*; total casualties were twenty-seven dead and over a hundred wounded. But President Grant supported Kellogg, and federal troops put down the insurrection peacefully, for the insurgents declined to resist federal force. Although the insurgents were temporarily repulsed, this was the beginning of the end for the Reconstruction government. In 1877, when the national government refused to use force to underwrite the regime, it collapsed.

The struggle to preserve the caste system did not end with the overthrow of Reconstruction. In the years of the Populist movement in the late 1880s and 1890s when the whites did split along class lines, blacks were able to participate in coalition governments and to hold public office again. In addition, a new generation of black people had arisen, the first born out of slavery and free of whatever internalized restraints slavery created. Whites met the challenge of the blacks with repressive violence.

To some extent it was large-scale. The whites of Wilmington, North Carolina, for example, infuriated by office-holding blacks, announced in 1898, "we will not live under these intolerable conditions. . . . We intend to change it, if we have to choke the current of Cape Fear River with negro carcasses!" The whites rioted, murdered blacks, and effected a *coup d'etat*. Increasingly, however, lynching became the preferred form of repressive violence. Between 1882 and 1927, about five thousand persons were lynched in the United States, seventy percent of them black. Many lynchings were by summary hanging or shooting, but many, in keeping with the desire to terrorize blacks into subordination, were spectacles of sadism. In 1899, at Palmetto, Georgia, excursion trains brought thousands on a Sunday afternoon to see a black man burned alive, but only after his ears, toes and fingers were cut off and passed to the crowd, his eyes gouged, his tongue torn out, and his flesh cut in strips with knives; afterward, his heart was cut out and slices of it were sold for souvenirs. In May, 1911, a black charged with murder was taken to the local opera house in Livermore, Kentucky, and tied on stage to a stake. Tickets were sold, and orchestra seats entitled men to empty their revolvers into the victim. Gallery seats gave them one shot apiece. In 1918 there was a five-day orgy of killing in Georgia, in which eight blacks died, one pregnant woman was slowly roasted alive, and her baby cut out and trampled. The charges on which such atrocities were based ranged from murder and rape to such offenses against the racial system as striking or talking back to whites, testifying against whites, making boastful remarks, or using offensive language.

With the coming of the twentieth century, lynching began its slow decline, and race riots became the main form of conflict between the dominant and subordinate groups. Increasingly, most outbreaks occurred in the North because blacks, spurred by the employment opportunities of two world wars, had migrated in enormous numbers to the North. Their coming posed a tremendous challenge to those whites in the lower rungs of the economy who had to confront increased competition for jobs, housing and recreational facilities. The challenge was sharpened by the increasing refusal of blacks, many of them veterans, to accept discrimination. A common white response was massive violent assaults on black communities.

At East St. Louis in 1917 employers broke strikes by hiring migrant blacks, and the fury and frustration of white laborers grew and was fanned by politicians. After a small riot failed to terrorize blacks into leaving, the whites resorted to all-out violence in July. Streetcars were stopped, blacks were pulled off, stoned, clubbed, kicked, shot, stomped and knifed. Mobs, thousands strong, roamed the streets chanting, "Get a nigger, get another." Most blacks were terrified into passivity, although at one point a hundred barricaded themselves in a building and shot it out with the mob. Nine whites and thirty-nine blacks were killed. In Chicago, the black population had doubled between 1916 and 1919. Beatings, bombings and murders marked the boundary line between white and expanding black territories. Then, on July 27, a black youth swimming in Lake Michigan floated past the imaginary boundary line separating white from black beach. He was stoned by whites and drowned. Blacks demanded that the police arrest the whites. Instead they arrested the complainants, touching off a riot that after seven days found twenty blacks and fifteen whites dead, over five hundred and thirty-seven injured, and about a thousand homeless. In 1921, in Tulsa, Oklahoma, blacks armed to protect an accused black rapist from the usual lynch mob. They clashed with police, and the white community, infuriated, organized a small army, led by American Legionnaires, that invaded the black district, burning and shooting. The entire area, one mile square, was burnt to the ground. Perhaps as many as a hundred and fifty men, women and children perished.

The 1940s brought another transformation in racial violence. With the exception of wartime riots in Detroit and Los Angeles, massive confrontations between black and white citizens ceased. Huge black ghettos developed, peopled with much more militant blacks. It was no longer safe to attempt forays into fortresses like Harlem. Whites themselves increasingly moved to suburban strongholds isolated from contact with blacks. Postwar prosperity alleviated many of the economic pressures on whites that had made them vulnerable to black advances. The burden of containing subordinate groups was left to one specialized segment of the white community: the police.*

Police violence is not "police brutality," a misleading term that implies that violent acts are aberrant phenomena, the product of a few sadists. Police violence in this instance is an outgrowth of the task that police have been assigned by the white community: to patrol the borders of the ghetto. The police treat blacks as a deviant or criminal group like, say, prostitutes, to be restricted to certain territories, black light districts if you will. By such procedures as "aggressive preventative patrols," roving task forces conduct intensive and indiscriminate stops and searches, obtaining dossiers on sizeable portions of the community; by using violence against blacks who in any way challenge their authority, they keep the subordinate group in line. James Baldwin summed up the system neatly when he said that the police

represent the force of the white world, and that world's real intentions are, simply, for that world's criminal profit and ease, to keep the black man corraled up here, in his place. The badge, the gun in the holster, and the swinging club make vivid what will happen should his rebellion become overt.

Lest anyone should assume that police violence is limited to southern sheriffs, let us remember that, at the time of this writing, twenty-eight members of the Black Panther party have met violent death at police hands. Thus are the perils of resistance made clear.

As the pattern of white repression changed, so did that of black resistance. A utilization of violence as protest developed in a fashion reminiscent of the European crowd violence that Rudé and Hobsbawm analyzed. The new style occurred first in Harlem in 1935. Ghetto conditions, aggravated by the Depression, brought organized protest, but attempts at producing change via the political process failed. A Jobs for Negroes campaign, which boycotted Harlem stores refusing to employ blacks, was broken by injunctions, and police violence against demonstrations was a commonplace. Harlemites finally erupted on hearing rumors of an incident of police violence. Policemen, symbols of white authority, were assaulted, and those

*There are two general exceptions to this. First is the white bombing campaign of the 1950s against blacks who tried to follow them to the suburbs. Second is the violent campaign against the civil rights movement of the late 1950s and 1960s in which dozens were killed and hundreds injured. Much of this violence was by private terrorist groups or individuals but, in line with the newer trend, much was by southern law enforcement agents; indeed, the two groups often had overlapping memberships.

stores that had been picketed unsuccessfully before were now burned to the ground. The commission that investigated the riot dismissed charges of Communist instigation and insisted that the riot was a protest against discrimination, unemployment and police violence. But the message failed to get through. Although there were some positive responses to the Harlem 1935 riot and to the hundreds that followed it in the 1960s, the basic situation of America's subordinate racial group has not changed; and a disturbingly characteristic response of dominant whites has been to develop more effective means of violent suppression.

We move now from racial violence to economic violence, from considerations of caste to considerations of class. Economic violence encompasses far more than the industrial violence that we usually associate with it. We have had, for example, food riots, bank riots, tollgate riots, Luddite violence, anti-rent disturbances, agrarian land riots, squatters' riots and anti-eviction riots. But considerations of space force me to restrict my focus to the more familiar field of relations between capital and labor.

Labor's challenge to capital began early in the nineteenth century. Workers were unable to better their conditions peacefully because the formation of unions was defined as criminal. Wildcat strikes, often accomplished by violence, were common. Outbursts against superintendents, business property or strikebreakers occurred in enterprises like railroads, canals, waterworks and mills. Ethnic communities, particularly Irish ones, provided the organizational basis. Thus canal workers rioted near Harrisburg in 1828, Irish workers on the Baltimore and Ohio Railroad beat up contractors and demolished their homes in 1829, and there were violent outbreaks on the Croton waterworks in 1840. These early communal outbursts were replaced by the more disciplined efforts of trade unions; when this happened, labor-initiated violence dropped sharply.

A major response of American capitalism to the challenge of labor, peaceful or not, was violence. Recently Philip Taft and Philip Ross found the pervasiveness of violence in American labor disputes "paradoxical" in light of the nonideological nature of our working class and their rejection of force as a method of achieving change. The "paradox" comes from looking in the wrong direction. The point is that the most moderate labor demands have called forth ferocious resistance; our "labor violence," in fact, might be more aptly renamed "capitalist violence."

From the first manifestations of unrest much effort went into developing effective means of repression. Increasingly, capitalists gained the assistance of the state. From the 1850s to the 1870s, according to a study in progress by Dennis Van Essendelft, militia units evolved from the traditional citizens' army into mobile compact forces that could deal with the rising disorders of urbanizing, industrializing America. Until 1877, the militia was supplemented by the Regular Army; as one Congressman found in 1878: "Generals commanding military departments, north, south and

east, report the employment, hundreds of times, of hundreds of detachments of the standing army in the suppression of strikes." After the Great
Strike of 1877, emphasis returned to the militia: William Riker has found
that states spent money on expanding the militia in direct proportion to the
amount of strike activity the state experienced. Armories sprouted in American cities to defend the better classes against the dangerous classes. New
York, for example, constructed armories in forty districts at a cost of twenty
million dollars.

American capitalists did not put all their eggs in the government's
basket, however. They developed private resources of violence: economic
Hessians like the Pinkertons, Baldwin-Felts, the Coal and Iron Police.
Often the line between public and private means of violence, already largely
meaningless, was effaced completely: employers' hired guns were transformed into a public force by having compliant sheriffs or marshals depu-
tize them, instantly cloaking them with the privileges and immunities of
the law.

The catalog of industrial violence is staggering. Many of the bloodiest
incidents occurred in the extractive industries, in the small coal towns or
silver mines, where the absence of limiting institutions led to straight-out
warfare. The spectacular affairs that took place in isolated mountain communities like Ludlow, Cripple Creek and Coeur D'Alene are well known.
But how many have heard of the violence at, say, Morewood Mine, Pennsylvania, where in 1891 sheriffs' deputies shot and killed eleven Hungarian
coal miners and wounded more than fifty of them? Or at Latimer, Pennsylvania, where over twenty died and over ninety were wounded; or the thirty
deaths at Mucklow, West Virginia, when Baldwin-Felts and militiamen used
armored trains to attack strikers?

Violence came to the cities as well. Some incidents are well known, like
the crushing of the 1877 railroad strike in which scores of workers were
killed, or the suppression of the 1919 strike against U.S. Steel, in which the
owners mobilized over twenty-five thousand armed men. But there were
hundreds of other incidents, such as transit strikes like the one in Chicago in
1905, in which fourteen strikers were killed, hundreds wounded and over
fifteen hundred arrested; or that in Denver in 1920 where federal troops
broke a strike at a cost of seven dead and eighty-one wounded. There were
strikes in the clothing industry, like Chicago's of 1910, in which forty thousand walked out, and private guards killed seven and wounded many more.

Violence came to the fields. In the South, where much of the rural
labor force was black, violence was particularly vicious—and effective. In
1887 nine thousand blacks working the Louisiana sugar plantations, together with a thousand whites, struck for one dollar a day. The planters
persuaded the governor to send in the militia, which shot into a crowd of
strikers at Pattersonville, killing several. Strike leaders were lynched. Finally, at Thibodaux, the "most prominent citizens" organized a private vigi-

lante force, massacred thirty-five strikers, and broke the strike. In 1919, when black Arkansas sharecroppers formed a union, their meetings were shot up; when the blacks fired back and killed some attackers, whites went on a week-long rampage, hunting out blacks in the countryside and killing them. Estimates of the murdered run from fifty to over two hundred.

Not all the violence was directed against organized labor or strikers. During depressions, when unemployed victims of the business cycle, either spontaneously or led by radical organizations, demanded bread and work, they were swiftly beaten into quiescence. In 1874, club-swinging police dispersed a mass meeting of seven thousand men, women and children gathered in Tompkins Square Park in New York City to back demands for a program of public works. The press enthusiastically commended repression of the unemployed, denounced their spirit as "communistic," and urged the authorities, should a similar spirit emerge, to "club it to death at the hands of the police or shoot it to death at the hands of the militia." In the depression of the 1890s, police tangled with the tramps and industrial (non-violent) armies and urban unemployed spawned by the hard times. In 1932, when unemployed workers organized by the Communist party marched on Henry Ford's Dearborn plant with a list of demands, the mayor, a relative of Ford's, told the chief of police, a former security chief of Ford's, to disperse them; this was done, with firehoses, pistols and a machine gun, killing four and wounding more.

Labor fought back when not hopelessly outmatched, or accepted defeat and tried again. But they seldom initiated violence against employers, except to destroy their property. Dynamite was a popular counterweapon at certain periods: in the 1880s, a virtual cult developed around it as the great equalizer. But the bulk of labor violence was directed against members of their own class. As workers climbed the economic ladder, they reacted violently against real or imagined threats to their hard-won positions. Massacres of scabs were all too common occurrences, often made easier by racial or ethnic antagonisms.

Probably the worst campaign of labor violence was that directed against the Chinese. Many incidents did not involve actual scabbing by the Orientals; rather, workers detested these men who worked for low wages, rejected American culture, and were hired in bulk in a fashion reminiscent of slavery. White workers responded with a blend of political action, leading to the legal restriction of Chinese immigration, and direct terrorism. The first major outburst came in Los Angeles in 1871, when eighteen Chinese, some children, were shot or hanged. Waves of riots and raids drove Chinese out of towns all over California in the 1870s; homes were destroyed, many persons were killed. This period was capped by riots in San Francisco and Chico in 1877. Even after the exclusion law was passed, anti-Chinese violence continued, particularly during depressions or periods of large-scale organizing. In 1885, members of a fledgling Knights of Labor local at

Rocksprings, Wyoming, furious because the Union Pacific hired Chinese to ward off strikes, killed twenty-eight Orientals in a gruesome massacre.

The massive series of violent confrontations between capital and labor continued for about sixty years and amounted to an industrial war. A truce was called in the 1930s, when labor's strength had grown to such proportions that violence became too expensive and counterproductive and the state withdrew from its role of arms supplier. But for three score years the use of violence was a commonplace in the struggle for economic power in America.

When we turn to ethnic conflict, we find a similar pattern of violent clashes. There are innumerable instances of armed encounters between ethnic groups to establish or contest control of territory; in the nineteenth century the formation of armed, ethnic self-defense groups was a commonplace. But the history of ethnic conflict differs significantly from the pattern of economic or racial violence. While the bulk of ethnic violence was repressive, as dominant, established immigrant groups resisted newcomers, the wavelike character of the migrations and the multiplicity of groups prevented the formation of a rigid ethnic hierarchy; that is, there was never an overwhelmingly predominant group for very long. Ethnic conflicts were thus seldom as lopsided as economic or racial clashes.

Another consequence of this relative balance of power was that no single ethnic group controlled the state in the way that whites and capitalists did. The state came close to being what it was supposed to be in theory: open to control by any group mustering sufficient electoral strength. And it was a prize worth competing for. It could enforce the cultural norms of any group by legislative fiat. Much ethnic violence resulted from such state action, as when Germans in Chicago rioted in 1855 over the closing of beer halls on Sunday or when, in 1844, the decision of Philadelphia authorities to allow the use of non-Protestant bibles in public shools so aroused the native population that two riots against Irish Catholics ensued, in which dozens were killed.

In addition to direct ecological warfare, and reactions to state policies, there was a third type of ethnic violence, the election riot, in which groups fought to gain control of the state. This extraordinary phenomenon was a blend of constitutionalism and insurrectionary violence that may have been peculiarly American. Ethnic groups—too constitutional to resort to ethnic coups, and too eager to limit themselves to constitutional methods—hit on the procedure of keeping opponents away from the polls. They did so by force, by terror or by murder. Yet no matter how violent the election, the outcome was considered valid. Groups fought to control the polls at least as early as the Bloody Election of 1742 in Philadelphia, but the election riot reached its peak as immigrants packed into the cities in the 1840s and 1850s. Scores were killed in riots at Louisville, New Orleans, Cincinnati, New

York and Philadelphia. Marines were called out in 1857 to put down an attempted nativist seizure of the Washington polls by groups carrying blacksmith sledges, revolvers, bowie knives, slingshots and cannon.

But the art was raised to its highest in Baltimore where innumerable ethnic street gangs became politicized after 1854 and turned out en masse on election day. They devised a whole panoply of methods for eliminating opponents. The Blood Tubs, for example, threw venturesome Irishmen into tubs of blood obtained from local butchers, then chased them down the street with knives. This was a most potent deterrent to would-be voters. Another strategy was to strap sharp shoemakers' awls to knees and gouge holes in persistent opponents. These tactics inevitably provoked retaliation, and full-scale street warfare would begin. The Know Nothing groups in Maryland, representing the established Protestants, were spectacularly successful, winning local and state contests and, in 1856, the presidential election; in many districts, not a single immigrant managed to cast a ballot.

Such riots did not end in the 1850s. They were common during Reconstruction, when they served a racial function, and they were characteristic of the South long after the 1870s. Catholics and Protestants fought on election days in the heyday of the American Protective Association in the 1890s, and the Klan and its opponents occasionally struggled for control of the polls in the 1920s. In sum, election riots were one of the primary ways in which ethnic groups battled for hegemony.

Much of America's violence, then, has been between groups struggling for power: conflicts have repeatedly skidded out of the normal political process. Much of the violence took the form of direct confrontation, although in many instances the state did aid one of the contending sides, almost always the dominant one. And American violence has been characteristically repressive: the great bulk of it was used by dominant groups defending their positions of privilege. Strikes have been crushed, slave revolts put down, peaceful growth of black communities blocked, abolitionists mobbed or killed, civil rights workers beaten or killed, thousands of blacks lynched, ethnic newcomers mobbed and kept from the polls, and radical labor organizations broken up.

This is not to deny a tradition of violence by the oppressed in our history. We have had slave revolts, agrarian rebellions (particularly in the colonial period when even *formal* opposition was considered illegitimate), and labor violence like that of the Molly Maguires. But three things are striking about such violence: its relative scarcity (our bread riots and Luddite violence were faint echoes of vigorous European traditions, for example); its characteristically low level (subordinate groups have engaged far more often in acts of force than of violence, and even their violence has been primarily directed against property rather than persons); its lack of challenge to the legitimacy of the state (such revolutionary violence as has occurred has come from the *right,* from displaced dominant groups, as during Reconstruction and the Civil War).

But this poses an important question. Why has there been so little expressive or revolutionary violence by subordinate groups throughout our history? I do not presume to have a simple explanation, but I offer a series of suggestions. It is best to start with the most obvious. To be subordinate is not automatically to be rebellious. I think that, on a gross level, Louis Hartz's notion of a Lockean consensus is largely correct: most groups at the bottom of the social and economic scale have not raised *fundamental* objections to the nature of bourgeois, capitalist America. They have attempted to become part of it, to get "more," in Samuel Gompers' words. Violence, therefore, would have been a most inappropriate tactic. Those who do not want to overthrow, but to be admitted, generally avoid violence. Still, there has been no lack of dissatisfied, angry groups who might readily have turned to violence to better their lot, so this explanation is not sufficient.

One reason why the anger was not turned against the *state* grows out of the peculiar nature of our repressive violence: the informal, nongovernmental nature of much of it. Subordinate groups have often suffered more violence from dominant groups than from the state. In race riots, lynchings, strike-smashing by private armies, massacres of scabs and Chinese by laborers, ethnic clashes, election riots, actions against civil rights workers, and vigilante terrorism, the state was simply not responsible for the bloodshed. It could not, therefore, be easily blamed, or become the focus for violent response. But often the state did actively engage in violence without producing lasting resentment against itself. Why was this so? Why were workers who were crushed by troops not turned into potential revolutionaries? Again there are many explanations, including the realities of power, the ethnic and racial divisions among the working class, and the vitiating effects of bourgeois ideology, but perhaps one explanation is that the state was considered to be a satellite, firmly within the orbit of some dominant social group. This may partly account for why it was seldom held directly and primarily responsible.

This dismissal of the state is a deeply ingrained American trait. It is the essence of the vigilante tradition that when there is serious work to be done, the community does it itself: it "takes the law into its own hands." Partly this attitude is a product of the weakness of the early American state, particularly on the frontier, but also in urban areas, where police forces were slow to develop. Partly it is due to the fragmentation of the American state into nation, state, county, town and city governments, many of them often at odds with one another. More directly, the dismissal of the state is related to the way decisions have been made in this country. A large number of critical decisions about the allocation of power and privilege have been in private arenas. Determinations about control of the economy, ethnic hegemony, and racial power have often been made not in legislatures, but in the marketplace, if you will. Subordinate groups have not been accustomed to looking at the *laissez-faire* national state as a potential source of remedial action. Labor, for example, organized not parties to influence the state, but unions to confront capitalists directly. Perhaps anti-state violence has also seemed irrelevant to subordinate groups accustomed to thinking of the state as amorphous and secondary.*

Two traditional explanations for nonviolence by the discontented I have space only to mention. There is the important fact that the bulk of the white male population was integrated into the *formal* political process quite early in the nation's history. We had a voting proletariat before we had an organized proletariat. Secondly, individuals belonging to a discontented subordinate group in, say, an economic capacity might belong to a dominant racial group, and thus feel represented by the state in at least some manner. Both these facts would lessen the likelihood of anti-state violence.

A final, seemingly simple explanation for the relative nonviolence of the oppressed is that our subordinate groups have been *minorities*. They have been outnumbered. They have been outgunned. The relatively pacific history of Afro-Americans, for example, can most readily be explained in terms of the realities of power. They have been only ten or fifteen percent of the population. And while blacks occasionally did resort to violence against great odds, particularly during slavery, they have consistently avoided *revolutionary* action, and with good reason. Even if they successfully overthrew the government they would only have to rule the other hostile eighty-five or ninety percent. The direction that angry blacks have taken is either emigration, or the formation of some kind of autonomous structure within the larger community, in which they would be, at the least, a clear majority.

The question of numbers cuts deeper than mere tactical considerations, however: it goes to the root of the nature of our violence. America is peculiar in that our dominant groups have been, for the most part, *majorities*. American history has been a great success story (in purely material terms) for a large proportion of the population. Because the majority of the people (and "majority" includes *elites* as well as *masses*) has benefited from the economic structure of the nation, they have been conservative, determined to hold what they have. They have repeatedly seen attempts to partake of that success by those excluded—the poor, the blacks, the ethnic minorities, the unions—as imperiling their own position. They repeatedly repressed such challenges. And because they were majorities, in a nation that exalted the power of the majority and placed only feeble restrictions in

*Perhaps, also, this is changing, as blacks and radicals now clearly perceive the national state as a source of both oppression and possible relief. Perhaps the assumption by the state of the task of repressing blacks that was previously performed by masses of whites might yet elicit an even more direct antistate response than the antipolice violence of the rebellions of the 1960s.

its path, there was little to stop them from resorting to violence if they chose to; and little to keep even that violence within "civilized" boundaries, once employed.

I would like to suggest the relevance here of the worn idea that tyranny is a product of unchecked power, and particularly of Tocqueville's application of that dictum to majorities. Listen to his fears voiced more than a hundred and thirty years ago, and apply them to the plight of the black man, of that day or this:

> When an individual or a party is wronged in the United States, to whom can he apply for redress? If to public opinion, public opinion constitutes the majority; if to the legislature, it represents the majority and implicitly obeys it; if to the executive power, it is appointed by the majority and serves as a passive tool in its hands. The public force consists of the majority under arms; the jury is the majority invested with the right of hearing judicial cases; and in certain states even the judges are elected by the majority. However iniquitous or absurd the measure of which you complain, you must submit to it as well as you can.

What has much of our violence been but the ultimate form of the tyranny of the majority? Certainly this has been true of our racial history. The vigilante impulse has been central to the white American mind.

Our industrial violence is more complicated. It is true that union members, and even the poor, have been a minority in this country, but industrialists have been numerically even fewer than workers. The crucial fact is that the values of the capitalists were accepted by a majority of the country: a sufficiently monolithic consensus existed to ensure that the interests of the economic elite would be respected. The widespread diffusion of property, and the Horatio Alger mythology (which assured those who did not have a stake in the existing order that they eventually would), bolstered the power of the industrialists. They were able to transmute a defense of privilege into a defense of something more abstract, more acceptable to the majority: the defense of law, order and property. Unions, particularly when largely composed of aliens, were branded as dangers to the existing order; labeling them anarchist or Communist helped isolate them. As a consequence, the majority did not check, but indeed acquiesced in, the resort to repressive violence by the economic elite.

The absence of restraint is a critical factor. Here again the work of Louis Hartz is illuminating when he speaks of the absence in America of powerful institutions that were Europe's inheritance from feudalism. Stanley Elkins applied this insight to the nature of American slavery, arguing that the absence of institutional checks of profit-oriented masters produced a particularly harsh system. We need not agree with all of Elkins' thesis to suspect that the idea is important for the character of American industrial capitalism. For its growth was essentially unchecked, certainly unchecked by a state that for much of our history accepted the principle of *laissez-faire* when it came to regulating business, but that, when it came to assisting it, became so integrated with the economy as to be almost indistinguishable from it. Industrialists developed a logical ruthlessness, and a disregard for human life that is perhaps the inevitable outgrowth of virtually unchecked power.

I am aware that I have passed over a host of ambiguities and subtleties. I am convinced, however, that when they are all taken into account, the pattern I have sketched, at this level of generalization, remains unchanged. It may be objected, for example, that the groups I have discussed are far from monolithic. Of course, there are many varieties of capitalists: industrialists, merchants, financiers, and so on; and divisions among them are important in determining the time, intensity, duration and nature of violent episodes. But capitalists are capitalists; their differences often dissolve in the face of a common enemy. For all practical purposes, on the broad question of dealing with labor during the industrial war, they were in substantial agreement; dissenters didn't affect the course of events significantly. It may be objected that there are difficulties in measuring intentions and purposiveness, particularly when dealing with crowds. But to avoid generalizations because in specific cases we lack direct evidence of the mind of participants is to be unnecessarily fastidious. We are dealing, after all, with *patterns* of events, as the lynching of blacks by whites, thousands of times, often in a public ritual fashion, for transgressions against the caste system. Granting that many crowd (or elite) actions are undisciplined, and at times partake of the psychopathological, the overall pattern clearly bespeaks social intentionality. Crowds are not irrational herds, nor are they mechanistic bodies reacting reflexively to stimuli like "relative deprivation": they are acting politically—with passion perhaps, but usually with a clear sense of what they are about.

Finally, if it be objected that I have not discussed many other types of purposive violence, I would agree. We are just beginning to probe this area. There are many kinds of domestic violence to be considered: vigilantism; the repression of antiwar groups, political and cultural radicals, and abolitionists; crime; our own war of national liberation, the greatest single incident of purposive violence, the Civil War. I have not discussed our use of violence against other people: the Indian and Mexican wars, by which we gained our continent, the wars by which we gained our empire, or the interventions all over the world, including Vietnam, by which we seek to maintain it. There are intriguing questions about the *interaction* between our domestic and exported violence that have been passed over. Why is it, for example, that almost without exception the greatest outbreaks of racial violence in our history have come in wartime—in 1863, 1917–19, 1943, 1964–68, with lesser outbreaks in other war periods, like 1740 and 1898? Conversely, how has America's pervasive racism and readiness to use violence against Indians and blacks affected our imperialist ventures? In our repression of the Philippine insurrection, our rationalization for violence was that the Filipinos were an inferior race that we had a duty to civilize. (It is noteworthy that in those lynching days our troops, including officers, habitually referred to the Filipinos whom they killed and tortured, and whose huts they burned, as "niggers.") And when all these aspects of our violence have been explored, it will remain to be seen how our history compares with that of other countries, but it is not too early to suggest that the use of violence has been a fundamental and grim characteristic of the American past.

Pauline Maier

POPULAR UPRISINGS AND CIVIL AUTHORITY IN EIGHTEENTH-CENTURY AMERICA

Mob violence has exerted a powerful influence throughout American history. For more than three centuries, mobs were involved at some stage in almost every crucial development leading to the formation of the American nation and the transformation of the United States from a rural agrarian state to an urban industrial world power.

To a large extent, the impact of mobs on a particular period or event has been determined by the specific political, social, economic, and intellectual context within which they occur. Revolutionary uprisings, such as the Stamp Act riots, were in some ways different from the antiabolition mobs of the next century and the contemporary rioters who recently exploded in the cities or protested the war in Vietnam. At the same time, according to some scholars, these mobs are linked together by certain common characteristics regardless of century. They argue that the process by which mobs are formed tends to be the same and that their activities are roughly similar. Responding to real or imagined grievances or dangers, mobs usually pursue limited action against a selective target, see their action as legitimate and necessary, and are generally noninsurrectionary.

In the article that follows, Pauline Maier examines eighteenth-century uprisings within a political environment that accepted such tumult as an appropriate expression of community interest and control. Her analysis distinguishes features of these insurgencies that are parallel to and different from those mob activities described elsewhere in this volume.

From *William and Mary Quarterly*, 3d ser., 27 (1970): 3–35. Reprinted by permission of the author.

It is only natural that the riots and civil turbulence of the past decade and a half have awakened a new interest in the history of American mobs. It should be emphasized, however, that scholarly attention to the subject has roots independent of contemporary events and founded in long-developing historiographical trends. George Rudé's studies of pre-industrial crowds in France and England, E. J. Hobsbawm's discussion of "archaic" social movements, and recent works linking eighteenth-century American thought with English revolutionary tradition have all, in different ways, inspired a new concern among historians with colonial uprisings.[1] This discovery of the early American mob promises to have a significant effect upon historical interpretation. Particularly affected are the Revolutionary struggle and the early decades of the new nation, when events often turned upon well-known popular insurrections.

Eighteenth-century uprisings were in some important ways different than those of today—different in themselves, but even more in the political context within which they occurred. As a result they carried different connotations for the American Revolutionaries than they do today. Not all eighteenth-century mobs simply defied the law: some used extralegal means to implement official demands or to enforce laws not otherwise enforceable, others in effect extended the law in urgent situations beyond its technical limits. Since leading eighteenth-century Americans had known many occasions on which mobs took on the defense of the public welfare, which was, after all, the stated purpose of government, they were less likely to deny popular upheavals all legitimacy than are modern leaders. While not advocating popular uprisings, they could still grant such incidents an established and necessary role in free societies, one that made them an integral and even respected element of the political order. These attitudes, and the tradition of colonial insurrections on which they drew, not only shaped political events of the Revolutionary era, but also lay behind many laws and civil procedures that were framed during the 1780's and 1790's, some of which still have a place in the American legal system.

I

Not all colonial uprisings were identical in character or significance. Some involved no more than disorderly vandalism or traditional brawls such as those that annually marked Pope's Day on November 5, particularly in New England. Occasional insurrections defied established laws and authorities in the name of isolated private interests alone—a set of Hartford County, Connecticut, landowners arose in 1722, for example, after a court decision imperiled their particular land titles. Still others—which are of interest here—took on a broader purpose, and defended the interests of their community in general where established authorities failed to act.[2] This common characteristic linked otherwise diverse rural uprisings in New Jersey and the Carolinas. The insurrectionists' punishment of outlaws, their interposition to secure land titles or prevent abuses at the hands of legal officials followed a frustration with established institutions and a belief that justice and even security had to be imposed by the people directly.[3] The earlier Virginia tobacco insurrection also illustrates this common pattern well: Virginians began tearing up young tobacco plants in 1682 only after Governor Thomas Culpeper forced the quick adjournment of their assembly, which had been called to curtail tobacco planting during an economic crisis. The insurrections in Massachusetts a little over a century later represent a variation on this theme. The insurgents in Worcester, Berkshire, Hampshire, Middlesex, and Bristol counties—often linked together as members of "Shays's Rebellion"—forced the closing of civil courts, which threatened to send a major portion of the local population to debtors' prison, only until a new legislature could remedy their pressing needs.[4]

This role of the mob as extralegal arm of the community's interest emerged, too, in repeated uprisings that occurred within the more densely settled coastal areas. The history of Boston, where by the mid-eighteenth century "public order . . . prevailed to a greater degree than anywhere else in England or America," is full of such incidents. During the food shortage of 1710, after the governor rejected a petition from the Boston selectmen calling for a temporary embargo on the exportation of foodstuffs one heavily laden ship found its rudder cut away, and fifty men sought to haul another outward bound vessel back to shore. Under similar circumstances Boston mobs again intervened to keep foodstuffs in the colony in 1713 and 1729. When there was some doubt a few years later whether or not the selectmen had the authority to seize a barn lying in the path of a proposed street, a group of townsmen, their faces blackened, levelled the structure and the road went through. Houses of ill fame were attacked by Boston mobs in 1734, 1737, and 1771; and in the late 1760's the *New York Gazette* claimed that mobs in Providence and Newport had taken on responsibility for "disciplining" unfaithful husbands. Meanwhile in New London, Connecticut, another mob prevented a radical religious sect, the Rogerenes, from disturbing normal Sunday services, "a practice they . . . [had] followed more or less for many years past; and which all the laws made in that government, and executed in the most judicious manner could not put a stop to."[5]

Threats of epidemic inspired particularly dramatic instances of this community oriented role of the mob. One revealing episode occurred in Massachusetts in 1773-1774. A smallpox hospital had been built on Essex Island near Marblehead "much against the will of the multitude" according to John Adams. "The patients were careless, some of them wantonly so;

and others were suspected of designing to spread the smallpox in the town, which was full of people who had not passed through the distemper." In January 1774 patients from the hospital who tried to enter the town from unauthorized landing places were forcefully prevented from doing so; a hospital boat was burned; and four men suspected of stealing infected clothes from the hospital were tarred and feathered, then carted from Marblehead to Salem in a long cortege. The Marblehead town meeting finally won the proprietors' agreement to shut down the hospital; but after some twenty-two new cases of smallpox broke out in the town within a few days "apprehension became general," and some "Ruffians" in disguise hastened the hospital's demise by burning the nearly evacuated building. A military watch of forty men were needed for several nights to keep the peace in Marblehead. [6]

A similar episode occurred in Norfolk, Virginia, when a group of wealthy residents decided to have their families inoculated for smallpox. Fears arose that the lesser disease brought on by the inoculations would spread and necessitate a general inoculation, which would cost "more money than is circulating in Norfolk" and ruin trade and commerce such that "the whole colony would feel the effects." Local magistrates said they could not interfere because "the law was silent in the matter." Public and private meetings then sought to negotiate the issue. Despite a hard-won agreement, however, the pro-inoculation faction persisted in its original plan. Then finally a mob drove the newly inoculated women and children on a five-mile forced march in darkness and rain to the common Pest House, a three-year old institution designed to isolate seamen and others, particularly Negroes, infected with smallpox. [7]

These local incidents indicate a willingness among many Americans to act outside the bounds of law, but they cannot be described as anti-authoritarian in any general sense. Sometimes in fact—as in the Boston bawdy house riot of 1734, or the Norfolk smallpox incident—local magistrates openly countenanced or participated in the mob's activities. Far from opposing established institutions, many supporters of Shays's Rebellion honored their leaders "by no less decisive marks of popular favor than elections to local offices of trust and authority." [8] It was above all the existence of such elections that forced local magistrates to reflect community feelings and so prevented their becoming the targets of insurrections. Certainly in New England, where the town meeting ruled, and to some extent in New York, where aldermen and councilmen were annually elected, this was true; yet even in Philadelphia, with its lethargic closed corporation, or Charleston, which lacked municipal institutions, authority was normally exerted by residents who had an immediate sense of local sentiment. Provincial governments were also for the most part kept alert to local feelings by their elected assemblies. Sometimes, of course, uprisings turned against domestic American institutions—as in Pennsylvania in 1764, when the

"Paxton Boys" complained that the colony's Quaker assembly had failed to provide adequately for their defense against the Indians. But uprisings over local issues proved *extra-institutional* in character more often than they were anti-institutional; they served the community where no law existed, or intervened beyond what magistrates thought they could do officially to cope with a local problem.

The case was different when imperial authority was involved. There legal authority emanated from a capital an ocean away, where the colonists had no integral voice in the formulation of policy, where governmental decisions were based largely upon the reports of "king's men" and sought above all to promote the king's interests. When London's legal authority and local interest conflicted, efforts to implement the edicts of royal officials were often answered by uprisings, and it was not unusual in these cases for local magistrates to participate or openly sympathize with the insurgents. The colonial response to the White Pines Acts of 1722 and 1729 is one example. Enforcement of the acts was difficult in general because "the various elements of colonial society . . . seemed inclined to violate the pine laws—legislatures, lumbermen, and merchants were against them, and even the royal governors were divided." At Exeter, New Hampshire, in 1734 about thirty men prevented royal officials from putting the king's broad arrow on some seized boards; efforts to enforce the acts in Connecticut during the 1750's ended after a deputy of the surveyor-general was thrown in a pond and nearly drowned; five years later logs seized in Massachusetts and New Hampshire were either "rescued" or destroyed. [9] Two other imperial issues that provoked local American uprisings long before 1765 and continued to do so during the Revolutionary period were impressment and customs enforcement.

As early as 1743 the colonists' violent opposition to impressment was said to indicate a "Contempt of Government." Some captains had been mobbed, the Admiralty complained, "others emprisoned, and afterwards held to exorbitant Bail, and are now under Prosecutions carried on by Combination, and by joint Subscription towards the expense." Colonial governors, despite their offers, furnished captains with little real aid either to procure seamen or "even to protect them from the Rage and Insults of the People." Two days of severe rioting answered Commodore Charles Knowles's efforts to sweep Boston harbor for able-bodied men in November 1747. Again in 1764 when Rear Admiral Lord Alexander Colville sent out orders to "procure" men in principal harbors between Casco Bay and Cape Henlopen, mobs met the ships at every turn. When the *St. John* sent out a boat to seize a recently impressed deserter from a Newport wharf, a mob protected him, captured the boat's officer, and hurled stones at the crew; later fifty Newporters joined the colony's gunner at Fort George in opening fire on the king's ship itself. Under threat to her master the *Chaleur* was forced to release four fishermen seized off Long Island, and when that ship's captain went ashore at New York a mob seized his boat and burned it in the Fields. In the spring of 1765 after the *Maidstone* capped a six-month siege of Newport harbor by seizing "all the Men" out of a brigantine from Africa, a mob of about five hundred men similarly seized a ship's officer and burned one of her boats on the Common. Impressment also met mass resistance at Norfolk in 1767 and was a major cause of the famous *Liberty* riot at Boston in 1768. [10]

Like the impressment uprisings, which in most instances sought to protect or rescue men from the "press," customs incidents were aimed at impeding the customs service in enforcing British laws. Tactics varied, and although incidents occurred long before 1764—in 1719, for example, Caleb Heathcote reported a "riotous and tumultuous" rescue of seized claret by Newporters—their frequency, like those of the impressment "riots," apparently increased after the Sugar Act was passed and customs enforcement efforts were tightened. The 1764 rescue of the *Rhoda* in Rhode Island preceded a theft in Dighton, Massachusetts, of the cargo from a newly seized vessel, the *Polly,* by a mob of some forty men with blackened faces. In 1766 again a mob stoned a customs official's home in Falmouth (Portland), Maine, while "Persons unknown and disguised" stole sugar and rum that had been impounded that morning. The intimidation of customs officials and of the particularly despised customs informers also enjoyed a long history. In 1701 the South Carolina attorney general publicly attacked an informer "and struck him several times, crying out, this is the Informer, this is he that will ruin the country." Similar assaults occurred decades later, in New Haven in 1766 and 1769, and New London in 1769, and were then often distinguished by their brutality. In [1769] a Providence tidesman, Jesse Saville, was seized, stripped, bound hand and foot, tarred and feathered, had dirt thrown in his face, then was beaten and "almost strangled." Even more thorough assaults upon two other Rhode Island tidesmen followed in July 1770 and upon Collector Charles Dudley in April 1771. Finally, customs vessels came under attack: the *St. John* was shelled at Newport in 1764 where the customs ship *Liberty* was sunk in 1769—both episodes that served as prelude to the destruction of the *Gaspee* outside Providence in 1772. [11]

Such incidents were not confined to New England. Philadelphia witnessed some of the most savage attacks, and even the surveyor of Sassafras and Bohemia in Maryland—an office long a sinecure, since no ships entered or cleared in Sassafras or Bohemia—met with violence when he tried to execute his office in March 1775. After seizing two wagons of goods being carried overland from Maryland toward Duck Creek, Pennsylvania, the officer was overpowered by a "licentious mob" that kept shouting "Liberty and Duck Creek forever" as it went through the hours-long rituals of tarring and feathering him and threatening his life. And at Norfolk, Virginia, in the spring 1766 an accused customs informer was tarred and feathered, pelted with stones and rotten eggs, and finally thrown in the sea where he nearly drowned. Even Georgia saw customs violence before independence, and one of the rare deaths resulting from a colonial riot occurred there in 1775. [12]

White Pines, impressment, and customs uprisings have attracted historians' attention because they opposed British authority and so seemed to presage the Revolution. In fact, however, they had much in common with many exclusively local uprisings. In each of the incidents violence was directed not so much against the "rich and powerful" [13] as against men who—as it was said after the Norfolk smallpox incident—"in every part of their conduct . . . acted very inconsistently as good neighbors or citizens." The effort remained one of safeguarding not the interests of isolated groups alone, but the community's safety and welfare. The White Pines Acts need not have provoked this opposition had they applied only to trees of potential use to the Navy, and had they been framed and executed with concern for colonial rights. But instead the acts reserved to the Crown all white pine trees including those "utterly unfit for masts, yards, or bowsprits," and prevented colonists from using them for building materials or lumber exportation even in regions where white pine constituted the principal forest growth. As a result the acts "operated so much against the convenience and even necessities of the inhabitants," Surveyor John Wentworth explained, that "it became almost a general interest of the country" to frustrate the acts' execution. Impressment offered a more immediate effect, since the "press" could quickly cripple whole towns. Merchants and masters were affected as immediately as seamen: the targeted port, as Massachusetts' Governor William Shirley explained in 1747, was drained of mariners by both impressment itself and the flight of navigation to safer provinces, driving the wages for any remaining seamen upward. When the press was of long duration, moreover, or when it took place during a normally busy season, it could mean serious shortages of food or firewood for winter, and a general attrition of the commercial life that sustained all strata of society in trading towns. Commerce seemed even more directly attacked by British trade regulations, particularly by the proliferation of customs procedures in the mid-1760's that seemed to be in no American's interest, and by the Sugar Act with its virtual prohibition of the trade with the foreign West Indies that sustained the economies of colonies like Rhode Island. As a result even when only a limited contingent of sailors participated in a customs incident officials could suspect—as did the deputy collector at Philadelphia in 1770—that the mass of citizens "in their Hearts" approved of it. [14]

Because the various uprisings discussed here grew out of concerns essential to wide sections of the community, the "rioters" were not necessarily confined to the seamen, servants, Negroes, and boys generally described as the staple components of the colonial mob. The uprising of

Exeter, New Hampshire, townsmen against the king's surveyor of the woods in 1754 was organized by a member of the prominent Gillman family who was a mill owner and a militia officer. Members of the upper classes participated in Norfolk's smallpox uprising, and Cornelius Calvert, who was later attacked in a related incident, protested that leading members of the community, doctors and magistrates, had posted securities for the good behavior of the "Villains" convicted of mobbing him. Captain Jeremiah Morgan complained about virtually universal participation of Norfolkers in an impressment incident of 1767, and "all the principal Gentlemen in Town" were supposedly present when a customs informer was tarred and feathered there in 1766. Merchant Benedict Arnold admitted leading a New Haven mob against an informer in 1766; New London merchants Joseph Packwood and Nathaniel Shaw commanded the mob that first accosted Captain William Reid the night the *Liberty* was destroyed at Newport in 1769, just as John Brown, a leading Providence merchant, led that against the *Gaspee.* Charles Dudley reported in April 1771 that the men who beat him in Newport "did not come from the . . . lowest class of Men," but were "stiled Merchants and the Masters of their Vessels"; and again in 1775 Robert Stratford Byrne said many of his Maryland and Pennsylvania attackers were "from Appearance . . . Men of Property." It is interesting, too, that during Shays's Rebellion—so often considered a class uprising—"men who were of good property and owed not a shilling" were said to be "involved in the train of desperado's to suppress the courts." [15]

Opposition to impressment and customs enforcement in itself was not, moreover, the only cause of the so-called impressment or customs "riots." The complete narratives of these incidents indicate again not only that the crowd acted to support local interests, but that it sometimes enforced the will of local magistrates by extralegal means. Although British officials blamed the *St. John* incident upon that ship's customs and impressment activities, colonists insisted that the confrontation began when some sailors stole a few pigs and chickens from a local miller and the ship's crew refused to surrender the thieves to Newport officials. Two members of the Rhode Island council then ordered the gunner of Fort George to detain the schooner until the accused seamen were delivered to the sheriff, and "many People went over the Fort to assist the Gunner in the Discharge of his Duty." Only after this uprising did the ship's officers surrender the accused men. [16] Similarly, the 1747 Knowles impressment riot in Boston and the 1765 *Maidstone* impressment riot in Newport broke out after governors' request for the release of impressed seamen had gone unanswered, and only after the outbreaks of violence were the governors' requests honored. The crowd that first assembled on the night the *Liberty* was destroyed in Newport also began by demanding the allegedly drunken sailors who that afternoon had abused and shot at a colonial captain, Joseph Packwood, so they could be bound over to local magistrates for prosecution. [17]

In circumstances such as these, the "mob" often appeared only after the legal channels of redress had proven inadequate. The main thrust of the colonists' resistance to the White Pines Acts had always been made in their courts and legislatures. Violence broke out only in local situations where no alternative was available. Even the burning of the *Gaspee* in June 1772 was a last resort. Three months before the incident a group of prominent Providence citizens complained about the ship's wanton severity with all vessels along the coast and the colony's governor pressed their case with the fleet's admiral. The admiral, however, supported the *Gaspee's* commander, Lieutenant William Dudingston; and thereafter, the *Providence Gazette* reported, Dudingston became "more haughty, insolent and intolerable, . . . personally ill treating every master and merchant of the vessels he boarded, stealing sheep, hogs, poultry, etc. from farmers round the bay, and cutting down their fruit and other trees for firewood." Redress from London was possible but time-consuming, and in the meantime Rhode Island was approaching what its governor called "the deepest calamity" as supplies of food and fuel were curtailed and prices, especially at Newport, rose steeply. It was significant that merchant John Brown finally led the Providence "mob" that seized the moment in June when the *Gaspee* ran aground near Warwick, for it was he who had spearheaded the effort in March 1772 to win redress through the normal channels of government.[18]

II

There was little that was distinctively American about the colonial insurrections. The uprisings over grain exportations during times of dearth, the attacks on brothels, press gangs, royal forest officials, and customsmen, all had their counterparts in seventeenth- and eighteenth-century England. Even the Americans' hatred of the customs establishment mirrored the Englishman's traditional loathing of excise men. Like the customsmen in the colonies, they seemed to descend into localities armed with extraordinary prerogative powers. Often, too, English excisemen were "thugs and brutes who beat up their victims without compunction or stole or wrecked their property" and against whose extravagances little redress was possible through the law.[19] Charges of an identical character were made in the colonies against customsmen and naval officials as well, particularly after 1763 when officers of the Royal Navy were commissioned as deputy members of the customs service,[20] and a history of such accusations lay behind many of the best-known waterfront insurrections. The Americans' complaints took on particular significance only because in the colonies those officials embodied the authority of a "foreign" power. Their arrogance and arbitrariness helped effect "an estrangement of the Affections of the People from the Authority under which they act," and eventually added an emotional element of anger against the Crown to a revolutionary conflict otherwise carried on in the language of law and right. [21]

The focused character of colonial uprisings also resembled those in England and even France where, Rudé has pointed out, crowds were remarkably single-minded and discriminating. [22] Targets were characteristically related to grievances: the Knowles rioters sought only the release of the impressed men; they set free a captured officer when assured he had nothing to do with the press, and refrained from burning a boat near Province House for fear the fire would spread. The Norfolk rioters, driven by fear of smallpox, forcefully isolated the inoculated persons where they would be least dangerous. Even the customs rioters vented their brutality on customs officers and informers alone, and the Shaysite "mobs" dispersed after closing the courts which promised most immediately to effect their ruin. So domesticated and controlled was the Boston mob that it refused to riot on Saturday and Sunday nights, which were considered holy by New Englanders. [23]

When colonists compared their mobs with those in the Mother Country they were struck only with the greater degree of restraint among Americans. "These People bear no Resemblance to an English Mob," John Jay wrote of the Shaysites in December 1786, "they are more temperate, cool and regular in their Conduct—they have hitherto abstained from Plunder, nor have they that I know of committed any outrages but such as the accomplishment of their Purpose made necessary." Similar comparisons were often repeated during the Revolutionary conflict, and were at least partially grounded in fact. When Londoners set out to "pull down" houses of ill fame in 1688, for example, the affair spread, prisons were opened, and disorder ended only when troops were called out. But when eighteenth-century Bostonians set out on the same task, there is no record that their destruction extended beyond the bordellos themselves. Even the violence of the customs riots—which contrast in that regard from other American incidents—can sometimes be explained by the presence of volatile foreign seamen. The attack on the son of customsman John Hatton, who was nearly killed in a Philadelphia riot, occurred, for example, when the city was crowded by over a thousand seamen. His attackers were apparently Irish crew members of a vessel he and his father had tried to seize off Cape May, and they were "set on," the Philadelphia collector speculated, by an Irish merchant in Philadelphia to whom the vessel was consigned. One of the most lethal riots in the history of colonial America, in which rioters killed five people, occurred in a small town near Norfolk, Virginia, and was significantly perpetrated entirely by British seamen who resisted the local inhabitants' efforts to reinstitute peace. [24] During and immediately after the Revolutionary War some incidents occurred in which deaths are recorded; but contemporaries felt these were historical aberrations, caused by the "brutalizing" effect of the war itself. "Our citizens, from a habit of putting . . . [the British] to death, have reconciled their minds to the killing of each other," South Carolina Judge Aedanus Burke explained.[25]

To a large extent the pervasive restraint and virtual absence of bloodshed in American incidents can best be understood in terms of social and military circumstance. There was no large amorphous city in America comparable to London, where England's worst incidents occurred. More important, the casualties even in eighteenth-century British riots were rarely the work of rioters. No deaths were inflicted by the Wilkes, Anti-Irish, or "No Popery" mobs, and only single fatalities resulted from other upheavals such as the Porteous riots of 1736. "It was authority rather than the crowd that was conspicuous for its violence to life and limb": all 285 casualties of the Gordon riots, for example, were rioters.[26] Since a regular army was less at the ready for use against colonial mobs, casualty figures for American uprisings were naturally much reduced.

To some extent the general tendency toward a discriminating purposefulness was shared by mobs throughout western Europe, but within the British Empire the focused character of popular uprisings and also their persistence can be explained in part by the character of law enforcement procedures. There were no professional police forces in the eighteenth century. Instead the power of government depended traditionally upon institutions like the "hue and cry," by which the community in general rose to apprehend felons. In its original medieval form the "hue and cry" was a form of summary justice that resembled modern lynch law. More commonly by the eighteenth century magistrates turned to the *posse commitatus,* literally the "power of the country," and in practice all able-bodied men a sheriff might call upon to assist him. Where greater and more organized support was needed, magistrates could call out the militia.[27] Both the *posse* and the militia drew upon local men, including many of the same persons who made up the mob. This was particularly clear where these traditional mechanisms failed to function effectively. At Boston in September 1766 when customsmen contemplated breaking into the house of merchant Daniel Malcom to search for contraband goods, Sheriff Stephen Greenleaf threatened to call for support from members of the very crowd suspected of an intent to riot; and when someone suggested during the Stamp Act riots that the militia be raised Greenleaf was told it had already risen. This situation meant that mobs could naturally assume the manner of a lawful institution, acting by habit with relative restraint and responsibility. On the other hand, the militia institutionalized the practice of forcible popular coercion and so made the formation of extralegal mobs more natural that J. R. Weston has called the militia "a relic of the bad old days," and hailed its passing as "a step towards . . . bringing civilization and humanity into our [English] political life."[28]

These law enforcement mechanisms left magistrates virtually helpless whenever a large segment of the population was immediately involved in the disorder, or when the community had a strong sympathy for the rioters. The Boston militia's failure to act in the Stamp Act riots, which was repeated in nearly all the North American colonies, recapitulated a similar refusal during the Knowles riot of 1747. [29] If the mob's sympathizers were confined to a single locality, the governor could try to call out the militias of surrounding areas, as Massachusetts Governor William Shirley began to do in 1747, and as, to some extent, Governor Francis Bernard attempted after the rescue of the *Polly* in 1765. [30] In the case of sudden uprisings, however, these peace-keeping mechanisms were at best partially effective since they required time to assemble strength, which often made the effort wholly pointless.

When the disorder continued and the militia either failed to appear or proved insufficient, there was, of course, the army, which was used periodically in the eighteenth century against rioters in England and Scotland. Even in America peacetime garrisons tended to be placed where they might serve to maintain law and order. But since all Englishmen shared a fear of standing armies the deployment of troops had always to be a sensitive and carefully limited recourse. Military and civil spheres of authority were rigidly separated, as was clear to Lord Jeffery Amherst, who refused to use soldiers against antimilitary rioters during the Seven Years' War because that function was "entirely foreign to their command and belongs of right to none but the civil power." In fact troops could be used against British subjects, as in the suppression of civil disorder, only upon the request of local magistrates. This institutional inhibition carried, if anything, more weight in the colonies. There royal governors had quickly lost their right to declare martial law without the consent of the provincial councils that were, again, usually filled with local men. [31]

For all practical purposes, then, when a large political unit such as an entire town or colony condoned an act of mass force, problems were raised "almost insoluble without rending the whole fabric of English law." Nor was the situation confined to the colonies. After describing England's institutions for keeping the peace under the later Stuarts, Max Beloff suggested that no technique for maintaining order was found until nineteenth-century reformers took on the task of reshaping urban government. Certainly by the 1770's no acceptable solution had been found—neither by any colonists, nor "anyone in London, Paris, or Rome, either," as Carl Bridenbaugh has put it. To even farsighted contemporaries like John Adams the weakness of authority was a fact of the social order that necessarily conditioned the way rulers could act. "It is vain to expect or hope to carry on government against the universal bent and genius of the people," he wrote, "we may whimper and whine as much as we will, but nature made it impossible when she made man." [32]

The mechanisms of enforcing public order were rendered even more fragile since the difference between legal and illegal applications of mass force was distinct in theory, but sometimes indistinguishable in practice. The English common law prohibited riot, defined as an uprising of three or more persons who performed what Blackstone called an "unlawful act of violence" for a private purpose. If the act was never carried out or attempted the offense became unlawful assembly; if some effort was made toward its execution, rout; and if the purpose of the uprising was public rather than private—tearing down whore houses, for example, or destroying all enclosures rather than just those personally affecting the insurgents— the offense became treason since it constituted a usurpation of the king's function, a "levying war against the King." The precise legal offense lay not so much in the purpose of the uprising as in its use of force and violence "wherein the Law does not allow the Use of such Force." Such unlawful assumptions of force were carefully distinguished by commentators upon the common law from other occasions on which the law authorized a use of force. It was, for example, legal for force to be used by a sheriff, constable, "or perhaps even . . . a private Person" who assembled "a competent Number of People, in Order with Force to suppress Rebels, or Enemies, or Rioters"; for a justice of the peace to raise the *posse* when opposed in detaining lands, or for Crown officers to raise "a Power as may effectually enable them to over-power any . . . Resistance" in the execution of the King's writs. [33]

In certain situations these distinctions offered at best a very uncertain guide as to who did or did not exert force lawfully. Should a *posse* employ more force than was necessary to overcome overt resistance, for example, its members acted illegally and were indictable for riot. And where established officials supported both sides in a confrontation, or where the legality of an act that officials were attempting to enforce was itself disputed, the decision as to who were or were not rioters seemed to depend upon the observer's point of view. Impressment is a good example. The colonists claimed that impressment was unlawful in North America under an act of 1708, while British authorities and some—but not all—spokesmen for the government held that the law had lapsed in 1713. The question was settled only in 1775, when Parliament finally repealed the "Sixth of Anne." Moreover, supposing impressment could indeed be carried on, were press warrants from provincial authorities still necessary? Royal instructions of 1697 had given royal governors the "sole power of impressing seamen in any of our plantations in America or in sight of them." Admittedly that clause was dropped in 1708, and a subsequent parliamentary act of 1746, which required the full consent of the governor and council before impressment could be carried on within their province, applied only to the West Indies. Nonetheless it seems that in 1764 the Lords of the Admiralty thought the requirement held throughout North America. [34] With the legality of impressment efforts so uncertain, especially when opposed by local authorities, it was possible to see the press gangs as "rioters" for trying *en masse* to perpetrate an unlawful act of violence. In that case the local townsmen who opposed them might be considered lawful defenders of the public welfare, acting much as they would in a *posse*. In 1770 John Adams cited opposition to press gangs who acted without warrants as an example of the lawful use of force; and when the sloop of war *Hornet* swept into Norfolk, Virginia, in September 1767 with a "bloody riotous plan . . . to impress seamen, without consulting the Mayor, or any other magistrate," the offense was charged to the pressmen. Roused by the watchman, who called out *"a riot by man of war's men,"* the inhabitants rose to back the magistrates, and not only secured the release of the impressed men but also imprisoned ten members of the press gang. The ship's captain, on the other hand, condemned the townsmen as "Rioters." Ambiguity was present, too, in Newport's *St. John* clash, which involved both impressment and criminal action on the part of royal seamen and culminated with Newporters firing on the king's ship. The Privy Council in England promptly classified the incident as a riot, but the Rhode Island governor's report boldly maintained that "the people meant nothing but to assist [the magistrates] in apprehending the Offenders" on the vessel, and even suggested that "Their Conduct be honored with his Majesty's royal Approbation."[35]

The enforcement of the White Pines Acts was similarly open to legal dispute. The acts seemed to violate both the Massachusetts and Connecticut charters; the meaning of provisions exempting trees growing within townships (act of 1722) and those which were "the property of private persons" (act of 1729) was contested, and royal officials tended to work on the basis of interpretations of the laws that Bernhard Knollenberg has called farfetched and, in one case, "utterly untenable." The Exeter, New Hampshire, "riot" of 1734, for example, answered an attempt of the surveyor to seize boards on the argument that the authorization to seize logs from allegedly felled white pine trees in the act of 1722 included an authorization to seize processed lumber. As a result, Knollenberg concluded, although the surveyors' reports "give the impression that the New Englanders were an utterly lawless lot, . . . in many if not most cases they were standing for what they believed, with reason, were their legal and equitable rights in trees growing on their own lands."[36]

Occasions open to such conflicting interpretations were rare. Most often even those who sympathized with the mobs' motives condemned its use of force as illegal and unjustifiable. That ambiguous cases did arise, however, indicates that legitimacy and illegitimacy, *posses* and rioters, represented but poles of the same spectrum. And where a mob took upon itself the defense of the community, it benefited from a certain popular legitimacy even when the strict legality of its action was in doubt, particularly among a people taught that the legitimacy of law itself depended upon its defense of the public welfare.

Whatever quasi-legal status mobs were accorded by local communities was reinforced, moreover, by formal political thought. "Riots and rebellions" were often calmly accepted as a constant and even necessary element of free government. This acceptance depended, however, upon certain essential assumptions about popular uprisings. With words that could be drawn almost verbatim from John Locke or any other English author of similar convictions, colonial writers posited a continuing moderation and purposefulness on the part of the mob. "Tho' innocent Persons may sometimes suffer in popular Tumults," observed a 1768 writer in the *New York Journal,* "yet the general Resentment of the People is principally directed according to Justice, and the greatest Delinquent feels it most." Moreover, upheavals constituted only occasional interruptions in well-governed societies. "Good Laws and good Rulers will always be obey'd and respected"; "the Experience of all Ages proves, that Mankind are much more likely to submit to bad Laws and wicked Rulers, than to resist good ones." "Mobs and Tumults," it was often said, "never happen but thro' Oppression and a scandalous Abuse of Power." [37]

In the hands of Locke such remarks constituted relatively inert statements of fact. Colonial writers, however, often turned these pronouncements on their heads such that observed instances of popular disorder became *prima facie* indictments of authority. In 1747, for example, New Jersey land rioters argued that "from their Numbers, Violence, and unlawful Actions" it was to be "inferred that . . . they are wronged and oppressed, or else they would never *rebell agt. the Laws.*" Always, a New York writer said in 1770, when "the People of any Government" become "turbulent and uneasy," it was above all "a certain Sign of Maladministration." Even when disorders were not directly levelled against government they provided "strong proofs that something is much amiss in the state" as William Samuel Johnson put it; that—in Samuel Adams's words—the "wheels of good government" were "somewhat clogged." Americans who used this argument against Britain in the 1760's continued to depend upon it two decades later when they reacted to Shays's Rebellion by seeking out the public "Disease" in their own independent governments that was indicated by the "Spirit of Licentiousness" in Massachusetts. [38]

Popular turbulence seemed to follow so naturally from inadequacies of government that uprisings were often described with similes from the physical world. In 1770 John Adams said that there were "Church-quakes and state-quakes in the moral and political world, as well as earthquakes, storms and tempests in the physical." Two years earlier a writer in the *New York Journal* likened popular tumults to "Thunder Gusts" which "commonly do more Good than Harm." Thomas Jefferson continued the imagery in the 1780's, particularly with his famous statement that he liked "a little rebellion now and then" for it was "like a storm in the atmosphere." It was, moreover, because of the "imperfection of all things in this world," including government, that Adams found it "vain to seek a government in all points free from a possibility of civil wars, tumults and seditions." That was "a blessing denied to this life and preserved to complete the felicity of the next." [39]

If popular uprisings occurred "in all governments at all times," they were nonetheless most able to break out in free governments. Tyrants imposed order and submission upon their subjects by force, thus dividing society, as Jefferson said, into wolves and sheep. Only under free governments were the people "nervous," spirited, jealous of their rights, ready to react against unjust provocations; and this being the case, popular disorders could be interpreted as "Symptoms of a strong and healthy Constitution" even while they indicated some lesser shortcoming in administration. It would be futile, Josiah Quincy, Jr., said in 1770, to expect "that pacific, timid, obsequious, and servile temper, so predominant in more despotic governments" from those who lived under free British institutions. From "our happy constitution," he claimed, there resulted as "very natural Effects" an "impatience of injuries, and a strong resentment of insults."[40]

This popular impatience constituted an essential force in the maintenance of free institutions. "What country can preserve it's [sic] liberties if their rulers are not warned from time to time that their people preserve the spirit of resistance?" Jefferson asked in 1787. Occasional insurrections were thus "an evil . . . productive of good"; even those founded on popular error tended to hold rulers "to the true principles of their institution" and generally provided "a medecine necessary for the sound health of government." This meant that an aroused people had a role not only in extreme situations, where revolution was requisite, but in the normal course of free government. For that reason members of the House of Lords could seriously argue—as A. J. P. Taylor has pointed out—that "rioting is an essential part of our constitution"; and for that reason, too, even Massachusetts's conservative Lieutenant Governor Thomas Hutchinson could remark in 1768 that "mobs a sort of them at least are constitutional."[41]

III

It was, finally, the interaction of this constitutional role of the mob with the written law that makes the story of eighteenth-century popular uprisings complexity itself.[42] If mobs were appreciated because they provided a check on power, it was always understood that, insofar as upheavals threatened "running to such excesses, as will overturn the whole system of government," "strong discouragements" had to be provided against them. For eighteenth-century Americans, like the English writers they admired, liberty demanded the rule of law. In extreme situations where the rulers had clearly chosen arbitrary power over the limits of law, men like John Adams could prefer the risk of anarchy to continued submission because "anarchy can never last long, and tyranny may be perpetual," but only when "there was any hope that the fair order of liberty and a free constitution would arise out of it." This desire to maintain the orderly rule of law led legislatures in England and the colonies to pass antiriot statutes and to make strong efforts—in the words of a 1753 Massachusetts law—to discountenance "a mobbish temper and spirit in . . . the inhabitants" that would oppose "all government and order." [43]

The problem of limiting mass violence was dealt with most intensely over a sustained period by the American Revolutionary leadership, which has perhaps suffered most from historians' earlier inattention to the history of colonial uprisings. So long as it could be maintained—as it was only fifteen years ago—that political mobs were "rare or unknown in America" before the 1760's, the Revolutionaries were implicitly credited with their creation. American patriots, Charles McLean Andrews wrote, were often "lawless men who were nothing more than agitators and demagogues" and who attracted a following from the riffraff of colonial society. It now seems clear that the mob drew on all elements of the population. More important, the Revolutionary leaders had no need to create mob support. Instead they were forced to work with a "permanent entity," a traditional crowd that exerted itself before, after, and even during the Revolutionary struggle over issues unrelated to the conflict with Britain, and that, as Hobsbawm has noted, characteristically aided the Revolutionary cause in the opening phases of conflict but was hard to discipline thereafter. [44]

In focusing popular exuberance the American leaders could work with long-established tendencies in the mob toward purposefulness and responsibility. In doing so they could, moreover, draw heavily upon the guidelines for direct action that had been defined by English radical writers since the seventeenth century. Extralegal action was justified only when all established avenues to redress had failed. It could not answer casual errors or private failings on the part of the magistrates, but had to await fundamental public abuses so egregious that the "whole people" turned against their rulers. Even then, it was held, opposition had to be measured so that no more force was exerted than was necessary for the public good. Following these principles colonial leaders sought by careful organization to avoid the excesses that first greeted the Stamp Act. Hutchinson's query after a crowd in Connecticut had forced the resignation of stampman Jared Ingersoll—whether "such a public regular assembly can be called a mob"—could with equal appropriateness have been repeated during the tea resistance, or in 1774 when Massachusetts *mandamus* councillors were forced to resign. [45]

From the first appearance of an organized resistance movement in 1765, moreover, efforts were made to support the legal magistrates such that, as John Adams said in 1774, government would have "as much vigor then as ever" except where its authority was specifically under dispute. This concern for the maintenance of order and the general framework of law explains why the American Revolution was largely free from the "universal tumults and all the irregularities and violence of mobbish factions [that] naturally arise when legal authority ceases." It explains, too, why old revolutionaries like Samuel Adams or Christopher Gadsden disapproved of those popular conventions and committees that persisted after regular independent state governments were established in the 1770's. "Decency and Respect [are] due to Constitutional Authority," Samuel Adams said in 1784, "and those Men, who under any Pretence or by any Means whatever, would lessen the Weight of Government lawfully exercised must be Enemies to our happy Revolution and the Common Liberty." [46]

In normal circumstances the "strong discouragements" to dangerous disorder were provided by established legislatures. The measures enacted by them to deal with insurrections were shaped by the eighteenth-century understanding of civil uprisings. Since turbulence indicated above all some shortcoming in government, it was never to be met by increasing the authorities' power of suppression. The "weakness of authority" that was a function of its dependence upon popular support appeared to contemporary Americans as a continuing virtue of British institutions, as one reason why rulers could not simply dictate to their subjects and why Britain had for so long been hailed as one of the freest nations in Europe. It was "far less dangerous to the Freedom of a State" to allow "the laws to be trampled upon, by the licence among the rabble . . . than to dispence with their force by an act of power." Insurrections were to be answered by reform, by attacking the "Disease"—to use John Jay's term of 1786—that lay behind them rather than by suppressing its "Symptoms." And ultimately, as William Samuel Johnson observed in 1768, "the only effectual way to prevent them is to govern with wisdom, justice, and moderation." [47]

In immediate crises, however, legislatures in both England and America resorted to special legislation that supplemented the common law prohibition of riot. The English Riot Act of 1714 was passed when disorder threatened to disrupt the accession of George I; a Connecticut act of 1722 followed a rash of incidents over land title in Hartford County; the Massachusetts act of 1751 answered "several tumultuous assemblies" over the currency issue and another of 1786 was enacted at the time of Shays's Rebellion. The New Jersey legislature passed an act in 1747 during that colony's protracted land riots; Pennsylvania's Riot Act of 1764 was inspired by the Paxton Boys; North Carolina's of 1771 by the Regulators; New York's of 1774 by the "land wars" in Charlotte and Albany County. [48] Always the acts specified that the magistrates were to depend upon the *posse* in enforcing their provisions, and in North Carolina on the militia as well. They differed over the number of people who had to remain "unlawfully, riotously, and tumultuously assembled together, to the Disturbance of the Publick Peace" for one hour after the reading of a prescribed riot proclamation before becoming judicable under the act. Some colonies specified lesser punishments than the death penalty provided for in the English act, but the American statutes were not in general more "liberal" than the British. Two of them so violated elementary judicial rights that they were subsequently condemned—North Carolina's by Britain, and New York's act of 1774 by a later, Revolutionary state legislature. [49]

In one important respect, however, the English Riot Act was reformed. Each colonial riot law, except that of Connecticut, was enacted for only one to three years, whereas the British law was perpetual. By this provision colonial legislators avoided the shortcoming which, it was said, was "more likely to introduce *arbitrary Power* than even an *Army* itself," because a perpetual riot act meant that "in all future time" by "reading a Proclamation" the Crown had the power "of hanging up their Subjects wholesale, or of picking out Those, to whom they have the greatest Dislike." If the death penalty was removed, the danger was less. When, therefore, riot acts without limit of time were finally enacted—as Connecticut had done in 1722, Massachusetts in 1786, New Jersey in 1797—the punishments were considerably milder, providing, for example, for imprisonment not exceeding six months in Connecticut, one year in Massachusetts, and three years in New Jersey. [50]

Riot legislation, it is true, was not the only recourse against insurgents, who throughout the eighteenth century could also be prosecuted for treason. The colonial and state riot acts suggest, nonetheless, that American legislators recognized the participants in civil insurrections as guilty of a crime peculiarly complicated because it had social benefits as well as damages. To some degree, it appears, they shared the idea expressed well by Jefferson in 1787: that "honest republican governors" should be "so mild in their punishments of rebellions, as not to discourage them too much." [51] Even in countering riots the legislators seemed as intent upon preventing any perversion of the forces of law and order by established authorities as with chastising the insurgents. Reform of the English Riot Act thus paralleled the abolition of constituent treasons—a traditional recourse against enemies of the Crown—in American state treason acts of the Revolutionary period and finally in Article III of the Federal Constitution. [52] From the same preoccupation, too, sprang the limitations placed upon the regular army provided for in the Constitution in part to assure the continuation of republican government guaranteed to the states by Article IV, Section IV. Just as the riot acts were for so long limited in duration, appropriations for the army were never to extend beyond two years (Article I, Section viii, 12); and the army could be used within a state against domestic violence only after application by the legislature or governor, if the legislature could not be convened (Article IV, Section iv).

A continuing desire to control authority through popular action also underlay the declaration in the Second Amendment that "a well regulated Militia being necessary to the security of a free State," citizens were assured the "right . . . to keep and bear Arms." The militia was meant above all "to prevent the establishment of a standing army, the bane of liberty"; and the right to bear arms—taken in part from the English Bill of Rights of 1689—was considered a standing threat to would-be tyrants. It embodied "a public allowance, under due restrictions, of the *natural right of resis-*

tance and self preservation, when the sanctions of society and laws are found *insufficient* to restrain the *violence of oppression.*" And on the basis of their eighteenth-century experience, Americans could consider that right to be "perfectly harmless. . . . If the government be equitable; if it be reasonable in its exactions; if proper attention be paid to the education of children in knowledge, and religion," Timothy Dwight declared, "few men will be disposed to use arms, unless for their amusement, and for the defence of themselves and their country." [53]

The need felt to continue the eighteenth-century militia as a counter-weight to government along with the efforts to outlaw rioting and to provide for the use of a standing army against domestic insurrections under carefully defined circumstances together illustrate the complex attitude toward peacekeeping that prevailed among the nation's founders. The rule of law had to be maintained, yet complete order was neither expected nor even desired when it could be purchased, it seemed, only at the cost of forcefully suppressing the spirit of a free people. The constant possibility of insurrection—as institutionalized in the militia—was to remain an element of the United States Constitution, just as it had played an essential role in Great Britain's.

This readiness to accept some degree of tumultuousness depended to a large degree upon the lawmakers' own experience with insurrections in the eighteenth century, when "disorder" was seldom anarchic and "rioters" often acted to defend the law and justice rather than to oppose them. In the years after independence this toleration declined, in part because mass action took on new dimensions. Nineteenth-century mobs often resembled in outward form those of the previous century, but a new violence was added. Moreover, the literal assumption of popular rule in the years after Lexington taught many thoughtful Revolutionary partisans what was for them an unexpected lesson—that the people were "as capable of despotism as any prince," that "public liberty was no guarantee after all of private liberty." [54] With home rule secured, attention focused more exclusively upon minority rights, which mob action had always to some extent imperiled. And the danger that uprisings carried for individual freedom became ever more egregious as mobs shed their former restraint and burned Catholic convents, attacked nativist speakers, lynched Mormons, or destroyed the presses and threatened the lives of abolitionists.

Ultimately, however, changing attitudes toward popular uprisings turned upon fundamental transformations in the political perspective of Americans after 1776. Throughout the eighteenth century political institutions had been viewed as in a constant evolution: the colonies' relationship with Britain and with each other, even the balance of power within the governments of various colonies, remained unsettled. Under such circumstances the imputations of governmental shortcoming that uprisings carried could easily be accepted and absorbed. But after Independence, when the form and conduct of the Americans' governments were under their exclusive control, and when those governments represented, moreover, an experiment in republicanism on which depended their own happiness and "that of generations of unborn," Americans became less ready to endure domestic turbulence or accept its disturbing implications. Some continued to argue that "distrust and dissatisfaction" on the part of the multitude were "always the consequence of tyranny or corruption." Others, however, began to see domestic turbulence not as indictments but as insults to government that were likely to discredit American republicanism in the eyes of European observers. "Mobs are a reproach to Free Governments," where all grievances could be legally redressed through the courts or the ballot box, it was argued in 1783. They originated there "not in Oppression, but in Licentiousness," an "ungovernable spirit" among the people. Under republican governments even that distrust of power colonists had found so necessary for liberty, and which uprisings seemed to manifest, could appear outmoded. "There is some consistency in being jealous of power in the hands of those who assume it by birth . . . and over whom we have no controul . . . as was the case with the Crown of England over America," another writer suggested. "But to be jealous of those whom we chuse, the instant we have chosen them" was absurd: perhaps in the transition from monarchy to republic Americans had "bastardized" their ideas by placing jealousy where confidence was more appropriate.[55] In short, the assumptions behind the Americans' earlier toleration of the mob were corroded in republican America. Old and new attitudes coexisted in the 1780's and even later. But the appropriateness of popular uprisings in the United States became increasingly in doubt after the Federal Constitution came to be seen as the final product of long-term institutional experimentation, "a momentous contribution to the history of politics" that rendered even that most glorious exertion of popular force, revolution itself, an obsolete resort for Americans.[56]

Yet this change must not be viewed exclusively as a product of America's distinctive Revolutionary achievement. J. H. Plumb has pointed out, that a century earlier, when England passed beyond her revolutionary era and progressed toward political "stability," radical ideology with its talk of resistance and revolution was gradually left behind. A commitment to peace and permanence emerged from decades of fundamental change. In America as in England this stability demanded that operative sovereignty, including the right finally to decide what was and was not in the community's interest, and which laws were and were not constitutional, be entrusted to established governmental institutions. The result was to minimize the role of the people at large, who had been the ultimate arbiters of those questions in English and American Revolutionary thought. Even law enforcement was to become the task primarily of professional agencies. As a result in time all popular upheavals alike became menacing efforts to "pluck up law and justice by the roots," and riot itself gradually became defined as a purposeless act of anarchy, "a blind and misguided outburst of popular fury," of "undirected violence with no articulated goals." [57]

NOTES

1. See the following by George Rudé: *The Crowd in the French Revolution* (Oxford, 1959); "The London 'Mob' of the Eighteenth Century," *Historical Journal,* II (1959), 1-18; *Wilkes and Liberty: A Social Study of 1763 to 1774* (Oxford, 1962); *The Crowd in History: A Study of Popular Disturbances in France and England, 1730-1848* (New York, 1964). See also E. J. Hobsbawm, *Primitive Rebels: Studies in Archaic Forms of Social Movement in the 19th and 20th Centuries* (New York, 1959), esp. "The City Mob," 108-125. For recent discussions of the colonial mob see: Bernard Bailyn, *Pamphlets of the American Revolution* (Cambridge, Mass., 1965), I, 581-584; Jesse Lemisch, "Jack Tar in the Street: Merchant Seamen in the Politics of Revolutionary America," *William and Mary Quarterly,* 3d Ser., XXV (1968), 371-407; Gordon S. Wood, "A Note on Mobs in the American Revolution," *Wm. and Mary Qtly.,* 3d Ser., XXIII (1966), 635-642, and more recently Wood's *Creation of the American Republic, 1776-1787* (Chapel Hill, 1969), *passim,* but esp. 319-328. Wood offers an excellent analysis of the place of mobs and extralegal assemblies in the development of American constitutionalism. Hugh D. Graham and Ted R. Gurr, *Violence in America: Historical and Comparative Perspectives* (New York, 1969), primarily discusses uprisings of the 19th and 20th centuries, but see the chapters by Richard M. Brown, "Historical Patterns of Violence in America," 45-84, and "The American Vigilante Tradition," 154-226.

2. Carl Bridenbaugh, *Cities in the Wilderness: The First Century of Urban Life in America, 1625-1742* (New York, 1964), 70-71, 223-224, 382-384; and Carl Bridenbaugh, *Cities in Revolt: Urban Life in America, 1743-1776* (New York, 1964), 113-118; Charles J. Hoadly, ed., *The Public Records of the Colony of Connecticut . . .* (Hartford, 1872), VI, 332-333, 341-348.

3. See particularly Richard M. Brown, *The South Carolina Regulators* (Cambridge, Mass., 1963). There is no published study of the New Jersey land riots, which lasted over a decade and were due above all to the protracted inability of the royal government to settle land disputes stemming from conflicting proprietary grants made in the late 17th century. See, however, "A State of Facts concerning the Riots and Insurrections in New Jersey, and the Remedies Attempted to Restore the Peace of the Province," William A. Whitehead *et al.,* eds., *Archives of the State of New Jersey* (Newark, 1883), VII, 207-226. On other rural insurrections see Irving Mark, *Agrarian Conflicts in Colonial New York, 1711-1775* (New York, 1940), Chap. IV, V; Staughton Lynd, "The Tenant Rising at Livingston Manor," *New-York Historical Society Quarterly,* XLVIII (1964) 163-177; Matt Bushnell Jones, *Vermont in the Making, 1750-1777* (Cambridge, Mass., 1939), Chap. XII, XIII; John R. Dunbar, ed., *The Paxton Papers* (The Hague, 1957), esp. 3-51.

4. Richard L. Morton, *Colonial Virginia* (Chapel Hill, 1960), I, 303-304; Jonathan Smith, "The Depression of 1785 and Daniel Shays' Rebellion," *Wm. and Mary Qtly.,* 3d Ser., V (1948), 86-87, 91.

5. Bridenbaugh, *Cities in Revolt,* 114; Bridenbaugh, *Cities in the Wilderness,* 196, 383, 388-389; Edmund S. and Helen M. Morgan, *The Stamp Act Crisis,* rev. ed. (New York, 1963), 159; Anne Rowe Cunningham, ed., *Letters and Diary of John Rowe, Boston Merchant, 1759-1762, 1764-1779* (Boston, 1903), 218. On the marriage riots, see *New-York Gazette* (New York City), July 11, 1765—and note, that when the reporter speaks of persons "concern'd in such unlawful Enterprises" he clearly is referring to the husbands, not their "Disciplinarians."

On the Rogerenes, see item in *Connecticut Gazette* (New Haven), Apr. 5, 1766, reprinted in Lawrence H. Gipson, *Jared Ingersoll* (New Haven, 1920), 195, n. 1.

6. John Adams, "Novanglus," in Charles F. Adams, ed., *The Works of John Adams* (Boston, 1850-1856), IV, 76-77; Salem news of Jan. 25 and Feb. 1, 1774, in *Providence Gazette* (Rhode Island), Feb. 5, and Feb. 12, 1774.

7. Letter from "Friend to the Borough and county of Norfolk," in Purdie and Dixon's *Virginia Gazette Postscript* (Williamsburg), Sept. 8, 1768, which gives the fullest account. This letter answered an earlier letter from Norfolk, Aug. 6, 1768, available in Rind's *Va. Gaz. Supplement* (Wmsbg.), Aug. 25, 1768. See also letter of Cornelius Calvert in Purdie and Dixon's *Va. Gaz.* (Wmsbg.), Jan. 9, 1772. Divisions over the inoculation seemed to follow more general political lines. See Patrick Henderson, "Smallpox and Patriotism, The Norfolk Riots, 1768-1769," *Virginia Magazine of History and Biography,* LXXIII (1965), 413-424.

8. James Madison to Thomas Jefferson, Mar. 19, 1787, in Julian P. Boyd, ed., *The Papers of Thomas Jefferson* (Princeton, 1950-), XI, 223.

9. Bernhard Knollenberg, *Origin of the American Revolution: 1759-1766* (New York, 1965), 126, 129. See also, Robert G. Albion, *Forests and Sea Power* (Cambridge, Mass., 1926), 262-263, 265. Joseph J. Malone, *Pine Trees and Politics* (Seattle, 1964), includes less detail on the forceful resistance to the acts.

10. Admiralty to Gov. George Thomas, Sept. 26, 1743, in Samuel Hazard *et al.,* eds., *Pennsylvania Archives* (Philadelphia, 1852-1949), I, 639. For accounts of the Knowles riot, see Gov. William Shirley to Josiah Willard, Nov. 19, 1747, Shirley's Proclamation of Nov. 21, 1747, and his letter to the Board of Trade, Dec. 1, 1747, in Charles H. Lincoln, ed., *The Correspondence of William Shirley . . . 1731-1760* (New York, 1912), I, 406-419; see also Thomas Hutchinson, *History of the Province of Massachusetts Bay,* ed. Lawrence S. Mayo (Cambridge, Mass., 1936), II, 330-333; and *Reports of the Record Commissioners of Boston* (Boston, 1885), XIV, 127-130. David Lovejoy, *Rhode Island Politics and the American Revolution, 1760-1776* (Providence, 1958), 36-39, and on the *Maidstone* in particular see "O. G." in *Newport Mercury* (Rhode Island), June 10, 1765. Bridenbaugh, *Cities in Revolt,* 309-311; documents on the *St. John* episode in *Records of the Colony of Rhode Island and Providence Plantations* (Providence, 1856-1865), VI, 427-430. George G. Wolkins, "The Seizure of John Hancock's Sloop 'Liberty,'" Massachusetts Historical Society, *Proceedings* (1921-1923), LV, 239-284. See also Lemisch, "Jack Tar," *Wm. and Mary Qtly.,* 3d Ser., XXV (1968), 391-393; and Neil R. Stout, "Manning the Royal Navy in North America, 1763-1775," *American Neptune,* XXIII (1963), 179-181.

11. Heathcote letter from Newport, Sept. 7, 1719, *Records of the Colony of Rhode Island,* IV, 259-260; Lovejoy, *Rhode Island Politics,* 35-39. There is an excellent summary of the *Polly* incident in Morgan, *Stamp Act Crisis,* 59, 64-67; and see also *Providence Gaz.* (R. I.) Apr. 27, 1765. On the Falmouth incident see the letter from the collector and comptroller of Falmouth, Aug. 19, 1766, Treasury Group 1, Class 453, Piece 182, Public Records Office. Hereafter cited as T. 1/453, 182. See also the account in Appendix I of Josiah Quincy, Jr., *Reports of the Cases Argued and Adjudged in the Superior Court of Judicature of the Province of Massachusetts Bay, between 1761 and 1772* (Boston, 1865), 446-447. W. Noel Sainsbury *et al.,* eds., *Calendar of State Papers, Colonial Series, America and the West Indies* (London, 1910), 1701, no. 1042, xi, a. A summary of one of the New Haven informer attacks is in Willard M. Wallace, *Traitorous Hero: The Life and Fortunes of Benedict Arnold* (New York, 1954), 20-23. Arnold's statement on the affair which he led is in Malcolm Decker, *Benedict Arnold, Son of the Havens* (Tarrytown, N.Y., 1932), 27-29. Gipson, in *Jared Ingersoll,* 277-278, relates the later incidents. For the New London informer attacks, see documents of July 1769 in T. 1/471. On the Saville affair see Saville to collector and comptroller of customs in Newport, May 18, 1769, T. 1/471, and *New York Journal* (New York City), July 6, 1769. On later Rhode Island incidents see Dudley and John Nicoll to governor of Rhode Island, Aug. 1, 1770, T. 1/471. Dudley to commissioners of customs at Boston,

Newport, Apr. 11, 1771, T. 1/482. On the destruction of the *Liberty* see documents in T. 1/ 471, esp. comptroller and collector to the governor, July 21, 1769.

12. On Philadelphia violence see William Sheppard to commissioners of customs, Apr. 21, 1769, T. 1/471; Deputy Collector at Philadelphia John Swift to commissioners of customs at Boston, Oct. 13, 1769, *ibid.;* and on a particularly brutal attack on the son of customsman John Hatton, see Deputy Collector John Swift to Boston customs commissioners, Nov. 15, 1770, and related documents in T. 1/476. See also Alfred S. Martin, "The King's Customs: Philadelphia, 1763-1774," *Wm. and Mary Qtly.,* 3d Ser., V (1948), 201-216. Documents on the Maryland episode are in T. 1/513, including the following: Richard Reeve to Grey Cooper, Apr. 19, 1775; extracts from a Council meeting, Mar. 16, 1775; deposition of Robert Stratford Byrne, surveyor of His Majesty's Customs at Sassafras and Bohemia, and Byrne to customs commissioners, Mar. 17, 1775. On the Virginia incident see William Smith to Jeremiah Morgan, Apr. 3, 1766, Colonial Office Group, Class 5, Piece 1331, 80, Public Record Office. Hereafter cited as C. O. 5/1331, 80. W. W. Abbot, *The Royal Governors of Georgia, 1754-1775* (Chapel Hill, 1959), 174-175. These customs riots remained generally separate from the more central intercolonial opposition to Britain that emerged in 1765. Isolated individuals like John Brown of Providence and Maximilian Calvert of Norfolk were involved in both the organized intercolonial Sons of Liberty and in leading mobs against customs functionaries or informers. These roles, however, for the most part were unconnected, that is, there was no radical program of customs obstruction *per se.* Outbreaks were above all local responses to random provocations and, at least before the Townshend duties, usually devoid of explicit ideological justifications.

13. Hobsbawm, *Primitive Rebels,* III. For a different effort to see class division as relevant in 18th century uprisings, see Lemisch, "Jack Tar," *Wm. and Mary Qtly.,* 3d Ser., XXV (1968), 387.

14. "Friends to the borough and county of Norfolk," Purdie and Dixon's *Va. Gaz. Postscrpt.* (Wmsbg.), Sept. 8, 1768. Wentworth quoted in Knollenberg, *Origin of American Revolution,* 124-125. Lemisch, "Jack Tar," *Wm. and Mary Qtly.,* 3d Ser., XXV (1968), 383-385. Shirley to Duke of Newcastle, Dec. 31, 1747, in Lincoln, ed., *Shirley Correspondence,* I, 420-423. Dora Mae Clark, "The Impressment of Seamen in the American Colonies," *Essays in Colonial History Presented to Charles McLean Andrews* (New Haven, 1931), 199-200; John Swift to Boston customs commissioners, Nov. 15, 1770, T. 1/476.

15. Malone, *White Pines,* 112. "Friends to the borough and county of Norfolk," Purdie and Dixon's *Va. Gaz. Postscrpt.* (Wmsbg.), Sept. 8, 1768; Calvert letter, *ibid.,* Jan. 9, 1772. Capt. Jeremiah Morgan, quoted in Lemisch, "Jack Tar," *Wm. and Mary Qtly.,* 3d Ser., XXV (1968), 391; and William Smith to Morgan, Apr. 3, 1766, C. O. 5/1331, 80. Decker, *Benedict Arnold,* 27-29; deposition of Capt. William Reid on the *Liberty* affair, July 21, 1769, T. 1/47l; Ephraim Bowen's narrative on the *Gaspee* affair, *Records of the Colony of Rhode Island,* VII, 68-73; Charles Dudley to Boston customs commissioners, Apr. 11, 1771, T. 1/482, and deposition by Byrne, T. 1/513, Edward Carrington to Jefferson, June 9, 1787, Boyd, ed., *Jefferson Papers,* XI, 408; and see also Smith, "Depression of 1785," *Wm. and Mary Qtly.,* 3d Ser., V (1948), 88—of the 21 men indicted for treason in Worcester during the court's April term 1787, 15 were "gentlemen" and only 6 "yeomen."

16. Gov. Samuel Ward's report to the Treasury lords, Oct. 23, 1765, Ward Manuscripts, Box 1, fol. 58, Rhode Island Historical Society, Providence. See also deposition of Daniel Vaughn of Newport—Vaughn was the gunner at Fort George—July 8, 1764, Chalmers Papers, Rhode Island, fol. 41, New York Public Library, New York City. For British official accounts of the affair, see Lieut. Hill's version in James Munro, ed., *Acts of the Privy Council of England, Colonial Series* (London, 1912), VI, 374-376, and the report of John Robinson and John Nicoll to the customs commissioners, Aug. 30, 1765, Privy Council Group, Class I, Piece 51, Bundle I (53a), Public Record Office. Hill, whose report was drawn up soon after the incident, does not contradict Ward's narrative, but seems oblivious of any warrant-granting

process on shore; Robinson and Nicoll—whose report was drawn up over a year later, and in the midst of the Stamp Act turmoil—claimed that a recent customs seizure had precipitated the attack upon the *St. John.*

17. On the Knowles and *Maidstone* incidents see above, n. 10. On the *Liberty* affair see documents in T. 1/471, esp. the deposition of Capt. William Reid, July 21, 1769, and that of John Carr, the second mate, who indicates that the mob soon forgot its scheme of delivering the crew members to the magistrates.

18. Malone, *White Pines,* 8-9, and *passim. Records of the Colony of Rhode Island,* VII, 60, 62-63, 174-175, including the deposition of Dep. Gov. Darius Sessions, June 12, 1772, and Adm. Montagu to Gov. Wanton, Apr. 8, 1772. Also, Wanton to Hillsborough, June 16, 1772, and Ephraim Bowen's narrative, *ibid.,* 63-73, 90-92. *Providence Gaz.* (R.I.), Jan. 9, 1773.

19. Max Beloff, *Public Order and Popular Disturbances, 1660-1714* (London, 1938), *passim;* Albion, *Forests and Sea Power,* 263; J. H. Plumb, *England in the Eighteenth Century* (Baltimore, 1961 [orig. publ., Oxford, 1950]), 66.

20. See, for example, "A Pumpkin" in the *New London Gazette* (Connecticut), May 14, 18, 1773; "O. G." in *Newport Merc.* (R.I.), June 10, 1765; *New London Gaz.* (Conn.), Sept. 22, 1769; complaints of Marylander David Bevan, reprinted in Rind's *Va. Gaz.* (Wmsbg.), July 27, 1769, and *New London Gaz.* (Conn.), July 21, 1769. Stout, "Manning the Royal Navy," *American Neptune,* XXIII (1963), 174. For a similar accusation against a surveyor-general of the king's woods, see Albion, *Forests and Sea Power,* 262.

21. Joseph Reed to the president of Congress, Oct. 21, 1779, in Hazard *et al.,* eds., *Pennsylvania Archives,* VII, 762. Five years earlier Reed had tried to impress upon Lord Dartmouth the importance of constraining Crown agents in the colonies if any reconciliation were to be made between Britain and the colonies. See his letter to Earl of Dartmouth, Apr. 4, 1774, in William B. Reed, *Life and Correspondence of Joseph Reed* (Philadelphia, 1847), I, 56-57. For a similar plea, again from a man close to the American Revolutionary leadership, see Stephen Sayre to Lord Dartmouth, Dec. 13, 1766, Dartmouth Papers, D 1778/2/258, William Salt Library, Stafford, England.

22. Rudé, *Crowd in History,* 60, 253-254. The restraint exercised by 18th century mobs has often been commented upon. See, for example, Wood, "A Note on Mobs," *Wm. and Mary Qtly.,* 3d Ser., XXIII (1966), 636-637.

23. Joseph Harrison's testimony in Wolkins, "Seizure of Hancock's Sloop 'Liberty,'" Mass. Hist. Soc., *Proceedings,* LV. 254.

24. Jay to Jefferson, Dec. 14, 1786, Boyd, ed., *Jefferson Papers,* X, 597. Beloff, *Public Order,* 30. John Swift to Boston customs commissioners, Nov. 15, 1770, Gov. William Franklin's Proclamation, Nov. 17, 1770, and John Hatton to Boston custom commissioners, Nov. 20, 1770, T. 1/476. The last mentioned riot occurred in November 1762. A cartel ship from Havana had stopped for repairs in October. On Nov. 21 a rumor spread that the Spaniards were murdering the inhabitants, which drew seamen from His Majesty's ship, *Arundel,* also in the harbor, into town, where the seamen drove the Spaniards into a house, set fire to it, and apparently intended to blow it up. A dignitary of the Spanish colonial service, who had been a passenger on the cartel ship, was beaten and some money and valuables were stolen from him. Local men tried to quell the riot without success. It was eventually put down by militiamen from Norfolk. See "A Narrative of a Riot in Virginia in November 1762," T. 1/476.

25. Burke and other to the same effect, quoted in Jerome J. Nadelhaft, "The revolutionary Era in South Carolina, 1775-1788" (unpubl. Ph.D. diss., University of Wisconsin, 1965), 151-152. See also account of the "Fort Wilson" riot of October 1779 in J. Thomas Scharf and Thompson Westcott, *History of Philadelphia, 1609-1884* (Philadelphia, 1884), I, 401-403.

26. Rude, *Crowd in History,* 255-257.

27. On the "hue and cry" see Frederick Pollock and Frederic W. Maitland, *The History*

of English Law before the Time of Edward I (Cambridge, Eng., 1968 [orig. publ., Cambridge, Eng., 1895]), II, 578–580, and William Blackstone, *Commentaries on the Laws of England* (Philadelphia, 1771), IV, 290–291. John Shy, *Toward Lexington: The Role of the British Army in the Coming of the American Revolution* (Princeton, 1965), 40. The English militia underwent a period of decay after 1670 but was revived in 1757. See J. R. Western, *The English Militia in the Eighteenth Century* (London, 1965).

28. Greenleaf's deposition, T. 1/446; *Providence Gaz.* (R.I.), Aug. 24, 1765. Western, *English Militia*, 74.

29. Gov. William Shirley explained the militia's failure to appear during the opening stages of the Knowles riot by citing the militiamen's opposition to impressment and consequent sympathy for the rioters. See his letter to the Lords of Trade, Dec. 1, 1747, in Lincoln, ed., *Shirley Correspondence,* I, 417–418. The English militia was also unreliable. It worked well against invasions and unpopular rebellions, but was less likely to support the government when official orders "clashed with the desires of the citizens" or when ordered to protect unpopular minorities. Sir Robert Walpole believed "that if called on to suppress smuggling, protect the turnpikes, or enforce the gin act, the militia would take the wrong side." Western, *English Militia,* 72–73.

30. Shirley to Josiah Willard, Nov. 19, 1747, Lincoln, ed., *Shirley Correspondence,* I, 407; Bernard's orders in *Providence Gaz.* (R.I.), Apr. 27, 1765.

31. Shy, *Toward Lexington,* 39–40, 44, 47, 74. Amherst, quoted in J. C. Long, *Lord Jeffery Amherst* (New York, 1933), 124.

32. Shy, *Toward Lexington,* 44; Beloff, *Public Order,* 157–158; Bridenbaugh, *Cities in Revolt,* 297; C. F. Adams, ed., *Works of Adams,* IV, 74–75, V, 209.

33. The definition of the common law of riot most commonly cited—for example, by John Adams in the Massacre trials—was from William Hawkins, *A Treatise of the Pleas of the Crown* (London, 1716), I, 155–159. See also, Blackstone, *Commentaries,* IV, 146–147, and Edward Coke, *The Third Part of the Institutes of the Laws of England* (London, 1797), 176.

34. Clark, "Impressment of Seamen," *Essays in Honor of Andrews,* 198–224; Stout, "Manning the Royal Navy," *American Neptune,* XXIII (1963), 178–179; and Leonard W. Labaree, ed., *Royal Instructions to British Colonial Governors, 1670–1776* (New York, 1935), I, 442–443.

35. L. Kinvin Wroth and Hiller B. Zobel, eds., *Legal Papers of John Adams* (Cambridge, Mass., 1965), III, 253. Account of the Norfolk incident by George Abyvon, Sept. 5, 1767, in Purdie and Dixon's *Va. Gaz.* (Wmsbg.), Oct. 1, 1767. Capt. Morgan quoted in Lemisch, "Jack Tar," *Wm. and Mary Qtly.,* 3d Ser., XXV (1968), 391. Munro, ed., *Acts of the Privy Council, Colonial Series,* VI, 374; Gov. Samuel Ward to Treasury lords, Oct. 23, 1765, Ward MSS, Box 1, fol. 58.

36. Knollenberg, *Origin of the Revolution,* 122–130; Albion, *Forests and Sea Power,* 255–258.

37. *N. Y. Jour.* (N.Y.C.), Aug. 18, 1768 (the writer was allegedly drawing together arguments that had recently appeared in the British press); and *N. Y. Jour. Supplement* (N.Y.C.), Jan. 4, 1770. Note also that Jefferson accepted Shays's Rebellion as a sign of health in American institutions only after he had been assured by men like Jay that the insurgents had acted purposely and moderately, and after he had concluded that the uprising represented no continuous threat to established government. "An insurrection in one of the 13. states in the course of 11. years that they have subsisted amounts to one in any particular state in 143 years, say a century and a half," he calculated. "This would not be near as many as has happened in every other government that has ever existed," and clearly posed no threat to the constitutional order as a whole. To David Hartley, July 2, 1787, Boyd, ed., *Jefferson Papers,* XI, 526.

38. John Locke, *The Second Treatise of Government,* paragraphs 223–225. "A State of Facts Concerning the Riots . . . in New Jersey," *New Jersey Archives,* VII, 217. *N. Y. Jour., Supp.* (N.Y.C.), Jan. 4, 1770. Johnson to Wm. Pitkin, Apr. 29, 1768, Massachusetts Histori-

cal Society, *Collections,* 5th Ser., IX (1885), 275. Adams as "Determinus" in *Boston Gazette,* Aug. 8, 1768; and Harry A. Cushing, ed., *The Writings of Samuel Adams* (New York, 1904–1908), I, 237. Jay to Jefferson, Oct. 27, 1786, Boyd, ed., *Jefferson Papers,* X, 488.

39. Wroth and Zobel, eds., *Adams Legal Papers,* III, 249–250; *N.Y. Jour. Supp.* (N.Y.C.), Aug. 18, 1768; Jefferson to Abigail Adams, Feb. 22, 1787, Boyd, ed., *Jefferson Papers,* XI, 174. C. F. Adams, ed., *Works of Adams,* IV, 77, 80 (quoting Algernon Sydney).

40. Jefferson to Edward Carrington, Jan. 16, 1787, Boyd, ed., *Jefferson Papers,* XI, 49, and Rev. James Madison to Jefferson, Mar. 28, 1787, *ibid.,* 252. Wroth and Zobel, eds., *Adams Legal Papers,* III, 250. Quincy's address to the jury in the soldiers' trial after the Boston Massacre in Josiah Quincy, *Memoir of the Life of Josiah Quincy, Junior, of Massachusetts Bay, 1744-1775,* ed. Eliza Susan Quincy, 3d ed. (Boston, 1875), 46. See also Massachusetts Assembly's similar statement in its address to Gov. Hutchinson, Apr. 24, 1770, Hutchinson, *History of Massachusetts Bay,* ed. Mayo, III, 365–366. This 18th century devotion to political "jealousy" resembles the doctrine of "vigilance" that was defended by 19th century vigilante groups. See Graham and Gurr, *Violence in America,* 179-183.

41. Jefferson to William Stephen Smith, Nov. 13, 1787, Boyd, ed., *Jefferson Papers,* XII, 356, Jefferson to Carrington, Jan. 16, 1787, *ibid.,* XI, 49, Jefferson to James Madison, Jan. 30, 1787, *ibid.,* 92–93. Taylor's remarks in "History of Violence," *The Listener,* CXXIX (1968), 701. ("Members of the House of Lords . . . said . . . if the people really don't like something, then they work our carriages and tear off our wigs and throw stones through the windows of our town-houses. And this is an essential thing to have if you are going to have a free country.") Hutchinson to [John or Robert] Grant, July 27, 1768, Massachusetts Archives, XXVI, 317, State House, Boston. See also the related story about John Seldon, the famous 17th century lawyer, told to the House of Commons in Jan. 1775 by Lord Camden and recorded by Josiah Quincy, Jr., in the "Journal of Josiah Quincy, Jun., During his Voyage and Residence in England from September 28th, 1774, to March 3d, 1775," Massachusetts Historical Society, *Proceedings,* L (1916-1917), 462–463. Seldon was asked what lawbook contained the laws for resisting tyranny. He replied he did not know, "but I'll tell [you] what is most certain, that it has always been the custom of England—and the Custom of England is the *Law of the Land.*"

42. On the developing distinction Americans drew between what was legal and constitutional, see Wood, *Creation of the American Republic,* 261-268.

43. *N.Y. Jour. Supp.* (N.Y.C.), Jan. 4, 1770; Wroth and Zobel, eds., *Adams Legal Papers,* III, 250, and C. F. Adams, ed., *Works of Adams,* VI, 151. Adams's views were altered in 1815, *ibid.,* X, 181. It is noteworthy that the Boston town meeting condemned the Knowles rioters not simply for their method of opposing impressment but because they insulted the governor and the legislature, and the Massachusetts Assembly acted against the uprising only after Gov. Shirley had left Boston and events seemed to be "tending to the destruction of all government and order." Hutchinson, *History of Massachusetts Bay,* ed. Mayo, II, 332-333. *Acts and Resolves of the Province of Massachusetts Bay,* III, 647. (Chap. 18 of the Province laws, 1752-1753, "An Act for Further Preventing all Riotous, Tumultuous and Disorderly Assemblies or Companies or Persons. . . .") This act, which was inspired particularly by Pope's Day violence, was renewed after the Boston Massacre in 1770 even though the legislature refused to renew its main Riot Act of 1751. *Ibid.,* IV, 87.

44. Arther M. Schlesinger, "Political Mobs and the American Revolution, 1765-1776," *Proceedings of the American Philosophical Society,* XCIX (1955), 246; Charles M. Andrews, *The Colonial Background of the American Revolution,* rev. ed. (New Haven, 1939), 176; Charles M. Andrews, "The Boston Merchants and the Non-Importation Movement," Colonial Society of Massachusetts, *Transactions,* XIX (1916-1917), 241; Hobsbawm, *Primitive Rebels,* III, 123-124.

45. Hutchinson to Thomas Pownall, [Sept. or Oct. 1765], Mass. Archives, XXVI, 157. Pauline Maier, "From Resistance to Revolution: American Radicals and the Development of Intercolonial Opposition to Britain, 1765-1776" (unpubl. PH.D. diss., Harvard University, 1968), I, 37–45, 72-215.

46. C. F. Adams, ed., *Works of Adams,* IV, 51; Rev. Samuel Langdon's election sermon to third Massachusetts Provincial Congress, May 31, 1775, quoted in Richard Frothingham, *Life and Times of Joseph Warren* (Boston, 1865), 499; Samuel Adams to Noah Webster, Apr. 30, 1784, Cushing, ed., *Writings of Samuel Adams,* IV, 305–306. On Gadsden see Richard Walsh, *Charleston's Sons of Liberty* (Columbia, 1959), 87.

47. *N.Y. Jour. Supp.* (N.Y.C.), Jan. 4, 1770; Jay to Jefferson, Oct. 27, 1786, Boyd, ed., *Jefferson Papers,* X, 488; Johnson to William Pitkin, July 23, 1768, Massachusetts Historical Society, *Collections,* 5th Ser., IX, 294–295.

48. *The Statutes at Large* [of Great Britain] (London, 1786), V, 4–6; Hoadly, ed., *Public Records of Connecticut,* VI, 346-348 for the law, and see also 332-333, 341-348; *Acts and Resolves of Massachusetts Bay,* III, 544–546, for the Riot Act of 1751, and see also Hutchinson, *History of Massachusetts Bay,* ed. Mayo, III, 6–7; and *Acts and Laws of the Commonwealth of Massachusetts* (Boston, 1893), 87–88, for Act of 1786; "A State of Facts Concerning the Riots . . . in New Jersey," *N.J. Archives,* VII, 211–212, 221–222; *The Statutes at Large of Pennsylvania . . .* (n.p., 1899), VI, 325–328; William A. Saunders, ed., *The Colonial Records of North Carolina* (Raleigh, 1890), VIII, 481–486; *Laws of the Colony of New York in the Years 1774 and 1775* (Albany, 1888), 38–43.

49. See additional instruction to Gov. Josiah Martin, Saunders, ed., *Colonial Records of North Carolina,* VIII, 515–516; and *Laws of the State of New York* (Albany, 1886), I, 20.

50. *The Craftsman* (London, 1731), VI, 263–264. Connecticut and Massachusetts laws cited in n. 45; and *Laws of the State of New Jersey* (Trenton, 1821), 279–281.

51. Jefferson to Madison, Jan. 30, 1787, Boyd, ed., *Jefferson Papers,* XI, 93.

52. See Bradley Chapin, "Colonial and Revolutionary Origins of the American Law of Treason," *Wm. and Mary Qtly.,* 3d Ser., XVII (1960), 3–21.

53. Elbridge Gerry in Congressional debates, quoted in Irving Brant, *The Bill of Rights, Its Origin and Meaning* (Indianapolis, 1965), 486; Samuel Adams, quoting Blackstone, as "E. A." in *Boston Gaz.,* Feb. 27, 1769, and Cushing, ed., *Writings of Samuel Adams,* I, 317. Timothy Dwight, quoted in Daniel J. Boorstin, *The Americans: The Colonial Experience* (New York, 1958), 353.

54. Wood, *Creation of the American Republic,* 410.

55. Judge Aedanus Burke's Charge to the Grand Jury at Charleston, June 9, 1783, in *South-Carolina Gazette and General Advertiser* (Charleston), June 10, 1783; "A Patriot," *ibid.,* July 15, 1783; and "Another Patriot," *ibid.,* July 29, 1783; and on the relevance of jealousy of power, see a letter to Virginia in *ibid.,* Aug. 9, 1783. "Democratic Gentle-Touch," *Gazette of the State of South Carolina* (Charleston), May 13, 1784.

56. Wood, *Creation of the American Republic,* 612–614.

57. J. H. Plumb, *The Origins of Political Stability, England 1675–1725* (Boston, 1967), xv, 187; John Adams on the leaders of the Shays's Rebellion in a letter to Benjamin Hitchborn, Jan. 27, 1787, in C. F. Adams, ed., *Works of Adams,* IX, 551; modern definitions of riot in "Riot Control and the Use of Federal Troops," *Harvard Law Review,* LXXXI (1968), 643.

Alden T. Vaughan

THE "HORRID AND UNNATURAL" REBELLION OF DANIEL SHAYS

Most American violence has pitted group against group and individual against individual rather than citizen against the state. For this reason the rebellion of sturdy country farmers and army veterans led by Daniel Shays against the Commonwealth of Massachusetts in 1786 is interesting. But the fact that the state was a target does not fully explain why this insurgency occupies a unique place in American annals. In many ways a typical eighteenth-century uprising, it occurred at a time of constitutional and political ferment in the newly independent United States. The Massachusetts turmoil forced many to ponder anew the relationship between liberty and authority under the Articles of Confederation, and undoubtedly the frightened reaction to this violence gave an emotional push to the events that culminated in the adoption of the U.S. Constitution.

In the following essay, Alden T. Vaughan traces the course and consequences of the Bay State insurrection. His conclusion poses an interesting paradox. On the one hand, violence such as Shays's Rebellion can result in positive change in a free society although on the other, the federal government under the Constitution is invested with the power to suppress such tumult if it should surface again. One issue to consider is whether the attitudes that supported mob violence as a quasi-legitimate part of the political process described by Pauline Maier were rendered obsolete in the new republic established following the Revolution.

October, 1786: "Are your people . . . mad?" thundered the usually calm George Washington to a Massachusetts correspondent. Recent events in the Bay State had convinced the General, who was living the life of a country squire at Mount Vernon, that the United States was "fast verging to anarchy and confusion!" Would the nation that had so recently humbled the British Empire now succumb to internal dissension and die in its infancy? To many Americans in the fall of 1786 it seemed quite possible, for while Washington was writing frantic notes to his friends, several thousand insurgents under the nominal leadership of a Revolutionary War veteran named Daniel Shays were closing courts with impunity, defying the state militia, and threatening to revamp the state government.

The uprising in Massachusetts was serious in itself, but more frightening was the prospect that it could spread to the other states. It had, in fact, already tainted Rhode Island, Vermont, and New Hampshire, and it showed some danger of infecting Connecticut and New York as well. By the spring of 1787, American spokesmen from Maine to Georgia were alarmed, Congress had been induced to raise troops for possible deployment against the rebels, and observers on both sides of the Atlantic voiced concern for the future of the nation. Even John Adams in London and Thomas Jefferson in Paris took time from their critical diplomatic duties to comment—the former, as might be expected, pessimistically; the latter with his usual optimism—on the causes and consequences of Shays' Rebellion. And well they might: the Massachusetts uprising of 1786–87 was to make a lasting contribution to the future of the United States by magnifying the demand for a stronger central government to replace the one created by the Articles of Confederation—a demand that reached fruition in the drafting and ratification of the Constitution in 1787–88. From the vantage point of the twentieth century, the rebellion of Daniel Shays stands—with the exception of the Civil War—as the nation's most famous and important domestic revolt.

The root of the trouble in Massachusetts lay in the economic chaos that accompanied political independence. The successful war against Great Britain had left the thirteen former colonies free to rule themselves, but it had also left them without the commercial ties that had done so much to promote colonial prosperity. While American producers, merchants, and shippers scurried after new goods and new markets to replace the old, the ill effects of economic independence crept across the nation.

Of all the American states, perhaps none felt the postwar slump so grievously as did Massachusetts. Its $14 million debt was staggering, as was its shortage of specie. Bay Staters once again swapped wheat for shoes, and cordwood for help with the plowing. They suffered too from the ruinous inflation that afflicted the entire nation as the value of Continental currency fell in the three years after 1777 to a ridiculous low of four thousand dollars in paper money to one dollar in silver or gold. But in addition, Massachusetts caught the full brunt of England's decision—vengeful, the Americans considered it—to curtail trade between the United States and the British West Indies. To New Englanders, more than half of whom lived in Massachusetts, the new British policy threatened economic disaster. Gone was their dominance of the carrying trade, gone the booms in shipbuilding, in distilling, in food and lumber exporting, and in the slave trade. Gone too was New England's chief source of hard cash, for the West Indies had been the one place with which New England merchants enjoyed a favorable balance of trade.

Most residents of Massachusetts were probably unaware of the seriousness of their plight until it came close to home. By the early 1780's the signs were unmistakable. Men in debt—and debt was epidemic in the late seventies and eighties—saw their farms confiscated by the state and sold for as little as a third of what they considered to be the true value. Others, less fortunate, found themselves in the dark and filthy county jails, waiting helplessly for sympathetic friends or embarrassed relatives to bail them out of debtors' prison. As the economic crisis worsened, a gloomy pessimism spread among the farmers and tradesmen in the central and western parts of the state.

The economic problems of Massachusetts were difficult, but probably not insoluble. At least they could have been lessened by a wise and considerate state government. Unfortunately for the Bay Staters, good government was as scarce as good money in the early 1780's. After creating a fundamentally sound framework of government in the state constitution of 1780, the voters of Massachusetts failed to staff it with farsighted and dedicated servants of the people. "Thieves, knaves, and robbers," snorted one disgruntled citizen. With mounting grievances and apathetic legislators, the people increasingly took matters into their own hands.

As early as February, 1782, trouble broke out in Pittsfield in the Berkshires, and before the year was over, mob actions had disrupted the tranquility of several other towns in the western part of the state. The immediate target of the Pittsfield agitators was the local court, which they temporarily closed by barring the door to members of the bench. A court that did not sit could not process foreclosures, pass judgments on debts, or confiscate property for defaulted taxes. In April, violence broke out at Northampton, where a former Connecticut clergyman named Samuel Ely—branded by one early historian as "a vehement, brazen-faced declaimer, abounding in hypocritical pretensions to piety, and an industrious sower of discord"—led the attack on the judges. Ely harangued a Northampton crowd to "go to the woodpile and get clubs enough, and knock their grey wigs off, and send them out of the world in an instant." Ely was promptly arrested and sentenced to six months in prison, but a mob soon freed him from the Springfield jail. The ex-parson found refuge in Vermont.

Instead of recognizing the validity of such protests, the Massachusetts legislature countered with a temporary suspension of habeas corpus and imposed new and higher court costs as well. And while the government did bend to the extent of authorizing certain foodstuffs and lumber to be used in lieu of money, the net effect of its measures was to rub salt into wounds already smarting. Currency remained dear, foreclosures mounted, the shadow of debtors' prison continued to cast a pall, and the state's legal system remained unduly complicated and expensive. Many citizens of western Massachusetts now began to question the benefits of independence; a few even concluded that the patriot leaders of 1776 had deluded them, and cheers for King George III were heard once again in towns that a few years before had cursed his name. And unrest continued to spread. In May, 1783, a mob tried to prevent the opening of the spring session of the Hampshire County Court at Springfield.

Perhaps the major outbreak of 1786 would have occurred a year or so sooner had it not been for a fortuitous combination of events that made the years 1784 and 1785 relatively easy to bear. In 1784 came news that a final peace had been signed with England; in 1785 Massachusetts farmers enjoyed their best harvest in several years, while the legislature, in one of its conciliatory if vagrant moods, refrained from levying a state tax. Although tempers continued to simmer, no serious outbreaks marred the period from early 1783 to midsummer 1786.

The episodes of 1782–83 and those that followed held a particular appeal for veterans of the Revolution. Even more than their civilian neighbors, the former soldiers nursed grievances that they could attribute to incompetent, if not dishonest, government. They had left their farms and shops to fight the hated redcoats, but they could not even depend on the paltry sums their services had earned for them. Inflation had made their Continental currency almost worthless, and now the government set up by the Articles of Confederation was delaying payment of overdue wages and retracting its promises of lifetime pensions to officers.

One lesson of the Revolution not lost on the Massachusetts veterans was that in times of necessity the people could reform an insensitive government by force of arms, and many of them still had in their possession the weapons they had used so effectively against the British and Hessian troops. Old habits and old weapons increasingly took on new meaning to the men of Massachusetts as the economic and political crisis of the 1780's deepened. The veterans of the Bay State knew where to find leadership, too, for among those hard-pressed by the economic problems of the decade were many who had served as officers during the War for Independence.

By 1786 several of these officers had emerged as acknowledged leaders in their own localities, although not until the final stages of the rebellion would any single commander claim the allegiance of more than a few hundred men at most.

In the eastern part of the state the most prominent leader was Captain Job Shattuck of Groton, a veteran of the French and Indian War as well as of the Revolution. Now in his fifties, Shattuck had been protesting vehemently, and sometimes violently, since 1781. His principal lieutenant in Middlesex County was Nathan Smith of Shirley, a tough veteran of both wartime and peacetime conflict—with a patch over one eye as testimony to his involvement in the latter. It was the burly Smith who on one occasion gave his hearers the unhappy choice of joining his band or being run out of town.

Farther west the rebels looked to other leaders. In Springfield and neighboring towns it was to Luke Day, said by some to be "the master spirit of the insurrection." A former brevet major in the Continental Army, Day seems to have had the inclination as well as the experience necessary to command a rebellion. In the dismal eighties he was often found grumbling his discontent in West Springfield's Old Stebbin's Tavern or drilling his followers on the town common.

But it was not upon Shattuck or Smith or Day that the final leadership devolved, with its mixed portions of glory and infamy, but on Captain Daniel Shays of Pelham. In some respects Shays was an improbable leader for a popular revolt, for he seems to have been a reluctant rebel in the first place; as late as the fall of 1786 he insisted: "I at their head! I am not." And even after he had assumed command of the bulk of the rebel army, he expressed eagerness to accept a pardon. But at the same time, Shays had attributes that made him a likely prospect for gaining the loyalty of the insurgents. Unlike the others, Shays presented a calm moderation that inspired confidence and respect. He also had a penchant for military courtesy and protocol, a quality that would have undoubtedly been repugnant to the veterans if overdone, but one that was essential if the "mobbers," as they were often called, were to acquire the discipline and organization necessary to resist the forces of government.

Daniel Shays also attracted confidence through his impressive Revolutionary War record. Joining the Continental Army at the outbreak of hostilities, he fought bravely at Bunker Hill (where his courage earned him a promotion to sergeant), served under Ethan Allen at Ticonderoga, helped thwart Gentleman Johnny Burgoyne at Saratoga, and stormed Stony Point with Mad Anthony Wayne. For recruiting a company of volunteers in Massachusetts Shays ultimately received a commission as their captain, a position he seems to have filled adequately if not outstandingly. And before leaving the service, Shays suffered at least one wound in battle.

Shays resigned from the army in 1780 and turned his hand to farming in the small town of Pelham, a few miles east of the Connecticut River. There his popularity, undoubtedly enhanced by his military reputation, won him election to various local offices. At the same time, Shays learned at first hand the problems that can beset a returned veteran. He had already sold for cash the handsome ceremonial sword that the Marquis de Lafayette had presented to him in honor of the victory at Saratoga. On long winter evenings at Conkey's Tavern, Daniel Shays listened to his neighbors' tales of distress. In 1784 he was himself sued for a debt of twelve dollars; by 1786 he was deeply involved in the insurrection. Like so many other men in western and central Massachusetts, Shays had been maneuvered by events of the postwar period into actions that he would hardly have contemplated a few years earlier.

The relative calm that followed the outbreaks of 1782–83 was abruptly shattered in 1786. To make up for the low revenue of the previous year, the legislature in the spring of 1786 imposed unusually heavy poll and property taxes, amounting to one third of the total income of the people. In 1774 taxes had been fifteen cents per capita; in 1786 they leaped to $1.75—a hefty sum for heads of families in frontier areas where a skilled laborer earned thirty to fifty cents a day. Protested one poor cobbler, "The constable keeps at us for rates, rates, rates!" Besides, the new tax schedule was notorious for its inequity, placing heavy duties on land without regard to its value —a palpable discrimination against the poorer farmers. The new schedule also worked injury on the least affluent classes by seeking almost forty per cent of its revenue through a head tax, asking equal amounts from pauper and merchant prince. As court and jail records poignantly testify, many people in the central and western parts of the state could not pay both the new taxes and their old debts. Worcester County, for example, had four thousand suits for debt in 1785–86 (double the total of the preceding two years), and the number of persons imprisoned for debt jumped from seven to seventy-two during that period. In 1786 debtors outnumbered all other criminals in Worcester County prisons 3 to 1.

The new taxes would probably have caused considerable anger by themselves, but when added to old grievances they were sure to bring trouble. During the summer of 1786, conventions met in several western counties—in Worcester, in Hampshire, in Berkshire—and even as far east as Middlesex, only a few miles from Boston. From these quasi-legal meetings came resolutions to the Massachusetts legislature calling for a variety of reforms: reduction of court and lawyers' fees, reduction of salaries for state officials, issuance of paper money, removal of the state capital from Boston (where it was deemed too susceptible to the influence of eastern commercial interests), reduction of taxes, redistribution of the tax load, and many similar changes. A few protests called for still more drastic reforms, such as abolition of the state senate and curtailment of the governor's appointive power, while some petitioners insisted on a state-wide convention to amend the constitution of 1780, now barely six years old. But on the whole the petitions demanded evolution, not revolution. This was a tempered and healthy challenge to an administration that had shown itself insensitive and incompetent.

In the protests about the government, two categories of citizens were singled out for criticism by the petitioners. First were the merchants and professional men, who enjoyed an unfair advantage within the tax system. Second were the lawyers, who seemed to be conspiring with judges and creditors to force the debtor still further into obligation. Perhaps not all lawyers were so harshly judged, but the condemnation was certainly meant to apply to those whom John Adams called "the dirty dabblers in the law," men who often created more litigation than they resolved. In contrast to the turbulent days before the Revolution, the new era in Massachusetts did not find lawyers in the vanguard of the movement for reform.

But in one respect, at least, the 1780's bore resemblance to the years before Lexington: peaceful protest soon gave way to more forceful action. In late August, following a Hampshire County convention at Hatfield, a mob of 1,500 men "armed with guns, swords, and other deadly weapons, and with drums beating and fifes playing" took command of the county courthouse at Northampton and forced the judges of the Court of Common Pleas and General Sessions of the Peace to adjourn sine die. During the next few months, similar conventions with similar results took place in Middlesex, Bristol, and Worcester counties. By early fall, mobs armed with muskets or hickory clubs and often sporting sprigs of hemlock in their hats as a sign of allegiance to the rebel cause moved at will through the interior counties.

The rebels did not go unopposed. In each county there were some citizens who looked askance at the growing anarchy and did their best to thwart it. In Worcester, seat of Worcester County, Judge Artemas Ward showed the mettle of those who would not succumb to mob rule. When on the fifth of September two hundred armed men blocked his path to the courthouse, the aging but still impressive ex-general defied the bayonets that pierced his judicial robes and for two hours lectured the crowd on the dangers of anarchy and the meaning of treason. A heavy downpour finally silenced the judge, though not until he had intoned a timely plea that "the sun never shine on rebellion in Massachusetts." But neither rain nor words had got the judge and his colleagues into the courthouse.

Elsewhere the story was much the same: a few citizens tried to stem the tide of rebellion but in the end were swept aside. At Great Barrington, in Berkshire County, a mob of 800 stopped the court, broke open the jail and released its prisoners, and abused the judges who protested. At Springfield, Daniel Shays and Luke Day made sure that the courthouse doors remained shut, while at Concord, less than twenty miles from Boston, Job Shattuck, aided by Nathan Smith and his brother Sylvanus, prevented the sitting of the Middlesex County Court. Only at Taunton, in Bristol County did a sizable mob meet its match. There Chief Justice (and former general) David Cobb was ready with a field piece, thirty volunteers, and a determination to "sit as a judge or die as a general." The Bristol court met as scheduled.

Governor James Bowdoin and the legislature responded to the latest outbreaks with a confusing mixture of sternness, concession, and indecision. In early September, the Governor issued his first proclamation, condemning the mobbers' flirtation with "riot, anarchy and confusion." In October the legislature suspended habeas corpus, but it also authorized some categories of goods as legal tender for specified kinds of public and private debts, and it offered full pardon to all rebels who would take an oath of allegiance before the end of the year. Yet the government failed to find solutions to the major complaints. No significant reforms were made in court procedures, the tax load was not reduced, officials' salaries were not lowered, the capital was not moved, and no curbs were placed on lawyers' machinations.

As mob violence continued through the fall of 1786, spokemen in the Bay State and elsewhere voiced a growing fear that the anarchy of Massachusetts might infect the entire nation. Several months earlier John Jay had predicted a crisis—"something I cannot foresee or conjecture. I am uneasy and apprehensive; more so than during the war." Now Secretary of War Henry Knox, Massachusetts statesman Rufus King, and others began to have similar apprehensions. They wrote frantic letters to one another, asking for news and predicting disaster. Abigail Adams, then in London, bristled at the "ignorant and wrestless desperadoes," while reports of the uprising helped prod her husband John into writing his ponderous *Defence of the Constitutions.* Even General Washington lost his equanimity. "[For] God's sake, tell me," he wrote to his former aide-de-camp, David Humphreys, in October, "what is the cause of all these commotions? Do they proceed from licentiousness, British influence disseminated by the tories, or real grievances which admit of redress? If the latter, why were they delayed 'till the public mind had been so much agitated? If the former, why are not the powers of Government tried at once?"

Fearful that the powers of state government would not be sufficient to thwart the rebellion, Governor Bowdoin and Secretary of War Knox hatched a scheme for employing federal troops should the need arise. Knox discussed the matter with Congress: the outcome was a call for 1,340 volunteers for the federal army (which then numbered only 700), most of them to be raised in Massachusetts and Connecticut. The additional troops were ostensibly to be used against the Indians of the Northwest, but in secret session Congress acknowledged the possibility that they might be sent instead against the self-styled "regulators" in New England, and that they might be needed to protect the federal arsenal in Springfield—a likely target for the rebellious veterans. Meanwhile the Massachusetts Council authorized a state army of 4,400 men and four regiments of artillery, to be drawn largely from the militia of the eastern counties.

Command of the state forces fell to Major General Benjamin Lincoln, a battle-tested veteran of the Revolution, and a man of tact and humanity as well as martial vigor. But before taking the field, Lincoln served a brief stint as fund-raiser for his own army, for the cost of a thirty-day campaign had been calculated at about £5,000, or about $20,000, and the impoverished state treasury could offer nothing but promises of eventual reimbursement to any who would lend cash to the government. In less than twenty-four hours General Lincoln collected contributions from 130 of Boston's wealthy citizens, including £250 from Governor Bowdoin.

By the time Lincoln's army was equipped for action, the rebellion was over in eastern Massachusetts. It had never been strong there, but in November of 1786 a mob tried to halt the Middlesex County Court. This time the militia was alert. After a brief skirmish in which Job Shattuck received a crippling wound, the Groton leader and two of his lieutenants were captured. While Shattuck languished in the Boston jail, his followers drifted west to join other rebel groups.

The situation now grew more alarming in Worcester, where the Supreme Court was scheduled to meet on December 5; by late November, mobs of armed men drifting into town had closed the Court of Common Pleas and made it obvious that no court could meet without an army to back it up. Local officials looked on helplessly. Even bold Sheriff Greenleaf, who offered to help alleviate the high court costs by hanging every rebel free of charge, was powerless in the face of such numbers, and he became a laughingstock to boot when he strode away from the courthouse one day unaware that someone had adorned his hat with the symbolic hemlock tuft.

At first the rebels at Worcester suffered from lack of a universally recognized leader. Then in early December Daniel Shays rode in from Pelham, mounted on a white horse and followed by 350 men. He had not come to do battle if he could avoid it; to a friend he confided: "For God's sake, have matters settled peaceably: it was against my inclinations I undertook this business; importunity was used which I could not withstand, but I heartily wish it was well over." Still, as a showdown with the judges approached, Shays increasingly assumed the role of spokesman for the disparate forces. And it was just as well; with milling crowds of disgruntled veterans and a frightened and divided populace, violence might well have erupted. Instead, choosing wisdom as the better part of valor, the rebels put their energies into drafting a petition to the legislature for a redress of grievances and into several wordy defenses of their own actions. Violence was scrupulously avoided. And their immediate point, after all, had been won; the Worcester court gathered meekly in the Sun Tavern and adjourned until January 23. The insurgents then gave way before the more impressive force of winter blizzards and dispersed to the west. Friends of the rebels were not greatly heartened, however, for the basic grievances remained. Friends of the government rejoiced at the retreat of the rebels, and chanted:

Says sober Bill, ''Well Shays has fled,
And peace returns to bless our days!''
''Indeed,'' cries Ned, ''I always said
He'd prove at last a fall-back Shays,
And those turned over and undone
Call him a worthless Shays, to run!''

But Shays was only running to a new scene of action. The Hampshire County court, scheduled to meet in Springfield in late January, should be stopped. Besides, the federal arsenal in that town had the only cache of arms the rebels could hope to capture, and without weapons the rebellion must collapse.

General Lincoln was preparing to defend the January session of the Worcester court when news reached him of the crisis in Springfield. The arsenal there boasted a garrison of some 1,100 militia under General William Shepard, but surrounding the troops were three rebel forces: Daniel Shays commanded 1,200 men at Wilbraham, eight miles to the east; Eli Parson had 400 at Chicopee, three miles to the north; Luke Day led another 400 at West Springfield, just across the Connecticut River to the west. There was every reason to believe they could overwhelm Shepard's garrison if they were willing to risk some bloodshed. General Lincoln headed for Springfield on the double.

Had Shays and his cohorts carried out their original plan they would in all likelihood have had possession of the arsenal before Lincoln arrived with reinforcements. The attack had been set for January 25: Shays was to have led a frontal assault from the southeast while Day directed a flanking movement from the west. But at the last minute Day decided to wait until the twenty-sixth, and his note informing Shays of the change was intercepted by Shepard's men. When Shays moved forward on the afternoon of the twenty-fifth, Shepard confidently grouped his full strength against the lone attack. But not much strength was needed. Shepard fired only three cannon shots. When two warning volleys failed to turn back the rebels, Shepard aimed the third into their midst. Three insurgents fell dead in the snow, a fourth lay mortally wounded. The remainder fled in confusion. It was a shattered band that Shays succeeded in regrouping a few miles from the scene of conflict.

At this point General Lincoln arrived and took position between Day and Shays. Both rebel armies at once broke camp and headed for safer territory—Day's men so hastily that they left pork and beans baking in their ovens and discarded knapsacks strewn along their route. The main force, under Shays, beat a rapid retreat to the northeast, passing through Ludlow, South Hadley, Amherst, and Pelham. Lincoln followed in close pursuit, moving overland after Shays, while General Shepard marched up the frozen Connecticut River to prevent a reunion of the rebel army's eastern and western wings.

At Hadley, General Lincoln halted his pursuit long enough to discuss surrender proposals with Shays. The rebel leader was willing to negotiate, but his insistence on an unconditional pardon for himself and his men was more than General Lincoln was authorized to grant. With no agreement likely, Shays suddenly shifted his men to the relative security of Petersham, a center of regulator sentiment which lay in terrain easier to defend. It was midwinter—an unusually cold and stormy winter—and deep snow blanketed the Connecticut Valley. Perhaps the militia would not bother to follow.

But Shays reckoned without General Lincoln. Ever since 1780, when he had surrendered Charleston, South Carolina, and its garrison of 5,400 men to the British in the most costly American defeat of the Revolution, Benjamin Lincoln had had to endure charges of cowardice and indecision. Although he had been officially exonerated, a few critics persisted; in a vigorous suppression of the Shaysites General Lincoln could perhaps fully restore himself in the public's esteem. With superb stamina and determination, Lincoln marched his men the thirty miles from Hadley to Petersham through a blinding snowstorm on the night of Saturday, February 3, arriving at Petersham early the next morning. Taken completely by surprise, the insurgents were routed: some 150 were captured; the rest, including Shays, escaped to the north. Lincoln then moved across the Connecticut River to disperse rebel nests in the Berkshires. By the end of February only scattered resistance remained. What the legislature had recently condemned as a "horrid and unnatural Rebellion and War . . . traiterously raised and levied against this Commonwealth" had come to an inglorious end.

While the militia crushed the remnants of rebellion, the state government drafted a series of regulations for punishing the insurgents. In mid-February, two weeks after Shays' dispersal at Petersham, it issued a stiff Disqualifying Act, offering pardons to privates and noncommissioned officers, but denying them for three years the right to vote, to serve on juries, and to be employed as schoolteachers, innkeepers, or liquor retailers. Massachusetts citizens would thus be shielded from the baneful influence of the Shaysites. Not included in the partial amnesty were the insurgent officers, citizens of other states who had joined the Massachusetts uprising, former state officers or members of the state legislature who had aided the rebels, and persons who had attended regulator conventions. Men in those categories would be tried for treason.

The government's vindictive measures aroused widespread protest, not only from those who had sympathized with the rebel cause but from many of its active opponents as well. General Lincoln, among others, believed that such harsh reprisals would further alienate the discontented, and he observed to General Washington that the disfranchisement of so many people would wholly deprive some towns of their representation in the legislature. New outbreaks, he argued, would then occur in areas that had no other way to voice their grievances. In token concession to its critics, the legislature in March, 1787, appointed a special commission of three men to determine the fate of rebels not covered by the Disqualifying Act. General Lincoln served on the commission, and under his moderating influence it eventually extended pardons to 790 persons. But in the meantime, county courts apprehended and tried whatever rebel leaders they could find. In Hampshire County, with Robert Treat Paine serving as prosecuting attorney, six men were sentenced to death and many others incurred fines or imprisonment. In Berkshire County eight men were sentenced to die for their part in the uprising.

Had the government of 1786–87 remained in office, more than a dozen lives would have been lost to the hangman, hundreds of other men would have suffered disqualifications, and the fundamental causes of Shays' Rebellion might have lingered on to trigger new outbreaks. But however strongly the regulators might complain of the legislative and judicial shortcomings of Massachusetts, they had cause to be thankful that its constitution required annual elections and that the franchise was broad enough to let popular sentiment determine the tenor of government. The result of the April election revealed the breadth and depth of the sympathy in which the regulators were held by the citizens and the extent of popular revulsion at the ineptitude of the government. In the gubernatorial contest, popular John Hancock, recently recovered from an illness that had caused him to resign the governorship early in 1785, overwhelmingly defeated Governor Bowdoin. Only 62 of the 222 members of the legislature and 11 members of the 24-man senate were returned to their seats. In some instances the voters chose men who had actively participated in the rebellion, including Josiah Whitney, who had recently served sixteen days in the Worcester jail.

Within the next few months the new legislature sharply mitigated both the causes of unrest and the punishments assigned to the rebels. It repealed the Disqualifying Act, reprieved all men under sentence of death—some on the very steps of the gallows—and by the following summer it had pardoned even Daniel Shays, though he and a few other leaders were still precluded from holding civil and military offices in the state. Equally important, it enacted long-range reforms—extending the law that permitted the use of certain personal and real property in payment of debts, imposing a lower and more equitable tax schedule, and releasing most debtors from prison.

Now in truth the rebellion was over. Peace, and soon prosperity, returned to the Massachusetts countryside. Differences of opinion still lingered, of course, as was made clear one Sunday when the church at Whately christened two infants—one name after Daniel Shays, the other after Benjamin Lincoln. But the Shaysites made no further trouble for Bay State authorities, and Daniel Shays, the reluctant leader, soon moved on to New York State, where he eked out a skimpy existence on his Revolutionary War pension until his death in 1825.

Americans of the 1780's drew various lessons from the affair in Massachusetts. Some, like Washington and Madison, appear to have misinterpreted the event and ascribed to the rebels a more drastic program than the majority of them had ever advocated. Others, like Mercy Warren, the lady historian, and Joseph Hawley, the Massachusetts patriot, detected the hand of Great Britain behind the uprising. Still others sensed that the true causes of Shays's Rebellion were local in origin and primarily in fault of the state government. Baron von Steuben had correctly surmised that "when a whole people complains . . . something must be wrong," while Thomas Jefferson, then American Minister to France, thought the rebellion of no dangerous importance and preferred to set it in a broader perspective than had most Americans. "We have had," wrote Jefferson, "13 states independent 11 years. There has been one rebellion. That comes to one rebellion in a century and a half for each state. What country before ever existed without a rebellion? And what country can preserve its liberties if their rulers are not warned from time to time that the people preserve the spirit of resistance? . . . The tree of liberty must be refreshed from time to time with the blood of patriots and tyrants." But while observers were drawing these diverse conclusions from the episode in Massachusetts, an increasing number of Americans were concerned with how to make sure it would never happen again.

On May 25, 1787, less than four months after the rout at Petersham, the Constitutional Convention began its deliberations at Independence Hall, Philadelphia. Through a long hot summer the delegates proposed, argued, and compromised as they sought to construct a new and better form of government for the American nation. And among the knottiest problems they faced were several recently emphasized by Shays's Rebellion: problems of currency regulation, of debts and contracts, and of ways to thwart domestic insurrection. As the records of the federal Convention reveal, the recent uprising in Massachusetts lay heavily on the minds of the delegates. Although it is impossible to pinpoint the exact phrases in the final document that owed their wording to the fear of similar revolts, there is no doubt that the Constitution reflected the determination of the Founding Fathers to do all they could to prevent future rebellions and to make it easier for the new government to suppress them if they did occur. Significantly, the new polity forbade the states to issue paper money, strengthened the military powers of the executive branch, and authorized Congress to call up state militiamen to "suppress Insurrections" and enforce the laws of the land. Jefferson's first glimpse of the Constitution convinced him that "our Convention has been too much impressed by the insurrection of Massachusetts. . . ." Jefferson exaggerated, but it is clear that the movement for a stronger central government had gained immense momentum from the "horrid and unnatural Rebellion" of Daniel Shays.

By the summer of 1788 the requisite nine states had ratified the new Constitution, and in the following spring General Washington took the oath of office as President. In the prosperous and dynamic years that followed, the passions generated by the insurrection in Massachusetts were gradually extinguished. But the lesson and the impact of Shays' Rebellion are still with us. Because of it, important changes were made in the government of Massachusetts as well as in the government of the nation, changes that have stood the test of time. Perhaps this episode lends some ironic credence to Thomas Jefferson's suggestion that "the spirit of resistance to government is . . . valuable on certain occasions."

Gerald Carson

WATERMELON ARMIES AND WHISKEY BOYS

In 1794, frontiersmen in western Pennsylvania erupted into open rebellion against a tax levied on distilled whiskey by an act of Congress in 1791. To stop payment of the hated tax, angry insurgents intimidated tax collectors, aborted trials and used other methods of terrorism familiar to the eighteenth century. The uprising tested the capacity of the new federal government to enforce the law. According to the Constitution, Congress is empowered "to provide for calling forth the militia to execute the laws of the Union." Congress, in turn, had authorized the President to summon the state militia in such cases. But would President Washington risk issuing a call and would militiamen, including Pennsylvanians, rise to the summons and march against their countrymen?

What happened is described in the following article by Gerald Carson. Americans in almost every generation since have had to deal with the question of when, whether, and how, in a free society, it is appropriate to invoke public force against popular disturbances.

When one recalls that the President of the United States, the Secretary of War, the Secretary of the Treasury and the governors of four states once mobilized against the farmers of western Pennsylvania almost as large an army as ever took the field in the Revolutionary War, the event appears at first glance as one of the more improbable episodes in the annals of this country. Thirteen thousand grenadiers, dragoons, foot soldiers and pio-

From Gerald Carson, *The Social History of Bourbon.* Reprinted by permission of Curtis Brown, Ltd. Copyright © 1963 by Gerald Carson.

neers, a train of artillery with six-pounders, mortars and several "grass-hoppers," equipped with mountains of ammunition, forage, baggage and a bountiful stock of tax-paid whiskey, paraded over the mountains to Pittsburgh against a gaggle of homespun rebels who had already dispersed.

Yet the march had a rationale. President George Washington and his Secretary of the Treasury, Alexander Hamilton, moved to counter civil commotion with overwhelming force because they well understood that the viability of the United States Constitution was involved. Soon after he assumed his post at the Treasury, Hamilton had proposed, to the astonishment of the country, that the United States should meet fully and promptly its financial obligations, including the assumption of the debts contracted by the states in the struggle for independence. The money was partly to be raised by laying an excise tax upon distilled spirits. The tax, which was universally detested in the West—"odious" was the word most commonly used to describe it—became law on March 3, 1791.

The news of the passage of the measure was greeted with a roar of indignation in the back country settlements. The duty was laid uniformly upon all the states, as the Constitution provided. If the West had to pay more, Secretary Hamilton explained, it was only because it used more whiskey. The East could, if it so desired, forgo beverage spirits and fall back on cider and beer. The South could not. It had neither orchards nor breweries. To Virginia and Maryland the excise tax appeared to be as unjust and oppressive as the well-remembered Molasses Act and the tea duties of George III. "The time will come," predicted fiery James Jackson of Georgia in the House of Representatives, "when a shirt shall not be washed without an excise."

Kentucky, then thinly settled, but already producing its characteristic hand-made, whole-souled liquor from planished copper stills, was of the opinion that the law was unconstitutional. Deputy revenue collectors throughout the Bluegrass region were assaulted, their papers stolen, their horses' ears cropped and their saddles cut to pieces. On one wild night the people of Lexington dragged a stuffed dummy through the streets and hanged in effigy Colonel Thomas Marshall, the chief collector for the district.

Yet in no other place did popular fury rise so high, spread so rapidly, involve a whole population so completely, express so many assorted griev-ances, as in the Pennsylvania frontier counties of Fayette, Allegheny, Westmoreland and Washington. In these counties, around 1791, a light plume of wood smoke rose from the chimneys of no less than five thousand log stillhouses. The rates went into effect on July first. The whiskey maker could choose whether he would pay a yearly levy on his still capacity or a gallonage tax ranging from nine to eleven cents on his actual production.

Before the month was out, "committees of correspondence," in the old Revolutionary phrase, were speeding horsemen over the ridges and through the valleys to arouse the people to arm and assemble. The majority, but not all, of the men who made the whiskey decided to "forbear" from paying the tax. The revenue officers were thoroughly worked over. Robert Johnson, for example, collector for Washington and Allegheny counties, was waylaid near Pigeon Creek by a mob disguised in women's clothing. They cut off his hair, gave him a coat of tar and feathers and stole his horse.

The Pennsylvania troubles were rooted in the economic importance and impregnable social position of mellow old Monongahela rye whiskey. In 1825, for instance, when the Philadelphia Society for Promoting Agriculture offered a gold medal to the person in Pennsylvania who carried on large-scale farming operations without providing ardent spirits for his farm workers, the medal could not be awarded. There were no entries for the uncoveted honor.

The frontier people had been reared from childhood on the family jug of farmer whiskey. They found the taste pleasant, the effect agreeable. Whiskey was usually involved when there was kissing or fighting. It beatified the rituals of birth and death. The doctor kept a bottle in his office for his own use under the deceptive label "Arsenic—Deadly poison." The lawyer produced the bottle when the papers were signed. Whiskey was available in the prothonotary's office when the trial-list was made up. Jurors got their dram, and the constable drew his ration for his services on election day. The hospitable barrel and the tin cup were the mark of the successful political candidate. The United States Army issued a gill to a man every day. Ministers of the gospel were paid in rye whiskey, for they were shepherds of a devout flock, Scotch Presbyterians mostly, who took their Bible straight, especially where it said: "Give strong drink unto him that is ready to perish, and wine unto those that be of heavy hearts."

With grain the most abundant commodity west of the mountains, the farmers could eat it or drink it, but they couldn't sell it in distant markets unless it was reduced in bulk and enhanced in value. A Pennsylvania farmer's "best holt," then, was whiskey. A pack-horse could move only four bushels of grain. But it could carry twenty-four bushels if it was condensed into two kegs of whiskey slung across its back, while the price of the goods would double when they reached the eastern markets. So whiskey became the remittance of the fringe settlements for salt, sugar, nails, bar iron, pewter plates, powder and shot. Along the western rivers where men saw few shilling pieces, a gallon of good, sound rye whiskey was a stable measure of value.

The bitter resistance of the western men to the whiskey tax involved both practical considerations and principles. First, the excise payment was due and must be paid in hard money as soon as the water-white distillate flowed from the condensing coil. The principle concerned the whole repulsive idea of an internal revenue levy. The settlers of western Pennsylvania were a bold, hardy, emigrant race who brought with them bitter memories of oppression under the excise laws in Scotland and Ireland, involving invasion of their homes, confiscation of their property and a system of paid informers. Revenue collectors were social outcasts in a society which warmly seconded Doctor Samuel Johnson's definition of excise: "a hateful tax levied upon commodities, and adjudged not by the common judges of property, but wretches hired by those to whom excise is paid."

The whiskey boys in Pennsylvania saw it as simply a matter of sound Whig doctrine to resist the exciseman as he made his rounds with Dicas' hydrometer to measure the proof of the whiskey and his marking iron to brand the casks with his findings. Earlier, Pennsylvania had taxed spirits. But whiskey produced for purely private use was exempt. William Findley of Westmoreland County, a member of Congress at the time and a sympathetic interpreter of the western point of view, looked into this angle. To his astonishment, he learned that all of the whiskey distilled in the west was for purely personal use. So far as the state's excise tax was concerned, or any other tax, for that matter, the sturdy Celtic peoples of the Monongahela region had cheerfully returned to nature: they just didn't pay. About every sixth man made whiskey. But all were involved in the problem, since the other five took their grain to the stillhouse where the master distiller turned it into liquid form.

The state had been lenient. But now matters had taken a more serious turn. The new federal government in Philadelphia was dividing the whole country up into "districts" for the purpose of collecting the money. And the districts were subdivided into smaller "surveys." The transmontane Pennsylvanians found themselves in the grip of something known as the fourth survey, with General John Neville, hitherto a popular citizen and leader, getting ready to enforce the law, with a reward paid to informers and a percentage to the collectors, who appeared to be a rapacious set.

The first meeting of public protest against the 1791 federal tax was held at Redstone Old Fort, now Brownsville. The proceedings were moderate on that occasion, and scarcely went beyond the right of petition. Another meeting in August, more characteristic of others which were to follow, was radical in tone, disorderly, threatening. It passed resolves to the effect that any person taking office under the revenue law was an enemy of society.

When warrants were issued in the affair of Robert Johnson, the process server was robbed, beaten, tarred and feathered and left tied to a tree in the forest. As the inspectors' offices were established, they were systematically raided. Liberty poles reappeared as whiskey poles. The stills of operators who paid the tax were riddled with bullets in attacks sardonically known as "mending" the still. This led to a popular description of the Whiskey Boys as "Tom the Tinker's Men," an ironical reference to the familiar, itinerant repairer of pots and kettles. Notices proposing measures for thwarting the law, or aimed at coercing the distillers, were posted on trees or published in the *Pittsburgh Gazette* over the signature, "Tom the Tinker," nom de plume of the insurgent John Holcroft and other anti-tax agitators. Findley, who tried to build a bridge of understanding between the backwoodsmen and the central government, described the outbreak as not the result of any concerted plan, but rather as a flame, "an infatuation almost incredible."

An additional grievance grew out of the circumstance that offenders were required to appear in the federal court at Philadelphia, three hundred miles away. The whiskey-makers saw this distant government as being no less oppressive than one seated in London, and often drew the parallel. The Scotch-Irish of western Pennsylvania were, in sum, anti-federalist, anti-tax, and it may be added, anti-Indian. West of Pittsburgh lay Indian country. The men of the west held to a simple concept of how to solve the Indian problem: extermination. The Indians had the same program, in reverse, and were getting better results. The bungling campaigns, which generals Hamar and St. Clair had conducted in the early 1790's made the people of the fringe settlements despair of the ability of the Union to protect them.

Congress amended the excise tax law in 1792 and again in 1794 to lighten the burden on country distillers. A further conciliatory step was taken. To ease the hardships of the judicial process, Congress gave to the state courts jurisdiction in excise offenses so that accused persons might be tried in their own vicinity. But some fifty or sixty writs already issued and returnable to Philadelphia resulted in men being carried away from their fields during harvest time. This convinced the insurgents that the federalist East was seeking a pretext to discipline the democratic West.

One day in July, while the papers were being served, William Miller, a delinquent farmer-distiller, and political supporter of General Neville, saw the General riding up his lane accompanied by a stranger who turned out to be a United States marshal from Philadelphia. The marshal unlimbered an official paper and began to read a summons. It ordered said Miller peremptorily to "set aside all manner of business and excuses" and appear in his "proper person" before a Philadelphia judge. Miller had been planning to sell his property and remove to Kentucky. The cost of the trip to Philadelphia and the fine for which he was liable would eat up the value of his land and betterments. The farm was as good as gone.

"I felt my blood boil at seeing General Neville along to pilot the sheriff to my very door," Miller said afterward. "I felt myself mad with passion."

As Neville and the marshal rode away, a party from the county militia which was mustered at Mingo Creek fired upon them, but there were no casualties. When the General reached Bower Hill, his country home above the Chartiers Valley, another party under the command of John Holcroft awaited him there and demanded his commission and official papers. The demand was refused and both sides began to shoot. As the rebels closed in on the main house, a flanking fire came from the Negro cabins on the plantation. The Whiskey Boys were driven off with one killed and four wounded.

The next day, Major James McFarlane, a veteran of the Revolution, led an attack in force upon Neville's painted and wall-papered mansion, furnished with such marvels as carpets, mirrors, pictures and prints and an eight-day clock. The house was now defended by a dozen soldiers from Fort Fayette at Pittsburgh. A fire-fight followed during which a soldier was shot and McFarlane was killed—by treachery, the rebels said, when a white flag was displayed. The soldiers surrendered and were either released or allowed to escape. Neville was not found, but his cabins, barns, outbuildings and finally the residence were all burned to the ground. Stocks of grain were destroyed, all fences leveled, as the victors broke up the furniture, liberated the mirrors and clock, and distributed Neville's supply of liquor to the mob.

The funeral of McFarlane caused great excitement. Among those present were Hugh Henry Brackenridge, author, lawyer and one of the western moderates, and David Bradford, prosecuting attorney for Washington County. The former wished to find ways to reduce the tension; the latter to increase it. Bradford was a rash, impetuous Marylander, ambitious for power and position. Some thought him a second-rate lawyer. Others disagreed. They said he was third-rate. But he had a gift for rough mob eloquence. Bradford had already robbed the United States mails to find out what information was being sent east against the conspirators. He had already called for the people to make a choice of "submission or opposition . . . with *head, heart, hand and voice.*"

At Major McFarlane's funeral service Bradford worked powerfully upon the feelings of his sympathizers as he described "the murder of McFarlane." Brackenridge also spoke, using wit and drollery to let down the pressure and to make palatable his warning to the insurgents that they were flirting with the possibility of being hanged. But the temper of the throng was for Bradford, clearly revealed in the epitaph which was set over McFarlane's grave. It said "He fell . . . by the hands of an unprincipled villain in the support of what he supposed to be the rights of his country."

The high-water mark of the insurrection was the occupation of Pittsburgh. After the fight and the funeral, Bradford called out the militia regiments of the four disaffected counties. They were commanded to rendezvous at Braddock's Field, near Pittsburgh, with arms, full equipment and four days' rations. At the field there was a great beating of drums, much marching and counter-marching, almost a holiday spirit. Men in hunting shirts practiced shooting at the mark until a dense pall of smoke hung over the plain, as there had been thirty-nine years before at the time of General Braddock's disaster. There were between five and seven thousand men on the field, many meditating in an ugly mood upon their enemies holed up in the town, talking of storming Fort Fayette and burning Pittsburgh as "a second Sodom."

Bradford's dream was the establishment of an independent state with himself cast as a sort of Washington of the West. Elected by acclaim as Major General, he dashed about the field on a superb horse in a fancy uniform, his sword flashing, plumes floating out from his hat. As he harangued the multitude, Bradford received applications for commissions in the service of—what? No one quite knew.

Marching in good order, strung out over two and a half miles of road, the rebels advanced on August first toward Pittsburgh in what was hopefully interpreted as a "visit," though the temper of the whiskey soldiers was perhaps nearer to that of one man who twirled his hat on the muzzle of his rifle and shouted, "I have a bad hat now but I expect to have a better one soon." While the panic-stricken burghers buried the silver and locked up the girls, the mob marched in on what is now Fourth Avenue to the vicinity of the present Baltimore and Ohio Railroad station. A reception committee extended nervous hospitality in the form of hams, poultry, dried venison, bear meat, water and whiskey. They agreed to banish certain citizens obnoxious to the insurrectionists. One building on a suburban farm was burned. Another attempt at arson failed to come off. The day cost Brackenridge four barrels of prime Monongahela. It was better, he reflected, "to be employed in extinguishing the fire of their thirst than of my house." Pittsburgh was fortunate in getting the main body in and then out again without a battle or a burning.

All through the month of August armed bands continued to patrol the roads as a "scrub Congress," in the phrase of one scoffer, met at Parkinson's Ferry, now Monongahela, to debate, pass resolutions and move somewhat uncertainly toward separation from the United States. Wild and ignorant rumors won belief. It was said that Congress was extending the excise levy to plows at a dollar each, that every wagon entering Philadelphia would be forced to pay a dollar, that a tax was soon to be established at Pittsburgh of fifteen shillings for the birth of every boy baby, and ten for each girl.

With the terrorizing of Pittsburgh, it was evident that the crisis had arrived. The President requisitioned 15,000 militia from Pennsylvania, New Jersey, Virginia and Maryland, of whom about 13,000 actually marched. Would the citizens of one state invade another to compel obedience to federal law? Here one gets a glimpse of the larger importance of the affair. Both the national government and the state of Pennsylvania sent commissioners to the West with offers of pardon upon satisfactory assurances that the people would obey the laws. Albert Gallatin, William Findley, Brackenridge and others made a desperate effort to win the people to compliance, though their motives were often questioned by both the rebels and the federal authorities. The response to the offer of amnesty was judged not to be sufficiently positive. Pressed by Hamilton to have federal power show its teeth, Washington announced that the troops would march.

The army was aroused. In particular, the New Jersey militia were ready for lynch law because they had been derided in a western newspaper as a "Water-mellon Army" and an uncomplimentary estimate was made of their military capabilities. The piece was written as a take-off on the kind of negotiations which preceded an Indian treaty. Possibly the idea was suggested by the fact that the Whiskey Boys were often called "White Indians." At any rate, in the satire the Indians admonished the great council in Philadelphia: ". . . Brothers, we have that powerful monarch, Capt. Whiskey, to command us. By the power of his influence, and a love to *his person* we are compelled to every great and heroic act. . . . We, the Six United Nations of White Indians . . . have all imbibed his principles and passions—that is a love of whiskey. . . . Brothers, you must not think to frighten us with . . . infantry, calvalry and artillery, composed of your water-mellon armies from the Jersey shores; they would cut a much better figure in warring with the crabs and oysters about the Capes of Delaware."

Captain Whiskey was answered hotly by "A Jersey Blue." He pointed out that "the water-melon army of New Jersey" was going to march westward shortly with "ten-inch howitzers for throwing a species of mellon very useful for curing a *gravel occasioned by whiskey!*" The expedition was tagged thereafter as the "Watermelon Army."

The troops moved in two columns under the command of General Henry (Light Horse Harry) Lee, Governor of Virginia. Old Dan Morgan was there and young Meriwether Lewis, five nephews of President Washington, the governors of Pennsylvania and New Jersey, too, and many a veteran bloodied in Revolutionary fighting including the extraordinary German, Captain John Fries of the Bucks County militia and his remarkable dog to which the Captain gave the name of a beverage he occasionally enjoyed—Whiskey.

The left wing marched west during October, 1794, over General Braddock's old route from Virginia and Maryland to Cumberland on the Potomac, then northwest into Pennsylvania, to join forces with the right wing at Union Town. The Pennsylvania and New Jersey corps proceeded via Norristown and Reading to Harrisburg and Carlisle. There, on October 4th, President Washington arrived, accompanied by Colonel Hamilton. The representatives of the disaffected counties told the President at Carlisle that the army was not needed but Hamilton convinced him that it was. Washington proceeded with the troops as far as Bedford, then returned to Philadelphia for the meeting of Congress. Hamilton ordered a round up of many of the rebels and personally interrogated the most important ones. Brackenridge, incidentally, came off well in his encounter with Hamilton, who declared that he was satisfied with Brackenridge's conduct.

By the time the expedition had crossed the mountains, the uprising was already coming apart at the seams. David Bradford, who had been excluded from the offer of amnesty, fled to Spanish Louisiana. About two thousand of the best riflemen in the West also left the country, including many a distiller, who loaded his pot still on a pack horse or a keel boat and sought asylum in Kentucky where, hopefully, a man could make "the creature" without giving the public debt a lift.

The punitive army moved forward in glorious autumn weather, raiding chicken coops, consuming prodigious quantities of the commodity which lay at the heart of the controversy. Richard Howell, governor of New Jersey and commander of the right wing, revived the spirits of the Jersey troops by composing a marching song, "Dash to the Mountains, Jersey Blue";

> To arms once more, our hero cries,
> Sedition lives and order dies;
> To peace and ease then did adieu
> And dash to the mountains, Jersey Blue.

Faded diaries, old letters and orderly books preserve something of the gala atmosphere of the expedition. At Trenton a Miss Forman and a Miss Milnor were most amiable. Newtown, Pennsylvania, was ticketed as a poor place for hay. At Potts Grove a captain of the cavalry troop got kicked in the shin by his horse. Among the Virginians, Meriwether Lewis enjoyed the martial excitement, wrote to his mother in high spirits of the "mountains of beef and oceans of Whiskey"; sent regards "to all the girls" and announced that he would bring "an Insergiant Girl to se them next fall bearing the title of Mrs. Lewis." If there was such a girl, he soon forgot her.

Yet where there is an army in being there are bound to be unpleasant occurrences. Men were lashed. Quartermasters stole government property. A soldier was ordered to put a Scotch-Irish rebel under guard. In execution of the order, he ran said insurgent through with his bayonet, of which the prisoner died. At Carlisle a dragoon's pistol went off and hit a countryman in the groin; he too died. On November 13, long remembered in many a cabin and stump-clearing as "the dismal night," the Jersey horse captured various citizens whom they described grimly as "the whiskey pole gentry," dragging them out of bed, tying them back to back. The troopers held their prisoners in a damp cellar for twenty-four hours without food or water, before marching them off at gun point to a collection center at Washington, Pennsylvania.

In late November, finding no one to fight, the army turned east again, leaving a volunteer force under General Morgan to conciliate and consolidate the position during the winter. Twenty "Yahoos" were carried back to Philadelphia and were paraded by the Philadelphia Horse through the streets of the city with placards marked "Insurrection" attached to their hats, in an odd federalist version of a Roman triumph. The cavalry was composed, as an admirer said, of "young men of the first property of the city," with beautiful mounts, uniforms of the finest blue broadcloth. They held their swords elevated in the right hand while the light flashed from their silver stirrups, martingales and jingling bridles. Stretched over half a mile they came, first two troopers abreast, then a pair of Yahoos, walking; then two more mounted men, and so on.

The army, meditating upon their fatigues and hardships, called for a substantial number of hangings. Samuel Hodgson, Commissary-general of the army, wrote to a Pittsburgh confidant, "We all lament that so few of the insurgents fell—such disorders can only be cured by copious bleedings. . . ." Philip Freneau, friend and literary colleague of Brackenridge, suggested in retrospect—ironically, of course—the benefits which would have accrued to the country "If Washington had drawn and quartered thirty or forty of the whiskey boys. . . ." Most of the captives escaped any punishment other than that of being held in jail without a trial for ten or twelve months. One died. Two were finally tried and sentenced to death. Eventually both were let off.

Gradually the bitterness receded. In August, 1794, General Anthony Wayne had crushed the Indians at the Battle of Fallen Timbers. A treaty was concluded with Spain in October, 1795, clearing the Mississippi for western trade. The movement of the army into the Pennsylvania hinterland, meanwhile, brought with it a flood of cash which furnished the distillers with currency for paying their taxes. These events served to produce a better feeling toward the Union.

If the rising was a failure, so was the liquor tax. The military adventure alone, without ordinary costs of collection, ran up a bill of $1,500,000, or about one third of all the money that was realized during the life of the revenue act. The excise was quietly repealed during Jefferson's administration. Yet the watermelon armies and the Whiskey Boys made a not inconsiderable contribution to our constitutional history. Through them, the year 1794 completed what 1787 had begun; for it established the reality of a federal union whose law was not a suggestion but a command.

Richard Maxwell Brown

THE AMERICAN VIGILANTE TRADITION

The attempt to achieve justice illegally is a universal phenomenon. Not only the actors in this volume but participants in riot, rout, and tumult the world over, Palestinian terrorists and medieval peasants in revolt, have justified themselves in the name of right, whatever the dictates of civil law. But in the narrower sense, as described by Richard Maxwell Brown, "vigilantism" is a distinctively American phenomenon. And it is one that, recurring throughout most of our national history, reveals much about the frequent conflict between "law" and "order" in American society.

The vigilante tradition, in the classic sense, refers to organized, extra-legal movements which take the law into their own hands. The first vigilante movement in American history occurred in 1767. From then until about 1900, vigilante activity was an almost constant factor in American life. Far from being a phenomenon only of the far western frontier, there was much vigilantism in the Eastern half of the United States . . . . Although the first vigilante movement occurred in Piedmont, S.C., in 1767-69, most of the Atlantic Seaboard States were without significant vigilante activity. But beyond the Appalachians there were few states that did not have vigilante movements. There may have been as many as 500 movements, but at the present only 326 are known. [1]

American vigilantism is indigenous. There were "regulators" in early-18th-century London who formed a short-lived official supplement to London's regular system of law enforcement, [2] but there was no connection

From Hugh Davis Graham and Ted Robert Gurr, *Violence in America: Historical and Comparative Perspectives* (New York, 1969), pp. 154–226.

between London's legal regulators and South Carolina's back country "Regulators" of 1767 who constituted America's first vigilante movement. From time to time in European history there appeared movements or institutions (such as the *Vehmgericht* of Germany and *Halifax law* of the British Isles)[3] which bear resemblance to American vigilantism, but these phenomena did not give rise to a vigilante tradition either on the Continent or in the British Isles. European expansion in other areas of the world has, similarly, failed to produce anything like the American vigilante tradition. Perhaps the closest thing to it was the *commando* system (against marauding *kaffirs*) of the Boer settlers in South Africa; the *commandos,* however, were more like the Indian-fighting rangers of the American frontier than the vigilantes.[4]

Vigilantism arose as a response to a typical American problem: the absence of effective law and order in a frontier region. It was a problem that occurred again and again beyond the Appalachian Mountains. It stimulated the formation of hundreds of frontier vigilante movements.[5] On the frontier the normal foundations of a stable, orderly society—churches, schools, cohesive community life—were either absent or present only in rough, immature forms. The regular, legal system of law enforcement often proved to be woefully inadequate for the needs of the settlers.

Fundamentally, the pioneers took the law into their own hands for the purpose of establishing order and stability in newly settled areas. In the older settled areas the prime values of person and property were dominant and secure, but the move to the frontier meant that it was necessary to start all over. Upright and ambitious frontiersmen wished to reestablish the values of a property holder's society. The hurtful presence of outlaws and marginal types in a context of weak and ineffectual law enforcement created the spectre and, often, the fact of social chaos. The solution hit upon was vigilantism. A vigilante roundup of ne'er-do-wells and outlaws followed by the flogging, expulsion, or killing of them not only solved the problem of disorder but had crucial symbolic value as well. Vigilante action was a clear warning to disorderly inhabitants that the newness of settlement would provide no opportunity for eroding the established values of civilization. Vigilantism was a violent sanctification of the deeply cherished values of life and property.

Because the main thrust of vigilantism was to reestablish in each newly settled area the conservative values of life, property, and law and order, vigilante movements were usually led by the frontier elite. This was true of the greatest American vigilante movement—the San Francisco Vigilance Committee of 1856—which was dominated lock, stock, and barrel by the leading merchants of the city. Again and again it was the most eminent local community leaders who headed vigilante movements.

"Vigilance Committee" or "Committee of Vigilance" was the common name of the organization, but originally—and far into the 19th century—vigilantes were known by the now obsolete term of "regulators." Variant names for vigilante groups were "slickers," "stranglers," "committees of safety," and, in central Texas, simply, "mobs." (In this study "vigilante" will be used as a generic term to cover all phases of the general phenomenon of vigilantism.) The duration of vigilante movements varied greatly, but movements which lasted as long as a year were long lived. More commonly they finished their business in a period of months or weeks. Vigilante movements (as distinguished from ephemeral lynch mobs) are thus identifiable by the two main characteristics of (1) regular (though illegal) organization and (2) existence for a definite (though possibly short) period of time.

COLONIAL ORIGINS:
THE SOUTH CAROLINA REGULATORS, 1767-69

The first American vigilante movement—the South Carolina Regulators, 1767–69—did not occur until 160 years after the first permanent English settlement at Jamestown. The reason for the late appearance of the phenomenon was the slow pace of frontier expansion. It was well into the 18th century before the settlement of the Piedmont began on a large scale, and at the time of the Revolution the settlement of the Piedmont was just coming to a close. Thus frontier expansion proceeded at a snail's pace in the colonial period, and it was possible to provide adequate systems of law enforcement for the slowly proliferating pioneer communities. The one exception to this pattern of orderly frontier expansion occurred in the South Carolina Piedmont in the 1760's.

Newly settled and recently devasted by the Cherokee Indian War, the disorder in the South Carolina back country of the 1760's was typical of later American frontier areas. During the Cherokee War so many habitations were burned, so many homes were broken up, and so many individuals were killed that the orphaned and homeless became a problem. Many drifted into outlaw bands formed by war veterans who were too restless or brutalized to settle down to peaceful pursuits. Outlaws, runaway slaves, and mulattoes formed their own communities where they enjoyed their booty. South Carolina way stations in an intercolonial network of horse thieves were established. "Crackers" and other frontier lower class people aided and abetted the outlaws. By 1766 and 1767 the back country was in the grip of a "crime wave," and the outlaws were almost supreme. They abducted young girls to be their paramours in the outlaw villages. They robbed and tortured plantation masters and raped their wives and daughters.

Lacking local courts and sheriffs to enforce law, respectable settlers of average or affluent means organized as "Regulators" in late 1767. A 2-year vigilante campaign was successful. Subscribing to articles to end the problem of crime and disorder, the Regulators attacked and broke up the outlaw gangs. The idle and immoral were rounded up by the Regulators, given trials, and flogged. If thought hopelessly incorrigible, the miscreants were driven from the area: those the Regulators deemed reclaimable were subjected to a system of forced labor on back-country plantations.

The South Carolina Regulator movement was constructive in that it did rid the back country of pervasive crime. Order and stability were at last established after many years of social chaos. But the Regulators were vindictive, and there was a streak of sadism in their punishments. The increasingly arbitrary, extreme, and brutal Regulators bred an opposition movement of "Moderators." Brought to a standstill by the equally violent Moderators and appeased by the Provincial government's provision for district courts and sheriffs, the Regulators disbanded in 1769.[6]

An American tradition had begun, for, as the pioneers moved across the Appalachian Mountains, the regulator-vigilante impulse followed the sweep of settlement toward the Pacific. The model for dealing with frontier disorder provided by the South Carolina Regulators was utilized over and over by American settlers.

EASTERN VIGILANTISM

Geographically, American vigilantism divides into Eastern and Western halves. Eastern and Western vigilantism are similarly distinct in regard to chronology. Eastern vigilantism came to an end in the 1860's while Western vigilantism began in the 1850's. Eastern vigilantism was largely a feature of the first half of the 19th century and Western vigilantism of the second. Eastern vigilantism fell between the Appalachian Mountains[7] and the 96th meridian, while Western vigilantism stretched from the 96th meridian to the Pacific.[8] The humid Mississippi Valley, Great Lakes, and Gulf Coast regions furnished the main scenes of Eastern vigilantism; Western vigilantism took in the arid and semiarid Great Plains and the Rocky Mountains and the Pacific Coast. Eastern vigilantism was a response, chiefly, to frontier horsethieves, counterfeiters, and ne'er-do-well white people. West of the 96th meridian the vigilantes were concerned largely with disorder in mining camps, cattle towns, and the open ranges.

In early-19th-century America, horsethieves and counterfeiters seemed to go together always, and when they did a vigilante movement was not far behind. The vulnerability of the settler to horse theft needs no comment, but counterfeiting as a frontier evil is a bit less familiar. The money problem made itself felt at the national level in the Age of Jackson in a number of famous issues such as the Bank War, but it was no less a problem in the backwoods and border country. Not only did the frontier suffer from a money shortage which counterfeiters as well as wildcat bankers tried to fill, but the frontier felt the lack of money especially in regard to the purchase of Federal public land. Added to the lively demand for cash at the land office was the chaotic condition of the paper money system. The lack of an effective system of Federal paper money and the plethora of private bank notes meant that never before or since in our history was counterfeiting easier. [9]

Counterfeiting and horse stealing were linked. Horsethieves commonly organized into gangs, stealing horses in one area and disposing of them hundreds of miles away—preferably across state lines. [10] For obvious reasons, counterfeiting operations were best carried on in the same way, and it was simple to combine the two occupations. The link between counterfeiting and horse theft had an effect on the geographical distribution of regulator and vigilante movements. The latter tended to be found in wilderness areas, close to State lines, or near Indian borders—all were places favored by horsethieves and counterfeiters.

. . .

WESTERN VIGILANTISM

The nature of western natural resources determined the types of frontier disorder which gave rise to vigilantism. Repeated strikes of precious and valuable metals in the Sierras and Rockies set off mining rushes that brought miners and others into raw new camps and towns by the thousands. In such places the law was often absent or ineffectual with vigilantism the result. The other great natural resource of the West was the grassy rangeland of the Great Plains and mountain plateaus. The open range system afforded an irresistible attraction to cattle—and horse—thieves who, in turn, invited vigilante retaliation.

Beginning with the first significant outbreak of vigilantism in the gold-rush metropolis of San Francisco in 1849 and continuing for 53 years down to 1902 there were at least 210 vigilante movements in the West. No vigilante movements in American history were better organized or more powerful than the San Francisco vigilance committees of 1851 and 1856. The San Francisco movements had an immense impact on American vigilantism in general and upon California vigilantism in particular. During the 1850's, the San Francisco committees were copied all over the State in the new mining towns (Sacramento, Jackson, etc.) and in the old Spanish cities (Los Angeles, Monterey, etc.). Of California's 43 vigilante movements, 27 occurred in the 1850's. [11]

Montana was a most significant vigilante State. It had two of the most important movements in the history of the institution: the influential Bannack and Virginia City movement of 1863–65 (which gave the term "vigilante" to American English) [12] and the 1884 movement in northern and eastern Montana, which Granville Stuart led against horse and cattle thieves in a human roundup that claimed 35 victims and was the deadliest of all American vigilante movements. [13] In addition, Montana, from the 1860's to the 1880's, was in the grips of a Territory-wide vigilante movement with headquarters, apparently, in the territorial capital, Helena. [14]

Texas had 52 vigilante movements—more than any other State. There were two important antebellum movements (Shelby County in East Texas, 1840–44; San Antonio, 1857 ff.), but the majority (at least 27) occurred in violence-torn central Texas in the post-Civil War period from 1865 to 1890. [15] There were dozens and dozens of vigilante movements in most of the other Western States; only Oregon and Utah did not have significant vigilante activity. Colorado's 16 movements were headed by the Denver vigilantes of 1859–61. [16] New Mexico had three potent vigilante movements in Albuquerque (1871–82), [17] Las Vegas (1880–82), [18] and Socorro (1880–84). [19] The Butler County vigilantes who enlisted almost 800 members and claimed eight victims formed the most notable of Kansas' 19 movements. [20] Wyoming vigilantism began with two lethal movements in the wild railroad boomtowns of Cheyenne and Laramie (1868–69) [21] and came to a climax with vigilantism's most famous failure, the cattlemen's Regulator movement which precipitated the Johnson County War of 1862. [22]

. . .

Significant vigilante activity did not always take the shape of a formally organized movement with officers, trials, etc. By the latter half of the 19th-century the ritual-like action of organizing a vigilante movement had been carried out so many times in so many frontiers that to many settlers it often seemed an unnecessary delay to swift lynch-law justice. A local consensus in favor of immediate vigilante action without any of the traditional formalities produced *instant vigilantism.* Instant vigilantism was more prevalent in the West than the East. Many of the "one-shot" vigilante actions in Western states were the result of the impulse for instant vigilantism. Thus instant vigilantism existed side by side with more formally organized vigilantism. Instant vigilantism meant that the public mind had long since been made receptive to vigilante action when general conditions or a particular crime seemed to warrant it. The ritual process of organization had been gone through so many times, the rationale of vigilantism was so well understood, and the course of action so obvious on the basis of past precedents that the settlers readily proceeded to the lynching.

Instant vigilantism seems to have occurred in all Western states but Oregon and Utah. Instant vigilantism was particularly effective in California. In the Golden State, regular vigilante action took 101 lives, but the toll of instant vigilantism from 1851 to 1878 was almost as great in amounting to 79. [23] On a lesser scale the same thing occurred in other Western states where time and again precipitate lynchings were justified by the vigilante tradition.

COMMUNITY RECONSTRUCTION AND
VIGILANTISM

New settlers ordinarily desire new opportunities but not social innovation. Their main desire is to re-create the life they left behind them by reconstructing the communities from which they came. This is no great problem for entire communities that migrate en masse. There have been many examples of the latter. The Pilgrim settlers of Plymouth, Massachusetts, and the Mormon migrants to Great Salt Lake, Utah, are notable cases of "colonized" new communities.

More common have been the "cumulative" communities of inhabitants thrown together helter-skelter by the migration process.[24] The migrants to San Francisco, California, in 1849 and after furnish an example of the cumulative new community. The San Franciscans came from all over and were an immensely diverse lot. The only thing that united them, initially, was their desire to profit from the California Gold Rush.

Basic to the reconstruction of the community is the reestablishment of the old community structure and its values. To the extent that both are achieved, an orderly and stable new community life will be achieved. Although American frontiersmen of the 19th century came to their new localities from all points of the compass and were usually unknown and unrelated to each other, most came from essentially similar communities. The typical American community of the 18th and 19th centuries possessed a social structure of three levels:[25]

(1) The upper level consisted of the leading men and their families. Included were the well-to-do businessmen, the most eminent professional men, the affluent farmers and planters, and the prominent men of whatever occupation. This was the local elite, and in it were concentrated the community leaders.

(2) The middle level included the men of average means: farmers, craftsmen, tradesmen, and the less eminent lawyers, teachers, and other professionals. The industrious, honest middle level formed the core of the community. In this sector resided the legendary but real American yeoman.

(3) The lower level included the honest poor and also those who were either marginal to or alienated from the remainder of the community. In but not really *of* the community (and spurned by it) were the ne'er-do-well, shiftless poor whites. They constituted a true *lower people;* they were viewed with contempt and loathing by the members of the upper and middle levels who could not abide their slatternly way of life, their spiritless lack of ambition, their often immoral conduct, and their disorganized family life.[26]

The lower people were not outlaws but often tended to lawlessness and identified more with the outlaw element than the law-abiding members of the community. The outlaw element lived on the fringes of the community. In some cases they sprang from the lower people but were often men of good background who chose the outlaw life or drifted into it. They were alienated from the values of the community, although some occasionally joined respectable community life as reformed men.

A community has behavioral boundaries just as it has geographic boundaries. When a new community establishes its geographic boundaries it must also establish its behavioral boundaries. The latter represent the positive, mutual values of the community.[27] The values which supported the three-level community and the basis upon which it rested were the linked ideals of life and property. The American community of the 18th and 19th centuries was primarily a property-holder's community, and property was viewed as the very basis of life itself.

The vigilante leaders were drawn from the upper level of the community. The middle level supplied the rank-and-file. The lower people and outlaws represented the main threat to the reconstruction of the community and were the main targets of the vigilantes.

In the cumulative new communities of frontier America, the lower people and outlaws met the representatives of the middle and upper levels in social conflict. The outlaws and lower people wished to burst their lower level bounds and "take over" the new communities. In sociological terms the outlaws and lower people constituted a "contraculture."[28] They rejected the respectable values of life and property and wished to upset the social structure in which the upper and middle level men were dominant. The lack of social bonds in the new settlements was their opportunity. On the other hand, the men of the upper level background or aspirations were determined to reestablish the community structure in which they were dominant. In this they had the support of the middle level inhabitants, and with it they mounted vigilante campaigns to quell the insurgent outlaws and lower people.[29]

The danger of a takeover of newly settled areas by the alienated, outcast elements of society was a real threat. Whether or not the alleged Murrell conspiracy of the lower Mississippi Valley in the 1830's actually represented a concerted plot of white outlaws to raise a gigantic slave rebellion in the interest of an "underworld" dominion of the region, the phenomenon revealed the sensitivity of lawful society to large numbers, aggressiveness, and alienation of the outlaws of the region. In southern Illinois in the 1840's the "Flathead" element of horsethieves, counterfeiters, brigands, slave stealers, and Ohio River-bottom dwellers triggered a violent "Regulator" reaction.[30] In east Texas in the late 1830's a similar combine of horsethieves, counterfeiters, slave stealers and "land pirates" incited a Regulator countermovement.[31] By 1841 a group of outlaw gangs had virtually taken over the Rock River counties of northern Illinois until challenged by a Regulator movement in that year.[32] Much earlier, in South Carolina in the middle 1760's a disorderly mixture of demoralized Indian war veterans, "straggling" refugee whites, "crackers," mulattoes, and outlaw horsethieves and counterfeiters well-nigh ruled the back country until honest men reacted in the Regulator movement.[33] West of the Mississippi and Missouri in the raw, new mining camps, cattle towns, railheads, and open ranges, the same threat emanated from the professional "bad men" and outlaw gangs, the "black-leg" element, and the always troublesome "rustlers" and horsethieves. These and other challenges were thus met head on by the vigilantes.

The masonic lodge was often found in frontier communities, and the relationship between Freemasonry and vigilantism was frequently an intimate one. Typical was the situation in Bannack, Nevada City, and Virginia City, Montana, rough, new mining camps in 1863–64. There the leading members of the potent vigilante movement of the winter of 1863-64 seem to have initially formed a bond as a result of their common membership in the masonic lodge.[34] The like happened elsewhere. The same impulse—desire to participate in the upper level dominance of the community—often caused the same person to join the masonic lodge (usually an elite local organization) and enlist in a vigilante movement. In Montana, Texas, and elsewhere, Freemasonry was often the shadowy background for the organization of a local vigilante movement.[35]

Sometimes the members of the upper level did not wait for an overt crime outbreak but formed a vigilante organization as a preventive measure and to cement the three-level community structure. Thus Thomas G. Wildman of Denver, Colo., wrote back East on September 3, 1859:

> There is to be a Vigilance Committee organized in the town this evening. All of the leading men of the town has signed the Constitution, and its object is a good one. . . . It is thought that stabbing and drunkenness will be rampant here this winter, and we think that the rowdies and gamblers will be more careful when they find out that we are organized and that all the first men of the town are determined to punish crimes.[36]

To the men of Butler County, Kansas, in 1870–71, vigilante action was the cornerstone of community construction. After killing eight men they justified their action by declaring, "it has become a question whether honest men of the country shall leave, or this gang." Invoking "self preservation" as "the first law of nature," they asserted that "however much we deplore the further use of violence in order to secure life and property, . . . we shall not hesitate to do justice to the guilty if it is necessary."[37]

James Hall described the challenge which outlaws and lower people presented in the early years of Midwest settlement:

> We had whole settlements of counterfeiters, or horse thieves, with their sympathizers—where rogues could change names, or pass from house to house, so skillfully as to elude detection—and where if detected, the whole population were ready to rise to the rescue. There were other settlements of sturdy honest fellows, the regular backwoodsmen in which rogues were not tolerated. There was therefore a continual struggle between these parties—the honest people trying to expel the

others by the terrors of the law, and when that mode failed, forming *regulating* companies, and driving them out by force. [38]

An example of the problem was the bandit and "blackleg" community of the tamarack thickets and swamps of Noble County in northern Indiana. William Latta, William D. Hill, and George T. Ulmer were the pioneer founders and leaders of this illicit community which thrived for 25 years. The banditti and their blackleg allies were sworn to uphold each other. They robbed, murdered, stole, gambled, burned buildings, and made and sold counterfeit money. They exerted a pernicious influence on the sons and daughters of their respectable neighbors, leading hundreds of young men and women into lives of crime, debauchery, and prostitution. [39] Finally, in 1858, 2,000 Regulators rose and scattered the blacklegs and outlaws once and for all.

The loathing of upper level men for the lower element—the contra-culture—of the frontier was stated with feeling by Thomas Dimsdale, who cried that "for the low, brutal, cruel, lazy, ignorant, insolent, sensual and blasphemous miscreants that infest the frontier we entertain but one senti-ment—aversion—deep, strong, and unchangeable." [40] At times the deep aversion expressed itself in gruesome ways. Such an incident occurred in Rawlins, Wyoming, in 1881 where Dr. John E. Osborne (a future Governor of Wyoming) attended a hanging of the brutal Western outlaw, Big Nose George Parrott (or Parrotti). The next day Dr. Osborne, "skinned 'Big Nose' George and cut away the top of the skull, in order to remove the brain. The skin was tanned and made into a medical instrument bag, razor strops, a pair of lady's shoes, and a tobacco pouch. The shoes were dis-played in the Rawlins National Bank for years," and, in effect, constituted an upper level trophy in honor of the community values of life and property held by such men as Dr. Osborne. [41]

VIGILANTE CHARACTERISTICS

Vigilante movements varied in size from the smallest of 12 to 15 mem-bers (the Pierre, South Dakota, vigilance committee) to the 6,000 to 8,000 who belonged to the San Francisco vigilance committee of 1856. . . . Of the 326 documented vigilante movements, information has survived on the number of members in 50 of them. There were 13 movements of small size, ranging from 12 to 99 members. At the other extreme there were nine move-ments ranging from 700 to 8,000 members. Predominant were the 28 move-ments which ranged in size from 100 to 599 members. Thus the typical vigilante movement was one of from one hundred to several hundred mem-bers. Considering that the majority of American vigilante movements took place in new frontier localities of small population, the typical participation of from one to a few hundred members underscores the extent to which the community as a whole participated in them.

The characteristic vigilante movement was organized in command or military fashion and usually had a constitution, articles, or a manifesto to which the members would subscribe. Outlaws or other malefactors taken up by vigilantes were given formal (though illegal) trials in which the accused had counsel or an opportunity to defend himself. An example of a vigilante trial is found in the northern Illinois Regulator movement of 1841. Two accused horsethieves and murderers were tried by 120 Regulators in the presence of a crowd of 500 or more. A leading Regulator served as judge. The defendants were given a chance to challenge objectionable men among the Regulators, and, as a result, the number of Regulators taking part in the trial was cut by nine men. Two lawyers were provided—one to represent the accused, and one to represent the "people." Witnesses were sworn, an arraignment was made, and the trial proceeded. In summation, the prosecuting attorney urged immediate execution of the prisoners. The crowd voted unanimously for the fatal sentence, and, after an hour allotted to the two men for prayer, they were put to death.[42] The accused were almost never acquitted, but the vigilantes' attention to the spirit of law and order caused them to provide, by their lights, a fair but speedy trial.

The punishments of whipping and expulsion were common in the early decades of vigilantism, but, as time passed, killing—usually by means of hanging—became the customary punishment. Through 1849 there are only 88 documented fatal victims of vigilante action. . . . In the next decade 105 persons were killed by vigilantes, and it was at about this time—the 1850's—that the transition in the meaning of the term "lynching" from whipping to killing was occurring. The killing character of vigilantism, made firm in the 1850's, was accentuated during the remainder of the century; from 1860 to 1909 vigilantes took at least 511 lives. . . .

Of 326 known vigilante movements, 141 (43 percent) killed 729 victims. Of the movements by category (i.e., large, medium, or small), the large movements were, as might be expected, the most deadly, the medium movements less so, and the small movements hardly so at all. . . . Of the 81 large movements, 59 (73 percent) took a total of 544 lives (76 percent of all vigilante killings) with an average of 9.2 lives per movement. Of the 107 medium movements, a substantial majority, 63 (59 percent) were fatal in effect; they took 156 lives with an average of 2.5 per movement. There were 138 small vigilante movements in all; only 19 of these killed victims: 13 took single lives while six claimed double victims. Thus the overwhelming number of deaths attributed to vigilantism, 704 (or 97 percent of the total of 729) were exacted by 122 large and medium movements which, however, amounted to only 37 percent of all 326 vigilante movements. . . .

The tendency among the 141 vigilante movements taking lives was to stop after claiming four or fewer victims. Thus 98 movements (or 70 percent of the 141 movements) inflicted from one to four deaths. Only 17 of the 141 movements (12 percent) took more than 10 lives. The most lethal movement was that in Montana in 1884 led by Granville Stuart against the horse and cattle thieves of the eastern and northern part of the territory; its toll was 35 persons. [43]...

Although the trend was for the large movements to kill the most victims ..., it was not always necessary for a powerful movement to take a large number of lives. Often a vigilante movement could achieve its aims by taking only one or a few lives. The greatest of all vigilante movements (San Francisco, 1856) killed only four men. Two other significant movements—the northern Illinois Regulators of 1841 and the northern Indiana Regulators of 1858—executed only two men and one man, respectively. The fearful example of one or two hangings (frequently in conjunction with the expulsion of lesser culprits) was on many occasions enough to bring about the vigilante goals of community reconstruction and stability.

Vigilante leaders wished to reestablish the three-level community structure (in which they would be dominant) and the values of life and property that supported it. Specifically, they wished to check disorder and crime, but in some situations the threat of the latter was mild. In such cases their desire to use vigilantism underscored their basic, implicit goals of implanting community structure and values.

All this they wished to achieve as cheaply as possible. They were the typical frontier entrepreneurs. Their enterprize in commerce or land was often speculative, and they frequently skated on economic thin ice. The delicate balance of their own personal finances could be easily upset; hence, they had a lively awareness of the cost of public service and a yen to keep them down lest, as substantial taxpayers, their own circumstances suffer. No better resolution of the conflicting goals of public order and personal wealth could be found than vigilantism which provided a maximum of the former at minimum cost to the ambitious and well-to-do.

. . .

THE PROBLEM OF FRONTIER LAW ENFORCEMENT AND JUSTICE

In frontier areas, law and order was often a tenuous thing. Outlaws—singly or in gangs—headed for the new areas and took every advantage they could of the social disorganization stemming from the newness of settlement and the weakness of the traditional institutions of state, society, and church.

Law enforcement was frequently inadequate. Throughout most of the 19th century (and not just on the frontier) it was pinned down to the immediate vicinity of county seat, town, or township. [44] Localities lacked the economic resources to support constables, policemen, and sheriffs in long journeys of pursuit after lawbreakers. A really large expenditure of funds for the pursuit, capture, jailing, trial, and conviction of culprits could easily bankrupt the typical frontier county or town.

There was also the handicap of poor transportation. The mobility of sheriffs and others was only as rapid and flexible as their horses afforded them. A fugitive, having gained any sort of lead, was difficult to catch. The development of the railroad was a help but was not without its disadvantages. The officer was bound to the fixed route of the railroad. There were large gaps, also, between the railroad lines—gaps into which the fugitives unerringly made. In the hinterland stretches unserved by the railroads, the authorities were forced to make their way over poor roads and disappearing trails.

Linked with inadequate law enforcement was an uneven judicial system. Through fear, friendliness, or corruption, juries often failed to convict the criminal. [45] Lack of jails (in the early days) or their flimsy condition made it nearly impossible to prevent those in custody from escaping. [46] The system presented numerous opportunities for manipulation by outlaws who could often command some measure of local support. Whenever possible outlaws would obtain false witnesses in their behalf, pack juries, bribe officials, and, in extreme cases, intimidate the entire system: judges, juries, and law enforcement officials. [47] Such deficiencies in the judicial system were the source of repeated complaints by frontiersmen. They made the familiar point that the American system of administering justice favored the accused rather than society. The guilty, they charged, utilized every loophole for the evasion of punishment. Compounding the problem was the genuinely heavy financial burden involved in maintaining an adequate "police establishment" and judicial system in a sparsely settled and economically underdeveloped frontier area. [48]

For many a frontiersman, vigilantism was the solution to these problems. W. N. Byers, an old Denver, Colorado, vigilante of 1860 reminisced:

We never hanged on circumstantial evidence. I have known a great many such executions, but I don't believe one of them was ever unjust. But when they were proved guilty, they were always hanged. There was no getting out it. *No, there were no appeals in those days; no writs of errors; no attorneys' fees; no pardon in six months. Punishment was swift, sure and certain.* [49]

THE IDEOLOGY OF VIGILANTISM

Vigilantism could never have become the powerful force in 19th-century America that it did become without having gripped the minds and emotions of Americans. This it did through a system of ideas and beliefs that emerged as the ideology of vigilantism. There were many elements in it.

1.The 19th-century doctrine of "Vigilance" suffused America in a way that had not been the case before nor since. To be vigilant in regard to all manner of things was an idea that increasingly commanded Americans as the decades passed. The doctrine of vigilance provided a powerful intellectual foundation for the burgeoning of vigilante movements, and, in turn, vigilante movements reinforced the doctrine of vigilance.

Vigilance committees were formed early for a host of things having nothing to do with the problem of frontier disorder. In 1813–14 the leading men of Richmond, Virginia (headed by Chief Justice John Marshall), organized a Committee of Vigilance whose purpose was home-guard defense against a possible British attack during the War of 1812. [50] The attack never came, but the idea of vigilance did not die. In 1817 when Pensacola, Fla. (at that time still under Spanish rule but soon to become American), was threatened by a ship of Mexican filibusters, the citizens established a "Committee of Vigilance" for home defense which, however, like that of Richmond was never put to the test. [51] American settlers in Texas on the eve of the Texan Revolution founded Committees of Vigilance in Nacagdoches and other localities in 1835–36 by way of preparing for the looming hostilities with the Mexican mother country. [52]

The doctrine of vigilance had thus been utilized in regard to the early-19th-century crises of war and expansion; so, too, was it put to the service of sectional interests as the North and South moved toward confrontation in Civil War. Possibly the first "vigilance committee" involved in the sectional issue was that of the Ohio county of Meigs which lay across the Ohio River from western Virginia. In 1824 Meigs County men organized a vigilance committee to prevent Virginians from pursuing fugitive slaves. [53] . . . In the 1850's Northern vigilance committees of this sort became increasingly common as they proliferated in response to the Fugitive Slave Act in Boston, Syracuse, Springfield, and smaller cities. [54] The South, conversely, fostered the founding of antiabolition vigilance committees as early as 1835 in Fairfax County, Va. Such committees spread through the South in the 1840's and 1850's. [55] By that time in Dixie abolitionists constituted an illusory threat at best. But the antiabolitionist vigilance committees probably helped increase the sectional solidarity of the South.

The doctrine of vigilance was not restricted to the great issues of war and sectional controversy but impinged upon the prosaic world of commerce. Thus, in a presage of the modern Better Business Bureau, the Merchant's Vigilance Association of New York City was organized in 1845 "to investigate and expose abuses in trade" and "to prevent frauds." [56] In time, the doctrine of vigilance merged with the earlier regulator tradition (that went back to the South Carolina back country) and the result, by the 1840's and 1850's was the "vigilance committee" dedicated to the eradication of frontier crime and turbulence.

2. The philosophy of vigilantism.—While the doctrine of vigilance was the background for the organizing of many vigilante movements, the vigilantes, knowing full well that their actions were illegal, felt obliged to legitimize their violence by fashioning a *philosophy of vigilantism.* The philosophy of vigilantism had three major components:

(a) *Self-preservation.*—By midcentury *self-righteous* vigilantes in as widely separated locales as Washington Territory, Montana, Missouri, and Louisiana were routinely invoking "self-preservation" or "self-protection" as the first principle of vigilantism. Thus the June 1, 1856, Vigilance Committee of Pierce County, Washington Territory, justified its existence by citing "self-preservation [as] the first law of society, & the basis upon which its structure is built." [57] The French Acadians of the *Louisiana Comités de Vigilance* were no less sure of their ground when on March, 16, 1859, they declared, as a basis for taking the law into their own hands, that "self-protection is supreme." [58] The same note was struck by Thomas J. Dimsdale in his classic contemporary account when he stated that, for the honest Montana miners of Bannack and Alder Gulch (1863–64), the depredations of the "road agents" had narrowed the question down to "kill or be killed." Under the principle that "self-preservation is the first law of nature" the vigilantes "took the right side." [59] The very same language—"self-preservation is the first law of nature"—headed the resolutions of the Johnson County vigilance committee as it organized against post-Civil War horsethieves, murderers, and robbers in Warrensburg, Missouri, on February 28, 1867. [60]

(b) *Right of revolution.*—Vigilantes were well aware that their illegal action was, in effect, a blow at established authority. In order to deal with horsethieves and counterfeiters in Illinois in 1816–17 "the people," Governor Thomas Ford later wrote, "formed themselves into *revolutionary tribunals . . .* under the name of regulators. [61] Vigilante penmen cut right to the heart of the matter by unequivocally invoking the right of revolution. A Louisiana *Comités de Vigilance* proclamation of March 16, 1859, explicitly avowed its character as a "revolutionary movement." [62] The authorized historian of the *Comités,* Alexander Barde, cited the American Revolution as a justified popular insurrection and precedent for the movement he described. To condemn the vigilance committee in the context of intolerable conditions of lawlessness (analogous to the lack of justice that brought on the Revolution of 1776), said Barde, would be "to condemn our history" and to say "that if Nero governed us, we should submit to Nero." [63]

(c) *Popular sovereignty.*—Most vital to the philosophy of vigilantism was the democratic ideal of popular sovereignty. An additional reason for the failure of vigilantism to appear before 1767 was the lack, up to that time, of a mature belief in democracy. The complete transition from deferential to democratic social values in America was a process that took from the time of the Revolution to the Age of Jackson. By the latter era (which coincided with the firm establishment of the vigilante tradition) the rule of the people was acknowledged by all but the most skeptical and reactionary.

. . . The same idea was put a bit more pithily in 1902 when the following jingle was found pinned to the body of a man hanged by the vigilantes of Casper, Wyoming:

Process of law is a little slow
So this is the road you'll have to go.
Murderers and thieves, Beware!
PEOPLE'S VERDICT.[64]

"The *right of the people* to take care of themselves, if the law does not," said Professor Bigger of the local normal school to the Johnson County, Missouri, vigilantes in 1867, "is an indisputable right."[65] Hence, to 19th-century Americans the rule of the people was superior to all else—even the law. Vigilantism was but a case of the people exercising their sovereign power in the interest of self-preservation.

3. The economic rationale of vigilantism.—Although vigilantism rested on a bedrock democratic premise, the vigilante operation in practice was often not democratic. Ordinary men formed the rank and file of the vigilante organization, but, usually, its direction was firmly in the hands of the local elite. Local vigilante leaders were often the large local taxpayers. They had the customary desire to whittle down the tax rate and keep local expenses in check. From this point of view there was a persuasive economic rationale, for vigilante justice, was cheaper, as well as quicker and more certain, than regular justice. This was a theme that the vigilantes sounded time and again.

. . .

THE TWO MODELS OF VIGILANTISM

Two "models" of vigilante movements developed. One was the "good" or socially constructive model in which the vigilante movement dealt with a problem or disorder straightforwardly and then disbanded. The result was an increase in the social stability of the locality; the movement was, thus, socially constructive. The other was the "bad" or socially destructive one in which a vigilante movement encountered such strong opposition that the result was an anarchic and socially destructive vigilante war. Some movements, hence, behaved according to the ideal theory of vigilantism while others did not. Some were socially successful; others were not.

THE SOCIALLY CONSTRUCTIVE MODEL

The socially constructive movement occurred where the vigilantes represented a genuine community consensus. Here a decided majority of the people either participated in the movement or approved of it. Vigilantism of this sort simply mobilized the community and overwhelmed the unruly outlaws and lower people. The community was left in a more orderly and stable condition, and the social functions of vigilantism were served: the problem of community order was solved by the consolidation of the three-level social structure and the solidification of the supporting community values.

Although the methods used were often harsh and arbitrary, most vigilante movements—large and small—conformed to the socially constructive model. One of the best examples was the northern Illinois Regulator movement of 1841. The northern Illinois movement confronted a classic threat to community order: an agglomeration of outlaw gangs was nearing control of the area. With the regular government virtually powerless, the respectable leading men (the community upper level) took the law into their own hands with the help of the middle level farmers.

Since 1835 the situation in the Rock Valley of northern Illinois had gone from bad to worse. Several gangs of horsethieves and counterfeiters found the Rock River country a convenient corridor for illicit operations in Wisconsin, Illinois, Iowa, and Missouri. The Driscoll and Brodie gangs had made Ogle and De Kalb Counties a virtual fief. The Oliver gang dominated Winnebago County. The Bliss-Dewey-West ring waxed strong in Lee County, while the Birch gang of horsethieves ranged in all quarters. By 1840 the desperadoes were numerous enough to control elections in Ogle County and similarly threaten other counties. One summer the outlaws even went so far as to burn down the newly constructed courthouse at Oregon, Illinois.

Finally, in April 1841, 15 "representative men" of Ogle County formed the first Regulator company. In no time at all the counties were dotted with Regulator squads, but the most vigorous were those of Ogle. The Regulators embodied the social, economic, and political prestige of Ogle County: John Phelps was the county's oldest and wealthiest settler and the founder of the county seat, Oregon. Peter Smith combined a bank presidency with the ownership of 1,600 acres of land. The farmers who made up the bulk of the movement were substantial property holders; they had taken up Government land claims ranging from 240 to 600 acres. These solid citizens brooked no opposition. They burned the Rockford *Star* to the ground soon after it published an anti-Regulator editorial. But on the whole, the local elite kept the movement well under control. Having accomplished their purpose in a campaign of whipping, hanging, and firing squads, the Regulator companies disbanded. Socially they left the Rock Valley in a better state than before they organized.[66]

The northern Illinois Regulator movement exhibited the major characteristics of the successful frontier vigilante movement. It was organized in a rational way. Mass participation of respectable men was the mode, but the movement was dominated, clearly, by the social and economic elite of the area. The Regulators were implacable in their war on the outlaws and unrelenting in the face of opposition. Although the Rockford *Star* opposed the Regulators, no anti-Regulator coalition, as a whole, developed. The outlaw gangs were isolated and broken up. The vigilante leaders desired the assurance of their position at the upper level of their communitites but were not power mad. With the outlaw threat put down, peace and order reigned.

THE SOCIALLY DESTRUCTIVE MODEL

In the socially destructive model, anarchy was the result of the vigilante movement. Because there was no community consensus behind the vigilante movement, strong opposition appeared, and civil conflict flared. In the socially constructive model, opposition to the vigilantes was narrowly restricted to outlaws and lower people who could gain no support from the remainder of the community. For the vigilantes to be stymied a broad antivigilante coalition was necessary. The formation of an antivigilante coalition almost inevitably condemned the community to a chaotic internecine struggle between the vigilantes and their opponents.

Respectable men did not join the antivigilante coalition because of any great sympathy for the outlaws and lower people. They were impelled into opposition by things the vigilantes did or stood for. Sometimes two or three powerful local families would join the antivigilante movement. In some cases, these families had been carrying on a feud of sorts with leading vigilante families.[67] Sometimes a local political party or faction went into the antivigilante movement, because the vigilantes were dominated by the rival party or faction.[68] If the leading Democrats of a community, for example, were found among the vigilantes, the antivigilante coalition would probably attract the local Whigs. Political rivalries were often linked to vigilante strife, for in many instances vigilante leaders harbored political ambitions and were not above using the movement to promote their personal goals.[69] Economic rivalries among community leading men also were a factor in pro and con vigilante alignments; acute mercantile competition sometimes caused a leading storekeeper to go into the opposition if his rival was a vigilante.[70] Thus, personal, family, political, and economic antagonisms accounted for a readymade vigilante opposition in some communities.

At other times vigilante extremism drew into opposition decent men who otherwise probably would not have opposed them. The best of vigilante movements usually attracted a fringe of sadists and naturally violent types. Often these men had criminal tendencies and were glad to use the vigilante movement as an occasion for giving free reign to their unsavory passions. It was always a problem for vigilante leaders to keep these elements under control, and sometimes a movement was taken over or seriously skewed by these social misfits. Sadistic punishment and torture, arbitrary and unnecessary killings, and mob tyranny marked vigilante movements that had truly gone bad.[71] When this happened, many sound and conservative men felt they must oppose the vigilantes with whose original objectives they had probably felt no quarrel.

Examples of the socially destructive model did not occur as often as the constructive model, but when they did extremely violent conflicts tended to appear. Among the leading instances were the East Texas Regulators (versus the Moderators), 1840–44; the Southwest Missouri Slickers (versus the Anti-Slickers), 1842–44; and the Southern Illinois Regulators (versus the Flatheads), 1846–50.[72] Sometimes an antivigilante coalition arose which, although unable to match vigilante strength, possessed the potential of calling in outside help and, hence, could define the limits of vigilante power. The antivigilante Law and Order faction in San Francisco, 1856, played this role. The vigilantes there would have liked to have hanged Judge David S. Terry but did not dare do so, for the Law and Order faction would have almost certainly obtained Federal action against the vigilantes.[73] Similarly, the Moderators in the South Carolina back country, 1769, were not strong enough to overturn Regulator domination, but they did check the movement and bring its excesses to an end.[74]

As the career of the socially destructive model proceeded, the moral standing of the vigilantes and the opposing coalition tended to be increasingly compromised. As the struggle became more violent, the respectable men of the antivigilante coalition put a higher premium on the violent talents of the outlaw element with which they otherwise had nothing in common. So, too, did the original vigilantes themselves recruit and acquire a criminal fringe which they put to mercenary use. With the community descending bloodily into chaos, wise and prudent men left if they could. The opposing movements tended to fall more and more into the control of the worst and most extreme of their adherents. About this time the desperate neutral residents would beseech State authorities for the intervention of the militia, and the "war" would subside fitfully in the presence of the state troops.[75]

The Regulator-Moderator war of east Texas (1840–44) was representative of the degenerate, socially destructive vigilante situation. The scene was the redland and piney wood country of east Texas in the days of the Lone Star Republic. The center of the conflict was in Shelby County. Fronting on the Sabine River where it formed the boundary between Louisiana and Texas, Shelby County lay in an old border area that had never been known for peace and calm. In 1840 the Regulator movement arose as a quite honest and straightforward attack on a ring of corrupt county officials who specialized in fraudulent land transactions. The rise of the Regulators was probably inevitable in any case, for the county had long wilted under a plague of counterfeiting, horse thievery, Negro stealing, and common murder and mayhem. However, the Regulators overplayed their hand, especially after their original leader, Charles W. Jackson, was killed and replaced by the nefarious adventurer, Watt Moorman. Bad elements infiltrated both the regulators and their opponents, the Moderators, but by comparison the latter seemed to become less obnoxious. Although some honorable and level-headed citizens like John W. Middleton stayed with the Regulators to the end, an attitude of wild vengefulness came to be more characteristic of the band. The early ne'-er-do-well group among the Moderators dwindled. As more and more citizens were forced to take sides, many joined the Moderators in reaction to the sadism and vindictiveness of the swashbuckling Watt Moorman who affected a military uniform and blew great blasts on a hunting horn to summon his henchmen.

The original reasons for the founding of the Regulator movement were all but forgotten. The war became a thing in itself, a complexity of personal and family feuds that was consuming the area in blood lust. Several attempts to restore peace failed. Complete anarchy was the situation in 1844 when an all-out battle between two armies of several hundred men each was only forestalled by the dramatic intervention of Sam Houston and the militia. After 4 years, 18 men had been killed and many more wounded. A stream in the vicinity was called "Widow's Creek." The killing of so many leaders and the exhaustion of the survivors probably explain why the war was not revived after Sam Houston and the militia withdrew. Ex-Regulators and ex-Moderators warily fought side by side in separate companies in the Mexican War, but for 50 years east Texans were reluctant to discuss the episode lest old enmities be rekindled.[76]

VIGILANTISM AS A PARALLEL STRUCTURE

Vigilantism characteristically appeared in two types of situations: (1) where the regular system of law and order was absent or ineffective, and (2) where the regular system was functioning satisfactorily. The first case found vigilantism filling a void. The second case revealed vigilantism functioning as an extralegal structure of justice that paralleled the regular system.

Why did vigilantes desire to erect a parallel structure when the regular one was adequate? There were a number of reasons. By usurping the functions of regular law enforcement and justice or, at times, duplicating them—

the cost of local government was greatly reduced. As taxpayers the vigilante leaders and the rank and file benefited from the reduction in public costs. Second, the process of community reconstruction through the re-creation of social structure and values could be carried on more dramatically by a vigilante movement than was possible through the regular functioning of the law. A vigilante hanging was a graphic warning to all potentially disruptive elements that community values and structure were to be upheld.

The sort of impression that vigilantes wanted to make was that received by young Malcolm Campbell who arrived in Cheyenne, Wyoming, in 1868 at the age of 28. No sooner had he arrived than there were four vigilante hangings. "So in rapid succession," he recalled, "came before my eyes instances which demonstrated the strength of law [as carried out by vigilantes], and the impotence of the criminal. Undoubtedly, these incidents went far in shaping my future life and in guiding my feet properly in those trails of danger where I was later to apprehend some of the most dangerous outlaws of the plains."[77] (Campbell later became a leading Wyoming sheriff.)

Finally, the vigilante movement sometimes existed for reasons that were essentially unrelated to the traditional problems of crime and disorder. The San Francisco vigilance committee of 1856 is one of the best examples of the vigilante movement as a parallel structure. The San Francisco vigilantes spoke of a crime problem, but examination of the evidence does not reveal a significant upsurge of crime in 1855–56. The regular authorities had San Francisco crime well under control. Fundamentally, the San Francisco vigilantes were concerned with local political and fiscal reform. They wished to capture control of the government from the dominant faction of Irish Catholic Democrats. The vigilantes actually left the routine enforcement of law to the regular police and intervened only in a few major cases. The parallel structure of the vigilante movement was utilized to organize a reform political party (the People's Party) and to shatter the Irish Catholic Democratic faction by exiling some of its leading operatives.[78]

Sometimes the regular and parallel structures were intertwined. Law enforcement officials often connived with vigilantes. Here a sheriff or police chief was not taken by surprise when a vigilante force bent on a lynching converged upon his jail, for he had helped plan the whole affair. Appearances were preserved, usually, by a token resistance on the part of the law officer, but it was well known in the community that he had shared in the vigilante plot.[79]

Why would men violate their oaths and subvert their own functions as officers of the law? For some men the reason was that they were little more than hirelings of the local vigilante elite to whom they were beholden for office. Other officers were of higher social status but, as large landholders or businessmen themselves, they shared the vigilante desire to keep down governmental costs. Little interested in legal niceties, the vigilante-minded law officers were happy to have a nefarious bad man disposed of quickly, cheaply, and permanently by a lynching.

. . .

A host of distinguished Americans—politicians, capitalists, lawyers, writers, and others—supported vigilantism by word or deed. Some of them were personally involved in vigilante movements; usually this was when they were younger men, but in later life they never repudiated their action.

. . .

Frontier vigilantes were headed, thus, by the frontier elite—men who, in turn, gained the highest political positions in territory, state, and nation. Men who were actually vigilantes or had expressed strong approval of specific vigilante movements included two Presidents of the United States (Andrew Jackson, Theodore Roosevelt), five U. S. Senators (Alexander Mouton, Louisiana; Francis M. Cockrell, Missouri; Leland Stanford, California; William J. McConnell, Idaho; Wilbur Fisk Sanders, Montana); eight Governors of states or territories (Alexander Mouton, Louisiana; Augustus C. French, Illinois; Leland Stanford, California; William J. McConnell, Idaho; Fennimore Chatterton and John E. Osborne, Wyoming; Miguel A. Otero and George Curry, New Mexico); one Congressman (George Curry); and one minister to a foreign country (Granville Stuart). At one time—in 1890—four ex-vigilantes served in the U. S. Senate; they were Francis M. Cockrell, Leland Stanford, William J. McConnell, and Wilbur Fisk Sanders.

Literary men were often outspoken in their support of vigilantism. Hubert Howe Bancroft, who wrote many volumes on Western history and who built his San Francisco publishing house into one of the leading businesses on the Pacific Coast, wrote a vigorous and highly favorable account of the San Francisco vigilance committees in his massive two-volume work, *Popular Tribunals* (1887).[80] Thomas J. Dimsdale, the Oxford-educated Montana superintendent of public instruction, wrote a popular and highly laudatory account of *The Vigilantes of Montana* in 1886[81] as did, later, Nathaniel Pitt Langford, the father of Yellowstone National Park.[82] Owen Wister, the socially prominent Harvard graduate and scion of an aristocratic Philadelphia family, in his immensely popular novel, *The Virginian* (1902),[83] strongly praised vigilantism and in so doing summed up the opinion of elite Americans. Andrew D. White, U. S. Minister to Germany, spoke for many when he maintained that "there are communities in which lynch law is better than any other."[84]

. . .

AN EVALUATION OF AMERICAN VIGILANTISM

In shortrun practical terms, the vigilante movement was a positive facet of the American experience. Many a new frontier community gained order and stability as the result of vigilantism which reconstructed the community structure and values of the old settled areas while dealing effectively with a problem of crime and disorder.

From a longer perspective, the negative aspects of vigilantism appear. Although the era of classic vigilantism came to an end in the 1890's, the tradition lived on. In fact, it was extended into areas of American life where it was wholly inappropriate. Thus arose the latter day phenomenon of neovigilantism.

Neovigilantism grew mainly after the Civil War and was largely a response to the problems of an emerging urban, industrial, racially and ethnically diverse America. The transition from the old to the new vigilantism was heralded by the San Francisco Vigilance Committee of 1856. The latter represented a blending of the methods of the old vigilantism with the victims of the new. Virtually all the features of neovigilantism were present in the San Francisco movement of 1856. Neovigilantism was to be frequently urban rather than rural, and that was the case in San Francisco. The old vigilantism had been directed mainly at horsethieves, counterfeiters, outlaws, bad men, and lower people. Neovigilantism found its chief victims among Catholics, Jews, immigrants, Negroes, laboring men and labor leaders, political radicals, and proponents of civil liberties. The actions and overtones of the San Francisco movement were strongly imbued with the passions and prejudices that came to feature the neovigilantism.

The San Franciscan vigilantes were ethnically biased; their ire focused on one group: the Irish.[85] The vigilantes were anti-Catholic; their hero and martyr was the anti-Romanist editor, James King of William, and most of their victims of 1856 were Catholics. Although their ranks included laborers and mechanics, there was a distinct class tinge to the 1856 movement: middle and upper class merchants were aligned against the lower class adherents of the San Francisco Democratic machine. Last but not least was a disregard for civil liberties. Angered by the arguments of John Nugent of the San Francisco *Herald* in favor of regular justice, the merchant vigilantes of '56 quickly organized an advertising boycott that transformed the *Herald* overnight from the strongest to the weakest of the city's major dailies.

Allegedly concerned with a crime problem, the San Francisco vigilantes of 1856 were in actuality motivated by a desire to seize control of the municipal government from the Democratic political machine that found the nucleus of its support among the lower class Irish Catholic workers of the city. Basic to the vigilante movement was the desire to establish a business-oriented local government which would reduce expenditures, deprive the Irish Catholic Democrats of access to municipal revenues, and lower taxes. To a considerable extent, the San Francisco vigilante episode of 1856 represented a struggle for power between two blocs of opposed religious, class, and ethnic characteristics. Thus, the vigilante leadership of upper and middle class, old American, Protestant merchants was aligned against a political faction based upon Irish Catholic lower class laborers. Such were the social and economic tensions that typically enlisted the violence of neovigilantism.

The protean character of neovigilantism precludes an extensive discussion of it at this time. Only significant tendencies may be noted. Negroes have been the targets of three distinct Ku Klux Klan movements over a 100-year period going back to 1867.[86] Catholics and Jews were singled out for verbal attack by the second Ku Klux Klan (of the 1920's), but the bulk of Klan violence in the 1920's seems to have been leveled against ne'er-do-well white Anglo-Saxon Protestants who did not measure up to the puritanical Klan moral standards[87] and was similar to the White Cap movement which violently regulated the immoral and shiftless from 1888 on into the 20th century.[88] Immigrants were repeatedly the victims of neovigilantism. One of the most spectacular instances was the lynching of 11 Sicilians in New Orleans in 1891.[89] Laboring men and labor union organizers (many of whom were immigrants) were frequently the subjects of vigilante violence when on strike or attempting to organize.[90]

Political radicals have often undergone vigilante harassment; one of the most striking examples was the arrest of thousands of Communists and radicals in the "Red raids" of January 1, 1920.[91] The raids were carried out under the color of law, but the whole action resembled nothing so much as a giant vigilante roundup. Proponents of civil liberties have at times fallen afoul of a quasi-vigilante spirit manifested in such waves of intolerance as the "McCarthyism" of the early 1950's. In contrast to the old vigilantism not even a pragmatic justification can be made for neovigilantism, whose efforts have been wholly pernicious. As an index of the tensions of America in an age of transition, neovigilantism is revealing, but as an attempt to apply vigilante methods to the solution of the complex social problems of urban, industrial, diverse America it has been a massive failure.

Neovigilantism is one phase of a larger American failing to which vigilantism has significantly contributed—the spirit of lawlessness. Americans have long felt that intolerable conditions justify defiance of law and its extension, revolution. In large part the spirit of American lawlessness (equal in importance to the spirit of lawfulness) goes back to the American Revolution where Americans learned a lesson that has never been forgotten: that it is sometimes good and proper to rebel and that rebellion succeeds.

Powerfully nurturing American lawlessness has been the vigilante tradition. A part of the historical heritage of hundreds of American communities from the Piedmont to the Pacific, vigilantism—like the American

Revolution—has taught the lesson that defiance of law pays. The typical vigilante took the law into his own hands sincerely (but paradoxically) in the interest of law and order. He desired social stability and got it. But was it purchased at too high a cost?

Yes, said the principled opponents of vigilantism who hammered home a philosophy of antivigilantism that went as far back as the opposition to the original South Carolina movement of 1767-69. From the very beginning antivigilante theorists cogently argued that due process of law was a precious Anglo-American legacy, that true law and order meant observing the law's letter as well as its spirit, and, finally, that the only way to obtain real and lasting law and order was to pour all one's energies and substance into making the regular system work.

One trenchant opponent of the San Francisco Vigilance Committee of 1856 noted that "if the same energy which prompted the formation of the Committee and organized the armed force that assaulted the jail had been directed to strengthen the regular course of justice as public opinion can do it, there would have been no need for the [vigilante] outbreak." "The precedent is bad, the law of passion cannot be trusted, and the slow process of reform in the administration of justice is more safe to rely on than the action of any revolutionary committee, no matter how great may be the apparent necessity," he continued. "Better to endure the evil of escape of criminals than to inaugurate a reign of terror which to-day may punish one guilty head, and tomorrow wreak its mistaken vengeance on many innocent lives," he concluded. [92]

Aside from the danger of vigilante action veering off into extremism, the critics of vigilantism were upset by its fundamentally subversive character. A southern Illinois opponent of the Regulator movement in Pope, Johnson, and Massac Counties, Richard S. Nelson, charged in 1847 that by attacking citizens and taking their property the Regulators had violated "those great principles of civil liberty" upon which the Illinois State constitution was based. Nelson also turned the vigilante justification of popular sovereignty against them by noting that in forcing elected county officials to leave the county or surrender their offices the Regulators had "made a direct attack upon the sovereignty of the people." [93] There is no doubt, however, that, for all the plausibility of Nelson's invocation of popular sovereignty against vigilantism, the appeal to popular sovereignty was made much more often by vigilantes than by their opponents.

Occasionally, vigilante opponents got at the sociological causes of the crime and turbulence which led to vigilantism. The Reverend William Anderson Scott was a courageous opponent of the powerful San Francisco vigilantes of 1856. In a sermon entitled "Education, and not Punishment, the True Remedy for the Wrong-Doings and Disorders of Society," Scott called for industrial education for the lower classes and for urban eleemosynary institutions as means of eradicating the root sources of crime.

"You may depend upon it," he insisted, "the stream of blood will never be staid [*sic*] while men take the law into their own hands.[94]

Americans have for generations been ambiguous in their attitude to law. In one sense, Americans are a law-abiding people of exemplary character. But the many organized movements in our history which have openly flouted and ignored the law (Revolutionary Whigs, Northern abolitionists, Southern filibusters, regulators, vigilantes, Ku Klux Klansmen, White caps, lynch mobs, etcetra.) are an indication that lawlessness has been rife. In 1837, the young Abraham Lincoln delivered an address on "The Perpetuation of Our Political Institutions" and found that the chief threat came from "the increasing disregard for law which pervades the country—the growing disposition to substitute the wild and furious passions in lieu of the sober judgment of courts, and the worse than savage mobs for the executive ministers of justice."[95]

Basic to American lawlessness has been our proclivity to pick and choose the laws we would obey, respecting those which we approve and defying those with which we disagree.[96] Our arbitrary attitude toward law reflects a fundamental and deep-seated disrespect for law, or, to put it another way, reveals only a superficial allegiance to law. Perhaps the most important result of vigilantism has not been its social-stabilizing effect but the subtle way in which it persistently undermined our respect for law by its repeated insistence that there are times when we may choose to obey the law or not.

NOTES

1. It will probably be impossible to ever obtain a definitive count of American vigilante movements; many small movements undoubtedly left no traces in historical sources. The latter seems to have been especially true in the Old Northwest and Old Southwest in the first 20 or 30 years of the 19th century. . . .

2. [Charles Hitchin], *The Regulator* . . . (London: W. Boreham, 1718), and Christopher Hibbert, *The Road to Tyburn* . . . (Cleveland and New York: World Publishing Co., [1957]).

3. Hubert Howe Bancroft, *Popular Tribunals* (2 vols.; San Francisco: History Co., 1887), vol. I, pp. 2–6.

4. James G. Leyburn, *Frontier Folkways* (New Haven: Yale University Press, 1935), p. 219.

5. There have been, indeed, urban as well as rural vigilante movements. The greatest of all American vigilante movements—the San Francisco Vigilance Committee of 1856—was an urban one. Vigilantism has been by no means restricted to the frontier, although most typically it has been a frontier phenomenon.

6. Richard Maxwell Brown, *The South Carolina Regulators* (Cambridge: Harvard University Press, 1963).

7. Aside from the South Carolina Regulators there was little vigilante activity in the original 13 States of the Atlantic seaboard. The North Carolina Regulators (1768–71) did not constitute a vigilante movement, but, rather embodied a violent agrarian protest against corrupt and galling local officials and indifferent provincial authorities.

8. The 96th meridian coincides, approximately, with both physiographic and state boundaries. Physiographically it roughly separates the humid prairies of the East from the semiarid Great Plains of the West. The States of Minnesota, Iowa, Missouri, Arkansas, and Louisiana fall into the province of Eastern vigilantism. The States of North and South Dakota, Nebraska, Kansas, and Oklahoma mainly fall into the area of Western vigilantism. In Texas the 96th meridian separates east Texas from central and west Texas, hence east Texas vigilantism was a part of Eastern vigilantism, while central and west Texas vigilantism properly belongs to the Western variety. For the sake of convenience, however, all of Texas vigilantism (along with that of the Dakotas, Nebraska, Kansas, and Oklahoma) has been included under the heading of Western vigilantism. . . .

9. Lynn Glaser, *Counterfeiting in America* . . .(New York: Clarkson N. Potter [1968]), ch. 5. On the relationship between counterfeiting and the frontier money shortage, see Ruth A. Gallaher, "Money in Pioneer Iowa, 1838-1865," *Iowa Journal of History and Politics,* vol. XXXI (1934), pp. 42-45. The use of counterfeit money for public land purchases is revealed in *Counties of Warren, Benton, Jasper and Newton, Indiana: Historical and Biographical* (Chicago: F. A. Battey, 1883), p. 458.

10. See, for example, Randall Parrish, *Historic Illinois* . . . (Chicago: A. C. McClurg, 1906), pp. 405-406. Charles Edward Pancoast, *A Quaker Forty-Niner* . . . , Anna P. Hannum, ed. (Philadelphia, University of Pennsylvania Press, 1930), pp. 103-104.

11. See, especially, Bancroft, *Popular Tribunals,* vol. I, pp. 441 ff. . . .

12. Thomas J. Dimsdale, *The Vigilantes of Montana* . . . (Virginia City, Mont.: Montana Post Press, 1866). Nathaniel Pitt Langford, *Vigilante Days and Ways* . . . (2 vols.; Boston, J. G. Cupples, 1890). Hoffman Birney, *Vigilantes* (Philadelphia: Penn Publishing Co., 1929).

13. Granville Stuart, *Forty Years on the Frontier,* Paul C. Phillips, ed. (2 vols.; Cleveland: Arthur H. Clark, 1925), vol. II, pp. 195-210. Michael A. Leeson, *History of Montana: 1739-1885* (Chicago: Warner, Beers & Co., 1885), pp. 315-316.

14. Montana Territory Vigilance Committee, *Notice!* (broadside, Helena, Mont., Sept. 19, 1865). Leeson, *History of Montana,* pp. 303-316.

15. Among the many vigilante movements of Central Texas . . . were those of Bastrop County, 1874-83. (C[harles] L. Sonnichsen, *I'll Die before I'll Run* [New York: Devin-Adair, 1962], pp. 167-187), Shackelford County, 1876-1878 (*ibid.,* pp. 150-166), San Saba County, 1880-1896 (*ibid.,* pp. 206-231), and the German "Hoodoo" vigilantes of Mason County, 1875 (Sonnichsen, *Ten Texas Feuds,* p. 87 ff.). Ten counties with major vigilante activity were Bell, Comanche, Coryell, De Witt, Eastland, Gonzales, Hill, Llano, Montague, and Young. Virtually all of the many other Central Texas counties had vigilante activity of one sort or another in this troubled period. In addition to contemporary newspapers, Central Texas vigilantism can best be explored in dozens of county histories done as M.A. theses at the University of Texas. Some of these have been published; see, for example, Zelma Scott, *A History of Coryell County, Texas* (Austin: Texas State Historical Association, 1965), ch. V, and pp. 135, 143. Among the many unpublished M.A. theses, one of the best on vigilantism is Billy B[ob] Lightfoot, "The History of Commanche County, Texas, to 1920" (unpublished M.A. thesis, University of Texas, 1949).

16. Among many sources, see Jerome C. Smiley, *History of Denver* . . . (Denver: Denver Times/Times-Sun Publishing Co., 1901), pp. 338-350.

17. Albuquerque *Republican Review,* Feb. 18, 1871. *Santa Fe Weekly New Mexican,* Nov. 13, 22, 1879. Victor Westphal, "History of Albuquerque: 1870-1880" (unpublished M.A. thesis, University of New Mexico, 1947), pp. 34, 64-65. Bernice A. Rebord, "A Social History of Albuquerque: 1880-1885" (unpublished M.A. thesis, University of New Mexico, 1947), pp. 34, 64-65, and *passim.*

18. Miguel Antonio Otero, *My Life on the Frontier* (2 vols.; New York and Albuquerque: Press of the Pioneers and University of New Mexico Press, 1935-1939), vol. I, pp. 181-206; vol. II, pp. 2-3. *Sante Fe Daily New Mexican,* Mar. 12, 25-26, Apr. 13, 1881.

19. Erna B. Fergusson, *Murder & Mystery in New Mexico* (Albuquerque: Merle Armitage [1948]), pp. 15–32. Chester D. Potter, "Reminiscences of the Socorro Vigilantes," Paige W. Christiansen, ed., *New Mexico Historical Review,* vol. XL (1965), pp. 23–54.

20. On the Butler County vigilantes, see A. T. Andreas, *History of the State of Kansas . . .* (2 vols.; Chicago: A. T. Andreas, 1883), pp. 1431–1432, and Correspondence of Governor J. M. Harvey, File on County Affairs, 1869–1872 (MSS in Archives Department of Kansas State Historical Society, Topeka). Materials on Kansas vigilantism are also to be found in Nyle H. Miller and Joseph W. Snell, *Why the West Was Wild . . .* (Topeka: Kansas State Historical Society, 1963), and Genevieve Yost, "History of Lynching in Kansas," *Kansas Historical Quarterly,* vol. II (1933), pp. 182–219. See, also, Robert R. Dykstra, *The Cattle Towns* (New York: Alfred A. Knopf, 1968).

21. J. H. Triggs, *History of Cheyenne and Northern Wyoming . . .* (Omaha: Herald Steam and Book Job Printing House, 1876), pp. 14, 17–18, 21, 23–27. J. H. Triggs, *History and Directory of Laramie City . . .* (Laramie: Daily Sentinel, 1875), pp. 3–15.

22. The classic (but far from flawless) contemporary account by the anti-Regulator Asa Shinn Mercer was *The Banditti of the Plains . . .* (Cheyenne: privately printed, 1894). A very good recent study is Helena Huntington Smith, *The War on Powder River* (New York, London, and Toronto: McGraw-Hill, 1966). General treatments of Western vigilantism are found in Bancroft, *Popular Tribunals,* vol. I, pp. 593–743; Wayne Gard, *Frontier Justice* (Norman: University of Oklahoma Press, 1949), ch. 14; and Carl Coke Rister, "Outlaws and Vigilantes of the Southern Plains," *Mississippi Valley Historical Review,* vol. XIX (1933), pp. 537 ff.

23. The figure of 79 killings was gained from an analysis of Bancroft's narrative in *Popular Tribunals,* vol. I, pp. 515–576.

24. This distinction between "colonized" and "cumulative" new communities was formulated by Page Smith in *As a City upon the Hill: The Town in American History* (New York: Alfred A. Knopf, 1966), pp. 17–36.

25. The following sketch of the three-level American community structure is based upon my own research and recent studies of American society. Among the latter are Jackson Turner Main, *The Social Structure of Revolutionary America* (Princeton: Princeton University Press, 1965), and for the 19th century: Stephan Thernstrom, *Poverty and Progress: Social Mobility in a Nineteenth Century City* (Cambridge: Harvard University Press, 1964); Ray A. Billington, *America's Frontier Heritage* (New York, Chicago, and San Francisco: Holt, Rinehart & Winston, [1966]), ch. 5, "The Structure of Frontier Society"; and Merle Curti, *The Making of an American Community* (Stanford, Calif.: Stanford University Press, 1959), pp. 56–63, 78, 107–111 ff., 126, 417 ff., 448.

26. On the marginal "lower people" of the South (where they have been labeled "poor whites," "crackers," etc.), see Brown, *South Carolina Regulators,* pp. 27–29, and Shields McIlwaine, *The Southern Poor White from Lubberland to Tobacco Road* (Norman: University of Oklahoma Press, 1939), a literary study. For lower people in the North, see Bernard De Voto, *Mark Twain's America* (Boston: Little, Brown, 1932), pp. 54–58, and George F. Parker, *Iowa Pioneer Foundations* (2 vols.; Iowa City: State Historical Society of Iowa, 1940), vol. II, pp. 37–48.

27. Kai Erikson, *Wayward Puritans: A Study in the Sociology of Deviance* (New York: John Wiley & Sons, 1966), ch. 1.

28. J. Milton Yinger, "Contraculture and Subculture," *American Sociological Review,* vol. XXV (1960), p. 629, holds that a contraculture occurs "wherever the normative system of a group contains, as a primary element, a theme of conflict with the values of the total society . . ." See, also, David M. Downes, *The Delinquent Solution: A Study in Subcultural Theory* (New York: Free Press [1966]), pp. 10–11.

29. See, for example, De Voto, *Mark Twain's America,* pp. 58–62, and Parker, *Iowa Pioneer Foundations,* vol. II, pp. 37–48, 247–265.

30. See Howard, *History of Virgil A. Stewart,* and Miles, "Mississippi Slave Insurrection Scare" on the alleged Murrel plot. On the Flatheads, see Brumbaugh, "Regulator Movement," pp. 28–65; Rose, Papers Relating to Regulator and Flathead Trouble; Charles Neely, *Tales and Songs of Southern Illinois* (Menasha, Wis.: George Banta, 1938), pp. 7, 35, 41; and Norman W. Caldwell, "Shawneetown: A Chapter in the Indian History of Illinois," *Journal of the Illinois State Historical Society,* vol. XXXII (1939), pp. 199–200.

31. See note [76] below.

32. See note [66] below.

33. Brown, *South Carolina Regulators,* pp. 27–37.

34. Langford, *Vigilante Days,* vol. I, pp. 320–324. Howard A. Johnson, "Pioneer Law and Justice in Montana," Chicago Corral of the Westerners, *Brand Book,* vol. V (1948–49), p. 10.

35. About frontier masons in Texas, the late Walter Prescott Webb wrote, that "they believed in the law and aided in preserving order, often in ways best known to themselves." James D. Carter, *Masonry in Texas . . . to 1846* (Waco, Tex.: Committee on Masonic Education and Service for the Grand Lodge of Texas A.F. and A.M., 1955), p. xviii.

36. Thomas and Augustus Wildman, Letters, 1858–1865 (MSS in Western American Collection, Beinecke Rare Book and Manuscript Library, Yale University, New Haven).

37. *Cowley County Censor* (Winfield, Kans.), Jan. 7, 1871.

38. David Donald, ed., "The Autobiography of James Hall, Western Literary Pioneer," *Ohio State Archaeological and Historical Quarterly,* vol. LVI (1947), pp. 297–298.

39. Mott, *Regulators of Northern Indiana,* pp. 6–7, and *passim.*

40. Dimsdale, *Vigilantes of Montana,* p. 116.

41. Fred M. Mazzulla, "Undue Process of Law—Here and There," *Brand Book of the Denver Westerners,* vol. XX (1964), pp. 273–279. Dr. Osborne became Governor of Wyoming in 1893.

42. Brumbaugh, "Regulator Movement," pp. 18–20.

43. Although at present I know of only 729 vigilante killings, it is surely possible that American vigilantism took as many as a thousand lives and perhaps more. In general, the statistics in this paper are tentative. Future findings might alter some of the figures, but it is not very likely that the broad trends revealed by the statistics in this paper would be significantly changed.

44. See, for example, Anthony S. Nicolosi, "The Rise and Fall of the New Jersey Vigilant Societies," *New Jersey History,* vol. LXXXVI (1968), pp. 29–32.

45. "Uses and Abuses of Lynch Law," *American Whig Review,* May 1850, p. 461. Pan Pancoast, *Quaker Forty-Niner,* pp. 103–104. Brumbaugh, "Regulator Movement," pp. 9–11.

46. Dwyn M. Mounger, "Lynching in Mississippi, 1830–1930" (unpublished M.A. thesis, Mississippi State University, 1961), p. 9.

47. Brumbaugh, "Regulator Movement," pp. 10–11.

48. James Stuart, *Three Years in North America* (2 vols.; Edinburgh: Robert Cadell, 1833), vol. II, pp. 212–213. Williams, "Crime and Punishment in Alabama," p. 26.

49. Smiley, *History of Denver,* p. 349. Emphasis mine.

50. "The Vigilance Committee: Richmond during the War of 1812," *Virginia Magazine of History and Biography,* vol. VII (1899–1900), pp. 225–241.

51. Harris G. Warren, "Pensacola and the Filibusters, 1816–1817," *Louisiana Historical Quarterly,* vol. XXI (1938), p. 816.

52. See, for example, Documents relating to the Committee of Vigilance and Safety of Nacogdoches, Texas, Jan. 3, 1835, to Dec. 5, 1837 (transcripts in University of Texas Archives, File Box B 15/40).

53. *Hardesty's Historical and Geographical Encyclopedia . . . of Meigs County, Ohio* (Chicago and Toledo: H.H. Hardesty & Co., 1883), pp. 273–275.

54. Wilbur H. Seibert, *The Underground Railroad from Slavery to Freedom* (New York: Macmillan, 1898), pp. 71 ff., 326 ff., 436–439. See, also, Larry Gara, *The Liberty Line: The*

Legend of the Underground Railroad (Lexington: University of Kentucky Press [1961]), pp. 99, 104–109.

55. John Hope Franklin, *The Militant South* (Cambridge: Harvard University Press, 1956), pp. 87–90. Gara, *Liberty Line,* pp. 157–158.

56. *National Police Gazette,* Sept. 17, 1845, p. 5.

57. Pierce County, Washington Territory, Vigilance Committee, Draft of Compact, June 1, 1856 (MS in Western Americana Collection, Beinecke Rare Book and Manuscript Library, Yale University, New Haven).

58. Griffin, "Vigilance Committees of Attakapas," pp. 153–155.

59. Dimsdale, *Vigilantes of Montana,* p. 107.

60. *History of Johnson County,* pp. 372–373.

61. Thomas Ford, *A History of Illinois from Its Commencement as a State in 1818 to 1847* [1854], Milo M. Quaife, ed. (2 vols.; Chicago: R. R. Donnelly & Sons, 1945–46), vol. I, pp. 10–11.

62. Griffin, "Vigilance Committees of the Attakapas," pp. 153–155.

63. Barde, *History of the Committees,* pp. 26–27.

64. Alfred J. Mokler, *History of Natrona County, Wyoming 1888–1922 . . .* (Chicago: R. R. Donnelly & Co., 1923).

65. *History of Johnson County,* pp. 372–373.

66. Brumbaugh, "Regulator Movement," pp. 3, 5–27. Bryant, *Letters of a Traveller,* pp. 55–68. Of the leading vigilante movements . . . , all but the following seem to have been socially constructive: Madison and Hinds Counties movements, Mississippi, 1835 (no. 8); East Texas Regulators, Shelby County, 1840–1844 (no. 12); Southwest Missouri Slickers, Benton and Hickory Counties, 1842 (no. 14); Southern Illinois Regulators, 1846–1849 (no. 16); San Saba County, Texas, Mob, 1880–1896 (no. 71); Johnson County, Wyoming, cattlemen Regulators, 1892 (no. 80); and the Sevier County, Tennessee, White Caps, 1892–1897 (no. 81). The evidence is ambiguous about the following movements: Central Kentucky Regulators, Marion and other counties, 1866–1871 (no. 48); Northern Florida Regulators, Madison and other counties, 1868–1870 (no. 55); Los Angeles Vigilance Committee, 1852–1858 (no. 23); San Francisco Vigilance Committee, 1856 (no. 25); Socorro, New Mexico, Vigilantes, 1880–1884 (no. 70); and New Orleans vigilantes, 1891 (no. 79). Although the Los Angeles, San Francisco, Socorro, and New Orleans movements produced at least temporary stability, they did so by attacking Mexican, Irish, Mexican, and Italian ethnic groups, respectively, and, in the long run, may have exacerbated rather than reduced tensions.

67. For example, the Turk family (Slickers) *vs.* the Jones family (anti-Slickers) in Southwest Missouri. Lay, *History of Benton County,* pp. 46–61.

68. For example, in the Southwest Missouri Slicker conflict the Slickers were mostly Whigs, and the anti-Slickers were mostly Democrats. Pancoast, *Quaker Forty-Niner,* p. 104. In the Southern Illinois Regulator-Flathead struggle, the factor of local political rivalry was important. Parker B. Pillow, Elijah Smith, and Charles A. Shelby, Regulators and political "outs," were in conflict with a Flathead "in" faction led by Sheriff John W. Read. Report of Governor Augustus C. French, Jan. 11, 1847, and *Sangamo Journal,* Jan. 28, 1847—both in Rose, Papers Relating to Regulator and Flathead Trouble. See, also, Brumbaugh, "Regulator Movement," pp. 66, 69. Political factionalism also contributed to the Regulator-Moderator strife in Shelby County of East Texas where a political "in" faction of old pre-Texas Revolution settlers (Moderators) was opposed by a political "out" faction of post-Revolutionary newcomers (Regulators). Neill, Shelby County" (unpublished M.A. thesis, Stephen F. Austin State College, 1950), pp. 75–77.

69. For example, in later years San Francisco's 1856 vigilance committee leader, William T. Coleman, criticized Charles Doane (the vigilantes' grand marshal) for running for sheriff on the People's Party ticket. Coleman felt that vigilante leaders such as Doane should not run for office. William T. Coleman, Vigilance Committee, 1856 (MS, ca. 1880, in Bancroft Library, University of California, Berkeley), p. 139.

70. In New Mexico's Lincoln County War of 1878–79, the McSween-Tunstall-Brewer mercantile faction organized (unsuccessfully) as Regulators against the dominant Murphy-Dolan mercantile faction. William A. Keleher, *Violence in Lincoln County: 1869–1881* (Albuquerque: University of New Mexico Press [1957]), pp. 152–154. Maurice Garland Fulton, *History of the Lincoln County War,* Robert N. Mullin, ed. (Tucson: University of Arizona Press, 1968), pp. 137–142 ff.

71. In addition to the East Texas Regulators (see below), other movements which fell into sadism and extremism were, most notably, the Southern Illinois Regulators and the Southwest Missouri Slickers. There were other movements of this stripe; even in well controlled movements the elements of sadism and extremism often crept in in a minor way. The problem was inherent in vigilantism.

72. See also note [66], above.

73. See San Francisco *Daily Town Talk,* Aug. 8–9, 1856. Political factionalism was a factor in the 1856 San Francisco vigilante troubles. By and large, the vigilante leaders were composed of old Whigs and Know-Nothings who were in the process of becoming Republicans. The political "ins" who controlled San Francisco and whom the vigilantes attacked were the Irish Catholic Democrats led by David C. Broderick. The "Law and Order" antivigilante faction tended to draw its strength from the Southern oriented wing of the California Democratic Party. Unlike most San Francisco vigilante leaders, William T. Coleman was a Democrat, but as a native Kentuckian he maintained a lifelong devotion to the principles of Henry Clay, and, hence, had much in common with the many vigilante leaders who were also oriented to Henry Clay nationalism.

74. Brown, *South Carolina Regulators,* ch. 6. Down to about the 1850's opponents of regulators and vigilantes were often called Moderators.

75. For a contemporary paradigm of vigilante movements gone bad, see "Uses and Abuses of Lynch Law," pp. 462–463.

76. Sonnichsen, *Ten Texas Feuds,* ch. 1. Neill, "Shelby County," pp. 77–153, and *passim.*

77. Robert B. David, *Malcolm Campbell, Sheriff* (Casper, Wyo.: Wyomingana Inc. [1932]), pp. 18–21.

78. See Brown, "Pivot of American Vigilantism" and this paper, below.

79. Clear examples of local officials who collaborated with vigilantes include: (1) The sheriff in Omaha, Nebr., 1858. Bryan T. Parker, "Extra-Legal Law Enforcement on the Nebraska Frontier" (unpublished M.A. thesis, University of Nebraska, 1931), pp. 58–59. (2) The county attorney of Vernon County, Mo., 1867. *History of Vernon County,* pp. 348–349. (3) The sheriff of Platte County, Nebraska, 1867. A. T. Andreas, *History of the State of Nebraska . . .* (2 vols.; Chicago: Western Historical Co., 1882), vol. II, pp. 1265–1266. (4) The bailiff, deputy sheriff, and other officials of Brown and Erath Counties, Tex., 1872. *Report of the Adjutant-General of the State of Texas* (for 1872), pp. 22, 121–123. (5) The sheriff of Wilbarger County, Tex., 1882. Torrence B. Wilson, Jr., "A History of Wilbarger County, Texas" (unpublished M.A. thesis, University of Texas, 1938), p. 97. (6) The territorial governor and judges of Illinois who in 1816–17 "winked at and encouraged the proceedings of the regulators." Ford, *History of Illinois,* pp. 10–11. (7) Governor William Pitt Kellogg of Louisiana who in 1872 advised Vermillion Parish vigilantes to use their own judgment in dealing with a "horde of cattle thieves" with the result that they hanged 12. Houston (Texas) *Telegraph,* Oct. 3, 1872. (8) The Governor, Mayor, and Sheriff who (in one of the most flagrant instances of implicit official collaboration with vigilantes) were all in New Orleans in 1891 when vigilantes lynched 11 Italians and who did nothing whatsoever to prevent the action for which there had been ample advance warning. John E. Coxe, "The New Orleans Mafia Incident," *Louisiana Historical Quarterly,* vol. XX (1937), pp. 1067–1110. John S. Kendall, "Who Killa De Chief," *ibid.,* vol XXII (1939), pp. 492–530.

80. See John W. Caughey *Hubert Howe Bancroft* (Berkeley and Los Angeles: University of California Press, 1946).

81. On Dimsdale, see pp. 5–8 of the edition of *The Vigilantes of Montana* (Helena, Mont.: State Publishing Co., 1940?), edited by A. J. Noyes.

82. Langford, *Vigilante Days*. On Langford, see *Dictionary of American Biography, s.v.*

83. *The Virginian* (New York: Macmillan, 1902), especially pp. 433–436. On Wister, see Fanny K. Wister, ed., *Owen Wister Out West* (Chicago: University of Chicago Press [1958]). Among the many lesser 19th-century and early 20th-century novelists who portrayed vigilantism favorably were James Weir, *Lonz Powers: or, the Regulators: A Romance of Kentucky* (Philadelphia: Lippincott, Grambo & Co., 1850), and Harris Dickson, *The House of Luck* (Boston: Small, Maynard & Co., [1916]). The enthusiastic reception of Walter Van Tilburg Clark's antivigilante *The Ox-Bow Incident* (New York: Random House, 1940)—the best novel ever written on American vigilantism (upon which a classic film was based)— marked an important shift in public attitudes, from favoring to condemning vigilantism.

84. Quoted in Emerson Hough, *The Story of the Outlaw . . .* (New York: Outing Publishing Co., 1907), p. 399 ff.

85. The following interpretation of the San Francisco vigilante movement of 1856 is based upon Brown, "Pivot of American Vigilantism."

86. On the first Ku Klux Klan, see Stanley F. Horn, *Invisible Empire . . .* (Boston: Houghton Mifflin, 1939). On the second K.K.K., see David M. Chalmers, *Hooded Americanism* (Garden City, N.Y.: Doubleday, 1965).

87. *Ibid.,* and two works by Charles C. Alexander, *The Ku Klux Klan in the Southwest* (Lexington: University of Kentucky Press, 1965), and *Crusade for Conformity: The Ku Klux Klan in Texas, 1920–1930* (Houston: Texas Gulf Coast Historical Association, 1962).

88. The White Cap movement is discussed in my paper, "Historical Patterns of Violence in America" [in Graham and Gurr, *Violence in America*].

89. In one sense the mass lynching was a classic vigilante response to a crime problem (the Italians had apparently been Mafia members and seem to have been involved in the killing of the New Orleans chief of police), but the potent element of anti-Italian ethnic prejudice was crucial to the episode and typical of neovigilantism. See Coxe, "New Orleans Mafia Incident," and Kendall, "Who Killa De Chief."

90. For example, in 1917 in Tulsa, Okla., vigilantes attacked 17 I.W.W. members who were attempting to organize oil field workers. *The "Knights of Liberty" Mob and the I.W.W. Prisoners at Tulsa, Okla. (November 9, 1917)* (pamphlet; New York: National Civil Liberties Bureau, 1918). In this incident the police apparently connived with the vigilantes.

91. See William Preston, *Aliens and Dissenters* (Cambridge: Harvard University Press, 1963), which contains examples of neovigilante attacks upon workers, immigrants, and radicals. See also John W. Caughey, ed., *Their Majesties the Mob* (Chicago: University of Chicago Press [1960]), pp. 1–25, 100–205.

92. Editorial in the New York *National Democrat* quoted in Bancroft, *Popular Tribunals,* vol. II, pp. 554–555.

93. *Illinois State Register* (Springfield), Jan. 1, 1847 (transcript in Rose Papers Relating to Regulator and Flathead Trouble).

94. William Anderson Scott, *A Discourse for the Times Delivered in Calvary Church, July 27, 1856* (pamphlet; San Francisco: N.p., 1856). On Scott, see Clifford M. Drury's aptly subtitled work, *William Anderson Scott: "No Ordinary Man"* (Glendale, Calif.: Arthur H. Clark, 1967).

95. John G. Nicolay and John Hay, eds., *Complete Works of Abraham Lincoln* (revised edition, 12 vols.; New York: Lamb Publishing Co. [1905]), vol. I, pp. 35–50. The quotations are from pp. 35 and 37. In his address Lincoln dwelled upon the ubiquity of "mob law" in the 1830's and specifically cited the Mississippi vigilante actions in 1835 in Madison and Hinds Counties and Vicksburg as well as a case of lynch law in St. Louis, Mo., *Ibid.,* pp. 38–39.

96. See, for example, James Truslow Adams, "Our Lawless Heritage," *Atlantic Monthly,* vol. XLII (1928), pp. 732–740.

Elizabeth M. Geffen

VIOLENCE IN PHILADELPHIA
IN THE 1840s AND 1850s

*No period in the history of American cities was more tur-
bulent than the three decades beginning about 1830. The rate of
urban growth was sharper than at any other time before or
after. A giant transportation network, principally involving the
newly invented steam railroads, was being built to connect the
cities with each other and the countryside, sharpening economic
competition. The Industrial Revolution unsettled previous
means of production and distribution, but not fully enough to
provide new employment or security for all. And both social and
political flux and uncertainty were added to economic. Much of
the incoming urban population was composed of unskilled,
rural Irish, fleeing poverty and famine at home, unused to their
new condition and resented by their new countrymen. The
looming threat of the Civil War, which would break out in
1861, meanwhile heightened all tensions among groups.*

    *Elizabeth Geffen provides a lively account of these years
in Philadelphia, then the second largest city in the country.
Although the specific events she describes were peculiar to the
ironically-named "City of Brotherly Love," overlapping conflicts between whites and blacks, Catholics and Protestants,
Whigs and Democrats, militiamen and fire companies were
common to all of the major eastern centers. So were the solutions sought, notably the formation of full-time professional
police forces, created here and elsewhere during these violent
decades to deal most immediately with the problem of riot.*

From *Pennsylvania History* (October 1969): 381–410. Reprinted by permission of the
author and publisher.

Violence is an old story in Philadelphia, although the city has been fantastically successful in concealing its wild side from the rest of the world. Never has one city fooled so many observers for so many centuries. ". . . [Philadelphia] is Quaker all over," Thomas Hamilton, a visiting Englishman, decided in 1843. "All things, animate and inanimate, seem influenced by a spirit of quietism as pervading as the atmosphere."[1] The city produced in Hamilton a peculiar tendency in the region of his mouth, "which ultimately terminated in a silent but prolonged yawn."[2] He epitomized what may with some fairness be considered a rather widespread reaction. Another English traveler, Captain Frederick Marryat, a few years earlier had noted with some surprise, "The first idea which strikes you when you arrive at Philadelphia is that it is Sunday."[3]

Actually, the Sabbath had been a favorite day for organized and spontaneous mayhem in Philadelphia at least since 1702, when a grand jury reported that young men and servants were taking the "licenceus liberty" of robbing orchards and "committing unruly actions, especially on the first day of the week, commonly called the Lord's Day."[4] By the mid-1840's, the *Public Ledger* found it so unusual as to be worthy of a special announcement in the newspaper when a certain March 31 was a "QUIET SUNDAY."[5]

Respect for the religious persuasion of the founder, even knowledge of the Greek roots of Philadelphia's name, must not blind one to the truth that the Quaker city of brotherly love has throughout its history erupted again and again into bloody violence. Some of the uproar originated in unlikely sources. Rival clergymen have occasionally battled with each other and with dissident factions of their congregations for control of churches, as, for example, did the two contending pastors of the German Reformed Church on Race Street near Fourth in 1750, a contest conducted with "some beating and bruising, . . . much to the scandal of religious profession."[6] Women have shattered the public peace, as in the "Dutch Riot" of the early 1780's, when several hundred of the weaker sex tore up all the posts and fence rails around a grain field on Callowhill Street between Third and Fourth, and set the whole square ablaze, after severely beating the owner, over the shooting of three foraging hogs.[7] On the other hand, juvenile delinquency has been endemic. One youthful outbreak of particular piquancy was that "strange freak [that] seized the minds of some of the young citizens" in 1761, when "The insulting of several women in the streets, by cutting their gowns and petticoats with a razor, rendered it dangerous for them to appear therein without protection, as also breaking of knockers and bells, cutting the spouts, &c., . . . nightly committed."[8]

Philadelphians have never hesitated to express political opinions with clarity and emphasis. In 1773, for instance, when the Common Council proceeded with the building of a new market in High Street between Third and Fourth against the will of the local constituency, the latter simply "tore down the market as fast as it was erected, demolishing by night what was built by day."[9] In 1798, popular indignation over the XYZ affair waxed so furious that President John Adams believed "The multitude in Philadelphia . . . was . . . ripe to pull me out of my house," and the Governor had to send a military patrol to quiet Adams' nerves.[10] Even the simple casting of ballots in the city's frequent elections often led to arson and murder.

Economic problems also produced violence. The city's workmen, especially its journeymen, early took to the barricades of labor organization, to meet in unequal combat the forces of their employers. The bourgeoisie, however, according to one observer, outclassed all others, for "The most disgraceful riots that occur[red] in Philadelphia [were] those which [were] produced by the opening of the books of subscription for a new bank."[11]

Every facet of the city's life has exhibited uproarious tendencies from time to time. The never entirely quiescent violence grew steadily stronger, more deadly, and more frequently eruptive, during the early part of the nineteenth century, reaching a horrifying climax of racial and religious warfare in the 1840's, the very decades when Thomas Hamilton was yawning, "The Philadelphians are no traffickers in extremes of any sort. . . ."[12] A native Philadelphian, the author Charles Godfrey Leland, testified to the contrary:

Whoever shall write a history of Philadelphia from the Thirties to the era of the Fifties will record a popular period of turbulence and outrages so extensive as to now appear almost incredible. These were so great as to cause grave doubts in my mind whether the severest despotism, guided by justice, would not have been preferable to such republican license as then prevailed in the city of Penn.[13]

All history begins with geography. Philadelphia's troubles began when William Penn located his metropolis on the peninsula formed by the Delaware and Schuylkill Rivers, midway between what were to be the two extremes of England's American colonies. The keystone of the colonial arch, the most southern of northern cities, Philadelphia ultimately found itself caught in the crossfire of two opposing forces which by the 1830's had already begun open warfare. The South was by this time Philadelphia's best customer. Not only were some of the city's best friends slaveowners but many of its blood relations as well, as social ties were forged concomitantly with trade. On the other hand, the first formal protest against slavery in the United States had come from Pastorius in the Philadelphia suburb of Germantown in 1688; and "The Pennsylvania Society for promoting the Abolition of Slavery, for the relief of free Negroes, unlawfully held in Bondage, and for improving the Condition of the African Race," founded in Philadelphia in 1775, was the first antislavery society in the United States. In 1780 Pennsylvania became the first state to legislate the gradual emancipation of its slaves. The preeminence of Philadelphia in the abolition movement together with the city's central location made it a natural meeting place for national organizations, and of the twenty-four antislavery conventions held in the United States from 1794 to 1828, twenty were held in Philadelphia. William Lloyd Garrison organized the American Anti-Slavery Society there in 1833. [14]

All of these factors combined to make the city a mecca for black people, both free and slave, escaping from Southern bondage. In 1847 an inquiry revealed that 47.7% of the Negro population of Philadelphia had been immigrants to Pennsylvania. [15] A reverse traffic from North to South, created by slave-catchers and kidnappers, had provided a major target for the Pennsylvania Abolition Society from its founding in 1775, but the passage of the Fugitive Slave Act of 1820 had so stimulated this illegal trade that the Pennsylvania Assembly had passed laws against it in 1826 and 1827. [16] The kidnapping of Negro children for sale in the South became so frequent in the same decade that Philadelphia City Councils passed a resolution in 1827 offering $500 reward for the arrest and conviction of anyone involved in such a crime. [17] Stronger than such terrors, however, the Philadelphia abolitionist tradition, the numerous charitable organizations widely known for their generosity to all unfortunates, the lure of the city's burgeoning economy, continued to attract more and more black people to Philadelphia.

Unfortunately, Philadelphia turned out to be something less than the Promised Land. The condition of the city's Negroes indeed improved statistically. They established many small businesses, engaged in trades of all kinds, and by 1838 held $322,532 in city and county real estate. [18] However, this economic well-being did not extend to all black people, most of whom were wretchedly poor. In 1837, although only 7.4% of the population, they provided 14% of the inmates of the County Almshouse. [19] The black population of Philadelphia County had grown from 2,489 in 1790 to 19,833 in 1840. [20] In 1790 approximately one-half of them had lived between Market and South Streets, from Fifth to Eighth Streets, mostly in the alleys between Lombard and South, while another 25% lived between Market and Vine Streets, east of Ninth. They had begun to push northward in the mid-1790's, only to be forced back by hostile whites, until by the 1840's they were effectively segregated in four wards centering at Sixth and Lombard Streets, in Moyamensing and Southwark. [21] Here they lived in extreme wretchedness, overcrowded into run-down tenements or hovels in back alleys and courts. Of 302 Negro families living in Moyamensing, from Fifth to Eighth Streets, South to Fitzwater, in 1847, 176 owned a total of $603.50 worth of personal property, or $3.43 per family. [22] Meanwhile, additional immigrants continued to pour in from the South, ignorant, poverty-stricken, unused to urban living. Such conditions inevitably produced a high rate of vice and crime. For the period 1830–1850, Negroes, constituting less than 1/14 of the population, were held responsible for about one-third of the serious crimes.[23] This fact provided a favorite excuse for white violence directed against Negroes, while the black community's physical concentration in one area made it tragically vulnerable.

The first major attack upon the Negro quarter occurred in 1829, in reaction to the increased influx of refugees from [the South]. . . . So bitter was public hostility at this time that Quakers advised against the sending in of any more fugitives until those already in the city had been accepted.[24] The mood of much of the white community in its relationship to Negroes and the question of their emancipation had changed radically from the general benevolence of the eighteenth century to open hostility by the 1830's.[25] The quality of Negro life had admittedly deteriorated as overcrowding and unassimilable immigration had diluted the effectiveness of normal social controls. Paradoxically, those black men who fought their way out of the depths—and they owned real estate in the city and county with an estimated value of $531,809 by 1848—irritated many whites even more than did their impoverished fellows, for success was interpreted as a claim for social equality.[26] Political recognition of the change in black-white relations was made when the Pennsylvania Constitutional Convention in 1838 added the word "white" to the qualifications for voters, thus depriving free Negroes of civil rights which had been theirs in Pennsylvania since 1790.[27]

Long, hot summers filled with rioting are no innovation of the mid-twentieth century. Philadelphia had them as long ago as the 1830's and probably for many of the same reasons that produce them today.[28] The heat in the city is alone enough to turn peaceful men to violence. Dirty, ugly, crowded slums outraged human sensibilities and dulled human decency, while the gap between the promise of the American Dream and the reality suffered by the poor produced frenzied frustration in both white and black men, then as now. The major difference between the 1960's and the pre-Civil War decades is that the Negroes were the target of white rioting a century ago.

In a typical incident, in August 1842 a white mob from Southwark, "chiefly Irish," beginning with an attack upon a procession of the Negro Moyamensing Temperance Society, laid completely waste the Negro area from Fifth to Eighth Streets near Lombard, assaulting black people on the streets, looting their homes, burning down a Negro hall and church.[29] When the police made arrests, the mob attacked the police in efforts to rescue those arrested. The following day Irish laborers in coal-yards on the Schuylkill River attacked Negroes working nearby, repelling a *posse* of sixty men led by the Sheriff. The mob then moved on to Moyamensing and attacked Negroes in the general area between South and Fitzwater Streets, from Thirteenth Street eastward, being driven off only by the muskets and artillery of the militia, which was not called into action, however, until the rioters had accomplished their purpose. Hundreds of Negroes, including women and children, the elderly and the sick, fled the area, some to the police station for protection, others crossing the river to the woods and swamps of New Jersey, where some were sustained by charitable farmers, while others starved. [30]

The general disorder surrounding the election of October 9, 1849, turned into an anti-Negro riot when a mob including members of two Moyamensing gangs, the Killers and Stingers, armed with stones, clubs, knives, and pistols, attacked California House, a hotel on St. Mary Street (below Lombard) between Sixth and Seventh, frequented by Negroes and operated by a mulatto married to a white wife. [31] The battle raged for a night and a day. The hotel and many adjacent houses burned down in a twelve-hour blaze attended by firemen fighting each other while the mob fought the firemen, cut fire hoses, and dragged fire engines away. Tearing up paving stones and bricks and also using guns, the blacks defended themselves vigorously, but the unarmed city police were run off by the mob. Once more the militia had to be summoned, and a strong force of infantry, cavalry, and artillery finally occupied the district, remaining for two days. The toll was nine whites and sixteen blacks taken to the hospital, three whites (including two firemen) and one Negro killed.

George Lippard, perhaps the first American muck-raking novelist, professed to "tell it as it was" in his phenomenally successful novel, *The Quaker City,* published in 1844. Two of his cutthroat characters discussed the Philadelphia racial situation:

"Why you see, a party of us one Sunday afternoon, had nothin' to do, so we got up a nigger riot. We have them things in Phi'delphy, once or twice a year, you know? I helped to burn a nigger church, two orphans' asylums and a school-house and happenin' to have a pump-handle in my hand, I aksedentally hit an old nigger on the head. Konsekance wos he died. . . ."

"And you was tried for this little accident?"

"Yes, I was. Convicted, too. Sentenced, in the bargain. But the Judge and the jury and the lawyers, on both sides, signed a paper to the Governor. He pardoned me. . . ." [32]

The census figures eloquently summarize one result. From 1840 to 1850, while the white population of Philadelphia and the surrounding area increased from 238,204 to 389,001, the Negro population declined slightly, from 19,833 to 19,761. [33]

Meanwhile, demographic developments contributing to violence were also occurring outside the Negro ghetto. Both centrifugal and centripetal patterns of growth caused trouble. The city of Philadelphia until 1854 officially included only the two square miles incorporated under the original charter granted by William Penn in 1701, between the Delaware and Schuylkill Rivers, from Vine Street on the north to Cedar (South) Street on the south. In 1840 a population of 93,665 lived within these limits, while "spill-over" into the adjoining area making up Philadelphia County totalled 164,372. By 1850 the City's residents numbered 121,417, the County's 238,121, with the center of the area's population no longer in the city itself but north of Vine Street, where 206,885 persons lived between the two rivers as compared with 188,802 who lived south of Vine. [34] An estimate of the rate of increase made in 1854 for the preceding decade foretold still greater disparity, for while the city's population had increased 29½% since 1844, the northern district of Spring Garden had grown 111½% and Kensington, in the northeast, 109½%, with only slightly lesser rates in the other neighboring communities. [35] In 1854 the city was surrounded by nine incorporated districts, six boroughs, and thirteen townships. The relationship between them was an unhappy one. As one Philadelphian pointed out in 1853, "The parent city . . . often evinced an illiberal policy toward her surrounding children, which they . . . more than requited by a spirit of retaliation." [36] In direct contrast to twentieth century patterns of urban growth, most of the "best people" of Philadelphia in the early part of the nineteenth century lived, at least part of the time, in the original heart of the city, south of Market Street and east of Seventh, while the "suburbs" to the north and south of this enclave housed the great bulk of the poorer classes. [37] City elections were usually dominated by Whigs, the surrounding districts by the Democrats, so that any effort to consolidate city and suburbs was immediately rejected by the city Whigs as a Democratic plot. [38]

With the city's jurisdiction restricted between the two rivers, Vine and South Streets, the maintenance of public order was impossible, since up to 1850 lawbreakers needed only to dash across the narrow limits of the city to become immune from arrest and punishment, while even within the city the provisions for law enforcement were inadequate. Under the Ordinance of 1833 twenty-four day policemen and 120 night watchmen were appointed, but the daytime force was later reduced because it was considered both too expensive and "unsatisfactory." [39] The districts' systems were worse, many having a single law officer, to whom no funds were given for hiring or arming citizen *posses,* nor was there any way in which volunteers could be forced to serve. Innumerable organized gangs, such as the Killers, Stingers, Skinners, Blood-Tubs, and Rats, terrorized their neighborhoods. [40] Events moved to a climax in 1844.

In February, the Board of Commissioners of Moyamensing received petitions "setting forth the riots and disorders which have disturbed the Township, and asking for the appointment of a police officer whose special duty it should be to preserve the peace by arresting all rioters, and dispersing all unlawful assemblages." [41] The Moyamensing Board of School Directors complained at the same time about "the collection of mobs, and the perpetration of outrages" in the neighborhood of Sixth and Catharine Streets. [42] Later in the same month a letter to the editors of the *Public Ledger,* signed "Many Subscribers," called attention of the authorities to "the gang of outlaws and desperadoes (all of whom appear to be at least 21 years of age) who nightly assemble at the N.W. corner of Christian and Second Streets, insulting in the most obscene and profane language, indiscriminately, all persons passing, in particular unprotected females, going and returning from Church on Sabbath evenings. . . ."[43] In April the *Ledger* reported that for some time past the neighborhood of Franklin Street and Germantown Road had been the scene of "great outrages by large mobs of boys, whose conduct on some occasions, in throwing stones and other missiles, has made it unsafe for persons to pass anywhere near them."[44] A letter published in the *Ledger* on April 9 announced that the writer was moving across the river, where people were more orderly, for he found it useless any longer to try to live in Southwark. Not only were property values depreciating because of the widespread disorder, but "In fact, the whole district pass their lives 'in terroram' of supernumerary, would-be firemen, half-grown blackguards, and young rowdies."[45]

From the earliest years of the city, increasing population and rising land values had encouraged the subdivision of Penn's original spacious plan, wherein each square was rimmed by individual houses, each with its own garden. During the eighteenth century both the center of the city and the surrounding neighborhoods had gradually developed a maze of alleys and courts where by 1840 thousands of the poor, white as well as black, were jammed into miserable hovels without light, air, or sanitation of any kind. Gradually, as many of the well-to-do had begun to move westward, many of the better houses they vacated were razed to be replaced by commercial construction; others deteriorated under absentee landlordism, often converted into multi-family tenements.[46]

Into this rapidly worsening situation came not only great numbers of Negroes but also increasing numbers of Europeans, the latter reaching flood proportions in the 1840's with the advent of the Southern Irish fleeing from the famine in their homeland. Most of them were forced by lack of housing in the city to seek homes in the outlying districts. There these new arrivals, impoverished, unskilled, and Catholic, immediately confronted an ancient enemy, the Protestant Scotch-Irish, longtime resident in Philadelphia, proud of their "in" status, mostly skilled workers, and ready, eager, and able to renew the political, economic, social, and religious feuds of the old country. During the 1830's they had organized an Orange Society for that express purpose.[47]

Still another factor adding to the explosive potential of Philadelphia's demography was the steady trend cityward from the rural hinterland, encouraged by the economic developments of the Industrial Revolution. Although farmers traditionally regarded all cities with suspicion, many of their sons and daughters came to Philadelphia seeking jobs and remained there even when the jobs failed to materialize.

The birth rate was high for all social and economic groups. The death rate, although high enough to keep everyone in a state of chronic apprehension, still permitted a net growth of population in excess of that which the economy could adequately support. A special grand jury investigating the "Mysteries and Miseries of Philadelphia" reported on January 21, 1853, "[t]he existence of such a scene of destitution in our midst [as] had never entered the mind of any of our body."[48] Typical was one house on Baker Street below Seventh in Moyamensing, containing a number of small rooms, without windows or other ventilation, in which the numerous occupants of both sexes huddled together, half naked, with no furniture, not even straw to lie upon. Casper Souder, Jr., a reporter for the *Evening Bulletin,* conducted his own investigation of "the infected districts" with a guide and guard, and found conditions so terrible that he felt unable adequately to describe them.[49] Within a few blocks of the most fashionable section of town he found an estimated 4,000 to 5,000 "miserable wretches," many of them homeless, others crowded into tenement rooms rented for 12½ cents a day, with spaces on the floor sublet at two cents each. Slum shops begged for food at the back doors of the wealthy and then sold it for one cent per meal. Such was one extreme of the economic spectrum, but every segment of the population experienced to some degree the profound disturbance produced in every phase of Philadelphia's life by the Industrial Revolution.

Equipped to become an industrial leader by natural resources and steadily augmented technological developments, Philadelphia had begun to fulfill that potential by 1840. The $8,896,998 invested in manufacturing that year increased to $33,737,911 by 1850, to $73,087,852 in 1860.[50] Anthracite coal sent to the port of Philadelphia, beginning with 365 tons in 1820, had increased to 5,490,146 tons by 1853.[51] New private fortunes accumulated, and in 1845 the anonymous author of *Wealth and Biography of the Wealthy Citizens of Philadelphia* reported that there were in the city at that time ten fortunes of $1,000,000 or more, eleven between $500,000 and $1,000,000, nineteen between $250,000 and $500,000, and 205 between $100,000 and $50,000, the latter being the minimum which entitled one to be classified as "wealthy."[52] In the same year, however, a salesman could be employed for $450 per annum and at the bottom rung of the mercantile ladder a bright lad could "prove" himself by working six days of twelve to fourteen hours each per week for a cash stipend of 75 cents.[53] A common male laborer could earn 80 cents for a 14-hour day, female labor 40 cents.[54] Paradoxically, while Jacksonian political orators assured the voters that the Age of the Common Man had come and equalitarianism was here to stay, the cleavage between the socio-economic classes began to widen to an unprecedented degree. The development of the corporate form of enterprise not only by its very nature limited individual responsibility but added insult to injury by its inevitable depersonalization of the relationship between employer and employee.

With Jackson's defeat of Biddle in the Bank War of the 1830's, Philadelphia had in 1837 fallen into an economic depression that, with periodic flurries of recovery, was to last for fifteen years. It plunged into the abyss in February, 1841, when Biddle's Bank under its Pennsylvania charter closed its doors for the last time.[55] "If a volcano had opened its fiery jaws in our midst," wrote Job R. Tyson in 1852, "or an earthquake had shaken the firmest edifices to their foundations, the popular terror could not have been more painful and pervading."[56] Boom-bust cycles had occurred throughout the Western world during the early nineteenth century, and Philadelphia had experienced recessions in 1824, 1829, and 1833. Always wage cuts and unemployment had caused misery among the working class, while in periods of recovery, prices had always out-run wages. The depression beginning in 1837 and reaching its lowest depths in 1841-42 lasted longer than any of its predecessors. The upper classes counselled optimism, one theory being that the sooner the bottom was reached, the sooner the upswing would begin. One clergyman quoted Bunyan to the effect that "He that is down needs fear no fall."[57] The clergy in general tended to remind the faithful that the economic order was the will of God. Other Philadelphians, however, remembered two early American teachings: the Lord helps those that help themselves, and in union there is strength.

The labor movements which had begun to organize local, single trade unions in Philadelphia in the 1820's tried political action through the Workingmen's Party, but without notable success.[58] During the 1820's and 1830's many strikes were called, demanding higher wages, shorter hours, and free public education. Employers retaliated with lock-outs, court actions, and sustained propaganda in the press, school, and pulpit. Professor Henry Vethake of the University of Pennsylvania stated in his best-selling textbook, *Principles of Political Economy,* in 1838: "No one will deny that the existence of all combinations of the nature of trades' unions is an evil, of no little magnitude. . . ."[59] The Rev. James W. Alexander in a book of advice for American mechanics in 1847 cautioned that trades unions, "that fearful system which is beginning to spread itself among our happy yeomanry," were *"the beginning of the end!"*[60] [Italics his] The degree of general confusion can be estimated from Vethake's conclusion: "Shew me a people who estimate highly the advantages of religion, of morals, and of education, and . . . I will shew you a people among whom wages are high."[61]

George Lippard established in Philadelphia in 1847 a labor organization with highly militant potential.[62] Calling themselves the "Brotherhood of the Union" and following a complicated secret ritual including ceremonial robes and countersigns, these workers began an organizational drive in 1849 with Lippard's issuance of a newspaper bearing the same name as his best-selling novel, *The Quaker City.* Lippard called upon labor "to go to War, in any and all forms—War with the Rifle, Sword and Knife!" if peaceful means failed, for "The War of Labor—waged with pen or sword— is a Holy War."[63] That no holocaust developed suggests that Lippard was too far ahead of his time—he fervently admired Fourier, Louis Blanc, and Michelet, although he was apparently unaware of Marx.[64]

The nationally organized Industrial Congress established in 1845-46 held its fourth meeting in Philadelphia in 1848. Prominent on its agenda was its discussion of the European revolutions of that year and the possible applicability of revolutionary methods to American problems.[65] Philadelphia's workers, however, felt they had won a major victory when, after two decades of agitation, Pennsylvania passed a ten-hour law in March 1848.[66] The continuing influx of unskilled workers and the increasing employment of women and children in factories contributed to the decision of the skilled workers in the 1850's to give up the idealistic drive for the betterment of all workers and to seek higher wages and better working conditions for themselves. By the mid-1850's the forty-one organized trades in Philadelphia specifically barred unskilled labor in general and a few barred women.[67] John Campbell, one of the city's prominent labor leaders, declared in 1850 that Philadelphia workingmen showed *"too much caution."*[68] [Italics his] Actually, they were typical of American labor in general at this time, barely conscious of their common cause and sharing middle class aspirations. Labor's chief problem in the 1840's and 1850's was the Industrial Revolution and they shared the general public ignorance of what to do about it.

Just as baffled as everyone else but angrier than most, some workers kept the city simmering with sporadic acts of unorganized violence. On August 26, 1842, for example, arsonists set fire to the wooden bridge of the Philadelphia and Reading Railroad Company at the Falls of the Schuylkill and totally destroyed it. This "diabolical Act," according to one commentator, was believed to have been done by the "lower classes, Irish probably," because their wages had been cut in the course of the Reading's "ruinous competition" with the Schuylkill Navigation Company for control of the anthracite coal trade.[69] In another area of the city the expression "riotous weavers" became by repetition practically one word in the annals of Philadelphia violence. "God knows some of the poor fellows had great cause to feel rebellious," stated one report.[70] "Empty stomachs and empty purses are not the best advocates of good order." Skilled hand weavers, owners of their own looms and working in their own homes, they stubbornly resisted the mechanization of the textile industry in which Philadelphia had been a leader since the 1820's. As early as August, 1828—during another long, hot summer, one can imagine—the weavers had erupted in an affray which killed one and wounded many.[71] In 1842 large numbers of them went on strike in protest against the inhuman conditions of their craft. In that year an average weaver, with the necessary full-time assistance of his wife or another relative, could in a 14-hour day weave twenty yards of cloth, for which he was paid the average rate of three cents per yard. Even this miserable sum was paid in store orders, which deducted eight to ten percent through overpriced merchandise. In the general economic distress of 1842, when some employers reduced wages still further, some workers were driven to accept what the *Public Ledger* called "the awful doctrine of 'blood or bread.'"[72] In August, 1842, and January,

1843, they rioted extensively in Kensington and Moyamensing, attacking in the streets those who refused to join them, raiding the homes of non-striking weavers, destroying looms and all the goods they could find, beating even the women and children of non-sympathizers. The climax came on January 11 and 12, 1843, when the mob forced the Sheriff's *posse* to flee, severely beat the Sheriff, and took control of the streets. Four companies of volunteers had to be called out, backed up by eight companies of General Cadwalader's brigade at their armories, before the riot ended. [73]

The many pressures combining to make life unpleasant, insecure, hazardous, and frightening for thousands of middle class and poor white Philadelphians did not enlarge the city's already limited capacity for religious tolerance. Of the city's 128 churches in 1840, 121 were Protestant, most of them convinced by the combined efforts of anti-Catholic journalists, politicians, clergy, and laity that they were about to be wiped out by an inundation of Catholicism. Philadelphia became a major center, during the 1840's, of what has been called "the Protestant Crusade." [74] The Union of Protestant Associations combined many local groups of anti-Catholic agitators and by 1842 established a Protestant Institute to distribute anti-Catholic literature. [75] Several newspapers began publishing with the same purpose. [76] Meanwhile, a new political coalition, to be called the Native American Party, was organizing, dedicated to the proposition that no immigrant should be admitted to full participation in the rights and privileges of American life until he had lived on American soil for twenty-one years. It held its first meeting in Germantown in 1837, finding many men happy to be given a scapegoat for their troubles in that depression year. [77]

On November 8, 1842, the American Protestant Association was organized, with ninety-eight Philadelphia clergymen ultimately appending their names to its constitution, pledging an unremitting war on Popery, through their own pulpits and in books, tracts, and pamphlets. [78] Most unfortunately, on November 14, 1842, the Right Rev. Francis P. Kenrick, Irish-born Bishop of Philadelphia's Roman Catholics, wrote a letter to the Board of Controllers of the Public Schools, asking that Catholic children be allowed to use their own Bible and be excused from other religious instruction while attending the public schools. [79] During the subsequent discussion of this subject by both Catholics and Protestants, the anti-Catholic agitation assumed the character of a holy war in defense of Sacred Writ. One contemporary Protestant critic commented that the crusade "arose in probably the least religious section of the city" [Kensington] and most of those inspired to fight for the cause "would not have known the difference between the Protestant and Catholic Bible if it had been placed in their hands." [80]

In December, 1843, political nativists organized the American Republican Association, which proceeded to set up branches in almost every ward and township of the city and county. [81] On May 3, 1844, one of their meetings in Kensington was broken up by a group of foreigners, mostly Southern

Irishmen, armed with clubs.[82] A continuation of this episode at the same place three days later ended with the wounding of eleven nativists and the fatal shooting of one of them, a young man named George Shiffler, who was promptly elevated to the status of martyr. That night a counterattack was made on a school of the Sisters of Charity at Second and Phoenix (Thompson) Streets, and two passersby were killed by shots fired in the melee. The battle continued back and forth, with thirty Irish homes destroyed by fire and many on both sides killed and wounded on May 7. The Sheriff called for volunteer troops but they refused to respond, apparently because they had not been paid for the last time they had served, among other reasons. Bishop Kenrick did what he could to stop the violence, having placards posted on all Catholic churches during the day, urging no retaliation, but nativists tore down the signs and made cocked hats out of them which they wore to battle.

The next day, May 8, the apex of fury was reached when the mob burned down St. Michael's Church and rectory at Second and Jefferson Streets, the Female Seminary of the Sisters of Charity at Second and Phoenix, St. Augustine's Church on Fourth Street below Vine, with an adjoining school, and several private homes of Irishmen. The troops finally brought into action were openly defied by the mob. Convinced that the weakness of law enforcement had encouraged the rioters, City Councils finally appropriated $20,000 for police to maintain the peace. "Peace police," civilians wearing white muslin badges around their hats, were organized in every ward for patrol duty and were given authority to fire upon the mob if necessary. Sporadic vandalism continued on May 9. A division of troops stayed on duty in the area for several days.[83]

On May 10 Bishop Kenrick had ordered that no public worship be held by Catholics until the city was safe and he had then left for a short visit to Baltimore. His departure angered not only the city fathers, who considered it a rebuke for their weakness, but also his more militant parishioners, who compared him unfavorably with Bishop Hughes of New York, who declared that if a single Catholic church was burned in his city, New York would become a second Moscow.[84] However, it would seem that Kenrick acted wisely, for Catholics were a weak, unorganized minority in Philadelphia, while Orangemen were numerous, well organized, and had many friends, police protection was inadequate, and the city had no jurisdiction over the district where the rioting had begun. The general mood of the city was reflected, moreover, in the Grand Jury's presentment on June 18, 1844, which blamed the riots on Bishop Kenrick's protest concerning Bible reading in the public schools. The toll of the riot was estimated at fifty wounded, three dead, and a property loss of $150,000.[85]

The Native American Party made enormous gains in membership as a result of the riot, increasing from approximately five hundred to many thousands, with members in every ward. When 4,500 of them paraded on July 4, 1844, with fifty ward and township associations represented, escorting the carriages of the widows and orphans of those killed in the May rioting, many feared a new outbreak. It did not erupt until the following day, when a mob moved on St. Philip de Neri's Church on Queen Street between Second and Third in Southwark.[86] The arrival of troops broke up this attack before any damage was done beyond sporadic firing of shots, fighting, and running through the streets. The troops remained on guard until Sunday morning, July 7, when most of them were withdrawn. The mob returned and forced an entry into the church with a battering ram. It now became clear that the Native American movement had attracted two different major groups of followers, one sincerely patriotic, believing that foreigners endangered the national welfare, while a second group, described by *The Spirit of the Times* as "the very dregs of society,"[87] simply wanted sanction for violence. A force of conservative Native Americans defended the Church on July 7, while the rowdies finally managed to precipitate a riot. The troops returned to the Church in the afternoon, were harassed by the mob, and by 8:30 p.m. soldiers and civilians were engaged in deadly conflict. Sheriff McMichael issued a proclamation.

Whereas, certain evil disposed persons have resorted to the use of firearms in open defiance of the laws; now therefore, this is to give notice that all such persons and all others aiding, abetting, assisting, or in any way giving an encouragement or countenance to such persons, are hereby declared in open rebellion to the laws, and will be dealt with as traitors and insurgents.[88]

More troops were ordered in by the Governor. Heavy discharges of cannon, firing of small arms in irregular reports and regular volleys continued throughout the night until two o'clock Monday morning, by which time two soldiers and thirteen civilians had been killed, eighteen soldiers and twenty-six civilians wounded. Complete order was not restored until July 9. The lead editorial of *The Spirit of the Times* that day declared:

We are in the midst of a civil war! Riot and anarchy are around us! Death and destruction stare us in the face; and for once we behold the strange anomaly in this country, of an open and regularly organized rebellion on the part of a certain faction against the constituted authorities of the law. . . .

Altogether an estimated 5,000 soldiers were on duty during this emergency. On July 19 the *Public Ledger* editorialized:

Our city and suburbs are now a garrison. Military companies are continually arriving from distant counties, to relieve those of our own and adjoining counties and we exhibit to a stranger almost every appearance of a town besieged or threatened with an attack from an invading army. . . . But we are in the midst of something still worse. The State is at war, and it is at war with treason, raising a parricidal hand against the law. This is worse, much worse, than a foreign war. [It indicates that] something is rotten in the state of Pennsylvania. Corruption is at work within us; the elements of mischief are among us, a part of ourselves.

The troops were gradually withdrawn within the next two or three weeks. On July 11 the City passed an ordinance providing for its own armed force if necessary. They eased their frustrations by bloody attacks upon more full troop of horse, subject to call when necessary, "to provide for the preservation of the peace of the city." [89] By September 26 the full complement was enlisted, consisting of 1,350 men. The State legislature recognized the seriousness of the situation when on April 12, 1845, it adopted an act requiring the provision of at least one police officer for every 150 taxable inhabitants of Philadelphia, the districts of Spring Garden, Northern Liberties, and Penn, and the township of Moyamensing. [90] This failed to pacify the area, and in 1849, during serious rioting in Moyamensing, an organized gang from a rival district was employed by the Moyamensing authorities to put down the disturbance. Even a critic who felt this was a bad policy, conceded that it was the only thing possible at the time, for the mayor and sheriff, being elective officers and needing votes, would not act against the rioters. [91]

The State Assembly acted more vigorously in 1850, creating a Philadelphia Police District with an organized police force under the direction of a police board consisting of a marshal and four lieutenants, which had authority not only in the city but also in the districts of Northern Liberties, Spring Garden, Kensington, and Richmond, and the townships of Southwark, Moyamensing, and Penn. [92] At a ratio of one policeman per 400 inhabitants, this force was independent of the old watch and the regular police of the city and districts. In spite of all of this, however, one citizen acidly remarked in 1852 that the police were "like angels' visits, few and far between." [93]

The special virulence sponsored by the Native American Party gradually died down in the city after its national convention was held in Philadelphia on July 4, 1845, although a Native American leader, Lewis C. Levin, was elected to Congress from Philadelphia three times between 1844 and 1848, a Native American was elected Sheriff in 1846, and the Party continued to elect minor city officials for several years. [94] However, other potent forces of disorder still remained in full operation.

On July 25, 1844, the *Public Ledger* noted that "frequent discharges of firearms have been heard in every quarter of the city and county. What does it mean?" The question can only have been asked for rhetorical purposes. The most indefatigable of all Philadelphia rioters had long been the volunteer firemen. Charles Godfrey Leland, remembering his boyhood in Philadelphia in the 1830's, recalled that the firemen were always "at deadly feud among themselves, and fighting freely with pistols, knives, iron spanners, and slung shot, whenever they met, whether at fires or in the streets." Leland charged that they included many incendiaries among their "runners" and hangers-on, permitted looting by their friends, and frequently blackmailed householders for "protection." [95] An investigating committee organized January 25, 1853, stated: "There is scarcely a single case of riot brought before the court that has not its origin in the fire companies, their members, or adherents."[96]

Sheer animal vitality and lack of anything legally permissible to do, plus an otherwise commendable pride in skill, must be granted as motivations for much of the volunteers' misbehavior. Probably no intent to desecrate the Sabbath prompted their uproarious performances on that day but simply the fact that this was their day of leisure. The expression "visiting firemen" might well have originated at this time, for volunteer companies from other areas did exchange visits, usually on Sunday, and the local hosts often set fires in order to entertain their guests as well as to show off their own extinguishing prowess. Unhappily, they fell victim to overweening pride, fought constantly and violently with each other, defied the law, terrified police and judges, and in general considered themselves above the law.

Volunteer companies had first been organized in Philadelphia in 1736 and until 1871 they provided the only regular fire protection the city had.[97] They had an honorable history, included in their membership many leading citizens, and performed a vital function, in many cases extremely well. Unfortunately, by the 1830's there were too many of them, many composed of what one gentleman called "the young and hardy of the lower classes."[98] By 1852 there were 35 engine, 33 hose, and two hook and ladder companies. Between 1826 and 1857 a total of 64 new companies were founded.[99] Competition for business produced an increasing number of false alarms, together with increasingly frequent bloody warfare between the companies, which often endangered innocent bystanders. The firemen became regularly involved in racial and religious rioting as well. Growing public protests secured regulatory legislation from City Councils in 1840 and 1844, but with little effect because of the firemen's alliance with ward politics. The close connection between the volunteer fire companies, local politics, and organized gangs is clearly illustrated in the career of William MacMullin, known as "Bull," leader of the Moyamensing Hose Company and of the gang called the Killers, later a lieutenant in the Marshal's police, and still later an alderman.[100] It was claimed that the firemen controlled all candidates for political office in 1843.[101]

Finding it impossible to get strong enough legislation through City Councils, reformers bypassed the local politicos and got the State legislature to pass a law on March 7, 1848, which included the provision that if convicted of riotous conduct a fire company could, for a first offense, be ordered out of service for six months and its firehouse closed, a second offense to be punished by the disbanding of the company and the prohibition of its reorganizing again.[102] Other provisions forbade the use of fire apparatus by minors and declared the destruction of fire company apparatus or property a felony, punishable by a prison sentence of six months to a year. By 1853 twenty-five companies had been put out of service under this law, but riots still continued, sixty-nine connected with firemen being started in 1852 alone. [103]

Many Philadelphians believed that peace had finally been won when the consolidation of the city with the outlying districts was accomplished in 1854 after many years of strenuous effort. [104] Enlarged police powers were given to the Sheriff of the County under the new charter and the police department was reorganized by an ordinance passed July 28, 1854, making each ward a separate police district, with a police station in each one and a central station in City Hall. [105] On January 30, 1855, City Council created a single Fire Department to have jurisdiction over the volunteer companies. Forty-seven companies immediately refused to comply, but many of them eventually capitulated, presumably with the intention of "boring from within," for they were shortly operating again almost as freely as before. Not until 1864 was effective action taken against false alarms, when the new Fire Marshal, Dr. Alexander M. Blackburn, began filling the jails with weekend offenders. However, technology and not legislation finally destroyed the volunteer system, for the new, sophisticated, steam-driven engines which began to arrive in 1859 required professional and full-time operators. This they got when the Philadelphia Fire Department became a full-time, paid organization under the City ordinance of March 5, 1871. [106]

As technology, the independent variable of social change, underwent the transformation of the Industrial Revolution, it demanded radical changes in the social order which was to administer the development and use of the new sources of energy now made available. Vigorous and enlightened leadership was needed, but Philadelphia's political establishment fell spectacularly short of what the times required. Both major parties were chronically split within their own ranks, fighting each other for various reasons at various times. As for the relationship between the two parties, according to one astute observer, Horace Binney, Whig and leader of the Bar, "there [was] no obvious characteristic difference in the nature of their respective bids." Both cared only for power, and "There [were] few or no sacrifices of constitutional principle that the Whigs [would] not make to gain power, as rapidly as the Democrats." [107] Philadelphia's social elite during this period notably withdrew from active politics, as many began to suspect that the business of America was business, and much of the best talent and energy of the city was directed toward the exploitation of economic resources and the accumulation of wealth made possible by the Industrial Revolution. [108]

The social adjustments demanded by the technological breakthrough were not made either promptly or thoroughly enough. The ideological machinery of churches, schools, colleges, the arts, communications media in general, failed to render either desirable, acceptable, or even comprehensible, to the public the upheaval in which they were involved. Individualism, *laissez-faire,* equalitarianism, optimism, romantic escapism and sentimentality, were offered as answers to the problems of living in a society characterized by the growth of corporations, the gradual development of government protection of industry, the increasing maldistribution of wealth, and the slow frustration of the hopes of the masses.

The violence of the 1840's and 1850's in Philadelphia testifies to the destructive force of that era's overpowering ignorance of social dynamics. The good people of Philadelphia were terrified by the spectacle of near-anarchy in their streets. They demanded law and order, imposed by military force if necessary. They eased their frustrations by bloody attacks upon scapegoats. But there was no peace. Only unendurable social misery, painfully, slowly, forced the social order to begin the necessary adjustments to the new technological facts of life. One hundred years later, many of the basic problems of the Industrial Revolution still remain unsolved. Now a new and infinitely greater revolution powered by atomic energy challenges the social order. Can man learn anything from History?

NOTES

1. Thomas Hamilton, *Men and Manners in America* (Edinburgh and London, 1843), 196. However, Carl and Jessica Bridenbaugh believed it was "an anachronism to speak of Philadelphia as the Quaker City" after 1735. Carl and Jessica Bridenbaugh, *Rebels and Gentlemen: Philadelphia in the Age of Franklin* (New York, 1962), 17.

2. Hamilton, *Men and Manners,* 193.

3. Frederick Marryat, *Diary in America,* ed. Jules Zenger (Bloomington, Indiana, 1960), 172.

4. J. Thomas Scharf and Thompson Westcott, *History of Philadelphia, 1609-1884* (Philadelphia, 1884), I, 180.

5. *Public Ledger and Daily Transcript* (Philadelphia), April 1, 1844, p. 2, col. 4. Hereinafter cited as *Public Ledger.*

6. John F. Watson, *Annals of Philadelphia . . .* (Philadelphia, 1944), I, 452.

7. *Ibid.,* II, 496.

8. *Ibid.,* I, 310.

9. Scharf and Westcott, *Philadelphia,* I, 266.

10. Charles Francis Adams (ed.), *The Works of John Adams* (Boston, 1856), IX, 279.

11. Cited by Nicholas B. Wainwright, *History of the Philadelphia National Bank . . .* (Philadelphia, 1953), 64.

12. Hamilton, *Men and Manners,* 196.

13. Charles Godfrey Leland, *Memoirs* (New York, 1893), 216.

14. For a general treatment of the history of the Negro and the abolition movement in Philadelphia see William E. B. DuBois, *The Philadelphia Negro* (Philadelphia, 1899) and Edward R. Turner, *The Negro in Pennsylvania* (Washington, 1911).

15. DuBois, *Philadelphia Negro,* 25, 304.

16. *Ibid.,* 25, 416; Scharf and Westcott, *Philadelphia,* I, 617.

17. *Ibid.,* I, 617.

18. DuBois, *Philadelphia Negro,* 180.

19. *Ibid.,* 270.

20. *Ibid.,* 47.

21. *Ibid.,* 37, 299-305.

22. *Ibid.,* 303. St. Mary Street and its courts, for example, had 80 families with 281 persons living in 35 houses.

23. *Ibid.,* 235–238. Negroes furnished one-third of all commitments for crime in 1837, one-half in 1847. *Ibid.,* 37. An interesting sidelight on crime and punishment, as well as the "humour" of the day, is provided by the case of a Negro boy arrested on August 21, 1842 for sitting in the "private back building" of a house at 51 South 3rd Street, "for which his Honor . . . gave him the privilege of the Moyamensing [prison] easement for 30 days." *Public Ledger,* August 23, 1842, p. 1, col. 6.

24. DuBois, *Philadelphia Negro,* 26–27; Scharf and Westcott, *Philadelphia,* I, 624.

25. DuBois, *Philadelphia Negro,* 25–31.

26. *Ibid.,* 180.

27. *Pennsylvania Inquirer and Daily Courier* (Philadelphia), January-February, 1838.

28. DuBois, *Philadelphia Negro,* 27–29; Scharf and Westcott, *Philadelphia,* I, 623, 637–638, 641–642, 654–655. The State Assembly passed an act in June, 1836, holding the County of Philadelphia liable for damages, "In case any dwelling house or any other building or property, real or personal, shall be injured or destroyed . . . in consequence of any mob or riot therein at any election, or at any other time. . . ." *Ibid.,* I, 639.

29. *Public Ledger,* August 2 and 3, 1842; Scharf and Westcott, *Philadelphia,* I, 660–661; DuBois, *Philadelphia Negro,* 29–30.

30. *Public Ledger,* August 3 to 11, 1842.

31. *Public Ledger,* October 10 to 12, 1849; Scharf and Westcott, *Philadelphia,* I, 692–693; DuBois, *Philadelphia Negro,* 32. The interracial marriage had marked this hotel as a special target.

32. George Lippard, *The Quaker City* (Philadelphia, 1876), 409.

33. DuBois, *Philadelphia Negro,* 32, 36.

34. Samuel Hazard (ed.), *United States Commercial and Statistical Register . . .* (Philadelphia, 1841), IV, 393; Eli K. Price, *The History of the Consolidation of the City of Philadelphia* (Philadelphia, 1873), 57.

35. Price, *History of The Consolidation,* 57.

36. *Ibid.,* 26. Incorporated districts: Belmont, Kensington, Moyamensing, Northern Liberties, Penn, Richmond, Southwark, Spring Garden, West Philadelphia,; boroughs: Aramingo, Bridesburg, Frankford, Germantown, Manayunk, Whitehall; townships: Blockley, Bristol, Byberry, Delaware, Germantown, Kingsessing, Lower Dublin, Moreland, Northern Liberties, Oxford, Passyunk, Penn, Roxborough. (Some names appear in more than one category. They refer to distinct, different areas.)

37. Sam Bass Warner, Jr., *The Private City: Philadelphia in Three Periods of Its Growth* (Philadelphia, 1968), 56–57.

38. Nicholas B. Wainwright (ed.), *A Philadelphia Perspective: The Diary of Sidney George Fisher Covering the Years 1834–1871* (Philadelphia, 1967), 179. Hereinafter cited as *Fisher Diary.*

39. Scharf and Westcott, *Philadelphia,* III, 1779.

40. *Ibid.,* I, 691. One picturesque departure from "horror" names was the gang called the Dock Street Philosophers. *Public Ledger,* April 13, 1846, p. 2, col. 4.

41. *Public Ledger,* February 6, 1844, p. 2.

42. *Ibid.*

43. *Public Ledger,* February 28, 1844, p. 1, col. 5.

44. *Public Ledger,* April 1, 1844, p. 2, col. 4.

45. *Public Ledger,* April 9, 1844, p. 1, col. 3.

46. The concentration of population within the city increased until the 1860's, when the organization of the street railway system made possible a large-scale exodus to the suburbs. Warner, *Private City,* 16.

47. Ray A. Billington, *The Protestant Crusade, 1800–1860* (New York, 1938), 61, 78; Hugh J. Nolan, *The Most Rev. Francis Patrick Kenrick, Third Bishop of Philadelphia, 1830–1851* (Washington, 1948), 307 *et seq.*; Scharf and Westcott, *Philadelphia,* I, 663–668.

48. Anon., *The Mysteries and Miseries of Philadelphia, as Exhibited and Illustrated by a Late Presentment of the Grand Jury . . .* (Philadelphia, 1853), 7.

49. *Ibid.,* 11–18.

50. Scharf and Westcott, *Philadelphia,* III, 2236, 2238.

51. *Twenty-first Annual Report of the Directors of the Philadelphia Board of Trade . . .* (Philadelphia, 1854), 37.

52. Anon., *Wealth and Biography of the Wealthy Citizens of Philadelphia* (Philadelphia, 1845), 5–23.

53. Joseph Sill, Diary, VI, 24, VIII, 13, HSP.

54. John R. Commons *et al., Documentary History of American Industrial Society* (New York, 1958), VII, 75.

55. Hazard, *Register,* IV, 96.

56. Job R. Tyson, *Letters on the Resources and Commerce of Philadelphia* (Philadelphia, 1852), 15.

57. James W. Alexander, *The American Mechanic and Workingman* (New York and Philadelphia, 1847), 197.

58. The labor history of this period is covered by the following: John R. Commons *et al., History of Labour in the United States* (New York, 1918), I, 169–218; Edgar B. Cale, *The Organization of Labor in Philadelphia, 1850–1870* (Philadelphia, 1940); Leonard Bernstein, "The Working People of Philadelphia from Colonial Times to the General Strike of 1835," *Pennsylvania Magazine of History and Biography,* LXXIV (July, 1950), 322–339; Louis H. Arky, "The Mechanics' Union of Trade Associations and the Formation of the Workingman's Movement," *Pennsylvania Magazine of History and Biography,* LXXVI (April, 1952), 142–176; William A. Sullivan, *The Industrial Worker in Pennsylvania, 1800–1840* (Harrisburg, Pa., 1955).

59. Henry C. Vethake, *Principles of Political Economy* (Philadelphia, 1838), 326.

60. Alexander, *American Mechanic and Workingman,* 123.

61. Vethake, *Political Economy,* 310.

62. Roger Butterfield, "George Lippard and His Secret Brotherhood," *Pennsylvania Magazine of History and Biography,* LXXIX (July, 1955), 285–301.

63. *The Quaker City,* September 29, 1849.

64. Butterfield, "George Lippard . . . ," 291. The Brotherhood eventually established branches in twenty-three states and survived into the twentieth century, but with modified aims. Butterfield considers it the parent of the Noble and Holy Order of the Knights of Labor, founded in Philadelphia in December, 1869, for the first Grand Mason of that organization was Uriah S. Stephens, who had been working as a tailor in Philadelphia in 1845 and knew Lippard well. *Ibid.,* 298.

65. Commons *et al., History of Labour,* I, 564.

66. *Ibid.,* I, 543.

67. *Ibid.,* I, 575, 596, 607.

68. *Ibid.,* I, 516.

69. *Public Ledger,* April 27, 1842, p. 2, col. 2; Still, Diary, IV, 79–80.

70. William A. Sullivan, "The Factory Operative in Pennsylvania," *Pennsylvania Magazine of History and Biography,* LXXVIII (October, 1954), 484.

71. Scharf and Westcott, *Philadelphia,* I, 623.

72. *Public Ledger,* August 29, 1842, p. 2, col. 2.

73. *Public Ledger,* August 19, 26, and 29, 1842, January 10 to 13, 1843; Scharf and Westcott, *Philadelphia,* I, 661.

74. Nolan, *Kenrick,* 311 *et seq.;* Billington, *Protestant Crusade,* Chapter IX.

75. *Ibid.,* 168.

76. *Ibid.,* 169, 218 n.; Nolan, *Kenrick,* 315 n.

77. Scharf and Westcott, *Philadelphia,* I, 663; Billington, *Protestant Crusade,* 132. It took the name "Native American Party" at its first national convention, held in Philadelphia on July 4, 1845. *Proceedings and Address of the Native American State Convention . . . February 22, 1847* (Philadelphia, 1847) includes the declaration and Principles of the 1845 organizational meeting bound in at the end of the volume.

78. *Address of the Board of Managers of the American Protestant Association; with the Constitution and organization of the Association* (Philadelphia, 1843), 5–12.

79. Anon. *The Truth Unveiled; or, A Calm and Impartial Exposition of the Origin and Immediate Cause of The Terrible Riots in Philadelphia, on May 6th, 7th and 8th, A.D. 1844* (Philadelphia, 1844), is composed of two pamphlets highly critical of the American Protestant Association, setting forth the Catholic side of the Bible-reading issue, by "a Protestant and Native Philadelphian." See also Nolan, *Kenrick,* 311–312.

80. Alexander K. McClure, *Old Time Notes of Pennsylvania* (Philadelphia, 1905), I, 203.

81. Henry R. Mueller, *The Whig Party in Pennsylvania* (New York, 1922), 104–105.

82. *Public Ledger,* May 4, 1844; Scharf and Westcott, *Philadelphia,* I, 663–668.

83. *Public Ledger,* May 4 to 10, 1844.

84. Nolan, *Kenrick,* 317–320; Billington, *Protestant Crusade,* 231–232.

85. Nolan, *Kenrick,* 324; Joseph Jackson, *Encyclopaedia of Philadelphia* (Harrisburg, 1931), I, 87–88.

86. *Public Ledger,* July 8 to 29, 1844; Scharf and Westcott, *Philadelphia,* I, 669–673. The Native American version is given in *Proceedings of the Native American State Convention, held at Harrisburg, Pennsylvania, February 22, 1845* (Philadelphia, 1845) and a view favorable to the Native Americans appears in *A Full and Complete Account of the late Awful Riots in Philadelphia* (Philadelphia, 1844).

87. *The Spirit of the Times,* July 9, 1844, lead editorial.

88. *Public Ledger,* July 8, 1844, p. 2.

89. Scharf and Westcott, *Philadelphia,* I, 673.

90. *Ibid.,* I, 674–675.

91. *Fisher Diary,* 226.

92. Scharf and Westcott, *Philadelphia,* III, 1779.

93. R. A. Smith, *Philadelphia As It Is in 1852* (Philadelphia, 1852), 369.

94. McClure, *Old Time Notes,* I, 89–91; Mueller, *Whig Party,* 108–111, 118–120, 155, 160–161, 163–164, 176, 198.

95. Leland, *Memoirs,* 216–217.

96. Andrew H. Neilly, "The Violent Volunteers: A History of the Volunteer Fire Department of Philadelphia, 1736–1871," Ph.D. dissertation, the University of Pennsylvania, 1959, p. 87.

97. *Ibid.,* 1.

98. *Fisher Diary,* 122.

99. Smith, *Philadelphia . . . 1852,* 395; Scharf and Westcott, *Philadelphia,* III, 1912.

100. Willis P. Hazard, *Annals of Philadelphia and Pennsylvania in the Olden Time . . .* (Philadelphia, 1900), III, 42; Neilly, 70–72.

101. Neilly, "Violent Volunteers . . . ," 62–64, 69, 70 *et seq.* William Welch made the statement referred to, speaking at the Spring Garden Institute's annual meeting, April 14, 1870. *Ibid.,* 72.

102. Hazard, *Annals,* III, 412; Scharf and Westcott, *Philadelphia,* I, 689; Neilly, "Violent Volunteers . . . ," 54, 90.

103. *Ibid.,* 87.

104. Price wrote *The History of the Consolidation of the City of Philadelphia* at the request of the Historical Society of Pennsylvania.

105. Price, *History of the Consolidation,* 90, 94.

106. Neilly, "Violent Volunteers . . . ," 55–57, 60–61, 93, 104.

107. Charles C. Binney, *The Life of Horace Binney . . .* (Philadelphia, 1903), 452.

108. E. Digby Baltzell, *Philadelphia Gentlemen: The Making of a National Upper Class* (Glencoe, Ill., 1958), 12, 88–89.

Michael Feldberg

THE CROWD IN PHILADELPHIA HISTORY: A COMPARATIVE PERSPECTIVE

Michael Feldberg, writing more recently than Elizabeth Geffen, deals with the same place and period, and some of the same incidents, from a somewhat different perspective. The reader may judge the degree to which his use of theoretical analysis helps to illuminate and explain the events she describes in more concrete detail.

In recent years, a growing number of scholars have become interested in American "pre-industrial" collective behavior.[1] Most acknowledge, to varying degrees, a debt to the European historians who first blazed a path in this area: notably George Rudé, Eric Hobsbawn, E. P. Thompson, and Charles Tilly.[2] Rudé, especially, has provided a model of European pre-industrial violence against which those who have studied violence on both sides of the Atlantic have measured the motives, beliefs, and behavior of crowds in history. In his careful studies of French and English uprisings in the period 1740–1848, Rudé had undermined the stereotyped image of the bloodthirsty and irrational "mob" created by such nineteenth-century critics as Hyppolite Taine and Gustave LeBon. Rudé has concluded that collective violence was a reaction by the disfranchised and relatively powerless "lower orders" against innovative technologies, government policies, and capitalist market relationships that threatened their security or stability. His insight has been refined and elaborated on by Tilly in particular, who has expanded it into the basis for a theory of modern European history that will be discussed below. Rudé's observations have also proven helpful in understanding the peculiar nature of American resistance to British author-

From *Labor History* (Summer 1974): 323–36. Reprinted by permission of the publisher and the author.

ity before the War of Independence.[3] But can his findings be applied to later periods of American history? In many ways, Jacksonian Philadelphia provides an even better test than Colonial America of the validity—and problems—of transferring the European model of pre-industrial collective violence to America.

Rudé focuses primarily on events in post-1770 England and Revolutionary France because it was during those periods in those two countries that pre-industrial, localized economies were becoming industrialized, and politically-centralized national units. Rudé argues, and Thompson, Hobsbawm, and Tilly generally agree, that as France and England switched from one productive mode to another, their social and political structures were transformed. These changes, in turn, elicited violent responses from the "lower orders." Through their uprisings, urban and rural rioters struggled to preserve the traditional social and economic systems within which they had always lived. Professor Tilly has labelled these crowds "reactive," or backward-looking.[4] They were groups of wage-earning peasant or artisan protestors seeking to prevent a new capitalist commerical order from replacing their own vestigial medieval economic value systems. Their pre-industrial values, Thompson points out, provided the rioters with "legitimising notions,"[5] such as "natural justice" and "just price," in whose name they carried out so many bread riots and rick burnings. Theirs was violence to protect the old order, not to abolish it.

This backward-looking orientation among European pre-industrial crowds was fated to disappear. With the imposition from above of an industrial, capitalist, politically centralized social order, rioters ceased hoping to preserve a golden age.[6] All four historians argue—and it is a crucial hypothesis for us in our comparison between Europe and America—that after the triumph of liberal capitalism, the French and English lower orders became a working class. Their organization, goals, and violent tactics changed along with their status. Instead of rioting to regain such vanished ends as the assize of bread, or to prevent such innovations as power looms, the newly-unified masses began to organize politically and industrially to demand their fair share in—or, in some cases, control of—the new economic order. They continued to oppose unpopular policies with violence, but now with a new kind of mass violence, involving much larger crowds who were brought together not on the basis of neighborhood residence or craft but simply by their respective memberships in the new urban working class. Thus the crowd at the Champs de Mars sought not the restoration of fair prices by guarantees of political rights for artisans and shopkeepers; the Chartists defended neither "Church and King" nor outmoded handlooms, but rather sought to enfranchise millions of English workers. Violence by both working people and the state went hand in hand with union organization, strikes, and mass political agitation. And indeed, the more the dominant capitalist state used force against working-class organization, the more it encouraged working-class unity. For the English historians, then, resistance to authority was an indicator not only of changes in the economic and social structure, but of the emergence of working-class consciousness as well. [7]

Does this European schema apply to Jacksonian Philadelphia? Chronologically, in the two decades between 1830 and 1850, the city passed from its pre-industrial to an early industrial stage. [8] Factories and machines invaded such Philadelphia industries as textiles, clothing, and shoemaking, while they created others like machine tool and locomotive manufacture. These innovations led to dislocations and unemployment, especially among portions of the city's skilled artisan community. Philadelphia craftsmen had a reputation for turbulence, and when the factory system and machine production directly threatened their livelihoods such men did not passively accept these industrial innovations. Several times in this period violent strikes disturbed the city's peace. At the same time, Philadelphia's commerce was drawn by the new canal and railroad network into the emerging national market for food and manufactures. In this competition for outlets, New York took a predominant commercial position, while inland centers such as Buffalo and Cincinnati grew up at Philadelphia's expense. By the Jacksonian era, Philadelphia's trade was losing ground to other ports while cheap manufactures from New England flooded her shops. [9]

Between 1830 and 1850, Philadelphia's economy was generally in poor shape, a condition that only exacerbated the social tension growing out of non-economic conflicts among various groups in the city. To name just one problem, there was the race issue. Since Philadelphia bordered on the Upper South, it attracted significant numbers of free blacks and runaway slaves, much to the dismay of many white Philadelphians. Similarly, as a port-of-call for Atlantic traders, Philadelphia also received a steady flow of South Irish peasants, many before 1846, but a veritable flood after the potato famine struck in full force. Blacks and Irishmen in particular did not mix well with each other or with the native white population.

The period's economic and demographic strains were reflected in episodes of collective violence—the Jacksonian decades were the most turbulent in Philadelphia's history. To mention only the city's dozen or so largest riots in chronological order, natives fought Irish weavers in 1828, blacks fought whites in August 1834, and again in July 1835, and a turbulent dockworker's strike took place that same year. Eighteen thirty-five was also notable for an incident in which a "respectable" crowd dumped abolitionist literature into the Delaware River. This action foreshadowed the burning of abolitionist-built Pennsylvania Hall in May 1838. On the same night the hall was destroyed, a crowd also attacked the Friends' Shelter for Colored Orphans. Two years later, in June 1840, residents of Front Street, Kensington (in what is now North Philadelphia), rioted to prevent the construction of a railroad on their neighborhood streets, and continued to riot off and on for two years until the project was finally abandoned. The summer and fall of 1842 witnessed an Irish attack on black temperance marchers, followed by a protracted and often violent Irish handloom-weavers' strike. The strikers were bold enough to attack a *posse* and severely manhandle the sheriff. This flood of violence peaked in the great riots of 1844 that pitted Irish Catholics against native Protestants, most of them skilled artisans. The fighting occurred in two stages, the first in May, the second in July 1844. At least thirty were killed, an equal number seriously wounded, and scores more hurt. In the July episode, the nativists even fought a pitched cannon battle with a State militia company. In 1849, an election riot turned into a full-scale race war known as the "California House" riot. In addition to all this major bloodletting, Jacksonian Phila-delphia was also plagued by a near-constant scourge of increasingly brutal firemen's fights and gang wars. The gangs and fire boys had become so regularly disruptive by the mid-1840's that the Philadelphia *Public Ledger* took special pains to announce one Monday, with both irony and relief, that the previous day had actually been a *"Quiet Sunday."* A Sabbath had finally passed without the fireboys running to false alarms that they had set themselves in hopes of clashing with a rival company. [10]

Much of this disorder follows closely the standard European pre-industrial behavior patterns described by Rudé, Tilly, Hobsbawm, *et al.* According to Rudé, the hallmark of a European pre-industrial "mob," contrary to the very connotations of that term, was its restraint. Crowds proceeded with "remarkable single-mindedness and discriminating pur-posefulness." They rioted for "precise objects and rarely engaged in indis-criminate attacks on either property or persons." Most attacks were in fact limited to property, and when directed at persons rarely produced fatalities. While there was sometimes bloodshed, Rudé notes, "it was authority, rather than the crowd that was conspicuous for its violence to life and limb." [11] Collective violence for Rudé, as well as for Tilly, Hobs-bawm, Thompson, and many others, was less an irrational outburst of emotion than a consciously chosen form of protest against government policies or social conditions. Riots were intended as a means for the politi-cally powerless to express limited and well-defined protest, and were not intended to injure persons gratuitously.

This pattern of goal-oriented violence marked by restraint clearly characterized the Philadelphia handloom weavers' strike of 1842. It pre-sented a classic example of what Eric Hobsbawm has called "collective bargaining by riot." [12] The striking weavers used machine breaking, intim-idation, destruction of unwoven wool and finished cloth, house wrecking, and the threat of even worse destruction for two connected reasons: first, to force their employers to accede to their demands, and second to keep strike breakers from accepting work. Problems in the Philadelphia weaving community actually began with the economic depression of 1837, when local employers felt compelled to lower wages. The industry never fully recovered from the slump, or from the competition of New England's more efficient textile mills. When, in 1842, employers lowered piece rates yet again, this time below what the organized handloom weavers considered a subsistence level, they struck. Unfortunately, their solidarity was undermined by the severe hard times in the weaving trade, which meant that many men and their families needed desperately to work at almost any wage, and the influx of semi-skilled Irish immigrants into the industry willing to accept employment at a time when the journeymen weavers' association was trying to maintain solidarity and stop production. [13]

Thus the need to force production to shut down. Breaking into several factories and workshops in the fall of 1842, strikers tried to drive out "scabbing" workers and to punish employers for not restoring the higher piece rates that had previously prevailed. Since much of the handloom weaving in Philadelphia was done by outworkers, periodically the strikers would march with fife and drum to the homes of families taking work from recalcitrant employers, break into the house, wreck the worker's loom and ruin his wool skein, destroy some furniture, apologize to his neighbors for the disturbance, and march peacefully away. In late September 1842, a band of Kensington strikers concocted a scheme to destroy Kempton's water-powered weaving mill in suburban Manayunk which "manufactured, by a much cheaper process, an article of cotton goods . . . hitherto . . . made by the handloom weavers." While the attack was driven off, two constables were wounded when they intercepted the weavers on their way to burn the mill. [14]

Although the strike was to last until winter 1843, these wounded constables were the only seriously injured individuals in over a half-year of strikers' protest marches and demonstrations, loom smashings and factory attacks. The more normal pattern of confrontation between the weaver and either their employers, or scabs, or the authorities was the one illustrated by the humiliating defeat inflicted by strikers on the Philadelphia county sheriff that climaxed their walkout. On January 9, 1843, approximately 300 weavers turned out for a solidarity march in suburban Moyamensing, which along with Kensington was a center of the handloom weaving industry in the city. As always, they broke into scab weavers' homes and destroyed their looms and goods. When they reached the southern boundary of the city proper (Philadelphia County was divided into over thirty different jurisdictions in this period), the mayor and his police turned them back. Determined to march in Kensington, the weavers gathered there two days later. Once again parading and entering homes, the weavers were challenged by two aldermen who tried to arrest a striker for rioting. The officers were beaten for their efforts. At a rally that afternoon, the weavers vowed to punish any other authorities who interfered with internal affairs in the weaving community. The sheriff arrived soon afterwards, hoping to address the meeting. When his pleas for peaceable behavior were hooted down, he resolved to raise a *posse* and put an end to the strikers' freedom of action.

Returning with his friends in late afternoon, the sheriff met with a rousing reception by several hundred well-prepared strikers carrying bricks, clubs, and guns. A volley of stones dispersed the unarmed volunteers, who fled forthwith. Only the sheriff and three valiant friends remained to face the great mass of aroused weavers, and they were quickly overwhelmed. Knocked down and badly bruised by stones, the sheriff was allowed to escape before he sustained serious injury, save that to his pride. He then called on the State militia, who entered Kensington in large numbers and pacified the area. The soldiers then kept guard in the district while their commanding general oversaw deliberations between the weavers and their employers that ended the strike in favor of the latter. [15]

The Kensington anti-railroad riots, which began in 1840 and recurred sporadically until 1842, also reflected tensions between the new industrial order and older community values. The trouble began when the Philadelphia and Trenton railroad corporation persuaded the Pennsylvania legislature to grant it the right to lay tracks on the streets of Kensington. The legislature aspired to make Philadelphia an important entrepôt for the rail traffic between New York and the Deep South. Kensington's weaving and truckmen's community, as well as their landlords, would have nothing to do with the scheme. The early "iron horse" spewed hot coals directly from its smokestack and would have posed a fire hazard to surrounding wooden houses. Property values in general were likely to drop sharply if trains passed through the neighborhood. Furthermore, tracks on the street threatened to disrupt local wagon traffic, an important element in the district economy. Finally, there was the very real danger that pedestrians, and especially children, would be killed by passing trains. Despite the danger to life, property and commerce, opponents of the railroad, joined by several Democratic politicans seeking to profit from this David and Goliath confrontation between big business and a defenseless neighborhood, ultimately chose to make their strongest objections on ideological grounds: the notion of political rights and constitutional liberties. "A PUBLIC HIGHWAY CAN NOT BE LEGALLY OR PROPERLY CHARTERED OUT TO A PRIVATE CORPORATION!" they proclaimed. "NO MONOPOLY! FREE PASSAGE TO ALL! . . . THE CONSTITUTION PROTECTS THE PEOPLE IN THE USE OF THEIR HIGHWAYS." In this way the anti-railroad coalition translated Jacksonian anti-monopoly rhetoric into a set of "legitimising notions" that justified their violence. [16]

Behaviorally, the anti-railroad resistance was even more limited—and, as it turned out, effective—than the striking weavers' violence. No member of the railroad work crews was hurt, probably because they ran as soon as the first paving stones were thrown. Once a *posse* unsucessfully tried to guard a construction crew but it, too, was dispersed with a minimal show of force on the protestors' part. That night, demonstrators burned a local tavern that had been used as the *posse's* headquarters. The crowd may have known that the tavern's landlord was also the railroad's president. After four or five false starts, all of which provoked riots, the railroad abandoned its efforts and the state legislature finally repealed its grant. When the revocation was announced in June 1842, the neighborhood celebrated with two days of fireworks and block parties. [17]

Jacksonian Philadelphia also produced an example of yet another classic type of pre-industrial violence, the "Church and King Mob." This was a crowd that used violence to defend established values from unpopular minority groups whose beliefs seemingly challenged prevailing orthodoxies. Just as in 1780 the Gordon rioters turned on London's Catholics when Parliament lifted the traditional civil disabilities from that group, Jacksonian era Philadelphians almost unanimously turned on abolitionists whose doctrines and actions threatened the city's own prevailing mores. In 1838, a crowd composed of both well-dressed gentlemen and turbulent native and Irish workingmen moved to defend the city from the opening of Pennsylvania Hall, a convention center for the national abolition movement. The anti-abolition crowd that ultimately burned the hall was opposing the dual blight of radical political doctrines and racial "amalgamation" (the contemporary term for miscegenation). A flyer announcing an opposition rally just before the hall's burning warned that "a convention to effect the immediate emancipation of the slaves throughout the country is in session in this city, and it is the *duty* of citizens who entertain a proper respect for the Constitution of the Union and the right of property *to interfere, by force if necessary* [emphasis added]." Even those without concern for constitutional niceties could find ample grounds for outrage upon learning that the aboliton convention meeting at Pennsylvania Hall "presented, for the first time since the days of William Penn, the unusual union of black and white walking arm in arm in social intercourse." Since the law could do nothing to interfere with the abolitionists' rights of free speech and assembly, white citizens were "forced"—in their own minds—to defend society by direct, if extra-legal, action. This was quintessential "Church and King" behavior. Yet even righteous anger did not lead the Pennsylvania Hall crowd to lose its collective head: when firemen arrived to fight the blaze, they were compelled to play their hoses not on the hall but on adjoining buildings so that none but the abolitionists would suffer loss. No individual was attacked, not even the abolitionists. The crowd moved with a deliberateness and calm that was striking to all observers. Of course, since they were unopposed by either the hall's owners or legal authorities, there was really no need for the rioters to take hasty or ill-conceived actions. [18]

While the anti-abolition crowd's behavior kept within conventional bounds common to both European and American pre-industrial crowds, the nature of its hostility was characteristically American. The popular objections to abolitionism might have been constitutional and political, but the hostility to "amalgamation" was purely racist. And racism was not an important part of the European pre-industrial tradition. While the histories show that European pre-industrial crowds intensified their efforts as they developed class consciousness, the increase in racial and ethnic violence in Jacksonian Philadelphia occurred outside the consciousness of class. This is not to say that economic factors played no role in exacerbating racial or ethnic animosities, for indeed they did, but in America violent ethnic and racial conflict has, for the most part, cut across class lines. [19]

Race wars and ethnic clashes in America have never been limited to a particular economic or technological setting; they appear to be endemic. While they have done their greatest damage within lower- and working-class communities, they have never, unlike pre-industrial European conflicts, shown consistent respect for class distinctions, social distance, or "better" neighborhoods. Philadelphia's native artisans battled Irish immigrant laborers and weavers from the 1830's to the Civil War, at first partly for economic reasons; the semi-skilled Irish replaced skilled native workmen in some of the city's industries. Even after the pre-industrial distinctions between craftsmen and laborers disappeared, however, and both Irish and native-born Americans were merged into a single "wage earning class," the two groups never did manage to suppress their feud. Similarly, poor whites have fought poor blacks at all stages of our history, pre-industrial and industrial, in prosperous times as well as bad, in rural and urban settings, in the North as well as the South. And, again, ethnic and racial violence has known no class distinctions. The American Republican party, for example, whose political rallies led directly to the great Philadelphia Native American Riots of 1844, had a substantial middle-class leadership and rank-and-file. The crowd that burned Pennsylvania Hall was led by "gentlemen of property and standing." [20]

Even though ethnic and racial violence in Jacksonian Philadelphia cannot be fully explained by the European pre-industrial model, it does help illuminate certain aspects of some violent episodes in the period. A surprising degree of restraint characterized Philadelphia's ethnic conflicts. At the outset of the bloody Native American Riots, the nativists on first entering the Irish ward in Kensington to do battle came unarmed. Only when it became clear that they were caught in a planned crossfire did they go home to get their guns. Even when their counter-attack was successful, and they were in a position to retaliate against the entire neighborhood, they only destroyed those houses from which gunfire had emanated, deliberately passing by dwellings of the old, infirm, or neutral. It was the Irish who first broke the city's tradition of not using firearms in collective disorders. Fighting between the Irish and the nativists seems to have escalated to the use of weaponry on a permanent basis thereafter. Bloodshed and loss of life became a much more common feature of Philadelphia rioting after the 1840s. [21]

The pre-industrial model offers yet another insight into Philadelphia violence in the Jacksonian era. The preoccupation of Rudé, Tilly, and others with working-class rioters reminds us that even though there were middle- and upper-class faces in Jacksonian crowds, for the most part these crowds were drawn from the ranks of the city's artisans, sailors, and laborers. Indeed, just as ethnicity and race seem to have become Philadelphia's chief source of violence, so they became the chief sources of self and group identity for members of the working class. Thus ethnic and race wars satisfied individual competitive instincts and the need to "belong." But psychic rewards were not the only benefit that Philadelphia's workingmen gained from ethnic conflict. The many gang wars and fire fights, for example, also provided an opportunity for physical recreation. Fire fights most frequently occurred on Sundays or in the evenings, when young apprentices and journeymen had time off from their labors. [22] These battles took a form not so different from Eskimo football; each side brawled to attach its hose to a fire plug before the other, or to tip over the other's hose carriage. After all, what other outlets were there for hard-working youths in a city without public recreational facilities?

There were also good "hard" returns to the winners in ethnic and racial confrontations. Control of jobs, housing, and neighborhoods was often on the line. For example, the whites who invaded the black ghetto in 1842 were not drawn randomly from the white population; the crowd was spearheaded by Irish coalheavers who lived next door to the black ghetto. There is evidence that black and Irish coalheavers were competing directly for control of the city's docks. [23] Indeed, in several occupations Irish immigrants replaced long-established free Negroes, driving down the latter's standard of living. [24] Similarly, middle-class Irish politicians clashed with their native American counterparts in the Democratic Party over the division of political patronage. Around half of the Philadelphia American Republican Party was composed of native-born ex-Democrats who had left their old Party when, among other things, it began rewarding its Irish supporters with places on the night watch and the staff of the public markets in Democratic districts. The native Jacksonians also resented the Party's willingness to support the immigrants on such questions as temperance and Sunday licensing laws, just as they disliked the favorable response that Democrats offered to the plea by the Catholic Church to permit Catholic children to read their version of the Bible in the public schools. [25]

If, then, violence flowed out of ethnic, racial, cultural, and religious conflicts as well as the dislocations of modernization and industrialization, can we find among the works of scholars of European collective violence a theory more wide ranging than the technologically-bound notion that changes in the nature of collective violence in the nineteenth century reflected the transition from pre-industrial to industrial society? In this regard, Charles Tilly has moved beyond the influence of Rudé and Hobsbawm into the realm of political sociology. He has argued that, irrespective of the technological environment, violence will occur when competitive social groups are gaining or losing influence in the political structure. By politics here, Professor Tilly means the bargaining process by which groups divide and distribute the various economic and prestige rewards that a society has to offer. As he puts it, "Far from being mere side effects of urbanization, industrialization, and other large structural changes, violent protests seem to grow most directly from the struggle for established places in the structure of power." [26]

Applying this theory is most helpful in our own case: Philadelphia's working- and middle-class nativists were losing control of the Democratic Party to Irish Catholic immigrants; American-born craftsmen, and even laborers, were losing certain jobs to these same semi-skilled Irish hands or to machines manned by Irish men, women, and children. In the eyes of native-born Americans, control of the Democratic Party, their schools, or their jobs were prerogatives worth fighting for. The Irish, on the other hand, were agitating to remove the Protestant bias in the public schools while struggling to maintain their religious and cultural autonomy. At the same time, despite hostility from the native-born, the Irish *were* making substantial gains in the Jackson Party and capturing a lowly but acknowledged place in the city's economy. Seeing themselves as upwardly mobile, if only in a limited way, the Irish identified with, and even went beyond, Philadelphia's accepted hostility toward blacks. For lower-class Irishmen, physical attacks on their black rivals helped them feel equal to other white groups in the city and superior to the numerically smaller black community. This violence also had the added benefit of driving blacks out of certain Irish-dominated occupations. At the same time, Philadelphia's blacks did not passively accept their own downward mobility. When they fired guns at the Irish coalheavers invading their neighborhood in 1842, they were fighting for their jobs, fighting to keep the ghetto boundaries from being blocked by surrounding Irish expansion, and fighting for their dignity. [27]

And what were the respectable middle and upper classes doing to protect their standing in the community during this time of upheaval and disorder? In the 1840s, the merchant, manufacturer, and Quaker elite busily lobbied for a modern professional police force and a city-paid, locally-stationed militia company. In 1844, the two city councils voted funds for the militia company, and after the California House riot of 1849, the State authorized Philadelphia County to create a full-time, uniformed police department. Thus those at the top increased *their* ability to use violence in defense of their property and authority. One of the major themes in American urban history since the 1850s has been the struggle of municipal authorities and their business-class allies to gain a monopoly on the use of violence. The problem was not that elected officials lacked a monopoly on the use of legally authorized violence; rather, they struggled to convince turbulent portions of the populace that all other violence was illegitimate. [28]

In the Jacksonian era, Philadelphia's municipal officials had neither the physical capacity nor the recognized legitimacy to control fully public disorder. Before the 1850s, government machinery was weak, police forces almost non-existent, legal powers severely curbed. When public officials intervened in riots, it was usually (and reluctantly) to part the two fighting sides long after hostilities had gotten out of hand. On the contrary, in the many riots studied by Hobsbawm, Rude, and Thompson, the crowd almost always fought on one side and representatives of the state on the other. Not so in the American case, or at least not in the case of ethnic or racial violence. Often, when private groups fought each other, government would stand aside. In this era, law-enforcement officials served through popular election. Only exceptional politicians protect unpopular minorities from aroused majorities. In Jacksonian Philadelphia, public officials were at all times slow to separate fighting elements among the lower classes, but they were especially slow in responding to attacks on the black ghetto. If they moved at all, it was because the fighting or burning threatened respectable neighborhoods. When abolitionist Pennsylvania Hall was burned, the sheriff failed to rouse his *posse,* and told the crowd that he would not call out the militia. And when the army defended a Catholic church in Southwark from a nativist crowd in July 1844, it did so only because two months earlier, during the Kensington riots, upper-class critics were roused to a frenzy when a Catholic church in a respectable downtown neighborhood was burned. Although a church in the Irish ward of Kensington had also been put to the torch, much less was said about that. [29]

Jacksonian Philadelphia lacked strong or purposeful authority to mediate between groups or keep them from each other's throats; riot thus was easily employed as a direct-action method by which groups regulated their relations. Violence did not replace politics, but rather was a part of politics. Violent conflict was used by ethnic groups to win and distribute jobs or political power; laboring groups like the weavers used it to raise their wages; Irish coalheavers used it to drive black rivals from the docks; Kensington's anti-railroad rioters used it to control their streets and counteract the legislative influence belonging to a railroad corporation; and the anti-abolitionists used their force to purge the city of unwanted radicals. The use of violence was inseparable from the process of social bargaining by which groups measured each other's strength and distributed power and influence accordingly. [30]

NOTES

1. Among the most important contributions in this area are Leonard Richards, *Gentlemen of Property and Standing* (New York, 1970); Pauline Maier, "Popular Uprisings and Civil Authority in Eighteenth-Century America," *William and Mary Quarterly,* XXVII, 1 (1970), 3–35; Jesse Lemisch, "Jack Tar in the Street: Merchant Seamen in the Politics of Revolutionary America," *ibid.,* XXVV, 3 (1968), 371–401; Gordon S. Wood, "A Note on Mobs in the American Revolution," *ibid.,* XXIII, 4 (1966); John Runcie, " 'Hunting the Nigs'

in Philadelphia: The Race Riot of August 1834," *Pennsylvania History,* XXXIX, 2 (1972), 187–218.

2. Among the best-known works of these authors are numbered Rudé *The Crowd in History: A Study of Popular Disturbances in France and England, 1730–1848* (New York, 1964); Rudé and Hobsbawm, *Captain Swing* (London, 1969); Hobsbawm, *Primitive Rebels: Studies in Archaic Forms of Social Movement in the 19th and 20th Centuries* (New York, 1959); Thompson, *The Making of the English Working Class* (New York, 1963); and Tilly, "Collective Violence in European Perspective," in Hugh Davis Graham and Ted Robert Gurr, eds., *Violence in America: Historical and Comparative Perspectives* (New York, 1970), 4–45.

3. The best application of Rudé's ideas to the coming of the American Revolution is Wood, "Notes on Mobs," cited in note 1. For a different view of "mobs" in the Revolution, see Loyd Rudolph, "The Eighteenth-Century Mob in America and Europe," *American Quarterly,* XI (1959), 447–59.

4. Tilly, "Collective Violence in European Perspective," 16.

5. Thompson, *Making of the English Working Class,* 68.

6. In reality, this break was not so abrupt as this sketch implies. See, for example, Hobsbawm, *Primitive Rebels,* for the survival of archaic forms of backward-looking social protest.

7. This point is made explicit by Rudé, *Crowd in History,* 234.

8. For a description of Philadelphia's industrial transformation, see Sam Bass Warner, Jr., *Private City: Philadelphia in Three Periods of Its Growth* (Philadelphia, 1968), ch. iv.

9. For the impact of "internal improvements" and their relationship to industrialization, see George Rogers Taylor, *The Transportation Revolution* (New York, 1951) chs. ii, x–xiii.

10. For the interconnectedness of these riots, see Warner, *Private City,* ch. vii; and Elizabeth M. Geffen, "Violence in Philadelphia in the 1840s and 1850s," *Pennsylvania History,* XXXVI (1969), 381–410.

11. Rudé, *Crowd in History,* 253–57, 60, 224.

12. Hobsbawm, *Labouring Men,* 9.

13. For conditions among the handloom weavers, see David Montgomery, "The Shuttle and the Cross: Weavers and Artisans in the Kensington Riots of 1844," *Journal of Social History,* V, 4 (1972), 412 416.

14. Philadelphia *Public Ledger,* August 29; September 3, 8, 24, 26; October 27, 1842. For the attack on Kempton's mill, see *ibid.,* September 26, 1842.

15. *Public Ledger,* January 12, 13, 1843.

16. Reports of the anti-railroad riots appeared in the *Public Ledger* on March 3, 13, 14 and August 4, 1840, as well as June 22, 1842. The quotation is from the latter date. The resistors included several prosperous landlords and even a district constable who lived in the neighborhood. For the identity of landlords, see the tax assessors' ledgers for Kensington, 1844, preserved in the Philadelphia City Archives, City Hall, Philadelphia.

17. *Public Ledger,* June 22, 1842.

18. For the characteristics of "Church and King Mobs," see Rudé, *Crowd in History,* ch. ix; for the burning of Pennsylvania Hall, see Warner, *Private City,* 123–37.

19. David Montgomery, in his "The Shuttle and the Cross," argues that ethnic conflict between native-born Protestant artisans and Irish weavers destroyed the class-conscious labor movement that had been developed by Jacksonian Philadelphia's working population.

20. The last phrase is taken from Leonard Richards' excellent book, see *supra,* fn. 1.

21. For the sequence of gunfighting in Kensington, see Michael Feldberg, "The Philadelphia Riots of 1844: A Social History," unpublished doctoral dissertation (University of Rochester, 1970), ch. v.

22. Bruce Gordon Laurie, "Firemen and Gangs in Southwark, 1843–1853," *The Peoples of Philadelphia,* Mark H. Haller and Allen Davis, eds. (Philadelphia, 1973).

23. Laurie, "The Working People of Philadelphia, 1827–1853," unpublished doctoral dissertation (University of Pittsburgh, 1971), 113.

24. For a discussion of downward social mobility among Philadelphia's blacks in the Jacksonian period, see Theodore Hershberg "Slavery and the Northern City: The Case of Ante-Bellum Black Philadelphia," Haller and Davis, eds. *Peoples of Philadelphia.*

25. Laurie, "Working Peoples of Philadelphia," ch. vii.

26. Tilly, "Collective Violence in European Perspective," 10.

27. For black self-defense, see Warner, *Private City,* 140.

28. For the creation of the police, see *ibid.,* 155–57; Montgomery, "Shuttle and Cross," 437–39. On government's struggle for legitimacy, see Alan Silver, "The Quest for Order in Civil Society," *The Police: Six Sociological Essays,* David J. Bordua, ed. (New York, 1967), 1–24.

29. For the sheriff's behavior at Pennsylvania Hall, see Warner, *Private City,* 134. For the upper-class reaction to the church burnings, see Feldberg, "Philadelphia Riots," ch. vi, *passim.*

30. For violence as a method of community control and regulation in an earlier period of American history, see Maier, "Popular Uprisings and Civil Authority." Cf. H. L. Neiburg, *Political Violence* (New York, 1969), 5.

Clement Eaton

MOB VIOLENCE IN THE OLD SOUTH

In 1837 Abraham Lincoln deplored the growing violence of American life. "Outrages committed by mobs" were everyday news, he wrote, and "whatever then their cause may be, it is common to the whole country." The preceding articles by Elizabeth Geffen and Michael Feldberg explore the causes and meaning of this tumult in northern cities. In the following article, Clement Eaton analyzes the conditions peculiar to the Old South that fueled mounting mob activity in that section during the same period. The meaning and impact of southern violence on the pre-Civil War years and its relationship to the turbulence of subsequent decades need to be explored.

Mob violence is not a sectional phenomenon; it has been widespread throughout the United States. At the end of a decade of great mob violence against abolitionists, James G. Birney jotted down on one of the pages of his notebook the following notation:

1835, July, Danville, Ky. mob
October 21, Boston mob
" " Utica [N.Y.] mob
1836, July 28, Cincinnati mob
1837, Nov. 7, Lovejoy murdered
1838, May 17, Pa. Hall [Philadelphia] burnt.[1]

This list of mobs against abolitionists is a mere fraction of the acts of violence directed against the antislavery reformers, and it is surprising to

From *Mississippi Valley Historical Review*, XXIX (December 1942): 351–70. Reprinted by permission of the Organization of American Historians.

observe that Birney included only one Southern mob. Some of the most brutal and intolerant cases occurred in the Ohio Valley states, New York, and Pennsylvania. The mobbing of zealots like Theodore Weld, Samuel J. May, and William Lloyd Garrison in the Northern states did not crush out those irrepressible individuals who were preaching the doctrine that slavery was a sin. Rather, the cause of the abolitionists in the North became allied with the more fundamental American interest of preserving civil rights, freedom of speech, freedom of the press, and the right of petition. After the decade of the 1830's the mobbing of abolitionists gradually subsided at the North. But below the Mason and Dixon line mob violence reached a period of the greatest intensity in the last decade of the ante bellum period. Consequently in the land of Dixie mob violence attained a greater significance than in the other sections of the country because mobs and vigilance committees continued from 1831 to 1861 to serve as a powerful instrument in controlling public opinion.

These mobs of the middle period of Southern history should be clearly distinguished from the vigilantes or regulating bands of the frontier who developed lynch law because of the lack of adequate courts and jails.[2] Even after the frontier had passed, some of the traditions of frontier society lingered in large areas of the South, among which was the practice of violence and extra-legal action. Travellers below the Potomac River were impressed with the number of natives who carried pistols or knives with keen long blades called "Arkansas toothpicks."[3] The Southern states continued to be a poorly policed section of the country up to the Civil War, with jails far apart and of flimsy construction. At intervals mobs would arise, in the frontier tradition, and obtain a catharsis of violent emotion by a swift exercise of lynch law without waiting for the slow and uncertain action of the courts. In 1835, for instance, the people of Vicksburg and Natchez formed vigilance committees and ordered the gamblers that infested the river towns to leave. When a group of insolent desperadoes defied this order, a mob of enraged citizens hanged five of them.[4]

Besides the persistence of the frontier tradition in many Southern communities, there developed another custom that engendered a disregard of legal processes—the practice of dueling. Although most Southern states passed severe laws against dueling, public opinion nullified these laws and sanctioned dueling as a proper means of a gentleman to protect his honor. Col. Alexander McClung, a Whig leader of Jackson, Mississippi, was an extreme example of the effect of the *code duello* in producing a cavalier disregard of law. McClung had a quixotic sense of honor that made him swift to detect an insult and resort to a duel. He had a reputation of never fighting a bloodless duel; a funeral frequently followed his challenge. When he was appointed marshal of the Northern district of Mississippi, his advent was awaited with considerable fear, for he was the second best pistol shot in Mississippi. "When he did arrive," according to the testimony of a contemporary, "the landlord whose hotel he had chosen received him with profound obeisance, mortally fearful of receiving at every glance of his fierce eye a ball or a bowie knife. The boarders stared rather than ate, and when he rose to return to the sitting room, he always had a full passage and a wide berth. His first appearance on the streets called every dealer and shopkeeper to his window or door, and as they viewed his game figure and proud gait, his bold features, and nonchalant manner, their expression told that they were reading a confirmation of all that they had heard.''[5] Yet this violent figure, the murderer of half a dozen men, was a hero in Mississippi, a great favorite with the ladies, who would invite him to ride in their carriages in the cool of the evening. When he returned from the Mexican War to Natchez, the citizens prepared a great celebration, at which he delivered a flowery address in which he spoke of the laurel wreath of glory his regiment had won. Shortly after the death of Henry Clay in 1852, the legislature of Mississippi invited this blood-stained duelist to deliver a eulogy on the career of the great Whig statesman.[6]

Certain other aspects of Southern society prior to the Civil War were conducive to the emergence of mobs. The Southern states in 1850 had an illiteracy ratio among the native adult white population of 20.30 percent, the Middle States, 3 per cent, and New England, .42 per cent.[7] The illiterate minority in the South was more susceptible to panics of fear that bred mob violence, and less capable of analysis, than the more urban and sophisticated society of the North. The editor of the Virginia newspaper, the *Alexandria Gazette,* observed in 1835 that the best way to prevent mobs was to educate the people.[8] Recent studies of the lynching of Negroes in the postwar South indicate that mobs are more likely to originate in the rural districts than in cities and industrial areas.[9] The rural population tends to generate a higher emotional voltage over issues than the dwellers in cities who are less provincial and have greater opportunities to make comparisons. At the outbreak of the Civil War the rural districts were hot for assertion of Southern rights, while the city folk in general were for compromise and conciliation, not only because of a divergence of economic interests but because of less provincialism.[10] In the monotonous Southern villages, mobs afforded a thrill of excitement to the loiterers and reckless youth. The blacking of an abolitionist to resemble a Negro, shaving half of his head, decorating him with tar and feathers, forcing him to submit to the kisses and caresses of the darkeys, broke the tedium of rural life and offered an outlet for boredom. Corn whiskey and a primitive sadistic element in human nature also played a role in the formation of Southern mobs.

The chief cause for the recurrence of mobs in the ante bellum South, however, was the strong popular excitement that was engendered by the antislavery controversy. The program of the abolitionists, immediate abolition of slavery without compensation to the slaveholders, if adopted, would have meant an enormous property loss to Southerners, and would have disrupted the economic structure of Southern society. The decline of the planter class and the economic decay of the island of Jamaica after the

British Emancipation Act of 1833 were a solemn warning to Southerners of the dangers of emancipation.[11] But deeper than the economic motive, which aroused an opposition comparable to a modern intolerance of communist proposals, the Southerners feared the social effects of abolition, especially in destroying racial control of the Negro. The desire to keep the South a white man's country, as Professor U.B. Phillips observed, was an imperative motive that affected all classes of society from the top crust to the humblest poor white.[12] After 1831 the South was forced to take a defensive position in regard to slavery; at the gates the abolitionists were swinging their sledge hammers; within the citadel, there was a deep feeling of insecurity. Ever latent was the fear of servile insurrection; at the same time Southerners knew that world public opinion was against their institution of slavery; there was the danger that the non-slaveholders, the majority of Southern people, might be organized against the slaveholders; and finally there was an uneasiness of conscience among many sensitive Southerners in regard to holding black men as slaves.[13] The abolitionist attack against the civilization of the South would not have stung so painfully, unless it had coincided with a disturbing sense of insecurity and an internal doubt as to the rightness of the peculiar institution. These multiple fears of the Southern people undoubtedly constituted a major cause of the prevalence of mobs.

The first important wave of mob violence in the ante bellum South occurred in the summer of 1835. Public opinion was inflamed by the impact of antislavery literature, by the petition strategy of the abolitionists in Congress, and by the discovery of slave plots in Mississippi and Alabama. The abolitionists were very active in publishing antislavery propoganda during the critical years of 1835-36. At the annual meeting of the American Anti-Slavery Society in May, 1835, a forward move was determined upon in the enlarged printing of antislavery publications.[14] Lewis Tappan, president of the Society, made the following statement in regard to this campaign: "In July 1835 the American Anti-Slavery Society issued 175,000 copies of newspapers and pamphlets, of which 1000 were destroyed in Charleston. The rest are accomplishing the design throughout the United States."[15] Such periodicals as the *Emancipator, Human Rights,* the *Anti-Slavery Record,* the *Slave's Friend* were issued in large editions and "scattered unsparingly through the land."[16] The report of the Massachusetts Anti-Slavery Society announced the policy of sending tracts and periodicals to ministers of religion, Justices of the Peace, members of Congress, and of the several state legislatures, and to other men of standing in the Southern states.[17] Thus the Southern states were threatened with a deluge of fervid antislavery publications.

An analysis of this abolition literature reveals why it aroused such great resentment in the South and provoked mob violence. Many Southerners believed that if this radical literature were allowed circulation in the South it would eventually fall into the hands of slaves and incite them to an insurrection.[18] In addition to this danger, Professor Avery Craven has pointed out that the abolition crusade of the North was not only an attack on the evils of Southern slavery, but it broadened into a bitter and indiscriminate condemnation of Southern society and the Southern way of life. [19] The abolitionists represented the South as a land of the most unbridled lust, a modern Sodom, where the female slaves were the victims of their licentious masters. The slave codes were cited as proof of the cruelty of Southern people to Negroes. They attacked the most vulnerable features of Southern slavery, the internal slave trade with its separation of families, and the denial of educational opportunities to the slave. They maintained that on the great plantations of the South the slaves were worked to death and inadequately fed. They presented the concept of the South as a land of extremes, proud aristocrats disdainful of honest work, and ignorant, vicious, exploited poor whites. [20]

But the abolitionists particularly infuriated the South by their main contention that Southerners were continually living in sin. The Massachusetts Anti-Slavery Society Report of 1836 had a distinct glow of moral superiority when it declared: "But we conceive it to be our duty to distribute to all, who are guilty of slaveholding, our pamphlets exhibiting our views of the enormity and danger of so doing." [21] Theodore Weld, the great Ohio abolitionist, urged that the best technique for agitating the abolition of slavery in the South was to concentrate on portraying the moral evil of slavery. [22] He collected choice items of violence that he had culled from Southern newspapers in the New York Public Library and published a terrible indictment of Southern civilization entitled *Slavery As It Is*. [23] The Massachusetts Society defended the use of pictorial representations as a legitimate means to expose national wickedness. The *Anti-Slavery Record,* May, 1835, for example, carried an incendiary picture of a coffle of slaves going South. The slave-driver was represented as dangling a little Negro baby in one hand and brandishing a whip in the other. The mother was crouching, imploring mercy. Another picture (issue of January, 1836) showed a prostrate slave begging for his life, while a planter stood over him pointing a gun. [24]

In addition to this extreme propaganda, with which the abolitionists sought to deluge the South, they also aroused Southerners by their presentation of petitions to Congress to abolish slavery in the District of Columbia. In the session of 1835–36 antislavery petitions containing thirty-four thousand names, in which the names of women predominated, were presented to Congress. [25] John Quincy Adams became a leader in presenting these petitions, and his biting sarcasm and taunts of Southern congressmen added oil to the flames of resentment. [26] In 1836 Congress passed the gag resolution, tabling such petitions without discussion. The bitter feeling evoked in Southern breasts by the petition strategy of the abolitionists and by the debates on the gag resolution is revealed in the passionate words of Henry A. Wise, Congressman from Virginia, when only ten Senators voted against receiving abolition petitions: "The South lies low and bleeding. Oh God! for energy for the occasion!"[27]

In the summer of 1835 a mob headed by former governor, Robert Y. Hayne, entered the Charleston, S.C., post office and destroyed several sacks of mail containing abolition literature. A vigilance committee of twenty-one members was appointed to meet incoming ships and search them for incendiary publications.[28] In this same year numerous anti-abolition meetings were held throughout the South which established vigilance committees to deal with an extraordinary emergency. Some idea of the nature of these vigilance committees can be gained from a perusal of the resolutions of a meeting in Fairfax County, Virginia, adopted in August, 1835. The chairman of the assembly was ordered to appoint three men in each militia district of the county to form a local vigilance committee. Their duty was "to detect and to bring to speedy punishment all emissaries who may be found within the borders of our county, giving circulation to the papers or pamphlets put forth by the Abolitionist Association of the North, agitating the question of slavery, and therefore endangering the peace and tranquility of our land."[29] A committee of correspondence composed of twenty members was also established to keep in touch with like committees throughout the South. When Southerners emigrated to the West, they carried with them a knowledge of the technique of vigilance committees.

During the year 1835 four notable cases of mob action occurred in the upper South. There was an episode that reminds one of the burning of Jewish books in modern Germany. The vigilance committee of Louisa County, Virginia, heard that two gentlemen in the county had some copies of Rev. John Hersey's "An Appeal to Christians on the Subject of Slavery." The committee visited these gentlemen and requested them to give up the books for inspection. The committee judged the books to be of an inflammatory nature and burned them publicly in front of the court house.[30] Amos Dresser, a student at Lane Seminary, was traveling through Tennessee in 1835 with some antislavery publications in his carriage. He was arrested and tried by a vigilance committee of sixty citizens of Nashville, and sentenced to twenty lashes, which were administered by a city officer.[31] Dr. Reuben Crandall, who had been engaged to give lectures on botany at Georgetown University, brought some antislavery publications into the District of Columbia, marked "read and circulate." These publications, which were left in a store, caused a large mob to form to do violence to him, but he was saved by being arrested and taken to jail. After spending some months in jail, he was tried in Washington by a court and released.[32] The pressure of the mob was exerted to prevent James G. Birney from establishing an antislavery newspaper, the *Philanthropist* at Danville, Kentucky, in the summer of 1835. An orderly public meeting was held, in which threats of violence, of destroying any press used in publishing an abolitionist newspaper, so frightened the printer that he sold his press to a pro-slavery man.[33] The following year Birney began publishing the *Philanthropist* at New Richmond, Ohio, near Cincinnati, but a mob destroyed his press.[34]

While these mobs were forming in the upper South, the lower South was agitated by a pathological fear of servile insurrection. The people of Mississippi were terrified by a pamphlet published in 1835 by Virgil Stewart purporting to reveal the plot of an extensive slave uprising in the South led by white desperadoes, chief of whom was John A. Murrell.[35] A panic of fear swept the central counties of Mississippi, patrols were organized, frantic appeals were made to the governor to call out the militia, and vigilance committees were appointed to arrest emissaries of the Murrell gang.[36] The vigilance committee of Clinton in Hinds County wrote to the governor that it had been organized by "the mass of the community" for a twofold purpose: (1) "for the direction of the utmost energies of the community for its self defense in the midst of actual insurrection" and (2) "for the suppression of irregular and precipitate movements resulting from extreme excitement and the protection of suspected persons until the just and sure ascertainment of their guilt."[37]

An insight into the mob psychology of Southerners under the stress of fear is given by a letter of Henry Watson, Jr., a Northerner who had settled at Greensborough, Alabama. Writing to a friend in Connecticut, he observed:

You have read, too, of the proceedings at Clinton in Miss: & the neighboring counties—the insurrection contemplated was confined to a small neighborhood & I have no idea was dreamed of except in those few counties—But those proceedings, the Murrell pamphlet (of which you must have heard) and the presence of an occasional Abolitionist, has excited the people of the whole South. Two men were taken up here a few days since, on suspicion of having dropped some copies of the "Emancipator," and it was only upon the suggestion of one or two of the more prudent, that a committee waited upon them & had an investigation. They were found innocent & discharged with a certificate to that effect—But with an excited populace a man stands a poor chance. The punishment inflicted by the Law for the circulation of such papers is *death*—but *this* is not the way to dispense it. A public meeting was held yesterday & a committee appointed to try & examine similar cases hereafter; but the more intelligent succeeded finally in getting passed a resolution that the committee should in no case adjudge death—that is one point gained—I am astonished at the blindness of the propagators of the doctrines of abolition, and however much I may abominate slavery, I do believe that the circulation in the South of such publications as the abolition newspapers is like throwing a fire brand into a magazine. Luckily few of our slaves can read and the longer they are kept in ignorance the better for us.[38]

Before the popular frenzy had subsided, a number of white men and innocent Negroes were hanged. Henry S. Foote, later governor of Mississippi, but at this time a young lawyer in Mississippi, has vividly described the savage temper of the mob during this excitement over insurrection.

Foote received an urgent appeal to come to the aid of a Kentuckian who had been imprisoned by the vigilance committee of Livingston. The suspect was a poor man who had brought a load of corn to sell in Yazoo County. There was no real evidence against him except the testimony of two or three ignorant Negroes, "from whose reluctant lips certain disclosures had been coerced under the severest infliction of the lash." Foote tried to save him, but twenty minutes after he arrived the Kentuckian was hanged.[39] This excitement over slave plots produced a strong reaction in Mississippi against "the black hearted crew of abolitionists."[40] A leading newspaper of the state, the Jackson *Mississippian,* summed up the feeling of the community: "the white men who were engaged in the matter, and who instigated the few negroes to insurrection, who have been detected, have been hung—as all such wretches should be—without judge or jury, as examples to others who are disposed to tamper with our slaves."[41]

Ten years later a great mob assembled at Lexington, Ky., to suppress the publication of the *True American,* a newspaper devoted to gradual emancipation of the slaves.[42] This journal was edited by Cassius Marcellus Clay, scion of an aristocratic Kentucky family who had been educated at Yale. "Cash" Clay was an indomitable man, ready to fight with pistol or bowie knife for his convictions. He realized that he might encounter mob violence if he published an antislavery paper in the South, so that he fortified his office in an ingenious manner, with small brass cannon commanding the door to his printing establishment, a trap door in the roof for escape, and a keg of gunpowder with a fuse attached to blow up any invaders.[43] But when the crisis that he had foreseen arose, he was sick in bed and could not defend his property.[44] A large but orderly assembly of citizens met in Lexington on August 18, 1845, and resolved that no abolition press could be permitted to pollute the soil of Kentucky. A prominent lawyer, Thomas F. Marshall, addressed the gathering, in which he gave the principal rationalization offered by Southerners to justify mob violence. It was the argument, *Salus populi suprema lex,* that the safety of the people demanded the suppression of an abolition newspaper that might incite the slaves to bloody insurrection.[45] After listening to Marshall, the assembly chose a committee of sixty to remove the invidious press of the *True American.* The mayor notified this committee that they were violating the law, but that he was powerless to prevent their action. The committee dismantled the press, boxed the parts, and sent them to Cincinnati.[46]

At the same period mob violence arose in the Upper South over the division of the Methodist Church. When the Methodist Episcopal Church split (over the question of slavery) into a Northern and a Southern branch in 1844, a Plan of Separation was drawn up, by which churches on the border should decide by a majority vote their allegiance to the antislavery Northern church or to the proslavery Southern church. The result of this arrangement was a bitter factional fight, characterized by a house to house canvass of members, barricaded churches, lawsuits over church property, and the mobbing of rival preachers.[47] Reverend Valentine Gray of the Northern Methodist Church, for example, tried to preach in July, 1846, in the Methodist Church at Salem on the Eastern Shore of Virginia, despite the warning of pro-Southern members. When he refused to leave, he was dragged by a faction from the pulpit by his hair and clothes, and he was unable to obtain any redress from the county court. In this same year Reverend James Hargis attempted to preach at Guilford in Accomac County, but he was forced to desist by a mob, "shooting, throwing stones at the building and shouting."[48] At Parkersburg in the western part of Virginia, a house to house canvass showed that one hundred and two members of the Methodist Church desired to join the Northern conference while eighty-two favored the Southern conference. A preacher from the Ohio conference, Rev. John Dillon, was sent to Parkersburg, but was ordered out of town by a vigilance committee of sixty members appointed by a mass meeting of the citizens.[49] At the close of the ante bellum period the struggle between the Methodist Episcopal Church, and the Methodist Church, South, still continued, and Northern Methodist ministers, such as Rev. Wesley Smith, were mobbed by pro-slavery adherents.[50]

With the advent of the decade 1850–60, mobs and vigilance committees became more dangerous as a method of crushing the radical. The violent controversy over the Wilmot Proviso and the Compromise of 1850 led to acts of intolerance against anti-slavery men in the South. In September, 1851, a spectacular example of the swift action of a vigilance committee occurred in Grayson County in western Virginia. John Cornutt was believed to be "a backer" of a Northern antislavery preacher who had been preaching in the neighborhood. A mob of two hundred citizens of the county visited him on his farm and ordered him "to renounce his abolition sentiments." When he refused to conform, he was stripped of clothing, tied to a tree and severely whipped until he promised to sell his property and leave the state. *The People's Press,* printed in the quiet little Moravian town of Salem, N.C., justified this use of mob law. Referring to the Grayson County episode, the editor wrote: "We warn the citizens of this and other counties to be vigilant lest others, equally obnoxious as the Ohio incendiaries, whom we have frequently felt bound to notice may intrude themselves amongst us, and spread desolation and death in our midst. We hope that experience has taught us that a *summary process* is the only effective remedy to be resorted to in such cases."[51] Cornutt attempted to secure redress from the courts, but was unsuccessful.[52]

Several Wesleyan ministers from Ohio were engaged in preaching anti-slavery doctrines in some of the Piedmont counties of North Carolina during the bitter slavery controversy in Congress in 1850. Reverend Jesse McBride and Reverend Adam Crooks were arrested for circulating incendiary publications, after newspaper clamor had aroused the people against them. Crooks was acquitted but McBride was sentenced to a year in prison and a whipping of twenty lashes.[53] He appealed his case to the Supreme

Court and continued to preach until in the spring of 1851 he was intercepted on his way to a religious service by a vigilance committee who forced him to promise to leave the state and never to return. He was saved from personal violence by the efforts of some of the first citizens of the county.[54] Several months later an assembly of citizens of Guilford and surrounding counties met and appointed a vigilance committee to drive out "foreign" abolition emissaries. John H. Gilmer, Whig Congressman, was one of the committee appointed to draw up resolutions. The meeting resolved that Adam Crooks and J.C. Bacon, two of the Wesleyan preachers, were agents of the American and Foreign Anti-Slavery Society, that they had been instrumental in "running off" a number of slaves, and that these dangerous characters should be expelled from the state.[55] The leading newspapers of the state, the Raleigh *Standard,* the *Greensboro Patriot, The People's Press,* the *Ashboro Herald,* the *North State Whig* of Washington, N.C., upheld lynch law directed against abolitionists and were frequently direct inciters and initiators of mob violence.[56]

The presidential campaign of 1856 was provocative of mob violence in the South, because it marked the appearance of the Republican party with its freesoil platform as a serious contender for the control of the national government. The most notable case of mob violence in connection with this political campaign was the driving of Professor Benjamin Sherwood Hedrick from his professorship at the University of North Carolina because he announced his sympathy for John C. Frémont, the Republican candidate.[57] Again it was the clamor of newspapers, especially the Raleigh *Standard,* that was largely responsible for this act of intolerance. In those parts of Virginia, where Northern settlers had taken up abandoned tobacco lands and restored them, occurred the most numerous cases of conflict. Also the Panhandle section of Virginia, sandwiched between Pennsylvania and Ohio, was the scene of pro-slavery mobs attacking Frémont men.[58] In Clarke County, in western Virginia, John C. Underwood, a native of New York, was forced to abandon his farm, because he had the hardihood to attend the Republican National Convention, styling himself as delegate from Virginia. The fact that he was a cultured man, a graduate of Hamilton College, and that he married a Southern woman, a cousin of the later famous "Stonewall" Jackson, had no weight with a large mass meeting of the citizens of Clarke County who threatened him with violence if he returned to the state.[59]

Mob violence in the South reached a climax in 1859–1860 after the John Brown raid. So many acts of violence against antislavery men and Northerners in the South took place that Garrison could fill a large pamphlet with Southern atrocities in these two years, entitled *The New Reign of Terror in the Slaveholding States.*[60] Mobs and vigilance committees in the South arrested Northern travelers below the Mason and Dixon line, fruit tree peddlers, book agents, traveling salesmen, and Northern school teachers. The Council of State of North Carolina passed a resolution requesting the governor to require justices of the peace to examine strangers from the North, and if any persons appeared suspicious to require them to give bond.[61]

Two storm centers of mob violence in 1859 and 1860 were Kentucky and Texas. The tension of feeling against antislavery men had been growing in Kentucky during this last decade of the ante bellum period, because of the great loss of slave property through the operation of the Underground Railway.[62] The excitement aroused by the John Brown raid led a mob to destroy the press of an antislavery newspaper, *The Free South,* published at Newport, Kentucky, by a machinist named William S. Bailey. Also a mob, composed of the "wealthiest and most respectable citizens," rode to the little antislavery colony of Berea, where the school was attended without discrimination by black and white children, and ordered the Bereans to leave for the North. They appealed to Governor Magoffin to protect them, but he refused the aid of the law and advised them to heed the mob.[63] Before this last expulsion, the leader of the Berea colony, John G. Fee, had been mobbed twenty-one times, but always he would pray for the mobs or start preaching to them as they persecuted him.[64] In Texas during 1860 mobs were directed primarily against suspected followers of John Brown and anti-slavery preachers of the Northern Methodist Church, who were accused of engineering slave plots of insurrection.[65]

In addition to the mobs that lynched white men in the Old South because of their antislavery views, there were Southern mobs that lynched Negroes. Few Negroes were lynched on account of the crime of rape before the Reconstruction period. Black slaves were valuable property, which their masters tried to protect. Furthermore, the slave-owning class in the South did not share the poor whites' hatred of the Negro. Almost invariably the chief reason for lynching Negroes was the fear of servile insurrection or the brutal murder of a master or overseer by a slave. In 1856 and 1860, both presidential election years, numerous plots of slave insurrection were reported all over the South, and many slaves were killed by mobs in a horrible fashion.[66] During the insurrectionary scare of 1856 the Memphis *Eagle and Enquirer* estimated that not less than forty Negroes were executed.[67] Charges were freely made both in Northern newspapers, such as Horace Greeley's *New York Tribune,* and in some Southern newspapers that these insurrectionary panics were manufactured for political effect.[68] Neverthe-less, the fact that the fear of servile insurrection reached its greatest height in December after the elections were over tends to disprove this sinister suspicion.

No study of mob violence in the Old South would be complete without a recognition of the fact that many moderate Southerners strongly con-demned mobs. A good example of the attitude of high-minded Southerners to this abuse of the law is found in a letter by A.P. Hill, later to become one of Lee's great generals. He had just heard of a shocking case of lynching a poor Negro in his home town of Culpeper, Virginia, in 1850. A Negro named William Grayson was accused of murdering a white man in a horrible manner. He was brought to trial and convicted by a local jury, but his case was appealed to the Appellate Court of Virginia, which ordered a new trial on the grounds of insufficient evidence. Nevertheless the mob seized him and promptly hanged him. When Hill heard of this outrage he wrote a passionate letter saying that all the lynchers should be hanged.[69] A melancholy aftermath of this outburst of violence was the discovery that the crime had been committed by a white man. Some independent Southern editors, like George D. Prentice of the *Louisville Journal,* wrote vigorous editorials against the resort to lynching. Nevertheless, the Southern press as a whole, as an examination of many newspapers reveals, condoned, and in some cases actively encouraged, the mobbing of abolitionists who were suspected of "tampering with" the slaves.[70]

No safe generalization can be made concerning the personnel of Southern mobs in the ante bellum period. Some mobs were dominated by the lower orders of Southern society. The mob that beat Amos Dresser was started by mechanics and workmen in Nashville; in the case of the lynching of Lunsford Lane, the colored abolitionist of Raleigh, N.C., in 1842, the man who applied the first coat of tar was a journeyman printer, but another leader of the mob was the profligate son of a good family of Raleigh;[71] the irate group that lynched John Cornutt in the back-country of Virginia, was composed primarily of yeoman farmers. On the other hand, the mob that destroyed the abolition mail in Charleston, the assembly that suppressed the *True American* in Lexington, and the mob that drove out the inhabitants of Berea included the wealthy and well-educated planters. A North Carolina blacksmith, John Stafford, wrote to Judge Thomas Ruffin, that mobs and illegal tribunals were encouraged by members of the governor's council and by influential editors in the state.[72]

Mob violence in the South was not confined to any region, but it was more extensive in the border states. Here ran the routes of the Underground Railway that cost Southerners huge sums of money in the loss of slaves. The upper South, moreover, was the buffer region against the inroads of the abolitionists and the impact of abolition literature. Also in these states were colonies of Northerners, such as Ceredo in western Virginia, and Northern farmers who acquired cheap exhausted tobacco lands. Although it is impossible to arrive at accurate statistics, the evidence indicates that before the Civil War mobs were directed more frequently against white persons than Negroes, a phenomenon that was reversed as a result of Reconstruction policy which made the Negro a pawn in radical Republican politics. In an attempt to justify these violent lynch courts, Southerners arrived at several rationalizations, each of which contained a small measure of truth. They asserted that it was often impossible to convict abolitionists in the legal courts, because Southern laws prohibited the use of Negro testimony. They declared that the safety of the community was the supreme law, and that the slowness of the courts and the weak police system justified, in an emergency, the development of vigilance committees to supplement the regular system of justice. The large amount of illiteracy, the bad traditions of the frontier and the *code duello,* the practice of the planters in ignoring the law in administering an informal justice on their plantations, and the rancor of party politics contributed to the disregard of law, which was the basic pattern of mob violence.

The prevalence of mob violence in the Old South left deep scars on Southern society. The growth of liberalism was rendered difficult in an atmosphere, surcharged with emotion, which produced mobs and vigilance committees that enforced a uniformity of thought in the Old South on the most important question of the period. The prevalence of mobs below the Potomac was used as effective propaganda by editors and politicians in the North to produce a distorted picture of the South.[73] Having conveniently forgotten that the Northern states had earlier gone through a phase of intolerant mob violence, these agitators and politicians portrayed the South as a land where life and civil liberties were constantly imperiled by the reign of lynch law. Another pernicious result of mob violence in the Southern states was the impairment of respect for the orderly processes of the law. Relatively few cases involving the circulation of antislavery literature or the arrest of abolitionists came before the legal courts; the Southern people supplanted the courts with mobs and vigilance committees.[74] Indeed, one of the outstanding paradoxes of Southern life was the reverence for the Federal Constitution and the law of the Bible which Southerners displayed, while they frequently ignored the legal courts in dealing with abolitionists and Negro insurrectionists.[75] In the light of this background of violence, it is easy to see why Southerners turned so readily to the Ku Klux Klan and similar organizations during the Reconstruction period. Lynch law in the settled communities of the South has developed by waves, primarily the reactions of an emotional people to the dangers of white supremacy. From a high point in 1892, during the Populist movement, the tide of lynching has receded, as the South has become more urban and industrialized, until it has become practically extinct in states like North Carolina and Virginia.[76]

NOTES

1. James G. Birney MSS., in *James G. Birney Papers,* Library of Congress.

2. James E. Cutler, *Lynch-Law: An Investigation into the History of Lynching in the United States* (New York, 1905), 112; see also Thomas W. Page, "The Real Judge Lynch," *Atlantic Monthly,* LXXXVIII, 731–43.

3. James S. Buckingham, *The Slave States of America* (2 vols., London, 1842), I, 247; Sir Charles Lyell, *A Second Visit to the United States of North America* (New York, 1849), II, 31, 32, 60, 61.

4. *Southern Argus* (Columbus, Mississippi), July 25, 1835; *Niles' Weekly Register,* XLVIII, 401.

5. "Sketches of Our Volunteer Officers: Alexander Keith McClung," *Southern Literary Messenger,* XXI, 1855, p. 3; for a picture of Colonel McClung brandishing his hair-trigger pistols in a Jackson tavern and causing the patrons to flee, see Reuben Davis, *Recollections of Mississippi and Mississippians* (Boston, 1889), 216–18.

6. *Ibid.,* 213–20.

7. J. D. B. DeBow, *Compendium of the Seventh Census* (Washington, D.C., 1854), 153.

8. *Alexandria Gazette;* August 25, 1836. A complete file of this excellent Southern newspaper from 1820 to 1860 is preserved in the library of the American Antiquarian Society, Worcester, Massachusetts.

9. W. J. Cash, *The Mind of the South* (New York, 1941), 299–310; see also J. H. Chadbourn, *Lynching and the Law* (Chapel Hill, 1933), 4.

10. Eric F. Goldman, ed., *Historiography and Urbanization* (Baltimore, 1941), 51–54, 58–61.

11. Lowell J. Ragatz, *The Fall of the Planter Class in the British Caribbean, 1763–1833* (New York, 1928), chap. xii, "The Overthrow of the Tropical Labor Regime."

12. U. B. Phillips, "The Central Theme of Southern History," *American Historical Review* (New York), XXXIV, 1928, pp. 30–43.

13. Clement Eaton, *Freedom of Thought in the Old South* (Durham, 1940), chap. x, "The Free Lances of the Upper South."

14. *Second Annual Report of the American Anti-Slavery Society* (New York), May, 1835, pp. 48–53.

15. Letter from Lewis Tappan, August 19, 1835, *Niles' Weekly Register,* XLIX, 21, September 12, 1835.

16. *Fourth Annual Report of the Massachusetts Anti-Slavery Society* (Boston), January 20, 1836, pp. 17, 18; see also *The Quarterly Anti-Slavery Magazine* (New York), July, 1837, p. 348.

17. *Fourth Annual Report of the Massachusetts Anti-Slavery Society,* 18; *The Liberator,* Garrison's newspaper, which contained the most extreme abuse of the South, had a small circulation, almost entirely in the North. Its chief support became the free Negroes of Philadelphia, New York, and Boston.

18. Resolutions on Incendiary Publications, *Acts of the General Assembly of the State of North Carolina, 1835–1836* (Raleigh, 1836), 121, 122. These resolutions state a conviction of Southerners that the slaves were peaceful and contented and would not think of insurrection, unless incited by incendiary publications of abolitionists.

19. Avery O. Craven, *The Repressible Conflict, 1830–1861* (Baton Rouge, Louisiana, 1939), 61, 62, 79–86.

20. Many of these errors are exposed by Henry H. Simms, "A Critical Analysis of Abolition Literature, 1830–1840," *Journal of Southern History,* VI, 1940, pp. 368–82; by F. L. and H. Owsley, "The Economic Basis of Society in the Late Ante-Bellum South," *ibid.,* VI, 24–45; and by studies of slavery by U. B. Phillips, C. S. Sydnor, and R. B. Flanders.

21. *Fourth Annual Report of the Massachusetts Anti-Slavery Society,* 19.

22. Gilbert H. Barnes, *The Antislavery Impulse, 1830–1844* (New York, 1933), 79.

23. Theodore Weld, *Slavery As It Is: Testimony of a Thousand Witnesses* (New York, 1839); see also Harriet Beecher Stowe, *Key to Uncle Tom's Cabin* (Boston, 1853).

24. *Anti-Slavery Record* (New York), May, 1835, and January, 1836. Scattered issues in the Harvard University Library.

25. Barnes, *The Antislavery Impulse,* 131, 140, 141. A modern parallel is the practice of pressure groups who send a flock of telegrams to Congressmen.

26. Charles F. Adams, ed., *Memoirs of John Quincy Adams* (12 vols., Philadelphia, 1874–1877), IX, 451, 454, 455; X, 64, 65, 72.

27. Wise to a person in Gloucester County, Virginia (name torn from the letter), March 12, 1836, Henry A. Wise MSS., Library of Congress.

28. Theodore D. Jervey, *Robert Y. Hayne and His Times* (New York, 1909), 379–81.

29. *Alexandria Gazette,* August 29, 1835.

30. Richmond *Enquirer,* September 25, 1835.

31. Amos Dresser, *The Narrative of Amos Dresser, with Stone's Letters from Natchez* (New York, 1836); and *Narrative of the Arrest, Lynch Law Trial, and Scourging of Amos Dresser at Nashville, Tennessee, August 1835* (Oberlin, Ohio, 1849).

32. *Trial of Reuben Crandall, M.D., Charged with Publishing Seditious Libels by Circulating the Publications of the American Anti-Slavery Society* (New York, 1836). A pamphlet in the Library of Congress.

33. Dwight L. Dumond, ed., *Letters of James Gillespie Birney, 1831–1857* (2 vols., New York, 1938), I, 197–200, 204–10, 232–35; William Birney, *James G. Birney and His Times* (New York, 1890), 181.

34. Gilbert H. Barnes and Dwight L. Dumond, eds., *Letters of Theodore Dwight Weld, Angelina Grimké Weld, and Sarah Grimké, 1822–1844* (2 vols., New York, 1934), I, 324.

35. Augustus Q. Walton, Esq. (pseudonym), *A History of the Detection, Conviction, Life and Designs of John A. Murel, The Great Western Land Pirate: together with His Villany and Plan of Exciting a Negro Rebellion. Also a Catalogue of the Names of Four Hundred and Fifty-Five of His Mystic Clan Fellows and Followers* (Cincinnati, n.d.); also H. R. Howard, *The History of Virgil A. Stewart and his Adventure in Capturing and Exposing the Great Western Land Pirate and his Gang* (New York, 1839).

36. Thomas Shackelford, *Proceedings of the Citizens of Madison County, Mississippi, at Livingston, in July 1835, in Relation to the Trial and Punishment of Several Individuals Implicated in a Contemplated Insurrection in this State* (Jackson, Mississippi, 1836). A pamphlet in the Rare Book Room, Library of Congress.

37. A. Hutchinson and William Jones of the Committee of Safety of Clinton to Governor Hiram G. Runnels, July 11, 1835. *Executive Papers of Mississippi,* MSS. at Jackson, Mississippi.

38. Henry Watson, Jr., to Julius Reed, August 23, 1835. Henry Watson, Jr., MSS., Duke University Library.

39. Henry S. Foote, *Casket of Reminiscences* (Washington, D.C., 1874), 253–55.

40. *Southern Argus* (Columbus, Mississippi), July 18, 1835.

41. *The Mississippian* (Jackson), July 17, 1835.

42. For a fuller account of this episode of mob violence, see Clement Eaton, "The Freedom of the Press in the Upper South," *Mississippi Valley Historical Review,* XVIII, 1932, 491–95.

43. *The Life of Cassius Marcellus Clay; Memoirs, Writings, and Speeches* (2 vols., Cincinnati, 1886), I, 107.

44. C. M. Clay, *Appeal of Cassius Marcellus Clay to Kentucky and the World* (Boston, 1845).

45. W. L. Barre, ed., *Speeches and Writings of T. F. Marshall* (Cincinnati, 1858), 208.

46. *History and Record of the Proceedings of the People of Lexington and its Vicinity in the Suppression of the True American* (Lexington, August 25, 1845). Pamphlet in Library of Congress.

47. Charles H. Ambler, *Sectionalism in Virginia from 1776 to 1861* (Chicago, 1910), 282–99.

48. John N. Norwood, *The Schism in the Methodist Episcopal Church, 1844* (New York, 1923), 132–34.

49. *Niles' Weekly Register,* LIX, 90.

50. Reverend Wesley Smith, *A Defense of the Methodist Episcopal Church Against the Charges of Rev. S. Kelley and Others* (Fairmont, Virginia, 1855). Pamphlet in the State Library at Charleston, West Virginia.

51. *The People's Press* (Salem, North Carolina), October 4, 1851. Files of this paper are preserved in the Moravian Museum, Winston-Salem, North Carolina.

52. Raleigh *Daily Register,* October 1, 1851; *The People's Press,* September 27, 1851; *New York Tribune,* September 29, 1851.

53. *Salem Diary,* October 11, 1850, MS., Archives of the Moravian Church in America, Southern Province, Winston-Salem, North Carolina, translated from German for the writer by Miss Adelaide Fries; Raleigh *Daily Register,* October 23, 1850; Raleigh *North Carolina Standard,* October 23, 1850.

54. *Greensboro Patriot,* May 31, 1851.

55. *Ibid.,* August 2, 1851; *The People's Press,* August 2, 1851; *North State Whig* (Washington, North Carolina), October 9, 1850; *Carolina Watchman* (Salisbury, North Carolina), June 6, 1850; on the other hand, some editors of Southern newspapers condemned the resort to lynch law, for example, the *Flag of the Union* (Tuscaloosa, Alabama), August 22, 1835; Raleigh *Star,* September 19, 1838; Louisville *Weekly Journal,* June 15, September 3, 1845; Louisville *Daily Journal,* October 4, 1849; *Ceredo Crescent* (Ceredo, Virginia), July 3, 1858.

57. J. G. deR. Hamilton, "Benjamin Sherwood Hedrick," *James Sprunt Historical Publications,* X; and J. S. Bassett *Anti-Slavery Leaders of North Carolina* (Baltimore, 1898).

58. Wheeling *Intelligencer,* August 18, 1856. For example, a Dr. G.P. Smith, speaker at a Republican meeting, was roughly handled by a mob and had to be taken to jail for safety.

59. *New York Tribune,* September 12, 1856; *Kanawha Valley Star* (Charleston, Virginia), February 3, 1857; *The Liberator,* August 16, 1856; *Dictionary of American Biography,* XIX, 113-14.

60. William Lloyd Garrison, *The New Reign of Terror in the Slaveholding States for the Year 1859-60* (New York, 1860).

61. Tarboro *Southerner* (Tarboro, North Carolina), December 17, 1859. *Executive Papers of Virginia for 1859-1860,* box entitled, "In Re John Brown," (MSS. in Virginia State Library); these papers show an almost fantastic excitement and fear of abolitionists on the part of many Virginians.

62. J. Winston Coleman, Jr., *Slavery Times in Kentucky* (Chapel Hill, 1940), chapter viii, "Nigger Stealers."

63. *Autobiography of John G. Fee, Berea, Kentucky* (Chicago, 1891); and John A. R. Rogers, *Birth of Berea College* (Philadelphia, 1903).

64. Edwin Rogers Embree, "A Kentucky Crusader," *American Mercury,* XXIV, 1931, p. 102.

65. Austin *State Gazette,* July 28, 1860; Natchez *Daily Free Trader,* August 5, 1860; New Orleans *Daily Picayune,* August 19, 1860.

66. Harvey Wish, "The Slave Insurrection Panic of 1856," *Journal of Southern History,* V, 1839, p. 222; Ollinger Crenshaw, "The Psychological Background of the Election of 1860 in the South," *The North Carolina Historical Review,* XIX, 1942, pp. 260-79.

67. Memphis *Eagle and Enquirer,* December 30, 1856.

68. Austin *State Gazette,* August 25, September 5, 1860; *Brownlow's Knoxville Whig,* November 17, 1860; *Hinds County Gazette* (Raymond, Mississippi), November 7, 1868.

69. This letter is quoted in a manuscript life of Hill by William J. Robertson, editor of the *Easton Express* (Easton, Pennsylvania), entitled "A. P. Hill Comes Up," 80, 81.

70. *The Mississippian,* August 14, 1835, for example, said, "No law is so well adapted to such villains as *Lynch's.*"

71. Lunsford Lane, *Narrative of Lunsford Lane, Formerly of Raleigh, N.C.* (Boston, 1845).

72. J. G. deR. Hamilton, ed., *The Papers of Thomas Ruffin* (4 vols., Raleigh, 1918-1920), III, 66, 67.

73. H. C. Perkins, Jr., *Northern Editorials on Secession* (2 vols., New York, 1942), I, Section XII.

74. When cases were brought before Southern courts, the judges interpreted the laws in a moderate spirit; see Eaton, *Freedom of Thought in the Old South,* chap. v, "The Law and the Courts."

75. Charles S. Sydnor, "The Southerner and the Laws," *Journal of Southern History,* VI, 1940, pp. 3-24.

76. On the other hand, Mississippi and Georgia, predominantly rural states with a high proportion of Negroes, led the nation in the number of lynchings between the years 1882 and 1927. Walter White, *Rope and Faggot, A Biography of Judge Lynch* (New York, 1929), 234-35.

Stephen B. Oates

TO WASH THIS LAND IN BLOOD : JOHN BROWN IN KANSAS

A fierce national debate raged over the issue of extending slavery into the new territories acquired by the United States in the 1840s. By 1850 the controversy threatened to tear the nation apart. Frightened moderates, however, forged the Compromise of 1850, a political patchwork of wheeling, dealing, and principle, in a great effort to save the nation. Thousands of Americans, in both the North and the South, hailed their success and celebrated the compromise.

A surface calm prevailed for a few years, and then the compromise came apart. The slavery issue was revived by a torrent of events that inflamed old passions, polarized sectional differences, and provoked repeated instances of violence. Even though no single incident dominated the decade, in some respects the violent struggle between pro-slavery people and free-soilers in Kansas kept both the North and the South stirred up and reflected the most tragic currents of the time. In the following essay, Stephen B. Oates tells the story of John Brown and "Bleeding Kansas." His chilling narrative compels speculation about the social and political uses of violence in the hands of terrorists such as John Brown.

By his own estimation John Brown, aged fifty-five, was an old man when he left northern New York for Kansas in the summer of 1855. He was gaunt, grim-faced, and sickly, having suffered for years from recurrent attacks of the ague, a malarial-type fever attended by fits of shivering and blazing

From *The American West* magazine, July and November, 1969, copyright © 1969 by the American West Publishing Company, Cupertino, California. Reprinted by permission of the author and publisher.

temperature. His hair, which he combed straight back over his head, was coarse and grizzled. His mouth was an inflexible slit, and his gray eyes shone like polished steel. Yes, he had recently confessed to his older children, he was an old man, guilty of many sins before God and scarred by a lifetime of hardship and failure, which he knew at last was part of his trial on earth. Yet he had a sense of profound exaltation because his follies only made him realize how dependent he was on the one, true God and made him believe all the more in God's justice, His mercy, and the divine purpose of His plans. And the journey Brown was now undertaking to Kansas was part of God's design, he believed, a journey that might lead him out of his season of trial and perhaps to a special destiny.

All his adult life Brown had been an austere, unpredictable man with a strangely divided personality, flawed and somehow tragic. If he was extremely religious, he could also be cruel, selfish, and intractably self-righteous, with an imperial egotism and a vindictive nature that made him intolerant and unappreciative of others, especially his own sons. He could become obsessed with a single idea—now slavery, now land speculation, now a wool crusade in Massachusetts, now a Negro community in the Adirondacks—and pursue his current fad with a single-minded determination. He could be notoriously inept and even unscrupulous as a businessman, yet at other times, as honest as Moses. And he could be kind and gentle—extremely gentle. He would rock a baby in his arms; stay up all night caring for a sick child, or his ailing father, or his afflicted first wife; hold children on both knees and sing them the sad, melancholy refrains of Isaac Watts' old hymn, "Blow ye the trumpet, blow." He would stand at the graves of his four children who had died of dysentery, weeping and praising God in an ecstasy of despair. He could teach his children to fear God and keep the Commandments—and exhibit terrible anxiety when the older ones began questioning the value of religion. He could offer to take a Negro child into his home and educate him, deplore racial discrimination in northern churches, hide runaways, and feel an almost paralyzing bitterness toward slavery itself—that "sum of villainies," that "sin against God"—and toward all the wicked people, in the South and in the federal government, who sought to preserve and perpetuate it.

He was born in 1800 (the same year Thomas Jefferson, the Virginia slave owner, came to power) in a stark, shutterless farmhouse in West Torrington, Connecticut. His father, a cobbler and tanner, who soon moved the family to Ohio's Western Reserve, taught the boy to fear an austere Calvinist God and to oppose slavery and its defenders. His mother died when he was eight, a tragedy that left him devastated with grief. When his father remarried, Brown refused to accept his stepmother emotionally, and "pined after his own mother for years." He grew into an arrogant and contentious young man, who ordered others about, a brother remarked, like "A king against whom there is no rising up." Around girls, however, Brown was painfully shy, a quality which deprived him of "a suitable connecting link" between the sexes—and which, as he admitted himself, "might under some circumstances have proved my ruin." Although he dropped out of school at an early age, he read the Bible meticulously and committed its entire contents to memory, taking pleasure in correcting anybody who quoted wrongly from it. In 1816, having been admitted to membership in the Congregational Church in Hudson, Ohio, he aspired to become a minister and traveled east to study. But he had to abandon his plans when he developed an inflammation of the eyes and ran short of funds. Failure was a leitmotif that was to run throughout his life.

Returning to Hudson, he built his own tannery and overcame his fears enough to marry Dianthe Lusk, who was pious and "remarkably plain." Dianthe bore seven children, whom Brown rigorously disciplined with a whip in one hand and a Bible in the other. In western Pennsylvania, where they resided for ten years, he organized an Independent Congregational Society and frequently preached, drawing his sermons from the works of Jonathan Edwards, whose mystical Puritanism greatly influenced his own religious beliefs. In the late 1820's, however, there were signs that he was entering another season of trial. Dianthe showed symptoms of deep-rooted emotional troubles, and then she and two of their children died. He soon married again, this time to a large, reticent girl named Mary Ann Day. Mary Ann gave him thirteen children, seven of whom died in childhood. There were tragedies in his worldly concerns too—he was wiped out in the Panic of 1837, declared bankrupt in 1842. But like other frontier businessmen, Brown had a reckless, go-ahead spirit. Recouping his fortunes, he plunged into another business venture, and another. Everything ended in failure.

As he grew older, Brown became more self-righteous and fixed in his convictions than ever. He lectured his children about providential interpositions and their trial on earth, beseeching them to suffer the word of exhortation. He became increasingly disturbed by all the proslavery wickedness that prevailed in the United States. He worked on the Underground Railroad in Ohio, publicly opposed the state's "black laws," attempted to integrate a Congregational church he attended in Franklin Mills and was expelled for his effort. After that, he grew more violent in his denunciations of slavery. He would gladly lay down his life for the destruction of that institution, because "death for a good cause," he told a friend, was "glorious." While living in Springfield, Massachusetts, he not only chided Negroes for passively submitting to white oppression but worked out a secret scheme to run slaves out of the South through a "Subterranean Pass Way." He may also have indulged in bloody fantasies of inciting a slave insurrection in the South, such as his black militant friend, Henry Highland Garnet, advocated. In 1851 Brown exhorted Negroes to kill any southerner or federal officer who tried to enforce the Fugitive Slave Law and enlisted forty-four Springfield blacks into a mutual-defense organization called the

"Branch of the United States League of Gileadites," based on the story of Gideon in the Book of Judges.

After a monumental debacle in the wool business, Brown returned to Ohio and tried to make ends meet as a wool grower and farmer. Still, he remained deeply troubled by the slavery sickness that infected his country; and in January, 1854, he wrote a letter to *Frederick Douglass' Paper* (a Negro journal published in Rochester, New York) which castigated those "malignant spirits"—those "fiends clothed in human form"—who used the churches, the courts, and the national government to protect such an abomination, and advocated an immediate end to the corruption of "our truly republican and democratic institutions." But his words did no good: just four months later, on May 30, 1854, President Pierce signed the Kansas-Nebraska Bill into law, an act which eradicated the old Missouri Compromise line and decreed that henceforth the citizens of each territory would vote on whether to have slavery or not. At once, antislavery northerners decried the act as a southern conspiracy to extend slavery into the West—and maybe the North as well. The first step in the plot was to occupy Kansas. Salmon P. Chase of Ohio saw it; so did William H. Seward of New York. "Come on, then, gentlemen of the slave States," Seward cried; "since there is no escaping your challenge, I accept it in behalf of the cause of freedom. We will engage in competition for the virgin soil of Kansas, and God give the victory to the side that is stronger in numbers as it is in right."

In response Eli Thayer formed the New England Emigrant Aid Society and, with visions of making money in Kansas as well as saving it from the Slave Power, sent out a handful of colonists that summer. At the same time hundreds of pioneers from the northwestern states also started for Kansas to make new lives for themselves on a "free-soil frontier." That fall five of Brown's sons (Salmon, Owen, Frederick, Jason, and John, Jr.) decided to emigrate as well. Later, Brown made up his mind to follow them and seek work as a surveyor to investigate prospects for speculating in land, farming, and the selling of horses and cattle.

In the summer of 1855, he moved the remainder of his family to North Elba, in the Adirondack Mountains, where he received a series of letters from his sons that were to alter significantly his reasons for moving on to Kansas. Proslavery gangs from neighboring Missouri—John, Jr. wrote— were attempting to make Kansas a slave state "by means no matter how foul." Already they had formed "Annoyance Associations" to terrorize free-state settlements and drive abolitionists from the territory. Worse, John, Jr., had heard that "hundreds of thousands" of men—"desperate" men from every slaveholding state in the Union—were now massing along the border "to fasten slavery on this glorious land" through outright invasion. Many of the free-state settlers in the Pottawatomie vicinity, where the Brown boys had located, were afraid to resist. And the Missourians, hearing of such cowardice, boasted that "they could obtain possession of the polls in any of our election precincts without having to fire a gun." (Although John, Jr., did not say so, the Missourians *had* taken possession of Kansas polls: on March 30, no fewer than five thousand of them—"enough to kill every Goddamned abolitionist in the Territory," said one Missouri captain —had swarmed across the border to vote in the election for a territorial legislature. By using fists and threatening murder, unseating fair judges and counting illegal ballots, the intruders had elected an overwhelmingly pro-slavery legislature.)

What could be done to stop the proslavery menace? John, Jr., wanted to fight. "The Antislavery portion of the inhabitants should *immediately, thoroughly arm and organize themselves in military companies,*" John, Jr., declared, repeating virtually the same thing Brown had said when he organized the U. S. League of Gileadites. But antislavery Kansans were desperately short of guns, John, Jr., said, and he requested his father to gather a number of revolvers, rifles, and knives to bring along when he came to Kansas.

The letter aroused Brown's fighting spirit, and he set about zealously soliciting money and weapons from antislavery groups in New York and Massachusetts. As he did so, additional letters arrived, enflaming his passions further. "The storm every day thickens," John, Jr., wrote, "Its near approach is hourly more clearly seen by all." Now was the time to help in the cause, for he was convinced that "the great drama will open here, when will be presented the great struggle in arms, of Freedom and Despotism in America. Give us the arms, and we are ready for the contest."

Brown was ready to move. All his life he had believed in predestination and providential signs and the storm gathering over Kansas gave him a glimpse of his own destiny, of what Providence had foreordained for him all along: he saw himself with a sword, exhorting his men to fight for the Lord and John Brown out on the Kansas prairie, just as Gideon had implored the men of Israel to fight the Midianites.

He left North Elba in August and traveled to Ohio, where he solicited more money and weapons—including several artillery broadswords. His son Oliver and son-in-law Henry Thompson joined him later. Then they loaded all the "freight"—rifles, revolvers, knives, and swords—into a wagon; tossed in Brown's surveying instruments, a tent, and some blankets; and set out to "meddle directly with the peculiar institution" in Kansas.

When Brown arrived at "Brown's Station" on North Middle Creek, some six miles northwest of Dutch Henry's Crossing on the Pottawatomie, he was dismayed at what he found. His "children" (including the families of Jason and John, Jr.) were living in makeshift tents, "shivering over their little fires and exposed to the dreadfully cutting winds." All the men were so sick with the ague that, if the storm had broken then, they would not have had the strength to fight.

As head of the family, Brown took charge at once, unboxing and distributing the weapons, gathering in crops, and nursing his children back to health. As he did so, he doubtlessly inquired about what had taken place in Kansas politics since John, Jr., had written last. As it happened, the "bogus" proslavery legislature, meeting at Shawnee Mission in July, had legalized slavery in Kansas and provided severe punishment for anybody who asserted that slavery did not exist there, or denied a man's right to own slaves, or circulated abolitionist literature, or assisted runaways. Governor Andrew H. Reeder, a moderate trying to maintain a semblance of justice, vetoed all these laws, but the legislators defiantly overrode him—and some members even threatened his life. Finally, President Pierce dismissed him from office ostensibly because he had speculated in Indian lands, and sent out Wilson Shannon as the new territorial executive. A doughfaced Cincinnati lawyer and former governor of Ohio, Shannon recognized the Shawnee Mission legislature as legal, befriended the leaders of the Kansas proslavery party, and imbibed all their suspicions of the free-state settlers, who formed a majority of the population.

In open defiance, free-state men—under the leadership of Charles Robinson, James Henry Lane, and others—launched a movement to establish a rival government and to write a free-state constitution—a movement in which John, Jr., himself had been actively involved until the sickness and stormy weather had set in. An election for a free-state congressman, as well as for delegates to a constitutional convention to convene at Topeka, was scheduled for October 9. Free-state citizens in the Pottawatomie settlement expected trouble at the polls, perhaps another invasion of Missourians (150 of them had cast illegal votes in the election for a territorial legislature), or perhaps interference on the part of the local proslavery minority.

On election day Brown accompanied his sons down to the Pottawatomie Meeting House. They went "powerfully armed," but no enemy appeared. Evidently Brown did not vote in this or any other election while he was there. (He had staked out no claim and did not regard himself as a Kansas citizen.) Since no invasion had occurred, Brown believed that Missouri might be giving up on Kansas and that prospects of making it a free state were improving; yet he still wrote his wife and daughters: "I humbly trust we may be kept & spared; to meet again on Earth; *but if not* let us all endeavor earnestly to secure admission to that Eternal Home where will be no more bitter seperations [sic]; 'where the wicked shall cease from troubling; & the weary be at rest.' "

With no fighting to do at present, Brown set about putting Brown's Station in order. Working outside despite the "cutting cold winds and storms," he fashioned a shanty for Jason and Ellen, then constructed a log cabin for John, Jr., and his family. Brown spent Thanksgiving in the nearby town of Osawatomie, visiting a preacher brother-in-law named Samuel Adair. Adair later told a couple of neighbors his guest seemed "impressed with the idea that God had raised him up on purpose to break the jaws of the wicked.''

While Brown was at Osawatomie, he heard electrifying news from Lawrence, the chief free-state settlement in Kansas: an army of Missourians had invaded the territory and was now massing along the Wakarusa River to burn the settlement to the ground. Brown hurried back to North Middle Creek, gathered four of his sons, and took a wagon loaded with guns and swords to help defend the beleaguered town. Because of Brown's zeal ''in the cause of freedom, both before and after his arrival in the Territory,'' Robinson and Lane, the free-state leaders, gave the old man command of a volunteer company. Brown's sons later asserted that he wanted to steal up on the Missourians during the night and slaughter them in their sleep. But fighting of any sort was averted when Governor Shannon and the free-state leaders worked out a peace treaty in which the latter secretly agreed not to resist the bogus laws. Then the governor persuaded the Missourians to withdraw, and the so-called ''Wakarusa War'' came to an end.

Brown himself was probably disappointed that a general bloodletting had not taken place (he had not brought along those broadswords for the sake of appearances). Nevertheless, he returned to Brown's Station greatly excited. ''I did not see the least sign of cowardice or want of self-possession exhibited by any volunteer of . . . the free State Force,'' he wrote Mary Ann. Truly, in this heroic struggle between Good and Evil, they had all sustained ''the high character of the Revolutionary Fathers.'' His excitement remained high when Kansas voters ratified the free-state constitution drafted at Topeka and elections were scheduled in January for a free-state governor and legislature. ''What now remains for the Free State men of Kansas,'' Brown rejoiced, ''is to hold the ground they now possess, *and Kansas is free.*''

He changed his mind, however, when an ominous sequence of events indicated to him that a monstrous conspiracy was underfoot to force slavery on Kansas by subterfuge and violence, a conspiracy that in Brown's view involved not only the bogus territorial government and its Missouri and southern allies, but the Pierce administration and the United States Army as well.

First, President Pierce delivered a special address to Congress in January, 1856, in which he blamed all of Kansas' troubles on northern emigrant aid societies, upheld the bogus legislature, branded the free-state constitution as ''revolutionary,'' and warned that organized resistance on the part of free-state Kansans would be regarded as ''treasonable insurrection.'' Brown was convinced that Pierce intended ''to crush the men of Kansas,'' and angrily predicted that the President would ''find his hands full before it is over.''

Then word came to Pottawatomie that border Missouri was *not* going to give up on Kansas, that proslavery forces planned to incite a ''general disturbance'' there, and that Lawrence itself was threatened with attack. At the same time, reports arrived that a proslavery gang had brutally murdered a free-state man near Leavenworth and that free-state people in the vicinity had fled to Lawrence. For Brown, these were "shocking outrages," and he wrote his wife that "we may soon again be called upon to 'buckle on our Armor'; which by the help of God we will do."

Then, as the snows melted and wagon trains started arriving in Kansas from the North, the proslavery press launched an editorial crusade against the "abolitionist invasion" and called on the Deep South for help. "War! War!!" screamed the Missouri *Squatter Sovereign.* "Sound the bugle . . . over the length and breadth of the land, cried the *Kansas Pioneer,* "and leave not an Abolitionist in the Territory. . . ."

With proslavery forces threatening a war of extermination, could there be any doubt of a general proslavery conspiracy in Kansas? Thus when United States troops turned up in the Pottawatomie vicinity, for the "ostensible purpose of removing *intruders* from certain Indian lands," Brown became as paranoid as a southerner hearing the cry of insurrection on the wind. He dispatched a letter to Congressman Joshua H. Giddings of Ohio, charging that "the real object" of those troops was to enforce the *"Hellish enactments"* of the bogus legislature—laws which the Browns had repeatedly broken. Brown was certain that the next move "of the Administration and its Proslavery masters" would be to make Pottawatomie citizens submit to "those Infernal enactments" or to "assume what will be termed *treasonable grounds"* by shooting the soldiers. "I ask in the name of Almighty God; I ask in the name of our venerated forefathers; I ask in the name of all that is good or true men ever hold dear; will Congress suffer us to be driven to such 'dire extremities'? *Will anything be done?"*

Giddings replied that Pierce would not dare use federal troops "to shoot the citizens of Kansas"; but Brown was not convinced, and John, Jr., echoed the old man's sentiments: if proslavery forces continued their "aggressive acts" against Kansas, "the war-cry heard upon our plains will reverberate not only through the hemp and tobacco fields of Missouri but through the 'Rice Swamps,' the cotton and sugar plantations of the Sunny South." If "the first act in the Drama of insane Despotism is to be performed here, you may look elsewhere for the theatre of other acts."

At least one act in that "insane despotism" was to take place in Pottawatomie. Word came that copies of the bogus laws were now being circulated among territorial officers and that Judge Sterling G. Cato, a staunch proslavery man, would hold the U.S. district court session for Franklin County at Dutch Henry's tavern. Pottawatomie buzzed with anxious questions: Would the court enforce the laws? Would offenders be arrested, imprisoned? Brown grew terribly belligerent when he heard the news. "For once," he wrote his wife, "I have no desire (all things considered) to have the Slave Power cease its acts of aggression. Their foot shall slide in due time."

He started to leave Pottawatomie (perhaps to do some surveying for the Indians) only to change his mind after the arrival of both a deputy marshal, to subpoena jurors for Cato's court, and a tax assessor, who announced that all property would be assessed and taxed according to the laws. At a settlers' meeting in Osawatomie, Brown declared that he was an abolitionist and that he would rather see the Union drenched in blood than pay taxes to the proslavery government (even though he had no claim and would not have to pay taxes anyway). He swore that he would kill any officer of either the territorial or the U.S. governments who tried to make him obey the bogus laws.

The meeting was a stormy one, and was climaxed by a bolt of conservatives who wanted to submit to the laws. The remaining settlers adopted a set of resolutions warning that anybody who attempted to assess taxes or enforce the laws would do so at his "peril." Brown detected the presence of God in these and other developments in the territory. When he heard, for example, that a Congressional committee, headed by William A. Howard of Michigan, had arrived to investigate conditions in Kansas, Brown trusted that much good would grow out of the committee's work (two of its three members were antislavery), "but at all events God will take care of his own cause." At the same time, he was haunted by a constant ringing in his ears; it was "the despairing cry of millions whose woes none but God knows. Bless the Lord, O my soul, for he hears."

When Cato opened court at Dutch Henry's tavern on April 21, it was demonstrably a proslavery gathering. On the day the court opened, Brown went with the Pottawatomie Rifles, a volunteer home-defense organization commanded by John Brown, Jr., to present Cato with the free-state resolutions and to demonstrate on the parade ground. The court was unimpressed, and went on to indict Benjamin Cochran, Nelson King, and David Baldwin (all free-state men) for relatively minor crimes, two of which did not involve the slavery question at all. No arrests were made, however, nor were the Browns or anybody else who had actually violated the black laws indicted. On April 22, Cato moved his court to Anderson County, where it indicted James Townsley, a free-state man who resided on the North Fork of Pottowatomie Creek, for assault with intent to kill.

After the Cato court episode, tension grew worse on the Pottawatomie. Rumors continued that "a distant storm" was gathering, that any day now a Missouri horde would invade Kansas and exterminate every abolitionist there, as Missouri leaders had threatened to do for months. As the rumors and threats increased in intensity, open hostility must have broken out between free-state settlers on the creek and their proslavery neighbors—especially Allen Wilkinson, the Shermans, and the Doyles, who were members of the proslavery Law-and-Order Party. None of them owned slaves, but all championed the *right* of slavery, were active in proslavery politics, defended the bogus government, wanted Kansas to become a South-dominated state, and probably viewed most if not all their free-state neighbors as "Yankee extremists" and "fanatical abolitionists" for resisting the bogus laws.

Actually, most free-state men on the creek were not fanatical abolitionists at all. Fully two-thirds of them, like most antislavery settlers elsewhere in the territory, entertained considerable anti-Negro prejudice, and had voted in favor of a Negro-exclusion clause in the Topeka Constitution that would keep free blacks out of Kansas as well as slaves. They intended to make Kansas free all right, but free and white.

Only Brown and a handful of others were radical or ultra abolitionists. But again, the Shermans and their cohorts apparently saw little difference among their free-state opponents and made repeated threats "to shoot & exterminate" them, echoing the invective of the proslavery press. Whether or not Wilkinson, the Shermans, and the Doyles, planned to carry out their threats may never be known. What is known is that Brown himself grew to fear and detest these men, viewing them as part of the whole tapestry of evil which proslavery forces were now weaving over Kansas.

The signs multiplied that the long-expected storm was about to break. A lone assassin wounded a proslavery sheriff near Lawrence, and the proslavery press, exploiting the incident for everything it was worth, called for "War to the knife and knife to the hilt." As though inspired by such bloody headlines, drunken proslavery elements in Kansas murdered two free-state men and (for lack of tar and feathers) stripped and cottoned another. Then, on May 2, Jefferson Buford led a battalion of armed southerners into the territory, with banners proclaiming *"The Supremacy of the White Race"* and *"Alabama for Kansas—North of 36° 30'."* Was Buford's column the advance of a massive southern thrust against Kansas? Was actual war about to commence?

John Brown's conviction that the slavery issue was about to erupt into full-scale war in the Kansas prairie was strengthened when a company of Georgians encamped on the Miami Indian lands near Pottawatomie. There is a much debated story that he disguised himself as a government surveyor, visited the southerners' camp, and learned that, while they had come here to help themselves first and the South second, they still planned to annihilate "those damned Browns" and to stand by the proslavery decisions of Judge Sterling G. Cato "until every damned abolitionist was in hell." Whether Brown actually visited the southerners' camp is not important; for him, the invaders could have come only to burn and kill—a man did not have to talk with them to know that. At any rate, there can be little doubt that, gathering his unmarried sons around him on North Middle Creek, he girded himself for war.

Suddenly, the long-awaited storm broke. Trying to smash free-state resistance once and for all, a proslavery court in Leavenworth indicted a number of free-state leaders for "high treason." Then a proslavery United States marshal claimed that the town of Lawrence had resisted attempts to serve process on several men and called for all "law-abiding citizens of the Territory" to help him enforce the law. Here was the opportunity pro-slavery forces had been waiting for to wipe out Lawrence. On May 20 a "swearing, whiskey-drinking" horde of Missourians, reinforced by Kansas militia and Jefferson Buford's southerners, descended on Lawrence, vow-ing to wipe that "abolitionist hell hole" off the face of the earth.

Brown, hearing the news, organized his unmarried sons and his son-in-law Henry Thompson into "a little company by ourselves," then joined the Pottawatomie Rifles of John, Jr., and marched to the defense of Law-rence. But if Brown hoped that an armed conflict between freedom and despotism had finally begun, he was to be extremely disappointed. Mes-sengers encountered on the way reported that the Missourians had already sacked Lawrence, that free-state leaders there had not resisted, and that U.S. troops had arrived. One messenger advised the volunteers to return to their homes; Lawrence was drastically short of food, and anyway there was nothing they could do now.

Brown, outraged because the free-state party had not put up a fight, helped carry a vote for the Rifles to push ahead. But a short while later James Hanway proposed that they encamp to await reinforcements on their way from Osawatomie, and the volunteers voted to do so. Regarding this as a cowardly act, Brown became "extremely excited," Hanway recalled, "and remarked that he would rather be ground in the earth than passively submit to proslavery usurpation and wrong." The more Brown thought about the sacking of Lawrence and the inexcusable timidity of the free-state leaders, the more "frenzied" he became "at the condition of affairs." And in that state of mind, he decided to strike a retaliatory blow at certain pro-slavery men on Pottawatomie Creek, a blow that would avenge the Law-rence fiasco and compensate for the screaming threats, the murders, and all the other outrages that the Kansas proslavery party and its Missouri allies had perpetrated since this great struggle between good and evil had begun.

Can there be any doubt that he believed himself guided by an angry and vengeful god? He told Hanway that he was glad the volunteers had voted not to proceed to Lawrence, that it was a providential sign. "Some-thing must be shown that we, too, have rights," he told the other men, and called for volunteers to accompany him on a *"secret mission"* to "regulate matters on the creek."

Only Theodore Weiner (a huge, savage Austrian) and James Townsley agreed to go with the old man and his "little company"—his sons Owen, Frederick, Salmon, and Oliver, and Henry Thompson. They honed the artillery broadswords Brown had collected in Ohio to razor-sharp edges, then, on the afternoon of Friday, May 22, set out for Pottawatomie—Weiner on a horse, the others in Townsley's wagon. All day Saturday they hid in a stand of timber near the creek, listening to the old man vindicate the grisly work ahead. According to Townsley, Brown declared that it was time to "fight fire with fire," to "strike terror in the hearts of the proslavery people." He said it was "better that a score of bad men should die than that one man who came here to make Kansas a Free State should be driven out."

That night, as a damp wind blew, Brown's self-styled "Army of the North" dragged James Doyle and his two eldest sons out of their cabin and two of Brown's boys hacked them to death with broadswords (as Gideon's men had slain the Midianites, as related in the Book of Judges). Although Doyle was already dead, Brown shot him in the forehead with a revolver, to make certain work of it. They then stole on to Allen Wilkinson's place, took him out into the night in his stocking feet, and cut him down in some dead brush nearby. Ironically, it was early in the morning of May 24—Sunday, the Lord's Sabbath—when Brown's men summoned William Sherman from James Harris's cabin and hacked him to death like the others, throwing his mutilated body into the Pottawatomie. They would have got tavern-owner Dutch Henry, too, had he not been out on the prairie looking for stray cattle. Brown spared James Harris (a juror on Cato's court) and two others who were staying with him, because they declared that they had never assisted the proslavery party and had never harmed or threatened free-state settlers.

Confiscating a saddle and a horse that belonged to Dutch Henry, Brown's war party washed their cutlasses in the Pottawatomie, then started back over the California Road to rejoin John, Jr. The old man was silent, transfixed, as the wagon rattled up the road. The enemy had murdered six free-state men since the struggle had begun in Kansas. Now, in getting five slavery men, Brown and his boys had about evened the score.

War! War! raged the Westport, Missouri, *Border Times*. EIGHT PRO-SLAVERY MEN MURDERED BY THE ABOLITIONISTS IN FRANK-LIN COUNTY. Already a war of reprisal had commenced, as proslavery gangs ransacked the Osawatomie-Pottawatomie area in search of the killers and plunged the entire region into an extraordinary state of "fear & excitement."

Trying to restore order to the area, Governor Wilson Shannon dispatched a cavalry company to Osawatomie, requested that Fort Leavenworth send reinforcements to Lawrence, and wrote President Pierce about the murders, declaring that he feared the consequences unless the offenders were brought to justice. In the meantime, down in Paola in Lykins County, Judge Cato had issued warrants for the arrest of Brown and his band on May 28; and two days later the old man was indicted again, along with John, Jr., and eight others, for "treasonably" resisting the territorial laws. Brown escaped capture by fleeing to a secret campsite on Ottawa Creek, but John, Jr., Jason, and several other free-state men were apprehended and marched in chains "like a gang of slaves" all the way to Tecumseh, where they were given a preliminary hearing by a U.S. commissioner. The commissioner released Jason and four others, but bound John, Jr., and one H. H. Williams over to the U.S. marshal "on the charge of treason," to await the action of the grand jury (to convene in September).

Meanwhile, a "mingled and raging" guerrilla war had broken out in southeastern Kansas, as bands of armed men—one led by Brown himself—prowled the countryside, firing at one another and looting enemy homesteads. On June 2 Brown's company, with reinforcements from Prairie City, fought and captured a Missouri force under Henry Clay Pate at Black Jack—a victory that pleased Brown immensely. He wrote his wife that Black Jack was the "first regular battle fought between Free State & pro Slavery men in Kansas. May God still gird our loins & hold our right hands, & to him may we give the glory."

First the Pottawatomie Massacre, then the victory at Black Jack—Brown was now totally and irrevocably at war with slavery in Kansas. And because in his own mind this was a holy war, waged in the name of God against obstinately wicked men, he could justify many acts for the good of the cause—all the way from distortion, secrecy, and lies to terrorization, plundering, house-stealing, and midnight assassination. To the victor belonged the spoils anyway, for as God commanded Moses, as related in the Book of Deuteronomy (one of Brown's favorites): "But the women, and the little ones, and the cattle and all that is in the city, even all the spoil thereof, shalt thou take unto thyself; and thou shalt eat the spoil of thine enemies, which the Lord thy God hath given thee." As one of Brown's recruits put it, "A state of war existed and it was quite proper to despoil the enemy." And despoil the enemy they did: they raided Joab Bernard's store near the Franklin-Douglas county line, helping themselves to between three and four thousand dollars' worth of supplies and confiscating several horses and cows. They continued to steal horses and cattle throughout the summer. Brown, however, used none of this plunder for his personal gain; he mounted his men on some of the horses, sold the others in Lawrence and in Nebraska, and used the money and stolen supplies "for the continuation of the struggle."

On June 5 a company of U.S. troops discovered Brown's camp on Ottawa Creek. Perhaps because the commander was under orders only to disband irregular forces (free-state and proslavery alike), he did not arrest Brown but merely liberated his prisoners and compelled his company to disperse. Fearing that the Missourians themselves might return with reinforcements, Brown, his sons, and several others fled into the brush, where they hid "from our enemy," Brown said, "like the David of old, [finding] our dwelling with the serpants of the Rock, & wild beasts of the wilderness."

While Brown hid in the brush for twenty days, unbridled civil war raged in the territory. "An eye for an eye and a tooth for a tooth" was the war cry of both sides in bleeding Kansas as the murders and atrocities multiplied. In an effort to terrorize and starve out free-state settlements, proslavery forces cut off the Missouri River to free-state immigration, blocked all roads along the Missouri border, and then constructed forts and blockhouses in a wide-swinging arc around Topeka, Lawrence, and Osawatomie. At the same time, all across the North antislavery crowds gathered to discuss proslavery terrorism in Kansas and to pledge money and start armed emigrants for the embattled territory.

Did Brown, still hiding in the brush, know what was going on? He wrote Mary Ann that "we are not disheartened," even though "we are nearly destitute of food, Clothing, & money" and "Owen & Oliver are down with fever." For "God who had not given us over to the will of our enemies but has moreover delivered them into our hand; will we humbly trust still keep & deliver us." He directed Mary Ann that "if under God this letter reaches you so that it can be read, I wish it at once carefully copied in Ink. . . . I know of no other way to get these facts, & our situation before the world."

Was Brown contemplating some plan to expand his war against the "Philistines"—one that would involve Smith and other wealthy abolitionists in the East? Had he heard about the money and "Beecher's Bibles" which antislavery northerners were pledging for the defense of Kansas?

On July 1 he went to Lawrence and penned a reply to Pate's account of Black Jack, published in the St. Louis *Republican,* which accused Brown of violating the articles of war—and also called him the Pottawatomie murderer. Brown, ignoring the latter accusation, insisted in his own account that he had defeated Pate in a fair fight. He sent the piece to the New York *Tribune,* which published it on July 11. Was Brown only trying to set the record straight, or was this a deliberate effort to attract publicity for himself in the East? About July 2 he had a long conversation with William A. Phillips, a correspondent for the *Tribune,* and said things obviously for the correspondent's benefit. Brown remarked that the free-state party was run by "broken-down politicians" from the East (he meant Charles Robinson and former governor Andrew H. Reeder in particular) who would "rather pass resolutions than act" and who "criticized all who did real work"— such as Brown did. That was why Brown had broken with the free-state party and undertaken his own independent war against the proslavery forces. Anyway he was not "in the habit of subjecting himself to the orders of anybody. He intended to aid the general result, but in his own way."

Phillips was very impressed with this gruff, Bible-quoting soldier and his inflexible belief that "men were nothing, principles everything." And in a book he published later that year, entitled *The Conquest of Kansas by Missouri and Her Allies,* Phillips portrayed Brown as a courageous, God-fearing captain fighting in his own way to make Kansas free—"a strange, resolute, repulsive, iron-willed, inexorable old man" whom the Missourians both hated and feared. Such a portrait was bound to impress wealthy abolitionists in the East who were worried about the fate of Kansas.

In late July, Brown decided to leave Kansas and wrote John, Jr., still in prison, about his plans. "Am very Glad that you have started," John, Jr., replied, "as all things considered I am convinced you can be of more use where you contemplate going than here." Obviously Brown was up to something; but whatever his plans were, he did not reveal them to anybody besides John, Jr., and perhaps his other sons. In early August, they went to Nebraska City, one of the major stations on the "Lane Trail," which Kansas emigrants had recently opened through Iowa and Nebraska. There Brown encountered James Henry Lane's celebrated "Army of the North" —some four hundred colonists sent out under the auspices of the newly formed National Kansas-Aid Committee—and a company of Kansas volunteers under Samuel Walker. Brown talked at length with Lane and Walker. (Did they tell him they too were tired of conservative free-state leadership and were prepared to attack proslavery strongholds?) Brown now changed his mind about going on, and he and Frederick returned to Kansas with Walker, Lane, and about thirty others, ahead of the wagon trains. Henry Thompson and Brown's unmarried sons, however, went on to Iowa, where Owen mysteriously remained while the others headed for Ohio and New York. On August 10, Brown left the free-state column and alone headed for Topeka. There he wrote Jason (who had returned to Osawatomie) that "God still lives; & 'blessed be his great & holy name.' The boys may go on farther East; & may hold on for me to join them." *Now* what did Brown have in mind? There is evidence that he intended to liberate John, Jr., but if so, what did he plan to do after that? Did he plan to travel east, to solicit aid from the National Kansas Committee for his private war in Kansas—or for some larger scheme?

Brown's whereabouts during the next six days are not known. But contrary to reports in the Missouri press, he did not participate in the campaigns that occurred between August 12 and 17, when free-state forces raided slavery strongholds at Franklin, Fort Saunders, Treadwell, Washington Creek, and Fort Titus, once more plunging the smouldering border into a "raging fury." On or about August 17, Brown turned up in Topeka again, where he apparently received a letter from John, Jr., advising against a rescue attempt. A day or two later Brown left for Lawrence on an unknown mission.

On August 22, at some place in or near Lawrence, Brown initiated seven recruits into what he called the "Kansas Regulators" and had them pledge "their word and sacred honor" to fight "for the maintenance of the rights and liberties of the Free State citizens of Kansas." The "by laws of this association," which consisted of twenty-three articles of war, were tantamount to an official declaration of war against slavery.

Commander Brown had an immediate opportunity to go into action. He heard that Osawatomie was threatened with attack and took his company to help defend the town. When no attack was forthcoming, Brown joined with the companies of James B. Cline, Samuel T. Shore, and Samuel Anderson and raided proslavery settlements on Sugar Creek, a raid that netted the combined forces a number of horses, cattle and other property. Brown himself had personally "liberated" some "number one" proslavery beef from the plantation of a border ruffian, and herded all his "free-state" cattle onto the Crane Ranch across the Marais des Cygnes from Osawatomie.

Either before or just after the raid, Brown received a letter from his daughter Ruth, written on July 20 at North Elba, in the Adirondacks, where the women of the family still waited. She related that the family subscribed to the New York *Weekly Times,* and had read that John, Jr., has been driven insane because of the "inhuman treatment" he had received at the hands of U.S. troops (they had clubbed him with rifle butts, thinking him one of the Pottawatomie murderers). Everybody at North Elba was upset about John, Jr., but they did thank God that none of the boys had been killed and that Brown, too, had been spared (the *Times* at first reported that he had also fallen into the hands of the Missouri ruffians). Then, referring to Brown's account of Black Jack in one of his previous letters [which contained a deliberate distortion of facts], Ruth remarked that Brown "must have had very exciting times" in that battle—a statement unintentionally ironic. A few lines later she said: "Gerrit Smith has had his name put down for ten thousand dollars toward starting a company of one thousand men to Kansas." *One thousand men? Ten thousand dollars?* One can imagine what went through Brown's mind when he read this. If he could persuade abolitionist Smith to give him that kind of support, could he not, under God, wage a truly great war against Slave Power despotism?

The next morning (August 30) a messenger from Osawatomie ran into Brown's camp yelling that the border ruffians were attacking the town and that Frederick—Brown's son—and another free-stater, David Garrison had already been killed. Brown grabbed his gun, shouted to his men, and hurried into town, his recruits following in pairs and groups.

At Brown's recommendation, the town's defenders took up a position in the timber just northwest of Osawatomie only to see the Missourians wheel off the road and charge "down the hill in half-moon shape" with guns blazing. The fighting was hot and bitter, but at last the Missourians overran the free-state men and drove them across the Marais des Cygnes in panic and rout. Brown and his son Jason fled through the timber above Osawatomie, looking for a ford where they could cross the river and go to the cabin of his brother-in-law Samuel Adair, perhaps to find Frederick. At one spot on the riverbank, Jason pointed in the direction of town: smoke was billowing up over the trees. The Missourians were burning Osawatomie! Brown could hear their shouts and gunfire as they rode through the smoking settlement looting cabins and herding off the very cattle that free-state forces had stolen during the past few days. First the murder of Frederick and now this! "God sees it," the old man said, and stood there trembling with grief and rage. "I have only a short time to live—only one death to die," he told Jason, "and I will die fighting for this cause. There will be no more peace in this land until slavery is done for. I will give them something else to do than to extend slave territory. I will carry this war into Africa."

On September 7 Brown rode into Lawrence on his gray horse, with his gun across his saddle and a dazed expression on his face. The old man was well known in Lawrence, and as he moved down the street men cheered "as if the President had come to town, but John Brown seemed not to hear it and paid not the slightest attention." Somebody told him that a war council headed by hatchet-faced James Lane and James A. Harvey was then in session and was planning a raid against proslavery strongholds in and around Leavenworth. Brown, however, was not interested in either accompanying or leading the projected raid, and rode on. For several days he came and went, his mind busy with plots. One can only conjecture what visions played in his thoughts during these last days in Lawrence: perhaps a vision of striking a blow against "Africa" that would make the earth shake and tremble as the blood of evil stained this land, for one of his favorite biblical texts was Heb. 9:22: "And almost all things are by the law purged with blood; and without shedding of blood is no remission." Then was Brown mulling over the possibility that God now wished him to strike a blow at the Deep South itself, to incite an insurrection there as he perhaps had dreamed of doing for ten years now? According to an account by E. A. Coleman, who lived near Lawrence, Brown came to his house and told Coleman and his wife that God had used him as an instrument for killing men and would use him "to kill a great many more." Others heard him say that he had his mission just as Christ did—that God had appointed him "a special angel of death" to destroy slavery with the sword.

Certainly Brown was on the verge of something large in these mid-September days. He sent a letter to Mary Ann, notifying her of Frederick's death with scarcely a trace of emotion. In the exultant state he was in (for surely he viewed Frederick's death and the sack of Osawatomie, however tragic, as providential signs showing him what must be done), he seemed incapable of ordinary human emotions. In fact, he had not even had the presence of mind to bury Frederick after Osawatomie, but had merely taken the boy's cap and faded into the brush, leaving others to dig his grave. After writing Mary Ann, Brown then prepared an account of the Osawatomie fight for the press—obviously to publicize himself in eastern newspapers. Not insignificantly, he was soon calling himself "John Brown of Osawatomie."

Preoccupied with his visions and his riots, Brown played only a perfunctory role in the defense of Lawrence during the last Missouri invasion (September 13 and 14). Walking about the streets with his gun on his shoulder and a cloud on his face, the old man may have made some attempt to rally volunteers at the forts on the edge of town, but clearly his heart was not in it. The new governor, John W. Geary, soon arrived, and backed by United States troops, he persuaded the Missourians to withdraw. After that

Geary embarked on a pacification program that eventually brought an end to the guerrilla war which the sacking of Lawrence and the Pottawatomie Massacre had precipitated.

As Geary set about executing evenhanded justice, indicting free-state and proslavery "troublemakers" alike, he may have ordered the arrest of Brown as well. Brown himself seems to have thought so; he returned to Osawatomie where he made plans to leave the territory. Since fighting in Kansas had nearly ended (and since U.S. troops were allegedly prowling the countryside in search of him), Brown was ready to travel east and launch his "grand scheme." Sick with dysentery and a "Chill fever," the old man ordered his Kansas Regulators to continue terrorizing the enemy; then he took his sons and their families to hide out at a friend's place near Lawrence, trying to elude whatever troops were on their trail. Still ill in early October, Brown started the womenfolk for Ohio "by way of the River," then set out for Nebraska with John, Jr. (who had been released by the authorities on September 7) and two other sons. As the party headed across Nebraska, Iowa, and the northwestern states, Brown lay on a bed inside the wagon, his fevered mind filled with visions of carrying his war into Africa; and in December, he began writing down in a notebook, in his cramped, hurried style, the names of anybody (militant Negroes, "military" abolitionists) who might help in his mission to liberate the slaves.

To carry out his mission, Brown needed guns and money too—a great deal of money—and his experiences in the Kansas struggle were to prove invaluable in his efforts to get what he wanted. Indeed, without them Brown could never have embarked on his "grand scheme," for throughout his fund-raising campaigns in the East, he used Kansas as a blind, beseeching audiences to give money, guns, and supplies to save Kansas for freedom, when he secretly planned to use these for his larger mission in the South itself. However reprehensible such deception may seem, in Brown's mind it was perfectly justifiable because he believed his ends not only were right, they were the will of God. For Brown was convinced now that God was calling him to a greater destiny than the skirmishes he had been waging against slavery in the West, and (as he put it himself) he devoted "his whole being, mental, moral, and physical, all that he had and was," to the fulfillment of his divine task. And that task was to incite a slave insurrection in the South, one that in God's hands would either destroy slavery in a carnage of racial violence, or ignite a civil war in which slavery would die and the sins of this whole nation would be washed away with blood.

Lawrence Lader

NEW YORK'S BLOODIEST WEEK

AND

Adrian Cook

ARMIES OF THE STREETS: THE NEW YORK CITY DRAFT RIOTS OF 1863

The Great New York City Draft Riot of July 1863 was the largest single act of civil insurrection in our history. While recent research by historian Adrian Cook has established that the total killed was far less than the twelve hundred or so that people believed at the time, the event still holds first place in terms of numbers of participants, deaths resulting, and political fears aroused.

In some senses, the riot appears simply the last and biggest of the mid-century urban riots discussed in two earlier articles. Many of the same groups were involved, and exhibited many of the same ethnic and racial hatreds. The riot, too, was a spectacular and convincing test for the uniformed professional police force which, in New York as elsewhere, had been founded largely to deal with explosive mob situations of this kind, if not on this scale.

But careful reading reveals that despite these parallels with the earlier disturbances, both the apparent objectives and the behavior of the draft rioters were unique in many respects, just as they seemed uniquely threatening to the governing authorities at the time.

Lawrence Lader, in the first of the two selections that follow, provides a vivid account of the riot as a whole. Adrian Cook, in the second, looks more closely at the participants and their motives, and goes on to suggest some reasons why the event was the last of its kind. At the same time, he joins the

authors of several articles in this collection in the view that the
mechanisms which have held disintegrative violence in check
over the past century may not work in the future.

NEW YORK'S BLOODIEST WEEK

"We shall have trouble before we are through," George Templeton Strong,
a wealthy New Yorker and staunch friend of Lincoln, warned in his diary
one July morning in 1863. Yet the first nationwide military draft, authorized by Congress on March 3 to fill the critically depleted ranks of the
Union Army, began in a festive mood.

At 9 A.M. on Saturday, July 11, the provost marshal of the Ninth
Congressional District, first in the city to start its drawing, ascended the
platform in his office at 46th Street and Third Avenue. A revolving drum
with thousands of tightly rolled slips of paper was spun. The marshal's
blindfolded assistant drew the first name—William Jones. The crowd
laughed, and someone shouted, "Poor Jones!" Each succeeding name was
greeted with similar banter, that of a prominent alderman, undoubtedly
expected to buy his way out of the draft under the much-disputed $300
exemption payment, eliciting cries of "There's three hundred for sure!"

Such "good feeling" was the rule of the day, reported the New York
Tribune. There was no premonition of disaster; only slightly strengthened
police patrols at the draft offices. Yet by Monday morning, New York
would be torn by the bloodiest riot in its history and would stand on the
brink of revolution.

The portents had been gathering for months. New York's Copperhead
press—the *Day Book, Express, Freeman's Journal,* and *Daily News* among
others—had been attacking the draft furiously. Governor Horatio Seymour
himself abetted the attack by insisting the draft was unconstitutional. A
Democrat elected in 1862, he had kept faith with the Union by rushing
seventeen regiments of militia to Gettysburg. But his position was equivocal, and in repeatedly demanding that the draft be stopped, he came disturbingly close to the Copperhead line.

There was nothing equivocal, however, about Fernando Wood, former
mayor and now a congressman. Elected to Congress in 1863, Wood seized
on the draft as the perfect issue to rouse his supporters, mainly Irish immigrants from the Bowery, the docks, and the Five Points tenements. Wood
had no trouble inciting great segments of the city's workers. They were
already embittered by the two controversial exemption clauses in the Conscription Act. One clause allowed any drafted man to gain release by hiring
a suitable substitute. The other allowed any draftee to buy his way out of
the Army by paying $300 to the government.

Either escape was far beyond the reach of the average workingman.
Even in the inflationary cycle of 1863, he would be lucky to earn $500 a

year, making the $300 exemption virtually impossible, the hired substitute a dream. Quite logically, the draft made this "A rich man's war and a poor man's fight." One workingman's letter to the New York *Times* asserted ". . . that $300 has made us nobodies, vagabonds and cast-outs of society. . . . We are the poor rabble and the rich rabble is our enemy by this law. . . ."

The $300 exemption gave Lincoln weeks of agonizing indecision. Finally he drew up a memorandum, summing up the arguments in its favor. Quite clearly his own arguments failed to satisfy him, and in the end he buried the memorandum in his file. The controversial exemption clause was allowed to stand, a fateful monument to political expediency.

The provost marshal's decision to start the drawing in New York on a Saturday was clearly foolhardy. Thousands of workers, with a whole Sunday ahead of them to churn up their bitterness in every corner bar, woke up to find their names listed in the papers. What had seemed only an ominous threat—that very day Governor Seymour had promised to stop the draft by sending his adjutant general to Washington—now became harsh reality.

All that Sunday afternoon New York's East Side was crowded with angry, cursing men. First and Second Avenue bars were jammed. The volunteer fire companies, often unofficial headquarters for the local Democratic machine, were leading centers of unrest. Some companies raised pools to buy exemption for drafted members. Others, like Fire Engine Company No. 33 on 58th Street near Broadway, proudly called "The Roughs," promised more direct action, telling a *Herald* reporter that ". . . if Lincoln attempts to enforce the draft in New York in violation of state authority, there will be black eyes and bloody noses."

Sam Galligan, known as "The Bully Boy" and described by the *Times* as "a well-known wire-puller of the Ward," went from bar to bar, organizing his cronies. The employees of a contracting firm agreed to meet en masse in an empty lot near Central Park early Monday morning. The stevedores decided to join them. Southern agents with ready cash, pro-Administration papers claimed later, helped fan the revolt. John Andrews, an aristocratic-looking Virginian, rode a plodding gray mare up and down the East Side streets, corralling friends and giving impromptu addresses at busy corners.

At 10 A.M. on Monday, July 13, Captain Charles Jenkins, the provost marshal, reopened the draft. But there was no hilarity then, only catcalls and hisses as each name was drawn.

Jenkins had drawn about seventy names when a pistol was fired outside his window. Paving stones and brickbats were thrown into the room. The crowd inside grabbed tables and chairs and hurled them at the draft officers. The small police detail barely managed to help Jenkins and his aides escape through the back door. Then the police were overwhelmed. Reported the *Tribune:* "They were knocked down, were beaten with fists, with clubs, with stones. . . ." Cans of kerosene were splashed across the floor. A few minutes later the building was in flames, the fire spreading to adjoining buildings on Third Avenue whose upper floors were occupied by women and children.

The clanging fire bell on 51st Street brought Fire Chief John Decker and two loyal engine companies to the scene. They unrolled their hoses, but the howling mob fought them off, threatening to kill them. Decker pleaded with the mob to let him save the rest of the street. But it was more than an hour, and most of the houses were in ruins, before he could use his hoses.

Since ten o'clock emergency messages had been flooding Metropolitan Police Headquarters on Mulberry Street, at the lower end of the city. The police telegraph system connected Superintendent John Kennedy simultaneously with all 32 precincts, and he immediately summoned all reserve platoons to duty. But the mob had cut down the telegraph poles, rendering twelve miles of wire useless and putting Kennedy out of touch with most of the upper half of the city. He decided to drive uptown in his carriage to investigate.

Kennedy had no idea of the extent of the riot until he found himself in the middle of the mob. A handsome, powerfully built man of sixty, he was immediately recognized, attacked, and knocked to the ground. "The mob nearly killed him," the *Tribune* reported. "They beat him, dragged him through the streets by his head, pitched him into a horsepond, rolled him into mud-gutters, dragged him through piles of filth indescribable." Kennedy saved himself only by shouting to a prominent member of the community, John Eagen, on the fringe of the mob. Eagen managed to fight off the attackers while Kennedy raced across a vacant lot to high ground. Here he was cornered and beaten again. By the time a small squad of police arrived, the mob must have thought Kennedy dead. His body was placed on a passing wagon and taken to police headquarters, where he remained under medical care for the rest of the week.

The senior member of the Police Board, Thomas Acton, now took command, conferring immediately with Mayor George Opdyke at City Hall. The defense of the city actually rested in Acton's hands since the state administration in 1857 had vested all power in the Metropolitan Police Board. This turned out well for the city. A police force packed with Fernando Wood appointments might have offered only token resistance to the mob.

With only 800 men on duty that day against a mob that would soon number 50,000, Acton's strategy was to concentrate his force at police headquarters and City Hall to protect the banks, federal installations, major hotels, and stores in the lower half of the city. The futility of limited resistance was already being demonstrated at Third Avenue and 43rd Street, where 44 policemen under Sergeant McCredie of the fifteenth precinct clashed with the mob. Only 5 of the 44 came through unwounded. One officer, after being beaten almost to death with crowbars, was saved by John Eagen's wife, who flung her body on the policeman's to shield him from the mob.

A fifty-man company of the Army's Invalid Corps (wounded veterans now on guard duty, rushed into action because of the shortage of troops) was cut to pieces even more brutally. Marched up Third Avenue, they fired directly into the mob; no one seemed to know whether they used bullets or blank cartridges. Then, fighting with bayonets, the soldiers were surrounded and cut off by hundreds of rioters. A few soldiers tried to flee for their lives, "hunted like dogs," reported the *Times.* One was left dead in the gutter on 41st Street. Another fled to the high rocks near 42nd Street, where he was beaten "almost to a jelly," said the *Tribune,* and tossed over a precipice.

By noon the city was virtually in the hands of the mob. Major General John Wood, commander of the Department of the East, and Brigadier General Harvey Brown, who commanded federal troops in the city, sent desperate messages for help to the Brooklyn Navy Yard, Governor's Island, and federal forts as far away as Massachusetts. The few hundred federal troops in the city had to be stationed at vital points like the arsenal on Elm Street. By midnight the first uniformed reinforcements had arrived: several companies of marines with howitzers and cannon, 300 sailors from the Brooklyn Navy Yard with revolvers and cutlasses, and police reserves from Brooklyn. By early Tuesday morning there were still only a thousand federal troops in the city. Since at least half had to guard federal installations in the lower city, General Brown, who cooperated closely with Acton, could keep only a small force of soldiers at police headquarters to join the police in flying squads against the rioters uptown.

The anger of the mob was now turned in a new direction. Under John Andrews' leadership, they were attacking not only the draft but all symbols of authority and wealth. They swarmed down Lexington Avenue, screaming "Down with the rich!" At 46th Street they plundered three fine homes, then burned them to the ground.

Another group of rioters attacked the provost marshal's office at 29th Street and Broadway, first plundering an expensive jewelry store on the main floor. Another mob attacked the armory at Second Avenue and 21st Street, used by the government for the manufacture of rifles. The 35-man Broadway squad fought off the mob for an hour, but when the rioters started to set fire to the building, Acton ordered it abandoned. The police managed to escape by squeezing through a tiny hole in the rear wall and fleeing to the eighteenth precinct police station, where they stripped off their uniforms. The station was later burned to the ground.

The Negro population, numbering less than 15,000, suffered most of all. No Negro dared appear on the street. "Small mobs are chasing isolated Negroes as hounds would chase a fox," Major Edward S. Sanford of the U.S. Military Telegraph Service wired Secretary of War Stanton. Many hotels, fearful of being attacked, displayed large signs: "No Niggers in back!" Abraham Franklin, who supported himself and his mother as a coachman, managed to get to his mother's house on Seventh Avenue to make sure she was safe. They talked a few minutes, then decided to pray together. A group of rioters burst open the door, beat Franklin, and hanged him before his mother's eyes.

Peter Heuston, a 63-year-old Mohawk Indian and army veteran of the Mexican War, was mistaken for a Negro and beaten to death near his home on Roosevelt Street, leaving an orphaned daughter of eight.

The mob's savagery to the Negro sprang from complex motivations—economic, social, and religious. Most of its members were Irish. Comprising over half the city's foreign-born population of 400,000, out of a total of about 814,000, the Irish were the main source of cheap labor, virtually its peon class. Desperately poor and lacking real roots in the community, they had the most to lose from the draft. Further, they were bitterly afraid that even cheaper Negro labor would flood the North if slavery ceased to exist.

All the frustrations and prejudices the Irish had suffered were brought to a boiling point by the draft. At pitiful wages they had slaved on the railroads and canals, had been herded into the most menial jobs as carters and stevedores. Many newspaper ads repeated the popular prejudice: "No Irish need apply." An Irish domestic worker was lucky to earn seven dollars a month. Their crumbling frame tenements in areas like the Five Points were the worst slums in the city. Already pressed to the wall, the Irish could logically view the draft as the final instrument of oppression by the rich. One worker wrote the *Times:* "We love our wives and children more than the rich because we got not much besides them; and we will not go to leave them at home for to starve. . . ."

In an objective statement of the Irish role in the riots, *Harper's Weekly* later pleaded that it "be remembered . . . that in many wards of the city the Irish were during the late riot staunch friends of law and order. . . ." Many loyal fire companies were made up of Irishmen. Irish priests opposed the rioters at every step, on risking his life to succor Colonel Henry O'Brien as he was being beaten to death, another persuading a mob not to burn Columbia College at 49th Street and Madison Avenue. Most important of all, a large segment of the Metropolitan Police were Irishmen who fought the mob with a bravery and devotion probably unequaled in police history.

In the war itself, four New York Irish regiments made impressive records. A former Irish editor, Brigadier General Francis Thomas Meagher, commanded the Irish Brigade. The Irish distinguished themselves at Antietam and Fredericksburg, losing 471 wounded and dead in the latter battle. Of 144,000 Irishmen in the Union Army, over 51,000 were from New York.

But on that Monday afternoon, unfortunately, their pent-up hatred of the Negro exploded in its most savage form. Its object was the Orphan Asylum for Colored Children, a four-story building on Fifth Avenue and 43rd Street, where 233 children were housed.

"Clamoring around the house like demons," as the *Tribune* described it, the mob burst the door with axes. The children knelt with Superintendent William E. Davis to pray. Then a long line of frightened boys and girls, two of them infants carried in teachers' arms, followed Davis out the rear door.

The mob surged through the building, stripping it bare. Hundreds of beds were carried from the dormitory wing. Women and boys grabbed them and carted them down the avenue—a strange procession that one reporter estimated ran for ten blocks. Carpets, desks, chairs, pictures, books, even the orphans' clothes, were tossed out the windows to the waiting plunderers. Then the handsome building was set on fire.

Fire Chief Decker and two engine companies responded to the call, Decker racing alone into the building, struggling to extinguish the brands tossed by the mob. But rioters followed him, setting new fires. Decker went back, accompanied by six of his men, and put them out again.

This time two dozen rioters grabbed him and would have beaten him to death had not ten firemen rushed to his rescue and warned that their chief would be taken only over their dead bodies. Frustrated, the mob turned suddenly on the Negro children, who huddled in a circle on the corner watching their home go up in flame.

Twenty children were cut off from the main group. "There is little doubt that many and perhaps all of these helpless children would have been murdered in cold blood," reported the *Times.* But a young Irishman on the edge of the crowd, Paddy McCaffrey, aided by two drivers from the 42nd Street cross-town bus line and members of Engine Company No. 18, surrounded the children and fought off the mob. While rioters pelted them with stones, they managed to get the children to the thirty-fifth precinct station house. An hour later the orphan asylum was a mess of charred rubble.

Paddy McCaffrey's heroism was one more contradiction of the assumption that all Irishmen supported the rioters.

At the height of the riot that Monday evening, Commissioner Acton got word that the mob was marching on City Hall and police headquarters. Acton decided it was time for the first counteroffensive. He assigned 200 men to Inspector Dan Carpenter, "the Metropolitan war horse of grizzled locks and martial figure," as one paper described him. Carpenter, promising "to win this fight or never come back alive," led his main force up Broadway with two parallel columns of fifty men ready to strike from the side streets. The police caught the mob by surprise. "Men fell by the dozens under the sturdy blows of the police who had orders to 'take no prisoners,'" the *Times* reported. ". . . Broadway looked like a battleground thickly strewn with prostrate forms."

Another mob, meanwhile, had invaded the *Tribune* building across the park from City Hall. Acton had decided to make his second major attack. He combined a force of almost fifty men at City Hall with the first-precinct reserves and rushed them to the *Tribune* building. Then he ordered Carpenter's men to catch the rioters from the rear.

"We struck them like a thunder-bolt," one officer recalled later. The floors were heaped with bleeding rioters. Hundreds, fleeing down side streets, were caught by Carpenter. "It was a striking illustration of the cowardice of the mob when confronted by a handful of determined officers of the law," the *Times* exulted the next morning. More important, it had not only saved the *Tribune, Times,* and *Post* buildings from destruction but demonstrated that the police still controlled the lower city.

That night New York was in turmoil. A Negro cartman, trying to escape under cover of darkness, was caught by a gang of men and boys and hanged from one of the fine spreading chestnut tress on Clarkson Street. Only a few feet from the consecrated ground of St. John's Cemetery, they built a fire under him, dancing wildly around the roasting flesh.

Shortly after midnight, a deluge of rain drove the rioters temporarily from the streets. At 1:15 A.M. the indefatigable Inspector Carpenter set out with a small force to cut down the body of the Negro cartman. Then Acton received a message, warning of a new attack on police headquarters. Carpenter had to bring back his men.

Tuesday was hot and muggy; a heavy pall of black smoke rose from innumerable fires hanging over the city. Mobs filled the streets at dawn "increasing in power and audacity," noted Ellen Leonard, a young New Englander staying at her brother's house on Nineteenth Street.

News from Gettysburg sharpened the tension. Decisively beaten in the three-day battle there, General Robert E. Lee had withdrawn his battered army and on the night of July 13 had crossed the Potomac and gained comparative safety in Virginia. Northern jubilation over the victory was sharply tempered by the realization that Lee's army had, after all, escaped destruction, and when the government ordered New York National Guard regiments returned from Pennsylvania to New York City to deal with the riot it was commonly assumed that this played directly into Lee's hands. Actually, the escape had already taken place; the National Guard regiments had seen little combat service in the Gettysburg campaign, and their departure did not deprive the Union commander, General George G. Meade, of any essential support once the Confederates had gone south of the Potomac. Nevertheless, the fact that Union troops had to be sent to New York at a time when a dangerous Confederate army still needed attention was profoundly dismaying and the *Times,* not surprisingly, declared editorially that the New York rioters were "the left wing of Lee's army."

Although some reporters considered the mob a directionless rabble, others noted disturbing signs of organization—the well-constructed barricades, for example, on First Avenue between Eleventh and Fourteenth streets, used as fortress and virtual assemblyground by the mob.

John Andrews was still supplying leadership on the East Side. Ellen Leonard saw him on horseback that morning, noting that "crowds quickly gathered around him . . . from all the neighboring alleys and greeted him with shouts and cheers." The *Times* added, "We have not a doubt there are other men, agents direct from Richmond, now in the city. . . ." When the police later tried to identify one of the most daring mob leaders killed on Second Avenue, and found under his grimy work clothes a handsome vest and an expensive linen shirt, the suspicions seemed justified.

Pitched battles, even more furious than Monday's, raged all day. A company of soldiers faced one mob at point-blank range on Delancey Street, fought them off, and was attacked again on Pitt Street. A marine detachment was forced to retreat before another mob on Grand Street. Almost 5,000 rioters invaded the Union Steam Works at 22nd Street and Second Avenue, where thousands of government carbines were stored. A strong force of police under Inspector George Dilks stormed the building, piled the carbines on wagons, and marched quickly downtown to relieve Mayor Opdyke's house, which was under attack. Meanwhile the mob retook the Steam Works, and Dilks had to return and fight for it again, floor by floor.

Inspector Carpenter with 300 police battled a mob estimated at 10,000 on Second Avenue. In phalanx formation the police hammered their way through the rioters. But at 34th Street they stepped into a trap. Hundreds of rioters, placed on rooftops and in windows, picked off the police with guns and bricks. Colonel Henry O'Brien offered to rush a detachment of his Eleventh New York Volunteers, a new regiment still being organized, to clear the avenue with two fieldpieces while Carpenter's men methodically routed the rioters from each building.

Colonel O'Brien, who lived on Second Avenue near 35th Street, soon paid for his daring. An Irishman himself, he foolishly assumed that his name would protect him from retribution and returned home alone a few hours later, stopping at a neighborhood drugstore. A crowd quickly gathered outside the store. O'Brien stepped out boldly, sword in one hand, pistol in the other. A woman hurled a brick, he fired, and then the mob swallowed him up, beating him, the *Tribune* reported, with "every club that could be brought to bear, every kick or stone that could be thrown. . . ." He was dragged, still breathing, over the rough cobblestones to his own courtyard, where for hours women and boys, as well as men, danced around the body. They paused only to allow a priest to administer the last rites. When a neighboring druggist offered the dying man a glass of water, his store was sacked.

That same morning Governor Seymour arrived from Long Branch, New Jersey. From City Hall, after conferring with Opdyke, he issued a strong proclamation calling for the restoration of law and order. Then a large crowd gathered in the park, and Seymour went to the steps of City Hall to address them—a speech that has remained the most controversial act of his controversial career.

"Let me assure you that I am your friend," he told his listeners. "You have been my friends. And now I assure you, my fellow citizens, that I am here to show you a test of my friendship. I wish to inform you that I have sent my Adjutant General to Washington to confer with the authorities there and to have this draft suspended and stopped. . . ."

Seymour's supporters have always claimed his first responsibility was to calm the city—that nothing more was implied in his words. But Administration papers bristled at this offer of "friendship" and obvious appeasement of the rioters. "He was proclaiming with all the authority attaching to his character and official position," stated the *Times,* "that mob law ought under certain circumstances to over-ride that of Congress. . . ."

Mayor Opdyke now was harassed both by Seymour and the Peace Democrats who controlled his own Board of Aldermen and City Council. While Seymour was speaking, the aldermen and council were preparing a $2,500,00 Conscription Exemption Bond bill which would allow the city to give $300 to each drafted man to buy his way out of the service. They passed the bill on Wednesday, and Opdyke immediately vetoed it, stating, "I felt it would be purchasing the peace of the city too dearly to thus bow to dictation of the mob. . . ."

The real struggle was at the barricades on Eighth Avenue between 37th and 43rd streets and on First Avenue between Eleventh and Fourteenth streets. Commissioner Acton and General Brown combined strong forces of soldiers and police, and by midnight took the barricades. But fighting went on all night.

From her room Ellen Leonard watched the rioters still surging through Nineteenth Street and noted that her "neighborhood was wholly at the mercy of the mob. . . . Destruction and death were on every side." She tried to sleep "when a sudden rush and scream brought me again to my window . . . I distinctly heard dreadful cries and caught these broken words, 'Oh my brothers! My brothers! Save me!'"

Not many hours afterward, on Wednesday afternoon, Ellen Leonard and her household were to play a heroic role in one of the decisive battles of the week. That morning a mob of 5,000 had been cleared from Seventh Avenue and 32nd Street by a force of U.S. artillery firing grape at point-blank range and killing scores of rioters. But the mob collected again in greater strength at Nineteenth Street and First Avenue. Colonel Cleveland Winslow, with one of the few small infantry detachments available for street-fighting, and Colonel Edward Jardine, with a battery of two howitzers, marched to meet them.

As Winslow's men rushed forward, they were attacked from every window and rooftop by rifle fire and bricks. The infantry was cut to pieces. Winslow had to order an immediate retreat. Jardine, struck by a bullet in the leg, crumpled to the pavement.

The regimental surgeon helped Colonel Jardine and another wounded soldier escape down Nineteenth Street. Ellen saw them from her window. She rushed downstairs and begged them to take refuge in the house. The Colonel and the surgeon were hidden in the cellar, the soldier taken to the top floor where Ellen and her mother could nurse him. Ellen's brother was sent for help, escaping over the rooftops at the rear. "Mrs. P.," who lived downstairs, waited calmly in the sitting room.

The rioters were combing the street, house by house. "A few moments we waited in breathless silence," Ellen wrote later. "Then came a rush up the stairs and the bell rang violently." The mob demanded that the soldiers be given up. Mrs. P. answered them calmly. Yes, they had been here, but had escaped by the back yard. One man pointed a carbine at her head. She brushed it aside, saying, "You know I am a woman, and it might frighten me." They threatened to burn the house down. "My only son works as you do, and perhaps in the same shop with some of you, for seventy cents a day," she told them omitting the fact that he had left a few weeks before to join the Union Army.

The sentinel at the stairs, younger and better dressed than the others, drew Mrs. P. aside and warned her that it was better to let them search the house. She agreed, trying to remain calm while they rushed to the cellar. They found the surgeon first and dragged him upstairs, beating him viciously. But Colonel Jardine, lying wounded on the cellar floor, insisted he was an ordinary citizen accidentally hurt in the fray.

Four men pointed muskets at his head. He told them to shoot—he would be dead soon from loss of blood anyway. But he begged them to bring a priest first. The request seemed to disconcert them. Then they left the house as suddenly as they had come, not even bothering to search the upper floors.

The women waited fearfully all that evening. Not until after midnight did they hear the welcome tramp of marching feet. Ellen's brother had reached police headquarters, and returned with a large contingent of soldiers and police. The whole party was rescued and taken to the well-guarded St. Nicholas Hotel. Even the surgeon, they learned, had managed to escape.

In the early hours of Thursday morning, the mob attacked a government warehouse on Greenwich Street, where 20,000 muskets were stored. This cache might have given them control of the city if Acton had not learned of the plan in time and sent a large headquarters force to stop them.

It was almost dawn before the turning point arrived. The steady tramp of thousands of feet—the Tenth and Fifty-sixth regiments, New York National Guard—was heard along lower Broadway. At 4 A.M. the perfectly formed ranks of the crack Seventh Regiment wheeled up Canal Street. They were the first elements of the state militia rushed from Gettysburg. Nine more New York regiments as well as one Michigan regiment arrived in the next two days. The city was out of danger at last.

From Washington on Thursday the President announced that he was standing firm: the draft would be resumed in New York at the first practicable date. Late that morning a detachment of police broke into No. 10 East Eleventh Street and arrested John Andrews, "this howling fiend, this emissary and spy of the Rebels," as the *Tribune* called him, who ironically enough was found with his Negro mistress.

The mob was to make its last stand on the East Side. Five thousand desperate men attacked elements of the Seventh Regiment on Second Avenue in what the *Times* labeled "the most sanguinary fight of the whole riot." Bullets and bricks from the rooftops killed fifteen soldiers before another 700 troops arrived to clear the avenue with artillery and bayonet.

It was the decisive battle. On Friday morning, the Mayor could announce: "The riotous assemblages have been dispersed."

On Friday, also, John Hughes, Roman Catholic Archbishop of New York, made an address from the balcony of his house at 36th Street and Madison Avenue. A loyal supporter of the Union, he had traveled in Europe as Lincoln's personal agent, speaking for the Union cause in Rome, France, and Ireland. He had no love for abolitionists, but he did not like mob rule either, and on Thursday it had been announced that he would address "the men of New York who are now called in many of the papers rioters." The wording of this proclamation disturbed the New York *Times,* which wondered what other term could be applied to men who had burned down public buildings, but the speech was a firm one, and it served to tamp down the last embers of revolt.

While the riots disappeared from the headlines by the end of the week, their repercussions continued. The President appointed Major General John A. Dix, former governor of New York, to the eastern command, and set August 19 as the date for the resumption of the draft. But Seymour was intractable. In letter after letter he argued with Lincoln that the city's quotas had been unfairly set, that prejudiced officials would corrupt the drawing, that he could fill New York's quotas immediately with volunteers. Lincoln rejected each excuse patiently but firmly. The draft was completed —but at some expense to the campaign against Lee.

"As it is quite possible we may be obliged to detach some of your troops to enforce the draft and to bring on the drafted men," General in Chief Henry W. Halleck wired General George G. Meade, commander of the Army of the Potomac, on July 29, "I think it would be best to hold for the present the upper line of the Rappahannock without further pursuit of Lee." The necessity had to be met, and Meade told Halleck on August 16, "I have sent you my best troops and some of my best officers"—almost 10,000 soldiers from the Army of the Potomac.

Firm as he had been with Seymour, Lincoln squashed all attempts to link the New York riots and leading Peace Democrats with Richmond. When James R. Gilmore of the New York *Tribune* called on Lincoln and proposed an investigation of the riot's causes, the President refused, supposedly saying, "One rebellion at a time is about as much as we can conveniently handle."

The ironic conclusion to the riots was the 1863 draft itself. Of 79,975 men conscripted in New York State, 54,765 were exempted on physical and other grounds, 15,912 bought their way out for $300, 6,998 furnished substitutes, and only 2,300—not many more than had been killed and wounded in the riots themselves—were added to the Union Army. In the North as a whole, in fact, the four drafts of 1863 and 1864 produced about 52,000 troops.

Yet the value of conscription could not be measured solely by the number of men drafted. Each state was given a quota at each call for troops, and officials tried to meet the quotas ahead of time by swelling their voluntary enlistments. So the threat of a draft was an invaluable asset as a constant prod. States and cities that raised more than their share of men could credit the extras to their quota at the time of the next draft.

There was a further irony in the attention focused by the riots on the $300 exemption clause. During the debates on a new draft law early in 1864, a large block of senators and congressmen opposed the exemption as "class legislation." Lincoln himself, with an election only a few months off, joined the opposition in June, thus daring the political wrath of those in wealth and power who supported the exemption. The final bill, passed on July 4, established a new system of bounty payments in graduated amounts for one-year, two-year, and three-year volunteers.

But when the $300 exemption came to a vote, both Fernando and Ben Wood, the most frenzied opponents of the exemption as a crime against the poor, refrained from voting!

And to add to the complex irony, the War Department during the fall, 1864, draft was so intent on placating New York that 18,448 men who had enlisted in the Navy during the four preceding years were credited to the city. Thus was its quota virtually filled by paper logistics. Thus did sailors from Iowa or Michigan, who happened to have signed their Navy papers in New York, keep the specter of another draft riot from a city that had already known the worst explosion in the nation's history.

ARMIES OF THE STREETS:
THE NEW YORK CITY DRAFT RIOTS

Three hundred and fifty-two people can be identified as rioters. No information, except their names, is available on ninety-two of them. Of the remaining, 241 were male and nineteen female. Three of the latter were

From Adrian Cook, *Armies of the Streets: The New York City Draft Riots of 1863* (Lexington: University Press of Kentucky, 1974), pp. 195–209. Reprinted by permission of the publisher.

young girls: Mary Ann Carmody, 10; Honora Murphy, 11; and Catharine Waters, 12. [1] The age of 235 of the rioters can be ascertained: 66 were under 21; 87 were between 21 and 30 years of age; 40 were between 31 and 40; 27 were from 41 to 50 years of age; 13 were from 51 to 60; and two, Luke Featherston and Matthew Zweick, were over 60. The 63 males under 20 and the 29 over 45 years of age were not liable to the draft.

. . .

The occupation of 168 rioters can be determined. Five, perhaps eight, of them could be described as middle-class or professionals of some kind. The most distinguished rioter was R. S. McCulloh, professor of mechanics and physics at Columbia College. He had strong southern sympathies, and a few months later he crossed the lines to throw in his lot with the Confederacy. [2] . . . Forty-seven had occupations that required some skill or training: tailor, carpenter, plumber, blacksmith, boilermaker, stonemason, barber, cabinet maker, shoemaker, rope maker, brass-finisher, bricklayer, glass-cutter, gunsmith. [3] Fifty-seven rioters held jobs calling for no special skills: carman, peddler, barkeeper, cartman, housewife, washerwoman, domestic, street paver, gardener, hostler, milkman. [4] And fifty-six were laborers or factory workers. [5] Out of the eighty-three rioters questioned about their literacy, forty-three could not read or write. This was a mob of the industrial age, with the people at the bottom of the social pyramid predominating. [6]

An overwhelming percentage of the rioters were Irish. Out of 184 whose country of birth can be determined, 117 were born in Ireland, forty in the United States, sixteen in Germany, seven in England, and one each in France, Canada, Denmark, and Switzerland. [7] Most of the American-born were from New York.

. . .

Until July 1863, most of the rioters had led quiet, respectable lives. Very few had any records of involvement with the law. Some, like John Hussey, "the Terror of the Hook," may have had a reputation as brawlers, but only a handful of the rioters can be called professional criminals.

. . .

After the riots, Mayor Opdyke said that "while the riot was ostensibly a resistance to the draft, the rioters themselves were not, in general, persons liable to be drafted. A great proportion of them were persons under twenty years of age, and many were convicts, thieves, and abandoned characters, the scum of this great city, and the hasty importations from other cities." [8] There was a certain measure of truth in the first part of his analysis, but hardly any at all in the second. The rioters were a fair cross-section of New York's younger male working class.

Most of the roaming bands of rioters who looted stores, wrecked Negroes' homes, invaded brothels, and beat up Republicans were quite small, numbering from twenty to fifty people. . . . Typically, numbers of "half-grown boys" would tag along with the adult rowdies. The longer police or troops took to arrive at a place offering rich pickings, like Brooks Brothers' store or the Gibbons house, naturally the more people would join the looters, but the attacks were always initiated by small groups.[9]

The mobs who met the police and troops in pitched battle were larger, but it does not seem that there were more than three hundred hard-core street fighters gathered in one place at any time during the riots. The *New York Times* estimated that the whole number of real rioters was only from two to three thousand.[10] The crowds who filled the streets were mostly spectators,[11] though numbers of them might take a marginal part in the rioting: adolescent boys by throwing stones, women by shrieking obscenities and threats at the police and soldiers or, more rarely, by putting stones in their stockings to make slingshots.[12]

. . .

The Draft Riots were fundamentally an insurrection of anarchy, an outburst against any kind of governmental control by the people near the bottom of society. The temporary powerlessness of the authorities released a flood of violence and resentment that was usually kept repressed. As the hours went by, the riot itself created a devil-may-care mood of euphoria that led to more rioting. A wild melange of motives drove the mob on. Obviously, there was strong opposition to the draft and to the war. Rioters cheered for Jefferson Davis and planned to hang Horace Greeley if they could catch him. Enrolling officers and reporters for Republican newspapers were beaten. Revenge for the deaths caused by his troops was the motive for the murder of Colonel O'Brien, and after being roughly handled by the police, or fired upon by the troops, other rioters may well have felt the same way. Something for nothing is always an attractive proposition, especially if other people seem to be getting away with it. "I took said property because every one else took it," said Theodore Arnold when he was arrested for looting.[13]

Some took advantage of the breakdown in law and order to settle old grudges, . . . or to extort money.

. . .

One extremely strong and persistent motive was deep-rooted hatred of Negroes. Many of those arrested for attacks on Negroes or their houses knew their victims before the riots or lived close to them. The implication is clear that they had long been envious of some Negroes' relative prosperity or resented having to dwell in the same neighborhood.[14]

· · ·

At times, with the destruction of the street-sweeping machines and the grain elevators at the Atlantic Docks, the riots took on a Luddite aspect; at times, with the attacks on well-dressed "$300 men," they became class war.

Some people simply drifted into rioting, aided by liberal quantities of drink. . . . Martin Hart, who had arrived in New York from Ireland on June 1, went to live in Harlem and took a job laying gas pipes at Kingsbridge. On the morning of July 15, he went to the dock at 130th Street and Third Avenue, as usual, to take the riverboat to work. Because of the riots, the boat was not running, and after waiting several hours, Hart gave up and started for home. On the way, he fell in with a crowd of rowdies, had several drinks with them, "from the effect of which he became intoxicated and then danced several times for the amusement of the crowd." Eventually, they straggled into Harlem and began demanding money from storekeepers. A few moments later, Hart was in jail. [15]

· · ·

There was also a certain element of what can only be called sexual vigilantism present in the riots. Several of the Negroes who fell foul of the mobs were married to white women. "What made you marry a nigger?" Daniel McGovern asked Mrs. Martin. "I told him I could marry who I liked—That he could marry who he liked," Mrs Martin recalled. [16] . . . Bordellos and prostitutes catering to Negroes were attacked, and eventually this broadened into an attack on all brothels. [17]

Unlike most American outbreaks of mass violence, the Draft Riots were directed initially against the state. Occurring in the summer, in the middle of a heat wave, they followed a familiar pattern, but there were one or two unusual features about the Draft Riots. First, rioting tended to diminish as darkness fell, instead of becoming more intense. Second, during most disturbances, fighting rises to a crescendo during the early morning hours, when people are going to work, and in the late afternoon, when they are going home. Except on the afternoon of the first day, Monday, July 13, this was not true of the Draft Riots. The paralysis of economic activity was complete, and few Negroes were foolhardy enough to risk going to their jobs.

Thoughts of conspiracy and subversion seem reasonable in times of great internal conflict and uncertainty, and just as the Gordon Riots were attributed to the machinations of French and American agents, and as the Jacobites were blamed for stirring up the London riots of 1736 over cheap Irish labor and the Gin Act, so many Republicans assumed that the Draft Riots were the result of a Confederate plot. [18] . . . Needless to say, there is not the slightest evidence to support any of these paranoid fantasies.

· · ·

The argument, sometimes heard, that the riots were sparked and fueled by white workers' (especially longshoremen's) fears of competition from cheap black labor will not stand up to examination. Only three longshoremen can be identified as rioters, and none of them was involved in attacking Negroes. . . . Only one Negro longshoreman, William Johnson, is known to have been beaten during the riots. [19]

. . .

In fact, it was the Negroes of New York City who were being undercut by competition from cheap labor. Employers preferred to hire immigrants, especially Germans, who would work long hours for low pay. In the 1850s and 1860s, Negroes were even being forced out of menial positions traditionally assigned to them, such as waiters' and barbers' jobs.

. . .

The authorities did not show up well during the riots. Even allowing for the disruption of communications by bad weather, the federal government was lamentably slow in getting reinforcements to New York. General Sandford was utterly unfit to command. . . . The police were brave enough, but the riots showed clearly that their training was grievously inadequate. Well-disciplined police officers should be able to control crowds much larger than their own numbers; but the police never won a battle during the Draft Riots unless they were numerically equal or superior to the mob.

To the surprise of some and the relief of many, all but a very few of the large number of Irish Catholics on the Metropolitan force remained faithful and did their duty.

. . .

In the early 1870s, riots ceased in New York City. Though immigrants flooded in and poverty, misery, and overcrowding were worse than ever, there were no outbreaks of mass violence. Many reasons can be adduced to explain why this new state of peace came about. A professional fire department replaced the roistering volunteer fire laddies; compulsory education and child labor kept many potential adolescent rioters busy. Industrial expansion and long spells of prosperity meant that, until the 1890s, there were usually few unemployed in New York. The new immigrants of 1870–1914 came from countries where political police were powerful and political activity was repressed. The rise of professional baseball and football provided an alternative to rioting as a form of communal weekend entertainment, and the establishment of working-class amusement centers like Coney Island supplied another safety valve. "We have to have it," an English visitor was told, "yes, sir, without it New York itself would burn, the people would go mad, there would be nothing to work off the general cussedness; New York without an outlet like Coney Island would soon be an inferno."[20] Cheap transportation—the bicycle and rapid-transit lines—made it possible for tenement dwellers to escape from the city now and again. There are indications that the police adopted a policy of aggressive patrol in the late 1880s.[21]

All these developments helped in greater or lesser degree to keep the peace in New York City. But the main reason why New York was free of major civil disturbances in the last quarter of the nineteenth century and the first years of the twentieth is that in the mid-1870s Honest John Kelly put together on a permanent basis the machine that Fernando Wood had tried to create and that Boss Tweed had temporarily succeeded in building. Kelly and Croker broke up the ward gangs, which only strengthened the district leaders and made it possible for them to rebel against the Tammany leadership.[22] Under that leadership, the interests of the city's multifarious ethnic groups, the police, and the politicians were harmonized. The result was a corrupt, but peaceful, city, free of the violent conflicts of the mid-nineteenth century. Riots did not resume until the machine faltered and failed to adapt to the needs of a new wave of immigrants, a group harder to assimilate than the Irish and Germans, Italians and Jews who had gone before, and whose demands may yet prove American democracy to be a rope of sand.

NOTES

1. The others were Bridget Barrett, Maria Carroll, Ellen Clyne, Mary Corcoran, Maria De Lemastany, Ellen Doyle, Mary Fox, Julia Hennessey, Mary Kennedy, Mary McGovern, Ellen Perkinson, Sarah Pine, Ann Shandley, Ann Farrell, Maria Pilkin, and Mary Ann Driscoll.

2. John Torrey to Hamilton Fish, October 6, 1863, Fish Papers, Columbia.

3. And baker, harness maker, coach maker, machinist, tinsmith, butcher, pianoforte maker, painter, and basket maker.

4. And blacksmith's helper, butcher's boy, stage driver, teamster, drugstore clerk, sailor, junk dealer, tobacconist, hack driver, mattress maker, longshoreman, and storekeeper. In one or two cases, there is contradictory information about rioters' occupations. Henry Tilton described himself as a gardener, but a witness in his case said that he kept a small grocery store at 152 East 32nd Street. Theodore Osterstock called himself a circus rider, but he had apparently been unable to find any employer for his peculiar talents, and at the time of the riots he was proprietor of a lager beer saloon in Greenwich Street.

5. This includes James Shandley, who answered "work in fish market" when asked his occupation; Painter Springstein, who replied "anything I can get to do"; Patrick Merry, who was a cellar-digger, and Daniel Vaughan, a mason's laborer. The last two jobs might conceivably require some skill—the latter more than the former.

6. Dentist, 1; professor, 1; contractor, 1; merchant, 1; real estate agent, 1; lawyer, 1; actor, 1; tinsmith, 1; barber, 1; storekeeper, 2; longshoreman, 3; basketmaker, 1; carman, 5; housewife, 4; domestic, 3; sailor, 6; mattress maker, 1; drug store clerk, 1; butcher, 1; plumber, 3; harness-maker, 1; coach-maker, 1; shoemaker, 5; baker, 2; boilermaker, 5;

blacksmith, 4; painter, 3; cabinet maker, 2; physician, 1; glass-cutter, 1; brass finisher, 1; tailor, 3; rope maker, 1; barkeeper, 3; peddler, 5; driver, 1; grocer, 3; street paver, 1; tobacconist, 1; junk dealer, 1; hack driver, 1; hostler, 3; washerwoman, 2; stage driver, 1; teamster, 1; milkman, 1; gardener, 1; bricklayer, 3; gunsmith, 1; unemployed, 1; carpenter, 4; piano maker, 1; machinist, 1; stonemason, 1; butcher's boy, 2; cartman, 3; blacksmith's boy, 1.

7. The number of Irish among the rioters was actually even higher. At least eleven of those born in the United States had Irish parents of distinctively Irish names. The latter is also true of thirty-one of those whose birthplaces cannot be discovered.

8. Mayor's veto message, July 25, 1863, in Proceedings of the Board of Aldermen, Special Session, July 27, 1863, vol. 150, MARC.

9. See RC [Documents of the New York County Board of Supervisors, 1868, document no. 13], 1:87–89, 210–11, 304–5, 419–22, 424–25, 579–80, 591, 612–13, 730–33, 737–42, 805–9, 852–60; 2:82–83, 250–52, 330–40, 361–64, 367–68, 401–2, 503–4, 567, 601–2, 621–25, 785–86, 807–9. Case of John William Joyce, Grand Jury Dismissals, August 1863, CCB. It is by no means easy to find reliable testimony on the size of the mob, since many people were too scared to take any interest in how many rioters there were, and others used "hundreds" to mean "quite a few." I have relied on witnesses who show elsewhere in their evidence that they were level-headed and accurate observers of detail. Diary of George Templeton Strong, July 13, 1863, Columbia; Claim of Lewis Ward, RC, 1:618–21; Claim of Michael Newman, RC, 2:434–36; Claim of Joseph Hecht, RC, 1:583–85; see also Cases of John Leary, Sr., and John Leary, Jr., Indictments, October 1863, CCB; RC, 1:101–2, 192–94, 214–16, 303–4, 310–18; 581–83, 684–86, 755–57, 765–67; 2:112–13, 257–61, 761, 845–47; Case of James Fingleton, Grand Jury Dismissals, September 1863, CCB. RC, 1:242–43, 357–66, 381–85, 562–64, 714–17; 2:148–50, 252–53, 278–79, 352–53, 413–16, 815–16, 884–88; Claim of Philip Bick, Comptroller's Records.

10. Tuesday, July 21, 1863.

11. One good thing about television coverage of recent riots is that people stay home and watch the disorders, instead of going out into the streets to get in the way of the police and troops.

12. Unknown (probably Caleb Lyon of Lyonsdale) to Charles Sumner, August 1, 1863, Sumner Papers, Houghton Library, Harvard University; Thomas Addis Emmet, *Incidents of My Life. Professional-Literary-Social. With Services in the Cause of Ireland* (New York: G.P. Putnam's Sons, 1911), 184.

13. Case of Theodore Arnold, Indictments, August 1863, CCB.

14. Thus, William Cruise knew Alfred Derrickson before the riots; William Butney and William Williams served on the same ship; Henrady McGovern, and Cumiskie knew the Martins. Maria Pilkin and Mary Ann Driscoll, accused of looting Dr. William Powell's house at 2 Dover Street, lived nearby in Water Street. The Pines and Painter Springstein, arrested for looting in West 32nd Street, all lived in West 30th Street; Maria Carroll, charged with the same offense, lived in West 33rd Street. All the murderers of Abraham Franklin lived within a few blocks of the victim. "This house was attacked by the rioters, who mostly resided in the neighborhood," reported the examiner on the claim of Hannah Sears, RC, 2:144–45. Many of the white victims, of course, were also known to their attackers before the riots; Maria Lydig Daly, *Union Lady,* 251.

15. *New York Daily Transcript,* October 7, 1863; The People vs. Martin Hart, Court of General Sessions, Affidavits, August 1863, CCB.

16. Cases of Patrick Henrady, Thomas Cumiskie, and Daniel McGovern, Indictments, August 1863, CCB.

17. There were also sexual undertones in the indignities to which Negroes were subjected by the rioters, such as being stripped naked. When Patrick Butler pulled Abraham Franklin's body up and down the street, he grabbed hold of the dead man's genitals.

18. See David Brion Davis, *The Slave Power Conspiracy and the Paranoid Style,* The Walter Lynwood Fleming Lectures in Southern History (Baton Rouge: Louisiana State

University Press, 1970); George F. E. Rude, " 'Mother Gin' and the London Riots of 1736," *The Guildhall Miscellany* 10 (1959):61–63; "The Gordon Riots: A Study of the Rioters and Their Victims," *Transactions of the Royal Historical Society,* 5th Series, No. 6 (1956):101; J. P. De Castro, *The Gordon Riots* (London: Oxford University Press, 1926), 217–25; Hibbert, *King Mob,* 122, 169, 171–72.

19. According to the *New York Daily News,* July 23, 1863, white longshoremen beat Johnson, but this cannot be corroborated from any other source. Since the *News* was constantly trying to incite white labor against black, it cannot be considered thoroughly reliable on this matter.

20. Juvenal, *An Englishman in New York* (London: Stephen Swift, 1901), 249.

21. See Reports of Captains—Gangs and Loafers, Police, 1888, Mayor's Papers, Boxes 378, 379, MARC. Captain Thomas M. Ryan, 21st Precinct, to Superintendent William Murray, May 25, 1888, Box 378, and "A Gentleman" to Mayor Abram S. Hewitt, June 29, 1888, Box 379, are typical examples.

22. Alfred H. Lewis, *The Boss: And How He Came to Rule New York* (New York: A. A. Barnes, 1903), 168–69, 221.

Allen W. Trelease

RECONSTRUCTION: THE GREAT EXPERIMENT

The defeat of the Confederacy settled forever the issues of secession and slavery. But it also produced new questions and new problems. How was the Union to be restored and what was the status of the black freedman in America? Attempts to resolve these issues produced the bitter conflicts that made the Reconstruction era the nation's bloodiest period of civil violence. Unprepared to accept the revolutionary social implications of congressional reconstruction mandates, southern whites worked to restore the ante-bellum political, economic, and racial order by force and violence. Twelve years after Lee's surrender, the South was "redeemed" as southern conservatives were returned to power and Reconstruction ended without achieving a position of equality for blacks.

Although the full force of the government had been invoked to save the Union and ultimately to destroy slavery, no comparable effort was made to end Reconstruction violence and to impose a new political, social, and economic order in the South. In the following passage, Allen Trelease examines this tragic era and offers an explanation for the ultimate failure of these years. The result is still with us and, as subsequent essays note, continues to produce violence in our time.

Conservatives and Democrats attacked almost every aspect of Radical reconstruction from its inception. So far as it revolutionized the South politically, it displaced Conservative leaders. They were a kind of ruling class which regarded the Negroes, carpetbaggers, and scalawags as upstarts who had no right to rule and were out to plunder the South. This is the traditional reaction of old ruling classes to the revolutionaries who overthrow them. But Conservative hostility was inspired by more than resentment at the loss of power and prestige. Accustomed to "small government" that performed few public services, Southern whites begrudged much of the aid given by Radical governments to the poor of both races; above all they resented the high taxes levied to finance them. This led, in South Carolina, to taxpayers' conventions which protested Republican fiscal policies and demanded greater economy in government. It created opposition to the public school system in Mississippi and other places. Many Democrats favored government aid to railroads but wanted to give it in other ways or to different lines. And, of course, the whole reconstruction movement represented a victory of the North and Unionists over the South and ex-Confederates. Even when Republicans were elected to office by a clear majority of the local electorate, Democrats regarded them as agents of outside control. When Democrats won elections, they termed it a victory for "home rule."

By far, the greatest cause of Conservative opposition was the Radicals' policy of equal rights for Negroes. The Democrats were everywhere the party of white supremacy. When they did not refer to their opponents as Radicals, they called them "black Republicans." Most Southern whites never lost their outrage at the idea of Negro equality in general, and Negro voting and officeholding in particular. As we have seen, the Republicans made Negroes equal only in politics, and even there white men dominated nearly every state and local government. But for race-conscious Southerners there was no middle ground. One race had to rule; if the party of white supremacy was not in control, then the Negroes were. This is why the phrase "Negro rule" packed such an emotional charge and was so commonly bandied about. White leaders who knew better used the term in order to inflame public opinion and speed the overthrow of Republicans. Racist political demagoguery was a common stock-in-trade among Conservative politicians and newspaper editors. Some Democrats reconciled themselves to Negro jurors, legislators, congressmen, and the like, and they even nominated a few black men themselves in the hope of capturing Negro votes. But they were determined to control black officeholders in the interest of white supremacy. Neither racism nor any other simple formula was enough by itself to account for Conservative bitterness against Radical reconstruction, but racism was certainly the most consistent deeply felt emotion of the white population. Where racism was not strong already, political leaders deliberately stirred it up. It was the greatest handicap Republicans faced in trying to win over white voters who might otherwise have sympathized with Radical objectives.

Conservative opposition took many forms. Since ex-Confederates regarded the scalawags as traitors and the carpetbaggers as foreign plunderers and racial agitators, they treated them accordingly—in everyday life as well as on election days. Except where white Republicans were numerous and relatively well-to-do, they were often ostracized socially. No respectable person would invite them to his house or even talk to them on the street if he could avoid it. Republican businessmen were boycotted and sometimes found it impossible to get credit from banks or other merchants. Active or prominent Republicans as well as white teachers in Negro schools sometimes found it all but impossible to rent houses or rooms in hotels and boardinghouses. If they moved in with Negroes (who were often the only ones to welcome them), they lost status even further, for in Southern eyes it was only the lowest and most degraded whites who associated with Negroes on anything but a master-servant basis. And nothing was too evil to be believed of such persons. Small towns hummed with rumors or rang with outcries against the supposedly shameless Radicals who kept company with blacks and treated them as equals. These conditions did not prevail everywhere or all the time, but they were very common. The Republicans who refused to do more than vote with Negroes or who took no active part politically were apt to be better accepted. Some were openly received in society, but this was rare outside the Unionist areas where Republicans themselves constituted polite society.

Political opposition to reconstruction took various forms. During the first reconstruction elections, many Democrats went out of their way to win Negro support. This policy was not entirely hypocritical, although they continued to think of themselves as white supremacists and other Democrats refused to have any truck with the blacks. Upper-class whites in particular still thought of themselves as the Negro's best friends and protectors. Believing the Negro to be inherently childlike and incapable of fending for himself or attaining real equality, these Democrats were convinced that white Republican leaders deliberately misled him for their own advantage. Thus, the Democrats felt the Negro's own welfare in the long run depended on his allying with the old master class who knew and loved him best. If the Yankees insisted on the foolish notion of Negro suffrage, his old masters would make the best of it and win "Sambo" back to his true allegiance. All they had to do was convince him that he was being used by vicious political manipulators. This accomplished, they would demolish reconstruction with Negro votes, just as the Republicans had imposed it with Negro votes.

Thus, in most states the Democrats campaigned among Negroes and sometimes even nominated Negro candidates for lesser offices to make their ticket more attractive. Their basic commitment to white supremacy was never far from the surface, however. Blacks were often invited to Democratic campaign rallies, but they sat on one side of the hall while whites occupied the other. At Democratic picnics and barbecues, the Negroes either ate at separate tables or waited until the whites had finished. Negroes who gave speeches for the Democratic ticket or accepted places on it were usually servile "Uncle Tom" types, despised by most blacks as traitors to their race. Negro Democrats were subjected to much abuse and occasional violence from the black community. The truth is that the Negroes were not content to remain an inferior laboring class, and the Republicans offered them their only hope of improvement. Only on rare occasions, as in South Carolina in the 1870's, when Republican corruption became so open or Republican internal rivalry so bitter, did any significant number of Negroes support the Democratic party; and even then it never approached a majority. Better the Republicans even if dishonest, most Negroes believed, than the Democrats who still thought of them only as hewers of wood and drawers of water.

Democratic appeals to the Negro almost invariably failed, as most Democrats realized by the end of 1868. They persisted only in areas with Negro majorities, where no legal alternative seemed to exist if they hoped to win. In some black belt counties, the cause was so hopeless that Democrats virtually gave up campaigning. This same attitude prevailed statewide in South Carolina, Mississippi, and occasionally in other states. Where Democrats were a hopeless minority, they sometimes took advantage of divisions in the Republican party and endorsed the more conservative Republican faction. Thus, they supported Alcorn over Ames for governor of Mississippi in 1873. In South Carolina in 1870, they organized the Union Reform party, composed of Democrats and dissident Republicans, to oppose the regular Republican ticket under Governor Scott. Both of these attempts failed, but earlier, in 1869, Democrats helped elect a relatively conservative Republican, DeWitt C. Senter, as governor of Tennessee over a more radical Republican, and thus helped bring reconstruction to a close in this first reconstructed state.

In states and localities where the Negro vote was smaller, the Democrats seldom tried very hard to win it. Instead they were apt to make the race issue central to their campaign, trumpeting it from the rooftops. In large areas of the South, they won elections this way, retaining control of local governments in the first elections and capturing state governments (especially in the upper South) as early as 1870. In that year, they replaced Senter with one of their own, General John C. Brown, in Tennessee and won control of the legislatures in North Carolina and Georgia. Legislative control in turn enabled the Democrats, through the use or threat of impeachment, to drive the governors of those states from power.

Wherever Democrats found their political prospects hopeless—and often before they bothered to find that out—some whites resorted to intimidation and physical violence. This course came all too easily and naturally, given the heritage of slavery and the background of violence which most of the South shared with other parts of the country. Violence was a hallmark of reconstruction from its beginning. It was used to discipline Negroes who did not work or act as white men thought they should, and it was used to deter and punish those who did not vote as they should. "Uppity" Negroes continued to be beaten and occasionally killed. And prominent Negroes, especially those active politically, were continually subject to mob violence and assassination, as were white Republican leaders. The most unpopular were whites who had the closest association with blacks and exercised the greatest influence among them. Conservative whites perpetually feared that these men (and occasionally female schoolteachers) were inciting the blacks to insurrection. Every gathering of Negroes, every Republican rally, and especially every Union League meeting, was regarded by many as an inducement to revolt, if not an actual plotting session. The fear of a Negro uprising increased with emancipation and was seldom far in the background of white thinking. It had no more foundation in fact than before the war, but the danger was just as real to those who feared it. This great fear intermittently stirred up the white population to what they regarded as defensive measures, including mob violence, lynching, and murder.

Race riots, such as those of Memphis and New Orleans in 1866, continued to plague the South through Reconstruction and even afterwards. Large and small, riots occurred in the hundreds. Because race was central to reconstruction politics, such riots were nearly all political, at least indirectly. Whites were usually the aggressors, even if they thought of the violence as defensive. The Negroes fought back often, and occasionally shared responsibility for causing the disturbance. But the fact remains that blacks were usually outclassed in numbers and morale, and they almost always suffered most of the casualties. Sometimes these outbreaks arose on the spur of the moment or were precipitated by unforeseen events; many others were deliberately planned.

The Eutaw riot of 1870 in Alabama [is a] . . . case in point. The [riot] . . . arose during an Alabama state election campaign, and to all intents and purposes was a part of Democratic campaign tactics. Western Alabama had been the scene of much racial and political violence during 1869 and 1870. The life of Congressman Charles Hays of that district had been threatened so often that he refused to risk it by campaigning alone. On the other hand, this region had a large Negro majority and was potentially the strongest Republican district in Alabama. If the party neglected it, they might lose the state. Hays hoped that if the chief dignitaries in the state traveled there together they would not be molested and could get a large Negro turnout on election day. Accordingly he persuaded Governor William H. Smith (who was running for reelection), former Governor Lewis Parsons, and Senator Willard Warner to accompany him on a speaking tour through the district. Their speeches were announced beforehand, and they planned to use the courthouse steps or a similar place to address the crowds in each county they visited.

When the officials reached Livingston, the seat of Sumter County, a largely Negro crowd was on hand to hear them. The few whites present were unfriendly as usual, and interrupted constantly with jeers, catcalls, and hostile questions. (This was fairly acceptable campaign practice at the time, and speakers of both parties had to expect it.) Some of the whites were also armed, which was not unusual either. Governor Smith was the first speaker, and as soon as he began to talk, a dozen or more armed whites pushed their way to the front of the crowd. One of their leaders stationed himself only a few feet from the Governor and stood there throughout the speech, brandishing a large knife and looking as if he were going to use it on the Governor at any moment. Smith pretended not to notice and finished his speech with no more than verbal interruptions. The other speakers did likewise, except for Hays who was afraid that any effort on his part would provoke a riot. The white men seemed to be looking for an excuse to start a fight, and the speakers were careful not to provide it.

That night the visitors went on to Eutaw in nearby Greene County. They noticed that some of the same pistol-and-bowie-knife men followed them on the train. Next day others came in to Eutaw from all directions. By the time of the meeting, about 150 armed and belligerent white men—most of them young—had gathered at the courthouse with perhaps 2,000 Negroes. The number of whites grew after a Democratic meeting on the other side of the building adjourned while the Republican rally was still in progress. Warner and Parsons were the first speakers and drew the same kind of treatment they had received the day before. Then Congressman Hays (who lived in this county) was called to speak and climbed onto the table which was serving as a speakers' platform. He had hardly opened his mouth when some of the white toughs nearby pulled him to the ground and a gun was fired. Immediately gunfire broke out in all directions. Some Democrats later testified that the first shot had come from Hays himself; others said from Negroes responding to Hays's commands to shoot. Republicans, on the other hand, swore that the armed whites began the firing. In any case, the blacks had been perfectly orderly up to this point, as they had in Livingston the day before. The whites did most of the firing, and they carried most of the armament. As usual, the Negroes suffered most of the casualties. Even Democrats admitted that white men standing around the edge of the crowd and in the courthouse windows overhead tried to stampede the Negroes with gunfire directed overhead at first and then into the crowd itself. This aim was achieved, and in the process they shot 54 Negroes, wounding 4 of them mortally. Apparently no whites were hit. Some of the blacks rallied after fleeing a distance and began to march back, armed with poles, fence palings, and any other weapons they could lay their hands on. Before they reached the courthouse square again, they were stopped by soldiers who formed a line across the street to block their way. (The army detachment had been stationed just outside town and had remained in camp until the firing began.) The Eutaw riot ended with several Negroes, but no whites, under arrest for committing acts of violence. Next morning, the Sumter County boys returned home on the train, boasting that "they had been to Eutaw and cleaned out the damned Radicals." As a result of similar tactics around the state, the Negro vote fell off drastically in several counties on election day, and the Democrats won control of Alabama.

. . .

The details of the . . . Eutaw riots were unique, of course, but they conformed to a general pattern which was repeated over and over. Occasionally riots failed to achieve their purpose, but experience confirmed their general effectiveness. It was only a matter of time before the technique became so widespread that it began to topple state governments as well as local ones.

Less successful in the long run but more spectacular was the work of secret terrorist organizations such as the Ku Klux Klan. Southern whites used to make fun of Negro superstition and the black man's fascination with fancy uniforms, high-sounding titles, elaborate ceremonies, secret meetings, and mysterious oaths and rituals, like those of the Union League. Yet they formed dozens of societies of their own with the same characteristics. Some of these, such as college fraternities, Masonic lodges, and fraternal orders of various kinds, were perfectly harmless and even served useful social purposes. But the Ku Klux Klan, the Knights of the White Camellia, the Constitutional Union Guard, the White Brotherhood, the Knights of the Rising Sun, and others were political in character and embarked on careers of violence which bore no comparison to the Union League.

The Ku Klux Klan was the most prominent of these organizations and gave its name to the whole movement. It started off innocently enough in 1866 as a social club organized by six young Confederate veterans in Pulaski, Tennessee. Most of their amusement came from dressing in outlandish regalia, conducting secret meetings in which they subjected new recruits to weird initiation ceremonies, and generally mystifying the people around town. Playing practical jokes on themselves led quickly to playing them on others, especially Negroes, who either lacked the means of retaliating or were afraid to try. Some of the Klansmen took to riding around the countryside after dark, dressed in white sheets and pretending to be the ghosts of Confederate dead. A favorite trick was to ask a Negro for a drink of water, the Klansman explaining that he had not tasted water since he was killed at the Battle of Shiloh in 1862. When the black man obliged with a dipperful of water the Klansman drank it and sent him back for a bucketful more, which he quickly consumed; actually the water passed through a tube into a large rubber bag concealed within the Klansman's robe. Another device made a Klansman appear to be ten or twelve feet tall and sometimes with a removable head. Few Negroes seem to have fallen for these tricks, but the acts of violence which sometimes accompanied them made most blacks genuinely afraid of the Klan. From this arose the superstition among whites that Negroes thought the Klan were ghosts and thus scattered before them.

The power to terrify Negroes was immediately put to use in the interest of white supremacy. Whites used the Klan to frighten blacks into good behavior and submissiveness and to control their voting at elections. It was no coincidence that the Klan became more than a social club and spread from Pulaski in 1867, when Governor Brownlow's Republican regime gained a new lease on life by adopting Negro suffrage. Klansmen in disguise rode through Negro neighborhoods at night, warning the Negroes either to cast Democratic ballots or stay away from the polls. The Klan also sent notices to Republican officeholders, warning them on pain of death either to resign or leave the vicinity. Similar notices went to active Republicans of both races and often to the teachers of Negro schools as well. Sometimes these threats took imaginative forms, such as miniature coffins, marked "K.K.K.," left on doorsteps, or mysterious proclamations illustrated with skulls and crossbones. Increasingly, Klansmen (with or without prior warning) descended on Negro cabins in the middle of the night, called out or dragged out the sleeping inmates, and administered beatings of up to several hundred lashes. They usually used small tree branches for this purpose, but weapons of every kind were employed and many victims were shot. White Southerners tended to defend and even glorify the Klan as a preserver of white civilization; in fact, the greater part of its work was both cowardly and barbarous.

Klan activity created a reign of terror in many localities and sometimes had the desired effect of demoralizing Negroes and Republicans. Because white public opinion was either sympathetic or neutral, Klansmen were almost never punished. Even if they wanted to, law enforcement officials, and even many white Conservatives, were afraid to antagonize the Ku Klux by opposing them. Once this was recognized, Governor Brownlow responded by calling federal troops into the affected counties. The soldiers were seldom effective, however. Once a state was reconstructed, the army was limited to aiding local authorities only when they asked, and they seldom did. Besides, it was fruitless to arrest Klansmen, with or without army help, only to have the authorities refuse to prosecute them or the courts and juries refuse to convict them. Brownlow's next response was to call out the state militia, composed mostly of men from Unionist east Tennessee, where the Klan never developed. Although the Tennessee militia never exercised the powers of martial law which enabled them to try Klansmen in military courts, their presence was moderately effective in stamping out terrorism in many communities. Brownlow resorted to the militia twice, in 1867 and 1869.

In the spring of 1868, just as the new reconstruction governments were forming, the Klan spread throughout the South. The only state where it failed to establish itself was Virginia, which the Democrats partially controlled from the outset. On the other hand, it terrorized Negroes and Republicans in the border state of Kentucky for several years. Klan development in the South as a whole resembled that in Tennessee. Thousands of notices were issued. Often they were published in Democratic newspapers, which usually supported the Klan with approving editorials. The papers were full of accounts of Ku Klux highjinks, especially the water-drinking trick, which was usually told as if it were an original event. For a brief time, Klansmen seem merely to have galloped around the countryside in sheets, trying to scare the Negroes without committing actual violence. This was especially true during the state election campaigns of the spring and summer of 1868. But this stage never lasted long. The freedmen did not scare that easily, and Klan operations became more and more bloody. Some of the upper-class whites who joined the order at the beginning gradually dropped out, but Ku Klux membership first and last was drawn from all elements of the Southern white population.

The head of the Klan in Tennessee, after it expanded beyond Pulaski and became political, was General Nathan Bedford Forrest, the former Confederate cavalry commander. Like most Klansmen, he tried to keep his membership and activities secret, but did not succeed very well. Forrest was engaged in the life insurance and railroad businesses, both of which required considerable travel. On his trips, he seems to have encouraged Klan organization in other states. He too was taken aback eventually by the increasing violence in the order. In 1869, when Tennessee passed out of Radical hands, he ordered the Klan to dissolve. It seems to have done so in considerable measure in Tennessee, but in most other states it continued to grow and become more violent. The truth was that higher Klan leaders seldom exercised much power over the rank and file; local Klans (sometimes called dens, headed by an officer called the Grand Cyclops) were virtually independent of each other, and even individual members did much as they pleased.

Many local societies did not even call themselves Ku Klux Klans. The Knights of the Rising Sun was a local organization centered in Jefferson, Texas. The White Brotherhood and the Constitutional Union Guard were similar but separate orders in parts of North Carolina. Klansmen in many areas referred to their organization as the Invisible Empire. The Knights of the White Camellia was founded in Louisiana in 1867, and spread throughout that state as well as into Arkansas, Texas, and Alabama. The White Camellias had the same white-supremacy objectives as the Klan, but they seem to have been better disciplined and less violent. In many places they existed alongside the Klan. Since membership in all of these orders was supposed to be secret, it was not easy to keep their memberships entirely separate. Some men, in fact, belonged to more than one of them.

The terrorism assumed similar patterns wherever it developed. It appeared least often in overwhelmingly white or overwhelmingly Negro areas, and most often in regions where the two races or parties were almost evenly divided. Negroes and white Republicans were almost always the victims, white Democrats and the few Negro Democrats almost never. Although the majority of victims were poor and relatively obscure persons attacked at home in the middle of the night, Negro and Republican leaders at the local level were singled out for special attention.

One of the most famous cases was the murder of State Senator John W. Stephens of Caswell County, North Carolina, in 1870. Stephens was the Republican leader of the county, which had a Negro majority. Democrats were jealous of his influence in the black community and suspected that he was encouraging Negro acts of violence. There is no reason to believe that this was true. In fact, Stephens was trying to conciliate the Conservatives by asking one of their leaders, Frank Wiley, a former sheriff, to run for that office again on the Republican ticket. It was Wiley who lured Stephens to his death. Under pretense of talking about the sheriff nomination, he took Stephens into a small room in the courthouse. As soon as he entered the room, Stephens was seized, strangled, and stabbed to death by waiting Klansmen, who left his body on a woodpile. Conservatives then circulated rumors blaming the crime on the Negroes.

In neighboring Alamance County, the sheriff and all his deputies were Klansmen. In the midst of widespread terrorism throughout the county, a large band of them galloped into the town of Graham one night, captured the leading Negro Republican, and hanged him from a tree on the courthouse lawn. On another occasion, a Ku Klux band went after T.M. Shoffner, the Republican state senator from that county, whose offense had been to introduce a bill in the legislature empowering the governor to proclaim a state of insurrection and call in the militia whenever terrorism got out of hand in any county. In Shoffner's case, a friend and neighbor who was a Klansman warned him in time. Later he fled the state.

The lynching of Negro prisoners was another characteristic Klan activity. In Union County, South Carolina, bands of more than 100 Klansmen raided the local jail twice to lynch a group of Negro prisoners who were accused of killing an ex-Confederate soldier. The raiders had to return a second time because some of their prisoners managed to escape when they were taken from the jail earlier. On larger raids such as these, Klansmen were apt to display great organization and military discipline, drawn usually from wartime experience; but the smaller raids on individual homes more nearly resembled common gangsterism.

. . .

Occasionally, Republicans fought back in various ways. Negroes in some localities organized to burn barns and other farm buildings belonging to white men or did some raiding of their own in disguise. But they were poorly organized, and public opinion was against them. Unlike Klansmen, they were quickly arrested, tried, and convicted. Often the attempts at resistance by white Republicans were little more successful. Groups of them organized in parts of Tennessee, Alabama, North Carolina, and elsewhere to fight the Klan with its own methods. They were sometimes effective; but even when the Republicans were as numerous and well organized as the Klan, they often refused to be as ruthless. After a brief spell of counter-raiding they remained at home, only to find the Klan in full swing again. The only remedy seemed to be action at the state or national level which would have the sanction of law. Thus, Republicans, and even a few Democrats, increasingly called for effective state and federal action to stop the terror.

Governors responded to these appeals in different ways, depending on the racial and political character of their states as well as on their own personalities and outlooks. Their first response was almost invariably to appeal to local sheriffs and other officials to do their duty. When this failed, federal troops were summoned, with little effect. Only in Texas, where the military were still in control in 1869 and 1870, was the army able to stamp out Ku Kluxism by resorting to military courts. Most state legislatures passed anti-Ku Klux laws, which were remarkably strong on paper, but were no better enforced than the old laws against murder, trespass, and assault and battery.

As in Tennessee, the only remaining remedy was to call out the militia, preferably with the power to hold military trials. However in a few states, the militia had never been organized, and in the deep South they were seldom, if ever, used. The reason was that nearly all the white men in these states were Democrats who either sympathized with the Klan or belonged to it; to organize and arm these men to put down the Klan was absurd and even dangerous, for they might turn on the government which had mobilized them. Governors in these states could summon a loyal militia composed of Negroes, but most of them refused to do so. Negroes constantly showed the effects of their slave heritage in confrontations with white men. Even organized, armed, and uniformed, blacks lacked the knowledge, experience, and morale necessary to face down a white population which was at least as well organized and armed. Just as important, the sight of armed Negro militiamen redoubled white hysteria over the prospect of Negro insurrection, and the whites increased their terrorist activity to prevent it. In other words, Negro militia tended to increase terrorism rather than suppress it.

This was illustrated in South Carolina in 1870 and 1871, when Governor Robert K. Scott in desperation organized Negro militia companies in several counties terrorized by the Ku Klux Klan. Ku Klux activity became infinitely worse, as Klansmen raided the homes of militia members, beat them, seized their guns, and killed their officers. Finally, the Governor decided to disband the companies and take back the weapons still in their possession. Klan activity continued, nevertheless. Short of precipitating a race riot with incalculable results, the Governor had exhausted his powers.

. . .

By 1871, Republicans almost everywhere had the same sense of helplessness. The Klan had virtually disappeared west of the Mississippi and in Virginia, but elsewhere it continued as it had been or grew worse. Apparently, only the federal government had the power to suppress the organization and stop the terrorism which was its stock-in-trade. Radical Republicans, North and South, had been demanding drastic federal action for a long time, but the moderates had held back. Democrats, also North as well as South, either approved the Klan or refused to concern themselves about it and opposed any action. The dilemma of the moderate Republicans arose because they were equally disturbed by Klan outrages and by the necessity of extending federal jurisdiction further than they already had. Most of the crimes committed by the Klan—murder, assault, and intimidation—had always been state offenses and outside of federal jurisdiction. Congress, if it passed a law to punish Klan violence, would expand federal authority even further than it had by the Civil Rights and Reconstruction acts. But this objection gradually gave way to outrage over the steady succession of crimes being committed against Southern Republicans. Congress went part of the way in 1870 with a law to protect the civil rights of citizens. In the spring of 1871, it passed two others, the stronger of which was nicknamed the "Ku Klux Act." Although Democrats accused the Republicans of fostering despotism, the new law was long overdue and none too severe.

The Ku Klux Act outlawed many of the specific types of crime committed by the Klan, making them federal offenses, and gave the President power to order military arrests, but all trials had to be held in the regular federal courts. Most Republicans still hoped that the mere passage of the law would stop the terrorism, without the necessity of enforcing it. But such was not the case, and President Grant finally invoked the law in the fall of 1871. Making an example of South Carolina, he proclaimed a state of insurrection in the nine most terror-ridden counties and ordered the army to restore law and order in them. The soldiers immediately began rounding up Klansmen, as they did on a smaller scale in other states as well. By the end of the year, many hundreds of suspected terrorists were under arrest and awaiting trial in the federal courts. There were so many in fact that the court system simply could not handle them all. Some of the worst offenders were convicted and sentenced to terms in local jails or the federal penitentiary at Albany, New York. A few were acquitted. But the great majority never came to trial at all; their cases were postponed from one court term to another and eventually dropped. Very few Klansmen received the punishment they deserved. On the other hand, federal arrests and prosecutions so demoralized the Klan and similar organizations that by 1872 they all but disappeared.

The Ku Klux Klan was not successful by itself in overthrowing a single Republican state government. It had won partial victories, however, in Alabama, North Carolina, and Georgia, as well as many successes in individual counties around the South. Its death did not end Conservative opposition to Radical reconstruction, even by violent means. Violence continued in more conventional forms, without recourse to night riding in disguise. Here lay the greatest threat to the continuance of reconstruction.

. . .

As time passed, the federal government intervened less and less often to protect Republican regimes against violent overthrow. First, it had delayed passing and enforcing the Ku Klux Act, and then it failed to strengthen the courts so that they could do the job properly. In 1872, Congress refused to renew the military part of the law, and in 1873, the Grant administration virtually stopped enforcing it, even pardoning many of those already convicted. In several states, growing numbers of whites organized into semi-military companies for the purpose of overthrowing Republican rule Georgia style. In 1872, in a violent campaign, Louisiana Democrats claimed to have elected their candidate for governor, but Republicans disputed their claim and kept control. Two years later, the Democrats organized militarily, brought up cannon, and actually besieged Governor William P. Kellogg and his supporters in the New Orleans customs house. Federal troops were required to disperse them and restore Republican authority. Arkansas Republicans divided and fought a minor civil war over their governorship, with the Democrats supporting whichever faction promised them more at a given time. Smaller disturbances threatened Republican control in other states. One or both sides repeatedly appealed to President Grant for army support to prevent its overthrow. Through 1874, Grant continued to use the troops whenever he felt the facts justified it, as in supporting Governor Kellogg in Louisiana.

These crises never seemed to stop, and the federal government, reflecting growing Northern public opinion, grew increasingly tired of them. As early as 1872, a revolt developed within the Republican party nationally, in part over reconstruction policy. Certain party members were so offended at the corruption of the Grant administration that they refused to support him for reelection. Calling themselves Liberal Republicans, they held a separate convention and nominated Horace Greeley, the longtime editor of the New York *Tribune.* Part of the corruption they objected to lay in the Republican regimes in the South; Liberal Republicans felt that the support of Negro rights against white opposition was costing more than it was worth, and troops should no longer be used to settle political problems in that section. Although Greeley was also nominated by the Democrats, he lost the election by a wide margin. Hostility to Republican reconstruction policy continued to increase, however, as one Southern crisis followed another.

. . .

Thus, Republicans (like Northerners generally) retreated from the commitment to Negro political equality. They never admitted their withdrawal and continued to talk in favor of equal rights, law, and order. But they virtually abandoned serious activity to protect them. It is ironic that Congress in 1875 passed the last sweeping Civil Rights Act for almost a century, perhaps as a salve for sore consciences. It forbade racial discrimination in hotels, restaurants, railroads, steamboats, and other places of public accommodation. But almost no effort was made to enforce the law, and the Supreme Court declared it unconstitutional a few years later.

This was the climate of national opinion and policy when Mississippi held its state election campaign in 1875. Governor Ames had two years remaining in his term, but if the Democrats won control of the legislature, they could dispose of him as their fellows had Holden and Bullock. They prepared accordingly. Newspapers carried slogans on their mastheads proclaiming such sentiments as "Mississippi is a white man's country, and by the Eternal God we'll rule it," or "A white man's Government, by white men, for the benefit of white men." Democratic clubs all over the state announced that no jobs would be open next year to Negroes who voted Republican. Lists of Negro voters were prepared and checkers were appointed to attend the polls and note how each voted. After the election, the names of Republican voters were to be published in the newspapers so that appropriate action could be taken. Strong efforts were made to get Negroes to join Democratic clubs; those who did were promised employment and protection against any violence that might occur. Negro speakers were again hired to address rallies in behalf of the party of white supremacy.

All these things had been tried before with only indifferent success. The main reliance, therefore, was placed on intimidation and violence. Throwing caution to the winds, newspapers called for carrying the election "peaceably if we can, forcibly if we must." Young men formed military companies around the state, and some Democratic clubs armed themselves with repeating rifles. They made little effort to hide this activity. The more publicity they received, the further their cause was advanced. Preparations reached such a point in some counties that, as one newspaper boasted, "it was easy . . . to put seventeen hundred well-mounted horsemen into line . . . to say nothing of a thoroughly organized artillery company and a company of Infantry" armed with the latest weapons. There was a great show of drilling, parading, and firing of cannon. Negro Republican leaders were openly threatened with death, and Republican meetings were either forbidden or broken up by armed men. Armed whites also physically prevented Negroes from registering to vote.

Probably the most effective technique was the riot, already well tested at Meridian and elsewhere. In Yazoo County, a white Republican was killed, several Negroes were wounded, the sheriff was forced to flee, and armed whites took over, systematically killing Negro leaders in each division of the county. At Clinton, a white Republican and ten to thirty Negroes were killed, along with two Democrats. For four days following, whites combed the countryside killing black leaders. And so it went around the state. In nearly every case, Negroes were killed and wounded, while whites suffered few casualties or none. In many counties, the Republicans gave up campaigning. Negro officials were driven out, if not killed, and companies of armed whites assumed control.

Time and time again, Republicans called on Governor Ames for protection, but the Governor was helpless. When he turned to Washington for troops, the Attorney General responded, "The whole public are tired of these annual autumnal outbreaks in the South." With no troops forthcoming, Ames tried to organize a militia, which the whites boycotted. When he went on to arm Negro recruits, Democrats did what they could to frustrate him, even seizing some of the guns by force. Negro leaders themselves finally opposed the militia plan, believing it would lead to a race war which they could not win. Democratic leaders also feared the outbreak of such a conflict, lest it provoke the federal government into intervening and frustrating their plans. As a result they agreed with Ames to conduct a fair and peaceful election in return for his dropping all efforts to organize a militia. They had no intention of keeping this promise. Rather they hoped to keep to a middle road, relying on intimidation and the threat of force instead of its actual use. The terrorism had already gone far enough to guarantee a Democratic victory, they believed, and they tried therefore to slow it down. But other Democrats, particularly in Negro counties, were not so sure of the prospects of success in their localities and continued the terror with every means at their disposal. Some of them openly repudiated the agreement with Ames.

On election day, Negroes in some counties hid in the woods and did not try to vote; in other counties, they cast Democratic ballots. At Meridian, White Leaguers seized the polls and prevented any Negro from approaching unless he was accompanied by a white man. Around Aberdeen, armed whites picketed the roads to prevent blacks from coming into town to vote. And in several counties, Democrats fired into groups of Negro voters or used other means to drive them away from the polls. In some sections, Negroes did manage to vote in large numbers and relatively freely. But the intimidation was great enough to give the Democrats a statewide victory of about 96,000 votes to 66,000. When the new Democratic legislature met in January, 1876, it proceeded to impeach and remove the Lieutenant Governor, and then secured Ames's resignation as governor on the threat of the same treatment.

Thus was Mississippi "redeemed" by and for the benefit of its white minority. The federal government accepted the result. The "Mississippi Plan" was quickly adopted by Democratic leaders in Louisiana, Florida, and South Carolina. All three states elected governors and legislatures in 1876, as well as sharing in the Presidential vote that year.

. . .

The Republicans had brushed aside President Grant's interest in a third term in 1876 and nominated instead Governor Rutherford B. Hayes of

Ohio. The Democratic candidate, Samuel J. Tilden of New York, had recently won acclaim as a destroyer of the infamous Tweed Ring. Both men were reformers, pledged to clean up the corruptions of the Grant era. More importantly for the South, they were both pledged to end reconstruction. For Tilden and the Democrats this represented no change; for Hayes it meant carrying even further the tendencies of the Grant administration since 1872. Apart from the growing popular disillusionment with reconstruction and the Negro, the Republicans hoped to gain strength in the South by this course. If the Republican party in the South were not to go down in wreckage with the Negro, it had somehow to recruit more white members in that section. This could only be done by dropping the question of civil rights and leaving the South to settle its problems in its own way. Republicans never admitted that they were abandoning the Negro or their commitment to equal rights, although most of them ceased to press the issue. Instead, they held out the hand of friendship to upper-class Southern whites, especially members of the prewar Whig party. These men had long shared many of the same economic and political objectives with Republicans. They agreed substantially on the desirability of government aid to railroads and to business, generally in the interest of economic growth. A few Southern Whigs had become Republicans during Reconstruction, and the major issue keeping many more away was the race question. Republican politicians now proposed to remove this obstacle, at the Negro's expense.

The Presidential election of 1876 was one of the closest in American history. The popular vote came to 4,284,020 for Tilden; 4,036,572 for Hayes; and about 90,000 for minor-party candidates. Tilden had won a clear majority, if one overlooked the fact that many thousands of Southern Negroes had been bulldozed into voting the Democratic ticket or not voting at all. But, of course, Presidents are chosen by electoral rather than popular votes. The electoral vote was still closer. With a total of 369 votes to be cast, the winner needed a bare majority, or 185. Tilden got 184 to Hayes's 165. The remaining 20 votes were in dispute. Hayes needed all 20 of them to win, Tilden only 1. Of the 20, 19 came from the states of Louisiana, Florida, and South Carolina. The remaining vote was in Oregon, which Hayes had carried, but where one of the Republican electors was legally disqualified and the Democrats claimed the right to replace him. All three Southern states sent two sets of returns to Washington, one supporting Tilden and the other Hayes. Under the Constitution, Congress counts the electoral votes as they are reported from the states and then declares the winner. The Constitution says nothing about choosing between contested votes from a state, although Congress had exercised this power in earlier elections. It required the agreement of both houses, however, and that now seemed impossible, for the Senate was under Republican control and the House Democratic.

Congress was in recess until December, over a month after the election. During the interval, feelings ran high and men on both sides threatened to settle the issue with guns if they were cheated of the victory they felt was rightfully theirs. A fairly distinct difference in emphasis developed, however, between the Northern and Southern Democrats. Northern Democrats were much more bitter at the possibility of losing the Presidency. Southerners, on the other hand, were more interested in gaining control of their own states.

Hayes and his backers took advantage of this difference. They made it plain to Southerners that if Hayes were elected, he would not use troops to buttress Republican state governments in the South. In other words, Southern Democrats could topple the Republican regimes of South Carolina, Florida, and Louisiana, and retain the states they had already seized, without federal interference. Furthermore, various federal appointments were promised to Southern Democrats, including a seat in the President's Cabinet. And Republicans promised to look kindly on federal appropriations for railroads and other public improvements in the South. By means of this package deal, they hoped not only to secure Hayes's election with Southern white support but also to win over many of these Southerners permanently to the Republican fold.

When Congress met, it created a bipartisan Electoral Commission to decide which sets of electoral votes from the disputed states should be counted. This commission consisted of five senators, five representatives, and five Supreme Court justices. As originally intended, there were to be seven Democrats and seven Republicans, with the fifteenth member being Justice David Davis, who was nonpartisan. Davis was all-important, since he supposedly would exercise the deciding vote. But at the last minute, he accepted a seat in the United States Senate, and no longer qualified for service on the commission. Instead, a Republican justice, Joseph P. Bradley, was chosen. This proved fatal for Tilden. The commission decided every important question in favor of the Republicans by a vote of eight to seven. Northern Democrats in Congress now urged a filibuster to prevent counting the electoral votes, but the Republicans and most of the Southern Democrats agreed to accept the commission's verdict. Thus, only a few days before his term was scheduled to begin, Hayes was declared the winner by an electoral vote of 185 to 184. The Southerners, content with the arrangements they had made with Hayes's supporters, were noticeably quiet when Northern Democrats raised anguished cries at being cheated of the Presidency.

In perspective, it appears that the Democrats first stole the election of 1876 by a systematic and deliberate campaign of terrorism and violence in the South. Then, as the result of compromise between Republicans and Southern whites, the Republicans stole back the Presidency but allowed the Democrats to keep the South. The major victims in all this were not the supporters of Tilden but the Southern Republicans and above all the Negro freedmen whose rights were traded away as part of the bargain.

As the white South had fervently hoped, the Compromise of 1877 (as it was called) ended reconstruction. President Hayes appointed a number of

Southern Democrats and ex-Confederates to office as promised, including David M. Key of Tennessee as Postmaster General. More important, Hayes withdrew federal troops from the disputed states and allowed the Republican state governments to fall before superior force. Other parts of the bargain were not kept so well. Congress failed to appropriate as much money for the South as many Southerners wanted, and almost no Southern Democrats (ex-Whigs or otherwise) came over to join the Republicans. Instead, the "solid South"—overwhelmingly Democratic—became a settled feature of American politics for nearly a century. For Southerners, the Democratic party was confirmed as the party of states' rights and white supremacy. Republicanism by contrast was indelibly associated with Unionism, Yankeeism, and Negro equality. Southern whites seldom either cared or dared to leave the Democratic party in years to come, and when they did, it was usually to join the Greenbackers, Populists, or some other third party, rather than the Republicans. Within the Republican party nationally, debate continued for many years between men who believed that the surest basis of Southern strength lay with the Negroes or with the whites, respectively. Meanwhile, the Southern Republican party, deprived of the nourishment of Negro votes, quickly withered on the vine. The great experiment had ended.

Philip Taft and
Philip Ross

AMERICAN LABOR VIOLENCE:
ITS CAUSES, CHARACTER,
AND OUTCOME

Differences in economic interest, which observers from James Madison to Karl Marx have observed are the most fundamental in any society, have been expressed most clearly in violent clashes between workingmen and their employers. The following excerpts deal largely with the situation in the late nineteenth and early twentieth centuries, the period in which the American economy began to establish itself as the most productive in the world. It was a time of ruthless competition, of new technology and forms of organization. These developments typically resulted in the replacement of skilled labor by unskilled, shops by large factories, local marketing arrangements by national distribution systems. The conflict between capital and labor, at a time when no clear rules or restraints had been established, was often bitter and even bloody.

What complicates the issue is that, as in several other situations described elsewhere in this volume, conflicts arising from economic differences were often tangled with other possible sources of hostility. When unions were still young and weak, workers were pitted against each other as well as against employers. It was not usually owners or managers themselves who physically confronted angry strikers but rather hired guards or imported strikebreakers. Traditional craftsmen feared that hungry new immigrants, differing in life style or religion, might cost them their jobs by using simpler new techniques. Managers often used black strikebreakers to replace whites, or took advantage of the kaleidoscope of American ethnicity by employing

From Hugh Davis Graham and Ted Robert Gurr, *Violence in America: Historical and Comparative Perspectives* (New York, 1969), pp. 281–395.

traditionally hostile immigrant groups such as Greeks and Turks in the same factory. These efforts to blur the lines of class and inflame other differences often succeeded in making it difficult for workers to organize.

When united action did get under way, laborers often, although by no means always, found law and government hostile to their interests. As in the Whiskey Rebellion, when the federal authorities feared the use of Pennsylvania troops, and as in the New York Draft Riots when local authorities feared to use Irish police against their coreligionists, so in labor disputes state officials feared that local police might not act against workingmen from similar backgrounds. The result was the formation of two significant new agencies of force. The first was a strengthened national guard. The second was the state police, beginning with Pennsylvania in 1902. Unlike local officers, who were usually married taxpayers and residents encouraged to develop local ties, the state officers were deliberately segregated from the population, often living together in isolated barracks. And in their early years their primary purpose was to prevent the disruption of business by strikers.

After describing conditions in an age in which capital clearly dominated labor, Philip Taft and Philip Ross go on to conclude that the legislation of the New Deal in the 1930s marked a dramatic change in the nature of labor disputes by making strikes a legitimate part of a process carried out under a reasonably clear set of rules. And they do not hesitate to generalize not only about the effect of violence in the history of the American working class but its potential use by other groups seeking to advance their interests.

The United States has had the bloodiest and most violent labor history of any industrial nation in the world. Labor violence was not confined to certain industries, geographic areas, or specific groups in the labor force, although it has been more frequent in some industries than in others. There have been few sections and scarcely any industries in which violence has not erupted at some time, and even more serious confrontations have on occasion followed. Native and foreign workers, whites and blacks have at times sought to prevent strike replacements from taking their jobs, and at other times have themselves been the object of attack. With few exceptions, labor violence in the United States arose in specific situations, usually during a labor dispute. The precipitating causes have been attempts by pickets and sympathizers to prevent a plant on strike from being reopened with strikebreakers,[1] or attempts of company guards, police, or even by National Guardsmen to prevent such interference. At different times employers and workers have played the roles of aggressors and victims. Union violence was directed at limited objectives; the prevention of the entrance of strike-breakers or raw materials to a struck plant, or interference with finished products leaving the premises. While the number seriously injured and killed was high in some of the more serious encounters, labor violence rarely spilled over to other segments of the community.

Strikers, no matter how violent they might be, would virtually always seek to win the sympathy of the community to their side, and therefore attacks or even incitements against those not connected or aiding the employer would be carefully avoided. Such conduct was especially common in the organized strikes, those which were called and directed by a labor organization. Strike violence can therefore be differentiated from violence that is stimulated by general discontent and a feeling of injustice. Moreover, the unions were normally anxious to avoid violence and limit its impact because, simultaneously with the strike, the organization might also be operating under a contract and negotiating with other employers in an attempt to solve differences and promote common interests. Unions seek and must have at least the grudging cooperation of employers. No major labor organization in American history ever advocated violence as a policy, even though the labor organizations recognized that it might be a fact of industrial life.

Trade unions from the beginning of their existence stressed their desire for peaceful relations with employers. However, minority groups within the labor movement or without direct attachment to it advocated the use of violence against established institutions and also against leaders in government, industry, and society. The union leader might hope to avoid violence, but recognized that in the stress of a labor dispute it might be beyond the ability of the union to prevent clashes of varying seriousness. They might erupt spontaneously without plan or purpose in response to an incident on the picket line or provocation. Those who saw in violence a creative force regarded the problem differently; they had no objectives of immediate gain; they were not concerned with public opinion. They were revolutionaries for whom the radical transformation of the economic and social system was the only and all-consuming passion.

The most virulent form of industrial violence occurred in situations in which efforts were made to destroy a functioning union or to deny to a union recognition.

There is only a solitary example in American labor history of the advocacy of violence as a method of political and economic change. In the 1880's a branch of anarchism emerged that claimed a connection with organized and unorganized labor and advocated individual terror and revolution by force. The principle of "propaganda by the deed," first promulgated at the anarchist congress in Berne, Switzerland, in 1876, was based upon the assumption that peaceful appeals were inadequate to rouse the masses. This view could be interpreted as a call upon workers to create their own independent institutions, such as trade unions, mutual aid societies, and producer and consumer cooperatives. However, almost from the beginning this doctrine was interpreted to mean engaging in insurrectionary and putschist activities, and in terror directed against the individual.[2] Emphasis upon individual force gained added strength from the terroristic acts of members of the People's Will, an organization of Russian revolutionaries who carrried out campaigns of violence against persons, culminating in the assassination of Czar Alexander II in 1881.[3]

Not all anarchists approved these tactics. Many thought that social problems could be solved only by addressing oneself to the removal of evils, by changing institutions and the minds of men. In addition, the reaction against acts of terror, the arrests and imprisonment of militants, weakened the movement by depriving it of some of its more vigorous and courageous elements. Nevertheless, the London congress of 1881, which established the International Working People's Association as the center for the national anarchist federations, came out in favor of "propaganda by the deed" as a creative method for carrying on warfare against capitalist society and its leaders.[4]

Social revolutionary views were not widely accepted in the United States during the 1880's, but the difference between the moderates and the militants, which divided the European movement, was also in evidence here. . . . It was the issue of using arms which was largely responsible for the split in the Socialist Labor Party in 1880, and the more militant social revolutionaries gradually approached the anarchist position on politics and violence.

An attempt to unite the scattered groups of social revolutionaries was made by the Chicago conference of 1881 and was unsuccessful. The meeting adopted a resolution recognizing "the armed organizations of workingmen who stand ready with the gun to resist encroachment upon their rights, and recommend the formation of like organizations in all States."[5] This was only a prelude to the convention held in Pittsburgh in 1883, dominated by Johann Most, a German-born revolutionary who had served prison terms in a number of countries. . . .

In typically Socialist fashion, the congress explained the causes of the evils afflicting modern society. Since all institutions are aligned against him, the worker has a right to arm himself for self-defense and offense. The congress noted that no ruling class ever surrendered its privileges and urged organization for planning and carrying out rebellion. Capitalists will not leave the field except by force.[6] These ideas had some influence among a limited number of workers, largely immigrants. Most himself did not favor trade unions, regarding them as compromising organizations, and even refused to support the 8-hour movement in the 1880's. Anarchists, however, were active in union organizations and some regarded them as the ideal type of workmen's societies. Albert Parsons, August Spies, and Samuel Fielden, all of them defendants in the Haymarket Trial, had close connections with a part of the Chicago labor movement.

. . . Even at the height of their influence the anarchists had few supporters. Whatever violence took place in the United States cannot be traced
to the thinking of Most or any of his coworkers. In fact, even then it was
widely believed that the armed societies were engaged in playing a game,
and that they represented little danger to the community. It is quite certain
that violence in labor disputes was seldom inspired by the doctrine of
"propaganda by the deed," whose self-defeating nature convinced many of
its exponents of its fallacy. In this regard, experience was a more potent
force than moral considerations. Governments reacted to these terrorist
methods with savage repression. One of the few incidents of anarchist
violence in the United States was an attack by Alexander Berkman on
Henry Frick during the Homestead strike. The boomerang effect of this
action was to transform the hated Frick into a folk hero when, though
wounded, he fought off his attacker. The assassination of William McKinley by the anarchist Czolgosz is another example. Most did not repudiate
the tactic, but laid down conditions for its use that were critical of Berkman's conduct.

In France, Italy, and Spain anarchist-inspired violence was savagely
repressed, as were the few attempts in Germany and Austria. [7]

THE INDUSTRIAL WORKERS OF THE WORLD (IWW)

Unlike the other national federations such as the Knights of Labor,
the American Federation of Labor, and the Congress of Industrial Organizations, the IWW advocated direct action and sabotage. These doctrines
were never clearly defined, but did not include violence against isolated
individuals. Pamphlets on sabotage by Andre Tridon, Walker C. Smith,
and Elizabeth Gurley Flynn were published, but Haywood and the lawyers
for the defense at the Federal trial for espionage in Chicago in 1918 denied
that sabotage meant destruction of property. Instead Haywood claimed it
meant slowing down on the job when the employer refused to make concessions. [8]

It is of some interest that IWW activity was virtually free of violence.
The free-speech fight was a form of passive resistance in which members
mounted soapboxes and filled the jails. The IWW did not conduct a large
number of strikes, and aside from the one in McKee's Rock, Pa., a spontaneous strike which the IWW entered after it was called, the IWW strikes
were peaceful.

The two bloodiest episodes in the life of the IWW were in Everett and
Centralia, Wash., each connected with the attempt to organize lumber
workers. The Everett confrontation started when the Lumber Workers
Industrial Union No. 500 opened a hall in Everett in the spring of 1916, in
an effort to recruit members. Street meetings were prevented and the sheriff
deported the speakers and other members of the IWW to Seattle on a bus. It

is of some interest to note that a speaker who advocated violence at a meeting at the IWW hall in Everett was later exposed as a private detective. For a time the deportations were stopped, but they were resumed in October 1916. An estimated 300 to 400 members were deported by the sheriff and vigilantes from Everett. On October 30, 1916, 41 IWW men left Seattle by boat. They were met by the sheriff and a posse, seized, and made to run the gauntlet between two rows of vigilantes who beat their prisoners with clubs.

On November 5, 1916, the IWW in Seattle chartered a boat, the *Verona,* and placed an additional 39 men on another vessel. The chartered boat set out for Everett. Having been informed of the attempt of the IWW to land peacefully, the sheriff and about 200 armed men met the chartered vessel at the dock. The sheriff sought to speak to the leaders. When none came forward and the passengers sought to land, a signal to fire into the disembarking men was given by the sheriff. Five members of the IWW and two vigilantes were killed, and 31 members of the IWW and 19 vigilantes were wounded by gunfire. The *Verona* and the other vessel carrying members of the IWW returned to Seattle without unloading at Everett. Almost 300 were arrested, and 74 were charged with first-degree murder. The acquittal of the first defendant led to the dismissal of the case against the others. [9]

Another tragedy occurred in Centralia, Wash., a lumber town of almost 20,000 inhabitants. Several times the IWW sought to open a hall in that community, but in 1916 the members were expelled by a citizen's committee, and 2 years later the IWW hall was wrecked during a Red Cross parade. With dogged persistence the IWW opened another hall. When threats were made to wreck it, the IWW issued a leaflet pleading for avoidance of raids upon it. During the Armistice Day parade in 1919, members of the IWW were barricaded in their hall and when the hall was attacked, opened fire. Three members of the American Legion were killed, and a fourth died from gunshot wounds inflicted by Wesley Everest, himself a war veteran. Everest was lynched that night by a citizen mob. Eleven members of the IWW were tried for murder. One was released, two were acquitted and seven were convicted of second degree murder. A labor jury from Seattle that had been attending the trial claimed that the men fired in self-defense and should have been acquitted. [10] It is not necessary to attempt to redetermine the verdict to recognize that the IWW in Everett and Centralia was the victim, and the violence was a response to attacks made upon its members for exercising their constitutional rights.

A number of States, beginning with Minnesota in 1917, passed criminal syndicalist laws that forbade the advocacy of force and violence as a means of social change. On the basis of the theory that the IWW advocated force and violence to bring about industrial changes, several hundred men were tried, and 31 men served in the penitentiary in Idaho, 52 in Washington, and 133 in California. These convictions were not based upon acts of violence committed by those tried. [11]

THE PRACTICE OF VIOLENCE
IN THE 1870's AND 1880's

Repudiation of theories did not eliminate the practice of violence from the American labor scene. The pervasiveness of violence in American labor disputes appears paradoxical because the great majority of American workers have never supported views or ideologies that justified the use of force as a means of reform or basic social change, nor have American workers normally engaged in the kind of political activity that calls for demonstrations or for physical confrontation with opponents. Through most of its history, organized labor in the United States has depended largely upon economic organizations—unions—for advancement through collective bargaining, and upon pressure politics and cooperation with the old parties for achieving its political aims. Yet we are continually confronted with examples of violent confrontations between labor and management. Does industrial violence reveal a common characteristic with basic causes and persistent patterns of behavior, or is it a series of incidents linked only by violence? Labor violence has appeared under many conditions, and only an examination of the events themselves can reveal their nature and meaning.

THE STRIKES AND RIOTS OF 1877

The unexpected strikes and riots which swept over the United States in 1877 with almost cyclonic force began in Martinsburg, W. Va., after the Baltimore Ohio Railroad had announced its second wage cut in a relatively short period. The men left their trains and drove back those who sought to replace them. Governor Henry W. Mathews called upon President Rutherford B. Hayes for Federal assistance, and the latter, despite his reluctance, directed troops to be sent. [12] Federal troops had a calming influence on the rioters in Martinsburg, but 2 days later, on July 20, Governor John Lee Carroll of Maryland informed the President that an assemblage of rioters ". . . has taken possession of the Baltimore Ohio Railroad depot" in Baltimore, had set fire to it, and "driven off the firemen who attempted to extinguish the same, and it is impossible to disperse the rioters." Governor Carroll also asked for Federal aid. [13]

Order was restored immediately by Federal troops, but Governor Carroll then appealed for help in putting down a disturbance at Cumberland. Requests also were made for troops to be sent to Philadelphia, where the authorities feared outbreak of rioting. The most serious trouble spot, however, was Pittsburgh, where the attempt to introduce "double headers" was the cause of one of the more serious disturbances of the year. The change might have been accepted if they had not followed cuts in pay and loss of jobs—both caused by declining business. Open resistance began, and when a company of militia sought to quell the disturbance it was forced to retreat before the mob and take refuge in a railroad roundhouse where it was under constant attack. A citizens' posse and Federal troops restored order.

Railroads in Pennsylvania, New York, and New Jersey suffered almost complete disruption. The Erie, New York Central, the Delaware Lackawanna Western, and the Canada Southern operating in Ohio, Pennsylvania, and New York States were struck on July 24, idling about 100,000 workers. Federal and State troops were used to suppress rioting, and sometimes the State police were themselves the cause of violence. After 13 persons were killed and 43 wounded in a clash between militia and citizens in Reading, Pa., for example, a coroner's jury blamed the troops for an unjustified assault upon peaceful citizens.

In Ohio the railroads were blocked, but the Governor's plea for Federal aid was not met. "In the end the State authorities, assisted by the National Guard and the citizens' committees succeeded in quelling the disturbances at Zanesville, Columbus, Toledo, and Cleveland, but it was nearly the middle of August before order had been completely restored." The strikes and rioting moved westward and Indiana and Illinois were affected. In the face of a threatened strike, the Governor of Indiana refused to appeal for Federal troops and the latters' duties were limited to protecting Federal property and enforcing orders of the Federal courts. Work on the railroads entering Chicago was suspended, and rioting broke out in the city. On the 26th of July a bloody skirmish between the police, National Guardsmen, and a mob resulted in the killing of 19 and the wounding of more than 100 persons. It started with resistance of a mob to the attempts of the police to clear the streets, and it ended when the police and militia charged the crowd.

. . .

The riots of 1877 mirrored deeply felt grievances generated by several years of unemployment and wage cuts. All the rioting cannot be attributed to striking workmen and their sympathizers. Railroads, urban transportation systems, and trucking are among the industries that are almost completely exposed to attack during a labor dispute. They operate in the open, and it is difficult to prevent attacks by strikers and sympathizers upon working personnel and property. The strikes and riots of 1877 were, however, a violent protest against deteriorating conditions and the suffering and misery endured during a great depression. The widespread and ferocious reaction has no parallel in our history, but there are others of lesser magnitude that were important in shaping labor-management relations. [14]

There is no evidence that the riots of 1877 brought reforms in the handling of railroad disputes, which was the initial cause of the disturbances. They did demonstrate that the United States would not escape the trials and tribulations affecting other industrial nations, and that more attention must be given to the problems that industrial societies tend to generate. It was, however, more than a decade later that the first hesitant step was taken by the Federal Government to provide a method of adjusting labor disputes, a method that was never tried. Not until the Erdman Act of 1898 did the Federal Government provide a usable procedure for settling labor-management disputes on the railroads. An added provision guaranteeing railroad workers protection of the right to organize was declared unconstitutional by the U.S. Supreme Court when challenged by a carrier, *Adair v. United States,* 1908.

. . .

LABOR VIOLENCE IN THE 1890's

Not all violence was inspired by employers. While employer obduracy might lead to rejection of recognition, such conduct was in itself legally permissible. Had workers passively accepted such decisions, the level of violence in American labor disputes would have been reduced. Workers were, however, unwilling to watch their jobs forfeited to a local or imported strikebreaker. Employers could shut down their plants and attempt "to starve" their employees out of the union. Such a policy might have worked, but employers cognizant of their rights and costs frequently refused to follow such a self-denying tactic. As a consequence violence initiated from the labor side was also prevalent. In the 1890's violent outbreaks occurred in the North, South, and West, in small communities and metropolitan cities, testifying to the common attitudes of Americans in every part of the United States. While workers might react against the denial of what they regarded as their rights, the outcome of their violent behavior seldom changed the course of events. Serious violence erupted in several major strikes of the 1890's, the question of union recognition being a factor in all of them. As will be noted below, the Homestead strike, which was a defensive action on behalf of an existing and recognized union, and the Pullman strike, which was called in behalf of other workers denied recognition, also failed. Violence in the Coeur d'Alene copper area eventually led to the destruction of the Western Federation of Miners in that district. Violence was effective in the Illinois coalfields only because the community and the Governor of the State were hostile to the efforts of two coal producers to evade the terms of a contract acceptable to the great majority of producers in Illinois.

Although steelworkers in Pennsylvania and copper miners in Idaho had different ethnic origins and worked under dissimilar conditions, each reacted with equal ferocity to the attempts of their employers to undermine their unions.

HOMESTEAD

In Homestead, Pa., the domineering head of the Carnegie Steel Co., Henry C. Frick, used a difference over wages and a contract expiration date as an excuse for breaking with the union. When the union called a strike against the demands of Frick, the latter was ready to bring in a bargeload of Pinkerton operatives to guard his plant from the harassment of union pickets. Frick's plan became known, and the guards were met by several hundred steelworkers. In the battle to land the guards from the barges, two Pinkertons and two strikers were killed. Another attempt to land also ended in failure. Eventually the Pinkertons were forced to surrender and some were severely mauled by strikers and sympathizers. At the plea of the sheriff, the Governor ordered 7,000 troops to Homestead. Leaders were arrested, but juries refused to convict.

While the violence was temporarily successful in holding off the landing attempted on July 4, it was unable to change the outcome of the contest between the union and Frick. Under the cover of the protection given to him by the National Guard, he was able to open his mills. Furnaces were lit on July 15, and the company announced that applications for work would be received until July 21. The following day a large force of nonunion men entered the plant. Ultimately the union was defeated, and according to a leading student of the steel industry of another generation, John A. Fitch, the union never recovered from its defeat in Homestead. The steelworkers were fearful of Frick's attempt to break the union. The hiring of several hundred Pinkertons and their stealthy efforts to land convinced the strikers that a serious movement to destroy their organization was on the way, and the use of the hated Pinkertons sharpened their anger. An investigation by the U.S. Senate noted: "Every man who testified, including the proprietors of the detective agencies, admitted that the workmen are strongly prejudiced against the so-called Pinkertons and their presence at a strike serves to unduly inflame the passions of the strikers."[15]

COEUR d'ALENE

Organization of the metal miners in the Coeur d'Alene region in Idaho was followed by the mine operators' establishment of an association after the miner's union had successfully won a wage increase. A lockout was called several months after the miner's success, and every mine in the area was closed down. An offer of lower wages was rejected. The strikers were not passive. Strikebreakers were urged to leave or were forcibly expelled; court injunctions against violence were ignored. In July 1892 the situation deteriorated. A union miner was killed by guards, and it brought an attack by armed miners upon the barracks housing guards employed by the Frisco mill. It was dynamited, and one employee was killed and 20 wounded. An attack on the Gem mill followed and although five strikers were killed and more wounded, the mill surrendered. The guards gave up their weapons and were ordered out of the county. Armed with Winchesters, the armed strikers marched on Wardner, where they forced the Bunker Hill mine to discharge its nonunion contingent.

At the request of the Governor, who sent the entire National Guard, Federal troops were sent to restore order. The commanding general ordered all union men arrested and lodged in a hastily built stockade or bullpen. The commander of the State militia removed local officials sympathetic to the strikers and replaced them with others favorable to his orders. Trains were searched and suspects removed. Active union men were ordered dismissed from their jobs. The district was treated like a military zone, and companies were prohibited from employing union men. About 30 men were charged with conspiracy, and four were convicted, but subsequently released by the U.S. Supreme Court. Nevertheless, the miners were able to win recognition from all but the largest of the mining companies, which set the stage for a more spectacular encounter 7 years later. [16]

USE OF TROOPS IN MINOR DISPUTES

The use of State troops against strikers was common in the 1890's. In some instances it was in response to violence or to attempts to prevent interference with strikebreakers or to the closing down of the properties. In 1894 the United Mine Workers of America called a national strike in the bituminous coal industry and the strike became the occasion for intervention of troops in many coal-mining communities. When miners in Athens County, Ohio, interfered with the movement of coal trains, the militia was sent into the area to restore order. The Kansas National Guard also saw service. [17] However, the tendency of local police officers to seek the aid of State troops during industrial disturbances did not always depend upon the existence of disorder. Sometimes it was precautionary and designed to overawe the strikers. Reporting the activity of the Illinois National Guard for 1893 and 1894, the Adjutant General noted that it "has performed more active service than during its entire prior existence." At two points, the troops found no disorder and withdrew after several days. In others, militiamen prevented interference with the movement of coal, and in a third group of places, soldiers and miners staged a series of armed encounters. [18]

The tendency to order troops into coal-mining areas during a strike was not limited to Illinois. During the strike of 1894, troops were moved into the southwestern area of Indiana and into Mahaska County, Iowa. Fourteen companies of militiamen were on duty from 8 to 20 days in the Indiana coalfields. No report of violence was made by the authorities, and the sending of troops was evidently based on rumor or on hope that the presence of troops would intimidate the strikers. [19]

THE PULLMAN STRIKE

Railroad strikes have been among the more violent types of labor dispute. Normally, railroad workers are not more aggressive than other workers. However, railroads cover large open areas and their operations are always open to the rock thrower or the militant picket who may take it upon himself to discourage strikebreaking. A sympathy strike by the newly organized American Railway Union with the workers in the Pullman shops led to a widespread suspension of railroad service in 1894. What stands out in this bitter clash is the sympathy that the losing struggle generated among thousands of railroad workers. The refusal of the Pullman Co. to discuss the restoration of a wage cut with its employees was interpreted as an example of corporate arrogance. Like 1877, 1894 was a depression year, and many workers were without a job or income.

The strike started in May, and the American Railway Union, meeting in convention the following month, sought to bring about a settlement of the differences. When the American Railway Union imposed its boycott upon Pullman equipment, its action was challenged by the General Manager's Association, made up of the executives of the 24 railroads entering Chicago. Special guards were engaged, Federal marshals were appointed to keep the trains moving, and if an employee refused to handle Pullman equipment he was discharged. Attempts to operate with strikebreakers led to fearful resistance. Rioting was widespread, and at the request of the railroads and advice of Attorney General Richard Olney, Federal troops were sent to Chicago, over the protests of Governor John P. Altgeld. Every road west of Chicago felt the impact of the strike. Clashes between strikers and strikebreakers brought out Federal or State troops in Nebraska, Iowa, Colorado, Oklahoma, and California. Although the loss of life and property was not as serious as during the disturbances of 1877, the Pullman strike affected a wider area. An estimated 34 people were killed and undetermined millions of dollars were lost in the rioting connected with this conflict. President Grover Cleveland claimed "that within the states of North Dakota, Montana, Idaho, Colorado, Washington, Wyoming, California, and the territories of Utah and New Mexico it was impracticable to enforce federal law by the ordinary course of judicial procedure. For this reason, he revealed, military forces were being used."[20]

The immediate cause of the violence was the determination of the General Manager's Association to defeat the sympathy strike. When the boycott of Pullman cars was announced, the association declared that the employees of the railroads had no right to punish the carriers nor impose hardships upon the traveling public. The association declared "it to be the lawful right and duty of said railway companies to protect against said boycott, to resist the same in the interest of their existing contracts, and for the benefit of the traveling public, and that we will act unitedly to that end."[21] The extension of support by the union brought forth the support of the carriers for the Pullman Co. It is however, as has been noted, extremely difficult to avoid disorders in a strike in an industry whose operations are carried on over an open and extensive area. Any occurrence can attract hundreds and even thousands of people who because of sympathy or search for excitement or loot can expand a simple incident into a large-scale riot. The chief inciters to violence were not known, and the police and the officers of the railroads did not agree on whether union members or city toughs were the chief promoters of the turmoil.

The Federal Government hired marshals in numerous railroad centers to protect the property of the carriers. Attorney General Richard Olney stated that the extra funds expended for this purpose by the Federal Government amounted to at least $400,000.[22]

The responsibility for violence rests largely on the behavior of George Pullman. His attitude was similar to those held by many industrialists. He was unwilling to allow his workers the slightest influence upon the decisions of the company which greatly affected their welfare. Like other firms, the Pullman Co. was suffering losses of business as a result of the depression, and it may not have been able to meet the demands of its employees. It could, however, have conferred in good faith and explained its position instead of following a policy of peremptory rejection and dismissal of those who had asked for a reconsideration of a wage cut. Pullman's attitude, shared by many industrialists, tells us something about the cause of violence in labor disputes. Arrogant, intransigent, unwilling to meet with their employees, owners depended upon their own or the Government's power to suppress protest. Behind the powerful shield they could ignore the periodic outbreaks by their labor force; they knew that these seldom were strong enough to gain victory.

. . .

COAL MINERS' STRIKES

. . . Separate incidents involving coal-mining violence illustrate the fragility of peaceful methods in this industry. In two of the three cases, the use of force did not end in failure, but there were exceptional circumstances in each. Much depended upon the attitude of the authorities and the sympathies of the public. Free miners in Tennessee were able to control changes in the system of working convict labor in the coal mines. Leasing of convicts for work in the mines was begun in 1865, and the competition of these men, who had no influence on their working conditions or pay, was a threat to the free miners. Other grievances also played a role. Payment of wages by scrip, absence of checkweighmen at the mines, and the use of yellow dog contracts were sources of protest. When the free miners went on strike in 1891 the companies introduced convict labor as replacements. On July 21,

1891, hundreds of armed miners demanded that convict workers leave the mining camps at Briceville and Coal Creek. State troops were ordered into the area, but the governor agreed to the discontinuance of convict labor in the mines. [23]

Violence was also a factor in the settling of the coal miners' strikes in Alabama in 1894. A month after the strike started, miners in Johns, Adger, and Sumpter were ordered to leave the company houses. The company "strategy in breaking the strike was to import Negro labor to work in the mines. During the strike's first week, 100 Negroes were brought from Kansas." [24] On May 7, 1894, a band of armed men invaded the Price mine at Horse Creek "blowing up boilers, burning supplies and destroying property." On July 16, in a gunfight at Slope, 5 miles from Birmingham, three Negro strikebreakers and a deputy were killed. Troops were ordered into the area by the governor and remained there until August 14, when the strike was settled. [25]

. . .

THE 10 YEARS BETWEEN 1900 AND 1910

The first decade of the 20th century witnessed expansion of union membership, which increased opportunities for conflicts with employers. As in previous periods, strikes were on occasion marked by violence. The prospect of violence was heightened by rising employer resistance to union objectives. The signs of this new employer response consisted of the founding of many employer associations, the beginning of the open-shop campaign, and the use of Citizen Alliances as assault troops on union picket lines.

PENNSYLVANIA ANTHRACITE COALFIELDS

Violence in Illinois and in the Coeur d'Alene was carried out primarily by native or Americanized workers. Through the 1870's the Pennsylvania anthracite area was dominated by English-speaking workers: Americans, English, Scotch, Irish, and Welsh were the principal sources of labor. [26] By 1900, large numbers of Eastern and Southern Europeans had come into the area, and the English-speaking ratio in the population had dropped from 94 percent in 1880 to 52 percent in 1900. [27] With the destruction of the Knights of Labor and the Amalgamated Association of Anthracite Miners, no offset to the companies' power existed. Absence of checkweighmen, the existence of the company store, and the complete domination of the area by the coal companies were unrestrained evils. Nothing better demonstrates the abuse of power than an attack in 1897 upon miners who had struck against the high prices at the company store and were peacefully marching from Hazleton to Latimer. The sheriff and a force of deputies met the marchers on the road and ordered them to disperse. When they failed to obey instantly, the sheriff ordered his deputies to fire on the unresisting paraders. Eighteen were killed and 40 seriously wounded. Many of the killed and wounded were shot in the back. The sheriff and several deputies were tried for murder but were acquitted. [28]

In 1900, the United Mine Workers of America was able to challenge successfully the anthracite coal operators. Although the union had only about 7 percent of the miners in the area in the organization, it called a strike in September of 1900. There was only one serious clash between strikers and guards, which led to the death of a strikebreaker. Immediately 2,400 troops were sent into the area by the Governor. The strike was settled on terms not unfavorable to the union, and the single violent encounter played no role in the outcome. [29] Peace in the anthracite mines was brought about by political pressure but also by the skillful leadership of John Mitchell, the president of the United Mine Workers. Mitchell had always deplored the use of violent methods and constantly pleaded for negotiations as a peaceful means of settling labor disputes. He further recognized the importance of retaining public sentiment on the strikers' side, and he was determined to prevent the use of widespread prejudice against the Southern European immigrant worker to defeat them. This strike was, however, only a skirmish; the anthracite workers were to face a more serious trial 2 years later.

When negotiations between the operators and the union broke down in April 1902, it appeared that the strike would be more violent than the preceding one. A more aggressive spirit was evident among the men, and the companies appeared to be equally determined to scotch further progress of the union. Hundreds of commissions for iron and coal police to guard mining property were issued, and the companies decided to recruit strikebreakers and operate during the strike. An attack on a colliery at Old Forge on July 1 resulted in the killing of a striker; another was killed at Duryea the next day. Shootings and assaults became more common as the strike dragged on, and at the end of July the Governor ordered two regiments to Shenandoah, where the town was literally taken over by rioters. In this community a merchant suspected of supplying ammunition to deputies was beaten to death, and deputies and strikebreakers were assaulted. On August 18, troops were sent to Carbon County after a coal and iron policeman killed a striker. Trestles and bridges were dynamited and nonstrikers assaulted. The Governor, in September, sent troops into the three anthracite counties. Violence did not abate. On September 28, a striker was killed, and later in the day, 700 strikers assaulted and wrecked the Mount Carmel office of the Lehigh Valley Coal Co. and seized the roads leading to the colliery. In a summary of violence at the end of September, the *New York Tribune* claimed that in the disturbances arising out of the strike, 14 had been killed, 16 shot from ambush, 42 others severely injured, and 67 aggravated assaults had occurred; 1 house and 4 bridges were dynamited, 16 houses, 10 buildings, 3 washrooms around mines, and 3 stockades were burned; 6 trains were wrecked and there were 9 attempted wrecks, 7 trains attacked, and students in 14 schools went on strike against teachers whose fathers or brothers were working during the strike.[30]

Despite the extent of violence, it is doubtful whether it had any decisive effect on the outcome of the strike. In insisting that the strikers were prevented from working because of union intimidation, the operators claimed that the mines would be opened and fully manned if adequate protection were granted. The Governor of Pennsylvania sent the entire National Guard of the State into the anthracite area, but their presence did not increase the output of coal. This demonstration that the tieup was not the result of coercion but of the determination of the miners to bargain through a union ended the impasse.

What made the union victory possible was the conciliatory attitude of Mitchell. Firm on essentials, he was ready to compromise on details. Careful not to antagonize public opinion, he emphasized the justice of the miners' cause, the right of men to bargain collectively over the terms of employment. Although considerable violence developed during the second anthracite strike, none of it had the spectacular features of some of the battles in the Rocky Mountain area (see below). Mitchell and his subordinates always pleaded for peaceful behavior, and while the advice was often honored in the breach, neither he nor any other leaders could be attacked for advocating destruction of property or assaults upon persons which, had they done so, would have given employers a powerful argument with which to sway public sentiment.

THE COLORADO LABOR WAR

The use of force to settle differences was more common in the Western mining camps at the turn of the century than in Eastern manufacturing or even mining communities. In the West there was a tendency for violence to erupt on a larger scale. In 1894 Colorado's Governor, David M. Waite, ordered the dispersal of an army of company-employed deputies in a mining-labor dispute. Only the intervention of the troops prevented a battle between strikers and deputies.

Later, in 1901, after a successful walkout, the union miners deported a group of strikebreakers who had taken their jobs during the strike. The tendency for each side to resort to force to settle differences led to a gradual escalation of the level of violence, which reached a point where the Western Federation of Miners faced the combined power of the Mine Operator's Association, aided by the State government and a private employer's group, the militant Citizen's Alliance. It was an unequal struggle in which men were killed and maimed; union miners imprisoned in the bullpen; union halls, newspapers, and cooperatives sacked; and many strikers deported. There is no episode in American labor history in which violence was as systematically used by employers as in the Colorado labor war of 1903 and 1904. The miners fought back with a ferocity born of desperation, but their use of rifles and dynamite did not prevent their utter defeat.

The war opened in 1903. It started with a peaceful withdrawal from work in the Colorado City mill of the United States Reduction Refining Co., after demands for a wage increase and union recognition had been rejected. The strike quickly spread to the other mines and mills in the area. Although no reports of lawlessness had been made, the Governor sent in several companies of militia at the request of the sheriff. Although settlement was made, with the assistance of the Governor, the manager of the United States Reduction Refining Co. refused to accept its terms. District No. 1 of the Western Federation of Miners on August 3, 1903, called strikes in mines shipping ore to the refineries of the United States Reduction Refining Co. This was denounced by the Colorado Mine Owners Association as an "arbitrary and unjustifiable action" which "mars the annals of organized labor, and we denounce it as an outrage against both the employer and the employee."[31]

The association announced that it was determined to operate without the cooperation of the federation and, in response to a plea from the operators, State troops were sent to Teller County, where Cripple Creek was located, on September 3, 1904. At the same time a strike for shorter hours was going on in Telluride, and troops were sent into that area, although no reports of trouble were published. Active union men were arrested through September, lodged in a bullpen for several days, and then released. The militia officers took umbrage at an editorial in the *Victor Record,* and arrested its staff, who were held for 24 hours in the bullpen before they were released.[32]

The first significant violence attributed to the strikers was the blowing up of the Vindicator mine in Teller County, in which two were killed. Martial law was declared in Teller County and the military informed the editor of the *Victor Herald* that editorial comments would be censored. When the union secured a writ of habeas corpus directing the military to bring an arrested miner before a State court, the Governor suspended the writ "on the ground of military necessity."[33] Deportations of strikers were begun, and temporarily halted by an order from a State court. The military obeyed this court order. When 16 men were killed by the fall of a cage at the Independence mine at Victor, bitter feeling increased. Violation of safety rules was blamed by the union for the accident.

By February 2, 1904, conditions in Teller County were sufficiently close to normal for the Governor to withdraw troops. The mining companies then put into effect a "rustling-card" system that required applicants for employment in mines and smelters to obtain a card authorizing them to seek work. Each time a person changed jobs he had to procure a new card, which gave the mining companies an opportunity to blacklist all who did not meet their standards. The strike dragged on, and on June 6, 1904, while nonunion miners were returning from work, a charge of dynamite exploded under the Independence railroad station, killing 13 and seriously wounding 16. After the explosion, the Citizen's Alliance went into action. County and city officials sympathetic to the union were forced to resign, and a roundup of union members and sympathizers started. They were placed in a bullpen, and many of them were later deported to Kansas and New Mexico. The commander of the militia, General Sherman Bell, set up a commission to decide the fate of the prisoners held in the bullpen. A person's attitude towards the Western Federation of Miners determined whether he would be released or deported. On July 26, 1904, the Governor ended military rule and left the field to the Citizen's Alliance. During its tenure, since June 8, the commission examined 1,569 men, recommending 238 for deportation and 42 for trial in the criminal courts; the rest were released from the bullpen.[34] Gradually, normal conditions were restored, but the union continued its nominal strike until December 1907, when it was called off.[35]

Simultaneously with the Cripple Creek strike, the union was directing another in the San Juan area of Telluride County, Colo. The same scenario was played here. Troops were sent into the area soon after the calling of the strike in September 1903. Censorship, deportations, and arrests accompanied the troops. The union fought a losing battle, and the Telluride Miner's Association announced it would never employ members of the Western Federation of Miners. When the resistance of the strikers was broken, the Governor withdrew the State troops, but by that time the Citizen's Alliance could itself handle deportations and assaults.[36]

The effect of this organized violence upon the miner's organization is summarized by Sheriff Edward Bell of Teller County, and a leader in the campaign against that union. After the assaults and deportations had broken the back of the resistance, the sheriff announced:

The danger is all past. There are less than 100 of the radical miners left in the Cripple Creek district. The rest have been deported, or have left the district because they were unable to gain employment. They can never get work again. The mine owners have adopted a card system by which no miner can gain admittance to a mine unless he has a card showing that he does not belong to a union.[37]

The miners were no easy victims. They resisted as well as they could, but they faced the overwhelming power of the mine operators aided by the business community, the Governor, and the courts.[38]

. . .

SPECIAL POLICE

In Pennsylvania, every railroad in 1865 and every colliery, iron furnace, or rolling mill in 1866 was granted by statute liberty to employ as many policemen as it saw fit, from such persons as would obey its behests, and they were clothed with all authority of Pennsylvania, were paid such wages and armed with such weapons as the corporation determined—usually revolvers, sometimes Winchester rifles or both —and they were commissioned by the governor. [39]

Appointments under the Coal and Iron Police Act were made without difficulty. Corporations would file requests, and as a rule no investigation of the need for such appointments or restrictions on the behavior of those selected were made. In 1871 a fee of $1 was charged for each commission issued. From then until 1931, when the coal and iron police were abolished, the mining companies of Pennsylvania were able to utilize police under their own control in labor disputes. "There was no investigation, no regulation, no supervision, no responsibility undertaken by the State, which had literally created 'islands' of police power which was free to float as the employers saw fit." [40] The Pennsylvania system was not duplicated elsewhere. In its stead, in other States sheriffs and other local officials were authorized to appoint persons paid by the employer for strike and other private police duty.

On numerous occasions mercenaries were guilty of serious assaults upon the person and rights of strikers, and their provocative behavior was frequently an incitement to violence and disorder. Their presence, when added to the special deputies and company policemen and guards, increased substantially the possibility of sanguinary confrontations in strike areas. [41] Furthermore, the availability of private police figured in many events which have been ignored in American labor history. These would include the expulsion of organizers from a county, the forceful denial to union organizers of the opportunity to speak in company towns, and the physical coercion of individual employees because of their union affiliation or sympathies.

USE OF TROOPS UNDER PEACEFUL CONDITIONS

As we have seen, outbreaks of labor violence frequently required the intervention of State troops, whose activities in restoring order usually resulted in defeating the strike. This lesson was not lost to some employers who, with the connivance of local public officials, secured military aid in situations where violence was absent or insignificant. During the general strike of silk workers in Paterson, N.J., in 1902, it was claimed that the mills faced an attack by a mob. At the request of the sheriff, troops were sent to the city on June 19. They found no disorder, and left after 9 days. [42]

. . .

The same course of events took place in two other widely separate cases. In a strike at the National Fireproofing plant at Raritan, N.J., troops were sent during a strike in November 1908. Although no violent incident or threats had been made, the sheriff asked the Governor to send troops. His request was met, but they stayed only a few days. It may be that the sheriff feared that violence would follow, since the strikers were mostly Poles, Hungarians, and other Southern Europeans. [43] At almost the same time, State troops were summoned to a tunnel job in McCloud, Calif. The sheriff had informed the Governor that strikers had taken over the "powder house, undoubtedly for use as bombs or like service." The sheriff claimed the strikers threatened to kill anyone who went to work. Troops were sent and they helped the sheriff arrest the leaders of the strike. When this was accomplished, the troops left. [44]

CAMPAIGNS OF VIOLENCE BY UNIONS

Despite explicit repudiation of force as an accepted tactic, a number of unions pursued systematic campaigns against opponents. These campaigns were directed against workers who refused to join a given labor organization, against employers, or both. One such campaign was carried on by the Western Federation of Miners against mine managers, company agents, and public officials. Harry Orchard, a member of the federation, confessed to the commission of many crimes, including the murder of Governor Frank Steunenberg of Idaho on December 30, 1905, at the alleged orders of the chief union officers.

The outstanding example of a campaign of force is the one conducted by the International Association of Bridge Structural Iron Workers in the first decade of the century against some employers. When the National Erectors' Association decided in 1906 that it would no longer continue its agreement with the union, the latter turned to terror and dynamite. In the first few years of the open-shop fight, about 100 nonunion ironworkers and company guards were assaulted, three guards being killed. Between 1906 and 1911, about 100 structures were damaged or destroyed by charges of explosives. [45] Luke Grant, who studied this episode for the Commission of Industrial Relations, concluded "that the dynamite campaign was ineffective as far as it was directed against the National Erectors' Association and that it weakened the influence of the organization with some independent employers." Others believed that the campaign kept the small contractors in line. [46] Moreover, Grant was convinced that the dynamiting campaign did the union a great deal of harm. "It stirred the public mind as few labor wars have done." [47] The "main reason for the resort to dynamite is found in the uncompromising attitude of the open-shop employers. The American Bridge Co. offered to compromise in the early stages of the fight and the union representatives rejected the terms of the compromise." After that the attitude of the employers was unyielding. Every effort on the union side to bring about a conference, after it realized the mistake that had been made, proved unavailing.

. . .

INDUSTRIAL VIOLENCE 1911–16

These 6 years rank among the most violent in American history, except for the Civil War. Although the origins of violent encounters were not different from those in the past, they frequently attained a virulence seldom equaled in industrial warfare in any nation. This was as true of many small disputes as it was of the major confrontations in Michigan copper and the West Virginia and Colorado coalfields.

THE ILLINOIS CENTRAL SHOPMEN'S STRIKE

This strike differed from others in which serious violence took place in that union recognition was not the cause of the conflict. Single crafts had been recognized by this carrier for a number of years, but the carrier refused to negotiate a common contract with the system federation, a central body of several crafts. Following the establishment of the Railway Employees Department, the Illinois Central Railroad was requested, in June 1911, to deal jointly instead of singly with the Machinists', Steam Fitters', Railway Clerks', Blacksmiths', Boilermakers', and Sheet Metal Workers' Unions. The carrier refused, and a strike was called on the entire line of the Illinois Central. The railroad decided to replace the strikers. Violence was reported all along the right of way of the carrier. In Mississippi, one of the more important areas served by the Illinois Central, violence erupted at a number of points. When a train carrying strikebreakers arrived at McComb on October 3, 1911, it was met by about 250 armed men who opened fire on the new arrivals. Ten men were killed, cars were burned, and strikebreakers were afterward removed from the strike zone by militia called in by the Governor. Demonstrations against those working were also carried on. On January 17, 1912, five Negro laborers employed as helpers at McComb were fired upon while returning from work; three were killed, the others wounded. Strikebreakers were temporarily escorted out of the strike zone.[48] The shops at Water Valley, Miss., were attacked and the Governor ordered troops to that community on October 6, 1911. Serious violence was reported in New Orleans and a company guard was killed at Athens, Tex., and a guard and strikebreaker at the Illinois Central roundhouse at Houston, Tex. In Clinton, Ill., Carl Person, a leader of the strike, killed a strikebreaker who had brutally assaulted him. Person was tried for murder and acquitted on the ground of self-defense.[49] Despite the strike's formal continuance until June 28, 1915, it was in effect lost within several months after its start.

...IWW STRIKES

Despite its temporary advocacy of direct action and sabotage, the strikes of the IWW were not particularly violent. In 1912–13, the IWW led two textile strikes in the East, and an affiliate, the Brotherhood of Timber Workers, operating in Louisiana, struck for improved wages and working conditions in the Louisiana timber area. An exchange of gunfire between pickets and guards before the Gallaway Lumber Co. at Grabow, La., resulted in the killing of three union men and a company guard. A score of others were wounded. Several companies of troops were sent into the area and remained 3 days. A clash between strikers and strikebreakers at Merryville, on November 14, brought State troops into the area. The trouble ceased with their arrival, and the business community was anxious that the troops remain. More than 1,000 men were on strike, and "the people in the area were mostly in sympathy with the strike."[50] It was, however, insufficient to help the strikers win. Several of the leaders were indicted for murder, but they were later acquitted.

The textile strike in Lawrence, Mass., including more than 25,000 workers, was the most important IWW-led strike and made a deep impression on contemporary observers.[51] Refusal of employers to offset the loss of wages that followed the reduction of hours required for women workers by a recently enacted law was the cause of the walkout on January 11, 1912. As the workers belonged to no union, they invited the general organizer of the IWW, Joseph Ettor, to aid them. He succeeded in having specific demands formulated and presented to each employer of the strikers. Troops were sent into the city, and their number was increased as the strike continued. At the same time, the Governor of Massachusetts sought to have the State board of arbitration settle the dispute. The strikers were willing, but the American Woolen Co., the largest employer, refused to participate. A number of clashes between pickets and the militia took place, and in one a woman was killed. The strike continued until March 12, and was ended by the offer of a wage increase. Although the strike was a victory for the textile workers, the IWW was unable to gain a permanent foothold in Lawrence or in the textile industry. While arrests are not necessarily a measure of strike violence, it is interesting that in Lawrence during the strike, more than 350 arrests were made. Several were sentenced to 2 years in prison; 24 to 1 year; and 22 were fined.

The third strike of the IWW, one which was almost equal to Lawrence in the public attention it attracted, took place in the silk mills of Paterson, N.J. The IWW capitalized on dissatisfaction which other organizations were unable to use to their advantage. A strike called against one of the large mills on February 1, 1913, was later expanded to embrace all the silk mills and dye works. Mass arrests of pickets began quietly, early in the walkout, and the attorney for the IWW claimed that innocent strikers had been arrested. Many private detectives were employed by the firms on strike, and on April 18, a bystander was killed when between 16 and 20 shots were fired at pickets. There was considerable violence, much of it due to the behavior of the private guards and detectives hired by employers. The strike ended without victory after 22 weeks. During its course, 2,338 had been arrested, 300 held for the grand jury, and more than 100 sentenced to prison. [52]

While the IWW strikes in the East represented forays into geographical areas where the union had few members, the strike in the Wheatland, Calif., hop fields took place in the union's natural habitat. The workers in this strike were typical of the IWW membership. The strike began on August 13, 1913, as a spontaneous protest against the miserable conditions at the Durst brothers' ranch, where several thousand pickets had assembled awaiting the beginning of the season. Through extensive advertising, several thousand pickers had been attracted to the ranch in search of employment. Even by the standards prevailing in migrant-worker camps, living conditions were very bad there. Inadequate toilet facilities, charges for drinking water, absence of housing for many hundreds, and the low sanitary state of the campsite caused sufficient dissatisfaction that the migrants elected a negotiating committee. Richard Ford and Herman Suhr, members of the IWW, were on the committee. Demands for improvements in sanitation and an increase in the price of picking were made, and the committee, headed by Ford and Suhr, met with one of the Durst brothers. Durst flicked his glove across Ford's face and rejected the demands. The resident constable then tried to arrest Ford. When a warrant was insisted upon, the constable left and returned with the district attorney of the county and several deputy sheriffs. An attempt to arrest Ford led to an argument which ended in general shooting. The district attorney, a deputy sheriff, and two hop pickers were killed. The next day the militia arrived, but quiet had already been restored. [53] Ford and Suhr and two others were tried for murder, and the first two were convicted and sentenced to prison. The affair ended without improvements, although it stimulated a legislative investigation.

The IWW leadership of the spontaneous strike on the Mesabi iron range in Minnesota was by invitation, in that many of the strikers had been brought into the area in 1906 to replace predecessors who were then on strike against the same employers. Ten years later, in June 1916, the miners were sufficiently dissatisfied to go on strike. Early in July, a group of deputy sheriffs invaded a boardinghouse and tried to arrest one of the strikers. A fight started; a deputy and a passerby were killed and a striker wounded by gunfire. In the meantime, the U.S. Steel Corp., the major employer, would made no concessions nor meet with a strike committee.

Eventually the strikers returned to work, having gained nothing. Three leaders of the walkout and several strikers were arrested and charged with murder. The IWW leaders were released and left the range, and several of the strikers were convicted and given prison terms.

Although IWW strikes were not unusually violent, the reputation of the IWW made its members an easy target for repressive action by the authorities, but the harsh treatment accorded to strikers was unrelated to the organization to which they belonged. Prof. Henry F. Grady, commenting on the killing of two pickets in the 1916 San Francisco longshoremen's strike, said that "neither of these murders were provoked. When the gunmen were brought to trial, Chamber of Commerce lawyers were there to defend them. The labor man sees no essential difference between the violence he may use to protect his right to work and the conditions which he claims fair, and the violence of an armed guard who is paid to oppose him." [54] The strike was the result of the violation of contract by the longshoremen's union. The action was denounced by U.S. Secretary of Labor William B. Wilson. The strike had serious repercussions for it served as a pretext for the launching of the open-shop campaign in San Francisco. In the defense of acts of terror against pickets, the open-shop forces claimed that 38 nonunion men had been assaulted and only six union men had suffered similar experiences. [55]

. . .

THE IMPACT OF THE NATIONAL LABOR RELATIONS ACT UPON VIOLENCE

A fundamental purpose of the national labor policy, first enunciated by the Wagner Act and confirmed by its subsequent amendments in the Taft-Hartley and Landrum-Griffin Acts, was the substitution of orderly procedures for trials of combat. But in balancing the public interest in the peaceful settlement of industrial disputes with the freedom of labor and management to work out their problems in light of their needs and experience, the law did not outlaw the exercise of economic force. Indeed, by endorsing collective bargaining, the NLRA explicitly acknowledged that tests of strength, i.e., the infliction of economic harm, with all its costs and hardships, is superior to such alternatives as compulsory arbitration.

However, this approval of the strike, the picket line, and the maintenance of hard bargaining lines by employers and unions was limited by the establishment of specified rules of conduct imposed on all parties. Some subjects were removed as bargaining issues and are not subject to economic pressures. Foremost among these was the question of union recognition and with it the concomitant mutual obligation to bargain in good faith. The wishes of a majority of employees within an appropriate bargaining unit determined whether or not collective bargaining was to begin, and this determination could not be lawfully qualified or limited.

The workings of the majority-rule principle can best be appreciated by applying it to the major disputes of the past. Members of the bargaining committee that approached the Pullman company were fired and Pullman refused to deal with any committee of his employees. Charles Schwab, head of the Bethlehem Steel Co., announced during the 1910 strike, "I will not deal with union committees or organized labor," an attitude reiterated for the entire industry in 1919. This position was taken by employers in Michigan Copper, in the coal industry of Colorado and the major coalfields in West Virginia, and by others in the more violent strikes. Some employer associations were hostile to the principle of dealing with unions, and these groups included the leading firms in many industries. Because employer refusal to meet and deal with unions was the major cause of past violent labor strikes, the effective enforcement of the Wagner Act reduced sharply the number of such encounters.

This diminution of labor violence was not a temporary phenomenon but endured the strains of major and minor wars, a number of business cycles, and substantial changes in national and local political administrations. Moreover, the social and economic environment in post-New Deal America was scarcely conducive to the pacific resolution of disputes of any kind. The reconversion of American industry after World War II brought on the greatest strike wave in our history. Yet, these mammoth strikes were accompanied by virtually no violence, completely at variance with the experience after 1918.

The contribution of the NLRA in sustaining the reduction in the number and severity of sanguinary labor clashes went beyond prescribing enforcible bargaining behavior. The law supported the right to organize of labor unions, but only on condition of avoidance of violence. Violence on a picket line is always latent but tends to surface when the employer recruits replacements and attempts to operate. Today, as always, employers have the legal right to move goods and people freely across a picket line and the duty and practice of police has tended to safeguard this right. Moreover, employees who engage in violence forfeit the protection of the act, which is a restraining influence upon them. The diminution of violence on labor's side has correspondingly lowered the propensity of employers to resort to force as either a defensive or aggressive tactic.

SUMMARY AND CONCLUSIONS

The United States has experienced more frequent and bloody labor violence than any other industrial nation. Its incidence and severity have, however, been sharply reduced in the last quarter of a century. The reduction is even more noteworthy when the larger number of union members, strikes, and labor-management agreements are considered. The magnitude of past violence is but partially revealed by available statistics. One writer estimated that in the bloody period between January 1, 1902, and September 30, 1904, 198 persons were killed and 1,966 injured in strikes and lockouts.[56] Our own independent count, which grossly understates the casualties, records over 700 deaths and several thousands of serious injuries in labor disputes. In addition, we have been able to identify over 160 occasions on which State and Federal troops have intervened in labor disputes.

The most common cause of past violent labor disputes was the denial of the right to organize through refusal to recognize the union, frequently associated with the discharge of union leaders. Knowledge of workers' resentment at their inability to join unions encouraged employers to take defensive measures during strikes and lockouts. These measures often included the hiring of guards who, by their provocative behavior, often created the very conditions they had been engaged to minimize.

The melancholy record shows that no section of the United States was free from industrial violence, that its origin and nature were not due to the influence of the immigrant or the frontier, nor did it reflect a darker side of the American character. Labor violence was caused by the attitudes taken by labor and management in response to unresolved disputes. The virtual absence at present of violence in the coal and copper mines, breeding grounds for the more dramatic and tragic episodes, are eloquent testimony that labor violence from the 1870's to the 1930's was essentially shaped by prevailing attitudes on the relations between employer and employee. Once these were changed, a change accomplished partly by legal compulsion, violence was sharply reduced.

EMPLOYER VIOLENCE

Employers and unions were both guilty of violence. Employer violence frequently had the cover of law. No employer was legally bound to recognize the union of his employees. He has and always had the right to defend his property and maintain free access to the labor and commodity markets. In anticipation of trouble, the employer could call on the community police force, and depending upon size and financial ability, supplement them with protective auxiliaries of his own. Such actions usually had public support, for the employer was exercising a recognized right to self-defense, despite widespread recognition by many public leaders in and out of Government of the desirability, need, and justice of collective bargaining. In the absence of the authority and effective sanctions of protective labor legislation, many employers fought unionism with every weapon at their command, in the certainty that their hostility was both lawful and proper.

UNION VIOLENCE

Facing inflexible opposition, union leaders and their members frequently found that nothing, neither peaceful persuasion nor the intervention of heads of government, could move the employer towards recognition. Frustration and desperation impelled pickets to react to strikebreakers with anger. Many violent outbreaks followed efforts of strikers to restrain the entry of strikebreakers and raw materials into the struck plant. Such conduct, obviously illegal, opened the opportunity for forceful police measures. In the long run, the employers' side was better equipped for success. The use of force by pickets was illegal on its face, but the action of the police and company guards were in vindication of the employers' rights.

The effect of labor violence was almost always harmful to the union. There is little evidence that violence succeeded in gaining advantages for strikers. Not only does the rollcall of lost strikes confirm such a view, but the use of employer agents, disguised as union members or union officials for advocating violence within the union, testifies to the advantage such practices gave the employer. There were a few situations, in areas made vulnerable by their openness such as a strike in municipal transportation or involving teamsters, where violence was effective in gaining a favorable settlement. Even here, however, such as in the Teamsters strike in Chicago in 1905, the violence often failed. The most sensational campaigns of the Western Federation of Miners to bring their opponents to heel by the use of force were unsuccessful, and the union was virtually driven out of its stronghold. The campaign of dynamiting of the Iron Workers' Union ended in the conviction of the McNamaras. Subsequent convictions of a number of union leaders, including its president, who were convicted of transporting dynamite and of conspiracy in the Federal courts, almost wrecked the union. The campaign of violence carried on by the molders against the members of the antiunion National Founders Association failed to change the latters' policy. [57]

The right to organize was not retained in Homestead, or won in Pullman, the Colorado metal mines, Coeur d'Alene, or in the steel mills in 1919, although the sacrifice by union members, especially the rank and file members, was great. In fact, the victories gained by violent strikes are rather few, for the use of violence tends to bring about a hardening of attitudes and a weakening of the forces of peace and conciliation. A community might be sympathetic to the demands of strikers, but as soon as violent confrontations took place, the possibility was high that interest would shift from concern for the acceptance of union demands to the stopping of violence.

It is the violent encounters that have provided organized labor with its list of martyrs, men and women who gave their lives in defense of the union and collective bargaining. The role of martyrdom is not for us to assay, and may be useful in welding the solidarity of the group. The blood of the martyr may be the seed of the church, but in labor disputes it is doubtful if the sacrifices have been worth the results obtained. The evidence against the effectiveness of violence as a means of gaining concessions by labor in the United States is too overwhelming to be a matter of dispute.

Except for contemporary examples, we have not dealt with the numerous minor disturbances, some of them fairly serious, that were settled by the use of the normal police force. We have also generally avoided the many instances in which organizers and active unionists were denied their right to remain in communities or were the victims of local vigilante groups. We know that union organizers could not enter the closed coal towns, and that labor speakers could neither hire a hall nor speak in a public square in many communities. A number of coal counties in Kentucky and West Virginia built what amounted to an iron wall against the invasion of union organizers. The situation became worse during strikes. In the 1919 steel strike, the mayor of Duquesne, Pa., announced that "Jesus Christ could not hold a meeting in Duquesne," let alone the secretary-treasurer of the American Federation of Labor.

. . .

PERSISTENCE OF VIOLENCE

We are, however, confronted with a paradox in that violence in labor disputes persisted even though it seldom achieved fruitful results. With few exceptions, labor violence was the result of isolated and usually unplanned acts on a picket line, or occurred during a prohibited parade or demonstration protesting employer obduracy or police brutality. It might also start by attempts of pickets to prevent the transportation of strikebreakers or goods, and a clash would follow police intervention. Where the employer refused to deal with the union, the possibility of eventual violence was always high. The desire of the American worker for union representation took place in the teeth of employer opposition that was able to impose heavy sanctions for union activity. The reproduction of conditions in which violence is spawned inevitably was followed by outbreaks of violence. Violence could be successfully repressed by superior forces but it could not be eliminated until its causes were removed.

THE REDUCTION IN VIOLENCE

The elimination in 1933 of the most important single cause of violence, refusal to recognize the union for purposes of collective bargaining, came about at the time when union membership was lower than it had been for 15 years. The first step taken was the adoption of section (7) (a) in the National Industrial Recovery Act, which guaranteed workers in industries operating under codes of fair competition the right to organize and bargain collectively through their own representatives. This provision was only partially effective in protecting the right to organize, but it was a significant beginning. Its successor, the National Labor Relations Act, with its amendments, has now been on the books for 33 years, and it is 31 years since it has been upheld by the Supreme Court. The sharp decline in the level of industrial violence is one of the great achievements of the National Labor Relations Board.

It may have been a fortunate coincidence that the labor laws guaranteeing the right to organize were enacted at the time the character of business management was changing. The professional business executive, who has increasingly come to dominate management, is not inclined to regard his business in the same sense as the head of a family-developed firm. He is more flexible in his thinking and more responsive to social and political changes. It may not be an accident that some of the bitterest contemporary labor disputes—Kohler and Perfect Circle, for example—took place in family-held businesses. The professional business leader is more detached, more pragmatic in his reactions, and knows that American business has sufficient resilience to adapt itself to free collective bargaining. The performance of American industry since the end of World War II demonstrates that union organization and collective bargaining are not incompatible with satisfactory profits and a high rate of technological change.

Violence has greatly diminished, but it has not entirely ceased. Between 80 and 100 proven charges of violence or coercion are closed annually by the National Labor Relations Board. In addition, reports of violence of varying seriousness appear periodically in the press. The charges that come before the Board that we have examined are largely based upon threats and generally minor picket-line incidents. In none of them did deaths or serious injuries occur. Nearly all of them, if they had taken place prior to the 1930's, would have been ignored in our study. Had we taken note of all the threats and picket-line incidents prior to the 1930's, our study would have reached unmanageable proportions. Present-day violence is by and large the result of accidental and random events which occasionally erupt in a picket line confrontation.

PROSPECT OF REVERSION TO PAST PATTERNS OF VIOLENCE

Has widescale violence been permanently erased from American industry? The reduction in violence in labor disputes has been accompanied by sharp increases in violent behavior in other areas of American life. This is no accident. The conditions that gave rise to past labor violence have been eliminated and a restoration of these conditions would lead to a reversion in conduct. Any tampering with the complex mechanism that governs our contemporary labor policy is an invitation towards unharnessing of the forces of violence and hate that we have successfully mastered.

LABOR AND OTHER FORMS OF VIOLENCE

Can one draw more general conclusions from the labor experience, or are they peculiar to the problems of workers seeking to establish unions in industry? On many occasions the union operated in a hostile community, while minorities carry on their protests in their own friendly neighborhoods. Nevertheless, in both situations the reaction of the majority is likely to be decisive. There have been times where public sentiment was so strongly on the labor side that no matter what violence it committed, it ran no risk of estranging local public sentiment. Such was the case in Virden and in the far more questionable situation in Herrin. Usually, however, violence led to the alienation of public opinion and sometimes to a shift in public sentiment to approval of severe actions against the strike. The evidence is clear that the absence of violence committed by unions would not have retrieved many lost strikes. However, it appears highly probable that the advocacy or the practice of organized and systematic violence on the union side would have prevented the enactment of the New Deal labor legislation.

There is no evidence that majorities will supinely accept violence by minorities. The fact that rioters are fighting for a just cause or reacting to oppression has not, in the case of labor, led to the condoning of violence by the public. The desirability of collective bargaining had, prior to the 1930's, been endorsed by a number of public bodies, and all 20th-century Presidents of the United States. Such views were also sponsored by leading students in the field, legislators, clergymen, and others. Such approval did not save labor from severe repression.

It appears to us that it is a gross confusion of the problem to emphasize the creative character of violence as a guide to the behavior of minorities suffering from serious inequities and injustice. Creative violence obviously refers to the successful revolutions in England, the United States, France, and Russia. It appears to us that such a view is completely irrelevant if it is not vicious and highly misleading. We are concerned not with revolutionary uprisings, which such a view implies, but how a minority can achieve belated justice. Although we believe that minorities can obtain little through violence, we are also convinced, on the basis of labor experience, that violence will continue unless attention is paid to the removal of grievances.

In some respects the violence in the ghettos resembles the kind that surrounded labor disputes; it arises without prior planning and out of isolated instances that may not repeat themselves. It is also highly probable that violence of this kind will be unproductive or even counterproductive, in that it will antagonize many who would normally support the claims of minorities for equal justice and opportunity. Yet the labor analogy with racial minorities can be pushed too far. Labor's grievances were specific and could be met by single or groups of employers with concessions. The adverse effects of granting these concessions were small, injured few people, and employers could generally pass on any added costs to consumers. On the other hand, to the extent that the grievances of minorities are of a general nature and the meeting of their demands impinges upon the privileges of wide sections of the community, the resolution of their disputes is apt to be met with greater opposition.

NOTES

1. For a long period of time strikebreakers were not regarded as replacements.

2. Jean Maitron, *Histoire du Mouvement Anarchiste en France* (Paris: Societe Universitaire D'Editions et de Libraire, 1961), pp. 67-69.

3. Rudolf Rocker, *Johann Most, Das Leben Eines Rebellen* (Berlin: "Der Syndikalist," Fritz Kater, 1924), pp. 127-128.

4. Maitron, *op. cit.,* pp. 103-104; Henry David, *History of the Haymarket Affair* (New York: Russell & Russell, 1958), pp. 63-66.

5. Quotation is from David, *op. cit.,* p. 73; see also John R. Commons and associates, *History of Labour in the United States* (New York: The Macmillan Co., 1918), pp. 291-293.

6. David, *op. cit.,* pp. 98-100; Commons, *op. cit.,* pp. 294-296; Rocker, *op. cit.,* pp. 148-149.

7. See Maitron, *op. cit.,* 168-241, for description of the violence against persons and property and the reaction of the French Government.

8. During World War I many members of the IWW were arrested, and 165 leaders were indicted in the Federal courts in Chicago for conspiring to violate the espionage law. Similar indictments were found against a group tried in Sacramento, Calif., and at Kansas City, Kans. An examination of the record of the trial shows that the prosecution was able to present few instances in which the IWW was guilty of serious violence. Most instances were trivial and, moreover, showed no organized tendency in that direction. William D. Haywood, among others, denied that the IWW advocated such a principle. See Philip Taft, "The Federal Trials of the I.W.W.," *Labor History,* Winter 1962, pp. 57-92.

9. Walker C. Smith, *The Everett Massacre* (Chicago: I.W.W. Publishing Co., 1917), deals with the issue from the IWW point of view. Also, Perlman and Taft, *op. cit.,* pp. 390-392.

10. Ralph Chaplin, *The Centralia Conspiracy* (Chicago: I.W.W. Publishing Co., 1924); *The Centralia Case,* Joint Report on the Armistice Day Tragedy at Centralia, Wash., Nov. 11, 1919, issued by the Department of Research and Education of the Federal Council of Churches, the Social Action Department of the National Catholic Welfare Council, and the Social Justice Committee of the Central Conference of American Rabbis, 1930; Ben Hur Lampman, *Centralia Tragedy and Trial* (Tacoma, Wash., 1920).

11. Eldridge Foster Dowell, *A History of Criminal Syndicalism* (Baltimore: Johns Hopkins Press, 1939), p. 17.

12. The exchange of letters between Governor Mathews and the President are in *Federal Aid in Domestic Disturbances, 1877-1903.* S. Doc. 209, 57th Cong., 2d session, p. 315.

13. Letters in *Ibid.,* p. 317.

14. See Robert V. Bruce, *1877: A Year of Violence* (Indianapolis: Bobbs Merrill, 1959); J. A. Dacus, *Annals of the Great Strikes* (St. Louis: Schammell & Co., 1877); Edward Winslow Martin, *The History of the Great Riots* (Philadelphia: National Publishing Co., 1877).

15. Quotation is from *Investigation of Labor Troubles.* U.S.S. Rept. 1280, 52d Cong., 2d sess., pp. XII, XIV. See also *Employment of Pinkertons,* H. Rept. 2447, 52d Cong., 2d sess.

16. *Report of the United States Industrial Commission,* Washington, 1901, vol. XII, p. 490; George Edgar French, "The Coeur d'Alene Riots," *Overland Monthly,* July 1895, pp. 33-34; Selig Perlman and Philip Taft, *History of Labor in the United States* (New York: Macmillan Co., 1935), vol. IV, pp. 17-173.

17. *Annual Report of the Adjutant General to the Governor of the State of Ohio for the Fiscal Year Ending Nov. 15, 1894,* pp. 5-6; *Ninth Biennial Report of the Adjutant General of the State of Kansas, 1893-94,* p. 13.

18. *Biennial Report of the Adjutant General of Illinois to the Governor and Commander-in-Chief, 1893 and 1894,* pp. XII, XIII.

19. *Report of the Adjutant General of the State of Indiana for the Year Ending October 31, 1894*, p. 9; *Report of the Adjutant General to the Governor of Iowa for the Biennial Period Ending November 30, 1895*, pp. 19–21.

20. Quotation from Almont Lindsey, *The Pullman Strike* (Chicago: University of Chicago Press, 1942), p. 263. Also see *Federal Aid in Domestic Disturbances*, pp. 194–195. President Cleveland, who had sent troops to Chicago during the strike, believed that "a comparatively insignificant quarrel between the managers of an industrial establishment and their workmen was joined by the large army of the Railway Union. It was the membership of these workmen in the Railway Union . . . that gave it the proportions of a tremendous disturbance, paralyzing the most important business interests, obstructing the functions of the Government, and disturbing social peace." Grover Cleveland, *The Government in the Chicago Strike of 1894* (Princeton: Princeton University Press, 1913), p. 6.

21. Resolution of the General Manager's Association is found in the *Report on the Chicago Strike of June-July 1894 by the United States Commission* appointed by the President, July 25, 1894, under the provisions of sec. 6 of ch. 1063 of the laws of the United States passed Oct. 1, 1888. (Washington: Government Printing Office, 1895), p. 250.

22. *Appendix to the Annual Report of the Attorney General of the United States for Year 1896* (Washington: Government Printing Office, 1896), pp. 221–222.

23. A. C. Hutson, Jr., "The Coal Miners' Insurrection of 1891 in Anderson County, Tennessee," *The East Tennessee Historical Society's Publications*, No. 7, 1935, pp. 103–121.

24. Robert David Ward and William Warren Rodgers, *Labor Revolt in Alabama: The Great Strike of 1894* (Southern Historical Publications No. 9, University of Alabama, 1965), p. 68.

25. *Biennial Report of the Adjutant General of Alabama*, 1894, pp. 52, 62; Ward and Rodgers, *op. cit.*, p. 111.

26. The Molly McGuires, a terrorist organization that operated in the anthracite area at this time, was not a bargaining organization. Made up of Irish miners, it exercised vengeance against arrogant mine bosses of British origin and others who came into its disfavor. It did not direct demands for improvements in working conditions, although it issued warnings against oppressors. Whatever its connection with the labor movement may have been we know that this group was destroyed and many of its leaders hanged.

27. Frank Julian Warne, *The Coal Mine Workers* (New York: Longmans, 1905).

28. *New York World*, Sept. 11–12, 1897; Also see Edward Pinkowski, *The Latimer Massacre* (Philadelphia: Sunshine Press, 1950).

29. *New York Tribune*, Sept. 23, Sept, 27, 1900.

30. *New York Tribune*, Sept. 30, 1902; Perlman and Taft, *op. cit.*, p. 44; Robert J. Cornell, *The Anthracite Coal Strike* (Washington: Catholic University Press, 1957); Frank J. Warne, *The Slav Invasion and the Mine Workers* (Philadelphia: Lippincott, 1904); *Report to the President on the Anthracite Coal Strike of May-October, 1902*, Anthracite Strike Commission (Washington: Government Printing Office, 1903).

31. *A Report on Labor Disturbances in the State of Colorado from 1880 to 1904*, S. Doc. 122, 58th Cong., 3d sess., p. 112.

32. *Ibid.*, pp. 182–187.

33. *Ibid.*, pp. 192–193.

34. *Ibid.*, p. 295.

35. *Ibid.*, p. 325.

36. *Ibid.*, pp. 168–169, 200–201, 205.

37. *Ibid.*, p. 325.

38. See Vernon Jensen, *Heritage of Conflict* (Ithaca: Cornell University Press, 1950); Benjamin McKie Rastall, *The Labor History of Cripple Creek District*, University of Wisconsin Bulletin No. 198 (Madison, 1908).

39. *Labor Conditions in the Anthracite Regions of Pennsylvania, 1887-1888*, H. Rept. 4147, 50th Cong., 2d sess., pp. 136–167.

40. J. P. Shalloo, *Private Police* (Philadelphia: The American Academy of Political and Social Sciences, 1933), p. 61.

41. See report of the *Committee on Education and Labor Pursuant S. Res. 266* (74th Cong.), *S. Rept. 6. Part 2, 76th Cong., 1st sess.,* 1939; *Report of United States Commission on Relations, S. Doc. 415, 64th Cong., 1st sess.,* 1916, pp. 92–98.

42. *Report of the Adjutant General of the State of New Jersey for the Year Ending October 31, 1902,* p. 25.

43. *Report of the Adjutant General of the State of New Jersey for the Year Ending October 31, 1909,* pp. 15–16.

44. *Biennial Report of the Adjutant General of California,* 1910, pp. 50–51.

45. Luke Grant, *The National Erectors' Association and the International Association of Bridge and Structural Iron Workers* (Washington: U.S. Commission on Industrial Relations, 1915), especially pp. 107–148.

46. *Ibid.,* p. 125.

47. *Ibid.,* p. 130.

48. *Report of the United States Commission on Industrial Relations* (testimony of Charles F. Markham, president of Illinois Central), vol. X.

49. The violence is described in sections dealing with the Harriman and Illinois Central strikes in *Ibid.*

50. *Annual Report of the Adjutant General of the State of Louisiana for the Year Ending December 31, 1912,* pp. 7–8.

51. *Annual Report of the State Board of Conciliation and Arbitration in Massachusetts, 1912,* p. 31; *Report of Massachusetts Adjutant General for 1912,* p. 7; *Report on Textile Strike in Lawrence, Massachusetts,* S. Doc. 870, 62d Cong., 2d session; *Hearings on the Strike at Lawrence, Massachusetts,* H. Doc. 671, 62d Cong., 2d sess.

52. *Report of the United States Commission on Industrial Relations,* vol. 3, pp. 2534, 2547.

53. *Report of the Adjutant General of the State of California,* 1914, pp. 45–46; *Proceedings of the 15th Annual Convention of the Convention of the California State Federation of Labor,* 1914, pp. 72–73.

54. Henry F. Grady, "The Open Shop in San Francisco," *The Survey,* May 25, 1916, p. 193.

55. *Law and Order in San Francisco: A Beginning* (San Francisco Chamber of Commerce, 1916), pp. 8–11.

56. Slason, Thompson, "Violence in Labor Disputes," *World's Work,* Dec. 1904.

57. *Final Report and Testimony of the Commission on Industrial Relations,* S. Doc. 415, 64th Cong., 1st sess. (Washington: Government Printing Office, 1916), vol. 1, pp. 242–244.

John William Ward

VIOLENCE, ANARCHY, AND
ALEXANDER BERKMAN

*Beginning in the mid-1960s the murder and attempted
murder of public figures in America has focused attention on
this most dramatic form of political violence. But until the recent
past it could not have been claimed that assassination, although
it claimed the lives of several presidents, was an important part
of our political tradition; there is no common denominator to
the killings of Abraham Lincoln in 1865, James Garfield in
1881, and William McKinley in 1901 except that all of the perpetrators were unbalanced in some degree. Few Americans have
been able even to comprehend the motives of the calculating
political assassin who is at the same time legally sane and motivated not by the desire for immediate advantage but for promoting social change by deliberately shocking or galvanizing the
populace.*

*John William Ward, in analyzing the prison memoirs of
one such attempted assassin, the anarchist Alexander Berkman,
explains why even Berkman himself came to understand that his
action was useless in the context of late nineteenth-century
America. Ward then goes on more broadly to comment on the
special nature of social violence in a nation committed to the
ideals of democracy and individualism.*

On July 23, 1892, Alexander Berkman, an immigrant Russian Jew, ide-
alist, and anarchist, forced his way into the Pittsburgh office of Henry
Clay Frick in order to kill him. The assassination was, in the anarchist

From *New York Review of Books,* November 5, 1970. Reprinted by permission of the
author.

tradition, to be an *attentat,* a political deed of violence to awaken the consciousness of the people against their oppressors. Frick, manager of the Carnegie steel works while Andrew Carnegie was on vacation in Scotland, had crushed the Amalgamated Association of Iron and Steel Workers in the infamous Homestead strike, which ended in a fatal battle between Pinkertons and strikers. Berkman was there to continue the struggle between the workers and their capitalist oppressors. He failed. He failed to kill Frick. He failed to arouse the workers. The outcome, instead, was a book, a classic in the literature of autobiography, *Prison Memoirs of an Anarchist.*

Prison Memoirs is one of those great works which somehow get lost and wait for time to find again. First published in 1912 by Emma Goldman's Mother Earth press, the book has had an underground reputation, but not many people know it. Why it may now find an audience is obvious enough. From *Newsweek* to I. F. Stone's newsletter, one finds references to Narodniks and Nihilists and Anarchists in editorials on the arson and bombing and terrorism which afflict our daily lives. Inevitably, we have the customary American reflex, a plenitude of panels and commissions.

Violence is nothing new to American culture but, as Hugh Davis Graham has said, there has been a curious historical amnesia about the subject. The historical volume of the National Commission on Violence, of which Professor Graham was one of the editors, is the first major attempt to redress the balance and provoke our collective memory. At such a moment, one may guess that Berkman will find readers. He should. *Prison Memoirs of an Anarchist* allows us to experience violence from the inside, to identify with a man who idealistically accepts terrorism as a political instrument.

But more important, in his exploration of the human ambiguity and political complexity of the violence to which he commits himself, Berkman forces a question on us. Does the terrible violence which has characterized American culture throughout its history, along with our inability to understand it, derive from our best and noblest ideals about the meaning and the promise of American life? Is violence, rather than some mad aberration, an intrinsic and understandable part of America?

I

Berkman's style is that of the naïve, direct, simple, and seemingly artless. He writes in the first person, in a continuing present tense, generally in simple declarative sentences, perhaps because he writes in English and not in his native language. He apostrophizes often in an embarrassing way. Some of the set pieces in *Prison Memoirs* seem to come straight from a sentimental novel. But the sometimes mawkish manner cannot conceal a remarkable self-scrutiny and a sure juxtaposition of scene and image which express a supple imagination and a penetrating psychology.

On the first page, Berkman plunges directly into the news of Homestead, the bloody battle between the workers and the Pinkertons, the crushing of the Amalgamated Association, the single largest and most powerful union of the time, and starts on his train trip to Pittsburgh to assassinate Henry Clay Frick. The journey starts him also on the trail of his own memories, back to his student days in Russia, to his own youthful rebellion and groping attempts to understand, to his violent estrangement from his mother and her death in his arms before they are reconciled, before he can tell her that he is full of compassion and love for her. As he bows his head over his dead mother, the doctor puts his hand on his shoulder; at that instant, a coarse and swarthy laborer in the seat behind in the train reaches forward to speak to him, and we are back with Berkman on his fateful trip.

A collage of news, visual impressions, youthful memories, and idealistic aspirations overlay and run one into another. The effect, however, is single: to define the abyss between Berkman's ideal hopes for mankind and the grim reality of man's condition. He came to America hounded from Russia as a "wolf," he says, because "there, beyond the ocean, was the land of noble achievement, a glorious free country, where men walked erect in the full stature of manhood—the very realization of my youthful dreams." Like many native American writers, he renders the contrast between the dream and the reality through images of the landscape. Against the infernal present of Homestead with its stink and soot and cinders, Berkman places a vision of arcadian bliss, sunshine, "green woods and yellow fields."

This is not to say that Alexander Berkman, Russian Jew, immigrant and anarchist, had somehow attached himself to a native American pastoral tradition. Quite the contrary. As Paul Avrich, in his fine book *The Russian Anarchists,* has pointed out, the anarchist tradition in Russia stretches back to the seventeenth-century peasant revolts of Stenka Razin (whom Berkman explicitly invokes), and the myth of a world of free, uncoerced mutuality derives from the dream of a lost Golden Age located in the "primitive bliss of Medieval Russia, when, supposedly, there was 'neither Tsar nor state' but only 'land and liberty.'" One may find the same figurative pattern, with its theme explicit and programmatic, in Kropotkin's *Fields, Factories and Workshops* (1898). But if Berkman carried his dream of idyllic freedom with him from Russia, the American myth of an Eden of natural harmony where men walked erect in freedom twisted that dream into nightmarish shape.

II

Prison Memoirs of an Anarchist is divided into three unequal parts. The first short section gives us quickly the *attentat,* the attempted political assassination of Henry Clay Frick, the "Caesar" of American capitalism, a tyrant to be killed in order to awaken the oppressed, the glorious and beloved People. The last short section gives us Berkman's return to life, his deep despondency which brings him to the verge of suicide, before he finds "work" to do and achieves his resurrection from the living death of fourteen years in a Pennsylvania state penitentiary. Most of the book deals with the experience of prison. The continuous present tense gives *Prison Memoirs* the air of a continuing diary of Berkman's efforts to survive physically and mentally the brutal and degrading conditions of those long years. But we know, especially from Emma Goldman's account in *Living My Life*, that Berkman wrote his story after prison, looking back over the terrible years.

As bizarre as the circumstances of Berkman's life may be, *Prison Memoirs* belongs to the genre, if one cares to classify it, of the *Bildungsroman*, the story of the formation of a young man, his coming to maturity. The "I" of the story undergoes change and development; as he writes, Berkman leads us toward his altered conception of himself as he re-creates the experience which led to change. That change involves two major themes in the book: first, a change in Berkman's relation to other human beings, a change in his assumptions about human nature; second, a change in his understanding of the political meaning of the deed of violence.

At the outset, Berkman draws the conventional anarchist distinction between murder and political assassination:

Human life is, indeed, sacred and inviolate. But the killing of a tyrant, of an enemy of the People, is in no way to be considered as the taking of a life. . . . True, the Cause often calls upon the revolutionist to commit an unpleasant act; but it is the test of the true revolutionist—nay, more, his pride—to sacrifice all merely human feeling at the call of the People's cause.

Could anything be nobler than to die for a grand, a sublime Cause? Why, the very life of a true revolutionist has no other purpose, no significance whatever, save to sacrifice it on the altar of the beloved People. And what could be higher in life than to be a true revolutionist? It is to be a *man,* a complete MAN. A being who has neither personal interests nor desires above the necessities of the Cause; one who has emancipated himself from being merely human, and has risen above that, even to the height of conviction which excludes all doubt, all regret; in short, one who in the very inmost of his soul feels himself revolutionist first, human afterwards.

In Pittsburgh, Berkman adopts a pseudonym, Rakhmetov, taking the name from the arch-revolutionist in Chernyshevsky's novel, *What Is To Be Done?* But he rejects the need to prepare himself, as did his namesake, to withstand pain. He finds it a "sign of weakness. Does a real revolutionist need to prepare himself, to steel his nerves and harden his body? I feel it almost a personal insult, this suggestion of the revolutionist's mere human clay."

Berkman's celebration of the ideal revolutionary hero glorifies the man who, through commitment to a noble cause, transcends the limitations of being "merely human." Devoted to the cause of humanity, one transcends the human condition, is beyond good and evil, beyond the fear of death and the claims of mortality. The ideal is put to the test when Berkman shoots Frick. Fearful that Frick may be wearing an armored vest, Berkman shoots at Frick's head, hits him but fails to kill. Struggling free of the grasp of another man in Frick's office, he fires and hits the wounded Frick again. He is overpowered for a moment, but shakes himself free, his pistol misfires, and he crawls toward Frick and stabs him with a homemade dagger in the leg and thigh. Finally, clubbed with a hammer by a carpenter, Berkman is overcome:

An officer pulls my head back by the hair, and my eyes meet Frick's. He stands in front of me, supported by several men. His face is ashen gray; the black beard is streaked with red, and blood is oozing from his neck. For an instant a strange feeling, as of shame, comes over me; but the next moment I am filled with anger at the sentiment, so unworthy of a revolutionist.

That fleeting moment when Berkman sees Frick's bloodied face before him and hesitates, almost surrenders to the feeling of shame, that fleeting moment is intensely important because it illuminates the special kind of violence possible only to man, the human animal. The object of attack, in this instance, Frick, is deprived of his individuality and his humanity because Berkman has turned him into an object, a symbol of the repressive forces of capitalism. It is not Frick, the man, but Frick, the symbol, there before Berkman. Berkman must do the same to himself. He must deny his own humanity, his own feeling, and turn himself into an instrument of a cause, a symbol of a revolutionary ideology.

Berkman carries the same attitude with him into prison. His sentimental glorification of the People and Humanity (always in upper case) provides no room in his affections for ordinary, flawed human beings. He shrinks from familiarity with other prisoners. "They are not of *my*-world," he writes, sealed off from them by his idealized conception of himself as more than human. "I would aid them," he says, "as in duty bound to the victims of social injustice. But I cannot be friends with them. . . . By virtue of my principles, rather than their deserts, I must give them my intellectual sympathy; they touch no chord in my heart." The chaplain who is kind to Berkman is still just a "cog" in the prison machinery. He feels disdain for the petty pickpockets, the "dips," and revulsion for the entertaining homosexual who thinks Berkman might become his "kid."

Gradually, though, Berkman comes to realize that humanity is no grand abstraction. It is made up of pitiful, stunted, hurt human beings. The organized violence of the prison, the sadism of the guards, the self-degradation of compulsive masturbation and forced buggery, the horrors of the creeping insanity of "crank row," the economic and human corruption of unchecked power, all these make the prison a microcosm of the wretched civilization Berkman wishes to destroy; but they also make him realize that to do violence to a human being means simply that, to do violence to a human being. Berkman comes finally to recognize what he calls his "coldly impersonal" way. Of an aged, but still flippant, burglar, he thinks:

With the severe intellectuality of revolutionary tradition, I thought of him and his kind as inevitable fungus growths, the rotten fruit of a decaying society. Unfortunate derelicts, indeed, yet parasites, almost devoid of humanity. But the threads of comradeship have slowly been woven by common misery. . . . Not entirely in vain are the years of suffering that have wakened my kinship with the humanity of *les miserables.*

Again, when he hears of the assassination of the King of Italy by the anarchist, Bresci, Berkman approves, thinks Bresci did well, but then goes on: "Yet, I feel that the individual, in certain cases, is of more direct and immediate consequence than humanity. What is [humanity] but the aggregate of individual existences—and shall these, the best of them, forever be sacrificed for the metaphysical collectivity?"

The climax of Berkman's emotional and intellectual journey comes when he receives the news in prison of the assassination of President McKinley by Leon Czolgosz. When first taken by the police, Czolgosz said he was an anarchist. Although he later repudiated the statement, the hunt was on for all known anarchists, and Czolgosz's slender acquaintance with Emma Goldman led to her quick arrest in Chicago. While McKinley was dying, Emma said to a reporter that, although she was sympathetic to Czolgosz, she would gladly, as a nurse, care for McKinley. Berkman wrote Emma (the "girl" in *Prison Memoirs*) a clandestine letter:

You were splendid, dear; and I was especially moved by your remark that you would faithfully nurse the wounded man, if he required your services. . . . That remark discovered to me the great change wrought in us by the ripening years. Yes, in us, in both, for my heart echoed your beautiful sentiment. How impossible such a thought would have been to us in the days of a decade ago! We should have considered it treason to the spirit of revolution; it would have outraged all our traditions even to admit the humanity of an official representative of capitalism.

And Berkman draws the conclusion: "the stupendous task of human regeneration will be accomplished only by the purified vision of hearts that grow not cold."

Berkman never ceased to be an anarchist. As in Bruno Bettelheim's account in *The Informed Heart* of how one stays alive under conditions of total power and nearly total degradation, Berkman survives because the prison is always more than a prison to him. It is a testing ground for his theory. The remarkable thing is that he learns what it means to be human, that to love humanity means to love the least of men. As he moves from a cold and abstract idealism to a warm and sympathetic identification, even to an unembarrassed and untroubled acceptance of the reality of homosexual love, Berkman discovers what it means to be a man.

Closely related to the change in Berkman's attitude toward human nature is the change in his understanding of the political complexity of the violent deed. The second theme as well as the first finds its formal conclusion in the same long letter to Emma Goldman. After the fine phrase, "human regeneration will be accomplished only by the purified vision of hearts that grow not cold," Berkman goes on: "I share your view entirely; for that very reason, it is the more distressing to disagree with you in one very important particular: the value of Leon's act." Berkman then draws a distinction between an individual act and a social act, between the impulse of a tortured and demented individual like Czolgosz and the probable social effect.

"To prove of value," Berkman argues, acts of violence "must be motivated by social rather than individual necessity, and be directed against a real and immediate enemy of the people." He rejects the educational effect of the assassination of President McKinley because, he says, "the social necessity for its performance was not manifest." And he pursues the point: "That you may not misunderstand, I repeat: as an expression of personal revolt it was inevitable, and in itself an indictment of existing conditions. But the background of social necessity was lacking, and therefore the value of the act was to a great extent nullified."

Why Berkman thought the "background of social necessity was lacking" is crucial, but, first, it is necessary to point out the drastic qualification Berkman has made to the rationale for the anarchist deed of violence. We can measure how drastic by Emma Goldman's response. After the first emotional shock, Emma thought, "Why Sasha [Berkman] is using the same argument against Leon [Czolgosz] that Johann Most had urged against Sasha. Most had proclaimed the futility of individual acts of violence in a country devoid of proletarian consciousness and he had pointed out that the American worker did not understand the motive of such deeds."

Emma's recollection here deals with one of the more colorful moments in the sectarian history of anarchism. When Emma and Berkman first met, Johann Most was the acknowledged leader and inspiration of the tiny foreign anarchist movement in the United States. For a while, both Most and Berkman were Emma's lovers, which complicated matters beyond potential theoretical differences. When Berkman tried to assassinate Frick, Most repudiated the deed for precisely the reason that Emma names here: the American worker was not sufficiently advanced to understand the meaning of the deed. When Most spoke in New York City, and Emma heard he might repeat his attack on Berkman, she went to the meeting with a long bull-whip wrapped around her body beneath her coat, and when Most began his attack on her beloved Sasha, Emma leaped to the stage and whipped him out of the hall.

Now Emma found Berkman in the same position Most had taken ten years before. Berkman has introduced an element of pragmatic political calculation into his assessment of the wisdom of violence. In his idealistic youth, Berkman dreamed that to assassinate Frick would awaken the consciousness of the working class, would startle the worker out of his lethargic and repressed condition, and identify for him his enemy. The deed of violence would create the revolution.

But Johann Most was right. When Berkman went to prison, he discovered that no one could understand why he had tried to kill Frick, not even the Homestead workers there in prison themselves. Other prisoners thought there must have been some personal quarrel between Berkman and Frick, or some "business misunderstanding." Or they thought Berkman was simply crazy. Not only those in prison. The union in Homestead immediately dissociated itself from Berkman's act, and sent condolences to Frick with the message that they prayed for his speedy recovery.

But Berkman, in his letter to Emma, did not simply resign himself to misunderstanding. He understood with remarkable precision why conditions in America made all the difference.

In Russia, where political oppression is popularly felt, such a deed would be of great value. But the scheme of political subjection is more subtle in America. And though McKinley was the chief representative of our modern slavery, he could not be considered in the light of a direct and immediate enemy of the people; while in an absolutism, the autocrat is visible and tangible. The real despotism of republican institutions is far deeper, more insidious, because it rests on the popular delusion of self-government and independence. That is the subtle source of democratic tyranny, and, as such, it cannot be reached with a bullet.

By comparing Russia and the United States Berkman does not, of course, say that there is no oppression in the United States and that there is no need for conflict, but that the real repression in American society, what Berkman names "despotism," derives from the generally shared belief that one is independent, one is self-governing. Berkman points, in other words, to the ideology which is immune to revolution and violent action, which cannot be "reached with a bullet." He goes on to make a distinction between political and economic repression in order to insist upon the worth of his own deed of violence, perhaps because of the need to believe that his years in jail were not in vain, but then comes back to the act of political assassination: do these "rockets of iron," he asks, does this "lightning really illumine the social horizon, or merely confuse minds with the succeeding darkness?"

Along with his awareness that the revolutionist's dream may only sacrifice people to the myth of the "People," the collectivity which has no room for actual, concrete, living individuals, Berkman came to realize that violence, the decision to kill, finds no sanction in some transcendent ideal, but is finally to be justified only in relation to historical necessity which, in turn, demands political calculation and a pragmatic estimate of the consequences.

III

At this point, an unwary reader may breathe a sigh of relief, glad that Berkman has come to recognize the inhumanity of his revolutionary ideal and the political inconsequence of direct violence, especially in the United States. But that is a false moral and a sentimental conclusion to draw from *Prison Memoirs*. Berkman is not saying that violence has no place in American life. He is saying that violence cannot be understood by Americans because of the ideology which holds captive even those who are the oppressed. The American creed of an open, egalitarian society means that there can be no violent protest against the conditions of American society because there can be no real cause for it. The act of violence cannot be understood. It must be the act of a deranged and mad individual. It escapes historical understanding.

To say that because of our ideals violence should not happen here is not to say that it does not happen here. Statistically, both in individual and collective acts of violence, the United States far surpasses any other Western society. In the straightforward language of the final report of the National Commission on the Causes and Prevention of Violence, "The United States is the clear leader among modern stable democratic nations in its rates of homicide, assault, rape, robbery, and it is at least among the highest in the incidence of group violence and assassination." In that context, the use of the word "stable" may seem rather heavy-handed irony, but it points to a curious aspect of the phenomenon of violence in America: the violence which has marked our history has rarely been directed against the state. Our political institutions have been little affected by it. Which is what Berkman pointed out: violence has had no political meaning in American consciousness. Berkman hints at why this is so: Americans believe deeply that they enjoy self-government and personal independence.

When Americans insist that American society is free, they generally mean that American society is a society in which each individual, irrespective of extrinsic associations of family, neighborhood, class, race, or ethnic origin, is free to make of himself what he can. More is involved than classical liberalism or laissez-faire capitalism. As Emerson put it, "Government will be adamantine without any governor." That was the millennial promise of America, a benign anarchism in which each individual was to be the bearer of his own destiny and society no more than a collection of individual wills. It was that very dream which drew Berkman to America: "There, beyond the ocean, was the land of noble achievement, a glorious free country, where men walked erect in the full stature of manhood."

A society which believes that it is the result of the actions of free and equal and self-reliant individuals has, logically, no reason to suppose that the state and the institutions of society are important. To the degree one believes that America is a uniquely free society, that each person is unencumbered by forces beyond the determination of his own personality, to the degree such an ideal has power over one's mind and imagination, there is no way to understand violence except as irrational and aberrant. Our difficulty in understanding violence in America is, in part at least, a consequence of our insistence that ours is a society of equality and opportunity and individual freedom. To ask questions about the reality of violence would force us to ask questions about the reality of our ideals.

Furthermore, our ideology, to the degree it is believed in and acted upon, leads to intense frustration which easily spills over into violent behavior when the social situation, the daily, lived experience of actual people, blocks and prevents them from acting out what they are told is ideally possible. After the ghetto riots in Watts and Newark and Detroit, a study was made of those who could be identified as participants. In the Detroit study, blacks who were actors in the riot, that is, those who were apprehended in overt acts from breaking a window to sniping, were asked whether they believed that if one had sufficient will and desire he could make of himself what he wanted in American society. A majority of those ghetto blacks said yes. There is a fact. What is one to make of it?

Not too much, perhaps, without knowing more. Was it a white man or a black man who asked the question? The blacks who answered were in the hands of the police and might well have wanted to assure everyone of their benign disposition toward American society. But to accept the fact on its face, one conclusion is that the most aggressive blacks were precisely those who believed they were free to seize the advantages of American life and, when blocked from doing so, reacted with rage and violence. One sociologist put it, as sociologists like to put it, that violence varies inversely with the presence of avenues to status and power, and avenues of legitimate modes of protest.

At yet a lower level, as Herman Melville put it, our ideals and values are even more deeply involved in the high incidence of violence in America. The traditional American emphasis on individualism and self-determination entails a weakening of institutional forms of restraint with the consequence of a relatively high statistical incidence of aberrant behavior. To put it paradoxically, a liberal, free society must be a repressive society: Freedom from external restraint means that the individual must internalize the values of the culture, and restrain himself. He must be, as we say, self-governing; he must repress his antisocial impulses in order to remain free.

A society such as ours, which increasingly rejects the sanctions of tradition, the family, the church, and the power of the state, necessarily must create the kind of personality who is self-governing, self-restraining, self-repressive. The founding fathers, following the Roman model, defined the essential quality as virtue; Emerson called it character, the Protestant evangelical tradition named it benevolence. The tradition is a long one, and we may respond warmly to some of its phrases, but we should not in our self-congratulation ignore the enormous psychic burden such an ideal places upon the individual. Until we reach the millennium of American democratic hopes, we must accept the probable instability of our society, especially when it denies the opportunity and self-respect which its ideology constantly celebrates.

Most interestingly, the rejection of violence as somehow un-American blinds us to the forms of violence, both official and private, which have in fact dominated American history. Consider the occasion of Berkman's deed: the Carnegie Steel Company imported a private army of 300 Pinkertons, the *condottiere* of industrial warfare in the late nineteenth century. The company held back its ultimatum to labor until it completed an order for steel plate for the United States Navy, whose power was needed to shield American commercial expansion. A lynch mob, after Berkman's assassination attempt, pillaged and destroyed a utopian anarchist community outside Pittsburgh. Finally, the state militia, welcomed by the Homestead workers who believed that the state was a neutral umpire, broke the strike and escorted scabs back to work. Such particulars support an important generalization: violence has been used again and again to support the structure of authority in American society. We are only puzzled when violence is used to attack that structure.

Our ideals are involved even here. The insistence that all men are free and equal leads to the curious consequence of a mass conformity and a mood of intolerance for dissent in any form. Tocqueville provided the classic statement, which still holds, that the energetic individualism and the tyranny of the majority in America both derived from the ideal of equality. The necessary obverse of the belief that "I'm as good as you are" is acceptance of the fact that "You are as good as I am." The basis of one's own self-trust and self-sufficiency must be extended to all the equal others in society. So, if one is in a minority, one has no claim against a tyrannous majority. The very ideal of the equal worth of every man, which promises a world of manly, independent, and free men, perversely leads to the mind and mood of the mass man who is intolerant of any deviation from what he thinks. That majority may be silent, but it has throughout American history been ready always to wreak its own repressive violence on the rash individual who dares to challenge it or call into question the ideology which creates and sustains it.

The fault, as Berkman would have it, lies in American consciousness: "that is the subtle source of democratic tyranny, and, as such, it cannot be reached with a bullet." If that is so, the keepers of that consciousness, American intellectuals, have dismally failed in their responsibility to American society. One of the functions of the intellectual is to raise to consciousness the ambiguities inherent in the professed ideals of society, and to make clear the meaning of the social forces implicit in the actions of society which contradict those ideals. We have failed to see that the ugly violence of our society is not an aberration of an otherwise sound and healthy society, but the unintended and unforeseen consequence of our most cherished ideals. We must act on our ideals, or change our minds.

"The struggle," to use Barrington Moore's words, "concerns contemporary capitalist democracy's capacity to live up to its noble professions, something no society has ever done. . . . As one peers ever deeper to resolve the ambiguities of history, the seeker eventually finds them in himself and his fellow men as well as in the supposedly dead facts of history. We are inevitably in the midst of the ebb and flow of those events and play a part, no matter how small and insignificant as individuals, in what the past will come to mean for the future."

There is, in the alien experience of Alexander Berkman, as in all great books, much to discover about ourselves. We affect history in the attempt to understand it. In this sense, simply to read is inevitably a political act. As we attempt to understand the meaning of violence in the American experience, Berkman is not a bad prophet for the condition in which we find ourselves. He may at last have found the moment when we can hear what he is saying.

H.C. Peterson and Gilbert C. Fite

THE AMERICAN REIGN OF TERROR

Nearly one hundred and fifty years ago Alexis de Tocque-ville's classic study of Democracy in America *warned of the special tendency toward a "tyranny of the majority." There is no clearer example than the treatment of those who refused to fall into step with administration policy during World War I.*

The nation was deeply divided right up until the eve of our entry into the fighting in the spring of 1917. Few Americans understood the complexities of international politics, or the issues at stake for the belligerents. President Woodrow Wilson, while privately fearful of the effect on civil liberties, supported a patriotic propaganda effort to unite Americans behind his policies. Ironically many citizens, all across the spectrum of political opinion, later felt that we had been duped, in some degree, into participation in the hostilities. Our support for the allies against Germany seemed at the least badly timed, our war aims unrealistic and easily diverted. But despite this later change in attitudes, it was dangerous to express or even be accused of reservations of any kind in 1917-18. As often happens, bigotry against ethnic minorities and fear of working-class organizers, many of them opposed to all war on principle, were vented in the name of "American Ideals."

H. C. Peterson and Gilbert Fite, writing in the 1950s, another time in which anything less than "100 percent Ameri-canism" was often suspect, describe the atmosphere on the home front during the war to "Make the World Safe for Democracy." They discuss the reasons why social violence that is de-signed to smother dissent is especially dangerous to the Republic.

Printed by permission of the University of Washington Press from *Opponents of War, 1917-1918,* by H.C. Peterson and Gilbert C. Fite (1968), pp. 194-207, 297-301.

Spring, 1918, in the United States was a time when strident voices filled the air, when mobs swarmed through the streets, when violence of all kinds was practiced upon the opponents of the war. The words and actions were not unlike those of earlier months, but the tones were heightened, the tempo accelerated.

A preacher was quoted by the *Detroit Free Press* on March 4, 1918, as saying, "The person who claims to be neutral ought to be exported, jailed, interned, labeled, or . . . rendered powerless." An editor exclaimed, "For goodness sake, when is the firing squad to get busy?"[1] Other editors spoke of firing squads, stone walls at sunrise, and telegraph poles.[2] There were even those who almost regretted the "passing of the boiling-in-oil period of administering reprisal to traitors to their country."[3] On August 3, 1918, the *New Republic* declared, "This [hysterical] state of mind is being assiduously cultivated by many of our newspapers, many of our respected fellow citizens, and certain public officials. Those who do not encourage it certainly fail to protest against it."[4]

To guarantee orthodoxy, the prying into people's opinions continued unabated. An army official in South Carolina invited civilians to report to him any suspicious and disloyal activity, as well as any signs of sympathy for the enemy.[5] The state Councils of Defense were flooded with complaints against individuals of doubted loyalty. In Nebraska, for example, it was at first the practice of the Council to have a representative call on the accused, question him, and warn or threaten him if that seemed necessary. But the complaints grew so numerous that this procedure had to be changed and offenders were forced to come before the Council. An official of this body reported, "When we summon offenders before our committee . . . we do not permit them to be represented by attorneys, and we do not reveal to them the names of the men who make the complaints." The writer added, "We are partial to the tender touch, to the educational process, and as I have said we find that in most cases it works successfully. But we have had cases—many of them—where the 'iron hand' was necessary, and we have not hesitated to use it."[6]

The Councils of Defense in some other states carried on in much the same way. At one time in South Dakota, some thirty-five people were subpoenaed in order to find out if they were loyally supporting the war. A farmer and his wife, suspected of "anti-American" activities, fainted when the sheriff read the subpoena to them.[7] Suspects in a Florida town were made to repeat a catechism of loyalty.[8]

From the very beginning of the war there had been attacks upon things German. Now the cries of hate rose to a crescendo. Names of towns and individuals were changed. The lowly hamburger became the liberty sandwich, and sauerkraut was called liberty cabbage. Hymns, symphonies, and operas of German origin were looked upon with suspicion. And then, of course, there was hatred of the German language.

During the winter of 1917–18, there was a strong drive to abolish the teaching of German in the country's schools. Theodore Roosevelt backed it.[9] So did the state Councils of Defense. The American Defense Society urged the mayor of New York to discontinue teaching the "Kaiser's tongue" in the city schools.[10] At a national meeting on illiteracy, much of the session was given over to attacks upon the teaching of German.[11] The argument was advanced that the German language had no cultural or practical value and that to teach it gave aid and comfort to the enemy. *The Manufacturers Record* said that German had been emphasized not because of its "intrinsic value" but because it was part of the "political propaganda intended to wean the people of this country away from Anglo-Saxon and Anglo-Celtic origins and ideals and divide the national interest and national sympathy."[12] Professor Knight Dunlap of Johns Hopkins declared that the German language was a "barbarous tongue," lacking in cultural worth and without commercial importance.[13]

With these sentiments predominating, the desired results were soon obtained. The use of the German language was forbidden in the pulpits and schools of Montana. In Iowa, the Governor ruled that German could not be used on streetcars, over the telephone, or anywhere else in public.[14] News stories from all sections of the nation told of individual cities outlawing the use of German in public places and forbidding its teaching in the schools. On March 26, 1918, the Seattle *Post-Intelligencer* announced, "German Barred from Spokane's Public Schools." Again on April 9, the *Post-Intelligencer* headed a story, "Speech of Hated Hun Forbidden." As the Oklahoma schools dropped German from their curricula, the Tulsa *Daily World* declared, "German Deader than Latin Now."[15] On the basis of a poll taken by the *Literary Digest,* 149 schools had discontinued German language study by March, 1918.[16] Others were to follow.

On the same intellectual level was the move to burn German books. In Lewiston, Montana, a committee marched on the local high school and burned all the German textbooks it could find.[17] A book-burning was announced as a part of a Fourth of July celebration in Shawnee, Oklahoma.[18] Another was promised in Spartanburg, South Carolina.[19] In a small Indiana town, German books were thrown into a muddy ditch.[20]

A common punishment devised for people suspected of disloyalty or sedition was that of kissing the flag. The riot in Boston on July 4, 1917, was accompanied by flag-kissing. In December, a young man in Arkansas was compelled to wrap a flag about him, kiss it, and then salute army recruiting officers.[21] By 1918 flag-kissing had become so frequent that it was hardly first-rate news. In Trenton, New Jersey, two sisters working in a pottery plant were reported to have made disparaging remarks about American soldiers. Other workers gave them the choice of being ducked in a canal or kissing the flag and pledging allegiance to the United States. The two chose the flag-kissing punishment.[22] In California, the police forced a Russian to kiss the flag. [23] A foreigner in New York was arrested for failing to register. He swore that he would be a "slacker as long as he lived." He was forced to kiss the flag several times and then wave it above his head as he paraded up and down the corridor. [24] In New Jersey a man who refused to subscribe for a Liberty bond was compelled to go to his knees and kiss the flag. [25]

A young man in Montana, E. V. Starr, fell into the hands of a mob bent upon vindicating its peculiar standard of patriotism by compelling him to kiss the flag. In the heat of the argument, Starr remarked, "What is this thing anyway? Nothing but a piece of cotton with a little paint on it and some other marks in the corner there. I will not kiss that thing. It might be covered with microbes." [26] Starr was arrested under the state sedition act for using language "calculated to bring the flag into contempt and disrepute." He was fined five hundred dollars and costs, and given a long penitentiary sentence. In denying Starr a writ of habeas corpus, the district court said that he had been "more sinned against than sinning." The members of the mob, not Starr, "should have been punished," said the court. The judge then sharply criticized that brand of patriotism which descended to fanaticism. [27] But the court held that Starr had no legal recourse, except to apply for a pardon.

Along with flag-kissing came a great sensitiveness about respect for the national anthem. A Croatian by the name of Frank Horrath failed to stand in a Pittsburgh theater when the anthem was played. A policeman took him away from an angry mob and put him in jail. He was charged with disorderly conduct and fined ten dollars. [28] In Chicago an individual was fined fifty dollars for failing to stand when the "Star-Spangled Banner" was played. [29] Similar incidents occurred elsewhere.

As mentioned before, yellow paint was customarily used to single out those who were considered disloyal. Sometimes homes, offices, and churches were marked with it. Frequently, even individuals were painted. [30] For example, when some Nebraskans refused to participate in a Liberty Loan rally they were painted yellow, [31] as were three men who made adverse comments about the loans in Kansas City. [32] A grain elevator in Little Rock, Iowa, was painted yellow because the proprietor was accused of pro-Germanism. When he tried to locate those who had done the painting job by using bloodhounds to follow them, "loyal citizens" beat him and drove him out of town. [33]

Unique forms of violence were often devised by mobs to punish those charged with disloyalty or pro-Germanism. For instance, in San Rafael, California, a man had his hair clipped in the form of a cross, after which he was tied to a tree on the courthouse lawn. [34] A person of German birth in Salt Lake City was thrown into a bin of dough where he almost suffocated. [35] In Pennsylvania a man was taken from a hotel room, "severely beaten, made to walk up and down the street with a dog chain around his neck, forced to kiss the flag and doused into a large watering trough." [36] At

LaSalle, Illinois, Dr. J. C. Biemann, a pioneer physician, was ducked in a canal by several hundred men and boys. Then he was forced to kiss the flag and warned to leave the city. His "crime" was that he was supposed to have called Secretary of War Baker a "fat head."[37]

In Berkeley, California, a large canvas tabernacle used by the Church of the Living God was burned down by a mob of men and boys. The pastor, the Reverend Joshua Sykes, and two elders were ducked in the baptismal tank. Along with other leaders, they were shortly arrested for their pacifist activities. They were accused of having told members of their church that they were citizens of God's kingdom and not of the United States, and that they should not assist with the war. Sykes and others were also accused of urging members not to contribute to the Red Cross, to buy Liberty bonds, to display the American flag, or to participate in war work. They were sentenced to various terms in McNeil Island Penitentiary.[38]

. . .

During the spring of 1918 news stories from all sections of the country told of people being beaten by mobs of super-patriots. Sometimes it was for not displaying a flag, for objecting to the draft law, for criticizing American soldiers, or even soldiers of the associated powers; perhaps it was for not buying bonds, or for other reasons. But whatever the cause, the safest policy for one's physical well-being in many communities was to remain silent. Criticism of war aims and policies would not be tolerated.[39]

Besides beating their victims, American mobs frequently resorted to the use of tar and feathers. There were a number of such cases in the fall of 1917. Perhaps the most notable incident was that of the seventeen I.W.W.'s at Tulsa. But throughout the late winter and spring of 1918, there was a veritable rash of tar and feather incidents. A few examples from various sections of the nation will illustrate the situation.

Joe Polaras, a Mexican living in Seattle, was tarred and feathered because he was supposedly unpatriotic.[40] In Reno, Nevada, Elmer White was tied to a stake, lashed with a cat-o-nine-tails, tarred and feathered, and ordered out of town.[41] A superintendent of schools in a Colorado town was given a coat of grease and feathers—a slight variation.[42] At Emerson, Nebraska, Rudolph Schopke was tarred and feathered because he refused to contribute to the Red Cross.[43] In Oklahoma O. F. Westbrook, a farmer living near Altus, was dragged from his bed by a masked and heavily armed mob and taken to a wooded area. There he was forced to kiss the flag and take the oath of "eternal allegiance to the Knights of Liberty." He was then lashed with a blacksnake whip and given a coat of tar and feathers.[44] Similar incidents were reported in or near Muskogee, Wynnewood, Elk City, and Henryetta—all in Oklahoma. At Electra, Texas, a confectioner by the name of George Geanapolus was tarred and feathered and driven out of town by some two hundred businessmen.[45]

. . .

Mobs had not been on the march long before they threatened the very lives of their victims. A Pennsylvania mob, composed of women munition workers, attempted to lynch a man who was supposed to have made seditious remarks. [46] An Oregon supporter of the Russellites distributed a circular criticizing persons said to have suppressed the circulation of *The Finished Mystery*. For this a mob threatened to lynch him. [47] When an Austrian employee of the Erie Railroad was accused of a lack of patriotism, he was "hauled thirty feet above ground at the end of a rope . . . and a fire hose was played upon him. He was cut down an hour later by friends who found him alive." [48]

Those who committed such acts quite naturally prepared the way for other mobs to kill their victims. The precedent for mob killings was, of course, present in the United States. In the first six months of 1918 alone, there were thirty-five such events. The states of Alabama and Louisiana led in number of killings with eight each. [49] But these were mostly racial killings. The new mob killings were to be "patriotic" affairs; they were murder in the name of liberty and democracy.

On March 24, 1918, in the small town of Hickory, Oklahoma, a Bulgarian was shot and killed by a policeman. It was alleged that he had said something "seditious," and, according to the policeman, the victim had fired first. [50] On the same date an "operative" of the County Council of Defense in Tulsa shot and killed Joe Spring, a waiter in a restaurant. He accused Spring of making pro-German remarks. [51] Two days later the County Council of Defense issued a statement declaring that "any person or persons who utter disloyal or unpatriotic statements do so at their own peril and cannot expect the protection of the loyal citizenship of this nation." [52] On March 27, the Tulsa *Daily World* reported, "It wasn't S. L. Miller that was on trial for murdering Joe Spring yesterday. . . . It was the patriotism of Tulsa and the principle of a new unwritten law that makes it justifiable for a man to slay one who speaks out against the country that shelters and nurtures him." Miller was found not guilty. "The decision was received with cheers, and men, women, and children rushed to Miller to congratulate him, both for his patriotism and the outcome of the trial." On April 14, the *Daily World* reported that the policeman who had killed the Bulgarian was also acquitted. The presiding judge released the officer "after making a patriotic talk and warning pro-Germans not to speak their sentiments against the United States."

Southern Illinois was one of the most mob-ridden parts of the country. There was widespread discontent and unrest in the coal fields. Conflicts between employers and workmen were common. It was in this region that a labor lawyer and a union leader were tarred and feathered and driven out of town because they were causing "dissension among several thousand coal miners near Staunton."[53] At the same time, according to an account in the files of the American Civil Liberties Union, "more than one hundred persons were made to sign pledges of loyalty." This news stimulated stern measures in Worden, Mount Olive, Gillespie, Williamson, Hillsboro, and several other small towns. There were numerous instances of people being taken from their homes and forced to make public professions of loyalty. Some were forced to kiss the flag; others had to sing the national anthem or play patriotic tunes on musical instruments. To protest such actions was in itself considered disloyal. It was said that the American Defense Society was trying to make the district "100 percent American."[54]

In the town of Christopher, a Polish Catholic priest, the Reverend John Kovalsky, was accused of having remarked that "God is with the Kaiser and the Kaiser will win the war." In spite of his fervent denials he was taken by a mob, and, with three other men, was tarred and feathered. What the others were accused of was not specified.[55] In Benton Mrs. Frances Bergen got into an argument and apparently said some uncomplimentary things about President Wilson. Both Mrs. Bergen and Henry Baker, with whom she had argued, were arrested. While Baker's fine was paid by public subscription, the Loyalty League took Mrs. Bergen through town on a rail, forcing her to wave the American flag. One account stated, "At frequent intervals the procession paused, while Mrs. Bergen was compelled to shout praise for President Wilson."[56]

Labor organizers were especially unpopular. At Hillsboro three union organizers, L. B. (Dad) Irvin, and Frank and Joseph Zib, had done effective work with the laborers. Among other things they had helped to bring about a large increase in the accident compensation received by injured miners. After the draft was passed, the Zib brothers registered as conscientious objectors. Although the questionnaires were supposed to have been private, the local editor immediately wrote a scathing article against them, and the private information was made public. Within a short time a group of citizens decided to take action against Irvin and the Zibs. On March 8, 1918, the vigilantes assembled, prepared tar and straw, and went in search of their intended victims. A report to the Civil Liberties Union stated: "Not finding the Zibs or Irvin at home after all their preparations, they became more enraged and with that frantically seized every possession—clothing, trunks, furniture, typewriter—their library, everything, and pulled them down the steps into the street where they offered them, in the name of freedom, to the flames prepared by the others of the group." Continuing their search, members of the mob descended in force upon a house where Irvin was believed to be hiding. When they knocked on the door—the occupants of the house apparently did not understand the purpose of a visit from the mob—a shot was fired, and a wild melee followed. Four men were wounded, including policeman Seaton Emory and a young man named Clifford Donaldson. Donaldson died later. He was twenty-four years old and had just enlisted in the navy.[57]

The hysteria of the area spread into the small town of Collinsville just east of St. Louis. The local Council of Defense advocated "loyalty pledges," and there was severe criticism of a Baptist minister who felt that the church should not be used for Thrift Stamp meetings. [58] Miners expressed uneasiness because some of their fellow workers were of foreign birth. Conservative elements were disturbed by union agitation. Members of a Loyalty committee began to agitate for the suppression of "disloyalty." Loud accusations were made against Robert Paul Prager, a young man of German birth. A registered enemy alien, Prager was employed in a local bakery. He had applied for membership in a local miners' union at which time he was supposed to have talked to the men on the virtues of Socialism. [59] However, so far as is known, he was not guilty of directly opposing the war. He had made no seditious statements and no incidents had occurred. In fact, he had tried to enlist in the navy but was rejected because he had one glass eye.

Because of wild and irresponsible talk about disloyalty, the mayor ordered the saloons closed on April 4, thus throwing a group of idle, half-drunken men onto the streets. They began a search for Prager. When they found him, "his shoes were stripped off and members of the mob began pulling off his clothes, when someone produced an American flag. It was wrapped around him and tied."[60] In this condition, with only a flag to cover him, he was dragged barefooted, stumbling through the streets.

At this point, the police rescued Prager and placed him in the city jail. But the mob soon broke into the jail and took its victim out of town in search of a convenient tree. This may have happened after the police "insisted no violence be done inside the city limits."[61] Prager was asked if he were a German spy, and "if he had tried to blow up the Maryville mine." One member of the mob was reported to have struck Prager on the head and knocked him down. A participant in the mob action, Joseph Riegel, was quoted as saying, "All the time the crowd kept getting more excited and angry. Someone shouted, 'Well if he won't come in with anything, string him up.' A boy produced a handkerchief and his hands were tied. I might have been the man who did the tying. I was drunk, and because I had been in the army the crowd made me the big man in the affair, and I guess I was sort of puffed over that."[62] Before they hanged Prager, he was allowed to write a note to his mother and father. "Dear Parents:" he said, "I must this day, the fourth of April, 1918, die. Please, my dear parents, pray for me. This is my last letter or testament. Robert Paul."[63] He was then given a few minutes to fall on his knees and pray before members of the mob pulled him high in the air where he gasped his last breath. As a report in the *New York Call* of April 16, 1918, expressed it, "He was one, his pursuers were five hundred, who, after baiting him to their heart's content, deliberately murdered him." The *New York Times* of April 11 reported that his last request was to be buried with an American flag over him.

At last the excesses of the super-patriots had reached such heights that some people were jolted into realizing for the first time, how serious mob actions in the name of loyalty had become. That Prager had been guilty of no crime, or of any overt acts of disloyalty, made the deed even more dastardly. In referring to the case, Attorney General Gregory declared, "From all the facts I have been able to gather concerning the lynching of the man in Illinois, I doubt his having been guilty of any offense."[64]

There was widespread condemnation of the lynching, even by those who had previously spoken out most strongly against all aspects of disloyalty. Theodore Roosevelt and William Howard Taft both immediately condemned the action. The most outspoken critic was Senator Sherman of Illinois. He referred to the mob and to city officials as follows: "The police followed this drunken mob to the edge of the city. . . . There are four policemen in that town to preserve the peace. That magnificent constabulary followed to the city limits; they said they had no jurisdiction beyond it; and the mob was allowed to wreak its bloody purpose upon the helpless victim."[65] He also called the mayor a "poltroon" and a "renegade in public office."[66]

. . .

Some papers, however, were quite reserved in their criticisms. This was probably because they did not want to take a position which might be interpreted as in any way lacking in patriotism. Their attitude, however, indicates a fundamental problem posed by modern nationalism. How can one safely attack an evil action when it is clothed in "patriotism"? It is quite apparent that many papers felt it could, and perhaps should, not be done. After the Prager lynching nationalists tried to lay the blame for mob actions on the victims themselves. Some elements of the press even seemed to approve the action.[67] On April 12 the *Washington Post* commented, "In the East the public mind toward the war was much earlier divested of errors." Then it added, "In spite of excesses such as lynching, it is a healthful and wholesome awakening in the interior of the country."

Eventually a number of the leaders of the mob were indicted and tried. There was great difficulty in obtaining a jury, and the trial was a most unjudicial affair. Defendants wore red, white, and blue ribbons, and occasionally a band would play patriotic airs in the courthouse. The defense attorney's statement to the jury "was almost entirely a loyalty plea, mingled with an attack on the State for conducting the prosecution."[68] The defense argued that Prager's lynching was a "patriotic murder" which served as a means of home protection.[69] The jury returned the usual mob verdict of not guilty in twenty-five minutes. Those in the courtroom congratulated the defendants. There was cheering and handclapping, and one juryman shouted, "Well, I guess nobody can say we aren't loyal now."[70] But he was wrong. The New York *Evening Post* of June 3, 1918, said that the verdict was a "gross miscarriage of justice." Indeed, it was.

The sentiment of local patriots, however, was expressed in a story from Edwardsville, Illinois. It reported a feeling of "grim satisfaction" by the public in southern Illinois. Continuing, the account stated, "Having lynched an undesirable resident and escaped without unpleasant consequences, Madison County is ready for the next comer. Hanging is not an agreeable business and it may not be necessary to hang anybody else. That is entirely up to the other fellow. If a deserving victim should happen along there are other trees and plenty of unused rope." [71] The "unhung traitors" idea had gained wide popularity and acceptance. On April 13, the *Seattle Union-Record* ran an editorial which stated ironically, "If you don't like your neighbor, shoot him! . . . Then declare he made seditious or pro-German statements and rely on the patriotism of the people to see that you are not punished. That is, in effect, the advice of the yellow press." After referring to certain local newspapers, the editorial in the *Union-Record* continued, "As a result of similar utterances we have had during the past few weeks a regular terror of tar and featherings, hangings, and even burnings of alleged traitors." Such was the spirit and action of early 1918.

Prager's hanging capped the climax of violence performed under the guise of patriotism. But even this ghastly incident did not bring people to their senses. It did not create a popular demand which might say in effect, mob law will no longer be tolerated. It did not end further patriotic excesses. [72] Instances of violence in late April and early May of 1918 continued to be reported in all sections of the United States. When a Kentucky citizen later protested to President Wilson about "the persecution of a naturalized German-American in his town," a man who had bought war bonds liberally, Wilson commented to Tumulty, "I have no doubt that there are hundreds of cases like it." [73]

The Prager affair, as well as the less violent actions by nationalists, seemed to call for vigorous action by the federal Government to protect innocent people against lawless and irresponsible mobs. Many moderate Americans, and even some of the super-patriots, objected and were publicly critical of current happenings. Also, stinging criticism of what was called American barbarism began coming from abroad. The German Government lodged an official protest through the Swiss legation, and even offered to pay Prager's funeral expenses. [74] Needless to say, this offer was not accepted.

But President Wilson was distressingly slow in taking any forthright action. The Prager murder was discussed at the regular Cabinet meeting on the afternoon of April 5. Apparently, the President and his advisers decided to sidestep this touchy issue. The *New York Times* reported on April 6 that "from what was said after the meeting it was apparent that the President and his advisers decided that the federal Government had no warrant for interference." Speaking after the meeting, Attorney General Gregory said that it was a problem for Illinois to handle. To refuse to accept responsibility may have been an easy way out, but it did not satisfy a great many people.

On April 18 John Lord O'Brian of the Department of Justice prepared a memorandum which was sent to Wilson suggesting that some sort of statement should be issued by the Government "for the purpose of reassuring the people, quieting their apprehensions, and preventing so far as possible the spread of mob violence, evidence of which is now appearing in all parts of the country."[75] Still Wilson held off. He did write on April 22 that he was "very deeply concerned" about the treatment of people "whose offense is merely one of opinion." Wilson added that he had "a very great passion for the principle that we must respect opinion even when it is hostile. . . ."[85] But his silent concern did little good.

On June 11, a bulletin was issued by the Council of National Defense warning its local representatives against undertaking any repression unless they were "expressly requested or authorized by the . . . Department of Justice."[77] It was not until July 26, after the "patriotic" jury in Illinois had proclaimed members of the mob innocent, and after other incidents had occurred, that Wilson finally spoke out. A few days earlier, he had asked Creel to prepare the way for his statement. "My only object," he told Creel, "is to fix the attention of the people on this protest of mine in the way that will give it the greatest possible emphasis."[78] One observer stated that Wilson acted because of the "use made of the Prager case in the German Reichstag."[79]

The President's statement said:

There have been many lynchings, and every one of them has been a blow at the heart of ordered law and humane justice. No man who loves America, no man who really cares for her fame and honor and character, or who is truly loyal to her institutions, can justify mob action while the courts of justice are open. . . .

We proudly claim to be the champions of democracy. If we really are, in deed and truth, let us see to it that we do not discredit our own. I say plainly that every American who takes part in the action of a mob or gives any sort of countenance is no true son of this great democracy, but its betrayer, and does more to discredit her by that single disloyalty to her standards of law and right, than the words of her statesmen or the sacrifices of her heroic boys in the trenches can do to make suffering peoples believe her to be their savior. How shall we commend democracy to the acceptance of other peoples if we disgrace our own by proving that it is, after all, no protection to the weak? Every mob contributes to German lies about the United States, what her most gifted liars cannot improve upon by the way of calumny. They can at least say that such things cannot happen in Germany except in times of revolution, when law is swept away!

I therefore very earnestly and solemnly beg that the Governors of all the States, the law officers of every community, and, above all, the men and women of every community . . . will co-operate . . . to make an end of this disgraceful evil.[80]

The President spoke noble sentiments and, as usual, spoke them well. But his statement came too late to be very effective. Had he spoken out boldly a day or two after the Prager lynching, the weight of his words might have been felt. As it was, little was accomplished. It was only page seven news in the *New York Times.*

. . .

An important question is, did the American people learn anything from their World War I experiences? Did the widespread violations of freedom and civil rights teach any lessons? Did the repressions and demand for conformity cause American citizens to vow an eternal war against the repetition of such events?

If World War I is compared with World War II, it is evident that the latter was fought without the harsh and extensive attacks on freedom of speech and press which were so common in World War I.[81] It is true, of course, that some Americans suffered from government policies of restriction. Thousands of Japanese were interned simply because they were Japanese.[82] Some papers, including Father Coughlin's *Social Justice,* were denied mailing privileges. There were a few incidents in which repressive policies were employed against political and economic radicals, either to the right or the left. These things were all reminiscent of World War I.

However, there were not the lynchings or mob actions; not the convictions of people for criticizing the President; there were not the pressure and charges of disloyalty if one failed to buy bonds or subscribe to the Red Cross; German was not dropped from the curriculum of hundreds of schools and colleges; yellow paint as a mark of disloyalty was seldom if ever seen; tar and feather episodes so common as punishment for disloyalty during World War I were not in evidence; conscientious objectors received much better treatment than in World War I; manifestations of intolerance and repression so characteristic of 1917 and 1918 were much less common. Indeed, the American people seemed more concerned with the rights and opinions of others.

So far, so good. However, the picture presented here is, unfortunately, much less than the whole story. In fact, since World War II, and even before the United States entered that conflict, there have been successful demands for repression of thought and opinion. The demands for conformity have grown to dangerous proportions. They have arisen out of a popular fear of communism and have been fostered to a considerable degree by professional patriots and demagogs. Pages have been taken directly from the book of World War I, and new chapters of repression have been added. Conformity and loyalty were synonymous in World War I. Now loyalty is associated with the conformity demanded by those who oppose communism. The present [1950s] attack on individual rights and liberties can be summed up in the legislative investigations of individuals for loyalty, state and federal sedition laws, loyalty oaths for public officials and labor union leaders, acceptance of the principle of guilt by association, and even threats to those who dare to criticize government or its policies, especially those policies relating to loyalty.

. . .

In 1950 Congress, under a continuing fear of the Communist menace, took another long step down the road of repression when it passed the Internal Security Act, commonly referred to as the McCarran Act. Under this statute it is unlawful for any person to conspire with others "to perform any act which would substantially contribute to the establishment within the United States of a totalitarian dictatorship."[83] Furthermore, in a time of national emergency people may be detained if there is reasonable belief that a person "probably will commit or conspire with others to commit espionage or sabotage." This is a new type of repression which may punish an individual *before* any unlawful act has been committed. These laws, along with other aspects of the federal Government's loyalty program, raise some fundamental questions about civil rights and human freedoms.

Americans who either participated in or approved of the events recorded in the pages of this book believed that they were good patriotic citizens. The felt that their motive of achieving unity behind the war effort was of such supreme importance that they could not be held strictly accountable for the means used to accomplish it. In other words, the end justified the means. They rationalized their conduct by saying that war opponents were trying to injure the nation and thus did not merit the privilege of free speech, nor the physical safety and security that the law and the nation granted to people in normal times. What they were actually doing was repeating the age-old trick of deceiving themselves and others by sanctifying their pet project—a war, an economic fancy, a racial fantasy—by identifying it with God, with religion, or with the nation.

This specious thinking has turned up everywhere in recent times. It has been used to excuse the destruction of freedom within nations and to promote acts which have destroyed the peace between nations. It was the prime justification for those who killed the Archduke Franz Ferdinand, Jean Jaurès, Giacomo Matteotti, and innumerable nameless people in Germany and Russia within the last three decades. These assassins, like those in Butte, Montana, and Collinsville, Illinois, claimed to be patriots. They said that their victims were enemies of the state, had injured the state, or were planning to injure the state. Thus the punishment handed out to them was deserved, and the perpetrators of the acts were patriots. This type of thinking is all too prevalent in mid-twentieth century United States. Now the demand for repression comes in the name of a type of negative loyalty against communism. The test of loyalty is not acts or deeds so much as loud denunciation of communism and the acceptance of certain repressive policies to fight it. One is reminded of the hypocritical Pharisee of Jesus' time who demonstrated his piety by long public prayers.

Excited Americans who made up the vigilante groups, the loyalty leagues, and the defense councils in 1917–18 displayed American traits. They reflected the lurid qualities of the American press and the American theater. They also demonstrated a normal human willingness to sacrifice fundamental principles or long-range benefits in order to gain some immediate advantage.

Since the beginning of modern history there have been people ready to support the autocratic power of rulers and to limit or suppress the rights and freedoms of individual citizens. Supposedly, however, believers in democracy do not accept this principle. In the American democratic system the majority party is given the reins of government, but its authority is neither absolute nor permanent. Ultimate sovereignty remains in the citizenry and not in the government. Thus, the business of the public officeholder in this arrangement is not to "rule" but to advance the welfare of all citizens and to protect their freedoms, immunities, and sovereign power. Above all, this means the protection of those citizens in minority groups whose views are opposed to those of the majority.

But, as might be expected, even in democratic countries politicians and pressure groups have sometimes stirred uneasily under such limitations and restrictions. The yearning to get one's way is so strong, regardless of the political traditions of a nation, that some men will seek to break down this system. In times of crisis, such as the 1917–18 period, good people, well-intentioned people, "democratic" people will themselves advocate a policy of repression and the abolition of freedom. They argue that the nation's right to protect itself overrides the citizen's right to express himself.

But freedom is not a handicap placed on a democratic nation to humor people. As Henry Steele Commager has written, "We do not protect freedom to indulge in error. We protect freedom in order to discover truth."[84] Freedom is an advantage given to a nation; it is national life insurance. To prevent individuals from expressing their views, therefore, does not protect a nation; it weakens it.

A country in which there is freedom of expression is one which has freedom of action. Policies are not limited to those suggested by a ruler or a dominant party. They may be initiated or modified by the suggestions of any individual or group. In this way a nation's range of effectiveness is widened and serious errors, even tragic errors, may be avoided. Man is prone to err. No individual, no ruler, no legislature, no political party can avoid making mistakes. But where policies are subject to unrestricted debate, where actions must withstand unlimited criticism, blunders can be avoided. Under such a system protagonists can safely present the good points of their theories, and opponents can safely uncover their faults. As a result, the nation can change it policies at any time; it can make strategic retreats; it can reverse its course. Politics is the art of the pliable. No system other than one of free government allows a nation such flexibility or such stability.

NOTES

1. A quotation from the magazine, *Merchant Plumber and Fitter,* undated, Committee on Public Information files.

2. See the *Minneapolis Journal,* April 20 and 21, 1918. Judge James D. Elliott spoke of the "stonewall at sunrise." See April 21. See also Seattle *Post-Intelligencer,* March 10, 1918.

3. Richmond (Virginia) *Journal,* quoted in "Boloism in this Country," *Literary Digest,* LVI (March 2, 1918), 15.

4. "Mob Violence and War Psychology," *New Republic,* XVI (August 3, 1918), 6.

5. *Atlanta Constitution,* April 19, 1918.

6. Richard L. Metcalfe to E. D. Smith, February 6, 1918, Council of National Defense files.

7. *Minneapolis Journal,* April 22, 1918.

8. *Milwaukee Leader,* April 20, 1918, quoting the Tampa *Daily Times.*

9. Roosevelt in the *Kansas City Star,* p. 110.

10. *New York Tribune,* December 29, 1917.

11. See the Seattle *Post-Intelligencer,* April 4, 1918.

12. Quoted in "American Students Boycotting German," *Literary Digest,* LVI (March 30, 1918), 29.

13. *New York Times,* December 2, 1918. Such sentiments, however, were not unanimous. The editor of the *New York Globe* condemned the anti-German language campaign as narrowminded and childish. "Ignorance of the language and customs of our enemies harms us, not them," he wrote. Quoted in "American Students Boycotting German," p. 29.

14. Seattle *Post-Intelligencer,* June 9, 1918.

15. Tulsa *Daily World,* August 10, 1917.

16. "American Students Boycotting German," p. 30. This issue of the *Literary Digest* carried a very extensive report by states. See pp. 44, 46–50, 52, 54–55, 58, 61–64, 66, 70, 72–74.

17. New York *Evening World,* March 28, 1918.

18. Tulsa *Daily World,* July 3, 1918.

19. *Spartanburg* (South Carolina) *Herald,* September 12, 1918.

20. *Chicago Herald,* April 13, 1918.

21. Little Rock *Arkansas Gazette,* December 20, 1917. Arkansas had other instances of flag-kissing later. See the *Gazette* for April 2, 1918, and the *Memphis Press* for April 30, 1918. Beatings and tarring and featherings often accompanied the flag-kissing.

22. *New York Herald,* March 1, 1918. See also the Seattle *Post-Intelligencer,* March 1, 1918.

23. Seattle *Post-Intelligencer,* March 1, 1918.

24. New York *Evening Post,* March 4, 1918.

25. Camden (New Jersey) *Evening Courier,* May 1, 1918.

26. *Ex parte Starr,* 263 Fed. 145 (D. Mont. 1920).

27. *Ibid.* For other cases of flag-kissings see the *New York Tribune* for March 7 and 9, 1918; the Williamsport (Pa.) *Gazette and Bulletin,* July 3, 1918; Seattle *Post-Intelligencer,* March 22, 1918; Tulsa *Daily World,* March 26, 1918; *Pittsburgh Chronicle Telegraph,* March 14, 1918.

28. *Pittsburgh Post,* October 29. 1917.

29. Louis P. Goldberg and Eleanore Levenson, *Lawless Judges* (New York, 1935), p. 169.

30. See the *American* (New York), April 2, 1918.

31. *Milwaukee Journal,* April 14, 1918.

32. *Milwaukee Leader,* May 2, 1918. See also April 19.

33. Seattle *Post-Intelligencer,* March 19, 1918.

34. *San Rafael Chronicle,* May 7, 1918.

35. Unidentified newspaper clipping from Salt Lake City, April 11, 1918, American Civil Liberties Union files, LXX, 274.

36. Baltimore *Evening Sun,* April 8, 1918.

37. New York *American,* April 2, 1918. See the American Civil Liberties Union files for many other such incidents, especially LXX, 213. See also the *New York Times* index under "sedition."

38. *Sykes et al. v. United States,* 264 Fed. 945 (9th Cir. 1920). See also National Civil Liberties Bureau, *Wartime Prosecutions,* p. 8.

39. See the *New York Evening Call,* March 7, 1918; Little Rock *Arkansas Gazette,* March 29, 1918; *New York Tribune,* March 29, 1918; *Butte* (Montana) *Post,* May 25, 1918.

40. *St. Paul Dispatch,* May 23, 1918.

41. *New York Times,* March 21, 1918. See also the *New York Tribune,* April 9, 1918.

42. Clipping from unidentified newspaper reproduced in *Survey,* XL (April 27, 1918), 101.

43. New York *American,* April 2, 1918.

44. *Fort Worth Record,* March 20, 1918.

45. *Washington* (D.C.) *Post,* April 28, 1918.

46. New York *World,* April 16, 1918.

47. Seattle *Post-Intelligencer,* April 23, 1918.

48. *Boston Daily Advertiser,* May 7, 1918.

49. See the *Atlanta Constitution,* July 1, 1918. See also May 23 and 24.

50. *Springfield* (Missouri) *Daily News,* March 25, 1918.

51. Tulsa *Daily World,* March 24, 1918.

52. *Ibid.,* March 26, 1918.

53. See the American Civil Liberties Union files, LXX, 172.

54. See *ibid.*

55. St. Louis *Post-Dispatch,* March 23, 1918.

56. *New York Tribune,* March 26, 1918. See the *New York Times* for the same date.

57. See the letter from Edith M. Short to Roger N. Baldwin, July 28, 1918, American Civil Liberties Union files, XX, 122–27.

58. *Collinsville* (Illinois) *Herald,* May 18 and 22, and June 21, 1918.

59. *New York Times,* April 5, 1918.

60. *St. Louis Republic,* April 5, 1918. See also the *New York Call,* April 6, 1918.

61. *Chicago Daily News,* April 17, 1918.

62. From an undated *New York Tribune* clipping in the American Civil Liberties Union files, LXX, 1.

63. *Collinsville* (Illinois) *Herald,* April 5, 1918. See also "Mob Violence in the United States," *Survey,* XL (April 27, 1918), 101–2.

64. Quoted in *Cong. Rec.,* 65 Cong., 2 Sess., May 9, 1918, p. 6233.

65. *Ibid.,* April 8, 1918, p. 4769.

66. *Chicago Daily Tribune,* April 9, 1918.

67. See "The First War-Lynching," *Literary Digest,* LVII (April 20, 1918), 16–17.

68. *Collinsville* (Illinois) *Herald,* June 7, 1918. For an account of the Prager affair, including the trial, see the *New York Times* for April 5, 6, 8, 9, 11, 12; May 14, 27, 29; June 2, 3.

69. *New York Tribune,* May 17, 1918.

70. *Ibid.,* June 1, 1918. For a later account of the trial see Marguerite Edith Jenison, *The War-Time Organization of Illinois* (Volume V of Illinois in the World War; Springfield, 1923), p. 7. It was said that because it was dark when Prager was hanged, identity of the leaders could not be certain. Thus, the verdict of "not guilty."

71. Quoted in *New York Tribune,* June 15, 1918. Shortly after Prager was hanged S. J. Walker was shot and killed by an army officer in Hawaii for allegedly "condemning the course of the United States in entering the War," New York *Evening Post,* May 1, 1918.

72. For other instances of mob actions see *Sacramento Bee,* May 2 and 3, 1918; Tulsa *Daily World,* April 14, 1918; *Minneapolis Journal,* April 24, 1918; and *Collinsville* (Okla-

homa) *Star,* April 27, 1917. For a sample taken from different parts of the country see the *New York Times* index under "sedition."

73. Baker, *Wilson: Life and Letters,* VIII, 78.

74. See the *New York Times,* April 12 and June 13, 1918.

75. John Lord O'Brian, Memorandum for the Attorney General, April 18, 1918, Wilson Papers.

76. Wilson to Mrs. Anita McCormick Blaine, April 22, 1918, in Baker, *Wilson: Life and Letters,* VIII, 102–3.

77. Council of National Defense, Bulletin No. 99, June 11, 1918. Statement was signed by W. S. Gifford.

78. Wilson to Creel, July 21, 1918, in Baker, *Wilson: Life and Letters,* VIII, 289.

79. Lawrence Todd to Roger Baldwin, July 30, 1918, American Civil Liberties Union files, VIII, 1.

80. *New York Times,* July 27, 1918.

81. See Robert E. Cushman, "American Civil Liberties in Mid-Twentieth Century," in Robert K. Carr, ed., "Civil Rights in America," *The Annals of the American Academy of Political and Social Science,* CCLXXV (May, 1951), 8.

82. On this point see Zechariah Chafee, Jr., compiler and editor, *Documents on Fundamental Human Rights* (Cambridge, 1951), pp. 587–628.

83. 64 *U.S. Stat.* 987 (1950).

84. Henry Steele Commager, "The Pragmatic Necessity of Freedom," in Clair Wilcox, ed., *Civil Liberties Under Attack,* p. 10.

John Shover

THE FARMERS' HOLIDAY
ASSOCIATION STRIKE,
AUGUST 1932

From Shays's Rebellion to the 1970s agrarian protest has been ever present in American history. Insurgent farmers, often provoked by economic grievances, have dissented individually and through groups such as the Grangers and the Populist party for relief and reform. They have engaged in strikes, boycotts, riots, and even open rebellion.

In the following essay, John Shover examines the rural discontent that reached peak levels during the Great Depression of the 1930s. Following a pattern of protest common to many groups analyzed in this volume, angry farmers used force and violence to focus attention on their problems during a period of national crisis. With the enactment of New Deal legislation that promised better times, the protest quickly waned. This outcome according to Shover, suggests that concessions to some alienated groups may prevent rather than breed additional violence.

An economic crisis without parallel gripped the American countryside in the summer of 1932. For a decade preceding it, farm markets had contracted and prices had dropped, but the depression of the twenties was only a prelude to the most disastrous collapse in the history of American agriculture. Between 1929 and 1931 the price of wheat per bushel declined from $1.03 to 36¢; in 1932 the return for hogs fell from $11.36 to $6.14 per head, the sharpest drop ever recorded. The purchasing power of farm commodities was less than a third that of 1914. The only inheritance from the prosperous war years was a heavy and unchanging burden of debt. In Iowa, North Dakota, and South Dakota, nearly 6% of farms changed ownership during

From *Agricultural History* 39 (1965): 196–203. Reprinted by permission of the Agricultural History Society and the author.

1932 through bankruptcy or foreclosure; in 1933 the ratio rose to 8%. The emergency ensnared producers of all commodities, even corn-hog and dairy farmers who had been spared the worst economic vicissitudes of the past. [1]

The American farmer has never been politically inarticulate or slow to rise in his own defense. The response to the depression of the thirties was neither so widespread nor so prolonged as such political movements as the Populist Party or the Nonpartisan League, but it reached peaks of intensity unequalled in earlier protests. The farm strike of 1932 was the first episode in a neglected little rebellion in the American cornbelt. Before it had run its course a year later, at least 140 foreclosure sales had been halted by direct farmer action, [2] a strike of milk producers had exploded into violence on the highways of Wisconsin, [3] and the Farmers' Holiday Association of Milo Reno had once threatened and once attempted a general strike of farmers to force legislative concessions from Congress and the new national administration. [4]

The farm strike manifested a spirit of frustration and resentment that the depression had set astir in the countryside. Only indirectly was it guided by leaders of the Farmers' Holiday Association or directed toward the goals of that organization. What was originally designed as a peaceable withholding of produce from market erupted at its very beginning into a direct-action movement of a magnitude seldom equalled in the history of farmer protests. At its climax it was a spontaneous grassroots uprising seeking immediate redress of economic grievances. Except for a small core of participants, it was an irrational movement, too poorly organized and inchoate to achieve the remedies either leaders or participants sought. The effort achieved little, but it served to place a label "urgent" upon the necessity for some type of legislation to alleviate the economic plight of the American farmer.

The sequence of events that accelerated into the August farm strike was set in motion by the Farmers' Holiday Association, founded in Des Moines in May 1932. The Holiday Association was an offspring of the National Farmers' Union, produced by factional battles within that organization in the early thirties. Contending for control of the Farmers' Union were, first, a cooperative marketing group, consisting mainly of grain interests of the Northwest, friends and supporters of the Agricultural Marketing Act. In opposition was a political faction, largely representative of livestock areas where there was little to gain from the cooperative marketing features of the Hoover farm program. Led by Milo Reno of the Iowa Farmers' Union, the political group demanded of the National a vigorous program to win legislation guaranteeing cost of production prices for farmers. Reno had argued as early as 1927: "If we cannot obtain justice by legislation, the time will have arrived when no other course remains than organized refusal to deliver the products of the farm at less than production costs." [5] In the depression year of 1930 the political faction won control of the Union with the election to the presidency of John Simpson of Oklahoma. The transfer of power was accompanied by acrimonious charges by both sides of corruption, mismanagement, and diversion of Union funds for political funds for political projects. [6]

Milo Reno's proposal for a general withholding movement lay dormant for four years, but support reawakened as depression hardship pressed heavier in the cornbelt. Reno presented to the Farmers' Union convention of 1931 a resolution calling for a farm strike to begin January 1. Although Simpson was president and the political action wing in control, the resolution was defeated by a decisive majority. [7] This rejection should not be overemphasized. The Farmers' Union could *not* have sponsored a marketing strike. Given the strength of the minority cooperative faction, such a move could have permanently split the Union or lost the political faction its control. Moreover, extensive investments in cooperative facilities could have been jeopardized by too bold political action. When Reno proceeded through his own affiliate, the Iowa Farmers' Union, to carry forward his withholding plans independently, he was sustained and advised by John Simpson and E. E. Kennedy, the national secretary of the Farmers' Union. In every particular the program of the Farmers' Holiday Association and that of the Farmers' Union were parallel. The most extreme of the political activists simply shifted their pressure tactics outside the bounds of the parent organization. The Farmers' Holiday Association was a strong-arm auxiliary of the Farmers' Union.

Within weeks after the Farmers' Union convention, Milo Reno and his state Union chapter were mobilizing support for a withholding movement in Iowa. Glen Miller, president of the Iowa Union, [8] coined a term when he declared that if banks could do it, why shouldn't farmers call it a "holiday" where corn and meat and milk would be kept at home until legislators and the public alike learned the importance of the men who tilled the soil. [9] From February until May the pages of the *Iowa Union Farmer* contained little else but plans for the forthcoming withholding action. Farmers' Union leaders toured Iowa, often addressing two rural gatherings daily; Reno cultivated Union associates in Wisconsin, South Dakota, and Minnesota. [10]

The organizing drive culminated when 2000 farmers assembled in Des Moines on May 3 to launch the Farmers' Holiday Association as a national organization. Milo Reno, the inevitable choice, was named president. The convention resolved that a general withholding movement was to begin July 4 and continue for thirty days or until cost of production prices were realized. [11]

The objectives of the incipient farmers' movement were vague, the methods for achieving them ill-defined. There was a stress upon immediacy: implicit in the simple resolutions was the assumption that the goal of cost of production prices could be quickly achieved. [12] Nothing implied that the forthcoming withholding movement would be other than voluntary; there was no suggestion that coercion might be used against farmers who failed to cooperate. Neither was it clear how cost of production prices were to be achieved. Milo Reno, although sometimes ambivalent, seemed to insist they would be guaranteed by legislative action. [13] On the other hand, many local leaders as well as the press interpreted the farm strike as a self-help effort—farm produce would be held off of the market until shortages forced prices up to the cost of production level. [14]

Cost of production, the principal demand of the Union and the Holiday Association, was more a panacea than a concrete economic program. "Concede to the farmer production costs," Milo Reno predicted, "and he will pay his grocer, the grocer will pay the wholesaler, the wholesaler will pay the manufacturer and the manufacturer will be able to meet his obligations at the bank. Restore the farmers' purchasing power and you have reestablished an endless chain of prosperity and happiness in this country." [15] To compute cost of production, average expenses for producers of every commodity would be itemized and a price determined for products consumed domestically that would return to the average operator his costs, labor, and a reasonable profit. To have realized returns equal to cost of production in 1932 a farmer would have had to receive 92¢ per bushel for corn, 11¢ a pound for hogs, and 62¢ per pound of butterfat. Prevailing prices in June 1932 were 10¢ per bushel for corn, 3¢ per pound for hogs, and 18¢ per pound for butterfat. [16]

Throughout the summer months of 1932, evangelists of cost of production carried the message across the cornbelt. As momentum increased, state Farmers' Holiday Associations were launched in South Dakota, North Dakota, and Minnesota. [17] Organizers asked farmers to sign pledges to support the forthcoming withholding action. These enthusiasts had an inspired sense of numbers; they reported that half a million midwestern farmers had signed by August. [18]

Original plans called for withholding to begin July 4, but the day passed without incident in the cornbelt. Organization plans were not complete and the declining price trend had momentarily reversed in June. A few hopeful observers prophesied that the high tide of depression had passed. A price slump on July 13 destroyed sanguine hopes and the price index began a steady decline that was not arrested until December. [19] Indicating the confusion prevailing, the county Holiday chairmen in Iowa rescheduled the holding action for August 15, but then on August 10 the *Iowa Union Farmer* announced it had already commenced. [20]

The farm strike that began at Sioux City on August 12 was a different movement from that planned by the Farmers' Holiday Association. In all the preceding buildup there had been no mention of picketing, yet at the very inception of the withholding movement farmers in Woodbury and Plymouth counties patrolled highways and threatened noncooperating farmers who tried to market their produce. Milo Reno conceded in a private letter: "I have not favored, at any time in our farm strike movement, picketing, because of the danger of loss of life and property, although I do feel that the action of the boys on the picket line has done more to focus the attention of the powers that be to the real facts of the situation than any other thing."[21] By this time it had become apparent that the Farmers' Holiday was two movements. One was the formal organization headed by Milo Reno that planned a peaceful holding action to bring pressure for enactment of cost of production legislation. The second was a spontaneous social movement triggered into action by the Holiday but looking to immediate remedies and seeking redress of local grievances.

The focal point in this unanticipated movement was a group of counties in northwest Iowa surrounding the terminal market at Sioux City. In the vanguard were 250 local milk producers for whom the strike was the culmination of grievances that had been accumulating for ten years.

Dairy farmers were the striking force of the depression farmers' protest. They were in the first echelon in Iowa in 1932 and they instigated both the Wisconsin dairy strike and a spirited movement in New York state in 1933. Milk producers had a legitimate economic grievance; in Sioux City, for example, the farmer's price for butter had declined from 40 to 19 cents between 1927 and 1932.[22] It was simpler to organize dairy farmers than other producers. Since milk was highly perishable, a "milk shed" area extended for no more than 20 or 30 miles around an urban center. Milk producers were relatively few in number and their total supply was sold to a handful of local distributors. It was reasoned therefore that price increases could be forced more surely by a withholding action.

The J. R. Roberts Dairy Company, the largest in Sioux City, had gradually extended its milk-shed area, assuring a constant surplus and permitting the company to dictate its own price. An adjustment in 1932 had raised prices so the farmer received 2 cents and the consumer paid 8 cents for the same quart of milk. A Producers' Cooperative Association, organized in May 1932, had by August signed up 900 members, a sizable portion of those who shipped to the Sioux City market. The refusal of J. R. Roberts Dairy Company to negotiate and the boasts of the owner that he had broken cooperatives in the past forced the leaders to withhold as the only means for winning concessions.[23]

The campaign to form a milk producers' cooperative coincided with the organizing drive of the Farmers' Holiday; many were members of both groups. As the date for the beginning of the Holiday withholding movement approached, the milk producers voted to combine the two campaigns. On August 10 the organization presented to the distributors a demand for price increases, pledged to halt all shipments into Sioux City, and arranged for free milk distribution in order to avoid public inconvenience and embarrass the distributor's retail trade.[24]

On the night of August 11 fifteen trucks carrying milk were halted west of Sioux City and the milk of two of them was dumped on the pavement. By the succeeding evening farmers had extended the vigil to all roads entering the city from the east and north. Trucks carrying livestock were also halted and the drive of milk producers coalesced with a general attempt to seal the Sioux City market. On August 14, 1500 farmers distributed over five highways virtually blocked all shipments. Pickets leaped on the running boards of farm trucks or threw such obstacles as hay bales, logs, and threshing machine belts in the path of oncoming vehicles. There was little violence; most trucks simply turned back. One hundred deputies were recruited to keep the roads open, but no attempt was made to prevent the stopping of vehicles so long as the techniques remained persuasive only. The Producers' Cooperative claimed that 90% of the city's milk supply had been stopped and on Thursday, August 18, hog receipts were just half those of the preceding Thursday.[25]

As the selling holiday spread, farmers in South Dakota and Nebraska blocked access from the north and new picket lines sealed the southern route to Sioux City. "This movement," declared the mayor, "threatens to sweep the midwest like wildfire."[26] Local strike leaders claimed that 90% of farmers in the vicinity either joined picket lines or refused to sell produce. Had this been true there would have been no need for roadside blockades. Newspaper reports, although probably exaggerated, allow a better estimate. The number of pickets at any time or place was usually recorded as between 200 and 400. The largest number reported was the 1500 who supposedly guarded the northern access to Sioux City on August 14. Allowing for exaggeration and the presence of non-farmers on the picket line, the maximum figure would constitute representatives from about ⅕ of the farm families in Woodbury and Plymouth counties.[27]

Few farmers out of the total rural population expressed their resentment by such extremes as picketing highways or defying sheriff's deputies. Those who did were a type of farmer largely immune to previous agrarian movements. Farm insurgency in the past had won principal midwestern support in wheat-producing regions.[28] The unrest of the thirties was most evident in livestock and milk producing areas whose residents were considered more economically stable and less affected by vagrant price or weather fluctuations. The most enthusiastic support for the strike technique was in Iowa and Wisconsin; when it spread to Nebraska, South Dakota, and Minnesota, its greatest attraction was always in corn-hog and dairy regions.[29]

The farm strike centered in some of the most prosperous farming counties in the livestock and dairy belts. In Iowa, the state where activity was most intense, at least 300 incidents of protest were reported in August and September.[30] More than three-quarters of these occurred in seven counties in the Missouri River valley at the western fringe of the state. In this, the leading meat-producing sector of the state, gross income per farm was well above the state average. By contrast, the single area in Iowa least affected by the farm strike was the so-called "southern pasture" area touching the Missouri border where land values and gross income were the lowest in the state and home conveniences fewest.[31] Add to high gross income the fact that rate of foreclosure was apparently the highest in counties in northwest Iowa[32] and rainfall in 1931 and 1932 the least in the state[33] and a pattern emerges. The farm strike was a response of individuals whose level of expectation had been conditioned by better times and some immediate crisis, in this instance, foreclosure or drouth, threatened to deprive them of property or accustomed income. Bruce Bliven, a native Iowan reporting for the *New Republic,* concluded: "It's where the farmers had something a few years ago and have had it suddenly taken away, that the agitators find a responsive audience."[34]

The farmers' strike in Iowa might attract publicity to the farmers' plight; it could achieve little else. Two handicaps rendered success impossible. First, there was a lack of leadership and discipline. Second, the effort was ineffectively organized and support was too narrow to influence farm marketing or prices.

Any relationship of the spontaneous movement in northwest Iowa to the formal program or leadership of the Farmers' Holiday Association was incidental. Even local leaders, much less Milo Reno, were unable to govern the actions of pickets scattered over 100 miles of highway. Because of this, the farm strike rapidly deteriorated into chaos and violence.

The milk dispute was settled after ten days when the distributors agreed to a compromise price increase. The settlement put the discipline of the farm strike to a severe test. Many pickets still refused to allow milk trucks to pass.

Most explosive, however, was the situation 75 miles to the south at Council Bluffs where shipments to Omaha were being blocked from the Iowa side of the Missouri River. County law enforcement officials informed Clinton Savery, organizer of the blockade, that he would be personally responsible for any violence or property damage. When Savery attempted to call off the pickets, he was taunted with shouts of "sell out." "I have washed my hands of the entire mess. The strikers are beyond my control," he protested. When 43 pickets were arrested on August 24, a mob of 500 farmers, unimpressed by the armed deputies hastily recruited by the Pottawattamie county sheriff, swarmed over the courthouse lawn at Council Bluffs. Throughout a tense day they negotiated with law enforcement officials. A sympathetic farmer posted bail late in the afternoon and the release of the prisoners averted a situation perilously close to tragedy and bloodshed.[35]

A rapid succession of critical events in the last days of August broke the back of the farm strike. Deputies and pickets battled for three nights on the outskirts of Omaha[36]; in northeast Nebraska an interstate freight train was halted and livestock cars were uncoupled.[37] Woodbury County deputies arrested 87 pickets on August 26; four days later pickets at Cherokee were injured by shotgun blasts from a speeding auto. At Clinton, in eastern Iowa, another mob defied armed deputies by threatening to release jailed pickets.[38] Under duress of this sort, Reno and state Holiday leaders proclaimed on September 1 a "temporary truce" to begin immediately. Roland Jones, *New York Times* correspondent in Omaha, observed that the "national leadership blew up, frightened at the appearance of the ugly monster into which its innocent child had so unexpectedly grown."[39]

The second handicap was the ineffective organization and narrow support both for the strike action and the withholding movement. From a practical standpoint, a farmer could not long participate in a general embargo that deprived him of all income. To keep marketable hogs and cattle on the farm meant added costs and lower returns.[40] Even before the "temporary truce," Reno announced that the withholding action would be relaxed sufficiently to allow hardpressed farmers to market some of their products.[41]

The peaceful withholding movement, the major objective of the Farmers' Holiday Association, had been lost sight of in the flurry of dramatic activity around Sioux City. It had been a failure. Receipts of livestock had decreased only at Sioux City. There was an increase at neighboring markets. Indeed, prices for farm products dropped to the year's low while the farm strike was in progress.[42] Blockading a single market could not reduce the overall supply of agricultural products sufficiently to effect price changes. Even had a marketing boycott been successful, the accumulated produce released at its conclusion would have broken the bottom out of the farm price structure. Only the milk producers, who operated independently of the Holiday Association and were able to control a restricted market, could claim concrete benefits from the farm strike.[43]

Paradoxically, however, the strike achieved results better than the original organizers could have expected. The spontaneous movement in northwest Iowa publicized the farmers' plight and prompted political responses more effectively than any ill-organized withholding movement. Elected political officials in the Middle West and national candidates could not ignore such dramatic evidence of rural discontent. Exemplifying the political prestige of the Farmers' Holiday Association was a meeting of four midwestern governors in Sioux City in September in the wake of the farm strike. After listening to the declarations of Holiday leaders, they forwarded to President Hoover a suggested program to inflate the currency and restrict farm foreclosures.[44] Governor Roosevelt, campaigning in Sioux City, talked with Farmers' Union and Holiday leaders and promised that if elected he would devote more time to agriculture than to any other single problem.[45] Over the debates on a farm bill in 1933 and the implementing of the Agricultural Adjustment Act hung the threat of a renewed farm strike.[46] In the autumn of 1933 the Holiday Association was able to muster the support of five governors who bore to Washington a demand that the domestic allotment system be replaced by cost of production price guarantees.[47]

The political power of the Farmers' Holiday Association was illusory;

the organization had won an unearned increment of importance, largely because of the farm strike. The strength of the association certainly was not in numbers. Membership statistics were never revealed, but the financial receipts of the national office in August 1933 indicate that returns equal to the dues payments of only 4494 members had been received. [48] What strength the association had was a tempestuous and little-organized force whose allegiance was tangential. The peaceful withholding movement planned by the organization in 1932 had been a failure. In October 1933 when Milo Reno, driven to extremism by his opposition to the New Deal agricultural program, attempted to mobilize farmers on the highways to compel the federal government to replace the Agricultural Adjustment Act with cost of production guarantees and currency inflation, the attempt perished in a flurry of rioting and violence. [49] The spontaneous support of discontented men was an insecure base for a permanent organization.

Generalizations drawn from one specific episode are obviously limited by the circumscribed scope of the data. Yet, if made the basis for comparisons with other examples of similar phenomena and carefully tested for similarities and differences, such generalizations can form the bridge to broader and more useful concepts. The conclusions that follow are intended not only as summary but as reference points for possible comparison with other social movements in general and farmers' movements in particular.

First, the farm strike was not a movement from the social depths. Its highest incidence was in relatively prosperous areas where economic disaster threatened to deprive participants of status and livelihood. The fact the movement centered in corn-hog and milk producing areas calls into question those interpretations that establish an automatic equation between wheat farming and rural insurgency.

Second, although specific leaders may have set the protest in motion, the farm strike was a spontaneous effort pursuing immediate and sometimes irrational goals, different from those of the leaders. To view the Farmers' Holiday Association in terms of its formal program and through the perspective of the leadership would be misleading.

Third, ideology was of limited importance. Farmers who picketed highways and challenged legal authority did so in pursuit of immediate relief, not because they demanded such specific remedies as inflation or cost of production prices. [50] Attempts by Holiday leaders to perpetuate the battle for ideological goals after the adoption of the Agricultural Adjustment Act were futile. Milo Reno died in 1936, a disappointed and embittered man; the Farmers' Holiday disappeared in 1937, torn between followers of Popular Front liberalism and supporters of the Coughlin-Lemke Union party. The New Deal agricultural program brought farmers the immediate economic assistance they demanded and this was sufficient to quell the tempestuous spirit that nourished farm strikes and the Farmers' Holiday Association.

NOTES

1. U. S. Department of Agriculture, *Yearbook of Agriculture, 1928* (Washington, 1929), 670; *Yearbook of Agriculture, 1932* (Washington, 1932), 784; *Yearbook of Agriculture, 1935* (Washington, 1935), 567–68, 681; *The Farm Real Estate Situation, 1933–34* (U.S. Department of Agriculture, Circular 354, Washington, 1935), 31; Horace C. Filley, "Effects of Inflation and Deflation upon Nebraska Agriculture" (Ph.D. dissertation, University of Minnesota, 1934), 26–27.

2. This estimate of anti-foreclosure demonstrations is based upon a tabulation of incidents reported in six national and local newspapers, 1932 and 1933.

3. A. William Hoglund, "Wisconsin Dairy Farmers on Strike," *Agricultural History*, XXXV (January, 1961), 24–34.

4. Theodore Saloutos and John D. Hicks, *Twentieth Century Populism: Agricultural Discontent in the Middle West, 1900–1939* (Lincoln, n.d. [Madison, 1951], 448–451; Van L. Perkins, "The Triple-A and the Politics of Agriculture" (unpublished paper delivered at the Seventy-Ninth Annual Meeting, American Historical Association, Washington, December 28, 1964); John L. Shover, "The Farm Holiday Movement in Nebraska," *Nebraska History*, XLIII (March, 1962), 72–73.

5. W. P. Tucker, "Populism Up to Date: The Story of the Farmers' Union," *Agricultural History*, XXI (October, 1947), 206–207; Milo Reno, undated ms., "For Miss Prescott," Milo Reno Papers, Library of University of Iowa, Iowa City.

6. *Iowa Union Farmer,* (Columbus Junction, Iowa), July 29, August 23, 1931.

7. *Ibid.,* December 2, 1931.

8. Reno resigned the presidency of the Iowa Farmers' Union in 1930 to become head of the Union's extensive insurance business, but he remained the *de facto* head of the organization.

9. *Iowa Union Farmer,* February 10, 24, 1932.

10. *Ibid.,* March 9, 1932; Roland A. White, *Milo Reno: Farmers' Union Pioneer* (Iowa City, 1941), 74.

11. *Iowa Union Farmer,* May 4, 1932.

12. For a theoretical discussion of the characteristics of incipient protest movements, see Wendell King, *Social Movements in the United States* (New York 1956), 42–44.

13. Milo Reno, "Why the Farmers' Holiday?," radio address of July 20, 1932, in White, *Milo Reno,* 152.

14. John Chalmers, president of the Iowa Farmers' Holiday Association still insisted 29 years later that this was the purpose of the Farmers' Holiday and further argued that had the attempt been better organized it would have succeeded. Personal interview with the writer, October 21, 1961.

15. Reno, "Why the Farmers' Holiday?," 151.

16. Howard W. Lawrence, "The Farmers' Holiday Association in Iowa, 1932–33" (M.A. thesis, University of Iowa, 1952), 24–6; Saloutos and Hicks, *Twentieth Century Populism,* 443.

17. *Willmar* (Minnesota) *Tribune,* August 1, 1932; *Sioux City Tribune,* July 20, 1932.

18. *Willmar Tribune,* August 2, 1932.

19. Julius Korgan, "Farmers Picket the Depression" (Ph.D. dissertation, American University, 1961), 31–32; Lauren K. Soth, *Argricultural Economic Facts Basebook of Iowa* (Iowa Agricultural Experiment and Extension Service, Special Report No. 1, Ames, 1936), 22.

20. *Sioux City Tribune,* July 30, 1932.

21. Letter to Ben McCormack, November 8, 1933, Reno papers.

22. Frank D. Dileva, "Iowa Farm Price Revolt," *Annals of Iowa,* third series, XXXII (January, 1954), 172; Korgan, 34 *et passim.*

23. I. W. Reck, president and founder, Sioux City Milk Producers' Cooperative Associa-

tion, personal interview with the writer, March 12, 1962; Sioux City Milk Producers' Coopera-tive Association, *Record of Progress* (Sioux City, n.d.); *Unionist and Public Forum* (Sioux City), March 3, July 28, 1932.

24. *Sioux City Journal,* August 10, 1932; I. W. Reck, personal interview.

25. *Sioux City Journal,* August 12-15, 19, 1932; *Sioux City Tribune,* August 15, 1932.

26. *Sioux City Journal,* August 22, 1932.

27. U.S. Bureau of the Census, *15th Census of the U.S.,* Population, VI (Washington, 1933), 451-52. If this figure is even a fair approximation, this percentage of local participation is remarkably high, particularly when contrasted with the sitdown strikes or such modern social movements as the 1962 March on Washington or the Free Speech Movement at the University of California. It would seem even more so given the obstacles to communication and organization in rural areas.

28. This point is particularly stressed in Benton H. Wilcox, "An Historical Definition of North-Western Radicalism," *Mississippi Valley Historical Review,* XXVI (December, 1939), 384-86; Richard Hofstadter, *The Age of Reform* (New York, 1955), 99-100; Seymour M. Lipset, *Agrarian Socialism* (Berkeley, 1950), 10-11.

29. This can be explained, I believe, by three factors: (1) The depression of the 1930's was more severe in corn-hog and dairy areas than any preceding crisis; (2) the only existing federal remedy, the Agricultural Marketing Act, was geared to the needs of producers of non-perish-ables such as wheat and cotton and the funds of the farm board had already been absorbed in heavy purchases of these commodities when the worst crisis struck dairy and corn-hog regions; (3) perishable products such as meat and milk were more easily made the objects of withhold-ing actions.

30. This figure was computed on the basis of a tabulation of reports of protest activities from two leading area newspapers, the *Des Moines Register* and the *Sioux City Journal,* August and September, 1932. Each occurrence was classified by county, an event reported in both newspapers was recorded twice, avoiding purely local reporting and giving double weight to an incident important enough to have reached both. The actual total was 335. The nine counties that scored highest were in order: Woodbury, Plymouth, Pottawattamie, Polk, Harrison, Monona, Cherokee, Clay, and Black Hawk. Only Polk and Black Hawk are outside the northwestern meat producing area.

31. Soth, *Agricultural Economic Facts Basebook of Iowa,* 139, 10, 117, 114, 104-105, 160.

32. Reliable data on foreclosures is difficult to obtain. Authority for my statement is a listing of foreclosure suits pending by counties published in *Des Moines Register,* July 15, 1934, showing that in 1933 Woodbury County, the county with most strike activity, had three times more foreclosure suits pending (485) than any other Iowa county.

33. U.S. Weather Bureau, *Climatological Data, Iowa Section,* XLII (August, 1931), 99-100; XLIII (July 1932), 54; XLIII (August, 1932), 66.

34. Bruce Bliven, "Milo Reno and His Farmers," *New Republic,* LXXVII (November 29, 1933), 64. For a theoretical discussion of this type of interpretation, see James C. Davies, "Toward a Theory of Revolution," *American Sociological Review,* XXVII (February, 1962), 5-19.

35. *Sioux City Journal,* August 26, 1932; *New York Times,* August 26, 1932.

36. *Omaha World-Herald,* August 30, 31, September 1, 1932.

37. *New York Times,* August 24, 1932.

38. *Sioux City Journal,* August 26, 31, 1932; *Des Moines Register,* September 1, 1932.

39. *New York Times,* September 4, 1932.

40. Dan W. Turner, governor of Iowa in 1932, reports he received "hundreds of tele-phone calls, letters and personal calls from farmers all over [the] western half of Iowa to open up the roads." He notes as an example of the problem that hogs between 190 and 230 pounds were priced as bacon hogs; as they grew heavier they became lard hogs and the demand for lard

was diminishing. Dan W. Turner to the writer, October 15, 1961; *Sioux City Journal,* August 25, 1932.

41. *Ibid.,* August 31, 1932.

42. The number of hogs marketed in Iowa was 750,525 in July; 804,335 in August, 787,353 in September, 806,035 in October. Computed on the 1910–1914 base, the index numbers for Iowa hog prices were: July, 58; August, 53; September, 49; October, 41; November, 38; December, 33. Soth, *Agricultural Economic Facts Basebook of Iowa,* 22, 41.

43. The original demand of the Milk Producers' Cooperative was for an increase in the price of milk containing 3.5% butterfat from the prevailing $1.00 per cwt. to $2.50. The settlement set the price at $1.80.

44. *Sioux City Journal,* September 10, 11, 1932. Present were Governors Turner of Iowa, Green of South Dakota, Shafer of North Dakota, and Olson of Minnesota.

45. *Iowa Union Farmer,* October 5, 1932. The farm leaders attending the conference, probably overly optimistic, also alleged that Roosevelt agreed to press for legislation refinancing farm loans at a low rate of interest and guaranteeing to farmers cost of production prices.

46. John L. Shover, "Populism in the Nineteen Thirties: The Battle for the AAA," *Agricultural History,* XXXIX (January, 1965), 17–24.

47. Henry A. Wallace, *New Frontiers* (New York 1934), 56–58.

48. Reno, "For Miss Prescott," Reno papers.

49. *New York Times,* November 5, November 7, 1933.

50. Angus Campbell, *et al.,* The *American Voter* (New York, 1960), 402–440.

Arthur F. Raper

THE TRAGEDY OF LYNCHING
AND

John Dollard

CASTE AND CLASS IN A SOUTHERN TOWN

Perhaps the most broadly successful example of repressive social violence in American history is the means by which, until the past generation, whites maintained almost total power over blacks in the southern states. Before the Civil War, oppressive relations were fully sanctioned by law. Afterward, the effort to keep blacks "in their place" necessarily involved some resort to illegal violence.

Between the end of Reconstruction, with its own violent heritage described earlier, and the new era of militance that followed World War II, there were several serious attempts to improve the lot of black Americans. The National Association for the Advancement of Colored People, founded in 1909, demanded full equality from the start, and began almost at once to win legal battles in the courts. During and just after World War I, many blacks, especially veterans, sought to win the rights implied by participation in the "War to Make the World Safe for Democracy." But for the vast majority, living still in the rural South, there was little change in these decades.

The means of oppression were complex and interrelated. A variety of devices, such as sharecropping and the crop lien system, kept former slaves and their descendants economically dependent as debtors and tenants. Intimidation and legal maneuvering once Reconstruction was over kept them from the polls. Segregated into badly inferior schools and facilities of all kinds, few blacks had the opportunity to break out of poverty. And attempts to escape inferior status by asserting economic,

From Arthur F. Raper, *The Tragedy of Lynching* (Chapel Hill: University of North Carolina Press, 1933), pp. 1–24. Reprinted by permission of the publisher.

educational, or political ambition were often discouraged by force.

Lynching was the most spectacular form of force employed. And the two accounts below, written in the 1930s when the practice was still common, illustrate both the situation in the South and the difficulties involved in any simple analysis of violent action. Arthur Raper provides a straightforward description. The social psychologist John Dollard, using observations gathered in "Southerntown," attempts to probe more deeply. Both argue that the lynching phenomenon was not simply what the lynchers, and many others, claimed or even believed that it was. The contemporary image, North as well as South, was that white mobs typically acted to defend white "honor," often to avenge a white woman raped by a black man. Dollard in particular suggests that this rationale masked deeper psychological tensions, and served much wider social purposes.

THE TRAGEDY OF LYNCHING

The toll of the mob reckons not alone the victims but the lynchers themselves and the economic, social, and cultural meaning of their lawlessness. Three thousand seven hundred and twenty-four people were lynched in the United States from 1889 through 1930.[1] Over four-fifths of these were Negroes, less than one-sixth of whom were accused of rape. Practically all of the lynchers were native whites. The lynching rates have been highest in the newer and more sparsely settled portions of the South, where cultural and economic institutions are least stable and officers of the law are farthest apart, poorest paid, and most dependent upon local sentiment.

Of the twenty-one persons lynched in 1930, many were captured after extended man-hunts organized by undeputized armed men who used bloodhounds and conducted some type of mock trial before the lynching. Though two of the victims were unaccused, and there is grave doubt as to the guilt of many more, the findings of these mob trials were the lynchers' assurance that their victims were guilty of the crimes of which they were accused. The fact that a number of the victims were tortured, mutilated, dragged, or burned suggests the presence of sadistic tendencies among the lynchers; herein lies one of the most baffling phases of the mob situation. Though there were a few notable exceptions, most of the lynchers, chiefly young men between their late teens and twenty-five, were from that unattached group of people which exercised least public responsibility and was farthest removed from the institutions and agencies determining accepted standards of conduct. A number of middle-aged women figured prominently in some of the outbreaks; children, too, were present, making more difficult any effective resistance by officers.

Of the tens of thousands of lynchers and onlookers, the latter not guiltless, only forty-nine were indicted and only four have been sentenced. Chief among the factors rendering the courts ineffective was the prevalent indifference of peace officers and court officials and the apathy of the general white public concerning matters affecting Negroes. With but rare exceptions, leaders and members of the local religious and civic organizations were maneuvered by the pro-lynchers into a position of silent acquiescence.

And so the lynchers went unpunished and the communities paid the bills. Hundreds of thousands of dollars worth of property was destroyed with no insurance collectible; indirect financial losses accrued from the unfavorable publicity. Labor was disorganized and racial antagonisms were accentuated, forming the basis for further racial exploitation. The local and state governments were openly defied; the officials along with the general public, by winking at the lawlessness, rendered more difficult the realization of a community where the basic rights of human beings are respected.

. . .

The alleged crimes which caused the twenty-one lynchings of 1930 were: murder, five; rape, eight;[2] robbery or theft, three; attempted rape, two; bombing a house, one; no crime alleged, two.

All of the alleged crimes of the nineteen accused mob victims were against white people, one of whom was foreign-born. In eight instances the mob victims were accused of crimes involving women; in four, involving men and women; in seven, involving only men. In four instances, the alleged crimes were against members of small farm-owning families; in three, officers of the law; in three, farm tenants; in two, farm wage hands; in two, farm overseers; in two, factory workers; in two, motorists en route; and in one, a filling station operator. Ten of the lynched persons and three of their accusers had used guns or other concealed weapons in the altercations which precipitated the lynchings.

Two of the 1930 mob victims were innocent of crime (they were not even accused), and there is grave doubt of the guilt of eleven others. In six of these eleven cases there is considerable doubt as to just what crimes, if any, were committed, and in the other five, in which there is no question as to the crimes committed, there is considerable doubt as to whether the mobs got the guilty men.

. . .

Two-thirds of the lynchings occurred in the open country or in towns of less than 2,500 population; in five of these counties there were larger towns, but in no case was the actual lynching within six miles of it. Four lynchings were staged in towns of 2,500 to 15,000 inhabitants, and three in towns of 15,00 to 25,000. Sherman and Marion, in the 15,000 to 25,000 population group, are relatively regressive towns of Texas and Indiana and in many respects fall below the average of their respective states.

The measures available show that the counties where lynchings occurred in 1930 were economically below the average. In approximately nine-tenths of them the per capita tax valuation was below the general state average as was also the per capita bank deposit. In three-fourths of the counties the per capita income from farm and factory was below the state average, in many cases less than one-half; in nine-tenths, fewer and smaller income tax returns were made per thousand population than throughout the state. In over two-thirds, the proportion of farms operated by tenants was in excess of the state rate; and in nearly three-fourths of the counties, automobiles were less common than in their respective states. As would be expected from their poor economic rating, the educational facilities in many of these counties were far below the state average. Baptists and Methodists account for over three-fourths of all church members in nearly three-fourths of the counties, and two-thirds of them regularly poll Democratic majorities.

Mobs are capable of unbelievable atrocity. James Irwin at Ocilla, Georgia, was jabbed in his mouth with a sharp pole. His toes were cut off joint by joint. His fingers were similarly removed, and his teeth extracted with wire pliers. After further unmentionable mutilations, the Negro's still living body was saturated with gasoline and a lighted match was applied. As the flames leaped up, hundreds of shots were fired into the dying victim. During the day, thousands of people from miles around rode out to see the sight. Not till nightfall did the officers remove the body and bury it.

The Sherman mob also went to extreme lengths. The courthouse was fired. Many of the court officials and four Texas rangers escaped by second-floor windows. The accused Negro was placed in the second story of a large vault, where he remained while the courthouse burned to the ground. Members of the mob cut the water hose and thwarted the fire department's attempt to save the building. With evening, a small group of militiamen was driven from the courthouse grounds to the county jail. A little later, a larger unit of militiamen, just arrived from Dallas, was forced to retire to the protection of the jail. Shortly before midnight, with an acetylene torch and high explosives, a second-story vault window was blown open and the Negro's body was thrown to the crowd below. It was greeted by loud applause from the thousands who jammed the courthouse square. Police directed traffic while the corpse was dragged through the streets to a cottonwood tree in the Negro business section. There it was burned. Some Negro business properties valued at between $50,000 and $100,000 were fired, and the fire department was not allowed to throw water on them, though the mob permitted a hose to be trained on a white man's dwelling within fifteen feet of a burning Negro residence.

At Honey Grove the body of George Johnson was fastened by the feet to the back of a truck to keep the face down. In this position the corpse was dragged for five miles in and out of town, and later burned in front of a Negro church.

In most of the 1930 lynchings, there were evidences of a madness similar to that at Ocilla, Sherman, and Honey Grove. The roots of mob psychology might well be given extended study by competent scientists.

. . .

The credulity of the lyncher or pro-lyncher in taking at face value all rumors, and the development of the tradition of the absolute guilt of the mob's victims are both phases of the inability of the mass of white people to deal dispassionately with situations involving actual or potential racial conflict.

Many white people—particularly in the open country—assume that Negroes are prone to crimes against women and that unless a Negro is lynched now and then the women on the solitary farms are in danger. These assumptions have been kept alive by certain types of politicians who keep themselves in office by appeals to racial fear and antagonism. In a few cases church leaders have appealed to the same race fears in religious controversies. [3]

These assumptions underlie the traditional practice of Southern white men in arming themselves unofficially and hunting down an accused person. This method of mutual aid in policing an area, evolved on the frontier, persists in localities where police power is least adequate, or where the populace, for whatever reasons, insist upon dealing directly with crime and criminals. By its very nature the man-hunt operates through a highly selective process. In the first place, people who have regular work-hours and routine responsibilities are precluded from participating in all-day and all-night hunts. Again, those who have faith in the peace officers and courts, are not likely to take part. And, finally, the man-hunt tradition, an important element of which seems to be the lure of the chase, brings together the people who find lynching attractive.

The man-hunt provides an opportunity for carrying and flourishing firearms with impunity, a privilege which appeals strongly to the more irresponsible elements. Moreover, man-hunts and lynchings make it possible for obscure and irresponsible people to play the roles of arresting officers, grand jurors, trial jurors, judges, and executioners. An added attraction is that they often afford an avenue of emotional escape from a life so drab and unilluminated that any alternative is welcomed.

. . .

The identification of lynchers can usually be accomplished without great difficulty. The Commission's field workers secured fairly definite information about many of the persons who took active part in 1930's lynchings. With the exception of the case at Plant City, where a foreign-born white man was presumably lynched by other foreign-born whites, practically all of the lynchers were native whites. The majority of persons known to have taken an active part in the lynchings were unattached and irresponsible youths of twenty-five or less, many of them not yet out of their teens. Among them were older men who encouraged the youngsters. Drinking was in evidence in most of the mobs.

Only one of the known active lynchers had a technical or college education. He was a professional man who had been released from the State Insane Asylum but a few months before his mob participation. Few of the lynchers were even high school graduates. About half of them were not identified with any church, with many others inactive as to contributions and attendance. Most of the lynchers read but little, and were identified with but few or no organizations. In short, they were least susceptible to the ameliorating influences in the community.

As to the ownership of property, the known active lynchers were generally propertyless. In the majority of cases they were unemployed, rambling, irresponsible people, many of them with court records. In the rural communities, the more shiftless types of white farm tenants and wage hands were most in evidence. Being without property to tax or collect legal damage from, mob members recklessly destroyed property at a number of places. More than one of the Sherman rioters remarked when looking at the burning courthouse: "Let 'er burn down; the taxpayers'll put 'er back."

It would be erroneous, however, to leave the impression that all the lynchers were of the shiftless, irresponsible, propertyless type. At Scooba, Mississippi, where a double lynching occurred, the two men reported to have organized and engineered the mob from start to finish were leading people in the community and prominently identified with the local church, school, and other community activities. Generally speaking, the more backward the community, the more likely were the "best people" to participate in the actual lynching.

. . .

Women figured prominently in a number of the outbreaks. After a woman at Sherman had found the men unwilling to go into the courtroom and get the accused, she got a group of boys to tear an American flag from the wall of the courthouse corridor and parade through the courthouse and grounds, to incite the men to do their "manly duty." Later in the afternoon and evening, women joined in the throwing of missiles which resulted in the militiamen's retreating to the protection of the jail. Other women held their babies high over their heads and dared the soldiers to shoot. At Marion, several women were close in with the men who knocked down the jailhouse door and seized the accused Negroes. In several instances, mothers with children in arms were in the midst of the mob. Expectant mothers were also in evidence. It is reported that at Honey Grove the wife of one minister ran to the home of another minister and called to his wife: "Come, I never did see a nigger burned and I mustn't miss this chance." At Darien, Ocilla, and Thomasville the part played by the women seemingly inspired the mobs to greater brutalities.

At Sherman a grandmother called her two small grandsons out of bed and took them some blocks away to see the victim's body roasted. Not all of the children in the mobs, however, were taken by their elders. Children of all ages rushed in everywhere to see what was going on. The presence of women and children incited the men to action and at the same time made peace officials and militiamen less inclined to shoot.

Most of the women in the mobs who chided the men into action and shouted approval of what was going on were of middle age. Darien, where the sheriff's teen-age daughter became hysterical, was the single exception. In no mob were women in their twenties reported.

. . .

In every community where lynchings occurred in 1930, there were some people who openly justified what had been done. All walks of life were represented among the apologists—judges, prosecuting attorneys, lawyers, business men, doctors, preachers, teachers, mechanics, day laborers, and women of many types.

Most apologists for lynching, like the lynchers themselves, seemed to assume that the Negro is irredeemably inferior by reason of his race—that it is a plan of God that the Negro and his children shall forever be "hewers of wood and drawers of water." With this weighty emphasis upon the essential racial inferiority of the Negro, it is not surprising to find the mass of whites ready to justify any and all means used to "keep the Negro in his place." It is largely because of this that nothing will get larger headlines in the rural press, receive more discussion at cross-road stores, or draw a larger trial crowd, than some major conflict situation between a Negro and a white person. The vehemence with which the Negro's inferiority is declared is probably an indication that many of the whites base their claims on emotion rather than reasoned thought.

Regardless of the cause of a particular lynching, there were always those who defended it by the insistence that unless Negroes were lynched, no white woman would be safe, this despite the fact that only one-sixth of the persons lynched in the last thirty years were even accused of rape. Regardless of the accusation, an example must be made of the accused Negro for the sake of womanhood. Thus the apologist for lynching doubly betrays the Southern woman, first, in making her danger greater by exaggerating her helplessness, and second, in undermining the power of police and courts, her legitimate protectors.

. . .

NOTES

1. See "Negro Year Book, 1931–1932," and earlier editions of Year Book for sources of quantitative data on lynchings appearing in this volume.
2. The proportion of mob victims accused of rape was higher in 1930 than for any year since definite records have been kept.
3. See especially the arguments presented in the Methodist controversy over unification appearing in both secular and religious press.

CASTE AND CLASS IN A SOUTHERN TOWN

White aggression against Negroes and the social patterns which permit it are forms of social control; they are instrumentalities for keeping the Negro in his place and maintaining the supraordinate position of the white caste. We know now from our study that the whites do not fight for social superiority just for fun; on the contrary, they are attempting to minimize or eliminate Negro competition in the spheres of economics, sex, and prestige. Competition appears, when it does appear, in the form of aggressive demands or acts on the part of the Negro which are directed toward the modification of the superior advantages enjoyed by the white caste . . . . As is so often the case, attack is the better part of defense, and the aggressive manifestations permitted to white-group members are much more overt and decisive than those enjoyed by the Negroes. So far as conscious intent goes, white-caste members justify the measures they take against Negroes on the familiar principle of "safety first." It is said, for example, that it is safer to lynch Negroes than to endure a spreading epidemic of attacks on white women and murders of white men. The white group, intrenched in its caste position, attempts to appal and discourage the Negro and thereby to mute pressure for status advancement from his side. From the unconscious side, it is probably true that social patterns of the white caste permit sadistic pleasures to those in the population who are especially disposed to enjoy them.[1] The fear of being in the hands of such a sadistic person has a particularly terrorizing value for any victim, Negro or white.

It must not be supposed that the major or perhaps even the significant part of white aggression against Negroes consists of the few dramatic acts of lynching featured in the newspapers . . . . Much more important than the actual lynchings is the effect on Negro personality of the threat of lynching; this is as it is intended to be. One can never expect all of the members of a society or caste to refrain from savage and sadistic acts if social patterns

From John Dollard, *Caste and Class in a Southern Town* (Garden City, N.Y.: Doubleday and Co., 1957), excerpts from pp. 315–63. Reprinted by permission of the author.

condone them, although, surprisingly enough, many persons are so social-
ized that they do refrain.

. . .

In the end it seems . . . that white people fear Negroes. They fear
them, of course, in a special context, that is, when the Negro attempts to
claim any of the white prerogatives or gains. Since the wider American
social pattern, however, offers to the Negro the hope of personal advancement and so directs his striving that he is in continuous actual or potential
opposition to the caste system, the whites must constantly fear him. Negro
opposition to white gains can only be manifested in aggressive action; and
this is the source of white fear. This fear, of course, has a long history, fear
of revolt,[2] fear of Negroes' running away, and fear of isolated assault or
terrorism. Before the Civil War efficient policing institutions and the isola-
tion of plantation life reduced these fears, although even then the white
owner and overseer apparently watched Negro behavior very carefully for
signs of recalcitrance.[3] It is urged that, when the North interfered with
existing social and property relationships in the South, this fear became
much more intense and continuous. It is so to the present day, especially in
rural black-belt areas of the type in which Southerntown is located. White
people fear that Negroes actually will demand equal status, equal economic
opportunity, and equal sexual chances, including under the latter the right
to protect their homes and women from sexual aggression. By a series of
hostile acts and social limitations the white caste maintains a continuous
threatening atmosphere against the possibility of such demands by Negroes;
when successful, as these threats are now, the effect is to keep the social
order intact. . . . The Negro is allowed only the feeblest of efforts to realize
the American ideal of vertical social mobility; efforts that would be considered normal in others are experienced by white men as fabulously aggressive when they are made by Negroes.[4]

. . .

There is, however, another form of fear which must be discussed. This
is not based on real acts of aggression by Negroes or the expectation of
them; it is rather the unconscious expectation of retaliation for the hostile
acts of whites on Negroes. The justification for this assumption is the fact
that white people seem to be much more afraid of Negroes than there is any
real reason to be. The Negroes seem, in fact, to be rather well adjusted to
the situation and to have, by and large, renounced aggression and organization as means of changing their status. The fright shown by white-caste
members seems disproportionate to the threat from the Negro's side; in
such a case we may invariably postulate that unconscious mechanisms are
functioning, in this case a fear of retaliation for the gains aggressively
acquired by the white caste at the expense of the Negroes. Only on such a

basis may the unreasonable, often panicky, fears which the whites have toward the rather helpless Negroes be accounted for. . . . Real fear and neurotic fear are compounded to build up a permanent necessity for severe measures against Negroes on the part of the white caste.[5]

. . .

Reality fears of Negroes are based on the furtive, isolated attacks that were referred to in the preceding chapter. These may be feared from specific Negroes who have been injured by an individual white man; and there is always the danger that an individual white man or woman will be the target for a symbolic attack on the white caste by an enraged Negro. In the latter case, of course, it seems justifiable for the whites to act as a unified group in outlawing attacks by Negroes. We have noted, however, that among Negro forms of aggression direct attack plays a relatively small role, and it seems by no means to explain the apprehension of the white group.

The notion that white people fear Negroes is often ridiculed in times of race peace when there have been no recent "incidents." One white informant represented the situation as quite peaceful: Negroes are not afraid, whites are not afraid, whites do not feel the necessity to have guns, and there is no reason at all for apprehension, especially if the Yankess would let things alone. Such a statement is open to the objection that people generally attempt to deny their own aggressive tendencies and to minimize their fears of retaliatory action. Still there is much truth in what this informant said, so long as the caste taboos are strictly observed, so long as whites have little economic competition with Negroes, and so long as the whites have no irrational personal need to do violence to Negroes. But these are a lot of "ifs" and unfortunately such conditions seldom prevail. The alternative is the constant smolder of race hostility and the occasional hot flame of violence.

. . .

As everyone knows, the occurrence of rape is the excitation usually alleged by the whites as the cause of lynching. Nonsouthern white men and women must remember that these rapes actually do occur. They are not mere fictions or excuses. They are said to happen frequently enough so that they give a grounding of fact to the stereotyped belief. Let us realize also that rape is an exceedingly unpleasant affair, that it tends to arouse irrational passion to an extraordinary degree, and that murderous lusts will be found in any man whose woman or women are attacked in this manner. It is firmly established in our mores that sexual contacts may take place only by consent of both parties. What seems to be true is that in the North murderous rage on the part of an aggrieved man may not flow over into vengeful action, whereas in the South it may and does. Further, white-caste solidarity seems to function in the following way: every southern white man has a claim on every white woman, at least to the extent of defending her against a Negro, and he may experience and express his full hostility against the raper of another man's woman just as if she were his own. The point is that the emotions excited by rape are not peculiar to the South; but the caste situation, the special horror of rape,[6] and the permissive social patterns which allow vengeance are features of the southern regional culture.

There are some other considerations attending this crime. It has been suggested that it is not permissible for a white woman to have a conscious perception of sexual excitation in reference to a Negro man. This does not mean, however, that such excitations are not experienced. It is equally impossible for a southern white man to assume any such motive on the part of his idealized white woman; still he may unconsciously respond to the fact if it does exist. Some evidence has already been given that there is such excitation, even though it is not rationally experienced and ratified by social values. In this case the following state of affairs may exist: instead of punishing the white woman for any seductive tendencies that she may have, the white man refuses to face these tendencies and attributes the whole blame for the contact to the Negro man. The Negro is then punished both for his own aggressive share in the act of rape and for the fact that white women are not completely able to reject a Negro man unconsciously as well as consciously.[7] This view of the matter spares the white man some anguish since he is not brought into the position of hating his white woman for her share in the transaction, but instead vents the full measure of his rage against the Negro male.

There has been a little, though not much, thinking about the sexual aspects of the race problem among psychoanalysts, and the idea has, of course, been brought forward that the white man may experience jealousy in reference to the supposed or actual superiority of the Negro as a sexual being.[8] It can certainly be established that beliefs about the superior genital adequacy of Negroes are widespread among southern white men and it can also be shown that the attitude toward the rape problem is irrational and unrealistic. The notion that sexual jealousy is in part the reason for the extraordinary sadism accompanying lynchings is not absurd. The only satisfying evidence on this score would come from intimate life histories of white men; but we can learn on any street corner that sexual jealousy plays a part in white aggression against Negroes.

The difference between the statistics and the popular views of the causes of lynching is very illuminating. When explaining a lynching southerners almost invariably bring up a case where rape has occurred and they give the impression that this is the standard excitation. Of the 3,724 people lynched from 1889 through 1930, more than four-fifths were Negroes, and of these less than one-sixth were even accused of rape.[9] There is no explanation for this confusion on the level of overt social patterning since whites know perfectly well through immediate experience that most lynchings begin with other events than rape. Yet the belief is held and the disparity between belief and fact gives new point to the explanations offered above of jealousy and suspicion of unfaithful inclinations on the part of the white woman.

The irrational elements of jealousy and suspicion just indicated can receive their emotional support only from events far back in the life histories of the white individuals concerned. They gather so naturally around the Freudian conception of the Oedipus complex as to make it seem an inevitable mode of perception at this point. Individuals who emerge from the Oedipus ordeal as jealous adults will grasp more eagerly at the southern social patterns which permit revenge for a sexual affront; individuals with most doubt about the chastity of in-family women will be most certain of Negro guilt whenever a rape charge comes up. Confirmation of this hypothesis again will require minute study of suitable white informants; it is a study, however, which would be most illuminating from the standpoint of race prejudice and hostility. Just this prejudice which is the key fact in the caste situation is until now unexplained and unintelligible. For this reason we are justified in advancing any explanation that will aid in reducing the mystery that surrounds it.

. . .

One of the most effective checks on acts of violence by Negroes against whites is the reprisals which may follow against the family of the Negro man. If the man himself gets away, it has been known to happen that the white crowd will go to his home, perhaps rape the woman and shoot the woman and children, perhaps burn down the house or loot it and destroy the furniture. In such a case the Negro family often does not suspect why the white mob came. This would be another example of the now-familiar displaced aggression and of the dreadful need on the part of the mob to make an example of every case.

. . .

We cannot leave the subject of white aggression without calling attention to the generally threatening behavior of whites toward Negroes. We have already noted the cases in which punishment of a crime by a Negro is exemplary and symbolic. The posse wants to get the right man, of course, but it is not too serious a matter if it does not, since the warning is even more clear when it hangs the wrong one; i.e., the Negro caste is punished through one of its representatives. White people may or may not be very conscious of this threatening atmosphere in which Negroes live, but Negroes are extremely conscious of it and it is one of the major facts in the life of any Negro in Southerntown. I once asked a middle-class Negro how he felt about coming back down south. He said it was like walking into a lion's den; the lions are chained; but if they should become enraged, it is doubtful whether the chains would hold them; hence it is better to walk very carefully. Another Negro thought it was a shame that a Negro man had to shape his behavior so much according to the wishes of the whites and out of fear of what they will do; he has to be careful not only on his own account, but also on account of his family and even of all the Negroes in the community. He said that after the shooting or lynching of a Negro the Negro community is frightened and that the whites act as if to say, "Well, it may be you next." Every Negro in the South knows that he is under a kind of sentence of death; he does not know when his turn will come, it may never come, but it may also be at any time. This fear tends to intimidate the Negro man. If he loves his family, this love itself is a barrier against any open attempt to change his status. Informant said that Negro men are not cowards and do want to defend themselves; but most of the time they just take the easiest way out—accommodation.

. . .

It has been noted that the Civil War broke up the smooth accommodation relationships that had existed in slavery and substituted a less stable form of social organization in the caste system. It also increased the hostile manifestations toward Negroes, not only in the direct physical sense beginning with the secret orders [10] and continuing through lynching behavior, but also in all the less tangible forms of personal derogation and social exclusion described in this chapter. There was, of course, some fear and hostility before the [Civil] War, centering particularly around the danger of revolt, but it has obviously enormously increased since then. The intent of the postwar aggression, seen from the sociological standpoint, was to restore and maintain the superior position of the white caste. It was really this superiority which was attacked by the War, the War amendments, the Civil Rights Bill, and the military occupation of the South. It would seem, therefore, that the legitimate hostility of southern white people would be directed against the North, northern armies, the northern theories of social justice, and the leaders who attempted to put them into practice. This was indeed, and still is to some degree, the case. After the military defeat of the South, however, there was no possibility of effective aggression against the North. The defeat was, of course, a great damage to southern pride in addition to being an economic loss. This is probably the context in which increased hostility has been directed at Negroes since the War; the Negroes have been made the butt of the hatred aroused in the South by the interference of the North with its folkways. Hostility against the North, northern people, and their ideas of social justice still exists and is not a negligible factor in American life, present or future; but the military cause, at least, is lost. There remains a passionate insistence on maintaining regional social relations along traditional southern lines. In a larger sense, the War has been continued by this hostility against Negroes. [11] This is not offered as a single-strand explanation, but merely as one interpretation; it is equally obvious that the threat of Negro competition to the middle-class trustees of southern culture would also arouse, and appear to legitimate, aggression against Negroes.

NOTES

1. The reader must turn to Freud to learn how hostile acts against others may be experienced as pleasurable. See Sigmund Freud, *Three Contributions to the Theory of Sex* (New York, 1930), 21–23.

2. "The general trend of public expressions laid emphasis upon the need of safeguards but showed confidence that no great disasters were to be feared. The revolts which occurred and the plots which were discovered were sufficiently serious to produce a very palpable disquiet from time to time, and the rumors were frequent enough to maintain a fairly constant undertone of uneasiness. The net effect of this was to restrain that progress of liberalism which the consideration of economic interest, the doctrines of human rights and the spirit of kindliness all tended to promote." U.B. Phillips, *American Negro Slavery* (New York, 1918), 488; quoted by permission of D. Appleton-Century Co.

3. "It was the interest and business of slaveholders to study human nature, and the slave nature in particular, with a view to practical results; and many of them attained astonishing proficiency in this direction. They had to deal not with earth, wood, and stone, but with *men;* and by every regard they had for their safety and prosperity they had need to know the material on which they were to work. So much intellect as the slaveholder had round him required watching. Their safety depended on their vigilance. Conscious of the injustice and wrong they were every hour perpetrating, and knowing what they themselves would do if they were victims of such wrongs, they were constantly looking out for the first signs of the dread retribution. They watched, therefore, with skilled and practiced eyes, and learned to read, with great accuracy, the state of mind and heart of the slave through his sable face." Frederick Douglass, *Life and Times* (Hartford, Conn., 1882), 178.

4. Is the "aggressiveness" often believed to be a personality characteristic of Jews an illusion of the same kind?

5. Frank Tannenbaum, *Darker Phases of the South* (New York, 1924), 167.

6. *Race Problems of the South,* Report of the Proceedings of the First Annual Conference Held under the Auspices of the Southern Society for the Promotion of the Study of Race Conditions and Problems in the South (Montgomery, Alabama, 1900), 170–174.

7. "Though Professor Siegfried refers particularly to lack of physical repulsion of white men towards coloured women, much more disturbing is the suspicion that the absence of repulsion applies to both sexes of both races. There is no doubt that most of the inter-mixture has come from relations between white men and coloured women. But the suspicion that it is not confined to that class motivates to a large extent the sadistic features of many lynchings and burnings. It has caused the enactment in twenty-nine states of anti-intermarriage laws—legislation which would be most unnecessary if the boasted repulsion were really true." Walter White, *Rope and Faggot* (New York, 1929), 67–68; quoted by permission of Alfred A. Knopf.

8. "In my opinion the phenomenon of 'lynch law' against negroes can only be explained by supposing the idea of sexual intercourse between his women kind and a negro stirs in the depths of the white man's mind a fury that is the entire product of sexual jealously. It is a general belief that the negro not only possesses a larger penis than men of other races, but is capable of maintaining it in a state of erection for a longer period than is possible for a male of any other race. This sexual jealousy of the negro's potency drives the white man temporarily mad, to the end that he inflicts the most horrible retributions on his unfortunate rival." Owen A.R. Berkeley-Hill, "The 'Color Question' from a Psychoanalytic Standpoint," *Psychoanal. Rev.* (1924), XI, 251–252.

9. Raper, *op. cit.* [*The Tragedy of Lynching*], 1.

10. Robertson, *op. cit.* [*The Changing South*], 57-58.

11. "It took ten years of misrule and bitter humiliation to create the 'solid South,' but the work was done so thoroughly that it will in all probability persist for years to come. It is a familiar façt that social habits, especially when they become tinged with strong emotion, are the last to change. . . . It was most unfortunate for the Negro whose interests were so intimately connected with those of the white that during this period of crystallization of group feeling he was not only excluded, but was identified from the very start with the outside forces making for the coercion of the white." Mecklin, *op. cit.* [*Democracy and Race Friction*], 168; quoted by permission of the Macmillan Co.

Harvard Sitkoff

RACIAL MILITANCY AND INTERRACIAL VIOLENCE IN THE SECOND WORLD WAR

World War II marked a period of major change in the condition and prospects of America's black citizens. At the time of the attack on Pearl Harbor, in 1941, all of the southern states and several over the border segregated blacks by law as well as custom in a variety of situations. So did the federal government, in institutions as centrally important as the armed forces. In the South acute observers such as the authors of the previous selections saw no immediate hope for change. And the prospects for national political action were not much brighter. Although the economic benefits of the New Deal had caused many blacks to switch their voting allegiance from the party of Lincoln to the party of Roosevelt, the Democratic president was too dependent upon the white southern wing of his party to make any real commitment to civil rights. But then the war, with its heavy demand for manpower, black as well as white, disrupted old patterns of employment and settlement, and created social and political pressures for change.

Harvard Sitkoff describes the ways in which at every level from individual protest to mass organization blacks challenged the racial situation in wartime. At the same time, he assesses the relative promise of the tactics used. Blacks and other groups, from workingmen to feminists, have often had to choose between self-help and the use of outside allies, between direct action and regular politics, between militance and compromise. Sitkoff expresses strong views about why and how this particular set of decisions was made, in the 1940s, and with what results.

From *Journal of American History* 58 (December 1971): 661–81. Reprinted by permission of the Organization of American Historians.

World War II opened a quarter of a century of increasing hope and frustration for the black man. After a decade of depression, the ideological character of the war and the government's need for the loyalty and manpower of all Americans led blacks to expect a better deal from President Franklin D. Roosevelt. With a near-unanimity rare in the Negro community, civil rights groups joined with the Negro press and influential church, labor, and political leaders to demand "Democracy in Our Time!" [1] Individuals and organizations never before involved in a protest movement found it respectable, even expedient, to be part of the new militancy in the black community. [2] The war stimulated racial militancy, which in turn led to increased interracial violence that culminated in the bloody summer of 1943. Negro leaders then retreated, eschewing mass movements and direct action in favor of aid from white liberals for their congressional and court battles. While many of the goals of the early war years remained, the mood and tactics became increasingly conservative. [3] Paradoxically, the wartime violence which summoned forth the modern civil rights movement, enlisting in the struggle scores of liberal organizations and tens of thousands of whites previously blind or indifferent to American racism, also smothered the embryonic black movement for equality by tying it ever more closely to liberal interracialism, which all too easily accepted the appearance of racial peace for the reality of racial justice. By the end of the war two trends emerged which would shape the course of the next two decades. Jim Crow had stumbled badly enough to heighten the aspirations of many Negroes that they would soon share the American Dream; and leadership in the battle for civil rights had been taken over by various communist-front organizations, labor unions, religious groups fighting intolerance, and social scientists making a career of studying race relations. [4]

At the beginning of this war, unlike World War I, few Negro leaders asked blacks to close ranks and ignore their grievances until the war ended. [5] Rather, the very dependency of the government on the cooperation of the Negro intensified his demand for civil rights. "If we don't fight for our rights during this war," said one Harlem leader, "while the government needs us, it will be too late after the war." [6] Memories of the false promises of World War I stirred a reader of the *Amsterdam-Star News* to write: "Remember, that which you fail to get now you won't get after the war." [7] Some Negro columnists openly advocated a prolonged war as the best hope for destroying the racial status quo. And the Negro press proclaimed the "time ripe for a new emancipation" and mobilized a "Double V" campaign to fight fascism and racism both abroad and at home. [8]

The Negro press headlined evidence of blacks excluded from defense jobs, blood plasma segregated by the Red Cross, abused Negro soldiers, and white hostility and violence. Circulation increased 40 percent as the Negro newspapers, functioning primarily to foster race solidarity and prod increasing militancy, campaigned to embarrass America's war for democracy by publicizing America's jim-crow policies and practices. [9] Membership in the National Association for the Advancement of Colored People multiplied nearly ten times during the war, and the number of its chapters tripled. [10] The Congress of Racial Equality, organized in 1942, experimented with non-violent action to end segregation in the North, and stimulated students at Howard University and interracial groups in various cities to begin sitting-in and experimenting with other forms of direct confrontation. [11] To "demand the right to work and fight for our country," A. Philip Randolph labored to build his March-on-Washington Committee into an all-black mass protest movement. [12] Even Negro fraternal, business, and professional societies collaborated in the battle against oppression on the homefront. Everywhere he turned, the urban black found new Negro organizations enlisting in the crusade and new leaders and journals exhorting him to demand equality. Each concession wrested from the government and every sign of the weakening of white supremacy added new converts, made fund raising easier and stimulated greater confidence and higher hopes. [13]

The establishment of the United Nations, the anti-imperialistic pronouncements of government officials, and a steady stream of articles, books, letters, and speeches—especially those of Pearl S. Buck, Eleanor Roosevelt, Wendell Wilkie, and Henry Wallace—disputing the scientific basis of racism and urging America to practice what it preached, further augmented the militancy of black America. [14] The attempt to educate the public to stop discrimination and end prejudice reached its peak in 1944 with the publication of Gunnar Myrdal's *An American Dilemma.* Eschewing the socio-economic explanations popularized by American Marxists in the 1930s, Myrdal described the race problem as a moral problem for white America, brought about by the collision between the American Creed's promise of equality and liberty and the denial of them to the Negro. Woefully underestimating the extent and depth of American racism, Myrdal optimistically predicted that Americans would resolve their dilemma by ending discrimination and segregation. [15]

The growth of Negro political power also stimulated hope for change. The steady migration of blacks to the North and the return, after 1938, of many white Republicans to their traditional voting habits, prematurely led Negro leaders to believe that Franklin D. Roosevelt could be persuaded to support civil rights. [16] He refused to do so in 1940, but Wilkie's strong bid for the Negro vote and the inclusion of a solid civil rights plank in the Republican platform forced the President to approve an anti-discrimination clause in the Selective Service Act, promote Colonel Benjamin O. Davis as the first Negro brigadier general, and appoint William Hastie as civilian aide to the secretary of war and Colonel Campbell Johnson as executive assistant to the director of Selective Service. Black political pressure also opened the way for new Reserve Officer Training Corps units in Negro colleges and an air force aviation school for blacks at Tuskegee. [17] These actions barely affected black life in America, but as possible first steps to be lengthened as the Negro vote grew in the North, they showed Negro leaders the power of the vote and the need for coordinated efforts. Moreover, the fact that President Roosevelt did respond, if only with gestures, increased black expectations. But the paucity of the response further clarified the disparity between Negro goals and gains—between democratic myths and realities. [18]

The experience of living in jim-crow America led the Negro to be acutely conscious of his deprivations and impatient with all impediments to first-class citizenship. Magazines and newspapers at the beginning of the war charted his plummeting morale and increased assertiveness. [19] Only a few blacks, mainly the followers of Leonard Robert Jordan's Ethiopia Pacific League and Elijah Muhammad's Temple of Islam, actually flirted with treason; many simply, but loudly, held their loyalty in check. [20] A Harlem doctor driving through Manhattan with a large sign on his car reading, "IS THERE A DIFFERENCE? JAPS BRUTALLY BEAT AMERICAN REPORTER GERMANS BRUTALLY BEAT SEVERAL JEWS AMERICAN CRACKERS BRUTALLY BEAT ROLAND HAYES & NEGRO SOLDIERS," [21] expressed the bitterness of countless others, as did the black college student who asked: "The Army jim-crows us. The Navy lets us serve only as messmen. The Red Cross refuses our blood. Employers and labor unions shut us out. Lynchings continue. We are dis-franchised, jim-crowed, spat upon. What more could Hitler do than that?" [22] NAACP responded to the new mood by repeatedly comparing Hitlerism with American racism and urging its followers: "Now Is the Time Not to Be Silent." [23]

The changing of signs on hiring gates from "No Help Wanted" to "Help Wanted, White," most stirred the militancy of lower-class blacks. After being first-fired during the Depression, they now found themselves last-hired, discriminated against in government training programs, excluded from many unions, and forced into the dirtiest and lowest paying jobs. To make matters worse, as the Depression in white America officially ended, the federal government drastically slashed welfare appropriations despite the fact that most blacks remained unemployed or underemployed. [24] Negro leaders established new committees and attended conferences requesting action, but their polite, formal protests and negotiations failed to budge President Roosevelt or the nation's leading industrialists and unions. [25]

As black discontent deepened, the established civil rights groups turned to mass protest meetings and picketing. [26] At the same time, Randolph issued a call for 10,000 blacks to march on Washington to de-mand federal action on job discrimination. Throughout the spring of 1941 the March on Washington Committee mobilized lower-class blacks never previously recruited by any Negro organization. As his movement grew, NAACP, Urban League, and a score of staid, old-line Negro associations and leagues that had always shunned direct action hastily boarded Ran-dolph's bandwagon. [27] Randolph kept countering presidential indifference by threatening to raise the number of angry marching blacks to 50,000 and then 100,000. A week before the scheduled march Franklin Roosevelt capitulated, agreeing to issue an executive order establishing the first President's Committee on Fair Employment Practices (FEPC) in exchange for cancellation of the embarrassing march on the nation's capital. [28] Although neither the original order nor the authority of FEPC ever fully met Negro expectations, President Roosevelt's action buoyed the most optimistic hopes of Negro organizations for further federal assistance. Similarly, the March-on-Washington Movement's apparent success in stirring thousands of blacks never before touched by the civil rights movement and in threatening the government with direct action graphically demonstrated the potential of mass black militancy. [29] The Chicago *Defender,* which in February labeled Randolph's proposal as "the miracle of the century," heralded the death of "Uncle-Tomism" and the new age of mass protest in July. [30]

To oppose discrimination in the armed services and the lack of black combat units, the two most bitterly resented aspects of American racism during the war, some young blacks publicly refused induction. [31] Various individuals and organizations such as the Chicago "Conscientious Objectors Against Jim Crow" tried to fight military segregation and racial quotas in the courts. [32] Countless other blacks just never showed up for examination or induction. Those who served often did so sullenly. "Here lies a black man killed fighting a yellow man for the glory of a white man," became a popular saying for black draftees. [33] In Harlem, a white draft board member noted: "When colored draftees came to the board for induction last year, I used to give them a little patriotic talk to make them feel good. But they didn't. They only laughed at me. Now I bow my head as they come in for their induction." [34]

The publicized denigration of blacks in the armed services caused both frustration and militant protest. Army policy at the beginning of the war strictly limited the quota of Negroes to be inducted and rigidly confined them to noncombatant units. Naval policy excluded them from the marines and coast guard and restricted blacks to being messboys in the navy. [35] While political pressure and war manpower needs slowly forced the armed services to move from exclusion to segregation to token integration, the great mass of blacks served throughout the war in service units commanded by white officers. They trained in segregated base camps, mostly in the South, and found themselves barred or jim-crowed by USO, service centers, theaters, and post exchanges. [36] Most bases even provided segregated chapels; the sign listing the schedule of religious services at one camp post read: "Catholic, Jews, Protestants, and Negroes." [37] Blacks who protested were harassed and intimidated; those who persisted in their opposition were transferred, placed in the stockade, or dishonorably discharged. [38]

The most chafing practice of the army, however, was its refusal to protect Negro servicemen off the post and its use of white military police to control blacks. Throughout the South a Negro in uniform symbolized "a nigger not knowing his place." [39] White bus drivers habitually refused to transport blacks to and from their bases. White military police enforced jim-crow seating restrictions, and off-base bars and restaurants used them to keep blacks out. To avoid friction with the local community, base commanders continuously enjoined blacks to obey the local customs of segregation and some even prohibited blacks from securing leave.[40] Little wonder that blacks equated army law with "white" law. Many blacks responded with cynicism and despair, and the war department regularly received reports on the low morale of the Negro soldier and accounts of black suicides, mental "crack-ups, desertions, and AWOL's due to discrimination and racist brutality.[41]

Other blacks responded by fighting back. Racial friction, sporadic conflict, and finally outright rioting became commonplace at nearly every army base in the South, many in the North, and even at a few in Australia, England, and the South Pacific.[42] As the experiences of war shattered the Negroes' illusions about white sincerity and destroyed their fear of white authority, "thousands of spontaneous and individual rebellions went unrecorded and unnoticed." Although the war department systematically suppressed most evidence of black revolt and labeled most of the deaths due to race battles as combat fatalities or "motor vehicle accidents," army statisticians, nevertheless, reported an unusually high number of casualties suffered by white officers of Negro troops and at least fifty black soldiers killed in race riots in the United States.[43]

In 1941, army authorities found a black private, arms and legs bound, lynched at Fort Benning. Brutality by the military police in Fayetteville, North Carolina, led to a pitched gun battle with black soldiers. Forty-three blacks went AWOL to escape the harassment and terrorization by whites in Prescott, Arizona. Black soldiers at Fort Bragg, Camps Davis, Gibbon, and Jackson Barracks fought white soldiers and police.[44] Although complaints and protests from Negro soldiers, chaplains, NAACP, and National Lawyers Guild poured into the war department and White House, neither would publicly respond.[45] The quantity and intensity of racial violence at military bases accelerated in 1942. The attempt by a military policeman to arrest a drunken black soldier in Alexandria, Louisiana, sparked a race riot that resulted in the shooting of twenty-eight Negroes and the arrest of nearly 3,000.[46] Other race riots broke out in New Orleans; Vallejo, California; Flagstaff, Phoenix, Arizona; Florence, South Carolina; Fort Dix, New Jersey; and the air force training school in Tuskegee.[47] The war department even refused to intervene when Beaumont, Texas, city policemen clubbed and shot a black soldier, and when a Negro army nurse was brutally beaten and jailed for defying the jim-crow seating arrangements on a Montgomery bus.[48]

Stories of race riots at Camps Stewart and Shelby, Forts Bliss and Benning, and March Field dominated the front pages of the Negro press along with accounts of southern peace officers killing black soldiers. Numerous bases reported Negroes wrecking post facilities and off-base restaurants that refused to serve them. Accounts of Negro soldiers going "over the hill" and battling with white military police increased dramatically. The growing fear of retaliatory violence by blacks led the governor of Mississippi to request the war department to move Negro regiments out of his state, and forced officers at some southern bases to order the removal of firing pins from the rifles of Negro servicemen.[49] Finally, after a bitter summer of violence, the war department officially acknowledged the existence of a serious morale problem among Negro troops and urged all white officers to treat blacks with the utmost care and diplomacy.[50]

The tensions and violence within the military mirrored the mushrooming conflict on the homefront. Both blacks and whites blamed the other for racial problems and both self-righteously sought advantage in the crisis of war. Many whites intensified their efforts to keep the Negro "in his place," regardless of the changes wrought by the war.[51] Each new protest against discrimination was seen as a sign of Negro disloyalty, and many feared that "the more they get the more they want." The more Negroes demanded their rights, the more white resistance stiffened, which led blacks to become even more impatient with second-class citizenship and determined to assert themselves.[52] The increasing competition between the races and the many petty irritations of war—the rationing, shortages, overcrowding, and high prices—engendered frustration, supersensitivity, and belligerency. The fatigue of long work weeks with little opportunity for recreation, the anxious scanning of casualty lists, the apprehension over a new job and a strange city, and the desire of noncombatants to prove their masculinity all fed the boiling racial cauldron.[53]

Government officials at all levels feared intervening in this explosive situation, contenting themselves with vague appeals to national unity. President Roosevelt, preoccupied with diplomacy and military strategy, and deeply dependent on southern support in Congress for his postwar foreign policy, let two southern aides, Mobilization Director James Byrnes and political secretary Marvin McIntyre, handle most racial matters.[54] Symptomatic of its approach to bury racial problems as deeply as possible—a mixture of blindness, patchwork compromise, and faith that good public relations could gloss over prior errors—the White House refused to do anything to prevent the riot by white Detroiters to keep Negroes from entering the Sojourner Truth public housing project. Warned well in advance of the trouble brewing, McIntyre sought only to avoid letting the conflict be publicized.[55] After the riot, the Office of Facts and Figures noted that unless strong and quick intervention by some high official, preferably the President, was not taken at once, disorders would follow.[56] The President did nothing. With little government action to relieve racial anxiety or enforce new norms, whites and blacks moved closer toward violence.[57]

The intensification of interracial rancor prompted various forms of violence, including lynchings.[58] Less dramatic, but more immediately affecting the racial climate, were the almost daily fights and incidents on public vehicles. Most involved Negro soldiers from the North refusing to honor southern racial etiquette and southern white migrants to the North refusing to mingle closely with blacks on the overcrowded busses, trolleys, and trains of industrial cities. Verbal abuse, shovings, slappings, and stabbings became everyday happenings, signifying the heightened racial animosity. [59]

The chaos, despair, and frustration arising from the Negro's resentment of the slow pace of racial progress and his accelerating hope for a better day, plus the bewilderment and anger of whites determined to maintain the racial status quo—expressed in and nurtured by three years of racial friction and conflict—exploded in an epidemic of interracial violence in 1943. The Social Science Institute at Fisk University reported 242 racial battles in forty-seven cities. [60] Throughout the North, juvenile delinquency increasingly turned into racial gang fights. Italo-American and Negro teenagers fought week-long battles in Newark and Philadelphia, while black and Polish gangs battled in Buffalo and Chicago. [61] Other racial gang fights were reported in Cambridge, Massachusetts, and Brooklyn. [62] The worst of these "zoot-suit" riots occurred in Los Angeles. A mob of over 1,000 whites, mainly sailors and soldiers, freely roamed the city attacking and stripping zoot-suited blacks and Mexican-Americans, while the city police, shore patrol, and military police looked the other way. Making no attempt to inquire into the causes of the riot, the Los Angeles City Council further stirred racial emotions by ordering the arrest for "vagrancy" of those who had been beaten and by declaring the wearing of a zoot-suit a misdemeanor. [63]

In mid-June, the Christian American Association of Texas spread a rumor that a Negro had raped a young white mother in Beaumont. A white mob of over 3,000, mainly workers from the Pennsylvania Shipyard fearing that FEPC would give their jobs to blacks, stomped through the Negro ghetto burning, pillaging, and terrorizing those in their path. War production stopped, businesses closed, thousands of dollars of property was damaged, one black and one white died, and more than seventy-five people were injured. Only a declaration of martial law and the swift, impartial action of the combined forces of local and state police, volunteers, and Texas Rangers quelled the riot. [64] In Mobile, the attempt to upgrade twelve Negro workers as welders in the yards of the Alabama Dry Dock and Shipbuilders Company caused 20,000 white workers to walk off their job and riot for four days. The League for White Supremacy, organized in 1942 to thwart the FEPC demand to end discrimination in the shipyards, had been agitating for a year unhindered by either company or union officials. It answered the company's decision to comply with FEPC policy by spreading a rumor that a black worker had just killed a white woman. While plant guards and local police looked on, gangs of whites attacked Negro workers with crowbars and wrenches and then rioted throughout the city. Only the belated entrance of federal troops finally stopped the riot, and FEPC backed down and agreed to the continuation of segregation in the shipyards. [65] Similar fears of Negro economic competition led to a series of hate strikes against the hiring of black workers in Maryland, Michigan, New York, and Ohio, and a violent battle between blacks and whites in the Sun Shipbuilding Yard at Chester, Pennsylvania. [66] A white walkout stopped Philadelphia's transportation system for a week when the city hired eight Negroes as trolley motormen, and a group of blacks in New Iberia, Louisiana, were driven out of town for setting up a welding school for Negroes—"the white people didn't want the colored folks to learn to be anything but sharecroppers and servants." [67]

Other cities beset by rumors of impending racial violence began taking extraordinary precautions to prevent riots. In Washington, the federal government worked behind the scenes with local Negro leaders and the municipal police force to keep a demonstration against the Capital Transit Company for refusing to hire black bus drivers from turning into an open race war. [68] A score of other cities hastily secured reinforcements for local police to avert rumored riots and instituted interracial committees, curfews, cancellation of leaves for local servicemen, and prohibitions on liquor. [69] While columnists publicly pondered the "threat of a domestic Pearl Harbor," racial rumors swept the nation. [70] Loose talk of Negro troops seizing the *Queen Mary* in a mutiny, of "Eleanor Clubs" (where Negro domestics organized a boycott and vowed to get "every white woman in her kitchen by Christmas"), of Disappointment Clubs (where blacks pledged to harass white women by promising to come to cook or clean on certain days and then not showing up), combined with tales of shovers, pushers, and bumpers clubs, whose members plotted to devote one day every week to walking in crowded areas and shoving whites, and rumors of blacks buying guns and a white counteroffensive against "uppity, out of line Negroes," kept many cities on edge. [71]

No city expected racial trouble more than Detroit, and none did less to prevent it. Forced to accommodate the more than 50,000 southern Negroes and 500,000 whites rushing into the city for employment in defense industries, with severe shortages of housing, recreation, and transportation, and an over-abundance of agitators and extremists of every color and persuasion, Detroit, the "Arsenal of Democracy," seethed with racism and hatred. [72] Racial clashes in schools, playgrounds, and factories, fights on busses and trolleys, and cross burnings throughout the city became accepted everyday occurrences. [73] The city was described as "a keg of powder with a short fuse." [74] When the riot finally exploded, Detroit's mayor told reporters: "I was taken by surprise only by the day it happened." [75]

The riot began when thousands of Detroiters, seeking relief from the hot, humid city streets, crowded into the amusement park on Belle Isle on Sunday, June 20. Small fights all through the day combined with rumors of a race war erupted into a riot on the bridge connecting the park with the city. News of the riot spread swiftly to every section of Detroit. [76] In the crowded ghetto blacks, tired of moving to find the Promised Land, tired of finding the North too much like the South, tired of being Jim-Crowed, struck out against "whitey" and his property and symbols of authority. Black mobs stoned passing motorists, hurled rocks and bottles at the police, stopped streetcars to beat up unsuspecting whites, and smashed and looted many of the white-owned stores in the ghetto.[77] White mobs, unhampered by the police, retaliated on all Negroes caught in white sections.[78] Throughout the melee, fresh rumors sustained the frenzy. Tales of babies killed and women raped served to justify the violent expression of old hatreds, while the excitement of a car burning in the night, the screeching of an ambulance siren, plenty of looted liquor, and a feeling of being free to do whatever one wished without fear of police reprisal fed the riotous appetite of the angry city.[79]

While city and state officials feared to act or ask for help and appeared unable to control the violence, and the White House and war department refused to intervene, the riot raged.[80] By Monday evening, nineteen police precincts, covering 75 percent of the Detroit area, reported riot activity. Most transportation lines had suspended operation and the fire department could no longer control the city's fires. Injured rioters and spectators were entering hospitals at the rate of one every other minute.[81] By the time federal troops finally arrived late Monday evening, Detroit's riot toll recorded thirty-four killed, more than 700 injured, over two million dollars in property losses, and a hundred million man-hours lost in war production.[82] Only the continued presence of soldiers patrolling the streets and armed military vehicles escorting busses and trolleys on their usual runs kept the continuing racial hysteria from erupting again. Throughout the summer anxiety increased, isolated racial fights continued, and rumors of blacks and whites collecting knives and guns for "the next one" heightened the tense atmosphere.[83]

Less than two months later, despite the extensive efforts of New York officials to maintain racial calm, a rumor of a Negro soldier killed by a white policeman triggered the same combination of deep grievances and war-bred tensions that had sparked the Detroit riot into an orgy of looting and destruction in Harlem.[84] The protest against discrimination and segregation, unemployment and restricted housing, police brutality, mistreatment of black soldiers, and the white-owned, rat-and-vermin-infested black ghetto led to the death of five Negroes, 500 injuries, and an estimated five million dollars of property damaged.[85] Once the rumor of another police killing swept through Harlem, Walter White, executive secretary of NAACP, wrote, "blind, unreasoning fury swept the community with the speed of lightening." The young and the poor, goaded by the white-owned property they were powerless to possess, suddenly smashed the plate-glass windows of stores on all the main avenues in the ghetto, and "the Bigger Thomases of New York passed like a cloud of locusts over the stores of Harlem."[86]

Shocked by the extent of racial violence in the summer of 1943, and without a program to do anything about it, liberals and Negro leaders looked to the White House for leadership.[87] But President Roosevelt remained silent. Having been nurtured and elevated to power by the southern dominated and oriented Democratic party, he followed the century-old tradition of successful Democratic politicians by studiously avoiding interference with a state's right to control racial issues. Although Eleanor Roosevelt and some of the liberals in his administration cautiously urged him to support civil rights, the President continued to let his southern assistants— Byrnes, McIntyre, press secretary Stephen T. Early, and General Edwin "Pa" Watson, his military aide and secretary—handle all racial matters. They viewed civil rights issues as a danger to the fragile Democratic coalition as well as an unwarranted intrusion on the President's precious time, and the so-called Negro balance of power as far more expendable than southern votes in Congress. Consequently, they blocked all proposals for White House action and shuffled off complaints to David Niles, Jonathan Daniels, and FEPC—the Wailing Wall for minorities, virtually powerless to act but handy as a safety valve.[88] Secretary of War Henry L. Stimson and Secretary of the Navy Frank Knox took an even more standpat attitude on racial questions than Roosevelt's advisers. Both viewed the civil rights issue as an impediment to the war effort with which no compromise should be made. Both accepted notions of Negro inferiority and of black agitators, not even supported by their own people, unfairly taking advantage of a nation in the midst of war.[89] Even some of the President's liberal advisers, such as Harry Hopkins, failed to see civil rights as a major issue. Following Franklin Roosevelt's lead in replacing "Dr. New Deal with Dr. Win-the-War," they shelved their zeal for social reform for a new standard: "will it help to win the war? if not, the hell with it!"[90]

Moreover, the President would not respond affirmatively to the racial crisis because the congressional elections of 1942 increased his dependence on the southern Democrats and because the new pressures from the black community offended his sense of paternalism. With the Democrats receiving less than half the total major party vote for the first time since 1932, and the Republicans gaining forty-seven seats in the House, the southern bloc in Congress rode high, encouraging Roosevelt to weaken FEPC and pigeonhole all racial issues.[91] At the same time, the black demand for immediate change hampered his hope for a wartime consensus. To Roosevelt, the Negro always remained an unfortunate ward of the nation—to be treated kindly and with charity as a reward for good behavior. Nothing in his political past prepared him for the new black assertiveness. Throughout his administration he had worked with the conservative followers of Booker T. Washington in the South and the reliable Negro machine politicians of the North.[92] Despite the significant change in temper in the black community, Roosevelt continued to rely for advice on Negro matters on an elite coterie which included Lester Granger of the National Urban League; Dr. James Shepard, president of the North Carolina College for Negroes; Lester

Walton, the minister to Liberia; and such prominent southern white liberals as Daniels, Mark Ethridge, Frank Graham, and John Temple Graves. Steeped in the politics of gradualism, these men did little to help the President understand why blacks supported NAACP and the March-on-Washington Movement or why civil rights required new initiatives from the White House. They reinforced his inclination to avoid antagonizing southern politicians and to act only when he had a clear mandate from the people, and then only for the simplest, least fundamental solution. [93]

Maintaining an official silence throughout the summer of 1943, the administration hoped to defuse the racial issue by adhering to its standard policy of patronage, public gestures, and public relations. The President's aides first buried all pleas for a fireside chat on the riots and then killed plans to have Congress investigate the disorders. [94] Franklin Roosevelt's advisers then shelved all proposals for a governmental race relations commission in favor of the inoffensive appointment of Daniels to correlate personally all information on racial problems. [95] Even Marshall Field's innocuous plan to circulate pledges asking people not to spread rumors and to help to "win the war at home by combatting racial discrimination wherever I meet it," which the President liked, went unheeded. [96] Instead, new government films and press releases emphasized the recent gains of Negroes, and the government acted to handle future riots more efficiently by clarifying the procedure for calling in federal troops and approving Federal Bureau of Investigation Director J. Edgar Hoover's recommendation to grant draft deferments to members of urban police forces. [97] The following year Hoover announced his plan to round up the communist agitators causing racial unrest. [98]

The American left, however, did little to press a new racial policy on the White House. Most communist sympathizers continued to subordinate Negro rights to demands for a second front, and liberals, fearing continued violence, urged the Negro "to go slow," work with white allies, and avoid precipitating a white reaction. [99]

Social scientists who had earlier supported the more militant black leaders now began to work to divert aggression and control violence. [100] Scores of liberal organizations that had never before cared about the race problem suddenly awoke to the realization that they had to do something. Interracialism became an overnight fad: by the end of 1943 more than 100 local, state, and national commissions "to promote better race relations" had been established. [101] But since most of the liberals enlisting in the crusade for civil rights considered other issues more important, the committees floundered, doing nothing to attack the basic causes of racial unrest. Under the banners of ethnic democracy, interracial cooperation, and a more scientific understanding of group prejudice, most of the committees did little but broaden the channel of communication between Negro and white leaders, set up rumor-control bureaus and institute training sessions for police on human relations and effective handling of rioters. [102] Despite some worthy intentions, the committees functioned mainly as a buffer between blacks and their local government and widened the gap between bourgeois Negro leaders and the urban masses. [103] The more white liberals joined the movement, the more intent Negro leaders became in holding their support, by being accommodating, respectable, and a part of the larger progressive coalition. By the end of the war, interracialism had become the dominant tactic of the civil rights movement, while the committees which had spawned it, content to beget more committees, more surveys, and more reports, quietly faded away. [104]

The fear of continued violence by lower-class blacks and of an even greater period of violence after the war, like that following World War I, along with the emergence of interracialism, had a stunting effect on Negro militancy. Although the single greatest Negro victory since the Civil War, Executive Order 8802, had come because of an uncompromising, independent all-black effort, most of the old-line Negro leadership now retreated from their earlier militancy and began to entrust white liberals with the job of winning the Negro his rights. [105] Some did so because of their apprehension about controlling the aroused black masses or their jealousy of newly organized black groups, and some because they believed a minority without allies could never be successful once the war ended. [106] Moreover, the wartime prosperity of the Negro middle class demanded a movement that would conserve these gains, rather than one that might undo the progress made. Accordingly, by the end of 1943, almost all the Negro fraternal, labor, and professional groups once prominent in the militant battles against Jim Crow in the armed services and defense work, were supporting legislation for a permanent FEPC and "Hold Your Job" Campaigns. [107] The once angry Negro press, regularly featuring full-page advertisements for war employment, directed much of their critical fire toward "irresponsible" blacks advocating sit-ins and civil disobedience. [108] And NAACP, the largest and richest of the Negro civil rights organizations, increasingly urged its chapters to get the movement out of the streets and into the courtroom and voting booth, and to back the national office in its support of an anti-poll tax bill, an aid to education bill, and an increase in social security coverage. [109]

In 1944 and 1945 the number of racial incidents declined, convincing many of the value of moderation. Negro and liberal leadership equated the decrease in interracial violence and the vocal support of whites with racial progress. Gradual reform, through legislation and court decisions, became the order of the day; capitalizing on the conscience of white America, the major tactic; and integration, the most sought objective. [110] Without any support from the established organizations and newspapers, the March-on-Washington Movement slowly faded away. With it went Randolph's hope for an all-black, mass direct-action movement—an organization of the masses, built on racial pride, that would force the white majority to heed the demands of black America. Following the lead of NAACP, Randolph turned his energies to building up the Negro vote and campaigning for a permanent FEPC.[111] Other Negro leaders exhorted blacks to mind their manners, be patient, and support liberal organizations. [112] Every week, it seemed, some new program of intercultural education, or interracial good-will, or another council on unity and amity appeared.[113] Not since the Civil War period had Negroes heard so many whites talking about freedom and racial justice; never before were so many journals and radio programs fea-turing items on race relations.[114] Civil rights had become respectable, and as many whites flocked into the movement their views and needs predomi-nated. The old Negro fighters for equality were quietly relegated to secon-dary and token positions. Meanwhile the talk of a new day coming grew louder and louder, convincing many that it was just around the corner while hiding from most Americans the fact that little or nothing was actually being done to eradicate the basic causes of racial inequality. But the mass of lower-class blacks did not have to be reminded of what the Boston *Globe* told its readers:

We have read about it. We have talked about it. We have held meetings and appointed committees and had more talk. We have passed the buck in all our talk. We blame the home, blame the schools, blame the police, blame the war. But what have we done—except talk?[115]

NOTES

1. "Negro Organizations and the War Effort," Report from Special Service Division, April 28, 1942, Records of the Committee on Fair Employment Practice, RG 228 (National Archives); "Recent Factors Increasing Negro-White Tension," Special Service Division Memorandum, Nov. 2, 1942, Records of the Office of Government Reports, RG 44 (National Archives); Roy Wilkins to Walter White, March 24, 1942, Stephen J. Spingarn Papers (Harry S. Truman Library, Independence, Mo.); New York *Times,* Jan. 10, 1942.

2. Richard M. Dalfiume, *Desegregation of the U.S. Armed Forces: Fighting on Two Fronts 1939-1953* (Columbia, Mo., 1969), 123n; Benjamin McLaurin, "Memoir," 36 (Oral History Collection, Columbia University); Charles S. Johnson, *To Stem This Tide: A Survey of Racial Tension Areas in the United States* (Boston, 1943), 131-39; Howard W. Odum, "Social Change in the South," *Journal of Politics,* 10 (May 1948), 247-48.

3. Herbert Garfinkel, *When Negroes March: The March on Washington Movement in the Organizational Politics for FEPC* (Glencoe, 1959), 144; Adam Clayton Powell, Jr., *Marching Blacks: An Interpretive History of the Rise of the Black Common Man* (New York, 1945), 172. See also Rayford W. Logan, ed., *What the Negro Wants* (Chapel Hill, 1944).

4. Lester B. Granger, "A Hopeful Sign in Race Relations," *Survey Graphic,* XXXIII (Nov. 1944), 455-56; "To Minimize Racial Conflict: Committees To Work on Human Rela-tionships," *American Century,* LX (Jan. 1945), 80. See also Harold Cruse, *The Crisis of the Negro Intellectual* (New York, 1967), 163-64, 207-09, 299, 324, 534-35; "Education for Racial Understanding," *Journal of Negro Education,* XIII (Summer 1944).

5. Lester M. Jones, "The Editorial Policy of Negro Newspapers of 1917-18 as Com-pared with That of 1941-42," *Journal of Negro History,* XXIX (Jan. 1944), 24-31.

6. Charles Williams, "Harlem at War," *Nation,* 156 (Jan. 16, 1943), 88.

7. Quoted in Roi Ottley, *'New World A-Coming': Inside Black America* (Boston, 1943), 314.

8. George S. Schuyler, "A Long War Will Aid the Negro," *Crisis,* 50 (Nov. 1943), 328-29, 344; Pittsburgh *Courier,* Oct. 5, 1940, Feb. 14, 1942; Chicago *Defender,* Dec. 13, 1941, March 14, 1942; Norfolk *Journal and Guide,* March 21, May 2, 1942; and "Government Blesses Separatism," *Crisis,* 50 (April 1943), 105.

9. Ralph N. Davis, "The Negro Newspapers and the War," *Sociology and Social Research,* XXVII (May-June 1943), 373-80; P. L. Prattis, "The Role of the Negro Press in Race Relations," *Phylon,* VII (Third Quarter 1946), 273-83; Thomas Sancton, "The Negro Press," *New Republic,* 108 (April 26, 1943), 557-60; Ernest E. Johnson, "The Washington News Beat," *Phylon,* VII (Second Quarter 1946), 127.

10. Charles R. Lawrence, "Negro Organizations in Crisis: Depression, New Deal, World War II" (doctoral dissertation, Columbia University, 1953), 103; Roy Wilkins, "Memoir," 83-88 (Oral History Collection, Columbia University); Report of the Department of Branches, April 14, 1941, NAACP Papers (Manuscript Division, Library of Congress).

11. Garfinkel, *When Negroes March,* 135-37; George M. Houser, "We Say No to Jim Crow," *Fellowship,* XI (April 1945), 61-63; *CORE: A Brief History* (New York, 1949).

12. A. Philip Randolph, "Why Should We March?" *Survey Graphic,* XXXI (Nov. 1942), 488-89; A. Philip Randolph, "Keynote Address to the Policy Conference of the March on Washington Movement," Francis L. Broderick and August Meier, eds., *Negro Protest Thought in the Twentieth Century* (Indianapolis, 1965), 201-10.

13. Raymond Hatcher to John Dancy, Feb. 1, 1943, Detroit Urban League Papers (University of Michigan Historical Collections, Ann Arbor); Roscoe E. Lewis, "The Role of Pressure Groups in Maintaining Morale among Negroes," *Journal of Negro Education,* XII (Summer 1943), 464-73; Thomas Sancton, "Something's Happened to the Negro," *New Republic,* 108 (Feb. 8, 1943), 175-79; Howard W. Odum, *Race and Rumors of Race: Challenge to Crisis* (Chapel Hill, 1943), 32-38.

14. Horace R. Cayton, "The Negro's Challenge," *Nation,* 157 (July 3, 1943), 10-12; Carey McWilliams, *Brothers Under the Skin* (Boston, 1943), 17-20.

15. Gunnar Myrdal, with the assistance of Richard Sterner and Arnold Rose, *An American Dilemma: The Negro Problem and Modern Democracy* (2 vols., New York, 1944); Carl N. Degler, "The Negro in America—Where Myrdal Went Wrong," *New York Times Magazine* (Dec. 7, 1969), 152, 154, 160. Also see Charles S. Johnson, "The Present Status of Race Relations in the South," *Social Forces,* 23 (Oct. 1944), 27-32.

16. Pittsburgh *Courier,* June 29, 1940.

17. Will Alexander, "Memoir," 360 (Oral History Collection, Columbia University); Pittsburgh *Courier,* July 6, Aug. 24, 1940; Nancy and Dwight Macdonald, *The War's Greatest Scandal: The Story of Jim Crow in Uniform* (New York, 1943), 13-14; Henry L. Stimson Diary, Oct. 25, 1940, Henry L. Stimson Papers (Yale University Library).

18. Pittsburgh *Courier,* Nov. 2, 1940; White to Franklin D. Roosevelt, Nov. 4, 1940, PPF 1336, Franklin D. Roosevelt Papers (Franklin D. Roosevelt Library, Hyde Park).

19. Washington *Post,* March 26, 1944; Horace R. Cayton, "Negro Morale," *Opportunity: Journal of Negro Life,* XIX (Dec. 1941), 371-75; Kenneth B. Clark, "Morale of the Negro on the Home Front: World Wars I and II," *Journal of Negro Education,* XII (Summer 1943), 417-28; P. L. Prattis, "The Morale of the Negro in the Armed Services of the United States, *ibid.,* 355-63.

20. Roi Ottley, "A White Folks' War?" *Common Ground,* II (Spring 1942), 28-31; Alfred McClung Lee, "Subversive Individuals of Minority Status," *Annals of the American Academy of Political and Social Science,* 223 (Sept. 1942), 167-68; George Martin, "Why Ask 'Are Negro Americans Loyal?'" *Southern Frontier,* II (Feb. 1942), 2-3.

21. Ottley, *'New World A-Coming,'* 306-07.

22. Walter White, "What the Negro Thinks of the Army," *Annals of the American Academy of Political and Social Science,* 223 (Sept. 1942), 67.

23. "Nazi Plan for Negroes Copies Southern U.S.A.," *Crisis,* 48 (March 1941), 71; "Now Is the Time Not to Be Silent," *ibid.,* 49 (Jan. 1942), 7; Memorandum to NAACP State Branches, Dec. 12, 1941, NAACP Papers.

24. Garfinkel, *When Negroes March,* 17–21.

25. Robert L. Vann to Roosevelt, Jan. 19, 1939, June 13, 1940, OF 335; White to Roosevelt, March 13, 1941; and Edwin Watson to White, April 8, 1941, OF 93, Roosevelt Papers; McLaurin, "Memoir," 64–65, 295–96. Among the committees formed were the Pittsburgh *Courier's* Committee on Participation of Negroes in the National Defense Program; Adam Clayton Powell, Jr.'s, Temporary National Protest Committee on Segregation; John A. Davis' Citizens Non-Partisan Committee for Equal Rights in National Defense; Committee on Negro Americans in War Industries, established by Phelps-Stokes Fund; and the Committee on Discrimination in Employment.

26. Pittsburgh *Courier,* Jan. 25, 1941; Walter White, *A Man Called White: The Autobiography of Walter White* (New York, 1948), 186–87; Florence Murray, ed., *The Negro Handbook* (New York, 1942), 72.

27. McLaurin, "Memoir," 36, 299; Lester B. Granger, "The President, the Negro, and Defense," *Opportunity: Journal of Negro Life,* XIX (July 1941), 204.

28. A. Philip Randolph to Roosevelt, May 29, 1941; Watson to Roosevelt, June 14, 1941, OF 93, Roosevelt Papers; McLaurin, "Memoir," 300–05.

29. Dalfiume, *Desegration of the U.S. Armed Forces,* 118–22.

30. Chicago *Defender,* Feb. 8, June 28, 1941; Williams, "Harlem at War," 87.

31. McWilliams, *Brothers under the Skin,* 33–34; Dwight MacDonald, "The Novel Case of Winfred Lynn," *Nation,* 156 (Feb. 20, 1943), 268–70.

32. Minutes of the Board of Directors, Sept. 9, 1940, NAACP Papers; Chicago *Defender,* Jan. 11, 18, 1941; PM, July 18, 1942.

33. Edwin R. Embree, *Julius Rosenwald Fund: Review for the Two-Year Period 1942–1944* (Chicago, 1944), 2.

34. Earl Brown and George Leighton, *The Negro and the War* (New York, 1942), 8.

35. War Department Press Release, Sept. 16, 1940, OF 93; Confidential Memorandum from Steve Early to Watson, Sept. 19, 1940, PPF 2538, Roosevelt Papers; NAACP Press Releases, May 8, July 31, 1942, NAACP Papers. Ulysses Lee, *United States Army in World War II: Special Studies: The Employment of Negro Troops* (Washington, 1966), 21–87.

36. Lucille B. Milner, "Jim Crow in the Army," *New Republic,* 110 (March 13, 1944), 339–42; "Jim Crow in the Camps," *Nation,* 156 (March 20, 1943), 429.

37. W. Y. Bell, Jr., "The Negro Warrior's Home Front," *Phylon,* V (Third Quarter 1944), 272.

38. Macdonald and Macdonald, *The War's Greatest Scandal,* 9–12; Dwight MacDonald to editors, "The Case of Alton Levy," *Nation,* 157 (Nov. 6, 1943), 538; "The Social Front," *Monthly Summary of Events and Trends in Race Relations,* 1 (Nov. 1943), 9.

39. "Negroes in the Armed Forces," *New Republic,* 109 (Oct. 18, 1943), 542–43.

40. Milner, "Jim Crow in the Army," 339–42; "Personalities on the Spot," *Monthly Summary of Events and Trends in Race Relations,* 1 (Sept. 1943), 26.

41. Bell, "The Negro Warrior's Home Front," 276–77. Also see Grant Reynolds, "What the Negro Soldier Thinks," *Crisis,* 51 (Nov. 1944), 352–54.

42. Lee, *United States Army . . . : The Employment of Negro Troops,* 348–79.

43. Charles E. Silberman, *Crisis in Black and White* (New York, 1964), 62–64.

44. Minutes of the Board of Directors, Sept. 8, 1941, NAACP Papers; Macdonald and Macdonald, *War's Greatest Scandal,* 2; Powell, *Marching Blacks,* 144; Pittsburgh *Courier,* Jan. 31, 1942.

45. White to Roosevelt, Aug. 13, 18, 20, 1941, OF 25; Ira Lewis to Roosevelt, Aug. 19, 1941; Gloster Current to Roosevelt, Sept. 26, 1941, OF 93, Roosevelt Papers; Chicago *Defender,* Aug. 30, 1941.

46. *Southern Frontier,* III (Feb. 1942), 1; Washington *Post,* March 26, 1944.

47. Macdonald and Macdonald, *War's Greatest Scandal,* 2–3; Powell, *Marching Blacks,* 144–45; New York *Times,* April 4, 1942.

48. McWilliams, *Brothers under the Skin,* 39; Randolph to Roosevelt, Aug. 1, 1942; Marvin McIntyre to Randolph, Aug. 6, 1942, OF 93, Roosevelt Papers.

49. Minutes of the Board of Directors, May 10, 1943, NAACP Papers; Chicago *Defender,* June 12, 19, 1943; Pittsburgh *Courier,* June 19, 1943; Florence Murray, ed., *The Negro Handbook 1944: A Manual of Current Facts, Statistics and General Information Concerning Negroes in the United States* (New York, 1944), 225; Powell, *Marching Blacks,* 145; "The Social Front," *Monthly Summary of Events and Trends in Race Relations,* 1 (Aug. 1943), 8–9.

50. "Negroes in the Armed Forces," 544.

51. "White Attitudes Toward Negroes," Report from OWI, Bureau of Intelligence, Aug. 5, 1942, Records of the Office of Government Reports, RG 44; "Race Tension and Farm Wages in the Rural South," Agricultural Department, Sept. 22, 1943, in OF 4245, Roosevelt Papers; Odum, *Race and Rumors of Race,* 7–8, 25, 42–43, 47–50; "Cities, North and South: A Reconnaissance Survey of Race Relations," *Monthly Summary of Events and Trends in Race Relations,* 1 (Oct. 1943), 11–12.

52. Pauli Murray to McIntyre, June 18, 1943, OF 93C, Roosevelt Papers; Sancton, "Something's Happened to the Negro," 175–79.

53. Arthur I. Waskow, *From Race Riot to Sit-In, 1919 and the 1960s: A Study in the Connections between Conflict and Violence* (Garden City, 1966), 220–23; Walter G. Muelder, "National Unity and National Ethics," *Annals of the American Academy of Political and Social Science,* 244 (March 1946), 10.

54. Roosevelt to Edwin Embree, March 16, 1942, OF 93, Roosevelt Papers; McIntyre to Roosevelt, March 2; James Byrnes to McIntyre, March 9, 1943, Records of the War Manpower Commission, RG 211 (National Archives); I.F. Stone, "Capital Notes," *Nation,* 156 (Jan. 23, 1943), 115.

55. McIntyre to C. F. Palmer, Jan. 19, 1942, OF 93, Roosevelt Papers; NAACP *Annual Report,* 1942, pp. 22–23, NAACP Papers. See also McIntyre to Roosevelt, Dec. 11, 1942, OF 4245-G, Roosevelt Papers, for McIntyre's attitudes toward racial protest.

56. Quoted in PM, June 28, 1943.

57. Bucklin Moon, *The High Cost of Prejudice* (New York, 1947), 60–61.

58. Jessie Parkhurst Guzman, ed., *Negro Year Book: A Review of Events Affecting Negro Life 1941-1946* (Tuskegee, 1947), 307–09; Murray, ed., *Negro Handbook 1944,* 169–72.

59. A. L. Foster to Dancy, June 10, 1943, Detroit Urban League Papers; Robert Lee Eichorn, "Patterns of Segregation, Discrimination and Interracial Conflict" (doctoral dissertation, Cornell University, 1954), 61–64; Allen Grimshaw, "Urban Racial Violence in the United States: Changing Ecological Considerations," *American Journal of Sociology,* LXVI (Sept. 1960), 117. See also "The Social Front," *Monthly Summary of Events and Trends in Race Relations,* 1 (Sept. 1943), 9; Odum, *Race and Rumors of Race,* 113–31.

60. *Monthly Summary of Events and Trends in Race Relations,* 1, (Jan. 1944), 2; Thomas Sancton, "The Race Riots," *New Republic,* 109 (July 5, 1943), 9–13; *Michigan Chronicle,* July 3, 1943.

61. White to Frank Murphy, June 30, 1943, Frank Murphy Papers (University of Michigan Historical Collections); *Monthly Summary of Events and Trends in Race Relations,* 1 (Aug. 1943), 1.

62. Embree, *Julius Rosenwald Fund . . . 1942-1944,* p. 6.

63. "Zoot-Suit War," *Time,* XLI (June 21, 1943), 18–19; Chester B. Himes, "Zoot Riots Are Race Riots," *Crisis,* 50 (July 1943), 200–01; Carey McWilliams, "The Zoot-Suit Riots," *New Republic,* 108 (June 21, 1943), 818–20.

64. "The Social Front," *Monthly Summary of Events and Trends in Race Relations,* 1 (Aug. 1943), 6; Sancton, "The Race Riots," 10–11.

65. "Summary of a Report on the Race Riots in the Alabama Dry Dock and Shipbuild-

ing Yards in Mobile," National Urban League, Detroit Urban League Papers; Washington *Post,* July 20, 1943.

66. "The Industrial Front," *Monthly Summary of Events and Trends in Race Relations,* 1 (Aug. 1943), 4-5; *ibid.*, (Oct. 1943), 5; White, *A Man Called White,* 224-25; New York *Times,* Aug. 5, 1943.

67. "The Industrial Front," *Monthly Summary of Events and Trends in Race Relations,* 2 (Aug.-Sept. 1944), 6-7; Embree, *Julius Rosenwald Fund . . . 1942-1944,* p. 3.

68. Alexander, "Memoir," 167-68; Minutes of the Board of Directors, May 10, 1943, NAACP Papers.

69. Minutes of the Board of Directors, July 12, 1943, NAACP Papers; *Monthly Summary of Events and Trends in Race Relations,* 1 (Aug. 1943), 7-8.

70. Thomas Sancton, "Trouble in Dixie: I. The Returning Tragic Era," *New Republic,* 108 (Jan. 4, 1943), 11-14; Thomas Sancton, "Race Fear Sweeps the South," *ibid.* (Jan. 18, 1943), 81-83; Alexander, "Memoir," 696-99.

71. Odum, *Race and Rumors of Race,* 67-89, 96-103; Embree, *Julius Rosenwald Fund . . . 1942-1944,* p. 4; Johnson, "The Present Status of Race Relations in the South," 29.

72. Walter White, "What Caused the Detroit Riots"; "The National Urban League Report of the Detroit Riots," Detroit Urban League Papers.

73. Minutes of the Board of Directors, July 16, 1942, NAACP Papers; John Dancy Press Release, June 26, 1943, William Baldwin Memorandum, July 6, 1943, Detroit Urban League Papers.

74. Detroit *News,* Oct. 5-9, 1942; "Detroit Is Dynamite," *Life,* 13 (Aug. 17, 1942), 15-23.

75. PM, June 28, 1943.

76. Alfred McClung Lee and Norman D. Humphrey, *Race Riot* (New York, 1943); Robert Shogan and Tom Craig, *The Detroit Race Riot: A Study in Violence* (Philadelphia, 1964); Harvard Sitkoff, "The Detroit Race Riot of 1943," *Michigan History,* LIII (Fall 1969), 183-206.

77. Harold Kingsley, "Memorandum on Detroit Race Disturbance," June 23, 1943, Detroit Urban League Papers.

78. "Report of Thurgood Marshall, Special Counsel for the NAACP, Concerning Activities of the Detroit Police During the Riots, June 21, and 22, 1943," Mayor's Papers (Burton Historical Collection, Detroit Public Library).

79. Neil J. Smelser, *Theory of Collective Behavior* (New York, 1962), 71-73, 269.

80. Colonel R. G. Roamer, "Summary of Events in the Detroit Riot"; and Roamer-Lerch transcript, June 21, 1943, Records of the Office of the Provost Marshal General, RG 389 (National Archives).

81. William Guthner to F. W. Reese, Aug. 2, 1943, *ibid.*; Detroit *Free Press,* July 1, 1943.

82. Sitkoff, "The Detroit Race Riots of 1943," 192-96; White, *A Man Called White,* 226-27.

83. William Guthner, "Commander's Estimate of the Situation," Nos. I-IV, Records of the Office of the Provost Marshal General, RG 389; Fiorello La Guardia to Roosevelt, June 27, 1943, OF 93C, Roosevelt Papers.

84. White, *A Man Called White,* 233-41; Margaret Marshall, "Some Notes on Harlem," *Nation,* 157 (Aug. 21, 1943), 200-02.

85. Harold Orlansky, *The Harlem Riot: A Study in Mass Frustration* (New York, 1943), *passim;* Powell, *Marching Blacks,* 171-72.

86. Walter White, "Behind the Harlem Riot," *New Republic,* 109 (Aug. 16, 1943), 220-22.

87. Vito Marcantonio to Roosevelt, June 16, 1943; Philip Murray to Roosevelt, June 18, 1943; Douglas Horton to Roosevelt, June 27, 1943, OF 93C, Roosevelt Papers.

88. Malcolm MacLean to McIntyre, Feb. 24, 1942; Jonathan Daniels to Roosevelt, Sept. 28, 1944; and Frank Boykin to Watson, OF 93; David Niles to Daniels, Sept. 8, 1943; and A. V. Boren to Early, May 19, 1944, OF 4245-G, Roosevelt Papers. See also Helen Fuller, "The Ring Around the President," *New Republic,* 109 (Oct. 25, 1943), 563–65; "The Negro in Industry," *ibid.* (Oct. 18, 1943), 539; Joseph P. Lash, *Eleanor Roosevelt: A Friend's Memoir* (Garden City, 1964), 160, 217.

89. Stimson to Roosevelt, Feb. 16, 1942, OF 18, Roosevelt Papers; Stimson Diary, Sept. 27, Oct. 22, 23, 1940, June 18, 1941, May 12, 1942, June 23, 24, 1943, Stimson Papers.

90. Quoted in Arthur Krock, "Memoir," 86 (Oral History Collection, Columbia University).

91. Ed Pauley to Roosevelt, Dec. 14, 1942, PPF 1820, Roosevelt Papers; James A. Wechsler, "Pigeonhole for Negro Equality," *Nation,* 156 (Jan. 23, 1943), 122; "The Jim Crow Bloc," *New Republic,* 108 (Feb. 22, 1943), 240–41.

92. Roosevelt to George Foster Peabody, March 22, 1935, Dec. 12, 1935, PPF 660; Roosevelt to McIntyre, June 7, 1941, PPF 1248, Roosevelt Papers. See also Henry Stimson Memorandum on consultants on Negro Affairs, Feb. 18, 1943, Stimson Papers; Mary McLeod Bethune, "My Secret Talks with F. D. R.," *Ebony,* IV (April 1949), 42–51.

93. Mark Ethridge to Early, Aug. 20, 1941; Daniels to Samuel Rosenman, Sept. 9, 1943, OF 93; Daniels to Roosevelt, Sept. 24, 1943; and Daniels to Watson, Sept. 11, 1944, OF 4245-G, Roosevelt Papers. See also Thomas Sancton, "A Southern View of the Race Question," *Negro Quarterly: A Review of Negro Life and Culture,* 1 (Fall 1942), 197–200; John Temple Graves, "It's The Direction That Counts," *Southern Frontier,* III (April 1942), 2–3.

94. Many pleas for a presidential statement on the riots are in OF 93, Roosevelt Papers. Henry Wallace wanted the congressional plan to investigate the riots stopped because it "was bad from the standpoint of the 1944 election." Wallace to Roosevelt, July 7, 1943, PPF 1820, Roosevelt Papers. See also Roosevelt to Byrnes, Aug. 13, 1943, OF 88, *ibid.*

95. Harold L. Ickes to Roosevelt, July 15, 16, 26, 1943, OF 6; Francis Biddle to Roosevelt, July 15, Aug. 19, 1943, OF 93C; Biddle to Daniels, July 27, 1943; Daniels to Roosevelt, July 23, 1943; Daniels to Bishop Haas, July 28, 1943, OF 4245-G; Saul K. Padover, Memorandum, June 29, 1943, PPF 1820, *ibid.*

96. Marshall Field to Roosevelt, July 24, 1943, OF 93C, *ibid.*

97. Biddle to Roosevelt, July 15, 1943, OF 93C; and Daniels to Haas, Sept. 8, 1943, OF 4245-G, *ibid.*

98. J. Edgar Hoover to Daniels, Aug. 22, 1944, OF 4245-G, *ibid.*

99. See essays by Willard S. Townsend and Doxey A. Wilkerson in Logan, ed., *What the Negro Wants,* 163–92, 193–216; and James Boyd, "Strategy for Negroes," *Nation,* 156 (June 26, 1943), 884–87.

100. Gordon W. Allport, ed., "Controlling Group Prejudice," *Annals of the American Academy of Political and Social Science,* 244 (March 1946). See also Arnold M. Rose, *Studies in Reduction of Prejudice: A memorandum summarizing research on modification of attitudes* (Chicago, 1947); Goodwin Watson, *Action for Unity* (New York, 1947); Robert C. Weaver, "A Needed Program of Research in Race Relations and Associated Problems," *Journal of Negro Education,* XVI (Spring 1947), 130–35; Robin M. Williams, Jr., *The Reduction of Intergroup Tensions: A Survey of Research on Problems of Ethnic, Racial, and Religious Group Relations* (New York, 1947); Donald Young, "Techniques of Race Relations," *Proceedings of the American Philosophical Society,* 91 (April 1947), 150–61; and, in general, the work of Louis Wirth and his students at the Committee on Education, Training and Research in Race Relations at the University of Chicago.

101. *Monthly Summary of Events and Trends in Race Relations,* 1 (Jan. 1944), 2.

102. Embree, *Julius Rosenwald Fund . . . 1942–1944,* pp. 13–14; "Liberals and the Future," *New Republic,* 111 (Sept. 11, 1944), 310; *Monthly Summary of Events and Trends in Race Relations,* 1, (Sept. 1943), 1–2; *Monthly Summary of Events and Trends in Race Rela-*

tions, 1 (Dec. 1943), 2; Rebecca Chalmers Barton, *Our Human Rights: A Study in the Art of Persuasion* (Washington, 1955), 13.

103. A. A. Liveright, "The Community and Race Relations," *Annals of the American Academy of Political and Social Science,* 244 (March 1946), 106-07.

104. Langston Hughes, "Down Under in Harlem," *New Republic,* 110 (March 27, 1944), 404-05; Albert W. Hamilton, "Allies of the Negro," *Opportunity: Journal of Negro Life,* XXI (July 1943), 115-17; Lester B. Granger, "Victory Through Unity," *ibid.* (Oct. 1943), 148.

105. Sancton, "A Southern View of the Race Question," 199; Granger, "A Hopeful Sign in Race Relations," 455-56. Of the fourteen contributors to Logan's *What the Negro Wants,* only W. E. B. DuBois dissented from the general view that Negroes must avoid extralegal tactics and ally themselves with labor and liberals to secure first-class citizenship from the government.

106. Minutes of the Board of Directors, Sept. 14, 1942, NAACP Papers; *Monthly Summary of Events and Trends in Race Relations* 1 (Oct. 1943), 2; McWilliams, *Brothers under the Skin,* 42-43.

107. "Programs of Action on the Democratic Front," *Monthly Summary of Events and Trends in Race Relations,* 2 (Nov. 1944), 105; "Negro Women Organize for Unity of Purpose and Action," *Southern Frontier,* IV (Dec. 1943), 2; Alvin E. Dodd, "Negro Employment Opportunities—During and After the War," *Opportunity: Journal of Negro Life,* XXIII (April-June 1945), 59-62; E. Franklin Frazier, *Black Bourgeoisie* (Glencoe, 1957), 49-50.

108. Garfinkel, *When Negroes March,* 144; Pauli Murray, "A Blueprint for First Class Citizenship," *Crisis,* 51 (Nov. 1944), 358-59.

109. Wilkins to Rev. E. S. Hardge, Dec. 19, 1944; Minutes of the Board of Directors, Dec. 14, 1943, NAACP Papers. See also, "Negroes Fight on Four Major Fronts," *Southern Frontier,* V (Jan. 1944), 1-2.

110. "Racial Tensions Seem Easier," *Christian Century,* LXI (Aug. 30, 1944), 988; "To Minimize Racial Conflicts: Committees to Work on Human Relationships," *American Century,* LX (Jan. 1945), 80.

111. New York *Times,* July 4, 1943; Randolph to Wilkins, Jan. 31, 1944, NAACP Papers; Garfinkel, *When Negroes March,* 145-46; Cruse, *Crisis of the Negro Intellectual,* 208-09.

112. "The National Urban League Establishes Department of Public Education," *Opportunity: Journal of Negro Life,* XXII (Oct.-Dec. 1944), 184; "Negro Leader Supports White Liberals," *Southern Frontier,* VI (Nov. 1945), 2; Charles S. Johnson, "The Next Decade in Race Relations," *Journal of Negro Education,* XIII (Summer 1944), 442-44; Wilkins to White, Dec. 28, 1944, NAACP Papers. Significantly, White broke a thirty-five year old NAACP tradition of staying out of electoral politics by campaigning for Senator Robert Wagner. New York *Times,* Oct. 14, 1944.

113. Philip L. Seman, "Inter-faith—Inter-Race," *Monthly Summary of Events and Trends in Race Relations,* 2, (Aug.-Sept. 1944), 22; "Programs of Action on the Democratic Front," *ibid.* (Dec. 1944), 135; "Programs of Action on the Democratic Front," *ibid.* (Jan. 1945), 165-69.

114. "In the daily press and on the air," wrote Horace Cayton, "the Negro is getting more attention than he has enjoyed since the old Abolitionist days. And there is a growing awareness on the part of labor that the Negro problem requires action. In normal conditions all these things would be considered gains for the Negro. But they are *sporadic and unintegrated* and are insufficient to counteract the apparent inability of the government to set up a comprehensive plan." Quoted in McWilliams, *Brothers under the Skin,* 46-47. See also Liveright, "The Community and Race Relations," 106; "Institutes of Race Relations," *Monthly Summary of Events and Trends in Race Relations,* 2 (Aug.-Sept. 1944), 57-58; "The Negro: His Future in America: A Special Section," *New Republic,* 109 (Oct. 18, 1943), 535-50.

115. Boston *Globe,* Aug. 19, 1944. See also June Blythe, "Can Public Relations Help Reduce Prejudice?" *Public Opinion Quarterly,* 11 (Fall 1947), 342-60.

Robert Fogelson

VIOLENCE AS PROTEST

Following World War II and its immediate aftermath, two movements dominated the history of America's black population: the migration into northern cities and the continued drive for equal rights. The so-called "color line" was repeatedly breached by outstanding individuals in sports, politics, and the arts, while in 1954 the Supreme Court capped a half-century of legal action by declaring that school segregation—and by implication all denial of equal rights—was unconstitutional. It came thus as a surprise to many that the black masses in the cities still felt enough discontent, during the 1960s, to engage in destructively riotous activity, while some leaders threatened worse.

Robert Fogelson addresses several of the major questions that arose out of the urban riots of this period: how they compared with previous "race riots"; why they occurred not when blacks were most hopeless but after two decades of apparent progress; what was the point, if any, of the protest being made? As is often the case with violence of many kinds, it appears that many observers after the fact chose to interpret the riots to suit their own purposes, or to fulfill their own hopes and expectations.

On July 16, 1964, two weeks after Congress passed President Lyndon B. Johnson's civil rights bill, a white policeman shot and killed a black young-

"Violence As Protest" from the book *Violence As Protest: A Study of Riots and Ghettos* by Robert Fogelson. Copyright © 1971 by Robert Fogelson. Reprinted by permission of Doubleday & Company, Inc.

ster in New York City. Two days later, following a rally protesting police brutality, a crowd marched through Harlem and demonstrated before the 28th precinct headquarters. The police tried to disperse the demonstrators but succeeded only in arousing them, and that evening the first full-scale riots in two decades erupted in Harlem. From July 18 to July 20 blacks not only defied and attacked the police, but also assaulted white passers-by and looted and burned neighborhood stores. Moderate black leaders, including such national figures as James Farmer and Bayard Rustin, pleaded with the rioters to return to their homes, but to little avail. In the meantime the police department ordered all available personnel into Harlem to quell the rioting, and on July 21 order was restored. By then, however, the riots had spread to Bedford-Stuyvesant, the vast black ghetto in Brooklyn. And not until July 23—with one dead, over one hundred injured, nearly five hundred arrested, hundreds of buildings damaged, and millions of dollars of property destroyed—were both communities under control.[1]

A day later riots broke out in Rochester after the police arrested a black teen-ager outside a neighborhood dance. A crowd tried to free the prisoner, stoned the chief of police, and then rampaged through the ghetto, looting and burning, for two days. The rioting in this normally peaceful city was so widespread that Governor Nelson Rockefeller mobilized a thousand National Guardsmen.[2] Except for relatively minor disturbances in Jersey City the following weekend and in Elizabeth and Paterson, New Jersey, and Dixmoor, Illinois, a week later, the next month passed without serious incident. Then on August 28, when it seemed as if the worst were over, riots erupted in Philadelphia after two patrolmen arrested a black woman for blocking traffic at a busy intersection. Intoxicated and apparently angry at her husband, she resisted; and they dragged her out of the car. A crowd quickly gathered; it shouted abuse at the policemen, tossed stones and bricks at their reinforcements, and looted and burned nearby stores. Despite the efforts of the Philadelphia police and the appeals of moderate black leaders, the rioting continued for two more nights and finally subsided on August 31.[3] Leaving two dead, over three hundred injured, and another three hundred arrested, the Philadelphia riots climaxed the nation's most turbulent summer in twenty years.

Except for unreconstructed southerners and northern reactionaries who found reason for their racism that summer, most whites, and especially white liberals, were appalled and perplexed by the riots. Appalled because the conservatives were exploiting the rioting to discredit the civil rights movement and to bolster Barry Goldwater's presidential candidacy, and perplexed because the blacks had probably made more progress in the two decades preceding the riots than at any time since emancipation. The reasons for this progress—the Supreme Court's decisions outlawing segregation, the nation's sustained postwar economic boom, and the black migration from the rural South to the urban North—need not be considered at this point. Suffice to say, most blacks shared in the nation's wealth and influenced its decisions more in the 1960s than ever before.[4] And though these advances were long overdue and imperfectly realized, at no other time (and in no other administration) was there so strong a commitment to eradicate racial subordination and segregation.

Most whites were also bewildered because blacks were disavowing the principles and tactics of nonviolent protest applied so successfully in the South in the late 1950s and early 1960s. For blacks, after all, civil rights were battles to be won and not gifts to be taken. And to win them they had produced skillful, inspired leadership, maintained rigorous discipline and boundless patience, and abided by strict nonviolence.[5] By 1964, largely as a result of these efforts, most whites were convinced that subordination and segregation were wrong. Hence they found it hard to believe that, as the 1964 riots revealed, many blacks were unhappy with the pace of progress, black leadership, discipline, and patience were at the breaking point, and nonviolence was only one form of social protest. By themselves, however, the 1964 riots showed no clear pattern. And though Attorney General Robert Kennedy and others were aware of incidents in Cleveland, New York, and other cities which had foreshadowed the 1964 riots, it was still conceivable as late as mid-1965 that these disorders were just one summer's deviation from the mainstream of the civil rights movement.

The Los Angeles riots of August 1965, which devastated the Pacific coast's largest black ghetto, proved that this was not the case. These riots closely resembled the 1964 riots. In Los Angeles, as in Rochester, an ordinary arrest triggered the rioting; there, too, the rioters looted and burned stores and assaulted policemen and passers-by, the moderate black leaders failed to restrain the rioters, and the local police and National Guard eventually quelled the rioting. The Los Angeles riots were, however, the country's worst racial disorder since the East St. Louis massacre of 1917. By the time order was restored, thirty-four were dead, over a thousand injured, nearly four thousand arrested, hundreds of buildings damaged, and tens of millions of dollars of property destroyed.[6] Notwithstanding other disturbances in Chicago and San Diego, the summer of 1965 was less tumultuous than the summer of 1964. But so vast, so awesome, so devastating, and so widely reported were the Los Angeles riots—for a full week they received front-page coverage nationally and internationally—that henceforth there could be no doubt that a distinct pattern of summer violence was emerging in the black ghettos.

For this reason various governmental authorities took precautionary measures to head off rioting in 1966. The Justice Department instructed its Assistant United States Attorneys to report on conditions in a score of inflammable communities, and the Vice-President's Task Force on Youth Opportunity authorized its field representatives to investigate potential troublespots. Meanwhile, city officials devised emergency programs to employ and entertain black youths and otherwise keep them off the streets, and local and state police departments, aided by the F.B.I., prepared riot-control plans.[7] But these measures were not designed to alleviate ghetto conditions, only to prevent severe disorders; and so it was with mounting apprehension that local and federal officials awaited the summer. They did not have to wait long. Rioting erupted in Los Angeles, Chicago, and Cleveland in June, and, to list only a few of more than two dozen other places, in Omaha, Dayton, San Francisco, and Atlanta in July and August.[8] It battered cities previously stricken and cities hitherto spared, cities believed to be tense and cities thought to be quiet. None of these riots matched the Los Angeles riots in magnitude or intensity, but taken together they marked the summer of 1966 as the most violent yet.

By June 1967 other riots had erupted in Nashville, Cleveland, and Boston, and most Americans, white and black, expected another turbulent summer.[9] Stokely Carmichael and Martin Luther King, Jr., charging that the federal authorities had done little to alleviate ghetto conditions, predicted more riots. So did Senator Robert F. Kennedy of New York State, Mayor John V. Lindsay of New York City, Mayor Samuel W. Yorty of Los Angeles, and other national and local figures of various political persuasions.[10] Yet the riots which erupted that summer in Cincinnati, Buffalo, Newark, Detroit, and Milwaukee, to list only a few of the scores of stricken cities, far exceeded their worst expectations. Indeed, the Detroit riots, which left forty-three dead, over a thousand injured, over seven thousand arrested, and at least fifty million dollars of property destroyed, were the worst riots since the New York City draft riots a century ago.[11] By the end of the summer city officials, federal administrators, editors, politicians, and state and national commissions were all trying to explain why. Yet wherever criticism was directed and however blame was apportioned, one conclusion was clear: the Los Angeles, Newark, and Detroit riots had assumed a place in the history of American race relations no less important, if not more so, than the East St. Louis, Chicago, and Washington riots a generation ago.

This was made even clearer in April 1968 when the assassination of Martin Luther King, Jr., triggered major riots in Washington, Baltimore, and Chicago and minor riots in more than a hundred other cities. These riots, which closely resembled the previous riots, had a tremendous impact. For a full week the nation, which was already numbed by the assassination, reeled under the rioting; and not until National Guardsmen (and, in Washinton, federal soldiers) were summoned was order restored in urban America.[12] The summer of 1968 was relatively peaceful, and so was the summer of 1969; but what future summers hold remains to be seen, and in any event the country has not yet worn off the shock of six years of rioting. Even now there is no agreement among whites and blacks or liberals and conservatives about where the responsibility for the riots lies; nor is there agreement among the individuals in these groups. There is, however, substantial agreement that the 1960s riots confronted America with the greatest threat to public order since the dreadful industrial disputes of the late nineteenth and early twentieth centuries. And for this reason, if for no other, a scholarly attempt to interpret these riots is very much in order.

Some observers, including journalists who have written full-length accounts of the Harlem, Bedford-Stuyvesant, and Los Angeles disorders, have implied that the 1960s riots were the latest in a long series of American race riots.[13] There is indeed a tradition of interracial rioting in the United States. To mention only a few examples, race riots erupted in Cincinnati and Philadelphia during the ante-bellum period and in New York City and Detroit during the Civil War. They broke out immediately after the war in New Orleans and Memphis and around the turn of the century in Wilmington, North Carolina, New York City, Georgia, and Springfield, Illinois. They reached one peak around World War I in East St. Louis, Washington, and Chicago and another during World War II in Detroit and Los Angeles, only to subside later in the 1940s.[14] At a quick glance, moreover, the race riots resemble the 1960s riots: blacks played a prominent role in both types of disorders; so did excitement, rumor, violence, death, and destruction. Nevertheless, a closer examination of the race riots, and especially the 1917, 1919, and 1943 riots, reveals that the 1960s riots were not extensions of this tradition.

Unlike the recent riots, which were as a rule precipitated by routine police actions, the earlier riots were in the main triggered by black challenges to the racial status quo. The outbreak of the Chicago riots of 1919 was a case in point.[15] At a time of tension generated by black migration and white racism a black youth swam from a beach set aside by tacit understanding for blacks to a nearby beach reserved for whites. At the same time several blacks who had been forced to leave this beach earlier in the day returned determined to stay. Whites and blacks started brawling and throwing stones. The black swimmer, rocks falling around him, remained in the water, clinging to a railroad tie; but when a white youth swam toward him, he abandoned the tie, took a few strokes, and then drowned. The police made no arrests, infuriating the blacks, who retaliated by mobbing a patrolman. When gangs of whites counterattacked that evening, the worst interracial riots in the city's history were under way. Hence rioting was precipitated in Chicago in 1919 by the blacks' refusal to accept, and the white's determination to maintain, segregated recreational facilities and not by routine police actions.

By contrast with the black rioters, who looted and burned stores and only incidentally assaulted passers-by, the white rioters vented their hostility for the most part against people, not property. The violence of the East St. Louis riots of 1917 was characteristic.[17] Angered by the employment of black immigrants as strikebreakers, white mobs attacked blacks in downtown East St. Louis. The rioters dragged their victims out of streetcars, stoning, clubbing, kicking, and afterwards shooting and lynching them. They also burned houses and, with a deliberation which shocked reporters, shot black residents as they fled the flames. They killed them as they begged for mercy and even refused to allow them to brush away flies as they lay dying. The blacks, disarmed by the police and the militia after an earlier riot and defenseless in their wooden shanties, offered little resistance. And by the time the East St. Louis massacre was over the rioters had murdered at least thirty-nine blacks, wounded hundreds more, and, in pursuit of their victims, damaged hundreds of buildings and destroyed about a million dollars of property.

The goverment authorities, and especially the local police, did not attempt to restore law and order in the race riots with the firmness they exhibited in the 1960s riots. This was certainly true in their response to the Washington riots of 1919.[17] When several hundred sailors (and a few civilians), out to avenge an alleged insult to a mate's wife, rampaged through southwest Washington attacking blacks, the district and military police arrested only two whites (and eight blacks). And when the sailors, joined by soldiers, resumed their assaults the next evening, the police with a handful of reinforcements provided scant protection for the terrified blacks. Law enforcement in the capital broke down not just because the police were outnumbered but also because the policemen as individuals sympathized with the rioters. Not until the police lost control and the blacks armed themselves did the District Commissioners request the cooperation of the military authorities and restore order. Hence the whites rioted in Washington in 1919 with an impunity which was in marked contrast to the danger faced by the blacks a generation later.

Lastly, few responsible white leaders labored so valiantly, if vainly, to prevent the riots and restrain the rioters in 1917, 1919, and 1943 as the moderate black leaders (or at any rate the so-called black leaders) did in the 1960s. This was clearly the case in Detroit in 1943.[18] A host of fascist spokesmen, including Father Charles E. Coughlin and the Reverend Gerald L. K. Smith, and racist organizations, including the Ku Klux Klan and the Black Legion, had long fomented racial animosity there. And though Detroit's civic leaders did not support these agitators, they did not forthrightly oppose them or otherwise deal with the community's racial problems. Once the rioting was under way, Detroit's elected leaders responded ambivalently. Not that they sanctioned the violence; on the contrary, they deplored it, though always from a distance. But they so feared for their political futures and their city's reputation that they did not call for the National Guard until the rioting threatened the whole community and not just the black residents. Whether Detroit's white leaders could have intervened more effectively in 1943 than Los Angeles' black leaders did in 1965 is a moot question because with the exception of a few courageous ministers they did not try.

The distinctive character of the race riots emerges from these brief descriptions. The riots were interracial, violent, reactionary, and ultimately unsuccessful attempts to maintain the racial status quo at times of rapid social change. They were interracial because whites, first- and second-generation European immigrants in Chicago and uprooted southerners in Detroit, were the aggressors, and blacks, newcomers themselves, the victims. They were violent because the whites did not know how to achieve their goals— how to force the blacks to leave East St. Louis and how to keep them in their place in Washington—through legitimate means. They were reactionary because the whites hoped to deprive the blacks of freedom of movement, equal access to public accommodations, and other rights which inhere in Americans whatever their color.[19] And however effective in the short run, they were unsuccessful in the long run. And not simply because the economic, social, and political changes underlying the migration of southern blacks and the militancy of northern blacks were too powerful.

The differences between the race riots and the 1960s riots are so marked that it is only necessary now to note a few reasons why the tradition of interracial rioting has waned since World War II. First, the racial status quo has changed so much that the issues which precipitated the race riots are no longer at stake; also, the tremendous expansion of white suburbs and black ghettos has insulated the protagonists from one another. Second, many children of the first- and second-generation immigrants who rioted in 1917, 1919, and 1943 are now middle-class Americans who do not have to rely on violence to uphold their racial privileges. Third, the goverment authorities, and especially the local police, are so determined to maintain public order that except in the rural South few groups, white or black, can riot with impunity anymore.[19] And fourth, again except in the deep South, white leaders are so committed to orderly social change they cannot sanction rioting even on behalf of causes to which they are otherwise sympathetic.

These changes can be exaggerated. The American tradition of interracial violence is waning; but, as intermittent rioting—primarily, though not exclusively, in the South—in the 1950s and 1960s revealed, it is not yet moribund. On several occasions mobs of middle-class whites have forcibly resisted the movement of middle-class blacks into residential suburbs of Philadelphia, Chicago, and other northern metropolises.[21] And gangs of working-class whites, themselves bypassed in the suburban exodus, have violently protested the influx of working-class blacks into East New York and other ethnic communities.[22] Nevertheless, the authorities have restored order so swiftly and thoroughly in these disorders that few people have been injured and few buildings damaged. By such measurements as actual outbreaks, lives lost, arrests booked, and property destroyed, these disturbances are much less serious than the riots under consideration here. There are of course no assurances that whites will restrain themselves in the suburbs or that the blacks will confine their violence to the ghettos in the future. But until then interracial rioting must be considered a vestige of a waning American tradition.

Other observers, including left-wing radicals and, more recently, black militants, have insisted that the riots, far from being traditional race riots, were incipient colonial rebellions.[23] By this they mean two things. First, that the riots were manifestations of a world-wide struggle against colonialism, the determined attempt of colored peoples everywhere to overthrow their white masters. The situation of black people in the United States, the radicals assume, is essentially the same as the situation of colored people in Africa and Asia; the blacks are a colonial people, the whites a colonial oppressor, and the ghettos colonies. Second, that the riots were expressions of a widespread struggle against capitalism, the proletariat's historic effort to regain its manhood, dignity, and freedom through socialism. The blacks resorted to violence, the radicals presume, because they have no hope whatever to achieve meaningful equality under the existing economic and political system. This interpretation is certainly as much a vision as a definition. But it deserves careful consideration, particularly for its implication that the riots are political actions (and revolutionary ones at that).

There are, as the radicals argue, similarities between the 1960s riots and colonial uprisings. In Chicago, Cleveland, and Los Angeles as well as in Nigeria, Uganda, and Nyasaland somewhat earlier, colored people resorted to violence in order to force social change.[24] Afro-Americans and Africans alike rioted in protest against genuine grievances and treated the customary restraints on rioting with indifference and even outright comtempt. There are similarities between the racial problem and the colonial situation. In both cases white people have subordinated and segregated colored people and then justified their exploitation and victimization on the grounds of innate racial inferiority.[25] What is more, many blacks who have recently overcome the long-standing antipathy toward their color, ignorance of their origins, and shame about their race have responded by identifying closely with the world's colored people. Their racial pride enhanced by the emergence of independent African nations after World War II, these blacks are now convinced that their future in the United States is inextricably linked with the destiny of colored people everywhere.[26]

There are, however, profound differences between the 1960s riots and colonial uprisings. The differences between the recent rioting and terrorist activity against the British in Kenya, guerrilla warfare against the French in Madagascar, and abortive invasions of Portuguese Angola are obvious.[27] Less obvious but not less noteworthy are the differences between the 1960s riots and the colonial uprisings in Nigeria, Uganda, Nyasaland, and other places which took the form of riotous protests, The 1960s riots were spontaneous and unorganized, opposed by the moderate black leaders, confined almost entirely to the ghettos, and quelled with

)ut not without restraint by the authorities. The colonial uprisings, by
1st, developed out of nonviolent demonstrations against colonial ex-
tion; the African leaders led the demonstrations and then directed the
;ings. The rioters rampaged outside the native districts, attacking gov-
nent buildings as well as private holdings; and the authorities, relying
;ely on the military, responded relentlessly and ruthlessly.[28] Hence the
50s riots were more restrained than the colonial uprisings, a pattern which
;ggests that the stakes were higher and the frustrations deeper in Africa
1an in America.

The differences between the 1960s riots and the colonial struggle
reflect the differences between the racial problem and the colonial situation.
The blacks have greater opportunities to enter the middle class and exert
political power than colonial people do. But, by the same token, the blacks
are much more limited than colonial people in their ultimate aspirations;
a minority, they can belong to the nation but cannot take it over. Also, for
all their prejudice, white Americans, and especially their leaders, have a
more ambivalent attitude towards colored people than European colonial-
ists do. They subordinate and segregate blacks unevenly, as much by omis-
sion as by commission, and often against their own law and ideology.[29]
Lastly, the ghetto is not a colony—unless by a colony is meant nothing more
than a dependent neighborhood, a definition which would include most
parts of the modern metropolis. The ghetto is exploited, but not so much by
the whole society as by fragments of it, and not so much to oppress its
inhabitants as to avoid them. These differences do not mean that the racial
problem is less serious than the colonial situation, only that it is very different.[30]

There are also, as the radicals claim, analogies between the 1960s riots
and socialist struggles. Although the blacks have traditionally based their
pleas for social juctice on the sanctity of the law and consistently honored
the committment to orderly social change,[31] they are still the nearest group
to an American proletariat nowadays. By rioting for six summers now they
have not only broken the law and ignored this commitment, but, by looting
and burning stores, disobeying the police, and attacking patrolmen, they
have also destroyed private property and challenged public authority.
There are also many black militants who have lost all hope of achieving
meaningful equality under the existing system—and not only the members
of the Revolutionary Action Movement and other fringe groups. Before his
assassination Malcolm X (whose ideas on these and other matters were in
flux at the time) concluded that racism and capitalism were so intertwined
that the one could not be abolished without eliminating the other. And,
more recently, Eldridge Cleaver (and, by implication, the members of the
Black Panthers) insisted that the blacks cannot expect social justice under
the prevailing economic and political conditions.[32]

The analogies between the 1960s riots and the socialist struggle do not
withstand careful scrutiny, however. No doubt the rioters rejected a long-

standing strategy by resorting to violence. But there is no necessary connection between violence and socialism, certainly not in the United States; the race riots of 1917, 1919, and 1943 are all cases in point. Accordingly the test of the analogy lies, if anywhere, in the purposes of the rioters, that is, were they directed against private property and public authority? It would appear that they were not. The blacks looted to acquire goods enjoyed by most Americans and burned to even the score with white merchants; they did not attempt to undermine property rights in general. They assaulted patrolmen to express specific grievances against the local police and not, as the blacks' attitude toward the National Guard indicated, overall disaffection with public authority. Perhaps even more pertinent, the rioting was confined to ghettos; the rioters did not destroy private property elsewhere, nor did they attack schools, hospitals, or other government buildings.[33] If anything, these patterns reveal that the violence was directed against the system's abuses and not the system itself.

Hence the 1960s riots were attempts to alert America, not overturn it, to denounce its practices, not renounce its principles. They were not insurrections, and not because blacks lacked the numbers, power, and leaders but rather because they wanted a change in norms not in values. These conclusions are consistent with the most recent surveys of black opinion[34] and with the ideology of all but a small (though increasing) fraction of the black nationalist organizations. The Black Muslims, the largest of these groups, have no fundamental disagreement with capitalist America, only with white America; their utopia is strict, separate, and black, but otherwise quite familar. And most Black Power advocates are more concerned with procedures than substance; that they insist on self-determination is clear enough, but whether for capitalism, socialism, or something else is not. Indeed, even Malcolm X's tremendous appeal rested as much on his eloquence, courage, and blunt defiance of white society as on any particular ideology, anti-colonialist or anti-capitalist.[35] For the great majority of blacks, the American dream, tarnished though it has been for centuries, is still the ultimate aspiration.

To argue that the 1960s riots were not colonial rebellions is not to imply what future riots will be like. The situation is anything but promising. Black moderates are convinced, and rightly so, that current federal, state, and city programs will not materially improve the ghettos. Black extremists are prepared to intensify their opposition to the system; and rumors about terrorism and guerrilla warfare are spreading through many cities.[36] The riots have greatly stirred the black community too; so has the realization that rioting is a sure way to attract attention. Hence it is impossible to say what the future holds. But there is no certainty that the United States will not experience organized and premeditated violence, and not only inside the black ghettos. Nor is there any certainty that blacks will not direct their hostility against the system itself instead of its abuses. In other words, the

ry in their means, may develop into colonial rebel-
heir ends. For the time being, however, it can safely
riots were not colonial rebellions.

ers, including the mayors (or acting mayors) of
s, and many other cities, have insisted that the riots
ursts and not rebellions, colonial or otherwise.[37]
lenied that the riots were political expressions, no
fined. For these officials this interpretation is highly
s attempts to blame them for the rioting and also
leviate long-standing problems in the ghettos. Most
incere in their convictions; and so are most of their
constituents, who also consider the riots meaningless outbursts. Nevertheless, this interpretation is untenable, and for reasons other than the obvious
one that no social phenomenon is meaningless; and a brief analysis of these
reasons should help clarify the meaning of the riots.

The conception of the riots as meaningless outbursts is intimately related to the absence of a *tradition* of violent protest in America. Not that the
United States has been a peaceful country. Quite the contrary; for three and
a half centuries Americans have resorted to violence in order to reach goals
otherwise unattainable. The whites who assaulted blacks in Washington and
Chicago in 1919 were a case in point. So, to list only a few notorious examples were the Protestants who attacked Catholics in Boston in 1834, the
vigilantes who lynched lawbreakers in San Francisco in 1856, and the citizens who massacred the "Wobblies" in Centralia, Washington, in 1919.[38]
Indeed, it is hardly an exaggeration to say that the native white majority has
rioted in some way and at the same time against nearly every minority group
in America. And yet most Americans regard rioting not only as illegitimate
but, even more significant, as aberrant.[39] From their perspective, which
reflects a boundless confidence in orderly social change, riots, no matter
how frequently they erupt, are necessarily unique and wholly unrelated.

Under ordinary circumstances the absence of a tradition of violent
protest makes it difficult for Americans to perceive the riots as anything but
meaningless outbursts. And circumstances today are far from ordinary.
The demand for public order and the opposition to rioting and violence are
now greater than ever in the United States. This situation, as Allan Silver
has perceptively pointed out,[40] reflects not only the spreading consensus
that disorder does irreparable and intolerable damage to modern political
and economic mechanisms. It also reflects the growing awareness of the
spatial interdependence of American cities, the realization that the outbreak
of rioting in one neighborhood threatens the security of all the others. It
reflects, too, the increasing confidence in the ability of the governmental
authorities, and especially the police, to maintain public order in the face of
any challenge. And the demand for public order, which has intensified the
middle classes' fear of the lower and working classes (and, above all, the

lower- and working-class blacks), has made it even harder for most Americans to regard the riots as anything but meaningless outbursts (or left-wing conspiracies).

The absence of a tradition of violent protest makes it just as hard for lower- and working-class blacks to express the meaning of the riots. Except in Harlem and Boston, where the rioting erupted after organized demonstrations against police brutality and welfare abuses respectively, nowhere did the rioters prepare a formal statement of grievances. And whatever the meaning of "Burn, Baby, Burn!" the slogan of the Los Angeles riots, surely no one can argue that it is readily understood. Moreover, the racial problem, complex enough to begin with, is obscured because the nation is committed in principle to equality and, save in the rural South, white attitudes toward black people are marked as much by indifference as by hostility. For these reasons it was no mean task for blacks to explain the rioting. What is more, this situation was aggravated because almost without exception the moderate black leaders disapproved of the riots. No one spoke for the rioters as Martin Luther King, Jr., and the Montgomery Improvement Association spoke for the Montgomery bus boycotters.[41] Whatever the meaning of the riots, then, it has to be sought in the rioting itself, and even sympathetic observers might well have trouble finding it there.

The meaning is there, but only if the riots are viewed as violent protests. That they are violent is obvious. But it is not so obvious that they, like the Montgomery bus boycott and other civil rights demonstrations, are also protests, because most Americans regard a violent protest as a contradiction in terms. There is, however, a long, if declining, *history* of violent protest in western society, a history exemplified by the pre-industrial urban mob in eighteenth-century Europe.[42] The mob, which was composed mainly of common people, as opposed to the riffraff, communicated popular dissatisfaction to the authorities; it protested by rioting and otherwise resorting to violence and not by adopting radical ideologies. It also expected a response, and a favorable one, too, from the authorities. To list only a few examples from London: the mob rioting against the Excise Bill in 1733, the employment of Irish labor in 1736, the expulsion of John Wilkes in 1768, and the Catholic Emancipation Bill in 1780.[43] These riots were articulate not so much because the elites understood them as because, in view of the mob's potential for disorder, the violence was restrained and selective.

Ignoring profound differences in grievances and responses, it is fair to say that the 1960s riots were articulate protests in the same sense. On the basis of the available statistical data, it is evident that the black rioters were not primarily the unemployed, ill-educated, uprooted, and criminal. They were rather a substantial and representative minority of the young adults which was widely supported in the ghettos.[44] Also, far from rejecting the prevailing ideology, the rioters demanded that all citizens honor it; they insisted on changes in practices not principles. They made it extremely clear that most blacks do not want to overthrow American society, but simply to belong to it as equals. Moreover, the rioters indicated to reporters during the riots and to interviewers afterwards that they expected the rioting to improve their position by arousing white concern.[45] They could not know then (and indeed they may not know now) that though some whites are more concerned many are more intransigent. Put bluntly, the blacks delivered a protest, but most whites did not receive it.

Also, viewed from a distance, the riots seem unrestrained and indiscriminate, which is what observers probably mean by meaningless; the mob is overwhelming, the confusion complete. But at closer observation, where individuals are visible and patterns discernible, the opposite appears to be true. Although the rioters vented their rage on patrolmen and passers-by and showed little remorse after the attacks, they killed only a handful of the thousands of whites caught in the rioting and even released unharmed several reporters similarly trapped. This restraint was repeated too often to be considered exceptional.[46] Again, though the rioters damaged hundreds of buildings, destroyed millions of dollars of property, and devastated whole sections of the ghettos, they burned mainly stores that charged excessive prices or sold inferior goods (or did both) and left homes, schools, and churches unharmed. This selectivity was noted by more than one witness, too.[47] Indeed, restraint and selectivity were among the most crucial features of the riots. And it is in these features that the meaning of the disorders is to be found.

Now not all the rioters were restrained and selective. A few, especially the handful of snipers, intended to provoke confrontation, not to arouse concern. Nor were the rioters restrained and selective all the time. The looters did not always choose the merchandise with care, and the arsonists did not always pick the buildings with precision. Nonetheless, most of the rioters were restrained and selective most of the time. What is more, the overwhelming majority of blacks viewed the riots as protests. According to a nation-wide survey conducted for the Kerner Commission, 86 per cent of black men and 84 per cent of black women considered the riots at least in part protests against unfair conditions.[48] And in many cases the rioters' actions confirm these conclusions. During the Harlem riots they surrounded white reporters and instead of beating them told them to write the full story; and after the Los Angeles riots they boasted that they had finally brought the south-central ghetto to the attention of the authorities.[49] All things considered, it is fair to conclude that the riots were protests and, like the civil rights demonstrations of the previous decade, articulate protests, too.

It now remains to discuss what the blacks were protesting against and why they were protesting violently. To this end it is instructive to consider the 1960s riots in connection with the two earlier disorders which were their direct precursors, namely, the Harlem riots of 1935 and 1943. Given the circumstances, no two riots should have had less in common. The Great Depression was in its fifth year in the spring of 1935; its economic and political repercussions were evident everywhere, and nowhere more so than in Harlem. Fully half the residents were unemployed and on relief; many were standing in long soup lines, and a few were actually starving. Meanwhile, various left-wing groups—so vividly described by Ralph Ellison in *The Invisible Man*—were busily planning for a socialist or communist takeover.[50] How different everything was in the summer of 1943 when World War II was reaching its peak and most Americans, black and white, were mobilized. The nation's economy, stimulated by wartime production, was enjoying full employment and even facing manpower shortages. And the country's radicals were silent because of the emotional demands of wartime patriotism and the Nazi invasion of Soviet Russia.[51] These circumstances notwithstanding, the Harlem riots of 1935 and 1943 had a great deal in common.

Contemporaries were hard pressed to explain what it was, however. Most of them, including Mayor Fiorello La Guardia, black author Claude McKay, and the New York *Times,* realized that the Harlem riots were not, strictly speaking, race riots.[52] Quite correctly and not without pride, they cited the absence of interracial violence in 1935 and again in 1943, the year of the Detroit race riots. If they did not blame the Communists, they claimed that though there was no justification for the Harlem riots there were grounds for the blacks' complaints, particularly the suffering of ordinary blacks during the depression and the attacks on black soldiers during the war. Nevertheless, they did not define the Harlem riots more precisely. Rather, they seconded La Guardia's statements that the riots were criminal and thoughtless acts by hoodlums and other irresponsible people who were a minute fraction of New York's overwhelmingly law-abiding black community.[53] La Guardia, who was at his best quelling the rioting and at his worst analyzing it, exhibited the traditional American misconception of violent protest. But he did not have the benefit of the perspective provided by the 1960s riots, a perspective which highlights the common and distinctive features of the Harlem riots.

The Harlem riots, like the 1960s riots, were spontaneous, unorganized, and precipitated by police actions. The 1935 riots began in a Harlem department store when a youth was caught shoplifting and forcibly subdued by the employees. He was then taken to a back room and after a while set free by the police. The shoppers believed that the police were beating the boy, however, and their fears were confirmed by the arrival of an ambulance called by an employee bitten in the scuffle. A crowd quickly gathered and—when, by a remarkable coincidence, the brother-in-law of another employee parked his hearse nearby—concluded that the police had killed the youth. Nothing the police said or did could persuade the blacks otherwise, and the rumor swiftly spread throughout Harlem, setting off the 1935 riots.[54] The 1943 riots, which erupted in a more credible but basically similar way, started in a Harlem hotel when a white patrolman attempted to arrest a boisterous black woman for disorderly conduct. A black soldier intervened, grabbing the patrolman's nightstick and striking him with it, and then turned to leave. The patrolman ordered him to halt and, when he refused, shot him in the shoulder. A crowd soon formed in front of the hospital to which the soldier was taken and, though the wound was not serious, the word that a white policeman had killed a black soldier rapidly passed through the ghetto, triggering the 1943 riots.[55]

Once the rioting was under way, the Harlem rioters directed most of their aggression against property rather than people. Several thousand strong in 1935, the rioters first threw bricks and bottles at the department store windows and the policemen patrolling nearby. Later they roamed the streets, attacking white passers-by and looting and burning neighborhood stores, especially white-owned stores. By the next morning one was dead, over one hundred injured, another one hundred arrested, and several hundred buildings damaged.[56] The violence was worse in 1943, but the pattern was much the same. Once again the rioters, numbering many thousands, assaulted white passers-by, overturned parked automobiles, and tossed bricks and bottles at policemen. They also looted and burned food and liquor shops, haberdasheries, pawn and jewelry shops, and, again, mainly white-owned shops. By the following day six were dead, over five hundred injured, more than one hundred jailed, and a few million dollars of property destroyed.[57] Like the New York riots of 1964, the Harlem riots of 1935 and 1943 were so completely confined to the ghetto that life was normal for whites and blacks elsewhere in the city.

The official response was about as vigorous in the Harlem riots as in the 1960s riots, too. Early in the 1935 riots Police Commissioner Lewis J. Valentine sent policemen organized in special squadrons and armed with special guns to reinforce the mounted and foot patrolmen and radio-car crews at the department stores. And later on, while the police, fully armed and often firing, struggled with the rioters, Mayor La Guardia prepared and distributed a circular calling on law-abiding blacks to cooperate with the authorities.[58] This response, however vigorous, was dwarfed by the response to the 1943 riots. The police department's afternoon shift was kept on duty, freeing the night shift for riot control; and by morning fully five thousand policemen, supported by military police and regular troops, were patrolling Harlem. Another five thousand New York State Guards and fifteen hundred black volunteers were standing by. In the meantime La Guardia closed streets and diverted traffic around Harlem, concentrated subway patrolmen on the Harlem lines, issued a declaration denouncing the rioting, and, accompanied by two well-known moderate black leaders, toured the ghetto appealing for restraint.[59] By dint of the police department's tactics and the Mayor's virtuoso performance, order was restored the following day.

The moderate blacks disapproved of the Harlem riots almost, but not quite, as strongly as they disapproved of the 1960s riots. Few attempted to restrain the rioters in 1935; more grasped the opportunity to denounce racial discrimination. This reaction was not surprising: rioting lasted only one night, discrimination had gone on for several centuries. What was surprising was that none of these leaders, no matter how firmly committed to civil rights, sanctioned the rioting. [60] The moderate black leaders reacted far more forcefully in 1943. A few accompanied La Guardia on his tour of the ghetto, others advised him about riot-control strategies, and still others manned voluntary patrols. Even more impressive, many broadcast from sound trucks, denying the rumor that the white policeman had killed the black youth and urging the rioters to clear the streets. [61] And as the rioting was more violent and the nation more united in 1943 than in 1935, even the leaders who used the occasion to condemn racial segregation did so circumspectly. Nonetheless, these efforts (and the riots themselves) highlighted the inability of the moderate black leaders to channel rank-and-file discontent into legitimate channels and when necessary to restrain the rioters.

Even this short discussion of the Harlem riots and the 1960s riots reveals their striking similarities and essential characteristics. These riots were spontaneous and unorganized, triggered by police actions, and distinguished by looting and burning of neighborhood stores and assaults on patrolmen and white passers-by. In all of them, the governmental authorities responded vigorously to increase the risks in participating, and, save in 1935, the moderate black leaders labored valiantly, if vainly, to restrain the rioters. Hence the essence of the Harlem riots and the 1960s riots is an intense resentment of the police, an intolerable accumulation of grievances, the ineffectiveness of the customary restraints on rioting, and the weakness of moderate black leadership. It is against police malpractice and other grievances, especially economic deprivation, consumer exploitation, and racial discrimination, that the blacks were protesting; and it is because of the ineffectiveness of the customary restraints on rioting and the weakness of moderate black leadership that they were protesting violently. Needless to say, these conditions are among the fundamental features of life in the black ghetto.

Accordingly it is not surprising that these riots first erupted in Harlem rather than in Chicago or the other sites of the twentieth-century race riots. Harlem was the first black ghetto. Developed as a middle-class community around the turn of the century, it was promptly caught in a severe real estate crash; and instead of being quickly settled by whites, it was slowly filled by blacks. Rioting did not break out there during the turbulent postwar years, however. Rather than fight the black influx, as the working-class first- and second-generation European immigrants did in Chicago, the middle-class native Americans in New York quietly moved elsewhere, [62] leaving a black Harlem in their wake. It was during the 1910s and the 1920s, fully a generation before the massive migration from the South after World War II transformed urban America, that Harlem emerged as the nation's first black ghetto. It was in these decades that as the headquarters of the black renaissance it fascinated white Americans in their misguided quest for the exotic and the primitive.[63] And it was in these decades that the conditions developed which led the blacks in Harlem to protest, and to protest violently, in 1935 and 1943.

What emerges from this deliberately circuitous approach is a rather straightforward interpretation: the 1960s riots were articulate protests against genuine grievances in the black ghettos. The riots were protests because they were attempts to call the attention of white society to the blacks' widespread dissatisfaction with racial subordination and segregation. The riots were also articulate because they were restrained, selective, and, no less important, directed at the sources of the blacks' most immediate and profound grievances. What is more, the grievances are genuine because by the standards of the greater society the conditions of black life, physically, economically, educationally, socially, and otherwise, are deplorable. And nowhere in urban America are these conditions—economic deprivation, consumer exploitation, inferior education, racial discrimination, and so forth—more deplorable than in the black ghettos. Having offered this interpretation, . . . I would like to conclude by considering two closely related questions: namely, why did the 1960s riots erupt when they did and where they did?

The timing of the riots is baffling. The blacks' grievances were not developments of the 1960s, nor, for that matter, were the burdens of subordination and segregation. If anything, these grievances were probably less serious and these burdens less severe then than at any time in American history. Since World War II large numbers of blacks moved into highly skilled and well-paying jobs and gained positions of political influence. At the same time a large majority of whites grew fairly reluctant to measure a man strictly by the color of his skin. To add to this, a battery of Supreme Court decisions made it much harder for Americans, individuals and authorities alike, to practice racial discrimination.[64] Thus, for all the inequities and prejudices remaining, most blacks were probably better off in the 1960s than in any decade in the recent past. And yet it was in the 1960s— not in the 1940s when the armed forces were segregated, nor in the 1950s when a civil rights act was an occasion—that blacks rioted.

At the heart of this paradox was the unprecedented rise in the blacks' expectations. This rise began with the great migration north in the 1910s and 1920s, gathered momentum during World War II, and accelerated during the late 1950s and early 1960s. It accelerated not only because the nation as a whole enjoyed remarkable prosperity but also because some blacks fully shared in it and a few attained standards long reserved for whites only. It accelerated, too, because civil rights programs made progress, white attitudes about race changed for the better, and, even more important, black pride flourished as it had not since the Garvey Movement of the 1920s.[65] The results were momentous. Blacks were more conscious of their deprivations—indeed, deprivation had a whole new meaning for them; they were dissatisfied with conditions that their fathers and grandfathers would have found tolerable (or at any rate inevitable). The blacks were also less concerned about social constraints, more militant and aggressive, at the least impatient and, when frustrated time and again, dangerously desperate. This rise in expectations was self-perpetuating, too; each new gain generated a new goal, and by the 1960s the blacks would settle for nothing less than a complete equality.

What rendered these expectations so explosive in the 1960s were the dreadful conditions of ghetto life. And not only in Harlem. Although the working-class, first- and second-generation European immigrants in Chicago, Detroit, and other cities resisted the black influx in 1919 and 1943, they eventually conceded the issue. Like the middle-class native Americans in New York, they or their children fled before the massive black migration after World War II, leaving behind them the swelling black ghettos.[66] By the 1960s these ghettos were a full generation old, about as old as Harlem was in the 1930s and 1940s; and, in view of the blacks' expectations, conditions there, no matter how much improved, were intolerable. What is more, the blacks realized that these conditions could not be readily remedied. Nor, by virtue of their color, could they easily escape to the suburbs like white immigrants before them. A state of permanent subordination and segregation loomed as a distinct possibility.[67] And thus, as ghetto life intensified the group's grievances and undermined the society's restraints, the blacks rioted to protest their plight.

The location of the 1960s riots is baffling, too. With a few exceptions—notably the Atlanta (1966), Nashville (1966), Tampa (1967), and Miami, (1968) riots—they have occurred less in the South, where by any objective consideration the blacks have more reason for rioting, than in the North.[68] This paradox cannot be resolved by the explanation (which is true so far as it goes) that the riots are urban phenomena and that the South is the least urbanized region in the nation. Atlanta, Nashville, Tampa, and Miami are not the only southern cities, and among the others Birmingham, Charleston, Little Rock, New Orleans, and Jackson have thus far been spared rioting. Again, with a few exceptions the riots have occurred almost everywhere in the North, a pattern which is particularly perplexing for most Americans. It is one thing for blacks to riot in New York, Chicago, Philadelphia, Cleveland, Detroit, and Los Angeles, the nation's largest metropolitan centers. Of them Americans expect almost anything, especially in the sweltering summer months. But it is another thing for blacks to riot in Rochester, Dayton, Omaha, and Lansing, and many other normally peaceful, presumably content medium-sized cities. From them Americans expect an occasional scandal, but nothing as serious as full-scale rioting.

There are explanations for these paradoxes, however. The South has suffered fewer riots than the North not simply because southern blacks have lower expectations than northern blacks and southern policemen fewer inhibitions than northern policemen. The South, which has about as many blacks as the North, has far fewer ghettos. Blacks have traditionally been more heavily concentrated in northern cities than in southern cities, where the differences between white and black were so well defined that there was little reason for rigorous residential segregation.[69] Only recently, as the racial status quo has been vigorously challenged in the South, have southern whites, like northern whites before them, retreated to segregated suburbs and left black ghettos behind. Where this has happened, as in Atlanta and Miami, southern blacks, like northern blacks, are most resentful of their grievances and less concerned about society's restraints, more conscious of their strength and less reluctant to test it. This pattern now prevails only in Atlanta and a handful of other southern cities;[70] but the same nation-wide forces transforming the North are emerging in the South, and so the probability of further rioting there may well increase in the future.

This explanation applies to the North as well as to the South. Small cities as well as large metropolises have been devastated by riots largely because northern blacks are everywhere confined to ghettos. And for all the differences between Harlem and Chicago's West Side, Rochester's seventh ward and Cleveland's Hough district, Boston's Roxbury and Brooklyn's Bedford-Stuyvesant, and south-central Los Angeles and all the others, life varies little from one ghetto to the next. In each there are intense resentment of the police, high unemployment rates, exploitative mercantile practices, excessive levels of violence, widespread residential segregation, and, among other things, ineffective moderate leadership. And in the end the blacks' grievances are no more tolerable in Omaha, Dayton, Lansing, and Rochester than in Chicago, Philadelphia, Newark, and Cleveland. All of which is perhaps another way of saying that the blacks' frustration, resentment, and aggression are a function not of the size of the white communities but of the conditions in the black ghettos.

The interpretation of the 1960s riots as articulate protests against genuine grievances in the black ghettos helps explain why the riots erupted when and where they did. But it does not help explain why they erupted first in Philadelphia, Los Angeles, and Cleveland, later in Buffalo, Newark, and Detroit, and only recently in Washington and Baltimore. A few offhand explanations have been offered, but an extended examination of these explanations is beyond the scope of this introduction; and it would probably not be worth while anyway. For there is no convincing evidence that the blacks are materially worse in Philadelphia, Los Angeles, and Cleveland than in Buffalo, Newark, and Detroit, or Washington and Baltimore. Indeed, it is probably only a coincidence that the riots erupted in some cities before others (and not at all in still others, such as Oakland, whose turn will doubtless come). And if the interpretation of the 1960s riots offered here is correct, it indicates why they have broken out in nearly every American metropolis except some in the deep South, where the black ghettos are little developed, and others in the Pacific Northwest, where the black population is extremely small.

NOTES

1. Fred C. Shapiro and James Sullivan, *Race Riot: New York 1964* (New York, 1964).

2. P. W. Homer, City Manager, "Report to the Rochester City Council on the Riots of July 1964," April 27, 1965; Federal Bureau of Investigation, "Report on the 1964 Riots," September 18, 1974, 5–6.

3. Lenora E. Berson, *Case Study of a Riot: The Philadelphia Story* (New York, 1966), 13–22; F.B.I., "Report on the 1964 Riots," 1, 3–15.

4. Oscar Handlin, *Fire-Bell in the Night* (Boston, 1964), 8–22; Anthony Lewis, *Portrait of a Decade* (New York, 1964), 3–15.

5. Martin Luther King, *Stride Toward Freedom* (New York, 1958), chapters 3–9; Louis E. Lomax, *The Negro Revolt* (New York, 1963), 78–222; William Brink and Louis Harris, *The Negro Revolution in America* (New York, 1964), 19–77; Lewis, *Portrait of a Decade,* 15–103.

6. Jerry Cohen and William S. Murphy, *Burn, Baby, Burn! The Los Angeles Race Riot August 1965* (New York, 1966); Governor's Commission on the Los Angeles Riots, *Violence in the City—an End or a Beginning?* (Los Angeles, 1965), 10–25 (hereafter referred to as *McCone Commission Report*).

7. The reports of the Assistant United States Attorneys and files of the Vice-President's Task Force on Youth Opportunity were made available to me by the President's Crime Commission. See also Federal Bureau of Investigation, *Prevention and Control of Mobs and Riots* (Washington, 1965).

8. United States Commission on Civil Rights, "Location of Riots Involving Minority Group Members Chronologically from January 11, 1964 through June 1966 as reported by the New York *Times,*" August 11, 1966.

9. New York *Times* April 10, 17, May 2, June 3–5, 1967.

10. *Ibid.,* April 19, 27, 30, May 3, 1967.

11. *Report of the National Advisory Commission on Civil Disorders* (New York, 1968), 42–108 (hereafter referred to as *Kerner Commission Report*). See also Tom Hayden, *Rebellion in Newark* (New York, 1967).

12. Ben W. Gilbert *et al., Ten Blocks from the White House* (New York, 1968), chapters 1–7. See also Arthur T. Waskow, *From Race Riot to Sit-In: 1919 and the 1960s* (Garden City, N.Y., 1964), 1–174.

13. At least this is the implication of the titles of the books on the New York and Los Angeles riots; see Shapiro and Sullivan, *Race Riot,* and Cohen and Murphy, *Burn, Baby, Burn.*

14. Herbert Aptheker, *A Documentary History of the Negro People in the United States* (New York, 1963), I, 102, 220, 501–2, II, 552–59, 788–91, 813–15, 866–68; Waskow, *From Race Riot to Sit-In,* 9–10, 12–104, 219–20; Citizens Protective League, *Story of the Riot* (1900).

15. Chicago Commission Race Relations, *The Negro in Chicago* (Chicago, 1922), 4–5.

16. Elliot M. Rudwick, *Race Riot at East St. Louis, July 2, 1917* (Carbondale, Ill., 1964), chapters 4 and 5.

17. Waskow, *From Race Riot to Sit-In,* chapter 3.

18. Robert Shogan and Tom Craig, *The Detroit Race Riot* (Philadelphia, 1964), chapters 5 and 6.

19. Chicago Commission on Race Relations, *The Negro in Chicago,* chapter 1; Shogan and Craig, *Detroit Race Riot,* chapter 2; Rudwick, *Race Riot at East St. Louis,* chapters 2–4; Waskow, *From Race Riot to Sit-In,* chapter 3.

20. Waskow, *From Race Riot to Sit-In,* chapters 10 and 11.

21. Charles Abrams, *Forbidden Neighbors* (New York, 1955), chapters 8 and 19.

22. United States Commission on Civil Rights, "Location of Riots"; Assistant United States Attorneys Reports: Chicago, August 5, 1966; New York, August 19, 1966.

23. See "The Colonial War at Home," *Monthly Review,* May 1964, 1-13, "Decoloniza-tion at Home," *ibid.,* October 1965, 1-13; Stokely Carmichael's Chicago, July 28, 1966, speech, in Student Nonviolent Coordinating Committee, *Notes and Comments,* August 1968; and Eldridge Cleaver, *Soul on Ice* (New York, 1968), 128-37.

24. *Report of the Commission of Inquiry into the Disorders in the Eastern Provinces of Nigeria* (London, 1950); *Report of the Commission of Inquiry into the Disturbances in Uganda during April, 1949* (Entebbe, Uganda, 1950); *Report of the Nyasaland Commission of Inquiry* (London, 1959).

25. Frantz Fanon, *The Wretched of the Earth* (New York, 1966), 27-84. See also G. Balandier, "The Colonial Situation: A Theoretical Approach," in Immanuel Wallerstein, *Social Change: The Colonial Situation* (New York, 1966), 34-61.

26. Harold R. Isaacs, *The New World of Negro Americans* (New York, 1963), 80-96, 288-93; C. Eric Lincoln, *The Black Muslims in America* (Boston, 1961), 9-10.

27. Carl G. Rosberg, Jr., and John Nottingham, *The Myth of "Mau Mau": Nationalism in Kenya* (New York, 1966), chapter 8; Virginia Thompson and Richard Adloff, *The Malagasy Republic* (Stanford, Calif., 1965), chapter 4; James Duffy, *Portugal in Africa* (Baltimore, 1963), chapter 7.

28. *Report on the Disorders in Eastern Nigeria,* 32-46; *Report on the Disturbances in Uganda,* 17-53; *Report of the Nyasaland Commission of Inquiry,* parts 3 and 5.

29. Gunnar Myrdal, *An American Dilemma* (New York, 1944).

30. For a scholarly defense of the colonial analogy, see Robert Blauner, "Internal Colonialism and Ghetto Revolt," *Social Problems,* Spring 1969, 393-408.

31. Lomax, *The Negro Revolt,* 88.

32. George Breitman, ed., *Malcolm X Speaks* (New York, 1965), 68, 69, 75, 78, 89, 120-22; Cleaver, *Soul on Ice,* 128-37.

33. See Berson, *Case Study of a Riot,* 18; Cohen and Murphy, *Burn, Baby, Burn,* 133. It should be added, however, that rioters did burn houses in Detroit in 1967 and that demon-strators did attack schools in Boston a year later (New York *Times,* July 24-31, 1967, and Boston *Globe,* September 24-26, 1968).

34. Angus Campbell and Howard Schuman, "Racial Attitudes in Fifteen American Cities," in *Supplemental Studies for the National Advisory Commission on Civil Disorders* (Washington, D.C., 1968), 15-28.

35. New York *Times,* April 16, 1967; Lincoln, *Black Muslims in America,* chapter 5; Stokely Carmichael and Charles V. Hamilton, *Black Power* (New York, 1967), chapter 2; Breitman, ed., *Malcolm X Speaks,* 194-226.

36. New York *Times,* April 24, May 17, 1967. See also Gary Wills, *The Second Civil War* (New York, 1968), chapter 6.

37. *McCone Commission Report,* 4-5. See also New York *Times,* July 22, August 4, 1964; Newark *Evening News,* July 20, 1964; New York *Journal-American,* July 26, 1964; Cohen and Murphy, *Burn, Baby, Burn,* 130.

38. Oscar Handlin, *Boston's Immigrants* (Cambridge, Mass., 1959), 186-90; Edward McGowan, *McGowan vs. California Vigilantes* (Oakland, Calif., 1946); William D. Haywood, *Bill Haywood's Book* (New York, 1929), 352-58.

39. Allan Silver, "The Demand for Order in Civil Society: A Review of Some Themes in the History of Urban Crime, Police, and Riot," in David Bordua, ed., *The Police* (New York, 1967), 23; Louis Hartz, *The Liberal Tradition in America* (New York, 1955), chapter 1.

40. Silver, "The Demand for Public Order," 20-22. See also Daniel Bell, *The End of Ideology* (New York, 1962), 151-75.

41. King, *Stride Toward Freedom,* chapters 5, 7, 9; Lomax, *The Negro Revolt,* chapter 8; Lewis, *Portrait of a Decade,* chapter 5.

348   *Robert Fogelson*

42. E. J. Hobsbawm, *Primitive Rebels* (New York, 1959), chapter 8; Silver, "The Demand for Public Order," 15-20.

43. George Rude, *The Crowd in History* (New York, 1964), chapters 3, 13-16; Hobsbawm, *Primitive Rebels*, chapter 8; Silver, "The Demand for Public Order," 15-20.

44. Robert M. Fogelson and Robert B. Hill, "Who Riots? A Study of Participation in the 1967 Riots," in *Supplemental Studies for the National Advisory Commission on Civil Disorders*, 221-43.

45. John F. Kraft, Inc., "Attitudes of Negroes in Various Cities" (1967), 4-7, a report prepared for the U.S. Senate Subcommittee on Executive Reorganization; David O. Sears, "Riot Activity and Evaluation: An Overview of the Negro Survey" (1966), 1-2, an unpublished paper written for the U.S. Office of Economic Opportunity.

46. Shapiro and Sullivan, *Race Riot*, 77-78; Cohen and Murphy, *Burn, Baby, Burn*, 73; Hayden, *Rebellion in Newark*, 32-33.

47. Shapiro and Sullivan, *Race Riot*, 152-54; Berson, *Case Study of a Riot*, 40-42; Cohen and Murphy, *Burn, Baby, Burn*, 132; Bayard Rustin, "The Watts 'Manifesto' and the McCone Report," *Commentary*, March 1966, 29-30.

48. Shapiro and Sullivan, *Race Riot*, 77-78; Rustin, "The Watts 'Manifesto,'" 29-30; Robert Blauner, "Whitewash Over Watts," *Trans-action*, March/April 1966, 54.

49. Campbell and Schuman, "Racial Attitudes in Fifteen American Cities," 47.

50. Ralph Ellison, *The Invisible Man* (New York, 1947), chapters 13-20; Mayor's Commission on Conditions in Harlem, "The Negro in Harlem: A Report on Social and Economic Conditions Responsible for the Outbreak of March 19, 1935," chapters 3-5, New York City Municipal Archives.

51. Walter White, "Behind the Harlem Riot," *The New Republic*, August 16, 1943, 220-22; William C. Hendrick, "Race Riots—Segregated Slums," *Current History*, September 1943, 30-34; Oscar Handlin, *The American People in the Twentieth Century* (Boston, 1963), chapter 9.

52. Claude McKay, "Harlem Runs Wild," *The Nation*, April 3, 1935, 382-83; New York *Times*, March 21, 1935, August 3, 1943; *Time*, August 9, 1943, 19.

53. "This was not a race riot," the Mayor said. "There was no conflict between groups of our citizens. What happened was the thoughtless, criminal acts of hoodlums, reckless, irresponsible people" (*Time*, August 9, 1943, 19). The New York *Times* agreed (August 3, 1943).

54. New York *Times*, March 20, 1935; Mayor's Commission, "The Negro in Harlem," 1-6; Hamilton Basso, "The Riot in Harlem," *The New Republic*, April 3, 1935, 210-11.

55. New York *Times*, August 2, 1943; White, "Behind the Harlem Riot," 221.

56. New York *Times*, March 20-22, 1935; McKay, "Harlem Runs Wild," 382-83; Mayor's Commission, "The Negro in Harlem," 6-12.

57. New York *Times*, August 2-3, 1943; White, "Behind the Harlem Riots," 221.

58. New York *Times*, March 20-22, 1935; McKay, "Harlem Runs Wild," 382.

59. New York *Times*, August 2-3, 1943; White, "Behind the Harlem Riots," 222.

60. New York *Times*, March 21, 1935.

61. New York *Times*, August 2-3, 1943; White, "Behind the Harlem Riots," 222.

62. Gilbert Osofsky, *Harlem: The Making of a Ghetto* (New York, 1930), and Alain Locke, ed., *The New Negro: An Interpretation* (New York, 1925).

64. Handlin, *Fire-Bell in the Night*, chapter 2; Brink and Harris, *The Negro Revolution*, chapter 8; Lewis, *Portrait of a Decade*, chapter 13; Abrams, *Forbidden Neighbors*, chapter 21.

65. On the Garvey movement, see E. David Cronon, *Black Moses* (Boston, 1961); and on black nationalism, see E. U. Essien-Udom, *Black Nationalism* (Chicago, 1962).

66. Robert C. Weaver, *The Negro Ghetto* (New York, 1948).

67. Handlin, *Fire-Bell in the Night*, chapter 5.

68. U.S. Commission on Civil Rights, "Location of Riots."

69. Richard C. Wade, *Slavery in the Cities* (New York 1964), chapter 3.

70. Karl E. Taeuber and Alma F. Taeuber, *Negroes in Cities* (Chicago, 1965), chapter 3.

Richard Wade

VIOLENCE IN THE CITIES: A HISTORICAL VIEW

Written at the end of the turbulent 1960s, Richard Wade's overview retraces a number of incidents and events in an effort to place the black riots of that decade in proper historical perspective. The issue of race, he reminds us, is only one of many, some critical and others apparently trivial, that have touched off bloodshed in American cities. Most of the others have been outgrown or at least no longer find violent expression in the face of the more powerful levels of force available to the authorities as well as other more efficient means of social control. But he concludes, with many of the other authors in this collection, that the racial situation in America remains unsolved, and still poses the threat of tragic violence.

Violence is no stranger to American cities. Almost from the very beginning, cities have been the scenes of sporadic violence, of rioting and disorders, and occasionally virtual rebellion against established authority. Many of these events resulted in only modest property damage and a handful of arrests. Others were larger in scale with deaths running into the scores and damages into the millions. This paper attempts to survey briefly some of these outbreaks and to analyze their origins and consequences. We confine ourselves, however, to the larger ones, and omit any discussion of individual acts of violence or the general level of crime. In addition, to keep these remarks relevant to the present crisis, we have confined our analysis to disorders in urban areas.

From Charles U. Daly, ed., *Urban Violence* (Chicago: University of Chicago Press, 1969), 7–26. Reprinted by permission of the University of Chicago Center for Policy Study and the author.

There has been, in fact, a good deal more violence and disorder in the American tradition than even historians have been willing to recognize. The violence on the frontier is, of course, well known, and in writing, movies, and television it has been a persistent theme in our culture. Indeed, one of America's favorite novelists, James Fenimore Cooper, transformed the slaughter and mayhem of Indians into heroic, almost patriotic, action. As the literary historian David Brion Davis has observed: "Critics who interpret violence in contemporary literature as a symptom of a sick society may be reassured to know that American writers have always been preoccupied with murder, rape, and deadly combat." To be sure, violence is not "as American as cherry pie," but it is no newcomer to the national scene.

Though serious scholarship on this dimension of the American past is shamefully thin, it is already quite clear that disorder and violence in our cities were not simply occasional aberrations, but rather a significant part of urban development and growth. From the Stamp Act riots of the pre-revolutionary age, to the assaults on immigrants and Catholics in the decades before the Civil War, to the grim confrontation of labor and management at the end of the nineteenth century and its sporadic reappearance after World War I and during the depression, through the long series of racial conflicts for two centuries, American cities have known the physical clash of groups, widescale breakdown of established authority, and bloody disorder.

Nor is it hard to see why this early history had more than its share of chaos. American cities in the eighteenth and nineteenth centuries were very young. They had not yet the time to develop a system of orderly government; there was no tradition of habitual consent to local authority; there was no established police system. In addition, these cities grew at a spectacular rate. In the twentieth century, we have used the term "exploding metropolis" to convey the rapid pace of urbanization. It is not often remembered that the first "urban explosion" took place more than a century ago. Indeed, between 1820 and 1860 cities grew proportionately faster than they had before or ever would again. The very speed of this urban development was unsettling and made the maintenance of internal tranquillity more difficult.

The problem was further compounded by the fact that nearly every American city was born of commerce. This meant that there was always a large transient population—seamen engaged in overseas trade, rivermen plying the inland waters, teamsters and wagonmen using the overland routes, and a constant stream of merchants and salesmen seeking customers. At any moment the number of newcomers was large and their attachments to the community slight. Hence when they hit town, there was always some liveliness. After exhausting the cities' museums and libraries, sailors and teamsters would find other things to do. In the eighteenth and nineteenth century, transients comprised a significant portion of those who engaged in rioting and civil disorders.

In addition to being young, rapidly growing, and basically commercial, American cities also had very loose social structures. Unlike the Old World, they had no traditional ruling group, class lines were constantly shifting, and new blood was persistently pumped into these urban societies. One could say that up until the last part of the nineteenth century, mercantile leaders dominated municipal government; but even that commercial leadership changed continually. Later, immigrant groups shared high offices in municipal affairs, thus underlining the shifting nature of the social structure of most cities. Within this looseness there was always a great deal of mobility, with people rising and falling in status not only from generation to generation but within a single lifetime.

This fluid social system contrasted sharply with other, older societies, yet it contained a high incidence of disorder. For it depended on the constant acceptance of new people and new groups to places of influence and importance, and their incorporation into the system on a basis of equality with others. This acceptance was only grudgingly conceded, and often only after some abrasive episodes. The American social structure thus had a large capacity to absorb revolutionary tensions and avoid convulsive upheavals. But it also bred minor social skirmishes which were not always orderly. It is significant that in the pre-Civil War South, where slavery created a more traditional social structure, there was less rioting and civil disorder than in the North (though one ought not underestimate the individual violence against the slave built into institutional bondage).

The American social structure was also unique because it was composed not only of conventional classes, but also of different ethnic, religious, and racial groups. They had at once an internal cohesion that came from a common background and a shared American experience and also a sense of sharp differences with other groups, especially with the country's older stock. These groups, the Negro excepted, were initially both part of the system and yet outside of it. The resultant friction, with the newcomers pressing for acceptance and older groups striving for continued supremacy, was a fruitful source of disorder and often violence. Since it was in the city that these groups were thrown together, became aware of their differences, and struggled for survival and advancement, it would be on the streets rather than on the countryside that the social guerrilla warfare would take place.

If the internal controls in the American social structure were loose, the external controls were weak. The cities inherited no system of police control adequate to the numbers or to the rapid increase of the urban centers. The modern police force is the creation of the twentieth century; the establishment of a genuinely professional system is historically a very recent thing. Throughout the eighteenth and nineteenth century, the force was small, untrained, poorly paid, and part of the political system. In case of any sizable disorder, it was hopelessly inadequate; and rioters sometimes routed the constabulary in the first confrontation. Josiah Quincy, for example, in

Boston in the 1820's had to organize and arm the teamsters to re-establish the authority of the city in the streets. Many prudent officials simply kept out of the way until the worst was over. In New York's draft riots, to use another instance, the mayor wandered down to see what the disturbance was all about and nearly got trampled in the melee.

Moreover, since some of the rioting was political, the partisanship of the police led official force to be applied against one group, or protection to be withheld from another. And with every turnover in the mayor's office, a substantial and often a complete change occurred in the police. In Atlanta, for instance, even where there was only one party, each faction had its own men in blue ready to take over with the changes in political fortunes. In some places where the state played a role in local police appointments, the mayor might even be deprived of any control at all for the peace of the city. In New York in the 1850's there was an awkward moment when there were two police forces—the Municipals and the Metropolitans—each the instrument of opposing parties. At the point of the most massive confusion, one group tried to arrest the mayor and an armed struggle took place between the two competing forces.

The evolution toward more effective and professional forces was painfully slow. Separating the police from patronage proved difficult, the introduction of civil service qualifications and protection came only in this century, and the development of modern professional departments came even later. To be sure, after a crisis—rioting, widescale looting, or a crime wave—there would be a demand for reform, but the enthusiasm was seldom sustained and conditions returned quickly to normal. The ultimate safety of the city thus resided with outside forces that could be brought in when local police could not handle the mob.

These general considerations account in large part for the high level of disorder and violence in American cities over the past three centuries. The larger disorders, however, often stemmed from particular problems and specific conditions and resulted in widescale bloodshed and destruction. Though these situations varied from place to place and time to time, it is perhaps useful to divide them into a few categories. Some rioting was clearly political, surrounding party struggles and often occasioned by legislation or an election. Some sprang from group conflict, especially the resistance to the rising influence of immigrant groups. Still others stemmed from labor disputes. And the largest, then as now, came out of race conflict. A few examples of each will convey some of their intensity and scale.

Politics has always been a fruitful source of disorders. Indeed, one of the most significant groups of riots surrounded the colonial break with Great Britain. In Boston, Samuel Adams and other radical leaders led the otherwise directionless brawling and gang warfare around the docks and wharfs into a political roughhouse against British policy. The Stamp Tax Riots, the Townshend Duty Riots and, of course, the Boston Massacre were all part of an organized and concerted campaign by colonial leaders. The urban middle classes initially tolerated the disorders because they too opposed certain aspects of British policy; they later pulled back when they felt that radical leadership was carrying resistance beyond their own limited objectives. Yet for nearly a decade, rioting and organized physical force was a part of the politics of the colonies.

. . .

Attacks against immigrants comprise another theme in the story. Often the assault by older, more established groups was against individuals or small groups. But in other cases it would be more general. The string of riots against Catholic churches and convents in the nineteenth century, for example, represented an attack on the symbols of the rise of the new groups. In the summer of 1834, for instance, a Charlestown (Mass.) convent was sacked and burned to the ground; scuffles against the Irish occurred in various parts of nearby Boston; some Irish houses were set afire. At the outset, the episode was carefully managed; then it got out of hand as teen-age toughs got into action. Nor was this an isolated incident.

Characteristic of this period too was the resistance to the incorporation of immigrants into the public life of the city. "Bloody Monday" in Louisville in 1855 will perhaps serve as an illustration. Local politicians had become worried about the increase of the immigrant (German and Irish) vote. The Know-Nothings (a party built in part on anti-immigrant attitudes) determined to keep foreign-born residents away from the polls on election day. There was only a single voting place for every ward, thus numbering only eight in the entire city. Know-Nothing followers rose at dawn and occupied the booths early in the morning. They admitted their own reliables, but physically barred their opponents. The pre-election campaign had been tense and bitter with threats of force flying across party lines. By this time some on each side had armed themselves. Someone fired a shot, and the rioting commenced. When it was all through, "Quinn's Row," an Irish section, had been gutted, stores looted, and Catholic churches damaged. A newspaper which was accused of stirring up feelings only barely escaped destruction. The atrocities against the Irish were especially brutal, with many being beaten and shot. Indeed, some of the wounded were thrown back into the flames of ignited buildings. Estimates of the dead range from 14 to 100, though historians have generally accepted (albeit with slim evidence) 22 as the number killed.

Labor disputes have also often spawned widescale disorder. Indeed, at the turn of the century, Winston Churchill, already a keen student of American affairs, observed that the United States had the most violent industrial relations of any western country. Most of this rioting started with a confrontation of labor and management over the right to organize, or wages and hours, or working conditions. A large portion of these strikes found the workers in a vulnerable if not helpless position, a fact which has led most historians to come down on the side of labor in these early disputes. Moreover, unlike the disorders we have previously discussed, these were nationwide in scope—occurring at widely scattered points. There was no question of their being directed since a union was usually involved and it had some control over local action throughout the country. Yet the violence was seldom uniform or confined to strikers. It might flare up in Chicago and Pittsburgh, while St. Louis, where the issues would be the same, might remain quiescent. Often, as in the case of the railroad strike of 1877, the damage to life and property was large. In the Homestead lockout alone, 35 were killed and the damage (in 1892 dollars) ran to $2,500.00. In the 1930's the organizing steel, auto, and rubber unions brought a recrudescence of this earlier grisly process.

. . .

Of all the sources of civil disorder, however, none has been more persistent than race. Whether in the North or South, whether before or after the Civil War, whether nineteenth or twentieth century, this question has been at the root of more physical violence than any other. There had been some sporadic slave uprisings before emancipation, the largest being the Nat Turner rebellion in 1831. But most which moved from plot to action occurred on the countryside rather than in the cities. Yet even the fear of a slave insurrection took its toll; in 1822, for instance, Charleston, South Carolina, officials, acting on tips and rumors, hanged 37 Negroes and deported many more for an alleged plot to capture and burn the city. Seven years later, in a free state, whites invaded Cincinnati's "Little Africa" and burned and killed and ultimately drove half the colored residents from town. In the same period mobs also assaulted abolitionists, sometimes killing, otherwise sacking buildings and destroying printing presses.

Even the New York City riot against the draft in 1863 took an ugly racial twist before it had run its course. The events themselves arose out of the unpopularity of the draft and the federal government's call for more men as Lee headed into Pennsylvania. The situation was further complicated by a crisis in the police department as a result of the conflicting claims of command by a Republican mayor and a Democratic governor. The rioting broke out July 13 and the first target was the provost marshal's office. Within a short time 700 people ransacked the building and then set it afire. The crowd would not let the firemen into the area and soon the whole block lay gutted. Later the mob began to spill over into the Negro area where many blacks were attacked and some killed.

The police were helpless as the riot spread. The few clashes with the mob saw the police retreat; the crowd wandered about almost at will. Political leaders did not want to take the consequences for action against the mob, and soon it started to head toward the business district. Slowly the police reorganized, by Tuesday they began to win engagements with the rioters, and in a little while they were able to confine the action to the original area. The mobs were, however, better armed and organized and gave a good account of themselves in pitched battle. On the third day federal troops arrived and the control swung over to the authorities and quiet was restored. But in three days the casualties ran to at least 74 dead and many times that number wounded. The property damage was never accurately added up, but claims against the county exceeded $1,500,000 by 1865.

Emancipation freed the Negro from bondage, but it did not grant him either equality or immunity from white aggression. From the New Orleans riot of 1866, through the long list of racial disorders to the end of World War II with datelines running through Atlanta, Springfield, East St. Louis, Washington, Mobile, Beaumont, Chicago, Detroit, and Harlem, [all these riots] reveal something of the depth of the crisis and the vulnerability of American cities to racial disorders. These riots were on a large scale, involved many deaths, millions of dollars of property damage, and left behind deep scars which have never been fully erased. Most of these riots involved the resort to outside military help for containment; all exposed the thinness of the internal and external controls within our urban society.

In fact, the war had scarcely ended before racial violence erupted in New Orleans. The occasion of the outbreak was a Negro procession to an assembly hall where a debate over enfranchising the blacks was to take place. There was some jostling during the march and a shot fired; but it was only after the arrival at the convention that police and special troops charged the black crowd. In the ensuing struggle [the] Negroes were finally routed, but guns, bricks, and stones were generously used. Many Negroes fell on the spot; others were pursued and killed on the streets trying to escape. Later General Sheridan reported that "at least nine-tenths of the casualties were perpetrated by the police and citizens by stabbing and smashing in the heads of many who had already been wounded or killed by policemen." Moreover, he added that it was not just a riot but "an absolute massacre by the police . . . a murder which the mayor and the police . . . perpetrated without the shadow of necessity." Federal troops arrived in the afternoon, took possession of the city, and restored order. But 34 Negroes and 4 whites were already dead and over 200 injured.

Smaller places, even in the North, were also affected with racial disorder. In August 1908, for instance, a three-day riot took its toll in Springfield, Illinois. The Negro population in the capital had grown significantly in the years after the turn of the century, and some whites sensed a political and economic threat. On August 13th a white woman claimed she had been violated by a Negro. An arrest was made and the newspapers carried an inflammatory account of the episode. Crowds gathered around the jail demanded the imprisoned black, but the sheriff quickly transferred the accused and another Negro to a prison in a nearby town without letting the public know. "The crowd outside was in an ugly mood," writes an historian of the riot, "the sun had raised tempers; many of the crowd had missed their dinners, which added to their irritation; and the authorities seemed to be taking no heed of their presence. By sundown the crowd had become an ugly mob.''

The first target of the rioters was a restaurant whose proprietor presumably had driven the prisoners from jail. Within a few minutes his place was a shambles. They then headed for the Negro section. Here they hit homes and businesses either owned by or catering to Negroes. White owners quickly put white handkerchiefs in their windows to show their race; their stores were left untouched. A Negro was found in his shop and was summarily lynched. Others were dragged from streetcars and beaten. On the 15th the first of 5,000 national guardsmen reached Springfield; very quickly the mob broke up and the town returned to normal. The death toll reached six (four whites and two blacks); the property damage was significant. As a result of the attack, Springfield's Negro population left the city in large numbers hoping to find better conditions elsewhere, especially in Chicago.

A decade later the depredations in East St. Louis were much larger, with the riot claiming the lives of 39 Negroes and 9 whites. The best student of this episode points out that the 1917 riot was not a sudden explosion but resulted from ''threats to the security of whites brought on by the Negroes' gains in economic, political and social status; Negro resentment of the attempts to 'kick him back in his place'; and the weakness of the external forces of constraint—the city government, especially the police department.'' Tensions were raised when the Aluminum Ore Company replaced white strikers with Negro workers. In addition to these factors, race had become a political issue in the previous year when the Democrats accused Republicans of ''colonizing'' Negroes to swing the election in East St. Louis. The kindling seemed only to lack the match.

On May 28 came the fire. A Central Trades and Labor Union delegation formally requested the Mayor to stop the immigration of Negroes to East St. Louis. As the men were leaving City Hall they heard a story that a Negro robber had accidentally shot a white man during a holdup. In a few minutes the word spread; rumor replaced fact. Now it was said the shooting was intentional; that a white woman was insulted; that two white girls were shot. By this time 3,000 people had congregated and the cry for vengeance went up. Mobs ran downtown beating every Negro in sight. Some were dragged off the streetcars, others chased down. The police refused to act except to take the injured to hospitals and to disarm Negroes. The next day the National Guard arrived to restore order.

Two days later the governor withdrew troops although tension remained high. Scattered episodes broke the peace, but no sustained violence developed. The press, however, continued to emphasize Negro crimes and a skirmish broke out between white pickets and black workers at the Aluminum Company. Then on July 1 some whites drove through the main Negro neighborhood firing into homes. The colored residents armed themselves, and when a similar car, this time carrying a plainclothesman and reporter, went down the street the blacks riddled the passing auto with gunshot.

The next day was the worst. At about 10:00 A.M. a Negro was shot on the main street and a new riot was underway. An historian of the event asserted that the area along Collinsville Avenue between Broadway and Illinois Avenue became a "bloody half mile" for three or four hours. "Streetcars were stopped: Negroes, without regard to age or sex, were pulled off and stoned, clubbed and kicked. . . . By the early afternoon, when several Negroes were beaten and lay bloodied in the street, mob leaders calmly shot and killed them. After victims were placed in an ambulance, there was cheering and handclapping," Others headed for the Negro section and set fire to homes on the edge of the neighborhood. By midnight the South End was in flames and black residents began to flee the city. In addition to the dead, the injured were counted in the hundreds and over 300 buildings were destroyed.

Two summers later the racial virus felled Chicago. Once again, mounting tension had accompanied the migration of blacks to the city. The numbers jumped from 44,000 in 1910 to 109,000 ten years later. Though the job market remained good, housing was tight. Black neighborhoods could expand only at the expense of white ones, and everywhere the transition areas were filled with trouble. Between July 1, 1917, and March 1921, there had been 58 bombings of Negro houses. Recreational areas also witnessed continual racial conflict.

The riot itself began on Sunday, July 27, on the 29th Street Beach. There had been some stone-throwing and sporadic fighting. Then a Negro boy, who had been swimming in the Negro section, drifted into the white area and drowned. What happened is not certain, but the young blacks charged he had been hit by stones and demanded the arrest of a white. The police refused, but then arrested a Negro at a white request. When the Negroes attacked the police, the riot was on. News of the events on the beach spread to the rest of the city. Sunday's casualties were 2 dead and 50 wounded. On Monday, attacks were made on Negroes coming from work; in the evening cars drove through black neighborhoods with whites shooting from the windows. Negroes retaliated by sniping at any white who entered the Black Belt. Monday's accounting found 20 killed and hundreds wounded. Tuesday's list was shorter, a handful dead, 139 injured. Wednesday saw a further waning and a reduction in losses in life and property. Rain began to fall; the Mayor finally called in the state militia. After nearly a week a city which [had] witnessed lawlessness and warfare quieted down and began to assess the implications of the grisly week.

The Detroit riot of 1943 perhaps illustrates the range of racial disorders that broke out sporadically during World War II. There had been earlier conflicts in Mobile, Los Angeles, and Beaumont, Texas, and there would be some others later in the year. No doubt the war with its built-in anxieties and accelerated residential mobility accounted for the timing of these outbreaks. In Detroit, the wider problem was compounded by serious local questions. The Negro population in the city had risen sharply, with over 50,000 arriving in the 15 months before the riot; this followed a historical increase of substantial proportions which saw black residents increase from 40,000 to 120,000 in the single decade between 1920 and 1930. These newcomers put immense pressures on the housing market, and neighborhood turnover at the edge of the ghetto bred bitterness and sometimes violence; importantly, too, recreational areas became centers of racial abrasiveness.

On June 20 the riot broke out on Belle Isle, a recreational spot used by both races, but predominantly by Negroes. Fistfighting on a modest basis soon escalated, and quickly a rising level of violence spread across the city. The Negro Ghetto—ironically called Paradise Valley—saw the first wave of looting and bloodshed. The area was, as its historians have described it, "spattered with blood and littered with broken glass and ruined merchandise. The black mob had spared a few shops owned by Negroes who had chalked COLORED on their windows. But almost every store in the ghetto owned by a white had been smashed open and ransacked." Other observers noted that "crudely organized gangs of Negro hoodlums began to operate more openly. Some looters destroyed property as if they had gone berserk."

The next morning saw the violence widen. The police declared the situation out of control and the mayor asked for state troops. Even this force was ineffective, and finally the Governor asked for federal help. Peace returned under the protection of 6,000 men; and the troops remained for more than a week. The dead numbered 34, 25 Negroes and 9 whites; property damage exceeded $2,000,000. And almost as costly was the bitterness, fear, and hate that became part of the city's legacy.

This survey covers only some of the larger and more important disorders. Others reached significant proportions but do not fall into convenient categories. For example, in the eighteenth century a protest against inoculation led to widespread rioting; mobs hit the streets to punish men who snatched bodies for medical training. In times of economic hardship, "bread riots" resulted in ransacking stores; crowds often physically drove away officials seeking to evict tenants who could not pay rent.

Two disorders perhaps best suggest the miscellaneous and unpredictable character of this process. One is so bizarre that only its bloody climax has kept it from being among the most amusing episodes of American history. It revolved around the rivalry between two prominent actors, the American Edwin Forrest, and William Macready, an Englishman. Both were appearing in "Macbeth" on the same night, May 7, 1849, in New York City. Some rowdies, mostly Irish, decided to break up the Macready performance, and when he appeared on the stage they set up such a din that he had to retire. After apologies and assurances, the English visitor agreed to try again on the 9th. This time, the police extracted the troublemakers and Macready finished the play. But a mob gathered outside after the final curtain and refused to disperse on police orders. Finally, the edgy guard fired into the crowd, killing 25 persons.

Another dimension is revealed in the events of March 1884, in Cincinnati. They came in the midst of what the city's best historian has dubbed "the decade of disorder." Two men were tried for the murder of a white livery man. Though one was Negro and the other German, race does not seem to be at issue. When the German was found guilty of only manslaughter, a public campaign developed to avenge the decision. A meeting at Music Hall, called by some leading citizens, attracted 10,000 people, mostly from the middle class, who were worried about a general breakdown of law and order and thought the light sentence would encourage criminals. The speakers attacked the jury and the administration of justice in the city. Afterward a crowd headed for the jail. In the first encounter with the police, casualties were light. But the next day the militia moved in and hostility climbed. Finally, a pitched battle ensued in which 54 died and over 200 were wounded. Thus, a meeting called to bring about law and order wound up ironically in disorder and violence.

This survey, which is only suggestive and not exhaustive, indicates that widescale violence and disorder have been man's companion in the American city from the outset. Some generalizations out of this experience might be useful in the light of the present crisis.

First, most of the rioting has usually been either limited in objective or essentially sporadic. This, of course, is not true of racial conflict, but it is characteristic of a large number of the others. In those, the event was discrete; there was no immediate violent sequel. After a labor dispute, especially if it involved union recognition, bitterness and hate persisted, but there was no annual recurrence of the violence. Attacks on immigrants seldom produced an encore, though they might have an analogue in some other city in the same month or year. In short, though there was enough disorder and mob action to create a persistent anxiety, the incidence of overt conflict was irregular enough to preclude predictions of the next "long hot summer."

Second, this sporadic quality meant that the postmortems were usually short and shallow. It was characteristic to note the large number of teenagers who got involved; to attribute the disruption to outsiders (especially anarchists and communists); to place a large responsibility on the newspapers for carrying inflammatory information and spreading unfounded rumors; to blame the local police for incompetence, for prejudice, for intervening too soon or too late, or at all. After any episode, the urge to fix blame led to all kinds of analyses. The historian of the 1877 railroad violence, for example, observes that "the riots were variously ascribed to avarice, the expulsion of the Bible from the schools, the protective tariff, the demonetization of silver, the absence of General Grant, the circulation of the *Chicago Times* and original sin.'' Others saw in it a labor conspiracy or a communist plot. And the *New York Times* could assert after the Chicago riot in 1919 that: "The outbreak of race riots in Chicago, following so closely on those reported from Washington, shows clearly enough that the thing is not sporadic (but has) . . . intelligent direction and management. . . . (It seems probable) that the Bolshevist agitation has been extended among the Negroes.''

There were a few exceptions. After the Chicago race riot, for example, an Illinois commission studied the event in some detail and also examined the deteriorating relations between the races which lay at the bottom. Others occasionally probed beneath the surface [to get] at the deeper causes of unrest. But most cities preferred to forget as soon as possible and hoped for an end to any further disorder. Indeed, even the trials that followed most riots show how rapidly popular interest faded. The number of people brought to trial was small and the number of convictions extremely small; and, most significantly, there was little clamor for sterner measures.

Third, if the analyses of the riots were shallow, the response of cities and legislatures was not very effective. After quiet was restored, there would almost certainly be a discussion of police reform. Customarily little came of it, though in Louisville the utter ineptness and obvious partisanship of the police in 1855 prompted a change from an elective to an appointive force. Legislation usually emphasized control. As early as 1721, Massachusetts responded to growing disorders with an anti-riot act. And Chicago's Commerical Club made land available for Fort Sheridan after the events of 1877 in order to have troops nearby for the protection of the city. But most cities rocked back to normal as soon as the tremors died down.

Fourth, there was a general tendency to rely increasingly on outside forces for containing riots. Partly, this resulted from the fact that in labor disorders local police and even state militia fraternized with strikers and could not be counted on to discipline workers. Partly, it was due to inadequate numbers in the face of the magnitude of the problem. Partly, too, it stemmed from the fact that sometimes the police were involved in the fighting at the outset and seemed a part of the riot. The first resort was usually to state troops; but they were often unsatisfactory, and the call for federal assistance became more frequent.

Fifth, while it is hard to assess, it seems that the bitterness engendered by riots and disorders was not necessarily irreparable. Though the immigrants suffered a good deal at the hands of nativists, it did not slow down for long the process of their incorporation into American life. Ten years after Louisville's "Bloody Monday" the city had a German mayor. The trade unions survived the assaults of the nineteenth century and a reduction of tension characterized the period between 1900 and the depression (with the notable exception of the post-war flare-ups). And after the violence of the 1930's labor and management learned to conduct their differences, indeed their strikes, with reduced bloodshed and violence. It is not susceptible of proof, but it seems that the fury of the defeated in these battles exacted a price on the victors that ultimately not only protected the groups but won respect, however grudgingly, from the public.

At any rate, the old sources of major disorders, race excepted, no longer physically agitate American society. It has been many years since violence has been a significant factor in city elections and no widespread disorders have even accompanied campaigning. Immigrant groups have now become so incorporated in American life that they are not easily visible and their election to high offices, indeed the highest, signals a muting of old hostilities. Even when people organized on a large scale against minority groups—such as the Americans' Protective Association in the 1890's or the Ku Klux Klan in the 1920's—they have seldom been able to create major riots or disorders. And though sporadic violence occasionally breaks out in a labor dispute, what is most remarkable is the continuance of the strike as a weapon of industrial relations with so little resort to force. Even the destruction of property during a conflict has ceased to be an expectation.

Sixth, race riots were almost always different from other kinds of disorders. Their roots went deeper; they broke out with increasing frequency; and their intensity mounted rather than declined. And between major disorders the incidence of small-scale violence was always high. Until recently, the Negro has largely been the object of the riot. This was true not only in northern cities where changing residential patterns bred violence, but also in the South where this question was less pervasive. In these riots the lines were sharply drawn against the Negroes, the force was applied heavily against them, and the casualties were always highest among blacks.

Finally, in historical perspective, if racial discord be removed, the level of large-scale disorder and violence is less ominous today than it has been during much of the past. As we have seen, those problems which have produced serious eruptions in the past no longer do so. In fact, if one were to plot a graph, omitting the racial dimension, violence and disorder over a long period have been reduced. Indeed, what makes the recent rioting so alarming is that it breaks so much with this historical trend and upsets common expectations.

Yet to leave out race is to omit the most important dimension of the present crisis. For it is race that is at the heart of the present discord. Some analysts, of course, have argued that the problem is class and they emphasize the numbers caught in widening poverty, and the frustration and envy of poor people in a society of growing affluence. Yet it is important to observe that though 68 percent of the poor people in this country are white, the disorders stem almost wholly from black ghettos. The marginal participation of a few whites in Detroit and elsewhere scarcely dilutes the racial foundations of these disorders.

In fact, a historical survey of disorders only highlights the unique character of the present problem. For the experience of the Negro in American cities has been quite different from any other group. And it is in just this difference that the crisis lies. Because the black ghetto is unlike any ghettoes that our cities have known before. Of course, other groups knew the ghetto experience too. As newcomers to the city they huddled in the downtown areas where they met unspeakably congested conditions, occupied the worst housing, got the poorest education, toiled, if fortunate enough to have a job, at the most menial tasks, endured high crime rates, and knew every facet of deprivation.

The urban slum had never been a very pleasant place, and it was tolerable only if the residents, or most of them, thought there was a way out. To American immigrants generally the ghetto was a temporary stage in their incorporation into American society. Even some of the first generation escaped, and the second and third generation moved out of the slums in very large numbers. Soon they were dispersed around the metropolitan area, in the suburbs as well as the pleasant residential city wards. Those who remained behind in the old neighborhoods did so because they chose to, not because they had to. By this process, millions of people from numberless countries, of different national and religious backgrounds, made their way into the main current of American life.

It was expected that Negroes would undergo the same process when they came to the city. Thus, there was little surprise in the first generation when black newcomers did indeed find their way into the central city, the historic staging ground for the last and poorest arrivals. But the ghetto proved to be not temporary. Instead of colored residents dispersing in the second generation, the ghetto simply expanded. Block by block it oozed out into the nearby white neighborhoods. Far from breaking up, the ghetto grew. In fact, housing became more segregated every year; and the walls around it appeared higher all the time. What had been temporary for other groups seemed permanent to Negroes.

The growth of the Negro ghetto created conditions which had not existed before and which generated the explosiveness of our present situation. In the first place, the middle-class Negroes became embittered at their exclusion from the decent white neighborhoods of the city and suburbs. These people, after all, had done what society expected of them; they got their education, training, jobs, and income. Yet even so they were deprived of that essential symbol of American success—the home in a neighborhood of their own choosing where conditions would be more pleasant and schools better for their children. For this group, now about a third of all urban Negroes, the exclusion seemed especially cruel and harsh.

As a result they comprise now a growingly alienated and embittered group. The middle-class blacks are now beginning to turn their attention to organizing among the poor in the worst parts of the ghetto. Their children make up the cadres of black militants in the colleges. And when the riots come, they tolerate the activity even though they usually do not themselves participate. In short, the fact of the ghetto forces them to identify with race, not class. When the riots break, they feel a bond with the rioters, not white society. This had not been true of the emerging middle class of any immigrant group before.

If the ghetto has new consequences for the middle class, it also creates a new situation among the poorer residents of the ghetto, especially for the young people. They feel increasingly that there is no hope for the future. For other groups growing up in the ghetto there had always been visible evidence that it was possible to escape. Many before had done it; and everyone knew it. This produced the expectation that hard work, proper behavior, some schooling, and a touch of luck would make it possible to get ahead. But the young Negro grows up in increasing despair. He asks himself—"What if I do all they say I should—stay in school, get my training, find a job, accumulate some money—I'll still be living here, still excluded from the outside world and its rewards." He asks himself, "What's the use?" Thus, the hopelessness, despair, and frustration mounts, and the temperature of the ghetto rises. Nearly all of our poverty programs are stumbling on the problem of motivation. To climb out of the slum has always required more than average incentive. Yet this is precisely what is lacking in the ghetto youth.

The present riots stem from the peculiar problems of the ghetto. By confining Negroes to the ghetto we have deprived them of the chance to enter American society on the same terms as other groups before them. And they know increasingly that this exclusion is not a function of education, training, or income. Rather, it springs from the color of their skin. This is what makes race the explosive question of our time; this is what endangers the tranquillity of our cities. In the historian's perspective, until the ghetto begins to break, until the Negro middle class can move over this demeaning barrier, until the young people can see Negroes living where their resources will carry them and hence get credible evidence of equality, the summers will remain long and hot.

Roger Lane

THE SQUEAKY WHEEL GETS THE OIL: INDEPENDENT TRUCKERS AND THE OPEC EMBARGO OF 1973-74

In the nearly two hundred years since adoption of the Constitution much of the specific political analysis in James Madison's Tenth Federalist *has necessarily lost its force. The* Federalist *papers were written before the rise of modern industrial capitalism, at a time when the overwhelming majority of citizens still lived on small farms. The economic differences that concerned delegates to the Constitutional Convention involved debtors and creditors, farmers and merchants. Few envisioned future clashes between workingmen and their employers, and none the more recent competition between rival claimants for government contracts, programs, and favorable fiscal policies. The new United States in 1788 was already the most ethnically diverse nation in the Western world, and its political leaders were painfully aware of the divisive potential of slavery as an institution. But while several recent authors in this volume have seen racial differences, in their modern form, as the most dangerous internal threat to the republic, Madison, himself a slaveholder, never mentioned "race" as a major source of political difference. Living in a time in which geographic distance could be considered protection against the formation of national "factions," he could not foresee, either, the close-linked modern universe in which Americans are almost instantly affected by events half a world away.*

So far, however, the American political system has managed to survive all of the changes and challenges of these two centuries. Apparently new issues often turn out to be fundamentally similar to the old. And many of the mechanisms for checking, balancing, and containing hostilities can be adapted to minimize the effect of violent conflict in the twentieth century as well as the eighteenth.

The truckers' "strike" of 1973–74, as many violent incidents before it, combined new elements and old. At one level the problem was, in almost pure form, the simple economic factionalism about which Madison was most concerned. At another it involved new sources of dissension, perhaps beyond our ability to control, for which nothing in our history seems to have prepared us. Again, as in the past, the ultimate issue is whether the new challenge will overwhelm the traditional means and conditions for moderating conflict in America.

When it was all over, the winter of 1973–74 turned out to have been a warm one throughout the country. But no one could count on that at the time, and however mild the temperature the national temper was nervous and even nasty. Although it had not been a hard winter, it seemed a long one, as against a background of deepening recession the vice president of the United States was forced to resign and the president himself struggled desperately against disgrace. And in the lives of most ordinary Americans even these disturbing political events were less immediately worrisome, during the dreary season, than the fears and bitterness set off by the Great Oil Shortage. In the long run, too, the fuel crisis and the reaction to it—in particular the violent reaction of the nation's independent truckers—suggested future problems far more serious than those measured by either thermometers or political polls.

Many conservationists and economists, even before the summer of '73, had pointed out that the goods of Mother Earth were limited and that the compound increase in technology's appetite for fuel and metals threatened to exhaust the supply. It would thus be mistaken and perhaps catastrophic to continue to expect the kind of material progress that the Western world had come to take for granted. Perhaps a constantly dropping birth rate was a sign that at some level of consciousness millions of ordinary Americans were beginning to understand this newly apparent reality. It was no surprise to many when the Organization of Oil Exporting Countries, OPEC, began in May to test its new strength by raising the price of petroleum, one of the world's scarce resources. There was talk throughout the summer of possible shortages when cold weather hit. If that happened, the federal government might be forced to make hard choices about the proportions of crude oil that should be refined into heating fuels or gasoline, and to decide among the competing claims of private consumption, industry, and transportation. But no firm steps were taken. And it was the sudden shock of events beginning in October that really awakened Americans to the painful meaning of shortages in daily life.

Although the underlying causes went much deeper and farther back, the opening of the crisis state began with Egypt's "Yom Kippur Invasion" of Israel on the first Saturday of the month. It had long been obvious that, partly as a result of American aid to Israel, new trouble in the Middle East would threaten the oil supply. The Arab leaders of OPEC responded to the hostilities first by doubling the posted wellhead price of oil to $6 a barrel. Then, more drastically still, they announced a complex plan to reduce the available world supply, and to embargo exports to the United States entirely, until Israel withdrew back to the much smaller boundaries of 1967.

Most Western nations responded to this pressure with immediate expressions of support for the Arab position. In the United States, with its historic and bipartisan tradition of support for Israel, such a position was politically unthinkable. But it remained true that even though we were less totally dependent than the Japanese and Europeans, we still imported up to one-third of our daily oil consumption, one million barrels from the Middle East alone. And if the United States was going to be cut off, we would have to allocate what we had very carefully. Even before the final embargo announcement the president ended months of substantial inaction by calling for mandatory allocation of scarce propane gas, jet fuel, and certain heating oils; in effect, although the word was carefully avoided, this was the first peacetime rationing program in our history. After the OPEC action, caught without a comprehensive energy policy of its own, the administration moved hastily if reluctantly to adopt some of the proposals long advocated by Democratic critics in the Congress. A new Federal Energy Administration (FEA) was created, headed by former Treasury official William E. Simon. And on the first weekend in December, Richard Nixon himself preempted national television time to announce a range of new measures designed to save energy.

In concrete terms the most important of the presidential proposals called for a ban on Sunday sales of gasoline, cuts in the use of oil ranging from 10 to 25 percent if necessary, and a national speed limit of fifty miles an hour for automobiles and fifty-five for trucks and busses.

Americans reacted to these proposals in many ways. Wall Street, already unsettled by the administration's ineffective attempts to deal with simultaneous inflation and recession, suffered its biggest one-day drop in eleven years. The House of Representatives, reacting as in those wartime emergencies when Congress responds to executive initiatives whatever their wisdom, shouted through the new speed limits and other decrees. Many ordinary consumers at first went along with the voluntary guidelines that the president had assured them would ease the problem, turning down thermostats and driving more slowly. But the use of state power, instead of the impersonal workings of the price system, to decide who would get how much of what, necessarily involved favoring some segments of the economy over others. No democratic government wants to antagonize any of its constituents, and the distracted Nixon administration, during the week in which Spiro T. Agnew was being forced out of office by the threat of prosecution for bribery, was especially reluctant to take unpopular measures. Many groups geared up to plead for their special interests, but the most dramatic pressure came from an unexpected source, and over an unexpected issue. Almost immediately after the president's speech, in fact, independent truck drivers, quite spontaneously, began to pull off the roads all over the country in protest against the new speed limits.

The independent truckers had been overlooked largely because, unlike the salaried drivers affiliated with the powerful Teamsters' Union, they had no real organization capable of carrying out a coordinated protest. The men who drove their own long-haul trucks were estimated to number about 100,000. The big interstate rigs—eighteen-wheelers weighing in at thirty-five tons or so and costing as many thousands of dollars—were capital equipment that could earn an owner $20,000 or even $30,000 a year. The owners were, moreover, a fiercely competitive lot; steel haulers, for example, typically bid against each other for contracts to move metal from one point to another, and if they admitted to no masters, they had many rivals.

But however proud of their status as independent businessmen, the drivers did recognize problems in common. Subject to a maze of rules imposed by a variety of state agencies as well as the federal Interstate Commerce Commission, with most rates fixed firmly by law, all of them had similar complaints about red tape and government "interference" with the business of making profits. Those organizations that they did have, in addition to simple fraternal functions, were designed to represent their interests before these regulatory agencies. Whatever their differences with each other, or with the paid employees hired to drive company trucks, they shared the same enemies on the road, ranging from bad weather to zealous cops and inspectors. They tended to congregate, too, in the same truck stops, oases strung out along the interstates to furnish food, fuel, and a variety of other needs and pleasures. They were fully aware of their strategic position in the transportation network, as it was reckoned that the independents hauled some 70 percent of the nation's overland freight. With the newly popular citizens' band radios to help them communicate, during the long slow hours on the road, they found that the proposed energy program posed another common threat.

The steady rise in diesel prices, from around thirty to close to fifty cents between May and December, had been bad enough for men driving machines that only got about five miles per gallon. But that perhaps seemed to the truckers the result of international forces hard to control or even confront. The new speed limit was something else again. Since long-haulers were paid by the mile, the limit would cut earnings by the difference between their previous speeds and fifty-five miles per hour, perhaps several thousands annually off the handsome incomes to which they had become accustomed. And in this case there was a target; the Nixon administration had made the rule, and the Nixon administration could break it.

At first the men simply bitched about the new limit as they met in the roughly one thousand truck stops that served as the informal clubhouses of their loose fraternity. "The Great White Father back in Washington don't give a damn about truck drivers" was the typical complaint, and it implied the next step; hundreds of men decided to make their stops more permanent, feeling that "we've got to shut down this country to show 'em what this is doing to us." [1] Even without much formal organization, these wildcat stoppages proved easy to spread. Men who load freight tend to be big and blunt, and seven men who have decided over beer or coffee to quit hauling can easily persuade newcomers, one by one, to pull over and join in. An angry crowd of thirty, such as gathered in the Tomahawk station just east of Denver on Interstate 805, is nearly irresistible in "argument." Transport strikes have always enjoyed a high level of success simply because of the ever-present threat of violence. Unlike workingmen gathered into a single plant, strikebreaking drivers cannot easily be protected by police, troops, or company security. Spread out, alone, over miles of road, their cargoes, vehicles, and persons subject to attack from ambush, the men tend to get nervous. And as word of shotgun blasts, rocks thrown from overpasses, and scattered bombings filtered from the stops into dispatching centers, more and more decided to sit tight. In the East, especially along the great interstates that cross Ohio, Pennsylvania, and New Jersey, another illegal tactic was employed as numbers of the rigs were parked to block traffic not only into the diesel pumps at the truck stops but along the highways themselves. By Tuesday, December 4, traffic on Interstate 80, for example, was completely halted by 3,000 trucks tangled in a great gray mass centering on Stony Ridge, Ohio.

The official reaction to this was confused and variable. Many individual Teamsters were sympathetic, and others scared. Their union, however, was headed by Frank Fitzsimmons, the president's only ally in the ranks of organized labor; "Fitz" promptly denounced the action. So, predictably, did the American Trucking Association and others representing the industry. But spokesmen such as William J. Hill of the Fraternal Association of Steel Haulers, and even Mike Parkhurst, editor of *Overdrive* magazine, urged that the pressure be kept up, as small ad hoc delegations began to filter into various state capitals and Washington. While Secretary of Transportation Claude Brinegar dickered with these men, promising to "review" their situation, the president—ignoring criticism from those who remembered mass illegal arrests of peace demonstrators, earlier—denied all responsibility for maintaining law and order in this case. Despite blockage of interstate transportation, he contended that violence on the highways was "a matter for the states." The politically sensitive confrontation with angry truckers was left to individual governors, most of them Democrats; in Ohio,

Governor Gilligan had to call out both the national guard and the state police to break up the biggest and most stubborn group of blockaders.

At this point the lack of prior organization and coordination began to tell with the truckers. Faced with troopers in force, the majority preferred to move their own rigs rather than have windows smashed and brakes or gears burnt out by heedless towers. Back in the stops, as beer ran short and families called, most began to hit the road two or three days after they had first quit. But the movement was not quite over, and Mike Parkhurst, most militant of the spokesmen thrown up by the emergency, called for a second, prearranged, protest at the end of the following week, December 13 and 14.

Faced with this new threat, the administration vacillated for several days. To grant major concessions in the face of illegal violence would be a crippling public relations blow to the energy proposals at the very start. But the truckers were clearly tough. And as both businessmen and blue-collar "hard-hats," they were unique in representing the two groups to which the president was most fond of appealing when in political trouble. The new FEA chief, William Simon, worked twenty-hour days to come up with a comprehensive plan for oil distribution by December 12, but although it called for cuts elsewhere, it contained nothing special for the truckers. Thousands pulled out on the 13th, and more the next day. Although there were fewer reports of highway stoppages, the diesel pumps were blocked again in many states, and gunfire and bombings were reported especially from Ohio. Transportation Secretary Brinegar announced, on the 14th, that as a result of negotiations the latest allocation plan would grant truckers not a 10 percent cut in the fuel they had used in 1972, the base year from which everyone's share was being calculated, but a 10 percent *addition*, the only increase allowed any major group. And with this apparent victory, the men moved back onto the road a second time.

After the middle of December, then, with their demands at least partially met and others "under review," the drivers dropped out of the news. But the fuel shortage itself, together with the still swelling Watergate scandal, continued to dominate headlines over the next several weeks. The price of energy crept upward only when it was not leaping; on Christmas Eve it was announced that Persian Gulf oil had again doubled, to nearly $12 a barrel. Closed gas stations and long lines at open ones resulted in short tempers and even shootings. Homeowners who turned down their thermostats fretted when government offices were kept hot at the insistence of employees who refused to wear unfashionably heavy clothing. Governors from the North and West besieged the administration with demands for more gas or heating-oil allocations, complaining bitterly about unfairness. The oil-rich South and Southwest, long resentful of environmentalist curbs on energy, urged the president, or perhaps the Deity, to "Let the Bastards Freeze in the Dark," as one bumper sticker put it. Any chance that the nation would pull together in the crisis was undercut by two considerations.

Large numbers of Americans, first, came to believe that the oil companies themselves were not only exploiting the crisis but had deliberately provoked it for profit. And the administration, second, revealed its lack of prior planning by speaking not with one firm voice but with several shrill ones. No one was willing to go all the way into such unpopular measures as strict rationing. But Simon and others directly concerned with energy stressed that the problem was long-term and serious, while Budget Director Roy Ash and similar optimists, eager for both political and economic reasons to reassure the public, tended to smile away its significance. The president himself, on January 23, delivered a special energy message to the Congress, stressing not the painful need to cut back but the encouragement of new sources, including more domestic oilwells.

And on the next day the truckers reappeared, stronger and better prepared than before. On January 24, men from seventeen different organizations, some of them clearly new or newly vitalized, announced in Washington that the drivers they represented would quit in just one week if a new list of demands was not met in full. The importance of the speed limit, which had proved popular with safety groups and relatively painless for the general public, was not stressed this time. The new concerns revealed— many remained secret—were instead carefully chosen for their broad appeal to the whole population. These included: first, an immediate freeze on all petroleum prices; second, an immediate "audit" of all oil company reserves and refining capacity; and only third, a special request for a "rollback" in diesel prices to the levels of May 1973. No one was sure just how many independents were represented by leaders such as George Rynn of the National Council of Independent Truckers, which centered largely in Ohio, or just how accurately anyone spoke for the rank and file. But it was immediately clear that the large number of men on the road were impatient; thousands pulled off on the 25th rather than wait out the week, and shootings, slashed tires, and punctured radiators were reported the same day.

The Nixon administration did not at first appear to take this very seriously. Secret negotiations were entrusted to William J. Usery, special assistant to the president and head of the Federal Mediation Service. But no one from the many other government agencies involved, notably the FEA, showed up to talk. The government's first offer, involving adjustments in freight rates to be made only after the men had gone back to work, was overwhelmingly rejected by drivers voting in Ohio and Pennsylvania. Meanwhile, both the violence and the wildcat stoppages continued right up through the "official" opening. On the last day of January, in the Northeast and Midwest especially, scheduled efforts were aimed at specific targets chosen for their strategic value. There were no indiscriminate highway blockades to enrage motorists in general; efforts instead were concentrated at truck stops, in an attempt to force a halt to all major overland traffic, by independents and teamsters alike. In order further to help dry up the flow of goods, "sympathizers" picketed fuel delivery centers in particular. And in addition to the official activities—themselves largely illegal—scattered violence continued to rattle those unwilling to go along. On the very first day one nonstriking driver, Ronald Engst of Spring Grove, Pennsylvania, was killed by a rock thrown off an overpass on Route 22 near Allentown.

During the following week, negotiations at the Statler Hilton were carried on against a background of National Guard mobilizations, layoffs at unsupplied factories, and growing shortages of gasoline, fresh meat, and produce. As it became clear that the administration was unable to get things moving, Governor Milton Shapp of Pennsylvania, representing the Mid-Atlantic Governors' Conference, joined the parley and demanded action. At the same time, it became evident that the truckers for their part were exploiting the situation to win concessions not only on oil policy but a tangled host of ancient grievances involving load limits, fees and fines, and differences between regulated and unregulated carriers. Some of these, if granted, would have an immediately inflationary impact, to the concern of Treasury officials. But as operators moving out of the Peoria stockyards refused to drive eastward—most of the gunfire, outside of Texas, was heard east of the Mississippi—higher-level officials came to join the talks. Simon announced, on February 5, that the president himself had ordered a month-long freeze on petroleum prices, and he was prepared to allow truck stops to open Sundays. At the same time, Attorney General William Saxbe, who as a result of the complex Watergate situation remained largely independent of the rest of the administration, called for tougher action against the violence, while Teamsters and trucking company executives united in urging the government to stand firm. It took a small army of troopers, meanwhile, with helicopters overhead, to escort a sixty-eight-truck beef convoy from Iowa to Chicago, and when the drivers got there, they had to pile out of their motel in the dark in response to a bomb threat. One of them spoke for thousands of others when he concluded wearily that "It ain't worth it. I'm going home tomorrow."[2] By February 7 some 75,000 working people had been laid off, midwestern beef prices were the highest in twenty years, and as supermarket stocks shrank alarmingly, the pump gas shortage hit its nadir.

The protest was finally settled, or began to crumble, on that day. In addition to the diesel price freeze and Sunday sales, the drivers were promised an immediate rise in freight rates and several less measurable future actions, ranging from the oil "audit" to an Interstate Commerce Commission (ICC) "review" of their load and traffic complaints. These pledges seemed good enough, after two weary weeks, to the representatives at the Hilton. They did not, at first, to many of their fired-up "constituents" along the roads. Few of the truckers' groups had any mechanism, unlike real unions, for either taking strike votes or enforcing settlements, and the Washington representatives were embarrassed by a series of rejections in the nine states that did report more or less formal reaction by the operators. But the press, and then the president himself in a national address, urged the men back to work, and most did not seem really unhappy about picking up their loads and getting back to making a living. In fact they had won about all that they could have expected to win; the diesel "rollback" proposition was clearly impossible, and the various complaints with the ICC were too complicated and involved too many third parties in the transport business to win an easy solution. By Monday, February 11 what *The New York Times* called "the most serious manifestation of the energy crisis yet"[3] was substantially over, and it was business as usual on the highways.

What had been learned through all of this? In terms of the need for a comprehensive energy policy, neither the public nor the administration seemed to have learned much. The warm weather blew away earlier fears about cold homes and factories, and the pump gas shortage eased as February turned into March. At the end of the latter month, when OPEC nations finally called off their leaky embargo, the earlier sense of crisis was quickly forgotten. The oil spigot was opened wider than ever. And despite bold presidential promises of "energy independence" the nation grew daily more reliant upon foreign sources of a fuel that experts warned would in any case run out, all over the globe, in little more than a generation.

But the truckers, and any other interest group that witnessed their performance, had learned something, namely, that it is the squeaky wheel that gets the oil. And as George Rynn put it later, "It's amazing how easily you can shut down this country."[4] The activities of independent capitalists do not properly constitute a "strike"; perhaps "protest" or "stoppage" would be a better word. But however defined, most of their activities were illegal; although quitting work is perfectly legitimate, physically blockading others is against the law, quite apart from the occasional murder and other routine forms of intimidation that seemed essential to success. Yet there were no sustained prosecutions after the settlement. And despite the most rudimentary organization, the drivers were able to win virtually all that the administration could grant. In the right circumstances, then, the right amount of violence applied in the right places by the right group is a winning tactic.

For the wider society this is a dangerous condition. The real importance of the Great Oil Shortage is that it gave us a glimpse of the future— and it does not work. As population and technology grow worldwide, there will be other and worse shortages. Few situations are more explosive than those in which groups feel that gains or "rights" that they have long enjoyed, or at least foreseen, are suddenly threatened. And the United States may be especially vulnerable. Our historical experience has involved the sharing of prosperity rather than scarcity. Group conflict in the past has been eased not so much by the achievement of social justice, cutting the economic pie into more nearly equal pieces, as by the kind of growth that has kept the whole pie expanding, giving bigger pieces to all whatever their relative shares. As this growth slows or even reverses, we shall find ourselves without traditional solutions to which to turn.

And as economic circumstances change, our traditional political order may prove inadequate also. In a world of shortages there is no more important function for a central government than to make and execute firm and fair plans for the distribution of scarce resources. But our Madisonian system does not work well at transcending hostilities in the name of fairness or the common good. Rather, it assumes the inevitable existence of group conflict and neutralizes this by pitting one group against another. In a more interdependent world, one in which the weapons of conflict, whether physical or economic, are more potent than ever, we perhaps cannot count on this neutralizing mechanism to preserve state and society from disintegration. For many years we have been warned by social scientists and others that the explosive issue of race will set off "the fire next time," a fire that will consume us. Among the several interesting features of the truckers' strike is that the issue was nothing so dramatic, but simply a difference in economic interest, precisely the kind that Madison himself had seen as the most important source of "faction." Those who resorted to illegal violence were not young or black or ideologically alienated but solid middle-class capitalists, threatened not with destruction but with an income loss of 10 or 15 percent. That individuals such as this could mount so violent a challenge suggests something of our fragility. If in crisis more groups react like this, threatening lawful authority, the only perceived alternative to anarchy may be totalitarian rule. It may in short be essential to the survival of democracy that we have better planning, firmer resolve, and less vulnerability to violent protest than we had during that first test in the winter of '73–'74.

NOTES

1. *New York Times,* 5 December, 1973.
2. *Ibid.,* 7 February, 1974.
3. *Ibid.,* 5 February, 1974.
4. *Time,* February 18, 1974.

SELECTED BIBLIOGRAPHY

Since the events of the 1960s brought violence forcibly to the attention of social scientists, it has been clear that the resort to illegal force has been an integral part of our social and political history. The best accounts of violence, as a result, are often simply the best books in their field—Reconstruction, for example, or labor history. In addition there has been a great recent increase in works having violence as their specific focus. For both reasons, any bibliography of the subject can only be highly and sometimes arbitrarily selective and must rely on more recent or comprehensive studies to lead back to earlier and special ones.

The official reaction to the violent decade was the creation of a number of study commissions. A task force of the President's Commission on the Causes and Prevention of Violence produced *Violence in America: Historical and Comparative Perspectives* (Washington, D.C.: U.S. Government Printing Office, 1969), edited by Hugh Davis Graham and Ted Gurr, which is still in many ways the best collection. In addition to articles by Richard M. Brown, Philip Taft, and Philip Ross, excerpted in this volume, the most relevant include pieces by August Meier and Elliott Rudwick, Morris Janowitz, and James P. Comer, on racial aggression, Brown's American and Charles Tilly's European overviews, Ted Gurr's ambitious study comparing American with worldwide indexes of civil strife, Sheldon Levy's statistically flawed longitudinal study of political violence, Robin Brooks's assessment of the relation between war and domestic violence, and James E. Davies's attempt to define the preconditions of rebellion. *The Politics of Protest* (New York: Touchstone-Clarion, 1969), published by a task force of the same commission under the direction of Jerome H. Skolnick, concentrates more immediately on the racial, antiwar, and student protests, and the often violent police and official reaction, which inspired the whole effort. Among the many who believed that the success of past violence might be an appropriate model for modern alienated groups was one of Skolnick's contributors, Richard Rubenstein, whose *Rebels in Eden* (Boston: Little, Brown and Company, 1970) is the most comprehensive historical treatment of that view. Richard Hofstadter brilliantly expressed a more moderate reaction in the long essay that opens the documentary collection *American Violence: A Documentary History* (New York: Alfred Knopf, 1971), which he edited with Michael Wallace. James F. Short and Marvin Wolfgang combined a special edition of the *Annals of the American Academy of Political and Social Science* with some later pieces in editing *Collective Violence* (Chicago: Aldine-Atherton, 1972), a book with a more theoretical approach to the issues addressed in Skolnick's.

No aspect of political and social violence has been more thoroughly studied and revised in the past generation than mob behavior. The seminal work by George Rudé, *The Crowd in History: A Study of Popular Disturbances in France and England, 1730-1848* (New York: Wiley, 1964), has been echoed directly and indirectly throughout this volume. Two articles here are especially linked to Rudé. The notes to Pauline Maier's article refer to pieces by Bernard Bailyn, Gordon Wood, and, with a more radical twist, Jesse Lemisch, which apply Rudé's insights to the American colonies. Michael Feldberg's describes not only Rudé's but related theories about European developments that may be applicable to the United States.

The especial turbulence of the Jacksonian years has always attracted historians. Some possible psychological determinants behind intergroup violence are suggested in David Brion Davis's "Some Themes of Counter-Subversion: An Analysis of Anti-Masonic, Anti-Catholic, and Anti-Mormon Literature" [*Mississippi Valley Historical Review,* 47 (September 1960), 205-224], an insightful supplement to the traditional account in Ray Allen Billington's *Protestant Crusade: 1800-1860* (New York: Macmillan, 1938). Leonard L. Richards's *Gentlemen of Property and Standing: Anti-Abolition Mobs in Jacksonian America* (New York: Oxford University Press, 1970) is a significant special study. The considerable recent scholarship devoted to the city of Philadelphia is summed up in Michael Feldberg's *The Philadelphia Riots of 1844: A Study in Ethnic Conflict* (Westport, Conn.: Greenwood Press, 1975). Adrian Cook deals with *The Armies of the Streets: The New York City Draft Riots of 1863* (Lexington: University of Kentucky Press, 1974) in a definitive book, rich in background, that carefully settles a century of misapprehensions.

Richard Kohn's *Eagle and Sword: The Federalists and the Creation of the Military Establishment in America* (New York: Free Press, 1975) describes the way in which popular uprisings during the early republic played a role in strengthening the central military apparatus. The development of police as a response to riot is described in Roger Lane's *Policing the City: Boston, 1822-1885* (Cambridge: Harvard University Press, 1967) and

James F. Richardson's *The New York Police: Colonial Times to 1901* (New York: Oxford University Press, 1970). Wilbur Miller's *Cops and Bobbies: Police Authority in New York and London, 1830–1870* (Chicago: University of Chicago Press, 1977) is a study of legitimation; Richardson's *Urban Police in the United States* (Port Washington: Kennikat Press, 1974) explicitly applies historical scholarship to modern problems and has an extensive bibliography to match Miller's critical one. Martha Derthick's *The National Guard in Politics* (Cambridge: Harvard University Press, 1965), says little about the role of the guard in labor disputes, merely citing the fuller account in William H. Riker's *Soldiers of the States; the Role of the National Guard in American Democracy* (Washington: Public Affairs Press, 1950); there is as yet no full modern history of state police.

Richard Maxwell Brown's *Strain of Violence: Historical Studies of American Violence and Vigilantism* (New York: Oxford University Press, 1975) sums up his expertise in this field. *Vigilante Politics* edited by H. Jon Rosenbaum and Peter C. Sederberg (Philadelphia: University of Pennsylvania Press, 1976), contains some articles on recent American manifestations as well as cross-cultural and theoretical perspectives. In *Frontier Violence: Another Look* (New York: Oxford University Press, 1974), W. Eugene Hollon stresses the genocidal character of vigilantism as well as other forms of attack against Chinese, Mexicans, Mormons, and Indians in the West.

Indian warfare and massacre—although outside the scope of this volume—has attracted considerable attention in recent years. Dee Brown's popular and sometimes inaccurate *Bury My Heart at Wounded Knee* (New York: Holt, Rinehart, and Winston, 1971) culminates a long tradition of impassioned protest and is itself partially responsible for this new interest. Wilcomb E. Washburn's *The Indian in America* (New York: Harper and Row, 1975) is now the standard general history, while Francis Paul Prucha has performed a service with "Books on American Indian Policy: A Half-Decade of Important Work, 1970–1975" [*Journal of American History,* 63 (December 1976), 658–669].

On black revolts against slavery, Herbert Aptheker's *American Negro Slave Revolts* (New York: Columbia University Press, 1943) remains the most comprehensive book despite severe criticism for its one-dimensional and exaggerated character. Gerald Mullin's *Flight and Rebellion: Slave Resistance in Eighteenth Century Virginia* (New York: Oxford University Press, 1972) is a strong recent study. The enormous recent literature on resistance at every level, broadly defined, is sensitively discussed and cited in Eugene Genovese's *Roll Jordan Roll: The World the Slaves Made* (New York: Pantheon Books, 1974).

Violence in the Reconstruction era is best understood as part of an ongoing tradition. Two books by John Hope Franklin illustrate part of the link: *The Militant South* (Cambridge: Belknap Press, 1956) describes the atmosphere of violence that pervaded the region at every level from 1800 to 1861; *Reconstruction After the Civil War* (Chicago: University of Chicago Press, 1961) demonstrates the way in which it was harnessed to maintain white supremacy. The same point is made in Allen W. Trelease's *White Terror* (New York: Harper and Row, 1971), a history of the first Ku Klux Klan, and Otis A. Singletary's *The Negro Militia in Reconstruction* (Austin: University of Texas Press, 1957). C. Vann Woodward, in *Origins of the New South: 1877-1913* (Baton Rouge, La.: Louisiana State University Press, 1951), describes both the continuation of the tradition and the newer ways in which blacks were held down and intimidated. In addition to the work of Raper and Dollard represented in this volume, James E. Cutler's *Lynch Law: An Investigation into the History of Lynching in the United States* (New York: Longmans, Green, and Company, 1905) and Walter White's *Rope and Faggot: A Biography of Judge Lynch* (New York: Alfred A. Knopf, 1929) are the standard older sources on southern lynching.

Aside from biographical and special studies relating to individual victims, virtually the only books on assassination in American history were all published about 1970; the most authoritative is *Assassination and Political Violence* (New York: Praeger, 1970), edited by James F. Kirkham, which incorporates the work on that subject by the President's Commission on the Causes and Prevention of Violence. International as well as domestic terrorism, over the past several years, has come to affect American politics; two relevant books are Murray Clark Havens et al.'s *Assassination and Terrorism: Their Modern Dimensions,* revised edition (Englewood Cliffs, N.J.: Prentice-Hall, 1975), and Walter Laqueur's *Guerrilla* (Boston: Little, Brown and Company, 1977). Full journalistic accounts of the most famous American groups are included in *Weatherman,* edited by Harold Jacobs (San Francisco: Ramparts Press, 1970), *SDS,* by Kirkpatrick Sale (New York: Random House, 1973), and *The Voices of Guns,* by Vin McLellan and Paul Avery (New York: Putnam, 1977), the latter about the Symbionese Liberation Army.

There is no general history of violence undertaken to suppress dissent or difference, the closest thing being Gustavus Myers's *History of Bigotry in the United States,* revised edition (New York: Random House, 1960), first published in 1943. Many of the case histories concentrate on the period of World War I and its aftermath. Walter Preston, Jr.'s *Aliens and Dissenters: Federal Suppression of Radicals, 1903-1933* (Cambridge: Harvard University Press, 1963) is the most comprehensive. Among other noteworthy special studies see: Stanley Coben, "A Study in Nativism: The American Red Scare of 1919-1920," *Political Science Quarterly* 79 (March 1974), 52-75; Kenneth T. Jackson, *The Ku Klux Klan in the City: 1915-1930* (New York: Oxford University Press, 1967); and R.C. Myers, "Anti-Communist Mob Action: A Case Study," *Public Opinion Quarterly* 12 (Spring 1948), 57-67. See also the Peterson and Fite volume represented here and the articles on dissent during the 1960s in Skolnick's *Politics of Protest.*

The history of the labor movement is inseparable from the violence that has accompanied it. The enormous pioneering work of John R. Commons et al. in *The History of Labor in the United States,* 4 volumes (New York: Macmillan, 1918-1935), still contains much information. So does its almost equally monumental modern counterpart, written from a more consistently Marxist point of view, Philip S. Foner's *History of the Labor Movement in the United States,* 4 volumes to date (New York: International Publishers, 1947-1965). Among preunion movements, *The Molly Maguires* by Wayne G. Broehl, Jr. (Cambridge: Harvard University Press, 1965) is the most scholarly account of the secret society known for its murderous tactics in the Pennsylvania coalfields, while Arthur Lewis's *Lament for the Molly Maguires* (New York: Harcourt, Brace and World, 1964) is highly readable. The most tactically radical of American unions, and the one most tragically victimized by repressive violence, is best described in Melvyn Dubofsky's *We Shall Be All: The Industrial Workers of the World* (Chicago: Quadrangle Books, 1969). While there is no short general history, there are relatively good and recent bibliographies in John H. Laslett's *Labor and the Left, 1881-1924* (New York: Basic Books, 1970) and Jeremy Brecher's *Strike!* (San Francisco: Straight Arrow Books, 1972). Among the host of noteworthy special studies are Herbert Gutman's "The Tompkins Square 'Riot' in New York City: A Reexamination" [*Labor History* 6 (Winter 1965), 44-70]; Robert Bruce's popular *1877: Year of Violence* (Indianapolis: Bobbs-Merrill, 1959); Rhodri Jeffreys-Jones's "Violence in American History: Plug Uglies in the Progressive Era" [*Perspectives in American History* 8 (1974), 465-583]; Irving Bernstein's *The Turbulent Years: A History of the American Worker, 1933-1941* (Boston: Houghton Mifflin, 1970); and Sidney Fine's *Sit-Down: The General Motors Strike of 1936-1937* (Ann Arbor, Mich.: University of Michigan Press, 1969).

In recent years the literature on urban black protest and interracial violence in the twentieth century has begun to rival that on the labor movement in volume. Much had been done before the first ghetto riots in 1964. The Chicago Commission on Race Relations, *The Negro in Chicago: Race Riot in 1919* (Chicago: University of Chicago Press, 1922), is a classic in early social science. Elliott Rudwick's *Race Riot in East St. Louis June 2, 1917* (Carbondale, Ill.: Southern Illinois University Press, 1964), is an excellent study, and Allen D. Grimshaw's unpublished thesis was available long before he edited his *Racial Violence in the United States* (Chicago: Aldine Publishing Company, 1969). Arthur Waskow's survey *From Race Riot to Sit-In, 1919 and the 1960s* (Garden City, N.Y.: Doubleday, 1966), is flawed only by its failure to go past the protest movement in the South. Vincent Harding's "Black Radicalism: The Road from Montgomery" [in Alfred F. Young, ed., *Dissent: Explorations in the History of American Radicalism*

(DeKalb, Ill.: Northern Illinois University Press, 1968)] helps explain the transition from South to North, nonviolence to violence. The Watts riot of 1965 inspired the first major official report, *Violence in the City—An End or a Beginning?* (Los Angeles, 1965), by the Governor's Commission on the Los Angeles Riots. Known as the *McCone Report,* this exemplifies the traditional official reaction in viewing riot and rioters primarily as criminal, and slighting other possible interpretations. The *Report of the National Advisory Commission on Civil Disorders* (Washington, D.C.: U.S. Government Printing Office, 1968), or the Kerner Report, is later, far more complete, and more in line with modern social science on the nature of riot and mob activity. (Cf. also the articles already cited in Graham and Gurr, *Violence in America,* and Skolnick, *Politics of Protest.*) All individual studies written since have drawn on this officially gathered material; among a long list, Robert Fogelson's *Violence As Protest: A Study of Riots and Ghettos* (Garden City, N.Y.: Doubleday, 1971), represented in this volume, stands up best after seven somewhat cooler summers.

There is one comprehensive work that covers many of the special subjects mentioned previously: *Political Violence in the United States, 1875-1974,* by Jarol B. Manheim and Melanie Wallace (New York: Garland Publishing, Inc., 1975). Although it does not evaluate, it does list over 1,500 books and articles, alphabetically, under seven headings: "Strikes," "Race, Riots and Urban Violence," "Anarchism and Terrorism," "Assassination," "The Violent Response—Vigilantism, Lynching, Police Violence," "Gun Control," and "General and Miscellaneous."

The following books and articles, finally, are of special interest because of their quality or recency or both:

Auerbach, Jerold "Southern Tenant Farmers: Socialist Critics of The New Deal" *Labor History* 7 (Winter 1966), 3-18.

Grant, Donald L. *The Anti-Lynching Movement: 1883-1932* (San Francisco, R & E Research Associates, Publishers, 1975).

Gurr, Ted *Why Men Rebel* (Princeton: Princeton University Press, 1970).

Hoerder, Dirk *Crowd Action in Revolutionary Massachusetts, 1765-1780* (New York: Academic Press, 1976).

Holmes, William F. "Whitecapping: Agrarian Violence in Mississippi 1902-1906" *Journal of Southern History* 35 (May 1969), 163-185.

Lens, Sydney *The Labor Wars: From the Molly Maguires to the Sitdowns* (Garden City: N.Y.: Doubleday, 1974).

McMillan, Neil R. *The Citizens' Council; Organized Resistance to the Second Reconstruction, 1954-64* (Urbana: University of Illinois Press, 1971).

Schwartz, Michael *Radical Protest and Social Structure: The Southern Tenant Farmers' Alliance and Cotton Tenancy* (New York: Academic Press, 1976).

Shockley, John Staples *Chicano Revolt in a Texas Town* (Notre Dame, Ind.: University of Notre Dame Press, 1974).

Suggs, George G., Jr. *Colorado's War on Militant Unionism: James H. Peabody and the Western Federation of Miners* (Detroit: Wayne State University Press, 1972).

Toplin, Robert Brent *Unchallenged Violence: An American Ordeal* (Westport, Conn.: Greenwood Press, 1975).

Utley, Robert *Frontier Regulars: The United States Army and the Indian 1866-1891* (New York: Macmillan, 1973).

Van den Haag, Ernest *Political Violence and Civil Disobedience* (New York: Harper and Row, 1972).

Wechsler, James *Revolt on Campus* (Seattle: University of Washington Press, 1973).

Weems, John Edward *Death Song: The Last of the Indian Wars* (Garden City: N.Y.: Doubleday, 1976).

INDEX

ABOUT THE EDITORS

Roger Lane, professor of history at Haverford College, specializes in the history of police, crime, and violence in America. He has previously published articles on crime and criminal violence in the *Annals of the American Academy of Political and Social Science* and *Journal of Social History* as well as a book-length work, *Policing the City: Boston 1822-1885.*

John J. Turner, Jr., is professor of history at West Chester State College in Pennsylvania, specializing in American violence, revolution, and American political parties. He has contributed articles to *The Historian, The New-York Historical Society Quarterly,* and *New York History.*